FROM PRISONERS TO PIONEERS

A Genealogy of John Frawley & Mary Ann McGarry

From Prisoners To Pioneers: A Genealogy of John Frawley & Mary Ann McGarry
by Dr. Tracy Rockwell (1955)

Volume 5
of the Rockwell Genealogies

First Published in Australia in 2025
by Pegasus Publishing
PO Box 980, Edgecliff, NSW, 2027

Orders: pegasuspublishing@iinet.net.au
www.pegasus-publishing.square.site

Copyright © Pegasus Publishing
An Ashnong Pty Ltd Company

All rights reserved. No part of this publication may be reproduced, stored in a retrieval system, or transmitted in any form or by any means, electronic, mechanical, photocopying, recording or otherwise, without the prior written permission of the copyright owner.

A CIP catalogue record for this book is available from the National Library of Australia.

ISBN: 978-1-925909-19-7

Printed and sold on Demand through:
Pegasus Publishing - www.pegasus-publishing.square.site
Ingram Lightning Source - www.ingramspark.com

Volumes In The Series - 'The Rockwell Genealogies':

Vol. 1 - (Reserved for 'A Genealogy of Augustus Rockwell & Frances Austin')
Vol. 2 - To The Great South Land: A Genealogy of Robert Bantin & Mary Barrett
Vol. 3 - The Mahony's of Dunloe, County Kerry, Ireland
Vol. 4 - The Path That Few Travel: A Genealogy of James Mahony O'Sullivan
Vol. 5 - From Prisoners To Pioneers: A Genealogy of John Frawley & Mary Ann McGarry
Vol. 6 - The Long Road To Grafton: A Genealogy of Thomas Eastman Shoveller
Vol. 7 - To The Big River: A Genealogy of John Hann & Mary Matilda Thompson
Vol. 8 - Nostalgia For Naremburn: The Ancestors of Robert Archibald Rockwell & Octavia Corelli O'Sullivan
Vol. 9 - Passengers & Central West Pioneers: A Genealogy of Thomas Cummings & Ellen Sheehan
Vol. 10 - Boldness Be Our Friend: A Genealogy of John McDonald & Ann Selina Harvey
Vol. 11 - : The Ancestors of William Wallace Wardle & Mary Agnes Cummings
Vol. 12 - Robbers, Rascals & Royals: The Ancestry, Life & Times of Dr Tracy Rockwell

Front Cover: 'Employees on the Coolangatta Estate, Shoalhaven River, N.S.W, c.1891 (SLNSW- a3683017), over an image of original sandstone blocks at the Coolangatta homestead, photo by Tracy Rockwell (2021).
Back Cover Inset: The new township of Pambula, c.1870.

OPPOSITE: 'Wolumla, a township which developed 15km northeast of Pambula, around a watering place for bullock teams, was later buoyed by the discovery and mining of gold. (Merimbula-Imlay Historical Society).

FROM PRISONERS TO PIONEERS

A Genealogy of John Frawley & Mary Ann McGarry

Volume 5
of the Rockwell Genealogies

By
Dr Tracy Rockwell

Pegasus Publishing

CONTENTS & PLATES

Preface	xi
Acknowledgement, Abbreviations & Symbols	xiii
Introduction	xiv
Chapter 1 - Discovering the South Coast of NSW	21
Chapter 2 - Explorers of the Shoalhaven & Illawarra	41
Chapter 3 - The Frawley Ancestors [Paternal & Maternal Antecedents of JF]	55
Chapter 4 - Land Grants & Squatters	71
Chapter 5 - An Unwilling Pioneer [c.1816-1839]	89
Chapter 6 - Berry's Coolangatta Homestead	103
Chapter 7 - The McGarry Ancestors [Paternal & Maternal Antecedents of MAM]	119
Chapter 8 - Mary Ann McGarry, Convict [c.1815-1839]	133
Chapter 9 - John Frawley & Mary Ann McGarry [1840-1844]	147
Chapter 10 - Maneroo & Twofold Bay	163
Chapter 11 - Warragaburra Homestead	179
Chapter 12 - Pioneers of 'Pamboola' [1845-1860]	195
Chapter 13 - The Frawleys of Victoria	213
Chapter 14 - Property & Prosecutions	223
Chapter 15 - Frawleys Under Fire [1861-1874]	239
Chapter 16 - Final Days in Queensland [1875-1901]	255
Chapter 17 - Descendants of John Frawley & Mary Ann McGarry	277
Appendices	317
Index	333
The Author	343

LIST OF PEDIGREE CHARTS...

1. The Ancestors & Descendants of Robert & Octavia Rockwell of Naremburn, NSW	xviii
2. Descendants of Michael Frawley & Margaret McNamara, of Co. Clare	62
3. The Ancestors & Descendants of John & Mary Ann Frawley	272-273

LIST OF DESCENDANTS & FAMILIES...

4. Descendants of John Frawley Jr. & Sarah Little	280-281
5. Descendants of Ellen Frawley & James Mahony O'Sullivan	288-289
6. Descendants of Patrick Frawley/Marr & Eliza Quigg	306-307
App. Frawley Descendants That Served In Australian Military Forces	331

LIST OF MAPS...

M1. Johnston Large Antique Map of New South Wales & Victoria, c.1845.	xii
M2. Map of the Journey of the "Sydney Cove" survivors in 1797.	33
M3. Map of the Survey and Exploration of the Jervis Bay, Crookhaven & Shoalhaven Districts, by Lt. B. Kent & James Meehan (Feb 1805).	48-49
M4. Sir William Petty's 689 Map of County Limerick, Munster.	65
M5. Map of the Journey of George W. Evans from Jervis Bay through to the Shoalhaven district, NSW in 1812.	74
M6. Map of the route of George W. Evans' expedition from Shoalhaven to Illawarra and overland to Appin in 1812.	75
M7. Map of the landmarks of the Illawarra region from Coledale to Bass Point.	78
M8. Map of the route of George W. Evans expedition overland from Shoalhaven to Illawarra and Appin in 1812.	81
M9. Map of the Earliest Explorer & Pioneer Journeys of the Illawarra	81
M10. Map of Alexander Berry's Coolangatta Homestead.	114
M11. Map of Limerick City, showing 'English Town', c.1587.	121
M12. Map of the Illawarra Police District, showing the Coolangatta Estate in relation to the town of Wollongong in 1841.	159
M13. William Baker's 1841 map of the South Coast of Australia showing the districts of New South Wales beyond the 'Limits of Location'.	164
M14. William Baker's 1841 map of the District of Maneroo showing the location of Twofold Bay, Shoalhaven and the Illawarra.	180
M15. Contemporary map of the Bega District, showing the location of the Warragaburra Homestead.	182
M16. Map of Ennis, County Clare, and and surrounds, showing the location of Doora, and Quin in relation to the larger town of Limerick.	213
M17. Road map of the South Coast of New South Wales, showing the development since the few settled areas in 1840.	251
M18. Map of Pambula, showing the location of Bega Valley Genealogy Society.	253
M19. Squatting map of the Darling Downs District, Queensland.	257
M20. Map of the South Eastern portion of Australia, showing the boundaries of the 'Nineteen Districts', gazetted by Major Thomas Mitchell, in 1838.	327

From Prisoners To Pioneers

'A Family Tree', by Norman Rockwell (1959).

DEDICATION

This genealogy is dedicated to the memory of John Frawley and Mary Ann McGarry, whose courage and strength of character as irish convicts and pioneers carried them through the many hardships of early Australian life in the mid to late 19th century. Their resilience and determination laid the foundations for future generations.

"To the land we live in... and the land we left behind."

Giraldus Cambrensus, Welsh Chronicler (1146-1223)

PREFACE

This volume delves into the genealogy of John Frawley (c.1816–1901) and his wife, Mary Ann McGarry (c.1815–1889), both transported from Ireland as convicts who later became pioneers in what became the township of Pambula on the far south coast of New South Wales, and in Toowoomba, Queensland. It traces their ancestral lines, Frawley, Kenny, McGarry, and Heffernan, while also shedding light on the lives of their known forebears.

Although this is Volume 5, the 'Rockwell Genealogies' are fundamentally one extensive work. To improve readability, I have divided the manuscript into 12 volumes. A single comprehensive book would be unwieldy, so where possible, I have dedicated separate volumes to each of my great-great-grandparents, great-grandparents, and grandparents. This volume is a tribute to these ancestors, honoring their lives and legacies (see Chart 1).

The purpose of this genealogy is threefold: to uncover the life stories of our ancestors, to present history with accuracy, free from sentimentality or exaggeration; and to preserve family pedigrees, stories, verses, and traditions that might otherwise be lost. My hope is that these pages rescue fragments of history from the tide of time.

Even the greatest historians often share our struggle to fully capture the past. My primary motivation in undertaking this extensive research was to organize and compile over 40 years of genealogical investigation. Rather than leaving behind an indecipherable collection of notes, diagrams, and images, my goal has been to present the 'Rockwell Genealogies' in a structured and engaging format for future generations. A key concern has been to balance depth with accessibility, as "a wealth of information can create a poverty of attention." Genealogy is not an exact science, and some branches of the family tree are well-documented, while others remain shrouded in mystery.

Initially, my aim was simply to discover how our ancestors came to settle in Australia, a project I expected to span just one or two volumes. Given the country's relatively young history, I focused on understanding when, why, and how our forebears arrived. Documenting their lives not only revealed where and how they lived, but also acknowledged the hardships they endured and the contributions they made, without which none of us would be here today.

As my research expanded, I uncovered more distant ancestors and indirect relatives from various countries of origin, prompting me to explore their lives in greater detail. In pursuit of a deeper understanding, I have traveled to many of the towns, cities, and regions where these ancestors once lived. Walking in their footsteps has been a profound experience, as "they are now like little ghosts, forever ebbing very slowly away from us."

Tracy Rockwell
Dip. Teach; BSc; MSc; PhD

M1. The 1845 'Johnston Large Antique Map of New South Wales & Victoria, Australia Felix', showing the residential locations of John & Mary Frawley at Coolangatta, Pambula and Warragubera homestead, in relation to Sydney.

ACKNOWLEDGEMENTS

This book has been a pleasure to write, and I hope it is also a pleasure to read. A number of people and organisations have helped me write it, yet it would be impossible to acknowledge the assistance of each and every contributer. Of notable mention however, are the staff at the Bega Valley Historical Society, who pointed me in the right direction at the start of my research in the early days from 1980. Of invaluable support was the Society of Australian Genealogists in Sydney, the Mitchell and State Libraries of New South Wales, the Merimbula-Imlay Historical Society, the National Library of Australia and their online Trove digital newspaper and photography facilities.

Online websites and resources have also been extraordinarily helpful in researching content for this publication and my sincere thanks goes to the NSW Govt Registry of Births, Deaths and Marriages and the State Archives of NSW. In Ireland, I am thankful for the use of the Dictionary of Irish Biography; The Tithe Applotment Books; Catholic Parish Registers at the NLI; Irish Convicts to NSW by Peter Mayberry; Ireland - Modern and Contemporary Maps, Library of Ireland; Irish History, Genealogy and Culture; A Vision of Ireland through Time; and the Casey Collection Indexes (1545-1960). International websites were also consulted including the International Genealogical Index (aka IGI or Family Search), Ancestry, as well as Wikitree and Wikipedia, which have all been invaluable sources of information.

ABBREVIATIONS & SYMBOLS

The following abbreviations and symbols are used throughout this book to summarize the historical information. A legend is provided below to help interpret the various systems and codes used in its compilation. Unless otherwise stated, records of baptisms, marriages, and burials should be understood as coming from the parish register of the respective church where the ceremony took place.

Additionally, throughout the following pages, you will find escutcheons representing various ancestral families of John Frawley and Mary Ann McGarry. These are primarily included to distinguish family groups rather than to signify any official grant of arms or blazon.

Legend of Abbreviations & Symbols

BVHS	Bega Valley Historical Society.	bc.	born circa.
CF	Copyright free image.	bp.	baptised.
GS	Government Servant (convict).	c.	circa [*Latin*], about.
IGI	International Genealogical Index.	d.	died.
JF	John Frawley.	dc.	died circa.
MM	Maternal Maternal.	d.s.p.	decessit sine prole [*Latin*], died without issue.
MP	Maternal Paternal.		
NA	National Arch. of England & Wales.	dspm.	descessit sine prole mascula [*Latin*]; died without male issue.
PM	Paternal Maternal.		
PP	Paternal Paternal.	dv.	divorced
PRO	Public Record Office, London.	d.v.p.	decessit vitae patre [*Latin*], died in father's lifetime.
SSD	Sands Sydney Directory.		
SMH	Sydney Morning Herald.	fl.	flourished.
UV	Unverified.	m.	married.
▲	Served in Australian Military Forces	mc.	married circa.
*	died before adulthood.	r.	reigned.
b.	born.	s.	succeeded

INTRODUCTION

Every family has a story, and this is ours. Exploring family history is an addictive pursuit, offering the thrill of discovering ancestors and even uncovering connections to historical figures, aristocrats, or royalty. More than that, genealogy unlocks a deeper understanding of who we are.

Researching one's lineage is both rewarding and challenging. Just when you think you've uncovered every possible detail, new evidence emerges, revealing unexpected connections. Genealogy is an ongoing journey, and one that requires patience, persistence, and a willingness to embrace surprises.

My passion for this fascinating field began in the early 1980s while working as an international flight steward for QANTAS. During layovers in London on the QF1 route, I spent my free time poring over historical documents at Somerset House and the Public Record Office, searching for long-lost relatives.

This book is just one of twelve volumes in the Rockwell Genealogies series. The purpose of this collection is to systematically examine the ancestry of each of our great-great-grandparents, tracing their histories from paternal to maternal lines. The information is organized by family branches, following each lineage as far back as records allow.

Genealogical research presents unique challenges, particularly when dealing with common surnames in heavily populated areas. Tracing a Smith or Brown in London or New York can be a daunting task, whereas researching an uncommon surname in a rural village is often much easier. Fortunately, many of our ancestors bore distinctive surnames and lived in smaller communities, making their stories more traceable.

In former British colonies and the United States, having a recorded lineage is a source of pride, regardless of noble or humble origins. Unlike some European traditions, one need not belong to a titled family to find value in tracing ancestry. Descendants of colonial-era figures, whether esquires or artisans, often consider their heritage noteworthy. Of course, the possibility of discovering distinguished ancestry provides additional motivation.

Historically, inheritance laws played a significant role in shaping family structures. The principle of primogeniture, the right of succession belonging to the firstborn child, helped preserve family estates but often left younger sons with limited prospects, pushing them toward careers in the church, military, or government. Daughters, prior to the 20th century, were mostly seen as assets for strategic marriages.

But none of this history would be accessible without first identifying people. Surnames became essential as governments introduced personal taxation, such as England's Poll Tax. Over time, surnames evolved, often producing astonishing variations in spelling. The earliest records of births, marriages, and deaths in England were voluntarily maintained by local parish churches. Many of these have since been transcribed into the International Genealogical Index (FamilySearch), making them more accessible than ever.

The inconsistency of English parish records led to multiple efforts to standardize the system in the 18th and 19th centuries. The Marriage Act of 1753 sought to prevent clandestine unions by requiring formal entries signed by both parties and witnesses. Except for Jews, Quakers, and Catholics, all legal marriages had to follow the rites of the Church of England. The English Parochial Registers Act of 1812 further mandated standardized bound volumes for record-keeping. However, non-conformist records were not legally recognized in court, creating difficulties for many families.

By the early 19th century, concerns over poor record-keeping, especially its impact on property rights, led to calls for civil registration. The government also sought accurate demographic data to address public health and social welfare concerns, which became more urgent as the Industrial Revolution fueled overcrowded cities.

The solution came in 1836 when legislation established the civil registration of births, marriages, and deaths in England and Wales, taking effect on July 1, 1837. This system improved the accuracy of recorded lineages, allowed non-conformists to document their lives without relying on the Church of England, and provided crucial data for medical research.

Notably, our ancestor from separate branch Dr. John Shoveller, played an important role in this development, receiving letters patent from King William IV as a commissioner involved in the establishment of national registers. England and Wales were subsequently divided into registration districts, initially 619, rising to 623 by 1851, each overseen by a Superintendent Registrar. These districts were further divided into sub-districts managed by local Registrars. The system's success led to the introduction of compulsory registration in Scotland (1854), Australia (1856), and Ireland (1864). Though not every event was meticulously recorded, the framework established then remains in use today.

The advent of the internet has revolutionized genealogy, making records that once took weeks or months to access available in an instant.

This book is more than a collection of names and dates, genealogical exploration spanning borders and centuries. It brings to life the triumphs, struggles, and lasting influence of our ancestors, offering readers a compelling glimpse into how generations of Irish heritage have converged in one Australian lineage.

As always, I welcome feedback and corrections from fellow genealogists and family members who may have additional insights to contribute. Remembering that...

> "We are all the product of people we have never met and events we have never witnessed, but if even a single detail had changed in their lives, our very existence might have been forever altered".
>
> *Melanie Johnston*

From Prisoners To Pioneers

Rare colonial engraving of 'Berry's Homestead', now called Coolangatta Estate c.1884, by Arthur Collingridge de Tourcey (1853 - 1907), from the original edition of The Illustrated Sydney News. References: Gibbs & Shallard. Illustrated Sydney News. ISSN 2203-5397 (SLNSW).

John Frawley spent his seven years of servitude at Coolangatta, and it was here that he met his future bride, Mary Ann McGarry, who was like John was a native of Limerick, co. Limerick, in Ireland.

THE ROCKWELL GENEALOGIES

Pedigree Chart 1 - The Ancestors & Descendants of Robert & Octavia Rockwell of Naremburn, NSW

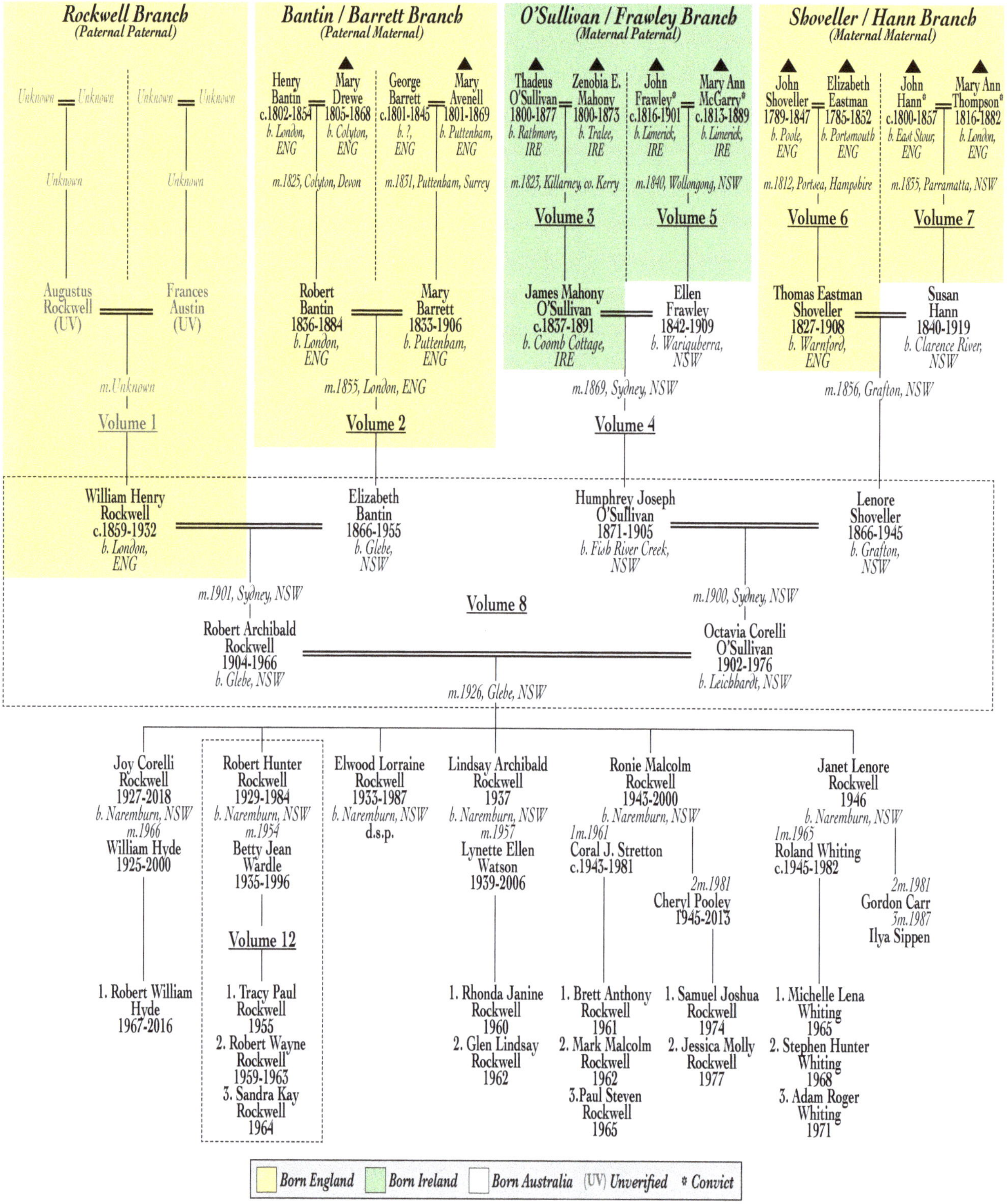

Rockwell Branch (Paternal Paternal)

- Unknown = Unknown
- Unknown = Unknown
- Augustus Rockwell (UV) = Frances Austin (UV)
  - m. Unknown
  - **Volume 1**
  - William Henry Rockwell c.1859-1932, b. London, ENG

Bantin / Barrett Branch (Paternal Maternal)

- Henry Bantin c.1802-1854, b. London, ENG = Mary Drewe 1805-1868, b. Colyton, ENG
  - m.1825, Colyton, Devon
- George Barrett c.1801-1845, b. ?, ENG = Mary Avenell 1801-1869, b. Puttenham, ENG
  - m.1831, Puttenham, Surrey
- Robert Bantin 1836-1884, b. London, ENG = Mary Barrett 1833-1906, b. Puttenham, ENG
  - m.1855, London, ENG
  - **Volume 2**
  - Elizabeth Bantin 1866-1955, b. Glebe, NSW

m.1901, Sydney, NSW

Robert Archibald Rockwell 1904-1966, b. Glebe, NSW

O'Sullivan / Frawley Branch (Maternal Paternal)

- ▲ Thadeus O'Sullivan 1800-1877, b. Rathmore, IRE = ▲ Zenobia E. Mahony 1800-1873, b. Tralee, IRE
  - m.1823, Killarney, co. Kerry
  - **Volume 3**
- ▲ John Frawley 1816-1901, b. Limerick, IRE = ▲ Mary Ann McGarry* 1813-1889, b. Limerick, IRE
  - m.1840, Wollongong, NSW
  - **Volume 5**
- James Mahony O'Sullivan c.1837-1891, b. Coomb Cottage, IRE = Ellen Frawley 1842-1909, b. Wariguberra, NSW
  - m.1869, Sydney, NSW
  - **Volume 4**
  - Humphrey Joseph O'Sullivan 1871-1905, b. Fish River Creek, NSW

Shoveller / Hann Branch (Maternal Maternal)

- ▲ John Shoveller 1789-1847, b. Poole, ENG = ▲ Elizabeth Eastman 1785-1852, b. Portsmouth, ENG
  - m.1812, Portsea, Hampshire
  - **Volume 6**
- ▲ John Hann* c.1800-1857, b. East Stour, ENG = ▲ Mary Ann Thompson* 1816-1882, b. London, ENG
  - m.1835, Parramatta, NSW
  - **Volume 7**
- Thomas Eastman Shoveller 1827-1908, b. Warnford, ENG = Susan Hann 1840-1919, b. Clarence River, NSW
  - m.1856, Grafton, NSW
  - Lenore Shoveller 1866-1945, b. Grafton, NSW

m.1900, Sydney, NSW

Octavia Corelli O'Sullivan 1902-1976, b. Leichhardt, NSW

Volume 8

m.1926, Glebe, NSW

Children:

- **Joy Corelli Rockwell** 1927-2018, b. Naremburn, NSW
  - m.1966 William Hyde 1925-2000
  - 1. Robert William Hyde 1967-2016

- **Robert Hunter Rockwell** 1929-1984, b. Naremburn, NSW
  - m.1954 Betty Jean Wardle 1935-1996
  - **Volume 12**
  - 1. Tracy Paul Rockwell 1955
  - 2. Robert Wayne Rockwell 1959-1963
  - 3. Sandra Kay Rockwell 1964

- **Elwood Lorraine Rockwell** 1933-1987, b. Naremburn, NSW
  - d.s.p.

- **Lindsay Archibald Rockwell** 1937, b. Naremburn, NSW
  - m.1957 Lynette Ellen Watson 1939-2006
  - 1. Rhonda Janine Rockwell 1960
  - 2. Glen Lindsay Rockwell 1962

- **Ronie Malcolm Rockwell** 1943-2000, b. Naremburn, NSW
  - 1m.1961 Coral J. Stretton c.1943-1981
    - 1. Brett Anthony Rockwell 1961
    - 2. Mark Malcolm Rockwell 1962
    - 3. Paul Steven Rockwell 1965
  - 2m.1981 Cheryl Pooley 1945-2013
    - 1. Samuel Joshua Rockwell 1974
    - 2. Jessica Molly Rockwell 1977

- **Janet Lenore Rockwell** 1946, b. Naremburn, NSW
  - 1m.1965 Roland Whiting c.1945-1982
    - 1. Michelle Lena Whiting 1965
    - 2. Stephen Hunter Whiting 1968
    - 3. Adam Roger Whiting 1971
  - 2m.1981 Gordon Carr
  - 3m.1987 Ilya Sippen

Legend: Born England | Born Ireland | Born Australia | (UV) Unverified | * Convict

The Rockwell Genealogies spans 12 separate volumes and includes the ancestors and descendants of Robert Archibald Rockwell & Octavia Corelli O'Sullivan, featuring the 'Bantin/Barrett' branch (#2), the 'Mahony's of Dunloe' (#3), the 'O'Sullivan/Mahony' branch (#4), the 'Frawley/McGarry' branch (#5), the 'Shoveller/Eastman' branch (#6), the 'Hann/Thompson' branch (#7) and the 'Rockwell/O'Sullivan' great grandparents & grandparents (#8). NOTE: Volume 1 is reserved for the 'Rockwell' branch if evidence ever emerges. Volumes not listed above detail the ancestors and descendants of Betty Jean Wardle and include William Wallace Wardle & Mary Agnes Cummings, which feature the 'Cummins/Sheehan' branch (#9), the 'McDonald/Harvey' branch (#10) and the 'Wardle/Cummings' great grandparents & grandparents (#11). The final volume features 'Robert & Betty Rockwell' (#12).

Chapter One

DISCOVERING THE SOUTH COAST OF NEW SOUTH WALES

The story of John Frawley is one of resilience, transformation, and legacy. Born in Limerick in 1816, he was just 17 years old when his life was irrevocably altered, sentenced to transportation to Australia for the minor crime of stealing clothes. Uprooted from his homeland, stripped of his future, and cast into the unknown, he became one of the 40,000 Irish convicts who were forcibly exiled from their homeland from between 1791 and 1867. Yet, rather than being merely a victim of history, John Frawley became a pioneering figure in colonial Australia, shaping the very land to which he was sent in chains.

This book chronicles the life and lineage of John Frawley (c.1816–1901), tracing his ancestry, his personal journey, and his enduring impact. Through meticulous genealogical research, we reconstruct his family's past, bringing to life the key individuals whose choices, struggles, and triumphs shaped his destiny.

But this is more than just a family history, it is a sweeping narrative that places John Frawley within the grand forces of his time. From the Napoleonic Wars to World War I, from the Industrial and Irish Revolutions to the Victorian era, his story is deeply intertwined with some of the most pivotal moments in modern history. Long before John Frawley's fateful transportation, the British had already begun their colonization of Australia, establishing the settlement of Sydney in 1788. By a twist of fate, Frawley would go on to forge a new life as a pioneer on the continent's rugged southeastern frontier, and to understand his remarkable journey, we must first explore the land he was forced to call home.

The exploration, mapping, and gradual opening of New South Wales to European settlement played a crucial role in shaping the world into which he arrived. The challenges, opportunities, and transformations of this frontier landscape would not only define his survival, but also his legacy.

However, before exploring John Frawley's personal odyssey, a story of endurance, adaptation, and survival; this book will first examine the key events that shaped a timeline of explorations and discoveries along Australia's Southeast Coast (*see Appendix A*). From the first European encounters to the rise of civilization in the decades before Frawley's arrival, this historical context helps illuminate how a young Irishman, exiled to an unfamiliar land, became not just a footnote in history but a pivotal part of Australia's story.

THE VOYAGE OF "HMS ENDEAVOUR"

Lt. James Cook (1728-1779)

The discovery of the east coast of Australia began with the arrival of that talented and able seaman Lieutenant James Cook, navigator, cartographer and later captain in the Royal Navy, and Fellow of the Royal Society. Cook became famous for his three voyages between 1768 and 1779 in the Pacific Ocean and to New Zealand and Australia in particular.

On the 25th May 1768, the British Admiralty commissioned Cook to command a voyage to the Pacific Ocean.[1] The purpose of the expedition wasn't to colonise new lands or subjugate 'inferior' races, but primarily to advance scientific knowledge by observing and recording the 1769 transit of Venus across the Sun, which when combined with observations from other places around the world, would help to determine the distance of the Earth from the Sun.[2] At age 39, Cook was promoted to lieutenant to grant him sufficient status to take command of the voyage.[3,4] For its part, the Royal Society agreed that Cook would receive a one hundred guinea gratuity in addition to his Naval pay.[5]

LEFT: Portrait of Lt. James Cook, commander of "HMS Endeavour", artist unknown. RIGHT: The expedition of "HMS Endeavour", departed from Plymouth, England, on the 26th August 1768.

"When Cook landed inside the southern headland of Botany Bay at a place known today as Kurnell, in April 1770, he was initially opposed by two Aboriginals brandishing spears. At first, Cook called the place 'Stingrays Harbour' for the number of stingrays they caught there, but later named it Botany Bay for the immense number of new botanical specimens that Joseph Banks and his colleagues were able to gather.

Aboard "HMS Endeavour", the expedition departed from Plymouth, England on the 26th August 1768.[6] After an eight month voyage Cook and his crew arrived at Tahiti on the 13th April 1769, where the observations of the transit were made.[7] However, the result of the observations was not as conclusive or accurate as had been hoped. Once his work there was completed, Cook opened his sealed orders, which were additional instructions from the Admiralty for the second part of his voyage, with dictates to search the south Pacific for signs of the postulated rich southern continent of Terra Australis.[8]

Cook then sailed to New Zealand where, with only some minor errors, he completely circumnavigated and mapped the two islands. With the aid of Tupaia, a Tahitian priest who had joined the expedition, Cook became the first European to communicate with the Maori.[9] Cook then voyaged west, reaching the southeastern coast of what they correctly assumed was New Holland, and in doing so his expedition became the first recorded Europeans to encounter the eastern coastline of Australia.

Cooks landfall was recorded in the ship's log as being sighted at 6 a.m. on Thursday 19 April 1770, but because the south-east coast of Australia is now regarded as being 10 hours ahead relative to Britain, that date is now called Friday, 20th April.[10] He named the point of contact as Cape Hicks, in honour of his second in command Lieutenant William Hicks (1788-1874), who had first sighted the mainland that morning.

Over the next seven days Cook sailed north, noting in his journal many prominent features of Australia's south east coast including Ram Head and Cape Howe, which he

"Sailors from the visiting French ship "Astrolabe" sharing their catch with the natives near Wollongong in early 1788 (lithograph, c.1833, From... Michael K. Organ, (1990). From... 'Illawarra & South Coast Aborigines 1770-1850' Univ of Wollongong, p.156a).

named after Richard Howe (1726-1799), 1st Earl Howe, a distinguished naval commander best known for his victory of the 'Glorious First of June' over the French, in 1794. Being 20km out to sea Cook missed Twofold Bay, but noted Mount Dromedary, Pigeon House Mountain and three or four small islands he called Bateman Bay, after Nathaniel Bateman (c.1723-1797), captain of the "Northumberland."[11]

If the sea was calmer Cook may have landed at Murramarang, but it was there that they glimpsed their first aboriginals, who they described in the following journal entry:

> "As we stood along shore we saw four or five of the Indians sitting near the fire; they appeared to be naked and very black, which was all we could discern at that distance."
>
> *Richard Pickersgill, Master's Mate*

Having failed to land on the 23rd April, Cook stood away from the shore passing present day Ulladulla at a distance of 20-25km, but he named Cape St George, noting also the existence of Jervis Bay although he did not name it. At that time a fresh gale blew up from the southwest and Cook could not take a closer look without beating up, which would have taken more time than he was willing to spare.

With the gale behind them the next day, Cook made good progress and attempted another landing near present day Bulli, putting off in the yawl accompanied by Joseph Banks (1743-1820), Dr Daniel Solander (1733-1782) and Tupaia, his interpreter, at a place where four or five natives gathered near the shore. Unfortunately the natives disappeared as the boat came near and no landing could be made because of the surf. That evening there was no wind and the "Endeavour" drifted within two km of the shore inside a line of breakers, which caused some concern. Fortunately a light breeze came off the land, which carried them out of danger. At daylight next day on April 29th, they sighted a large bay and entered it that afternoon, which he later named Botany Bay.

Cook landed at Kurnell, on the southern bank of Botany Bay, at what is now Silver Beach, and his arrival marked the beginning of Britain's interest in Australia and in the eventual colonisation of the new found 'southern continent'.[12] Initially the name 'Stingrays Harbour' was used by Cook and other journal keepers on his expedition, for the plentiful number of stingrays they caught,[13] a name which was also recorded on the Admiralty charts.[14] Cook's log for the 6th May 1770 records...

"The great quantity of these sort of fish found in this place occasioned my giving it the name of Stingrays Harbour". However, in the journal prepared later from his log, Cook wrote instead: (sic) "The great quantity of plants Mr. Banks and Dr. Solander found in this place occasioned my giving it the name of ~~Botanist~~ Botany Bay".[15,16]

Two Aboriginal men came down to the boat and Cook's party attempted to communicate their desire for water and threw gifts of beads and nails ashore. The two Aboriginals continued to oppose the landing and Cook fired a warning shot. One responded by throwing a rock, and Cook fired on them with small shot, wounding one of them in the leg. The crew then landed, and the Aboriginals threw two spears before Cook fired another round of small shot, when they retreated. The landing party found several children in nearby huts, and left some beads and other gifts with them. The landing party collected 40 to 50 spears and other artefacts.[17,18,19]

Cook and his crew remained at Botany Bay for a week, collecting water, timber, fodder, botanical specimens and explored the surrounding area. The indigenous inhabitants observed the Europeans closely, but generally retreated whenever they approached. Cook's party made several attempts to establish relations with the native people, but they showed

Painting of the English First Fleet in Table Bay at Cape Town, South Africa in late 1787, by Robert Dodd.

The principal cargo of the First Fleet was convicts. Above Black-eyed Sue, and Sweet Poll of Plymouth take leave of their lovers, who were being transported to Botany Bay in 1792.

no interest in the food and gifts the Europeans offered, and occasionally threw spears as an apparent warning.[20,21]

While Cook's chart of the southeast coast shows few major errors, it is interesting that nowhere in his original papers did he refer to the land as New South Wales. The first mention of that name appears in the account of Cooks voyage written-up by Dr John Hawksworth LLD (1715-1773), the officially appointed editor. At that time the map of the known world already showed a New Britain, New England, New Scotland, New Ireland and even a New North Wales, so Hawksworth apparently chose New South Wales as the best of what was left.

Transportation Beyond The Seas

Banishment or forced exile from a society has been used as a punishment since at least the 5th century BC in ancient Greece. The practice of banishment reached its height in the British Empire during the 18th and 19th centuries.[22] Penal transportation not only deterred crime, but removed the offender from society, mostly permanently, and was seen as being more merciful than capital punishment. This method was used for criminals, debtors, military and political prisoners. Penal transportation was also used as a method of colonization as from the earliest days of English colonial schemes, new settlements beyond the seas were seen as a way of alleviating domestic social problems committed by criminals and the poor, and at the same time it increased the colonial labour force, for the overall benefit of the new colony and the realm.[23]

Following the introduction of the Transportation Act into the House of Commons (1717), by the Whig government in 1717, transportation was legitimised as a punishment.[24] During an era of great inflexibility persons convicted of the most inconsequential of misdemeanors and crimes, saw offenders being commonly sentenced to 'transportation beyond the seas.' But where were these convicts sent and what purpose was fulfilled by transporting them to other destinations around the world? The story that follows explores why the colony of New South Wales was chosen as a prison, how that immense continent was explored and gradually became their new home.

After Cook departed from Botany Bay in 1770, it took 18 long years for the British to return. But why did they bother? What was it that motivated them to return to a place so foreign, destitute, and so very far away?

All the available evidence points to Botany Bay on the east coast of New South Wales as being selected for settlement for two main reasons. First and most important, was the need to establish a base in the Pacific as a strategic imperitive to counter French expansion;[25] and second, the American Revolution brought an abrupt end to the transportation of convicts to North America.[26]

John Montagu (1718-1792), the 4th Earl of Sandwich, together with the President of the Royal Society Sir Joseph Banks, the eminent scientist who had accompanied Lt. James Cook on his 1770 voyage, were among the first to advocate the establishment of a British colony at Botany Bay.[27,28] Under the guidance of Banks, American loyalist James Matra (1746-1806) accepted an offer to assist with "A Proposal for Establishing a Settlement in New South Wales", which was published on the 24th August 1783. Matra developed a set of reasons for a colony composed of American Loyalists, and Chinese and South Sea Islanders, but not convicts.[29] The final decision to establish a colony in New South Wales was made by Thomas Townshend (1733-1800), otherwise known as 1st Viscount Sydney, who was then the Secretary of State for the British Home Office.[30]

The First Fleet (1788)

Under the leadership of Capt. Arthur Phillip (1738-1814), who was also appointed the honour of being the very first governor of the fledgling colony, the 'First Fleet' left from Portsmouth, England on 13 May 1787.[31] En route they stopped at Rio de Janeiro in June,

'Arrival of the First Fleet at Botany Bay, New South Wales', on 18th January 1788, watercolour by Charles Gore (SLNSW 826105).

TOP: "HMS Sirius" and the convoy working in to Botany Bay, with "HMS Supply" and the Agents Division already in the Bay, on the 21st January 1788, by William Bradley (Drawings from his journal `A Voyage to New South Wales, 1802' (Mitchell Library - Safe 1/14 (412997)]). ABOVE (Left): The 'First Fleet' in Sydney Cove, 27th January 1788. (Right): Having dropped anchor after seven months at sea, the ships prepare to unload (artists unknown).

and again at Table Bay off the Cape of Good Hope to take on supplies in October, before Phillip transferred to the "HMAT Supply" on the 25th November 1787. Together with "Alexander", "Friendship" and "Scarborough", the fastest ships in the fleet, which were carrying most of the male convicts, "Supply" hastened ahead to prepare for the arrival of the rest. Phillip intended to select a suitable location, find good water, clear the ground and perhaps even have some huts and other structures erected before the others arrived. This was a planned move, discussed with the Home Office and the Admiralty prior to the Fleet's departure.[32] However, this "flying squadron" reached Botany Bay only hours before the rest of the Fleet, so no preparatory work was possible.[33] "Supply" reached Botany Bay on the 18th January 1788; the three fastest transports in the advance group arrived on the 19th January; and the slower ships, including "Sirius", arrived on the 20th January.[34] Although

ABOVE (Left): 'The Founding of Australia by Capt. Arthur Phillip, R.N. at Sydney Cove, 26th January 1788.' (Original oil sketch by Algernon Talmage R.A., 1937). (Right): With no time to waste, the camp was laid out, trees were felled and supplies brought ashore (artist unknown).

Phillip's initial instructions were to establish the colony at Botany Bay, he was authorised to establish the colony elsewhere if necessary.[35]

It was quickly realised that Botany Bay did not live up to the glowing account that Cook had provided.[36] The bay was open and unprotected, the water was too shallow to allow the ships to anchor close to the shore, fresh water was scarce, and the soil was poor.[37] First contact was made with the local indigenous people, the Eora, who seemed curious but suspicious of the newcomers. The area was studded with enormously strong trees. When the convicts tried to cut these down, their tools broke and the tree trunks had to be blasted out of the ground with gunpowder. The primitive huts built for the officers and officials quickly collapsed in rainstorms. The marines developed a habit of getting drunk and not guarding the convicts properly, whilst their commander Major Robert Ross (c.1740-1794), drove Phillip to despair with his arrogant and lazy attitude. Crucially, Phillip worried that his fledgling colony was exposed to attack from those described as 'Aborigines' or from foreign powers.

On the morning of the 21st January, Phillip and a party which included Capt. John Hunter (1737-1821), departed from Botany Bay in three small boats to explore other bays to the north. Phillip quickly discovered that a natural harbour, about 12 kilometres to the north, would be an excellent site for a colony with sheltered anchorages, fresh water and fertile soil. Cook had seen and named the opening Port Jackson, but had not entered it. Phillip's initial impressions of the harbour were recorded in a letter he sent to England lauding "the finest harbour in the world, in which a thousand sail of the line may ride in the most perfect security." The party returned to Botany Bay on the 23rd January.[38]

On the morning of the 24th January, the party was startled when two French ships, the "Astrolabe" and the "Boussole", were seen just outside Botany Bay. This was a scientific expedition led by Jean-François de La Pérouse (1741-c.1788). The French had expected to find a thriving colony where they could repair ships and restock supplies, not a newly arrived fleet of convicts considerably more poorly provisioned than themselves.[39] There was some cordial contact between the French and British officers, but Phillip and La Pérouse never actually met. The French ships remained until the 10th March before setting sail on their return voyage to France. However, they were never seen again and were later discovered to have been shipwrecked off the coast of Vanikoro in the present-day Solomon Islands.[40]

TOP (Left): 'Old Sydney Town' in 1789, drawn by Granger. (Right): 'Early Sydney Town' in 1796, drawn by Augustus Theodore.
ABOVE: The camp is laid out at Sydney Cove, 1788 (artist unknown).

Western view of Sydney Cove, c.1797, by Edward Dayes.

On the 26th January 1788, the fleet weighed anchor and sailed north for Port Jackson.[41] The site selected for the anchorage had deep water close to the shore, was sheltered, and had a small stream flowing into it. Phillip named it Sydney Cove, after Lord Sydney, the British Home Secretary.[42] This date is celebrated as Australia Day, marking the beginning of British and European settlement,[43] while the British flag was planted and formal possession was annexed. This was done by Phillip and some officers and marines from "Supply", with the remainder of her crew and the convicts observing from on board ship. The remaining ships of the fleet did not arrive at Sydney Cove until later that day.[44] Writer and art critic Robert Hughes popularized the idea in his 1986 book "The Fatal Shore" that an orgy occurred upon the unloading of the convicts, though more modern historians regard this as untrue, since the first reference to any such indiscretions is as recent as 1963.[45,46]

In the beginning the geographical features of Sydney and adjoining country, on which now stands the City of Sydney, consisted of a picturesque panorama of water, with hills clothed with dense scrub. Sydney Cove was at the head of the harbour, into which flowed a pure stream of fresh water they called 'the Tank Stream'. Eleven vessels, carrying not more during than 3800 tons aggregate, dropped anchor at this site in January 1788. The secretary to the governor, David Collins Esq. (1756-1810), one of the earliest chroniclers, reported:[47]

> "The confusion that ensued during the landing will not be wondered at, when it is considered that every man stepped from a boat literally into a wood. Parties of people were everywhere heard and seen variously employed, some in clearing the ground for different encampments, others pitching tents or bringing up some stores as were more immediately wanted; and the spot which had so recently been the abode of silence and tranquility was now changed to that of noise, clamour, and confusion."
>
> *David Collins Esq., Judge Advocate*

Collins went on to provide some interesting figures at the start of the colony:

"A south view of Sydney Cove, New South Wales" from an original picture in the possession of Isaac Clementson Esq., from a picture painted at the colony, by Edward Dayes.

"On 1st May, 1788, the number of live stock in Australia was 1 stallion, 3 mares, 3 colts, 2 bulls, 5 cows, 29 sheep, 19 goats, 49 hogs, 29 small pigs, 5 rabbits, 18 turkeys, 29 geese, 35 ducks, 142 fowls, 87 chickens." In the 'Illustrated London Library', an important publication of those days reported: "In April, 1788, two bulls and four cows wandered away from the 'pickpocket' herdsmen in the new settlement of New South Wales into the bush and were lost. They were undoubtedly the first discoverers of the several gorges leading down from the coast ranges to the sea."

EARLY EXPLORATIONS OF THE SOUTH COAST

Although Governor Phillip and his successor, Major Francis Grose (1758-1814) were too concerned with events in the near vicinity of Port Jackson to spare effort in exploring the southeast coast, some information did trickle in, so that as early as August 1794, David Collins apparently thought there was nothing unusual in a Mr. Melville going on a fishing (sealing?) trip to Jervis and Bateman Bays. The latter had been named by Cook, while Jervis Bay was discovered and named in August of 1791 by Lt. Richard Bowen (1761-1797).

Lt. Bowen & Capt. Weatherhead (1791)

Governor Phillip finished his term and embarked for England on 11th December, 1792, and settled at Bath on a pension granted by the British Government of £500 per year, which was where he died in 1814. Next to make signifant discoveries was Lt. Richard Bowen of the "Atlantic", a convict transport of the Third Fleet, who made an eye-draft of Jervis Bay and named Bowen Island to the south of the entrance in 1791. He found deep water and a good anchorage and named the bay in honour of Admiral Sir Richard John Jervis (1735-1823), later Lord St Vincent, under whom he had served.

Later that same year Captain Weatherhead of the "Matilda" entered Jervis Bay for minor repairs and made a second eye-draft, reporting "an exceedingly good anchorage with room for the largest ships to work in or out with great safety." For three years after

Governor Phillip's departure the settlement was practically a military despotism, but it is likely that unknown sealers and whalers visited the South Coast from that date forward. The government first devolved upon Major Francis Grose, and secondly on Capt. William Paterson (1755-1810), both senior officers of the New South Wales Corps, as Lt-Governor, where incompetency and militarism were blazed on the face of their every act.[48]

The official notification of the appointment of Capt. John Hunter, R.N., as Governor of New South Wales appeared in the "London Gazette" on the 5th February, 1794, and the commission passed the Great Seal on the following day.[49]

George Bass & Voyages of "Tom Thumb" (1796)

Dr. George Bass (1771-1803) attended Boston Grammar School and later trained in medicine at the hospital in Boston, Lincolnshire. At the age of 18, he was accepted as a member of the Company of Surgeons in London, and in 1794 he joined the Royal Navy as a surgeon. He arrived in Sydney aboard "HMS Reliance" on 7th September 1795.[50] Also on that voyage was his surgeon's assistant William Martin, Matthew Flinders (1774-1814), Capt. John Hunter, and Bennelong (c.1764-1813), who was returning to Sydney after five years in Britain. Bass had brought with him on the "Reliance" a small boat with an 8-foot (2.4m) keel and 5-foot (1.5m) beam, which he called the "Tom Thumb" on account of its size. The first "Tom Thumb" voyage occurred between the 26th October and 5th November 1795, which included Bass, Flinders and Bass's servant William Martin, as they explored the Georges River further upstream than had been done previously by the colonists. Their reports on their return led to the settlement of Banks' Town.[51]

LEFT: M2. Map of the journey of the "Sydney Cove" survivors in 1797. RIGHT (Top): 'Native hunters spearing fish in a canoe', by A.H. Fulwood. (Above): A number of the survivors of the "Sydney Cove" were murdered by Aboriginals.

Dr George Bass with his companions in the "Tom Thumb" in 1796, painted by John Charles Allcot.

On the 24th March 1796 the same party embarked on a second voyage in a slightly larger boat with the same crew, which they called the "Tom Thumb II."[52,53] During this trip they explored Port Hacking and sailed down the coast to Lake Illawarra, and named Tom Thumb Lagoon. Amongst other discoveries this voyage demonstrated to the colonists that indigenous Australians from different parts of the country spoke very different languages.[54] Later that year Bass discovered good land near Prospect Hill, and found lost cattle brought out with the First Fleet, but failed in an attempt to cross the Blue Mountains. It was on this journey that Matthew Flinders and George Bass feared for their safety when they encountered the fearsome native Dilba.

The "Sydney Cove" Survivors (1797)

Little official notice was reported about the South Coast until in 1797, three survivors from the wreck of the "Sydney Cove" were rescued by a fishing boat to the south of Botany Bay. Under Captain Guy Hamilton, the "Sydney Cove" with a crew of nearly 50, left Calcutta with merchandise for Port Jackson on the 10th November 1796, intending to follow the usual route south of Van Diemen's Land (Tasmania). They ran into continuous bad weather and developed a serious leak, becoming so waterlogged that they had to beach the ship on an isle in the Furneaux group in mid February 1797, at a place still called Preservation Island. They were fortunate that all made it safely ashore with provisions and arms as well as the ship's longboat. The next fortnight was engaged in preparing for a voyage to Port Jackson to seek help.

On 28 February 1797, leaving about 30 survivors with the wreckage, a party of 17 men set off in the ship's longboat to reach help at Sydney, which was some 400 nautical miles away. The party was led by first mate Hugh Thompson, and included William Clark (the supercargo), three European seamen, and twelve Indian lascars (sailors). But ill fortune struck again when the longboat was wrecked on the mainland at the northern end of Ninety Mile Beach in Victoria. Their only hope of survival was to walk along the coast all the way to Sydney, a distance of over 800 kilometres.

They had few provisions and no ammunition, and fatigue and hunger lessened their number as they marched. Along the way they encountered various aboriginal people, some friendly, some not. The last of the party to die on the march was killed by a man named Dilba and his people near Hat Hill, from a clan that had a reputation around Port Jackson for being ferocious.

By May of 1797, the three survivors of the march, William Clark, sailor John Bennet and one lascar had made it as far as the cove at Wattamolla and on the 15th May 1797, with their strength nearly at an end, they were able to signal a fishing boat, which took them on to Sydney.[55] On the march, Clark had noted coal in the cliffs at what is now called Coalcliff between Sydney and Wollongong, which was the second instance of coal being discovered in Australia.[56]

Bass & Flinders (1797)

On the 3rd December 1797, this time without Flinders, inthe same open whaleboat with a crew of just six, Bass sailed to Cape Howe, the farthest point of south-eastern Australia. From here he went westwards along what is now the coast of the Gippsland region of Victoria, to Western Port, almost as far as the entrance to Port Phillip, on the north shore of which is the site of present-day Melbourne. His belief that a strait separated the mainland from Van Diemen's Land, was backed up by his astute observation of the rapid tide and the long south-western swell at Wilson's Promontory.

On this voyage Bass visited the Kiama area and made many notes on its botanical complexity and the amazing natural phenomenon they called 'the Blowhole', noting the volcanic geology around the waterspout, which contributed much to its understanding. The journey was highly regarded at the time as one of the great feats of seafaring. The whaleboat was left on the shores of Sydney Harbour and was regarded, for many years as something of an icon by the locals. French naturalist Francois Peron recorded that "some snuff-boxes made from the wood of its keel form relics of which the possessors are as proud as they are careful".

The whaleboat voyage, along with Flinders' separate voyage to the Furneaux Islands on the "Francis" convinced the pair that Tasmania was an island, and they set out to prove their theory on the 7th October 1798, in the sloop "Norfolk", by attempting a circumnavigation

LEFT: Dr George Bass in the whaleboat they called "Tom Thumb II", which navigated to Western Port Bay in Victoria, in December 1797. RIGHT: In 1798, Dr George Bass and Lt. Matthew Flinders circumnavigated Van Diemans Land in the "Norfolk".

Governors of the Colony of New South Wales, 1788-1846

Captain Arthur Phillip, R.N.
Governor of NSW, 26 Jan 1788 - 10 Dec 1792.

Captain John Hunter, R.N.
Governor of NSW, 11 Jan 1795 - 27 Sep 1800.

Captain Philip Gidley King, R.N.
Governor of NSW, 28 Sep 1800 - 12 Aug 1806.

Captain William Bligh, R.N.
Governor of NSW, 13 Aug 1806 - 26 Jan 1808.

Major-General Lachlan Macquarie, R.A.
Governor of NSW, 1 Jan 1810 - 1 Dec 1821.

Major-General Sir Thomas Brisbane, R.A.
Governor of NSW, 1 Dec 1821 - 1 Dec 1825.

Lt.-General Ralph Darling, R.A.
Governor of NSW, 19 Dec 1825 - 22 Oct 1831.

Major-General Sir Richard Bourke, R.A.
Governor of NSW, 3 Dec 1831 - 5 Dec 1837.

Major Sir George Gipps, R.E.
Governor of NSW, 24 Feb 1838 - 11 Jul 1846.

of Van Diemen's Land. In the course of this voyage Bass visited the estuary of the Derwent River, found and named by Captain John Hayes in 1793,⁵⁷ where the future city of Hobart would be founded on the strength of his report in 1803. When the two returned to Sydney, Flinders recommended to Governor John Hunter that the passage between Van Diemen's Land and the mainland be called 'Bass Strait'.

> "This was no more than a just tribute to my worthy friend and companion," Flinders wrote, "for the extreme dangers and fatigues he had undergone, in first entering it in a whaleboat, and to the correct judgement he had formed, from various indications, of the existence of a wide opening between Van Diemen's Land and New South Wales."
>
> *Mathew Flinders*

The summer of 1798-9 was remarkable for one of the colony's first protracted droughts on record. For ten months scarcely a shower of rain fell. The drought finally ended with a disastrous flood in the Hawkesbury River, of which local weather conditions gave no warning. The banks were "overflowing with vast rapidity." The Government store and all the provisions it contained were swept away. The river was more than fifty feet above its common level, and the torrent was so powerful that it carried all before it. Settler's houses and furniture, live stock and provisions were alike swept away, and "the whole country looked like an immense ocean." About this time, Captain Hunter, who had taken up the governorship from August 7th, 1795, had a survey made of the coast south of Botany Bay, and the Shoalhaven River was also explored and named.⁵⁸

Lt. James Grant (1800)

The original "Lady Nelson" was built at Deptford, in England in 1799, for service to the Transport Office on the River Thames. She was designed with a sliding keel (centre

"This plate of the "Lady Nelson" was respectfully dedicated to Capt. John Schank of the Royal Navy, by his obediant servant Lt. James Grant, R.N."

Western view of Sydney Cove looking at the Government windmill in 1804, painted by John Eyre.

board), a device invented by Captain John Schank of the Royal Navy. On completion she was selected for exploration services in the colony of New South Wales and sailed for Port Jackson on the 18th March 1800 under the command of Lt. James Grant (1772-1833). As a man, Grant was upright and sincere with a mind of his own, as well as being a gallant and skilful officer.[59]

A brig of 60 tons, she carried a crew comprising the commander, two mates and 12 seaman. As she left the River Thames sailors on nearby ships ridiculed her because of her size and shape, calling her, as she sailed past, 'His Majesty's Tinderbox'. At Portsmouth on the 9th February 1800 she was fitted out with four brass carriage guns, three to four pounders, in addition to the two guns already on board. Because of the heavy load she was carrying, the "Lady Nelson" sat very low in the water, having only two feet nine inches of freeboard amidships. The ship finally left Portsmouth on 17th March 1800 as part of an East Indian convoy.

After leaving the convoy on 23rd March, the ship sailed on alone and arrived at St. Jago, Cape Verde Islands on the 13th April 1800, where two of the crew made off with one of the ship's boats. They were, however, soon captured by the Portuguese and brought back to the ship "both riding the one ass." Dissension and unrest amongst the crew had been stirred up by the second mate and Grant sent him back to England, with two young Portuguese men being signed on as replacement crew.

As she sailed into Table Bay, South Africa on the 8th July 1800, the crew of "Lady Nelson" saw a convoy of ships that had left England at the same time. These ships had suffered heavy damage from rough weather and yet the "Lady Nelson" had survived the journey without mishap. It was here that Grant received dispatches from William Bentinck, 3rd Duke of Portland (1738-1809), advising him of the discovery of a straight between New South Wales and Van Diemen's Land, and that he was to sail through it on his way to Port Jackson, instead of sailing around Van Diemen's Land.

On leaving the Cape on 7th October 1800, the ship took on board a Dr. Brandt, ship's surgeon who had been wrecked at Delagoe Bay some years earlier. Grant also secured a ship's carpenter for the journey, but had to refuse many offers from young seaman who wished to join the "Lady Nelson" on her journey of discovery. One of these was John Johnston (aka Jorgen Jorgenson, 1780-1841) and his is a fascinating tale of adventure,[60] which was later tied to the colony of New South Wales. However, Grant had to refuse a disappointed Johnston, and was obliged instead to take a fellow Dane and convict, who had to be transported to Port Jackson.

At daybreak on 3rd December 1800 in latitude 38° south, the crew first sighted the land of New Holland, near present day Mount Gambier. A few days later she sailed through the straight, becoming the first ship to sail from west to east through what was later named 'Bass Strait', charting the then unknown coastline. The "Lady Nelson" entered the heads at Port Jackson at six in the evening on the 16th December, after a passage of seventy-one days from Cape Town.[61] Grant spent little more than twelve months in Australian waters, but he played quite an important role as an explorer, being the first commander to traverse Bass Strait from west to east and to explore the Hunter River.

While skilled and determined explorers were expanding the boundaries of knowledge and British influence along the South Coast of New South Wales, events back in the British Isles were reshaping the empire in a very different way. Efforts to reduce British control, particularly in Ireland, culminated in the Act of Union of 1801, which merged the 'Kingdom of Ireland' with the 'Kingdom of Great Britain' to form the 'United Kingdom of Great Britain and Ireland.' This unification was largely a response to the 1798 Irish Rebellion, an event that undoubtedly impacted the ancestors of John and Mary Frawley.

Although John Frawley's story had yet to unfold, his family's history became deeply intertwined with the Shoalhaven, Illawarra, and Maneroo regions on the South Coast of New South Wales. To fully understand their journey, it is essential to first explore how this part of Australia was discovered and developed during the colony's first 50 years. For a timeline of exploration on the South Coast of New South Wales, see Appendix A.

References

1. Kippis, Andrew (1788). Narrative of the voyages round the world, performed by Captain James Cook; with an account of his life during the previous and intervening periods. Chapter 2. Archived from the original on 3 October 2018. Retrieved 3 October 2018.
2. Collingridge, Vanessa (2003). Captain Cook: The Life, Death and Legacy of History's Greatest Explorer. Ebury Press. ISBN 978-0-09-188898-5., p. 95.
3. Rigby, Nigel & van der Merwe, Pieter (2002). Captain Cook in the Pacific. National Maritime Museum, London. ISBN 978-0-948065-43-9., p. 30.
4. Beazley, Charles Raymond (1911). "Cook, James" . In Chisholm, Hugh (ed.). Encyclopædia Britannica. Vol. 7 (11th ed.). Cambridge University Press. p. 71.
5. Beaglehole, J. C., ed. (1968). The Journals of Captain James Cook on His Voyages of Discovery. Vol. I: The Voyage of the Endeavour 1768–1771. Cambridge University Press. OCLC 223185477., p. cix.
6. "The Sydney Morning Herald". National Library of Australia. 2 May 1931. p. 12. Retrieved 4 September 2012.
7. "BBC – History – Captain James Cook". Archived from the original on 16 October 2014. Retrieved 31 July 2017.
8. "Secret Instructions to Captain Cook, 30 June 1768" (PDF). National Archives of Australia. Archived (PDF) from the original on 27 April 2020. Retrieved 3 September 2011.
9. Salmond, Anne (1991). Two worlds : first meetings between Maori and Europeans, 1642–1772. Auckland, N.Z.: Viking. ISBN 0-670-83298-7. OCLC 26545658.
10. Arthur R. Hinks, "Nautical time and civil date", The Geographical Journal, 86 (1935) 153–157.
11. Pleaden, Ronald F. (1990). 'Coastal Explorers,' Milton/Ulladulla & District Historical Society, p.4.
12. Cook, James; Hawkesworth, John (1773). "Entrance of Endeavour River in New South Wales. Botany Bay in New South Wales" (Map). David Rumsey Historical Map Collection. State Library of Queensland. Retrieved 7 September 2012.
13. Wales, Geographical Name Board of New South. "Extract – Geographical Names Board of NSW". gnb.nsw.gov.au. Archived from the original on 7 November 2016. Retrieved 7 November 2016.
14. Beaglehole J. C., ed. (1968), op. cit., p. ccix.
15. Beaglehole J. C., ed. (1968), op. cit., p. ccix.
16. The strikethrough is in the Cook's original, reflecting a change of mind sometime after leaving the Bay in 1770.
17. Cook's Journal: Daily Entries, 29 April 1770". southseas.nla.gov.au. South Seas. Retrieved 25 October 2019 [https://webarchive.nla.gov.au/awa/20110403094436/http://southseas.nla.gov.au/journals/cook/17700429.html].
18. Blainey, Geoffrey (2020). Captain Cook's Epic Voyage: the strange quest for a missing continent, Viking (Australia). pp. 141-43.
19. Smith, Keith Vincent (2009). "Confronting Cook". Electronic British Library Journal (2009) [https://bl.iro.bl.uk/concern/articles/9740df81-e9c9-4776-b2fe-

5c5b862bacdb?locale=en].
20. FitzSimons, Peter (2019). 'James Cook : the story behind the man who mapped the world'. Sydney, NSW. ISBN 978-0-7336-4127-5. OCLC 1109734011.
21. Blainey (2020). op. cit., pp. 146-57.
22. Maxwell-Stewart, Hamish & Watkins, Emma (n.d.). "Transportation". Digital Panopticon. Digital Panopticon Project. Archived from the original on 8 January 2019. Retrieved 7 February 2019.
23. Ibid.
24. Beattie, J.M. (1986), Crime and the Courts in England 1660–1800, Oxford: Oxford University Press, p. 503.[ISBN 0-19-820058-7].
25. Cameron-Ash, Margaret (2021). Beating France to Botany Bay: The race to found Australia. Balmain: Quadrant Books. ISBN 9780648996125.
26. "Why were convicts transported to Australia". Sydney Living Museums. Archived from the original on 2 December 2013. Retrieved 16 December 2013.
24. Frost, Alan; Moutinho, Isabel (1995). The precarious life of James Mario Matra : voyager with Cook, American loyalist, servant of empire. The Miegunyah Press. ISBN 9780522846676., p. 110.
28. Gascoigne, John (1998). Science in the service of empire : Joseph Banks, the British state and the uses of science in the age of revolution. Cambridge, UK. p. 187. ISBN 0-521-55069-6. OCLC 39524807. Archived from the original on 18 July 2021. Retrieved 18 July 2021.
29. Carter, Harold B. (1988). "Banks, Cook and the Century Natural History Tradition". In Delamothe, Tony; Bridge, Carl (eds.). Interpreting Australia: British Perceptions of Australia since 1788. London: Sir Robert Menzies Centre for Australian Studies. pp. 4–23. Archived from the original on 29 May 2014. Retrieved 18 July 2021.
30. George Burnett Barton (1889). "History of New South Wales From the Records, Volume I – Governor Phillip – Chapter 1.4". Project Gutenberg of Australia. Charles Potter, Government Printer. Retrieved 25 April 2019.
31. Project Gutenberg Australia. "The First Fleet". Retrieved 24 November 2013, [https://gutenberg.net.au/first-fleet.html].
32. Frost, Alan (2012). 'The First Fleet: the real story'. Collingwood: Black Inc. ISBN 9781863955614., p. 174.
33. Frost, Alan (2012). op. cit., p.175.
34. "Timeline-1788". The World Upside Down: Australia 1788–1830. National Library of Australia. 2000. Retrieved 27 May 2006.
35. "Governor Phillip's Instructions 25 April 1787 (UK)". Museum of Australian Democracy. Retrieved 24 November 2013 [https://www.foundingdocs.gov.au/item-sdid-68.html].
36. Frost, Alan (2012). op. cit., p.177.
37. Parker, Derek (2009). 'Arthur Phillip: Australia's First Governor.' Warriewood: Woodslane P. ISBN 9781921203992., p.113.
38. Parker, Derek (2009). op. cit., pp.115–116.
39. Parker, Derek (2009). op. cit., p.118.
40. John Dunmore, "Introduction", The Journal of Jean-François de Galaup de La Pérouse, Vol. I, Hakluyt Society, 1994, pp. ccxix–ccxxii.
41. Project Gutenberg Australia. "The First Fleet", op. cit.
42. Parker, Derek (2009). op. cit., pp.115–116.
43. "About Our National Day". National Australia Day Council. Retrieved 25 November 2013.
44. Hill, David (2008). 1788: The brutal truth of the First Fleet: the biggest single migration the world had ever seen. North Sydney: Heinemann. ISBN 9781741667974.
45. Hughes, Robert (1986). 'The Fatal Shore'. Alfred A. Knopf. p. 88-89. ISBN 9780099448549.
46. Eamon Evans (November 2015). Great Australian Urban Legends. Affirm Press. p. 116-17. ISBN 9781925475241.
47. McCaffrey, Frank (1922). 'The History Of Illawarra And Its Pioneers,' John Sands Ltd, Sydney, p.10.
48. Pleaden, Ronald F. (1990). op. cit., p.10.
49. McCaffrey, Frank (1922). op. cit., p.11.
50. Scott, Ernest (1914). The Life of Captain Matthew Flinders, RN. Sydney: Angus & Robertson. p. 100.
51. Scott, Ernest (1914). op.cit., p. 86.
52. Flinders, Matthew. 'Narrative of expeditions along the coast of New South Wales, for the further discovery of its harbours from the year 1795 to 1799'. Archived from the original on 11 July 2011.
53. The Journal of Daniel Paine 1794–1797, p.39.
54. Museums Victoria, Collections, George Bass, Surgeon & Navigator (circa 1771-1803), [https://collections.museumsvictoria.com.au/articles/10413].
55. Wikipedia - Sydney Cove (1796 ship). [https://en.wikipedia.org/wiki/Sydney_Cove_(1796_ship).
56. "Timeline 1 (1791–1862)". www.illawarracoal.com. Retrieved 12 November 2015.
57. Roe, Margriet (1966). "Hayes, Sir John (1768–1831)". Australian Dictionary of Biography. Melbourne University Press. ISSN 1833-7538. Retrieved 17 October 2013 – via National Centre of Biography, Australian National University.
58. McCaffrey, Frank (1922). op. cit., p.11-12.
59. "Lady Nelson", Tasmania [https://www.ladynelson.org.au/history/short-history]).
60. Wikipedia - "Jorgen Jorgensen" [https://en.wikipedia.org/wiki/Jørgen_Jørgensen].
61. Wikipedia - "HMS Lady Nelson" (1798) [https://en.wikipedia.org/wiki/HMS_Lady_Nelson_(1798)}.

Chapter Two

EXPLORERS OF THE SHOALHAVEN & ILLAWARRA

The story of John Frawley and his family is closely tied to the Shoalhaven, Illawarra, and Maneroo regions on the South Coast of New South Wales. To fully appreciate their journey, it's important to understand how this part of Australia was discovered and developed during the colony's first 50 years.

In the early years of white settlement, exploration south of Sydney was limited and primarily conducted by sea. Land-based expeditions were rare, as the colony's early Governors prioritized defense, self-sufficiency, and expansion westward and southwestward, especially in their efforts to cross the Blue Mountains. The South Coast, considered largely barren at the time, remained a lower priority for exploration. However, the early 19th century marked the first significant attempts to chart the regions directly south of Sydney.

Governor Philip Gidley King, 1800-1806.

Captain Philip Gidley King, R.N. (1758-1808), was invested with civil and military powers in New South Wales when he took up the duties as governor on the 28th September 1800, which he continued to hold until the 12th August 1806. But he was a weak man in many respects, as his power over certain members of the military authorities was such that they did much as they liked. King was nervous and frightened of troubles coming on him

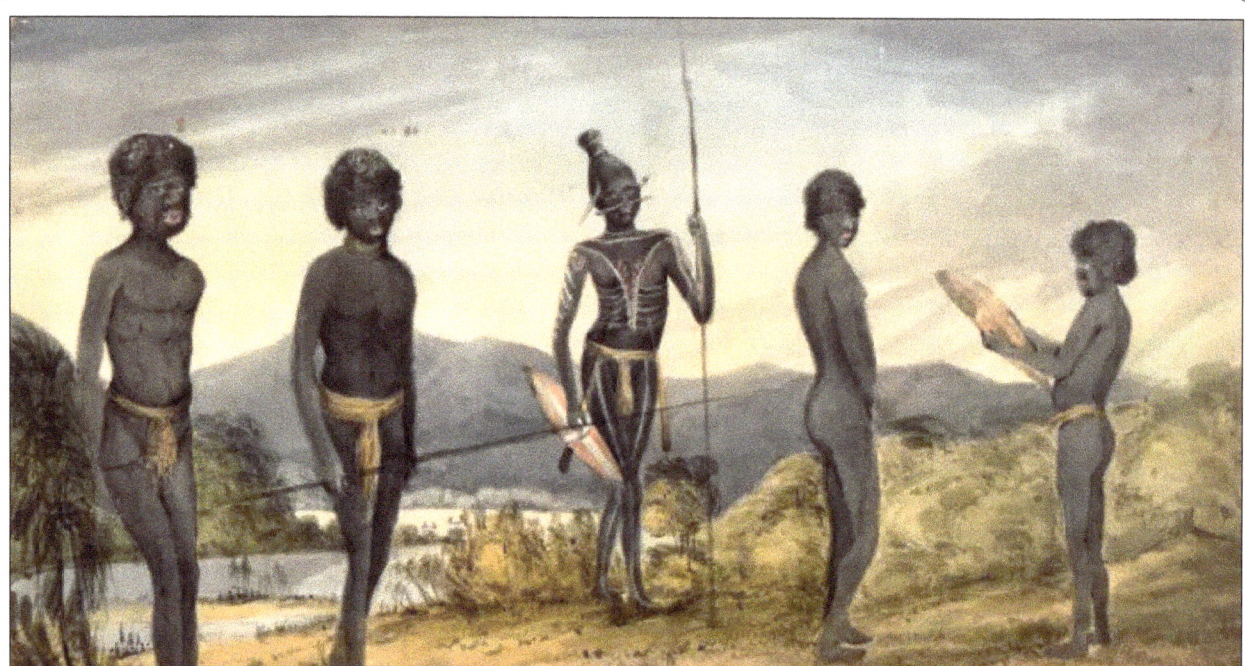
Aboriginals of the 'Hunter Region', as painted by James Wallis (State Library of NSW).

from within and from foreign parts. It was during his watch that a return of government held stock was conducted on 12th May 1804, "which included the holdings of five cattle stations of Parramatta, Toongabbie, Castle Hill, Seven Hills and Sydney that then comprised 17 bulls, 678 cows, 735 male calves, 672 female calves, 129 bullocks."[1]

Clash of Cultures

As the colony developed, so too did the number of vessels to Sydney increase, and some of these had reason to take shelter along the coast, which often involved unintended, but violent clashes with the Aborigines. These encounters often resulted in a collision of cultures between the technologically superior whites, and the innocent blacks, who like the kangaroos and koalas had been held captive and isolated in Australia since the land bridge to Asia had closed some 40,000 years previously.

One of the first of such clashes occurred in July of 1804, when the sloop "Contest" arrived in Sydney from Jervis Bay, with a report that the crew and a detachment of soldiers had been involved in a skirmish with the local Aborigines, with one native being killed.[2]

The next year brought news of the crew of the cutter "Nancy", which was wrecked to the south of Jervis Bay on the 18th April 1805. Eleven survivors reached that bay on the 20th April and guided by an Aborigine, they trekked overland to Sydney, whence they arrived on the 1st of May.[3]

In October of that year, after six persons had left from Sydney in a whaleboat making for Kings Island, a report was received of the spearing of a Mr Murrell by natives at Twofold Bay, with the killing of two natives there. The account given was as follows:[4]

"That everywhere along the coast the natives wore a menacing appearance, and manifested a wish to attack them. Upon making Twofold Bay, they percived a small group round a fire, who

> greeted them in a very friendly tone, but a flight of spears was soonafter thrown... with one of the weapons, most dangerously barbed, lodging in Mr Murrell's side. They made for the boat, leaving their inhuman assailants to express their joy of the barberous event by reechoed peals of mirth, and were soon out of reach. Unable to proceed for their destination they reversed their course, but could only reach Botany Bay, on account of contrary wind."

This was followed a month later by a report by Mr Rushworth, master of the "Fly", who received several spear wounds at Jervis Bay, and of Thomas Evans, who was killed.[5]

Then in January 1806, the sloop "George" was wrecked at Twofold Bay. After the vessel was beached a large party of Aborigines set the nearby grass on fire and threw spears, but were dispersed when Captain Birbeck and his men opened fire, killing several of them. A section of the crew later sailed to Sydney, whilst the remainder walked overland from Jervis Bay.[6] In April, further disagreeable accounts were received by the "Venus", another private colonial vessel, of the inimical disposition of the natives at Twofold Bay. The sealers were employed there in the hope of getting off the "George" or her iron-work, but they were obliged to act with the greatest caution for fear of assassination. The gang of 11 were soon attacked en-masse by a large group of natives, causing them to open fire and kill nine of their assailants, whereupon all the rest made off. "To intimidate them it was thought advisable to suspend those that fell on the limbs of trees, but before daylight the next morning they were taken down, and carried off."[7]

By May a report was received of the fate of some of the survivors of the "George" wrecked at Twofold Bay in January, who had travelled overland from Jervis Bay and were involved in a skirmish with the natives.[8]

> "About the 20th May, one of their party 'Yankey Cambell' went missing and had presumably fallen victim to native barbarity, with the white men later being attacked by a large group of Aboriginals on the beach, which was answered by musketry. The engagement continued with the intended victims of native animosity being rushed like a torrent, who fled to their boat of only 7 feet keel, which was only reached with extreme difficulty. Beyond the reach of their missiles,

'An Aboriginal Corroboree', painted by Samuel Elyard (1817-1910).

TOP (Left): The spearing of Governor Arthur Phillip by Willemering (c.1755 – c.1800), a man of the Eora people. This painting shows 'Capt. Henry Waterhouse endeavouring to break the spear after Governor Phillip was wounded… where the whale was cast on shore in Manly Cove on the 7th September 1790 (artist unknown). (Right): Aboriginals built gunyahs from bark, but in pursueing their nomadic lifestyle, they regularly moved on (artist unknown).
ABOVE: Aborigines resting by a camp fire near the mouth of the Hunter River, Newcastle, NSW, by Joseph Lycett (National Library of Australia).

> they watched as the stock were massacred and everything destroyed by their assailants, yet were thankful for their deliverance. They abandoned their boat at Jervis Bay and subsisted entirely on shellfish along the coast walk, but were assisted by two Sydney natives, which enabled them to complete their tedious and distressing travel in eight days."
>
> *Sydney Gazette & NSW Advertiser, 18 May 1806*

Another unfortunate incident was reported in 1808 when three of the crew of the colonial vessel "Fly", were murdered by Aborigines at Batemans Bay. The "Fly" had sailed for Kangaroo Island, but being overtaken by bad weather and contrary winds was obliged to take shelter at Batemans Bay, and to send on shore for water. The three unfortunate persons whose fate it was to fall under the barbarity of the natives, were sent on shore with a cask, but were confronted by a large group of natives. The three men quickly returned to their boat, but had no sooner put off from the shore than a flight of spears was thrown, which continued until all three fell from their oars. The natives immediately took and manned the boat, with a number of canoes preparing to attack the vessel, which only narrowly escaped their fury by cutting the cable and standing out to sea. The names of the murdered men were Charles Freeman, Thomas Bly and Robert Goodlet…[9] and relations with the Aborigines afterwards descended into a state of 'kill or be killed.'

Exploring the Shoalhaven

In the meantime, Governor King had despatched Capt. William Kent (1760-1812), with a number of labourers and ample provisions, to explore the coast as far south as the Shoalhaven. Captain Kent, of "HMS Buffalo", in company with James Meehan (1774-1826) returned on Sunday, 3rd March 1805, from a five week examination of the coast about Shoals Haven. After walking 18 miles they were fortunate to find a small boat lost in a gale of wind exactly at the place they wanted to make use of it, to trace the river 18 miles up when it became impassable. Unfortunately, they reported the entrance to the river was closed by a bar on which there is a constant surf.[10]

Following a stint at the Cape of Good Hope, George William Evans (1780-1852) was persuaded by Capt. Kent to go to New South Wales, and he arrived at Port Jackson in "HMS Buffalo" on 16 October 1802, where in August 1803 he was appointed acting surveyor-general. He commenced exploring and by September 1804 had discovered the Warragamba River, and penetrated upstream to the present site of Warragamba Dam.

Further troubles came upon the head of Governor King with droughts, cattle disease and floods. It is recorded that in the month of March, 1806, one of the heaviest floods occurred that up to that time had ever visited the Hawkesbury. It rained every day for a month, causing loss of life and property. The loss of property was estimated at £35,000, with several persons being drowned, and those who escaped with their lives had to face starvation.

LEFT: Lieutenant Kent explores the Shoalhaven in the "Anne" ('Ship News', The Sydney Gazette & NSW Advertiser, 10 March 1805, p.2). RIGHT: Mountain Pass from Jamberoo to Bong Bong, Illawarra, painted by Capt. Robert Marsh Westmacott.

'The Five Islands & Tom Thumb's Lagoon, Illawarra', painted by Capt. Robert Marsh Westmacott.

After 1800, ideas of settlement along the south east coast were temporarily shelved partly because of the unfavourable report furnished by George Bass and also at that time, the Hawkesbury and Hunter River districts provided enough land for expansion. Nevertheless, the government always had South Coast colonisation on its mind and by the end of 1804, Governor King was once again discussing the possibilities with London, writing to the Secretary of State, Lord Portland:

> "The next object of research will be the Shoalshaven, between this place and Port Jarvis."
>
> *Governor King, 6th January 1805*

Kent & Meehan at Shoalhaven (1805).

Almost immediately the acting Surveyor General, George Evans was instructed to carry out an investigation of the Shoalhaven with the following notice being published:

> "Acting Lieut. B. Kent of His Majesty's ship "Buffalo" and Mr. Evans, Surveyor, in the "Anne", Colonial cutter going to examine the entrance and course of the Shoal's Haven, 52 miles to the Southward of this place, are also detained by foul winds."
>
> *Sydney Gazette, 27th January 1805*

The notice was misleading as it is now known that Evans did not go, but instead sent his assistant James Meehan in his place. Meehan was at that time a convict on conditional pardon, and likely due to his lowly status, his name was ignored. The object of the expedition was the Shoalhaven River, not the Shoals Haven.

'Tom Thumb's Lagoon', painted by Capt. Robert Marsh Westmacott.

Lt. Kent and Meehan boarded the "Anne" on the 28th January 1805, but were unable to progress further than Botany Bay until the 4th February due to adverse winds. When they did arrive off the Shoalhaven River they were unable to enter due to the sandbar across the mouth and the heavy surf thrown up by the wind, whereupon the ship's boat was lost in the heavy seas. Kent continued south and entered Jervis Bay, where they spent several days putting the ship to rights after the rough passage, so it was not until the 11th February that Kent, Meehan and their small party of sailors landed near present day Callala Beach, and embarked on their expedition to the Shoalhaven River.

They travelled a track north, reaching the southern bank of the Crookhaven near Billy's Islands, where the river opened into a lagoon, with Meehan describing the country in derogatory terms as "sandy scrub, swampy, and bad ground". Walking north, by extraordinary good fortune they found the boat that had been lost at sea the previous week, which was still in a usable condition. The boat had been "hauled up by the natives and covered with bark exactly at the place where they wanted to make use of it." This enabled them to row out of the Crookhaven, along the coast and into the Shoalhaven River, thus renewing their original goal.[11]

During the next three weeks they explored the river system, assessing the possibilities of future farming and described the north bank of the Shoalhaven as "apparently good soil,

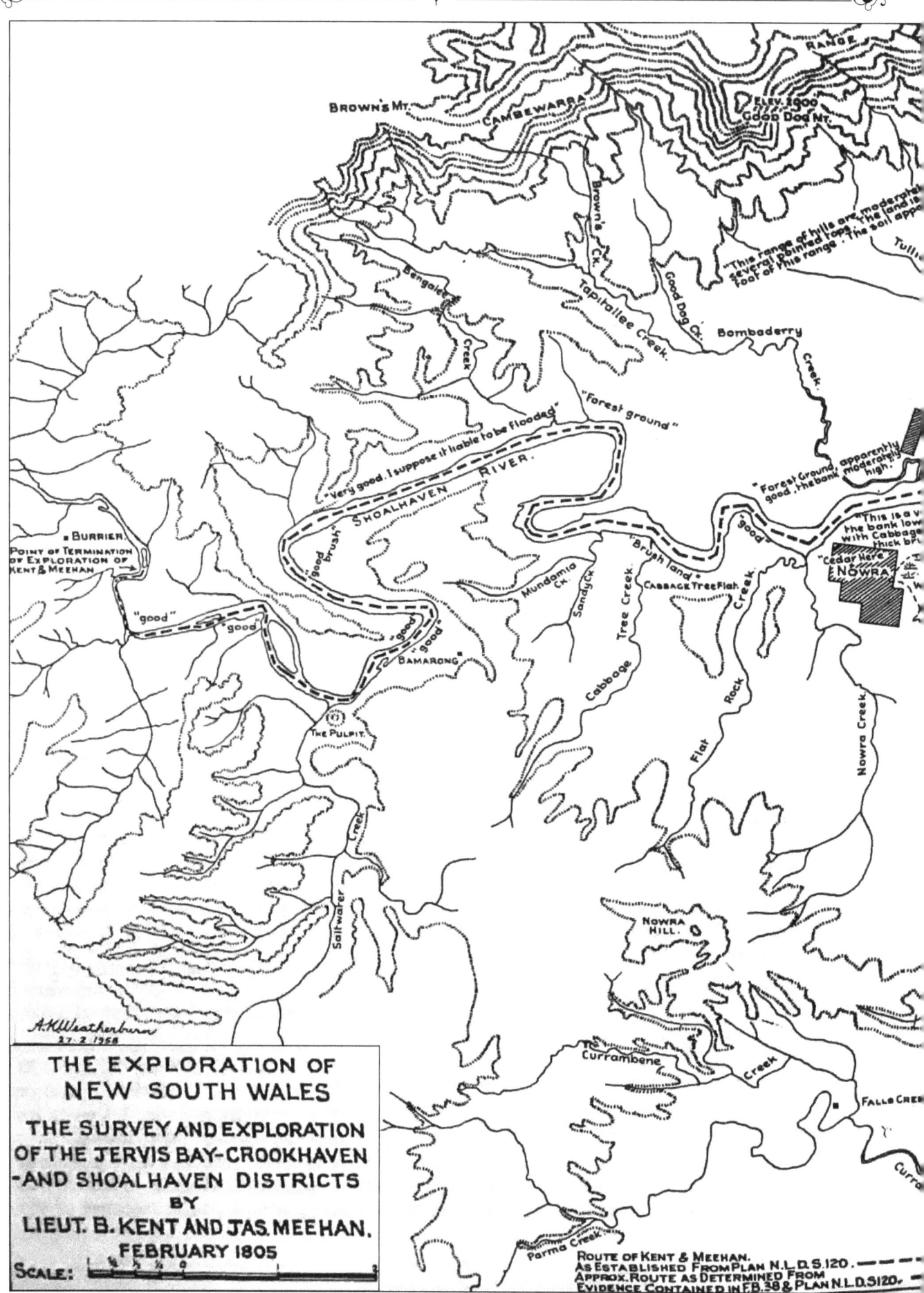

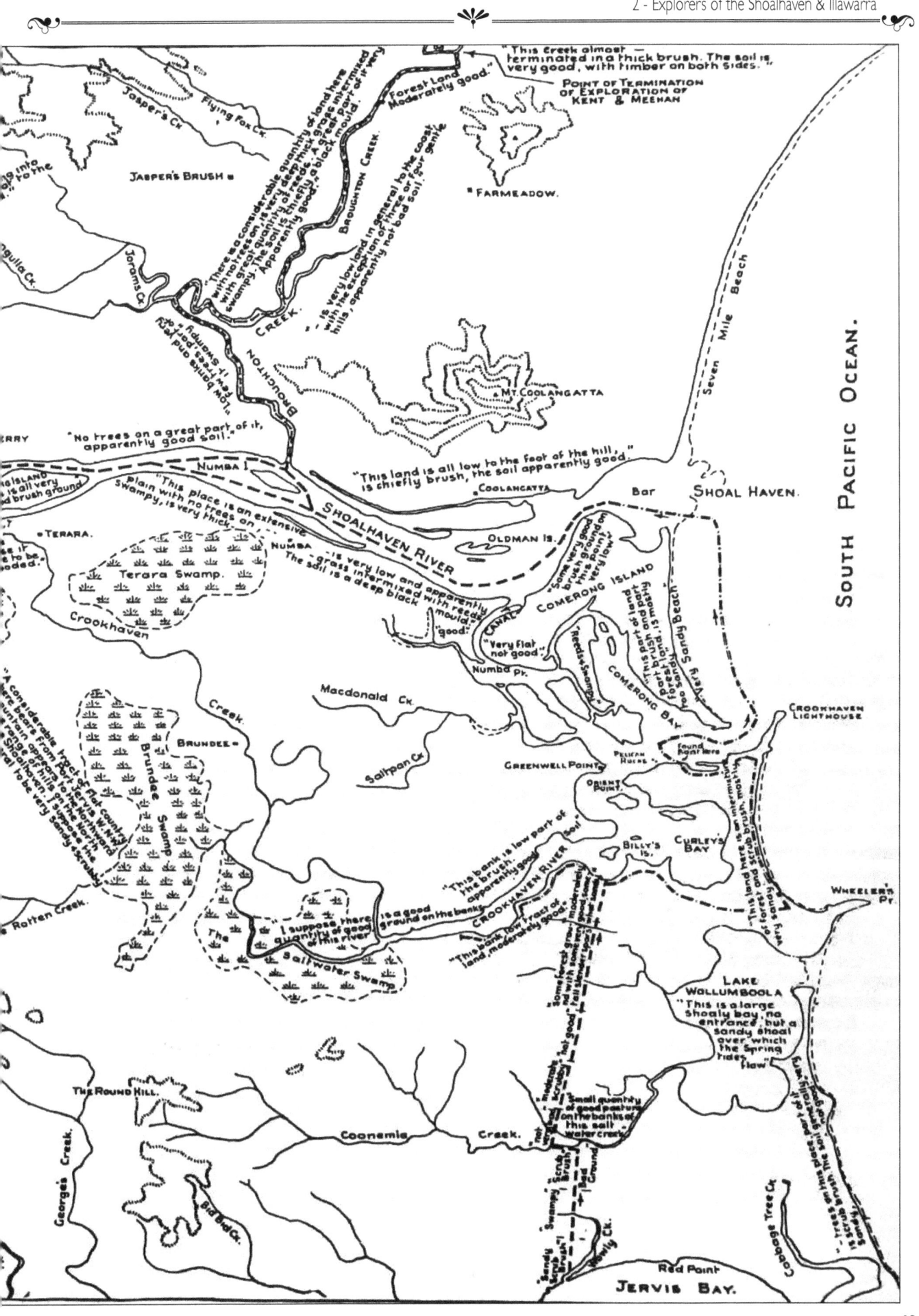

chiefly brush-covered, to the foot of the Coolangatta Mountain." The party penetrated as far west as the present day settlement of Burrier before turning back. They also followed what was later named Broughton Creek, nearly as far as the present day town of Berry. Kent and Meehan surveyed about 40km of the Shoalhaven River and 20km of Broughton Creek before returning to Jervis Bay and thence to Sydney. Kent's report appears to have been favourable, as Governor King relayed it to Charles Pratt, 1st Earl Camden in London:

> "The officer and surveyor who I sent to examine the country about Shoals Haven report much good land on the banks of the two small bar rivers, which will hereafter prove of great benefit to the extension of these settlements."
>
> *Governor King, 30th April 1805*

However, the matter rested there until some six years later when the incoming governor became interested in the area.[12] While sealers and whalers had been intermittently operating in these waters at least as far south as Jervis Bay, it was not until the arrival of Governor Lachlan Macquarie that possibilities of settlement were reconsidered. Macquarie visited Van Diemen's Land aboard the "Lady Nelson" in 1811 and had to take shelter in Jervis Bay on the outward journey due to bad weather. He spent two days there, walking with Mrs Macquarie on the mainland and being impressed by the 'stout well-made good looking natives.' The new governor was so impressed by the chances of settlement, that on his return to Sydney, he instructed the Deputy Surveyor George Evans to make a further examination.[13]

The 'Rum Rebellion' was brewing and King's real troubles were with the military authorities. These people went so far as to comment that…"the administration of Governor

'Five Islands Aborigines', painted by Edward Close, c.1815 (SLNSW).

King was barren of good fruit." This was no doubt owing to his great antagonism to the military 'ring' whose influence, owing to his previous concessions, he found himself powerless to break. It was said that "the influence of the officers of the New South Wales Corps shortened King's period of service in the colony."[14]

Whalers evidently became well acquainted with the seaboard of New South Wales during the years from 1800 to 1806. It was also known that many hundreds of acres of land was good open forest country, and that much land along the seaboard was free from timber and covered with native grass that was only kept in check by hordes of marsupials. The official returns for 1806 were given as follows... "Quantity of land occupied by Government or granted to private individuals - 125,476 acres; quantity of land cleared - 16,624 acres. Average production of land in wheat - 7118 acres; in barley, maize, etc. - 5279 acres; of wheat per acre - 18 bushels. Number of horned cattle - 3264; of sheep - 16,501; of pigs - 14,300; of horses - 458; and of goats - 2900."[15]

While we have a great deal of information in certain directions, stores of records and more than we know how to use, little that is precise and serviceable about those brave pioneers of the bush or open forest country, the bushmen who penetrated the dense scrubs in search of cedar, and the cattlemen who took up the open country adjacent to those dense scrubs to raise bullocks to haul the timber to market.

These hardy men penetrated the deepest gullies and ravines in search of cedar. The finest trees were at all times where vegetation was the most luxuriant, and where the scrubby undergrowths were always the thickest. Their position in such places was that of isolation not at all times of a voluntary nature. Many of these sawyers were half-fed, ill-clothed mortals, who had escaped from the iron gangs, stockades or penal settlements, dreading capture. Having experienced 'torture,' they were the prey of the more cunning members of the society, who used them for selfish ends. The heavy scrubs in many of the gullies and gorges were considered dank, damp, and unhealthy, consequently many of the early sawyers died off early owing to the want of sunlight. They left their records behind, and passed to the 'Great Beyond.'

Before his departure on 28th September 1806, Governor King gave the incoming governor, Captain William Bligh, R.N. (1754-1817), a grant of 1000 acres of land. In return, on taking command Bligh gave Mrs. King a grant of 1000 acres as a token of mutual friendship. At this time, the population of the colony was estimated at 9000, of which number 8472 were in New South Wales and 528 at Hobart Town.[16]

Governor William Bligh, 1806-1808

In 1788 when on a visit to Tahiti in command of the ship "HMS Bounty", by order of the British Government to transport the bread-fruit tree of the South Sea Islands to the West Indies, the sailors were allegedly harassed to such an extent by Bligh, that they mutinied, seized the ship, and set Bligh and his officers adrift in a launch. Bligh displayed such good seamanship that he covered 4,000 miles in the launch, and reached Timor safely. This drastic action was the means of making Captain Bligh an Admiral and a governor, as a few years later he was then considered a fit officer to rule the convict colony of New South Wales.

He was returned to England and was despatched again with two ships, the "Providence" and the "Assistant", and in due course landed in Van Dieman's Land, and spent 12 days there planting fruit-trees, acorns and vegetables. He was sometimes called "Bread Fruit Bligh," but he found trees did not flourish in Van Diemen's Land. His assistant botanist Mr. Brown however, landed at Adventure Bay, and planted the first apple tree on Tasmanian soil. Bligh's next visit to Tasmania was in 1808, immediately after the Rum Rebellion in Sydney. Between 1806 and 1808, Mr Brown made botanizing visits to beautiful Illawarra, and hence we have Mount Brown and Brown's Mountain.[17]

Exploring the Illawarra

The Illawarra consists of a grassy coastal plain, narrow in the north and wider in the south, bounded by the Tasman Sea on the east and the mountainous, almost impassable Illawarra escarpment, forming the eastern edge of the Southern Highlands plateau, to the west. In the middle of the region is Lake Illawarra, a shallow lake formed when sediment built up at the entrance to a bay. The district extends from the southern hills of the Royal National Park in the north to the Shoalhaven River in the south, and today contains the thriving city of Wollongong, the fourth largest urban area in New South Wales.

The Illawarra region was originally inhabited by the Dharawal indigenous Australians *(see Appendix B)*. While the first Europeans to visit the area were the navigators George Bass and Matthew Flinders, who landed at Lake Illawarra in 1796, a few people had unofficially visited the Wollongong area in the early 1800s.[18] Possibly as early as 1807, noted bushman Joe Wild was assisting bird collectors to enter the area.[19] And although others may have come before, the first settlers of the region were likely to have been the cedar cutters, who cut and shipped cedar from Illawarra as early as 1810.[20]

> "cedar was carried from the inner shores of Lake Illawarra, in small craft, during convenient periods to Sydney in 1810, and bullock teams were used to haul cedar logs and planks to the edges of the Lake, for years before any real settlement took place."

In the course of a few years the white settlers learned to follow the tracks of the blacks into the several valleys and gorges of the Illawarra and the Shoalhaven River districts, at a time when things were very unsettled under the regime of Governor Bligh.

During a drought in 1815 all the country around Liverpool was burnt up, consequently Charles Throsby [#] and a few others who had good cattle asked Governor King's leave to send cattle to Illawarra. Captain Nicholls, a relation of the old Major, brought them down in a boat and put them ashore at Five Islands, with two ex-convicts being placed in charge. The foregoing remarks are quite in keeping with statements that have been made by the descendants of the old time sawyers...

> "The chief point touched in the early history of Illawarra, goes to prove that our history is not a myth as it would appear to those who lived outside of the district. Most writers are compelled to study Illawarra from the outside, as the early Governors merely mentioned its existence, as viewed from the sea. It was not the case with the real settlers who took the risks and breathed the air of solitude. Such men saw instinctively what the authorities failed to understand."

The early pioneers of Illawarra did much to wear down the rage of governors, and saved and preserved hundreds of valuable cattle from the ravages of disease, droughts and floods. The region was circumscribed by natural barriers, hence its difficulties of ingress caused it to be nature's granary and a natural stockyard for a given number of cattle in all seasons.[21]

"We are all aware that no human skill known to the old pioneer of Illawarra could turn the barren rocky passes over the coast range into easy ways of ingress and egress for cattle, nor could they, with the material at their command, construct safe harbours. They had to take things as they found them. Yet, it is evident by such skill and forethought as they

Squatters established their claim by erecting rudimentary fencing and bark slab huts.

possessed, they employed their limited resources to the best advantage, and thereby turned even the privations of their day into such blessings, that in a short time they became a great power for good."

As the 19th century dawned, the embers of the 1798 Irish Rebellion still smoldered. Though the uprising had been crushed, its spirit lived on, with many Irishmen continuing to face arrest, conviction, and forced transportation to New South Wales. From the distant colony, these events may have seemed like echoes from another world, yet their impact shaped the Irish diaspora in ways both seen and unseen. While the rugged South Coast of New South Wales was gradually being explored, across the ocean, John Frawley's ancestors were navigating a very different struggle, one that would set the course for generations to come. Their story begins next...

References

1. McCaffrey, Frank (1922) 'The History Of Illawarra And Its Pioneers,' Johns Sands Ltd, Sydney, p.13.
2. Sydney Gazette & NSW Advertiser, 22nd July 1804.
3. Sydney Gazette & NSW Advertiser, 5th May 1805.
4. Sydney Gazette & NSW Advertiser, 27th October 1805.
5. Sydney Gazette & NSW Advertiser, 8th December 1805.
6. Sydney Gazette & NSW Advertiser, 16th February 1806.
7. Sydney Gazette & NSW Advertiser, 6th April 1806.
8. Sydney Gazette & NSW Advertiser, 18 May 1806.
9. Sydney Gazette & NSW Advertiser, 15th May 1808.
10. McCaffrey, Frank (1922). op.cit., p.13.
11. Pleaden, Ronald F. (1990). 'Coastal Explorers,' Milton/Ulladulla & District Historical Society, p.23-26.
12. Ibid.
13. Ibid, p.27.
14. Ibid.
15. Ibid.
16. Ibid.
17. McCaffrey, Frank (1922). op.cit., p.16.
18. Jervis, James, (1942). 'Illawarra: A Century of History' JRAHS, XXVIII, p.273.
19. Ibid..
20. Hagan, Jim & Andrew Wells, (ed, 1997). 'A History of Wollongong', University of Wollongong, Wollongong, p.24.
21. McCaffrey, Frank (1922). op.cit., p.21.

Chapter Three

THE FRAWLEY ANCESTORS
(Antecedents of John Frawley)

Although John Frawley was not born until 1816, his story begins long before then. This chapter traces the origins of the Frawley name and delves into the earliest known ancestors of the family, who appear to have lived at Doora, near Ennis in Co. Clare, in western Ireland. Understanding their history provides essential context for John Frawley's own life and legacy.

In addition to exploring the Frawley lineage, this chapter examines the broader historical landscape of Ireland, particularly in Limerick, between 1800 and 1816. This was a turbulent period marked by significant events that shaped the country's social, political, and economic fabric. The Act of Union (1801) formally united Ireland with Great Britain, dissolving the Irish Parliament and intensifying tensions between Irish nationalists and the British Government. The early 19th century also saw widespread hardship due to economic struggles, agrarian unrest, and the ongoing impact of the Penal Laws, which disproportionately affected Catholic families like the Frawleys.

Limerick, a city with deep political and economic significance, was particularly affected by these changes. The Napoleonic Wars (1803–1815) fueled both economic opportunities and challenges, as trade fluctuated and many Irishmen were recruited into the British Army. At the same time, secret societies such as the 'Whiteboys' and the 'Rockites' emerged in

'Limerick from across the River Shannon', the birthplace of John and Mary Ann Frawley, painted by Tom Greaney (Irish, b.1927)

response to oppressive landlord policies and rural poverty, leading to unrest in the region.

By weaving together family history with the broader historical backdrop, this chapter provides a foundation for understanding the world John Frawley was born into and the legacy he inherited.

Irish Australians have emerged as a distinct ethnic group, tracing their ancestry to Ireland. Since the late 18th century, they have played a significant role in shaping Australia's history. The first arrivals included both convicts, many of whom were prisoners of war from the 1798 Irish Rebellion, and free settlers seeking new opportunities. The great Irish Famine and the economic hardships that followed drove many more to Australia, where they made substantial contributions across various fields.

By the late 19th century, Irish Australians comprised up to a third of the country's population. According to the 2011 Australian Census, 2,087,800 people identified as having Irish ancestry, either alone or in combination with another heritage. This made Irish ancestry the third most commonly reported, after English and Australian, representing 10.4% of the total population. Additionally, the Australian Embassy in Dublin estimates that up to 30% of Australians have some degree of Irish heritage.

Limerick & Its History

The history of Limerick stretches back to its establishment by the Vikings as a walled city on King's Island, on the River Shannon in the year 812AD. Luimneach originally referred to the general area along the banks of the Shannon Estuary as 'Loch Luimnigh'. The original pre-Viking and Viking era settlement on Kings Island was known in the annals as 'Inis Sibhtonn' and 'Inis an Ghaill Duibh'. The earliest provable settlement dates from 812 however, history suggests the presence of earlier settlements in the area surrounding King's Island.[1]

Antiquity's map-maker, Ptolemy, produced in 150 the earliest map of Ireland, showing a place called "Regia" at the same site as King's Island. History also records an important battle involving Cormac mac Airt in 221 and a visit by St. Patrick in 434 to baptise an Eóganachta king, 'Carthann the Fair'. Saint Munchin, the first bishop of Limerick died in 652, indicating the city was by then a place of some note. In 812 the Vikings sailed up the Shannon and pillaged the city, burned the monastery of Mungret, but were forced to flee when the Irish retaliated and killed many of their number.[2]

The Normans redesigned the city in the 12th century and added much of its notable architecture, such as King John's Castle and St Mary's Cathedral. In early medieval times Limerick was at the centre of the Kingdom of Thomond, which corresponds to the present day Mid West region however, the Kingdom also included North Kerry and parts of South Offaly. One of the kingdom's most notable kings was Brian Boru, ancestor of the O'Brien's of the Dalcassian Clan. The word Thomond is synonymous with the region and is retained in place names such as Thomondgate, Thomond Bridge and Thomond Park.[3]

Limerick in the 16th and 17th centuries was often called the most beautiful city in Ireland. The English-born judge Luke Gernon, a resident of Limerick, wrote in 1620 that at his first sight of the city he had been amazed at its magnificence with "lofty buildings of marble, like the colleges in Oxford."[4]

During the civil wars of the 17th century the city played a pivotal role, besieged by Oliver Cromwell (1599-1658), in 1651 and twice by the Williamites in the 1690's. The 'Treaty of Limerick' ended the Williamite War in Ireland, which was fought between supporters of the Catholic King James II (Jacobites) and the Protestant King William of Orange (Williamites). The treaty offered toleration to Catholicism and full legal rights to Catholics that swore an oath of loyalty to William III and Mary II, which was of national significance as it

Painting of 'Baal's Bridge, Limerick' by William Bartlett (1840).

▲ TOP: Panorama of Thomond Bridge and King John's Castle, Limerick, photo by Tracy Rockwell (2018). ABOVE: The Shannon River from the Tower of Limerick Cathedral, Ireland about 1840, by T. Hughes.

ensured closer British and Protestant dominance over Ireland. However, the articles of the Treaty protecting Catholic rights were not passed by the Protestant Irish Parliament, which rather updated the Penal Laws against Catholics with major implications for Irish history. Reputedly the Treaty was signed on the Treaty Stone, an irregular block of limestone which once served as a mounting block for horses, and Limerick is sometimes known as the Treaty City. This turbulent period earned the city its motto: "Urbs antiqua fuit studisque asperrima belli", meaning an ancient city well studied in the arts of war.[5]

The peace that followed the turmoil of the late 17th century allowed the city to prosper mostly through trade in the 18th century. During this time Limerick established itself as one of Ireland's major commercial ports exporting agricultural produce from the 'Golden Vale', one of Ireland's most fertile areas, to Britain and America. This increase in trade

ABOVE: Sketch of the Thomond Bridge over the River Shannon, King John's Castle (centre) and St Mary's Cathedral at far right, in Limerick, Ireland, c.1830.

and wealth, particularly amongst the city's merchant classes saw a rapid expansion of the city as Georgian Limerick began to take shape. This prosperity gave the city its present-day look including the extensive terraced streets of fine Georgian townhouses, which remain in the city centre today. The Waterford and Limerick Railway linked the city to the Dublin–Cork Railway line in 1848 and to Waterford in 1853. The opening of a number of secondary railways in the subsequent decades developed Limerick as a regional centre of communications. However, the economic downturn from the European conflicts of the French Revolution and Napoleonic eras, and following the Act of Union (1801), as well as the impact of the Great Irish Famine of 1848 caused much of the 19th century to be a troubled period.[6]

THE FRAWLEY ANCESTORS

A historical connection has been suggested between Irish Australians and Aboriginal Australians, particularly those of mixed descent, based on their shared experience of British oppression. Whether arriving as convicts, settlers, or political exiles, Irish migrants laid deep roots in Australia, roots that would eventually lead to the 1816 birth of John Frawley, the 'boyo' from Limerick. What better way to begin this genealogy than by exploring the origins of the Frawley surname?

The Surname of Frawley

The Frawleys were the paternal ancestors of John Frawley. In Ireland, the Frawley surname comes from the Irish gaelic name O'Fearghail, which means 'man of valour' with its origin appearing in Leinster, Ireland. However, it tends to be generally a medieval English surname and is locational from various places called Fawley in the counties of Buckinghamshire, Hampshire, Herefordshire and Berkshire.[7] The surname Frawley derives

William Frawley

William Clement Frawley (February 26, 1887 – March 3, 1966), was born in Iowa, the second son of Michael A. Frawley (1857-1907). He was an American stage entertainer, screen and television actor best known for playing the landlord Fred Mertz in the famous American television sitcom 'I Love Lucy', as well as Bub in the television comedy series 'My Three Sons'.

Frawley began his career in vaudeville in 1914 with his wife, Edna Louise Broedt. Their comedy act, known as "Frawley and Louise", continued until their divorce in 1927. Frawley performed on Broadway multiple times and signed with Paramount Studios in 1916 to play in silent films. He appeared in more than one hundred feature films over 35 years.

Frawley had a reputation for being cantankerous and difficult, likely exacerbated by a drinking problem; he was once fired for punching another actor on the nose. When he got the call offering him the part of Fred Mertz on 'I Love Lucy', Desi Arnaz and Lucille Ball told him he would only get three chances before getting fired. Frawley died on March 3, 1966, from a heart attack.

LEFT: Profile of the Amercian actor, William Clement Frawley. RIGHT: 90 year old Tom Frawley runs P. Frawley's, the last traditional bar in the booming coastal town of Lahinch, County Clare, Ireland. The bar only has one tap and that's Guinness (the best pint around). Tom has one eye and says he hasn't been married yet. He was born in the bar and has lived there all his life (relationship unknown).

The original Thomond Bridge at Limerick was erected about 1185 as a lead from King John's Castle to the Clare side of the River Shannon. It has been rebuilt several times over the centuries. It is on the site of the oldest bridge in Limerick city, and was once the only bridge across the Shannon. The bridge of the 18th and early 19th century had fourteen arches, and is the scene for Limerick's tales from the Bard of Thomond, including "The Bishop's Lady" who the story tells us would toss late walkers over the bridge to be taken by the river. The bridge that stands today was completed in 1840, and was designed by the Pain Brothers, who designed many buildings in Limerick during this period, including the County Courthouse, and the Customs House. There is a benchmark in the centre of Thomond Bridge. The monument to the Treaty of Limerick (1691), which concluded the Siege of Limerick and ended the Williamite War in Ireland between the Jacobites and the supporters of William of Orange, can be seen at the top left. Photo by Tracy Rockwell (2018).

from the old English pre-7th century word 'filithe', meaning a hay field, with 'leah', a clearing in a forest, whilst Fawley in Buckinghamshire has for its first element the old English word 'fealg', meaning fallow land, although why a place would apparently be permanent fallow land doesn't seem logical. Fawley in Berkshire has the word 'felam' as its prefix, which possibly denotes a forest frequented by fallow deer. However, there is no such place recorded as Frawley, and the records suggest that the intrusive 'r' was probably added to Fawley in the London area as an aid to pronunciation.[8]

Examples of the surname taken from surviving registers of the diocese of Greater London include: Thomas Fowley, who married Jone Fletcher at St Margarets, Westminster, on May 27th 1543; Richard Fawly, a witness at the church of St Christopher le Stocks, on August 19th 1593; William Fawley who was christened on May 29th 1692 at St. Brides church, Fleet Street; and Andrew Frawley, the son of Andrew and Catherine Frawley, who was christened at Endell Street lying in hospital, on April 18th 1771.[9]

Research has shown that Frawley ancestors have appeared under many spelling variants ie. Fawley, Fraley, Frayley, Frewley, Frailey, Frauley, Fawly, Fowley, Frawly, and Frawley,

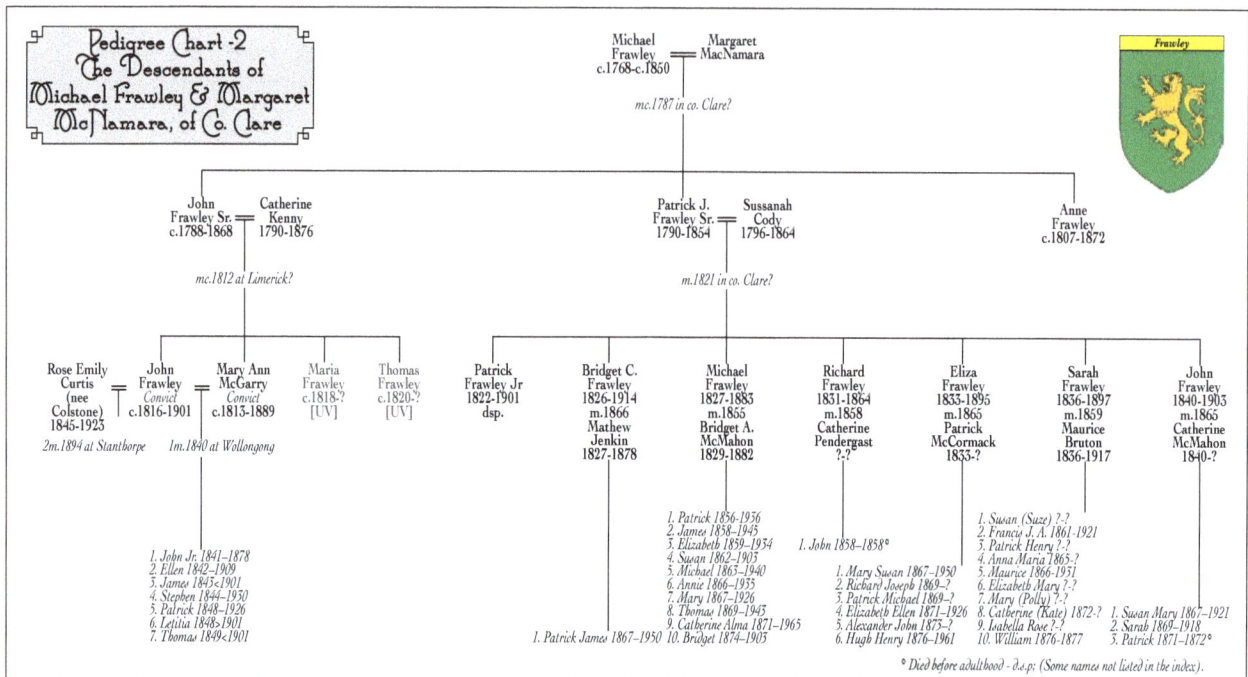

although the surname is generally uncommon. The distribution of families sharing the relatively uncommon name of Frawley at the time of the 1891 England and Wales Census was relatively small, ranging from only 48 to 113 family units. The main concentrations across England being in Lancashire, Yorkshire and London. However, the vast majority of Frawleys at this time resided in Ireland, was a concentration in and around the town of Doora and nearby Ennis, in County Clare.[10]

Famous & Notable Frawleys

William Clement Frawley (1887-1966, no known relation) found much work as a character actor with roles in comedies, dramas, musicals, Westerns and romances.[11] He was an American vaudevillian actor, best remembered for playing landlord 'Fred Mertz' in the American television sitcom "I Love Lucy", and 'Bub O'Casey' in the television comedy series "My Three Sons", as well as the political advisor to the judge character in the film "Miracle on 34th Street" (1947).[12]

James Joseph Frawley (1936-2019, no known relation) was an American director and actor. He was a member of the Actors Studio since around 1961, and was best known for directing "The Muppet Movie" (1979) and 'The Monkees' television series.[13]

While the surname Frawley likely originated in County Clare, Ireland, from the Gaelic name "O'Frailigh," meaning "descendant of Frailigh." This name could be linked to the early Irish nobility and may have arrived with Gaelic settlers during the early medieval period. The region's rich history of Viking invasions and Norman conquests also influenced the surname's presence, as these groups interacted with local populations, resulting in the assimilation of names and customs. The Frawleys may also have been part of the Gaelic Irish clans that thrived in County Clare, influenced by the region's agricultural economy and the significance of land ownership.

Additionally, the migration of Irish families to other regions during the Great Famine in the mid-19th century contributed to the dispersal of the Frawley surname globally. Unfortunately, little is known about our Frawley ancestors. The earliest confirmed mention of John Frawley's paternal ancestors is recorded on his 1894 second marriage certificate, to Rose Emily Curtis in Stanthorpe, Queensland. On that document, John Frawley identified his parents as John Frawley Sr., a clerk, and Catherine Kenny, both apparently residents of Limerick.

But due to a lack of records, no further details about John Frawley Sr. or Catherine Kenny have been found, making it difficult to trace their lineage with confidence. A possible record for a John Frawley Sr. suggests he may have died in Limerick, in 1868 at the age of 80, placing his birth around the year 1788. Unfortunately, this record does not provide information about his parents or an exact birthplace. Despite these uncertainties, the 1868 death notice remains the only registration in the International Genealogical Index (IGI) that aligns with the necessary timeframe for being the father of our ancestor John Frawley, who was born around 1816 and transported to Sydney as a convict in 1833.

Frawleys in Victoria

However, in a development in 2023, a family booking into Ribbon Gum Lodge (my holiday property in Katoomba), with guests bearing the uncommon name of Frawley, revealed somewhat of a breakthrough. I couldn't resist asking about their ancestry, to which they very kindly supplied a lengthy list of ancestors, and a modest booklet entitled "From Clare to Bungaree", by Ray Frawley, which provided a detailed coverage of the family of Patrick and Susan Frawley, and the emigration of their family to Victoria. This fortuitous incident established a clear family connection, which has enabled the addition of Michael Frawley (c.1768-1864) and his wife Margaret MacNamara as the paternal grandparents of our ancestor, John Frawley the convict, although at this stage, we know nothing more than their names (*see chapter 13*).

A photograph of residential Limerick during the early days of the 20th century.

THE KENNY ANCESTORS

Unfortunately, just as little is known about our Kenny ancestors. The earliest confirmed mention of John Frawley's maternal ancestors being the same 1894 second marriage certificate, to Rose Emily Curtis in Stanthorpe, Queensland. On that document, John Frawley identified his mother as Catherine Kenny, who was apparently residing with her husband John Frawley Sr, in Limerick. While we face the same frustrating lack of information about John Frawley's maternal ancestors, we can nevertheless dive into the origins of the Kenny surname and uncover its rich history.

The Surname of Kenny

As a surname, the eponym 'Kenny' is a diminutive of several different given names. In Ireland, the surname is an Anglicisation of the Irish Ó'Cionnaith, sometimes spelled Ó'Cionnaoith. It is also a name common from Waterford to Cork, which is derived from MacKenny. One bearer of the name was Cainnech of Aghadoe, better known in English as Saint Canice, a 6th century Irish priest and missionary after whom the city and county of Kilkenny is also named.[14] It is thought that the Ó Cionnaith sept was part of the Uí Maine kingdom, based in Connacht. Within this region, the name is associated traditionally with the counties of Galway and Roscommon.

The surname Kenny is ranked at number 76 in the list of most common surnames in Ireland. Other spellings include O'Kenny, Kenney, Kennie, Kinnie and Kinny. Kenny (or Kenney), now common in Britain as well as Ireland, can be of Scottish or Irish origin. In both cases the name is derived from the popular Gaelic personal name 'Cionaodha', thought to be made up of two elements 'cion', meaning love or affection, and 'Aodh', the name of the pre-Christian god of fire. It might therefore be translated as "cherished by Aodh" or, perhaps, "fiery love." In addition the purely Irish 'O'Coinnigh' and 'O'Coinne' have been anglicised as Kenny.[15]

The surname came into being independently in a number of places in Ireland, including Tyrone, Donegal/Leitrim and Down, where the original Irish was 'O'Coinne'. The most prominent family of this name however, arose in the area of east Galway and south Roscommon known in ancient times as 'Ui'Maine', where they were of the same stock as the Maddens, and it is in Galway and Roscommon that the name of Kenny is still most frequent today.[16]

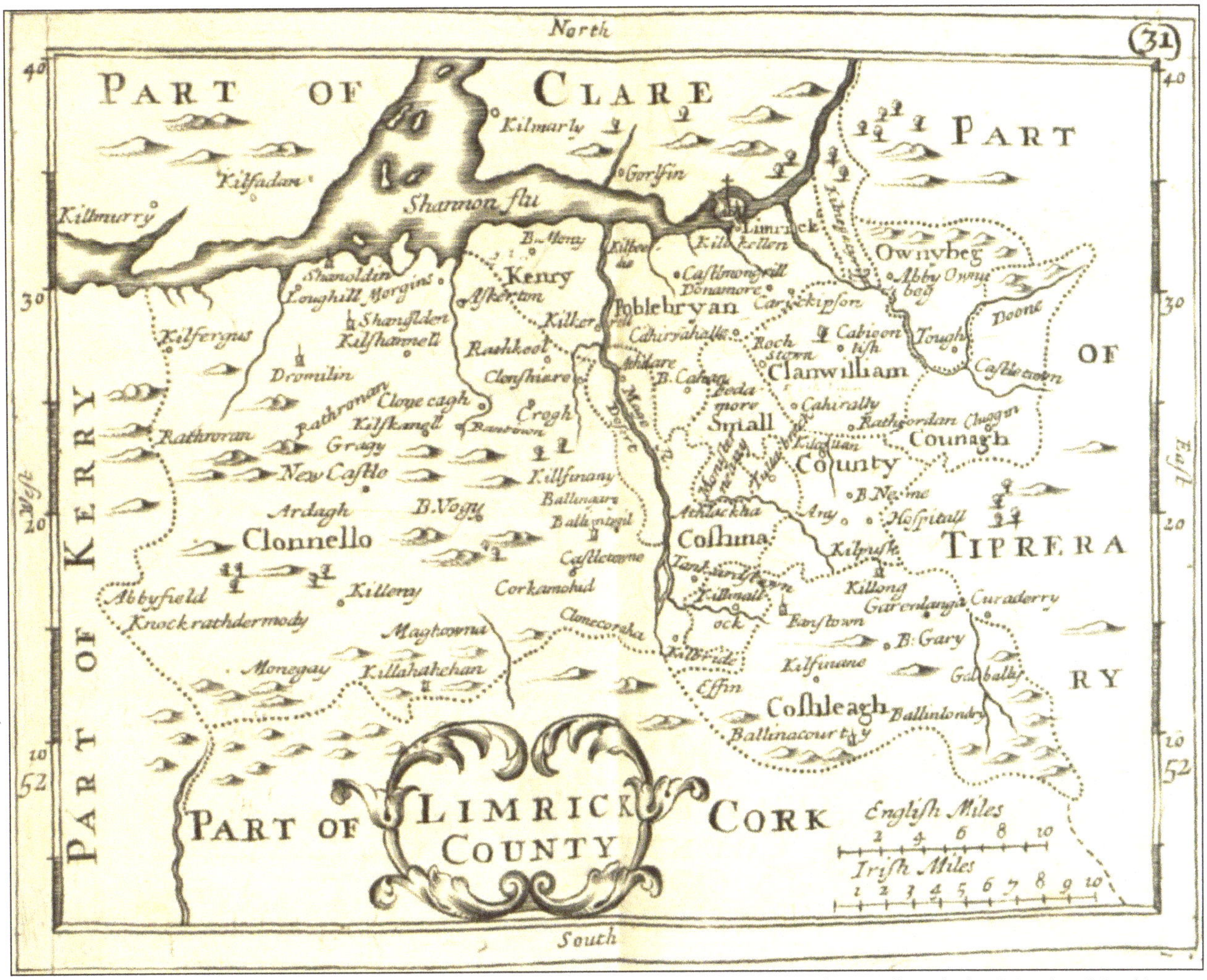

M4. Map of County Limerick, Munster (in Sir William Petty's, (1689) 'A Geographical Description of Ye Kingdom of Ireland', London, F. Lamb).

Famous & Notable Kennys

Born in Dublin, James Kenney (1780-1849, no known relation) was one of the most successful and prolific playwrights of his day, and author of more than 50 plays. His reputation has not prospered, but Lord Byron wrote of him: "Kenney's World - ah, where is Kenney's wit? - tires the sad gallery, lulls the listless pit."[17]

Sister Elizabeth Kenny (1886-1952, no known relation), was an Australian nurse who became widely known for the treatment she developed for paralysed children. Despite widespread opposition from the medical establishment, her methods, which involved stimulation and physiotherapy instead of casts and splints, eventually gained acceptance. The Kenny Institute in Minneapolis, USA is named after her.[18]

William Kenny (1846-1921, no known relation) QC, was an Irish judge and Liberal Unionist politician. Kenny was born in Dublin, the only son of Edward Kenny, solicitor, of Kilrush, County Clare, and his wife, Catherine (née Murphy). Kenny married Mary Coffey on 13 August 1873, and produced a family of eight children.[19]

JOHN FRAWLEY SR. & CATHERINE KENNY

John Frawley Sr. and Catherine Kenny lived in County Limerick during the late 18th and early 19th centuries, a period of immense social and political upheaval in Ireland. Born around the 1780s, they would have come of age amid the turmoil of the 1798 Irish Rebellion, when the United Irishmen, inspired by the American and French Revolutions, sought to overthrow British rule. While there is little recorded about their personal lives, they were undoubtedly shaped by the economic hardship and tensions of the time, as Limerick, an important port city, was deeply affected by trade restrictions, agrarian unrest, and growing nationalist sentiment. The Act of Union in 1801 further altered the landscape of Irish governance, binding Ireland to Britain and intensifying resentment among the rural poor, many of whom struggled under oppressive landlordism and rising rents.

Despite these challenges, John and Catherine endured, raising a family in a time when survival itself was an achievement. Their son, John Frawley (c.1816–1901), would later become entangled in the harsh realities of 19th-century Ireland, finding himself charged with stealing clothes and sentenced to transportation to Australia, a fate that befell many impoverished Irishmen. The early 19th century in Limerick saw the rise of secret societies like the Whiteboys, who resisted eviction and high tithes, suggesting that ordinary people like the Frawleys and Kennys navigated a world of quiet resistance and resilience. The Napoleonic Wars (1803–1815) brought both hardship and opportunity, as increased military demand temporarily boosted the economy but also conscripted Irishmen into service. Though we may never know the specifics of their daily lives, John and Catherine's survival through these tumultuous decades speaks to the strength and endurance of those who lived in the shadow of history's grand events, shaping the generations that followed them.

Birthdates from Family Search.org

For John Frawley Sr.

Death	Age	Place	Birth	Source
1865	80	Mallow	1785	IGI
1873	87	Killadysert	1786	IGI
1868	**80**	**Limerick**	**1788**	**IGI**
1869	80	Glin	1789	IGI
1875	86	Kilrush	1789	IGI
1896	103	Listowel	1793	IGI
1871	75	Ennistimon	1796	IGI
1887	90	Kilrush	1797	IGI

For Catherine Frawley (nee Kenny)

Death	Age	Place	Birth	Source
1877	84	Kilrush	1793	IGI
1879	84	Dublin North	1795	IGI
1874	75	Ennis	1799	IGI
1869	67	Rathkeale	1802	IGI

John Frawley
Ireland Civil Registration Indexes, 1845-1958

Name:	John Frawley
Event Type:	Death
Event Date:	1868
Event Place:	Limerick, Ireland
Registration Quarter and Year:	1868
Registration District:	Limerick
Age:	80
Birth Year (Estimated):	1788
Volume Number:	10

LEFT: Possible death registrations for John Frawley Sr., father of John Frawley (from Family Search.org). RIGHT: A possible death registration of 1868 for John Frawley Sr. at Limerick, Ireland (from IGI/Family Search.org).

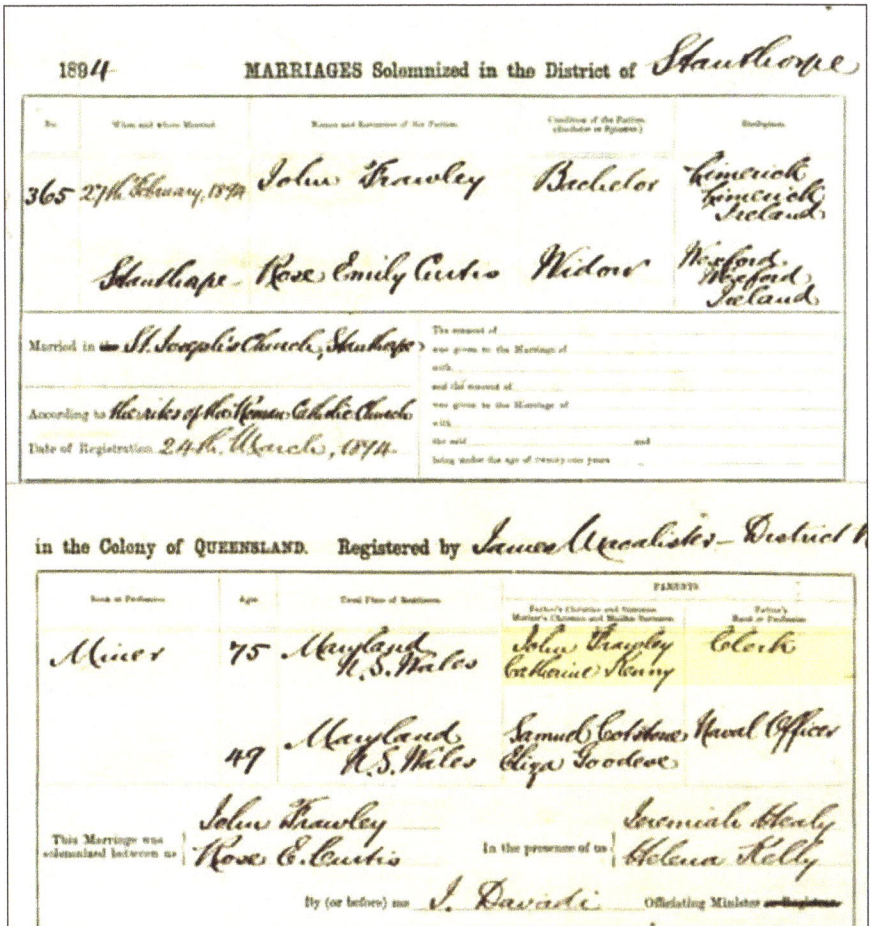

Marriage certificate for John Frawley (c.1816-1901) to Rose Emily Curtis on the 27th February 1894, showing the names of his parents.

John Frawley, the Patriarch

John Frawley Sr. and Catherine Kenny likely married in the aftermath of the 1798 Irish Rebellion, a time of great upheaval when Irish patriots took a stand against English rule. Their lives unfolded in the heart of Limerick, a city steeped in history and resilience.

What we do know of John Frawley Sr. is that he worked as a clerk and that the Frawley family called Limerick home. A possible death record found in Family Search (IGI) suggests that a John Frawley of Limerick was born around 1788, but without concrete evidence, we cannot confirm if he was the father of John Frawley (c.1816–1901).

Catherine Kenny, the Matriarch

The mother of John Frawley (c.1816–1901), Catherine Kenny, remains an elusive figure. Though records have been scarce, she was likely born between 1795 and 1800, possibly in Limerick. Despite exhaustive searches, no confirmed details about her marriage or death have surfaced, leaving her story largely untold. While no further details about John Frawley Sr. or Catherine Kenny have been found, their legacy, nevetheless lives on through their descendants, who continue to piece together the fragments of their past.

The 1798 Irish Rebellion [20]

The 1798 Irish Rebellion, which occurred around the time that John Frawley Sr. and catherine Kenny were residing in Limerick, was a defining moment in Ireland's history, and while its battles were fought primarily in Ulster and Wexford, its impact rippled across the entire country, including Limerick, where John Frawley Sr. and Catherine Kenny lived. The rebellion was driven by the Society of United Irishmen, a revolutionary group founded in 1791 and inspired by the American and French Revolutions. The society first emerged in Belfast, where Presbyterians predominated, and later expanded to Dublin, attracting a mix of Catholics and Protestants. Their goals were parliamentary reform based on universal male suffrage, full Catholic emancipation, and, ultimately, an end to British rule in Ireland.

By 1795, the movement had evolved into a secret, military-style organization, fueled by an alliance between radical Presbyterians and discontented working-class groups. Agrarian unrest was widespread, and many Irish peasants, already involved in secret societies of their own, joined the United Irishmen. Hoping for foreign support, the radical Irishman Theobald Wolfe Tone (1763–1798) traveled to France in early 1796 to seek aid. That same year, a French expedition led by General Lazare Hoche (1768–1797) set sail for Ireland. However, storms scattered the fleet, and though some ships reached Bantry Bay, County Cork, but no troops were landed, dashing hopes of a successful rebellion.

The British Government responded with force. In 1796, it passed the Insurrection Act and suspended habeas corpus, granting authorities sweeping powers to suppress dissent. In 1797, General Gerard Lake (1744–1808) launched a campaign in the north, confiscating private arms and shutting down 'The Northern Star', a radical Belfast newspaper. As tensions escalated in early 1798, both the United Irishmen and the government prepared for battle.

The rebellion erupted in May 1798, though it remained concentrated in eastern Ulster and Wexford. Northern rebels suffered defeats at Antrim and Ballinahinch, while in Wexford, the uprising took on a sectarian character, with Catholic rebels attacking Protestants, further deepening religious divisions. Though the Wexford insurgents won key victories, they failed to capture strategic towns like New Ross and Arklow. By mid-June, government forces under General Lake had gathered in Wexford, crushing the rebellion at Vinegar Hill on June 21.

Just as the uprising seemed over, a small French force landed near Killala, securing a brief

Catholic rebels in a muddled cause were defeated at the Battle of Vinegar Hill in June 1798.

"The charge of the 5th Dragoon Guards on the insurgents at Vinegar Hill on the 21st June 1798", a recreant yeoman in uniform having deserted to the rebels, is being cut down, painted by William Sadler (1782–1839).

victory at Castlebar before being surrounded and captured. The British response was ruthless with many Irish rebels were executed or transported to the penal colony of New South Wales.

For John Frawley Sr. and Catherine Kenny, the rebellion would have been impossible to ignore. As residents of Limerick, they lived in a city deeply affected by political turmoil. The extent of their involvement, whether in active opposition to the rebels or as mere witnesses to the unrest, remains uncertain. However, as a literate man working as a clerk, John Frawley Sr. may have had incentives to align with the British administration. Whether he quietly supported the status quo or merely sought stability in uncertain times is unknown, but what is certain is that he and Catherine Kenny married soon after, starting a family in post-rebellion Ireland. Their son, John Frawley (Jr.), was born in Limerick around 1816, and while his likely siblings were Patrick and Anne Frawley, it would have been unusual for John Frawley (Jr.) to be an only child.

The Irish Rebellion may have ended in 1798, but its effects lasted for generations. Whether as beneficiaries of British rule or cautious observers of the political landscape, the Frawleys of Limerick navigated a world forever changed by the struggle for Irish independence.

The first decade of the 19th century was a time of upheaval and hardship for John Frawley's parents as Ireland was wracked by social unrest, economic instability, and political turmoil. The aftershocks of the 1798 Rebellion lingered, with British rule tightening its grip and the effects of the Act of Union in 1801 reshaping the nation's future. For many, survival meant navigating poverty, land displacement, and the ever-present specter of transportation for even minor offenses. It was in this world of uncertainty and desperation that John Frawley's fate took a decisive turn.

Convicted and sentenced to transportation in 1833, John Frawley was cast into the vast unknown of the penal colony of New South Wales. What became of him upon his arrival, and how his story unfolded in a land so distant from his Irish roots, is central to this book. To understand the world he entered, we must first explore the early European incursions

LEFT: Photograph of Thomond Bridge and King John's Castle (right), by Tracy Rockwell, 2018. RIGHT: Memorial headstone for a John & Catherine Frawley, with their daughter Maria Frawley, from the townland of 'Monreel', and her brother Tom Frawley, potentially the parents and siblings of John Frawley that was transported to Australia in 1833. The monument was erected by Maria's son William, of New York City, at Ennistymon Cemetery, Ennistimon, County Clare, Ireland. Unfortunately, dates were not listed on the memorial.

along the South Coast of New South Wales. Long before organized settlement, the rugged shores of the Shoalhaven and Illawarra districts lured sealers, cedar-cutters, and squatters, each carving out a precarious existence in the untamed frontier. It is here, in the shadow of towering cliffs and dense forests, that the next chapter of this story begins.

References

1. Wikipedia - Limerick, op. cit.
2. Ibid.
3. Ibid.
4. Gernon, Luke (1620). 'A Discourse of Ireland', edited by C.L. Falkiner 1904.
5. Wikipedia - Limerick, op. cit.
6. Ibid.
7. Wikipedia - Limerick [https://en.wikipedia.org/wiki/Limerick].
8. Surname DB - Frawley [https://www.surnamedb.com/Surname/Frawley].
9. Ibid.
10. Ancestry - Frawley [https://www.ancestry.com/name-origin?surname=frawley].
11. Wikipedia - William Frawley [https://en.wikipedia.org/wiki/William_Frawley].
12. IMDB - William Frawley [https://www.imdb.com/name/nm0292433/].
13. D23 - James Joseph Frawley - Celebrate 40 Years of The Muppet Movie with These "Muppetational" Facts [https://d23.com/the-muppet-movie-facts/].
14. Surname DB - Kenny [https://www.surnamedb.com/Surname/Kenny.
15. Ibid.
16. Ibid.
17. Wikipedia - James Kenney (dramatist), [https://en.wikipedia.org/wiki/James_Kenney_(dramatist).
18. Wikipedia - Elizabeth Kenney [https://en.wikipedia.org/wiki/Elizabeth_Kenney].
19. Wikipedia - William Kenny (Irish politician) [https://en.wikipedia.org/wiki/William_Kenny_(Irish_politician)].
20. Brittanica - The 1798 Irish Rebellion [https://www.britannica.com/event/Irish-Rebellion-Irish-history-1798].

Chapter Four

LAND GRANTS & SQUATTERS

In 1833, John Frawley was torn from his homeland, sentenced to transportation, and cast adrift into the vast unknown of the New South Wales penal colony. What became of him in this distant land, so far from the green fields of Ireland, is a story of survival, reinvention, and fate. But to truly understand his journey, we must first step back into the world he entered.

Long before the first prison ships arrived, the rugged shores of the Shoalhaven and Illawarra districts beckoned the bold and the desperate. Whalers braved treacherous waters, cedar-cutters hacked their way through dense forests, and squatters laid claim to the untamed frontier, all in pursuit of fortune or survival. It was a land of opportunity and peril, where towering cliffs and ancient rainforests concealed both danger and promise. It was here that

Possible Aboriginal Meanings for Place Names of the Illawarra [27]

Bombo	from Thumbon (renowned head man)	**Kembla**	from Djembla (the wallaby)
Bong Bong	big swamp	**Kiama**	the father spirit of Eastern NSW
Coolangatta	splendid lookout or view		or fish caught from rocks; or where the seas roar
Gerringong	fearful noises on beach	**Minnamurra**	sheltered camping ground; or lots of fish
Elanora	home by the sea	**Moruya**	home of the black swan
Illawarra	high place near the sea	**Nowra**	Black cockatoo
Jamberoo	track or meeting place	**Wollongong**	sound of the sea; or hard ground near water.

Mt Keera [sic.], Belambi, painted by Capt. Robert Marsh Westmacott.

John Frawley stepped into the wild beauty and harsh realities of an unforgiving coast.

The land system from 1788, that is, from the foundation of the colony to the arrival of Governor Sir Richard Bourke (1777-1855), in 1831 is a matter of concern only to those who wish to study misfit administration. Up to the year 1824 the regulations for the disposal of land were left entirely in the hands of the governor for the time being. Land was, in the early days of the colony, bestowed on any man, bond or free, who could undertake to support himself. As the colony progressed in wealth and population, certain situations became valuable and were eagerly sought by parties of influence, but large portions were held, especially as pastures, under free licenses of occupation.

The Australian magnates emulated the white slave system by means of rum. Those who had grants of land bartered their holdings to the rum magnates. Hundreds of small land grants were allowed to pass unnoticed by the authorities into the possession of a few wealthy individuals. A keg or a bottle of rum purchased large and small holdings prior to 1831, not only in Sydney and its immediate surroundings, but north, south and west of the capital for at least a distance of one hundred miles. The Illawarra did not escape the rum traffic, sometimes a pig or a goat was substituted and many holdings could be pointed out as the result of purchase by a bottle or a keg of rum. So corrupted had the system become that the following edict was issued:

> "Lands granted from the Crown are prohibited to be sold, either directly or indirectly, for the term of five years, bearing date from June 8th, 1811."
>
> *By Command of His Excellency, J. F. Campbell Secretary, 1816* [1]

Governor Lachlan Macquarie, 1810-1821

Major General Lachlan Macquarie, CB (1762-1824)[2] was a British Army officer and colonial administrator from Scotland, who served as the fifth governor of New South Wales from 1810 to 1821, and played a leading role in the social, economic, and architectural development of the colony.[3] He is considered by historians to have had a crucial influence on the transition of New South Wales from a penal colony to a free settlement and therefore to have had a major role in the shaping of Australian society in the early 19th century.[4,5]

In 1812 a committee of the British House of Commons was appointed to examine the state of the colony of New South Wales. After examining a number of witnesses, including ex-Governors King and Bligh, a report was printed from which it appeared that the population amounted to a total of 10,454 persons, distributed in the following proportions:

> "The Sydney district - 6,158; Parramatta - 1,807; Hawkesbury - 2,389; Newcastle - 100; (of these, 5,513 were men and 2,200 women); military, 1,100; of the remainder, one-fourth to one-fifth were actually bond, the rest being free or freed from servitude by pardon. In addition, 1,321 were living in Van Diemen's Land, and 177 on Norfolk Island, but orders had been sent out to compel the voluntary settlers, who had adhered to that island after the Government establishment had been removed, to withdraw."

George Evans' Land Route to Sydney (1812)

Evans and his party left Sydney on the 26th March 1812 in the "Lady Nelson", and anchored in the shelter of Bowen Island at Jervis Bay the following day. On the 28th he commenced his survey at the south entrance and traversed the Bay's coastline, using chain

TOP: 'Lake Illawarra', painted by Samuel Elyard. ABOVE (Left): Early settlement in the 'Illawarra', painted by John Skinner Prout (1805-1876). (Right): 'Early Settler's In The Illawarra' (artist unknown).

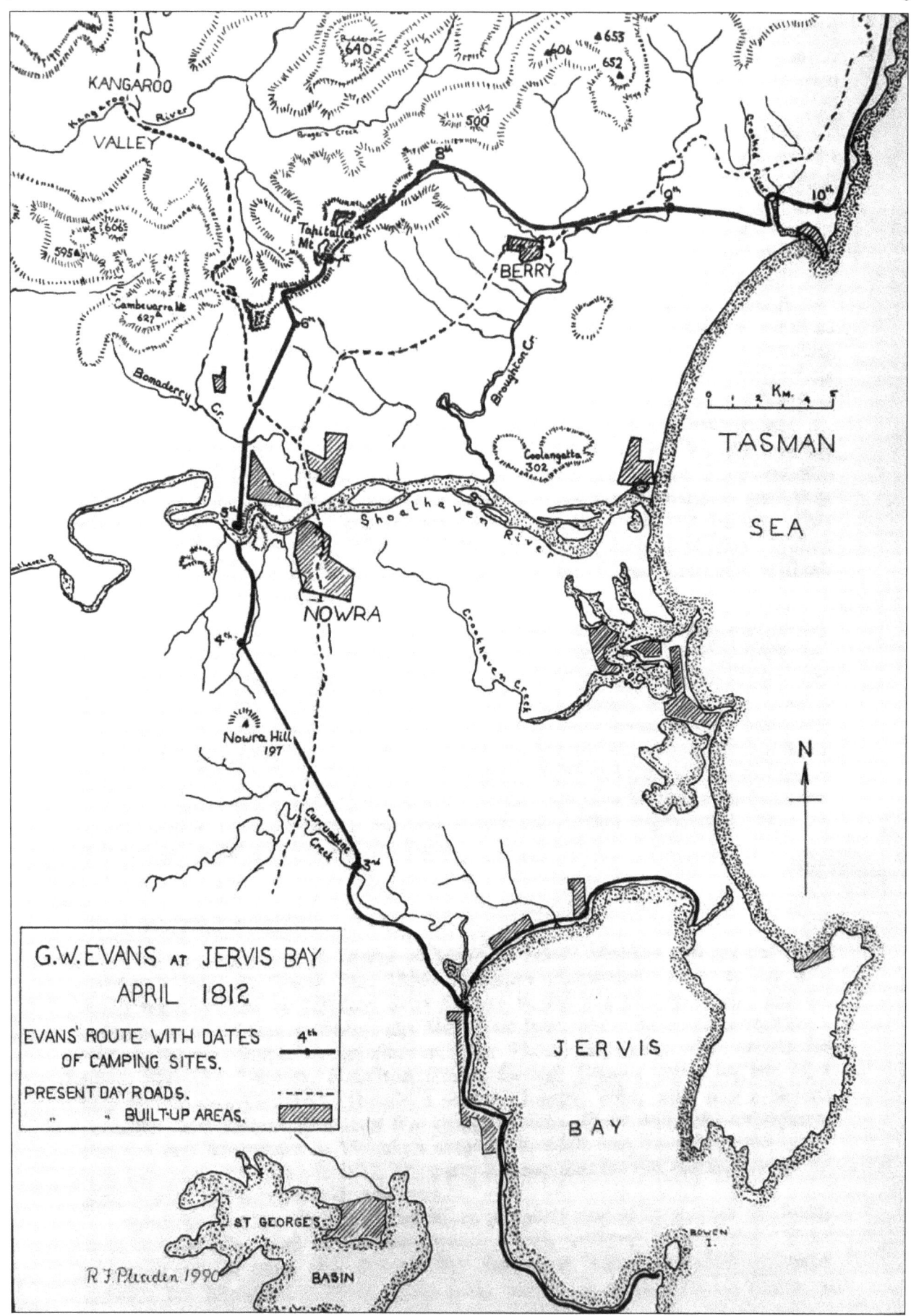

M5. The journey of George W. Evans from Jervis Bay through to the Shoalhaven district, NSW in 1812, by R.J. Pleaden, 1990.

4 - Land Grants & Squatters

M6. The route of George W. Evans' 1812 expedition from Shoalhaven to Illawarra and overland to Appin (From... '1812 Route of G.W. Evans' (From... McDonald, W.G., (1966). 'Earliest Illawarra by its Explorers & Pioneers', Illawarra Historical Society, Wollongong, 64p.)

and compass for about 30km. Despite being bitten by a snake, he set out on the 3rd April to survey a practicable land route from the Bay to Sydney. Skirting to the west of present day Nowra, Evans and his party ascended the Good Dog Mountain to a point just north of the present Cambewarra Lookout on the 7th April. The difficult ascent took over five hours. Having decided to make his way back to the coast Evans walked along the narrow neck of Cambewarra Mountain Range from Beaumont to Bellawongarah, sleeping overnight on top of Tapitallee Mountain. Looking west from here for nearly twenty kilometres Evans was the first recorded European to view Kangaroo Valley, and in the other direction the summit presented them with magnificent views back across the coastal plain:

> "One of the finest views I have ever seen; it would be impossible for a painter to beautify it; I took a sketch although I was much tired in travelling 3 miles."
>
> George W. Evans, 7th April 1812 [6]

Evans then found the way north west was just too difficult with vertical rock walls making further progress almost impossible. So they changed course on the 9th to pass north of present day Berry, noting the presence of cedar and commenting that "this part of the country would make a beautiful settlement." The party was travelling light and only carried rations for about a fortnight, so they likely didn't intend the survey to take long and by April 11th they were running out of food. After reaching the coast the party turned north and camped overnight on April 12th at the site of the future city of Wollongong, after which they turned inland, and finally arrived at Appin on the 17th April.[7]

After an interim period of farming, Capt. William Kent returned to survey the shores of Jervis Bay in March 1812, whence he led a small party overland on foot to Appin. This journey of two weeks was conducted under most arduous circumstances and resulted in the settlement of the Illawarra District during the drought years that soon followed. His success probably induced Governor Macquarie to select him for later tasks penetrating into the interior of New South Wales.[8]

'View on the coast of New South Wales at Illawarra', painted by Augustus Earle (1827).

Illawarra & Wollongong

Album of drawings of New South Wales view, by Georgiana Lowe c.1840s. TOP (Left): 'Illawarra'. (Right): 'Kembla, Illawarra'. ABOVE (Left): 'Mt Kiera, Illawarra 2'. (Right): 'Stockade, Illawarra'.

A year later, Capt. Collins in another vessel called the "Matilda" sailed from Port Jackson on the 25th March 1813 for the purpose of exploring the Shoal Haven. They arrived on Wednesday 29th and stood into Jervis Bay, which was about 24 miles to the southward of Shoals Haven. After two unsuccessful attempts, a party consisting of a naval and military officer, Mr Archer, Deputy Commissary and the commander of the "Matilda", with six of the Samarangs and three of the ship's company, set out with three natives as guides, who staid by the party just 24 hours. The party possibly reached the southern bank of the Shoalhaven River, but after being deserted by the natives at a distance of 12 or 14 miles from the vessel, they were reduced to the necessity of abandoning the project.[9]

It was by a simple means of organisation, a primitive form of co-operation that a few settlers were enabled to endure and overcome difficulties, in a spirit, and with a success, which could not otherwise be attained. All the movements of these men were neither hurriedly made nor done in a spirit of haphazardness as the Illawarra was opened up. Scouts and advance agents such as the more daring convicts, assisted by Aboriginals were employed to report on the line of march, and the place to which it should lead. There were also labourers who did much of this pioneering work, who lie here and there today, in unknown graves, whose duty it was to remove obstacles to allow the stock to pass along the narrow passes in dangerous places on the mountain range.

The halts and advances were to a great extent regulated by these men according to the amount of labour required to remove nature's obstructions. Let these considerations, therefore, be fairly weighed, as they will explain away much of the difficulties met with by

Landmark Map of the Illawarra

M7. Contemporary map of the landmarks of the Illawarra region stretching from Coledale in the north to Bass Point in the south.

LEFT: 'Pumpkin Cottage', the first home of Henry and Sarah Osborne of 'Marshall Mount', painted by Robert Hoddle, 1832. RIGHT: Early photograph of Charles Throsby Smith, 'father of the Illawarra'.

the early pioneers and the perilous positions they were often in, while engaged taking their stock to Illawarra by land.[10]

In 1816, the year of John Frawley's birth in Ireland, an inspired paragraph appeared in the New South Wales "Gazette" on the 28th September, and read as follows... "The natives of the new settlement at the Five Islands are described as being very amicably disposed to us, and the general mildness of their manners to differ considerably from the other tribes known to us. Several gentlemen have removed their cattle thither, as the neighbourhood affords good pasturing; and it is anxiously hoped that the stockmen in charge of their herds will be able to maintain the friendly footing that at present exists with them." Later on the following notification appeared in the 'Sydney Gazette,' under the heading Public Notices:

"Government House, Sydney, 16th November, 1816. Those gentlemen and free settlers who have lately obtained His Excellency the Governor's promises of grants of land, in the new district of Illawarra, or Five Islands, are hereby informed that the Surveyor-General and his deputy have received His Excellency the Governor's instructions to proceed thither in the course of the ensuing week to make a regular survey of the said district, to locate the several promised grants. And in order that the locations may be made accordingly, those persons who have obtained promises of allotments are hereby requested to avail themselves of the approaching occasion of the Surveyors on duty in Illawarra, to get their locations marked out to them. And for this purpose they are required to meet the Surveyor-General at the hut of Mr. Throsby's stock-men, in Illawarra, or the Five Islands district, at the hour of twelve noon, on Monday, 2nd day of December next, at which time he is to commence on locating the lands agreeable to the instructions which he will be officially furnished previous thereto."

By Command of His Excellency, J. F. Campbell Secretary, 1816 [11]

Exploration of the Illawarra

Shortly after the allocation of the first grants of land in Illawarra in 1817, the government formed a settlement at Red Point, Port Kembla with Dr. William Elyard Sr., R.N., he being the first government visiting officer, and superintendent of convicts stationed at Sydney. He came down in the "Snapper", and brought a sergeant, whose duty it was to count and record the strokes of the cat-o'-nine tails, and a flogger to administer the punishment. At that time the whole of the coast was policed by the military as far south as Jervis Bay.

Hence we have Barrack Point at Shellharbour and Kinghorn Point near Jervis Bay. However, the powers invested in men like Elyard were most arbitrary. It was in their power to hang delinquents on the spot, and punish others with up to 500 lashes. They moved from centre to centre with a few of the military and a flogger in order to deal with each case that came before them. But the sickening stories of the old regime could not withstand the light of day, and consequently were collected and burned.[12]

Throsby, Meehan, Hume & Others (1818)

The next exploration of the south east came from the west, after having been commissioned by Governor Macquarie to find a way overland from the Southern Tablelands to Jervis Bay. The party consisting of Charles Throsby, James Meehan, Hamilton Hume (1797-1873), and others departed from the Moss Vale area in March 1818, crossing the Wingecarribee River, they passed though Marulan and Bungonia Creek, but the expedition split with James Meehan's party discovering the Goulburn Plains. Charles Throsby's (1777-1828) party, who were guided by Aboriginals, explored Bundanoon Creek, Meryla Pass, Yarrunga Creek and came upon Kangaroo Valley. He reached the Kangaroo River at Bendeela and a day later, climbed out of the valley over the Bugong Gap and continued on to Jervis Bay, reaching the Shoalhaven River at Burrier, and Jervis Bay at Huskisson Hill before returning to Exeter.[13]

By 1818 William Emmett was in charge of the government station at Red Point, and although he was not a military man, he had the government cattle under his charge. In 1818 a general order was issued to begin on 1st January 1819, calling upon all persons, bond and free, who were engaged cutting cedar in Illawarra, to obtain permits to do so. About this time, Charles Throsby, who was born in England in 1777, was promised a grant of 1000 acres for finding a fresh track from the cow pastures to Bong Bong in 1815. His servants, Joe Wild (1750-1837) and Jack Waite received 100 acres each and another servant named Rowley got 200 acres. Joe Wild and Jack Waite understood the bush tracks in the years before the county of Camden was marked out in August of 1819. During that same year Surgeon D'Arcy Wentworth (1762-1827) was shipping cattle to his Peterborough Estate in Illawarra.[14]

Postcard of the magnificent scenery of the 'Illawarra, NSW', painted by A.H. Fulwood, c.1900.

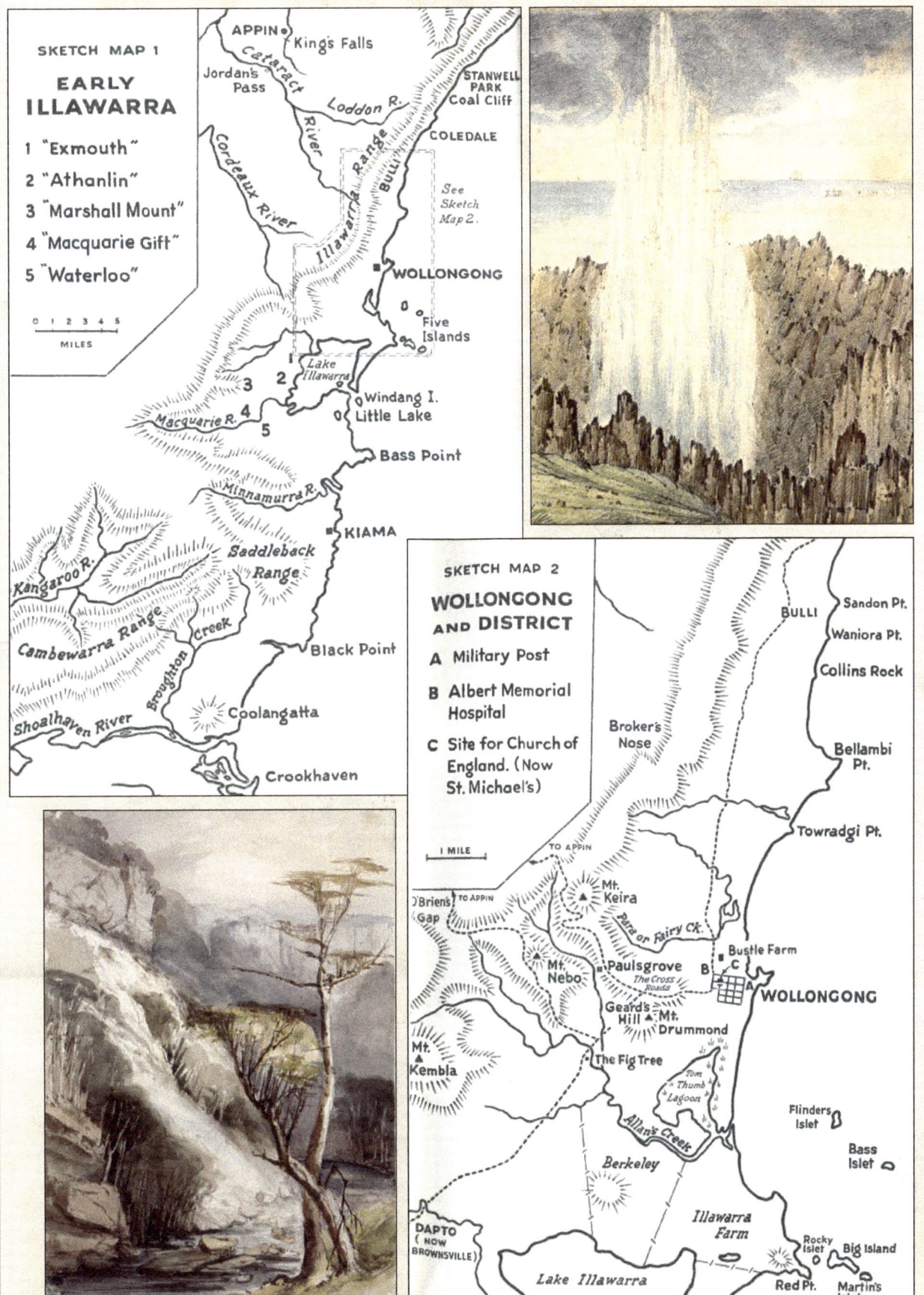

TOP (Left): M8. The route of G.W. Evans' 1812 expedition from Shoal Haven to Illawarra and overland to Appin (From... '1812 Route of G.W. Evans', in... McDonald, W.G., 1966). (Right): 'Kiama Blowhole' painted by Capt. Robert Marsh Westmacott, c.1840. ABOVE (Left): '50 Miles [South] from Sydney', painted by Georgiana Lowe, c.1840s. (Right): M9. 'Map of Earliest Illawarra by its Explorers & Pioneers', (in... McDonald, W.G., 1966, Illawarra Historical Society, Wollongong, p.64).

Early Settlers in the Illawarra by Charles Throsby Smith [28]

Judge Alfred McFarland (1824–1901), in his work on the Illawarra, records an account provided by Mr. Charles Throsby Smith of Wollongong, one of the region's earliest settlers. He recounts the gradual occupation and settlement of this fertile yet untamed land.

Early Settlement of Illawarra

In 1815, the county of Cumberland was suffering from a severe drought. Cattle were dying daily due to a lack of food and water. Dr. Charles Throsby, then residing at Glenfield near Liverpool, was an enterprising man. During one of his excursions, he encountered a group of Aboriginal people who told him of a land called the "Five Islands," where grass and water were abundant. Intrigued by their descriptions, he decided to see for himself.

Accompanied by two white men, two Aboriginal guides, and a packhorse loaded with provisions, Dr. Throsby set out. They spent their first night at Appin before continuing eastward. After four arduous days of carving a path through the dense bushland, they reached the mountain range's summit and caught their first glimpse of the vast ocean. The next day, they began the challenging task of cutting a track down the mountain, near what later became Bulli.

Upon arrival, they found an abundance of grass and water—more than enough to sustain livestock. Without delay, they returned to Liverpool to report their findings. Soon after, they drove a herd of cattle down into the Illawarra, making them the first cattle ever to enter the district. A stockyard was built near the site of the present-day Roman Catholic schoolhouse in Wollongong, with a hut erected nearby at what is now Smith Street.

As news of Dr. Throsby's success spread, other settlers followed. Colonel Johnston drove his cattle to what became known as Johnston's Meadows along the Macquarie River, while Samuel Terry settled on the opposite bank. Mr. Brown from Abbotsbury brought his livestock to the shores of Illawarra Lake, known to the local Aboriginal people as "Yalla." Captain Brooks sent cattle from Denham Court to the same area, near present-day Dapto. More settlers followed, including George Cribb, who established himself near Figtree, naming the location "Charcoal Creek" after his stockman, known as "Charcoal Will."

In 1817, the father of W.W. Jenkins arrived, guided down the mountain by Throsby Smith himself. He settled near what would later become Berkeley. Smith vividly recalled the event, particularly because Charcoal Will became extremely drunk that day. By this time, some of Dr. Throsby's cattle had grown remarkably fat. A small number were driven back up the mountain to Sydney, then still a fledgling town, and slaughtered at the Government abattoir where Dawes Battery now stands. The exceptional quality of the beef quickly made "Five Islands" meat famous, and before long, the region became overstocked with horses and cattle.

In 1820, Dr. Throsby relocated his cattle to Bong Bong. Throsby Smith assisted in the move and, around the same time, decided to settle permanently in the colony. In 1823, he selected the land where he now resided, drawn to its natural harbor. In those days, settlers chose land freely before surveys were conducted. With his wife and four assigned convicts, he began clearing the land, despite occasional conflicts with local Aboriginal people. However, through kindness and mutual respect, he quickly formed friendships with them.

That same year, another drought in Cumberland County drove more settlers into Illawarra. Among them was Hamilton Hume, the "Mungo Park of Australia," who oversaw sawyers cutting cedar on the mountain between Wollongong and Bulli—the first cedar felled in the colony. The timber was cut into boards, carried up the mountain, and carted to Parramatta. These sawyers, however, were often unruly, providing shelter to bushrangers—escaped convicts—who harassed settlers. The problem became so severe that Governor Macquarie dispatched soldiers to suppress both bushrangers and hostile Aboriginal groups.

Meanwhile, the government continued expanding its presence. Surveyor-General John Oxley and Commissary Allan established a stock station

The 'Harbour at Wollongong', painted by J.G. Sawkins, c.1852-53.

at Five Islands Point, while D'Arcy Wentworth, Sydney's Police Magistrate, acquired land south of Illawarra Lake. He later sold it to M. Badgery, who used it as a stock station. The estate, known as Peterborough, passed through several hands but remains in Wentworth's family today.

To maintain order, the government deployed around 30 soldiers under Captain Bishop of the 40th Regiment to Red Point. However, due to difficult conditions, they soon relocated to Wollongong, setting up tents on the site of the current courthouse. Captain Bishop was later replaced by Mr. Butler, and soon after, barracks and a commandant's residence were built. As convicts flooded the colony, authorities also commissioned a road down Mount Keira, completed under the supervision of Mr. O'Hanly and Captain Sheaffe.

A Police Magistrate's office was soon established, first led by Captain Allman and later by others, including Captain Plunkett. In early settlement days, a court was also held monthly in Shoalhaven.

Wollongong's Development

The first church built in Wollongong was a Roman Catholic chapel, pastored by Father Therry, on the site of the present Catholic schoolhouse. For Anglicans, Archdeacon Broughton provided a catechist, who initially led services in a rented barn before Rev. F. Wilkinson became their minister. He also held monthly services in Shoalhaven. The first schoolhouse, built on Market Street, later became the Church of England schoolhouse. The Presbyterian Church followed, built under Rev. J. Tait.

By this time, the settlement was beginning to take shape. Governor Bourke, Major Mitchell, Colonel Barney, and G.K. Holden visited and laid out the official plan for Wollongong. To support development, 300 convicts, accompanied by soldiers, were dispatched to construct the basin. They established a stockade on Flagstaff Hill, marking Wollongong's rapid transformation into a thriving township.

Industry followed. The first steam-powered flour mill was built near Para Creek by Peck and Palmer, with others soon appearing in Dapto and Wollongong. Dr. Grover became the first resident medical practitioner. Wilson Brothers opened the first significant store in Wollongong, while Mr. Hargraves, later famed for discovering gold, established the first country store in Dapto before leaving for California.

Land prices fluctuated. Under Governor Brisbane, land was briefly sold at five shillings per acre, and many settlers took advantage. One early farmer, Mr. Barrett, cultivated Herne Farm but perished at sea when his shipment of potatoes was lost. Later, James Shoobert acquired the Mount Keira estate and pioneered Illawarra's coal industry.

Meanwhile, roads continued to improve. Cornelius O'Brien, overseeing his uncle's cattle, discovered a new pass down the escarpment, now known as O'Brien's Road. It became the main route to the Five Islands until the Mount Keira road was constructed.

The Land and Its People

In the early years, Illawarra was densely forested, with towering trees, tangled vines, and thick undergrowth. Only a few natural clearings existed, such as the swamplands near Tom Thumb Lagoon and pockets of land around Macquarie River. The region boasted rich timber resources, including cedar, sassafras, ironbark, and stringybark, fueling a booming timber trade. However, much of it was wasted in the rush for settlement.

The Aboriginal people of Wollongong, numbering around 100, were generally peaceful. Their diet consisted of fish, kangaroos, possums, and wildfowl. The local chief, "Old Bundle," claimed Wollongong as his domain, often receiving food and supplies from settlers. Another leader, "Old Timberry," ruled the Berkeley area, though territorial boundaries were flexible. Though occasional conflicts arose, early settlers and Aboriginal groups often coexisted, sharing knowledge of the land that shaped Illawarra's future. Thus, the settlement of Illawarra was forged—through hardship, perseverance, and the meeting of two worlds.

The coastal escarpment at 'Bulli, Illawarra', painted by Capt. Robert Marsh Westmacott (National Library of Australia).

It was with a view to preventing horse and cattle stealing that Capt. Richard Brooks (1765-1833), undertook the great task of stocking the Kangaroo Valley country in 1818. To do so he used the path which led from Lake Illawarra, crossing the Macquarie Rivulet to the west of Johnston's Meadows, then up the range into the Pheasant Ground to a spot known today as Hoddle's Track, and from thence along the range to the valley below. The Kangaroo Ground could also be reached from the County of Argyle, by a path leading from Bong Bong, and by another path which led from Coura to Cambewarra. Jervis Bay and Coolangatta could then be reached by paths from the Kangaroo Ground, but it was the impression of old settlers that a convenient road could not be found to carry a wheel conveyance of any description in and out of the place.[15]

In 1819 Charles O'Brien was appointed government overseer of stock at Red Point, Illawarra, and Conor Wholohan was managing David Allan's farm at Five Islands. Among the places set apart for grants of land for small settlers was Coalcliff. Cedar cutting was at that time an important industry in the Illawarra and Hamilton Hume, took advantage of the neglect of those whose grants were there to take possession, and sent gangs of sawyers there from Appin to cut cedar in 1823. So extensive was this industry that the government decided to cease controlling the affairs of the Illawarra or Five Islands district from Sydney, and arrangements were made to send a detachment of military to build barracks at Red Point. This took some time to complete in even a rough manner, but in time Capt. Peter Bishop (?-1846), of the 40th Regiment of Foot, one sergeant, one corporal and 20 privates were duly quartered there.

When the military got going in Illawarra they were victualled by the ship "Snapper" for a short period, under the command of Lt. Robert Johnston (1792-1882). She was a government cutter of 40 tons, with dimensions of 43ft. 6ins (length), 15ft. 6ins (breadth) and 6ft. 1ins (depth). Built in New South Wales and launched on the 18th May 1821. She was originally designed as a revenue cutter and/or a dispatch vessel, but was used mainly for transporting convicts to Newcastle and as a survey vessel on discovery voyages to the South Coast of New South Wales, as well as Moreton Bay and New Zealand. The "Snapper" carried Alexander Berry (1781–1873), to the Shoalhaven River in 1822, and was transferred from colonial service to private ownership in June 1823 when she was purchased by Solomon Levey (c.1794–1833).[16]

The earliest register for marriages dates from June 16th, 1820, a marriage having been performed on that date at Liverpool. The register is in excellent order in the handwriting of some individual who copied the records of all those early marriages, nearly all of which were celebrated by Father John Joseph Therry (1790-1864).[17] Therry was a Catholic priest, the son of John Therry of Cork, and his wife Eliza, née Connolly, who was educated privately at St Patrick's College, Carlow in Ireland.

Dr. Charles Throsby (1777-1828) & Charles Throsby Smith (1798-1876)

It should not be overlooked that it was Dr. Charles Throsby Esq. (1777-1828), who was the first 'whitefella' to establish a settlement in the 'Five Islands' area in 1815, when "accompanied by a couple of men, two native blacks and a pack-horse carrying provisions, he started on his journey to move cattle into Illawarra and establish a stockyard and stockman's hut at Wollongong, creating the first official white settlement at the Illawarra."[18]

In 1819 Charles Throsby's nephew, Charles Throsby Smith (1798-1876) was given a land grant of 300 acres at the Five Islands that was to become known as Wollongong, where he would move to after his first marriage in 1822. The recollections of Mr. Charles Throsby Smith of Wollongong, one of the earliest settlers, was published in his Honor Judge McFarland's work on the Illawarra, and this account provides a detailed summary of the gradual occupation and settlement of the Illawarra.

LEFT: The first paddlesteamer to visit Wollongong was the "Sophia Jane" in 1831. RIGHT: Regular paddlesteamer services began in 1839 operated by the Illawarra Steam Packet Company - Schedule (The Sydney Monitor & Commercial Advertiser, 10 June 1839, p.3).

Land Grants in Illawarra

The earliest land grants in the Illawarra were made on the 24th January 1817 to Capt. Richard Brooks, George Johnston, Andrew Allan, Robert Jenkins and David Allan, who did not reside there, but ran cattle cared for by their employees.[19] These land grants were issued by several governors under the following conditions:

> "Each person to whom a grant was given received a number of convicts in accordance with the area of land bestowed by the Governor. These convicts were clothed and fed by the Government. Thus the landowners had absolutely free labour provided for them. This state of things was not altered much until the mid-thirties." [20]

Settlement commenced in the parish of Kembla west of the present day Wollongong running south to Dapto in 1817. When an area of 300 acres was granted to George Molle on the 11th September 1817.[21] Macquarie informed the Home Government on the 12th December 1817 of the discovery of new country at Five Islands known to the Aborigines as 'Illawarra'.[22] The first settlers in Jamberoo were two half-brothers, Messrs. John Ritchie and William Wright,[23] with other of the earliest Illawarra land grants following:[24]

- Wollongong (Berkeley) - 1,000 acres granted to Robert Jenkins; date, 24th January, 1817; quit rent, £1. Commencing 24th January, 1822. Granted by Lachlan Macquarie. Conditions: To cultivate 75 acres, and not to sell for five years.
- Wollongong (Illawarra Farm) - 1,500 acres granted to David Allan; date, 24th January, 1817; quit rent, £2.4.0 from 24th January, 1822. Granted by Lachlan Macquarie. Conditions: To cultivate 75 acres, and not to sell for five years.
- Jamberoo (Terry's Meadows) - 2,000 acres granted to Samuel Terry; date, 9th January, 1821; quit rent, £1, commencing from 9th January 1826 (Mount Terry) Granted by Lachlan Macquarie. Conditions: To cultivate 100 acres, and not to sell for five years.
- Kangaroo Ground (Exmouth) - 800 acres granted to Richard Brooks on or before 21st February, 1821; quit rent, £1. Granted by Lachlan Macquarie; Not to sell for five years.
- Coolangatta - 10,000 acres, granted to Alexander Berry and Edward Wollstonecraft, county of Camden; registered date of grant, 30th June, 1825. Granted by Sir Thomas Brisbane.
- Numbaa - 2,000 acres granted to Alexander Berry (Portion 8) on 30th June, 1825.
- Brundee and Numbaa, granted to William Elyard the younger, on 23rd April 1841, (Portion 4 - Brundee) being the land promised to William Elyard the elder, on or before 23rd April, 1829.

There was also a transfer of land at Greenwell Point from William Elyard to Alexander Berry, which was an exchange under government supervision, Berry taking the Greenwell Point property in exchange for Brundee. Anyone interested could possibly find the particulars in the Mitchell Library, where many of those peculiar transactions are stored.

The first grant of land on the south side of Lake Illawarra was given by Governor Macquarie to Lt-Col. Thomas Davey (1758-1813), generally known as 'Mad Davey,' situated at Barrack Hill, Shellharbour, in January of 1817, with others following:[25]

- Macquarie Rivulet (Macquarie's Gift) - 1,500 acres granted to George Johnston Esq., senr., on 24th January 1817; quit rent, £1.10s; quit rent commences 24th January, 1822, situated on the northern bank of the Macquarie Rivulet and later part of the estate known as 'Johnston's Meadows.'
- Macquarie Rivulet (Waterloo) - 700 acres granted to Allan Andrew, situated on the south bank of the Macquarie Rivulet, opposite the 'Macquarie Gift' grant.
- The Dunlop Vale Estate, near Lake Illawarra, was a grant from the Crown to Mr. John Wyllie, bearing date 1822. It comprised 2000 acres. It was approved by Governor Ralph Darling on 13th October, 1829, about which date Mr. Wyllie had it somewhat improved and stocked with many valuable Ayrshire cattle. Mr. Wyllie then went into the employ of Mr. Alexander Berry at Coolangatta, Shoalhaven.

Up to 1820, the last year of Macquarie's government, 400,000 acres had passed into the hands of private individuals. Macquarie was generous to his friends, and from him the settler frequently obtained with his grant, the use of a government gang, who not only cut down, but rolled the logs into piles and burnt and cleared the timber off land that would not pay the settler to clear with hired labour.[26]

Governor Macquarie's replacement Sir Thomas Brisbane (1773-1860) granted 180,000

LEFT: 'Rock Hill' at Shoalhaven, painted by Samuel Elyard. RIGHT: 'Shoalhaven River', painted by Samuel Elyard (Shoalhaven Regional Gallery, Nowra).

acres at a yearly quit rent of 2/- per 100 acres. Between December 1824, and the 19th May 1825, he sold 369,050 acres at 5/- per acre, giving long credit, with, in addition, 2/- per 100 acres, and he also granted in two years between 1823 and 1825, 573,000 acres at 15/- annual quit rent per 100 acres. But it must be noted that all these grants and purchases were accompanied by an allowance of a certain number of convicts per 30 acres to clear and till them, and that these convicts, as well as the settler and his wife, were rationed for a limited period at the expense of the government.

Governor Sir Ralph Darling (1772-1858), who ruled the convicts with a rod of iron, arrived as the new governor in December 1825, when the times of the 'first fleeters,' the irresponsible floggers, and the short allowance of coarse food were revived, and carried out in Illawarra. Some authorities have stated that his six years administration was singularly and deservedly unpopular. He was a man of forms and a precedent of the true red-tape school, and he continued to rule until the year 1831.

All the same, for years afterwards there were long lists of floggings ordered by the several naval and military magistrates who visited, first at Red Point, Port Kembla, then later at Wollongong and from thence south to Kiama, and then on Alexander Berry's Coolangatta Estate.

By 1830, the South Coast of New South Wales had been transformed from a rugged frontier into a patchwork of pastoral settlements, where European settlers carved out farms, built homesteads, and forged uneasy relationships with the land and its original custodians. The once-isolated coastline was now dotted with the odd whaling station, timber camp, and sheep run, as new arrivals sought their fortunes in an unfamiliar world.

But for some, the journey to this distant shore was not one of choice, but of punishment. Among them was a young Irishman, by the name of John Frawley, whose fate was sealed not by ambition, but by misfortune. Born in Limerick around 1816, John's life took a fateful turn when, while still just a teenager, he was convicted of stealing clothes, an offence that saw him torn from his family and sentenced to exile on the other side of the world. In 1833, he arrived in Sydney in chains, condemned to seven years of servitude, where the next chapter of his settlement in the great south land would begin.

References

1. The Sydney Gazette & NSW Advertiser, 8th June 1811, p.1.
2. McLachlan, N. D. (1967). 'Macquarie, Lachlan (1762-1824)', Australian Dictionary of Biography, Melbourne University Press. (ISSN 1833-7538 - via National Centre of Biography, Australian National University).
3. Davison, G., Hirst, J.B., & MacIntyre, S. (1998). 'The Oxford Companion to Australian History' (revised ed.). Melbourne, Vic: Oxford University Press, p.405 (ISBN 9780195515039).
4. Ward, R. (1975). 'Australia: a short history' (rev ed.). Ure Smith, p.37-38. (ISBN 978-0-7254-0164-1).
5. Molony, J.N. (1987). 'The Penguin History of Australia,' Ringwood, Vic: Penguin, p.47 (ISBN 978-0-14-009739-9).
6. Ibid, p.28.
7. Ibid, p.30.
8. Australian Dictionary of Biography - George William Evans [https://adb.anu.edu.au/biography/evans-george-william-2029].
9. The Sydney Gazette & NSW Advertiser, 17th April 1813, p.2.
10. Ibid.
11. McAffrey, Frank (1922). 'The History of Illawarra & Its Pioneers,' Sydney, John Sands Ltd., p.22.
12. McCaffrey, Frank (1922). op. cit., p.25.
13. Heritage Shoalhaven - Shoalhaven in the 19th centurey: Kangaroo Valley [https://heritageshoalhaven.wordpress.com/2018/01/23/shoalhaven-in-the-19th-century-2/].
14. Ibid.
15. McCaffrey, Frank (1922). op. cit., p.23-24.
16. Journeys in Time - "Snapper" from List of Ships [https://www.mq.edu.au/macquarie-archive/journeys/ships/list.html#s].
17. McCaffrey, Frank (1922). op. cit., p.24.
18. Organ, Michael (1990). 'Illawarra & South Coast Aborigines 1770-1850. Aboriginal Education Unit, The University of Wollongong, p.48.
19. Dowd, B.T. (1977). 'The First Five Land Grantees and the Grants in the Illawarra', Illawarra Historical Society, Wollongong, p.2.
20. Ibid.
21. Jervis, James, (1942). 'Illawarra: A Century of History' JRAHS, XXVIII, p.86.
22. Jervis, James, (1942). op. cit., p.65-6.
23. First Settlers of Jamberoo (The Kiama Independent and Shoalhaven Advertiser, 5 Aug 1939, p.2).
24. McCaffrey, Frank (1922). op. cit., p.26.
25. McCaffrey, Frank (1922). op. cit., p.27.
26. McCaffrey, Frank (1922). op. cit., p.26.
27. Kiama Library - First Nations Place Name Meanings [https://library.kiama.nsw.gov.au/History/First-Nations-Kiama#section-5].
28. Charles Throsby Smith - Early Settlers in Illawarra (Illawarra Mercury, 3 October 1876, p.4).

Further Reading

Andrews, G. (1984. South Coast Steamers. Maritime History Publications.
Bach, J. (1976). A Maritime History of Australia. Sydney, Pan Books.
Bateson, C. (1974). The Convict Ships 1787 – 1868. Sydney, Reed.
Cousins, A. (1994). The Garden of NSW: A history of the Illawarra and Shoalhaven districts. Wollongong: Illawarra Historical Society.
Cox. P. (1978). South Coast of New South Wales. Melbourne, Macmillan.
Elias, S. (Ed.) (1986). Tales of the Far South Coast. Vol.3., Bega Valley Shire Bi-Centennial Committee.
Flower, C. (1981). Illustrated History of NSW. Adelaide, Rigby.
Hawkins, I. (1977). Shipping Arrival and Departures Sydney 1826 – 1840: Volume 3, Canberra, Roebuck.

Chapter Five

AN UNWILLING PIONEER

The waves that had carried settlers and fortune-seekers to the south coast of New South Wales also bore the unwilling, the exiled, and the condemned. Among them was our ancestor John Frawley, a boy of barely seventeen, whose journey to this distant land was not driven by ambition, but by punishment.

Born in Limerick, Ireland, John's life was forever altered by a single act of desperation, a theft of clothes that saw him branded a criminal and wrenched from his family. His sentence was unforgiving: transportation across the seas to the convict colony of New South Wales. In 1833, he stepped off a prison ship onto the sun-scorched shores of Sydney, a world away from the damp green fields of his homeland. But exile was only the beginning. Assigned to the sprawling Coolangatta Estate on the South Coast, John Frawley would find himself thrust into the brutal rhythms of servitude, forging a life in a land both foreign and untamed. Though he had arrived in chains, the choices he made in this strange new world would shape not only his fate, but that of the generations to come.

John Frawley of Limerick

John Frawley was born and baptised a Catholic in Limerick, in Ireland.[1] Unfortunately, no birth or baptism records have been found, but information ascertained from his convict, marriage and death records mark his birth year to be around the year 1816.[2] A number of records attest to John's age and place of birth,[3] but the information he himself supplied on his second marriage certificate in 1894 substantiate this and would likely be most valid.[4]

Details about John Frawley's parents and early years are scarce. His father worked as a clerk and likely valued education, as John was able to read and write. He spoke the Limerick dialect, known for its sharp, nasal quality, which was often mocked for sounding rough.

The ancient entry door to St. Mary's Cathedral, Limerick, photograph by Tracy Rockwell (Oct, 2018).

Early morning breaks over the entrance to King John's Castle, Limerick (built 1200), photographs by Tracy Rockwell (2018).

Life in early 19th-century Limerick was harsh, and survival often required desperate measures. Like many others, young John likely took whatever work he could find. By the time of his arrest, he was employed as an errand boy.[5]

The City of Limerick

At this time, Limerick, located 125km west of Dublin, was and still is the principal city in the southwest of Ireland and is the Irish Republic's third largest city with it's most striking feature being the River Shannon, flowing majestically beneath the city's three bridges. The city received its charter in 1197, and is divided into three principal areas: English Town, on King's Island; Irish Town lying to the south of the river, which includes the oldest part of the city dating from the 9th century Norse settlement; and Newtown-Pery, to the south of Irish Town, dating from 1769. Historically Limerick is a city of many contrasts, containing a medieval core with a later Georgian addition. Of particular importance are King John's Castle, built on the orders of King John in the year 1200, and the cathedral, built about 1172.[6] Dominating the King's Island, which is the oldest part of Limerick City, is the enormous St. Mary's Cathedral, founded by the King of Munster, Donal Mor O'Brien, on a site where his palace once stood.

In view of the especially desperate and difficult situation many Irish folk found themselves in at this time, it is not surprising that young John Frawley fell upon difficult times. About the age of 16 he may have fallen in with a disreputable gang, or more likely found himself in a desperate situation. While the reasons why he committed his offence, without any former convictions, are unclear, evidence reveals that he was arrested, tried in court and convicted of 'stealing clothes' in Limerick, on the 5th of March 1833.[7]

During the course of the 18th century, when the death penalty came to be regarded as too severe a punishment for certain categories of capital offences, as an alternative there was frequent recourse to the transportation of convicts to colonies outside of Britain and Ireland. Initially, convicts were transported to North America, but after the American War of Independence, New South Wales was preferred as the first Australian penal colony.

Legislation to permit the transportation of convicts from Britain to New South Wales was passed in 1784. Equivalent Irish legislation, enacted in 1786 and with further legislation in 1790 to make transportation from Ireland more effectual, permitted the transportation of convicts from Ireland from 1791. Until the termination of the transportation system in 1853, some 160,000 persons were transported to Australia, approximately 26,500 of whom left from Ireland.[8]

In accordance with the strict laws of the time, crimes involving possessions or property were heavily dealt with and despite this being his first ever conviction, John Frawley's case was of this nature. For the crime of stealing clothes, he was duly sentenced to seven years penal service in the colony of New South Wales. Along with other convicted criminals, he was speedily transferred under guard by goal wagon from Limerick to the city of Cork in preparation for his transportation.

ABOVE: Painting of the 1820 'food riots' in Limerick, with crowds swarming on the opposite bank, the spire of St. Marys at far right. BELOW: Convict Indent for John Frawley (Jr).' transported on the "Java" in 1833 (NSW Convict Indents, Bound Indentures, 1788-1842)

LEFT: St Mary's Cathedral, Limerick was completed c.1194. It's inspiration came from the Cistercian monasteries, incorporating elements of both Romanesque and Gothic styles of architecture. RIGHT: A stylised Irish shamrock.

Cork City, County Cork

The city of Cork dates from a religious settlement founded there in 622AD by Saint Finbar, and is the seat of the county of Cork, located on the Lee River, at the head of Cork Harbour inlet and today, is the second largest city in Ireland. During the 11th century the Danes made it a trading station encircled with walls, then in 1172 Cork was subsumed into the Angevin Empire by King Henry II of England. By 1649 the city fell to Oliver Cromwell, Lord Protector of England during the English Civil War. The town changed hands once more in 1689 when it was captured by John Churchill (1650-1722), 1st Duke of Marlborough, for the English crown by forces loyal to King James II.[9]

Transportation to New South Wales

However, John Frawley wouldn't have spent much time in Cork as he was quickly embarked aboard the convict ship "Java", which was loaded with 206 male convicts and that ship sailed from Cork on the 24th July, 1833.[10]

Convicts under transportation were routinely handed over to the master of a ship for the duration of the voyage at the beginning of the voyage, and formally transferred at the other end, into the custody of the governor of the colony that was receiving them. Indents, or 'Indentures', were the documents used to record the transactions of transferring the convicts on arrival.

Although the convicts of the First Fleet arrived in relatively good condition, the same cannot be said for the many ships that followed over the next 60 years. The lengthy voyage,

TOP: Photograph of a warship anchored in Cork Harbour, about 1860. ABOVE: A convict ship sets sail from Ireland in foul weather, with most prisoners being seasick for the first few days.

cruel masters, harsh discipline, scurvy, dysentary and typhoid fever often combined to result in a substantial loss of life. During the voyage, convicts were housed below decks on what was known as the 'prison deck' and often further confined behind bars. In many cases they were restrained in chains and were only allowed on deck for fresh air and exercise. Conditions were very cramped and like the sailors, they mostly slept in hammocks. While little information is available about the usual layout of the convict ships, a few books do contain artist's impressions and reproductions of images held in library collections.[11]

After the English authorities began to review the system in 1801, convict transports were despatched twice a year, at the end of May and again at the beginning of September, to avoid the huge seas and dangerous winters of the southern hemisphere. Surgeons employed by the early contractors had to obey the master of the ship and on later voyages were replaced by independent Surgeon Superintendents, whose sole responsibility was for the health and well being of the convicts. As time went on, more successful routines were adopted and surgeons were supplied with explicit instructions as to how life on board ship should be organised. By then the charter operators were also paid bonuses if convicts were landed safe and sound at the end of the voyage.

By the time exiles were being transported in the 1840's and onwards, a more enlightened routine was in place, which even included the presence on board of an onboard Religious Instructor to educate the convicts and attend to their spiritual needs. The shipboard routines on some of the Western Australian transports during the 1860's have been transcribed in detail and are worth reading.

Another point of confusion that often arises with convict voyages is the route they sailed. The convict shipping lists usually indicated if a ship travelled via other ports. That was especially so in the early days when ships were smaller, took longer and had to put in for supplies and repairs along the way. In later years, after other Australian settlements had been established, the transports often stopped at more than one destination to land convicts. From England the transports may have stopped off at Gibraltar, a port in the West Indies, South America, the Cape of Good Hope and any one of the Australian penal settlements.

Voyage of the "Java" (1833)

The "Java", on which John Frawley journeyed, was built in 1813 in Calcutta and was a barque of 411 tons, the master being Jn. Todd.[12] During the voyage John Frawley reported to the ships surgeon with a complaint on the 21st August 1833. The ship's surgeon, Mr. Robert Dickson diagnosed him with having contracted pneumonia, which lasted until 25th August when he was discharged:

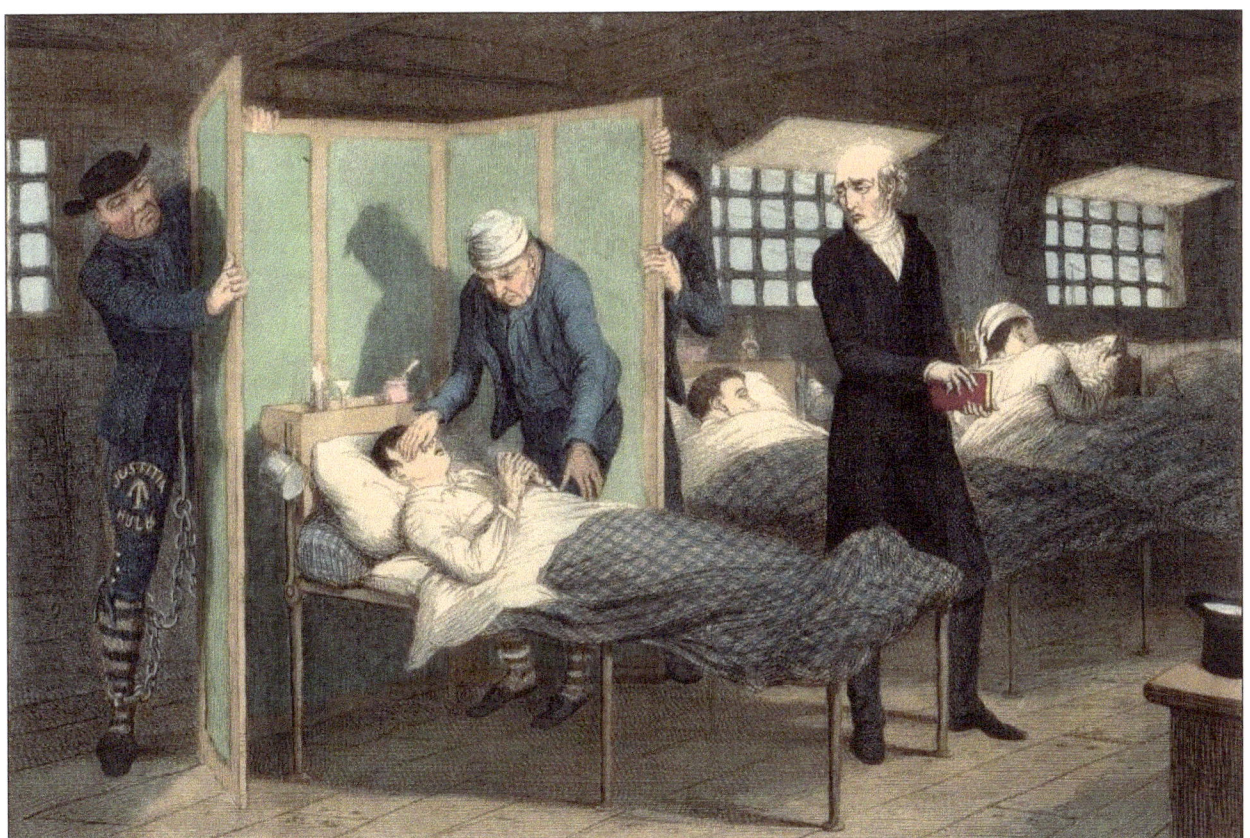

Death of a convict aboard the hulk "Justitia", attributed to George Cruikshank, by Rex Nan Kivell, 1830s, (nla.obj-135886659).

> Between the 24th day of July and the 3rd day of December, 1833. John Frawley, aged 17, pneumonia, from 21st to 25th August, discharged.
>
> *Journal of the "Java", Convict Ship* [13]

He apparently made a full recovery as no other mention of John Frawley was made on the voyage. The captain of the "Java" held regular Sunday church services for the convicts and all ships company on the way to Port Jackson. At journey's end the medical superintendant submitted his journal, which he was required to keep throughout the voyage.

> On the 22 July 1833 at the Cove of Cork, embarked on board, John Todd, master, 200 convicts, six military convicts and four free settlers, total 210, of whom three namely Daniel Sheehan, Patrick Burke and John Sullivan, did not appear in health. However, Sheehan landed at Sydney; Sullivan, the only person (a boy of 13 years) whom I objected to, after several physical attacks, rallied and landed in health; but of exceedingly delicate habit, Burke died. The embarkation of the convicts was more hurried than the surgeon had wished. The surgeon attributed the cause of so many bowel complaints to the sudden change from dry heat to cold moisture, choking perspiration and determining to the intestines. Also mentioned was that the Irish convicts, as these were, being so ill fed in their own country, do not bear the long passage or the vissitudes of climate so well as their more pampered neighbours. Included in the remark is the surgeon's (Robert Dickson) opinion of the way in which several naval surgeons have boasted of their great success in taking out convicts without losing a man, and instead of filling this journal with a repetition of successful cases the surgeon (Robert Dickson) inserted the most severe, and most fatal cases.
>
> *Surgeon's General Remarks from the "Java", 1833.* [14]

However, a critique was added to this journal by the inspector who checked it in Sydney.

"This is a very ill-written journal and by no account creditable in any respect to Mr. Dickson". [15]

After the penal colony of New South Wales became well established and permanent buildings had been erected, a routine for handling newly arrived convicts was set in place. Most convicts were assigned to settlers and emancipated convicts after an application for a convict servant or worker was lodged with the governor. Some married convicts were

Convicts being transported by ship in cages, c.1840 (artist unknown).

Voyage of the "Java" in 1833

Captain John Todd commanded the "Java", while Surgeon Superintendent Robert Dixon maintained a 'Medical and Surgical Journal' from June 30 to December 3, 1833. On July 22, 1833, 200 convicts were hastily embarked at the Cove of Cork. Alongside them, three free settlers, John McNamara, Michael McNamara, and Patrick McNamara also boarded. Additionally, six military convicts were taken on, including Robert Deighton, Michael Fox, James Fraser, Hugh McQuiggan, and Edward Standford.

The "Java" set sail from Cork on July 24th, just two days after embarkation. Among the convicts, three were already ill. A 13-year-old boy, John Sullivan, was also in poor health, but eventually recovered enough to be landed in a stable, though still fragile, condition. Surgeon Dixon attributed the high number of bowel complaints during the voyage to abrupt changes in temperature, from dry heat to cold moisture and excessive perspiration. He also believed that Irish convicts, being less well-fed than their English counterparts, were more susceptible to illness during the long passage and shifting climates. Several convicts did not survive the journey. Thomas Adams, aged 15, died on October 17; Patrick Burke on October 8; Robert Polly, 19, on October 11; James Crawley, 19, on October 30; and Michael Bercury on October 15.

After a 117-day voyage, the "Java" arrived in Port Jackson on November 18, 1833. The ship's guard comprised 29 rank-and-file soldiers from the 4th, 17th, and 21st Regiments, accompanied by five women and four children, all under the command of Lieutenant Wrixon of the 21st Regiment. Passengers included Mrs. Wrixon, Ensign Codd, and John Wrixon. The "Java" was scheduled to sail for Madras and Calcutta in December 1833.

List of 201 male convicts by the Ship
JAVA
John Todd – Master;
Robert Dickson – Surgeon.
Arrived from Cork November 18th, 1833.

Standing Convict No:	33-3093
Indent No:	169
Name:	Frawley, John (Jr.)
Age:	17
Education:	Read & Write
Religion:	Roman Catholic
Single or Married:	Single
Children:	None
Native Place:	County Limerick
Trade or Calling:	Errand Boy
Offence:	Stealing Clothes
Tried Where:	Limerick City
When Tried:	March 5th 1833
Sentence:	7 Years
Former Conviction:	None
Height:	5' 4.5"
Complexion:	Ruddy & Freckled
Hair Colour:	Brown
Eye Colour:	Grey
Marks or Scars:	Small scar left temple

TOP (Left): A convict ship making headway in a good breeze. (Right): Convict Indent for John Frawley (NSW Archives Convict Indents Fiche# 706, p.181; Film# 907, Shelf# X635) & (NSW Archives Convict Indents Fiche# 688, p.202; Film# 906, Shelf# 4/4018). ABOVE: Record of Convict Disposal, showing John Frawley's assignment to Alexander Berry, at Shoalhaven.

even assigned to their free spouses. Very few assignment registers have survived, but the Assignment Registers of 1821 to 1824 do exist. Martin Cash described his arrival in 1828 as follows:

> "On the 10th February, 1828, we arrived at Sydney, and on landing we were drafted to Hyde Park Barracks, which formed the general depot at that time for receiving prisoners. The assignment or hiring-out system had then come into operation, and myself, together with eighteen or nineteen of my companions in misery, were forwarded to different masters in Richmond."
>
> *Martin Cash, Convict* [16]

Hyde Park Barracks, Sydney [21]

The Hyde Park Barracks, Sydney is a heritage-listed former barracks, hospital, convict accommodation, mint and courthouse and now museum at Macquarie Street in the Sydney central business district of Sydney. Originally built from 1811 to 1819 as a brick building and compound to house convict men and boys, it was designed by convict architect Francis Greenway (1777-1837).

After his arrival in Sydney, Governor Macquarie had become increasingly disturbed by the male convicts' behaviour in the streets after work. Convicts had been allowed to find their own lodgings, however, Macquarie thought that barracks accommodation would improve the moral character of the men and increase their productivity. To this end, he requested convict architect Francis Greenway design a barracks for 600 men. Constructed by convicts, the foundation stone was laid by Macquarie on the 6th April 1817 and the barracks were completed by 1819. Macquarie was so impressed by Greenway's design that he granted him a full pardon shortly after its completion.[22] Convicted of forging signatures, Greenway was also known for his architectural skills and quickly advertised himself in the local places. The barracks were officially opened on the 4th June 1819, when 589 convicts were admitted.[23]

Internally, the four rooms on each floor were hung with two rows of hammocks, with a 0.9-metre (3-foot) passage. The room allowed for each hammock was 2.1 by 0.6 metres (7 by 2 feet). In this way, the long eastern rooms could sleep 70 men each, while 35 men slept in the smaller western rooms.[24]

Macquarie was happy to note that since the confinement of the male convicts to the Barracks at night "not a tenth part of the former Night Robberies and Burglaries" occurred.[25] Commissioner John Bigge (1780-1843), however, complained that the congregation of such a large number of "depraved and desperate characters" in one area had just condensed the problem.[26] Stealing was rife within the Barracks with items being passed over the walls to waiting accomplices for disposal. In an attempt to curb the thefts convicts were searched at the gates and broad arrows were painted on items of clothing and bedding.[27]

TOP: The 'Convict Barracks', Sydney, New South Wales. ABOVE (Left): A convict tied to the 'triangle' receives his allocation of lashings. (Right): Convicts were encouraged to marry rather than live in de facto relationships.

The accommodation soon proved inadequate as up to 1400 men were being housed in the Barracks at any one time. It has been estimated that perhaps 30,000 men and boys passed through the Barracks between 1819 and 1848.[28] The convict response to the Barracks was somewhat mixed: those that were able to pay for lodgings by working on Saturday were not happy about the confinement; others were happy to have a roof over their heads. In 1820, in order to ease the pressure on the crowded Barracks the reward of being allowed to live outside the facility was extended. Convicts found gambling, drunk, engaged in street violence or other unseemly behaviour had this freedom revoked and were returned to live in the Barracks - it had become a form of punishment. Loitering or idling on a Saturday was also punishable by confinement to the Barracks. Convicts had a peculiar mix of detention and freedom, they had to work for the government during the week, but were allowed to work for their own benefit on Saturdays. This was a privilege Governor Macquarie did not like to see abused.[29]

From 1830 convicts were brought to the site for sentencing and punishment by the Court of General Sessions sitting in northern perimeter buildings. Punishments handed down included floggings, which were carried out onsite, or terms on the treadmill or chain gangs. While one of the first agencies to encroach on the Barracks, but not the last - the Board for the Assignment of Servants operated from the Barracks between 1831 and 1841.[30]

Today, the Hyde Park Barracks is also known as the Mint Building and Rum Hospital; Royal Mint - Sydney Branch; Sydney Infirmary and Dispensary; Queen's Square Courts; and Queen's Square. The site is managed by the Sydney Living Museums, an agency of the Government of New South Wales, as a living history museum open to the public.

The site is inscribed on the UNESCO World Heritage List as one of 11 pre-eminent Australian Convict Sites as amongst "the best surviving examples of large-scale convict transportation and the colonial expansion of European powers through the presence and labour of convicts",[31,32] and was listed on the Australian National Heritage List on the 1st August 2007,[33] and on the New South Wales State Heritage Register on 2 April 1999.[34] The historic site was closed in January 2019 for $18 million restoration work to transform it into "a rich new, immersive visitor experience like no other in Australia" and reopened in February 2020.[35,36]

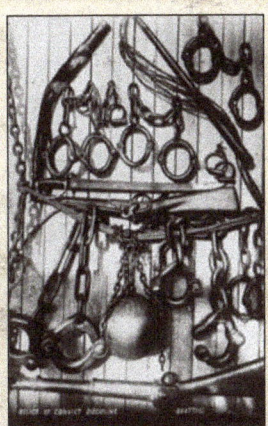

◀LEFT: Implements of oppression familiar to British convicts. RIGHT: 'The Barracks, Top of King St, Sydney.' ▲Broad arrows were painted on items of convict clothing and bedding. ▼

A government goal gang wait to be assigned to a work detail outside the Hyde Park Barracks, Sydney.

The worst type of convicts were assigned to hard labour in iron-gangs and set to work on the roads. Road gang reports (1827-1830) supplied convict number, name, ship, job, casualties, discharge details, the place stationed and the overseer. State Archives hold other records for Iron Gangs and Road Parties, and there is also a list of men in irons on Norfolk Island and Moreton Bay (1839-1840).

Musters, or head counts of prisoners were needed to keep a check on supply and demand upon the Government Stores. Usually they recorded the name, ship, sentence and residence of the convicts. Some also included the children of convicts and free persons. The 1828 Census of New South Wales is the most detailed and best surviving record of its type and is kept in most major libraries.[17] Divorce was not available to commoners until the late 1800's and was both scandalous and expensive. However, previously married convicts were permitted to remarry after seven year's separation as long as their spouse was abroad, even if they were still living. The government encouraged marriage between convicts as it was seen as a means of rehabilitation and more desirable than de facto relationships.

In the latter half of the voyage they experienced much wet, foggy weather, which saturated the decks, clothes and everything that moisture could reach. It was amidst the confusion of this convict driven society that John Frawley arrived in Port Jackson on the 18th of November 1833, after a journey of 117 days at sea. The prisoners were mustered on board the "Java" on the 22nd November 1833, which revealed that of 206 male convicts that embarked in Cork, five had died at sea and four were sent on shore sick on arrival at Sydney.

A convict ship arrives in Sydney Harbour around the same time as the arrival of John Frawley Jr. in 1833.

Convict chain gang on their way to work near Sydney NSW, c.1842 (E. Backhouse).

Upon disembarkation in Sydney all convicts were recorded by the authorities in the Convict Indents and the listing for John Frawley contains his details.[18] Oddly there were two convict indent listings for John Frawley with the only difference being the reported age of 17 in one and 19 the other. The other feature is that he is listed as being John Frawley Jr, so he obviously had a father, who was called John Frawley Sr.[19]

After being processed by the authorities, convicts were then either allocated to government service or assigned to the care of free settlers and land owners, who were required to support them in return for their work. This support included the provision of housing, clothing and food. After being held for a short stint in the Hyde Park Barracks, John Frawley was perhaps fortunate to be assigned to an established estate at Shoalhaven on the mid South Coast of NSW.

This property known as 'Coolangatta', was more than just a backdrop to John Frawley's seven years of servitude, it was a vast and ambitious estate shaped by one of early Sydney's most influential figures, Alexander Berry.[20] Understanding Berry's background and motivations provides crucial insight into the world Frawley inhabited, as it was here that he likely honed the skills and gained the experience that would shape his future. But how did this remote expanse of land become one of New South Wales' first great rural enterprises? And what obstacles did Berry overcome to bring his vision to life? Before we continue on John Frawley's journey, we must first uncover the story of Coolangatta and the man who built it.

References

1. NSW State Archives & Records. (1833). 'John Frawley off the "Java", arrived Sydney, 18th Nov. 1833, in 'Convict Indents.' (Fiche #706, p.181; Film #907, Shelf #X635) & (NSW Archives Convict Indents Fiche #688, p.202; Film #906, Shelf #4/4018).
2. Ibid.
3. John Frawley - Christening held on the 27th October, 1811 (International Genealogical Index (2000).
4. Queensland Dept of BDM. (1894). Marriage Certificate for John Frawley & Rose Emily Curtis, 27th February 1894, #1894/C/1672).
5. NSW State Archives & Records. (1833). 'John Frawley off the "Java," op. cit.
6. Wikipedia - Limerick [https://en.wikipedia.org/wiki/Limerick].
7. NSW State Archives & Records. (1833). 'John Frawley off the "Java," op. cit.
8. National Archives, Ireland [https://www.nationalarchives.ie/wp-content/uploads/2019/03/Ireland-Australia-transportation_DB.pdf].
9. Wikipedia, 'History of Cork.' [https://en.wikipedia.org/wiki/History_of_Cork]. Retrieved 8th June 2021.
10. Convict Records, 'Departure of the "Java", 24th July 1833.' [https://convictrecords.com.au/ships/java]. Retrieved 2nd March 2020.
11. Hawkins, I. (1977). 'Shipping Arrival and Departures Sydney, 1826-1840: Volume 3.' Canberra, Roebuck.
12. Bateson, C. (1974). 'The Convict Ships, 1787-1868.' Sydney, Reed.
13. Medical Journal of the "Java" convict ship from 30 June to 3 December 1833 by Robert. Dickson.The National Archives, Kew. (Public Record Office, 3198/ADM, 101/36.)
14. Ibid.
15. Ibid.
16. Cash, Martin (1961).The Bushranger of Van Diemen's Land in 1843-4: A Personal Narrative of His Exploits in the Bush and His Experiences at Port Arthur and Norfolk Island, Hobart. Convict Letters, Mitchell Library, Sydney.
17. NSW State Archives & Records.(1828). "1828 Census, New South Wales." Mitchell Library, Sydney.
18. NSW State Archives & Records. (1833). 'John Frawley off the "Java," op. cit.
19. NSW State Archives & Records. (1833). 'John Frawley off the "Java," op. cit.
20. NSW State Archives & Records. (1833). John Frawley, Assigned to Alex Berry at Shoalhaven 'Coolangatta.' Convicts Arrived, 1833-1834.
21. Wikipedia - Hyde Park Barracks, Sydney [https://en.wikipedia.org/wiki/Hyde_Park_Barracks,_Sydney].
22. "Mint Building and Hyde Park Barracks Group". New South Wales State Heritage Register. Department of Planning and Environment. H00190. Retrieved 13 October 2018. Text is licensed by State of New South Wales (Department of Planning and Environment) under CC-BY 4.0 licence.
23. ondinee (4 June 2019). "On this day: an 'excellent institution' opens". Sydney Living Museums. Retrieved 27 June 2019.
24. "Mint Building and Hyde Park Barracks Group", op.cit.
25. Cumberland County Council (1962). Historic Buildings: Central Area of Sydney, Volume II. 1962, p.6.
26. Cumberland County Council (1962). Historic Buildings: op.cit.
27. "Mint Building and Hyde Park Barracks Group", op.cit.
28. Lynn Collins, ed. (1994). Hyde Park Barracks, p.19.
29. "Mint Building and Hyde Park Barracks Group", op.cit.
30. "Mint Building and Hyde Park Barracks Group", op.cit..
31. "Australian Convict Sites". World Heritage Convention. United Nations. Retrieved 10 October 2015.
32. "Australian Convict Sites". Department of the Environment. Australian Government. Retrieved 10 October 2015.
33. "Hyde Park Barracks, Macquarie St, Sydney, NSW, Australia (Place ID 105935)". Australian Heritage Database. Australian Government. 1 August 2007. Retrieved 7 December 2018].
34. "Mint Building and Hyde Park Barracks Group", op.cit.
35. "'Work in progress': Hyde Park Barracks closes for $18 million transformation". The Sydney Morning Herald. 10 January 2019.
36. Dow, Steve (20 February 2020). "'Designed to wake people up': Jonathan Jones unveils major public work at Hyde Park barracks". The Guardian. Retrieved 20 February 2020.

Further Reading

1. Chapter 1 of Australian Government's "Australian Convict Sites" World Heritage nomination Archived 17 March 2011 at the Wayback Machine Accessed 5 August 2010
2. "Stories and Histories". Sydney Living History Museums. Archived from the original on 22 August 2010. Retrieved 10 October 2015.
3. "Australian Convict Sites". World Heritage Convention. United Nations. Retrieved 10 October 2015.
4. "Australian Convict Sites". Department of the Environment. Australian Government. Retrieved 10 October 2015.
5. "Hyde Park Barracks, Macquarie St, Sydney, NSW, Australia (Place ID 105935)". Australian Heritage Database. Australian Government. 1 August 2007. Retrieved 7 December 2018.
6. "Mint Building and Hyde Park Barracks Group". New South Wales State Heritage Register. Department of Planning and Environment. H00190. Retrieved 13 October 2018. Text is licensed by State of New South Wales (Department of Planning and Environment) under CC-BY 4.0 licence.
7. "'Work in progress': Hyde Park Barracks closes for $18 million transformation". The Sydney Morning Herald. 10 January 2019.
8. Dow, Steve (20 February 2020). "'Designed to wake people up': Jonathan Jones unveils major public work at Hyde Park barracks". The Guardian. Retrieved 20 February 2020.
9. ondinee (4 June 2019). "On this day: an 'excellent institution' opens". Sydney Living Museums. Retrieved 27 June 2019.
10. Cumberland County Council (1962). Historic Buildings: Central Area of Sydney, Volume II. 1962, p.6
11. Lynn Collins, ed. (1994). Hyde Park Barracks, p.19

Chapter Six

BERRY'S 'COOLANGATTA' HOMESTEAD

Nestled just north of the Shoalhaven River, the towering hill known as 'Cullunghutti' to the Jerrinja people offers a breathtaking lookout, providing expansive views over the surrounding landscape. In 1822, Alexander Berry, along with his partner Edward Wollstonecraft (1783-1832), who managed affairs in Sydney, set out to establish the first private European settlement on the South Coast of New South Wales. They chose Coolangatta Mountain in Shoalhaven as the site for their ambitious project. The sprawling property, named 'Coolangatta,' would become more than just a land transaction, it would develop into a pioneering estate, shaped by the vision and influence of one of early Sydney's most notable figures, the Scotsman Alexander Berry.

Berry's background and motivations offer crucial insight into the world in which our ancestor, John Frawley, lived and worked during his seven years of servitude. It was on this land, transformed by Berry's ambition, that Frawley likely gained the skills and knowledge that would define his future. But how did this remote stretch of land, far from the bustling life of Sydney, evolve into one of New South Wales' first great rural enterprises?

Berry faced numerous challenges in realizing his dream. From managing the vast property to navigating the difficulties of establishing a European settlement in such an isolated location, his journey was far from easy. However, his determination and foresight led to the creation of a thriving estate, which played a significant role in the early

'Summer Dawn, Farmland and the Sacred Mountain, Cullunghutti (Coolangatta), North East view', by Penny Sadubin (2018).

agricultural development of the region. The story of Coolangatta is more than just a tale of land acquisition, it is a testament to the pioneering spirit that helped shape the future of Australia's rural landscape.

Foundation of the Coolangatta Estate

Alexander Berry, a Scottish-born ship's surgeon, merchant, and explorer, sought a government land grant to develop an estate on the mid-south coast of New South Wales, alongside the Shoalhaven River. The government approved his request, estimating that by maintaining 100 convicts, Berry and his partner, Edward Wollstonecraft, would save authorities £16,000 over ten years.

Notwithstanding the trail-breaking role of the aforementioned explorers, Berry became the first European to establish a settlement in the Shoalhaven District. It was the colonial cutter "Snapper", under the command of Lt. Robert Johnston that first carried Berry to Jervis Bay and the Shoalhaven River in January of 1822. Berry was likely aware of the earlier expeditions, but it was this visit that convinced him to establish a settlement at the foothills of Coolangatta Mountain on the northern side of the Shoalhaven River, where he built his homestead that became the headquarters of his Coolangatta Estate.

Establishment of the Coolangatta Estate

On the morning of June 22, 1822, Alexander Berry embarked from Sydney Cove aboard the small, single-masted wooden ship "Blanche". He was heading to the northern bank of the Shoalhaven River to take up his government land grant. Alongside the crew, there were convicts, whom Berry insisted be called "government men", explorer Hamilton Hume, and an Aboriginal man named 'Charcoal Will', who was familiar with the area. The ship also carried provisions, tools, and eight pigs.

As the "Blanche" attempted to enter the Shoalhaven River, the large waves and shallow, narrow river mouth proved treacherous. A small boat sent out to assess the conditions capsized, resulting in the loss of two men. Berry then took command of the ship and sailed south to the Crookhaven River, where they anchored for the night.

The next morning, Berry had the convicts dig a channel through a sandbar between the Shoalhaven and Crookhaven Rivers, aiming to join the rivers and make navigation easier. This project, overseen by Hamilton Hume, kept the convicts busy for 12 days. The channel, known as 'Berry's Canal', became the first navigable canal in Australia and is still in use today. It altered the dynamics of the Shoalhaven River, making the original entrance to the river at Shoalhaven Heads accessible only during major floods. The canal also separated a landmass, creating Comerong Island. It became an essential route for transporting goods and people to Sydney.

The date 22 June 1822 has since been recognised as the first European settlement on the South Coast of New South Wales. Alexander Berry himself wrote:

> "For my headquarters I fixed on the north side of the river at the foot of a hill called by the natives 'Collungatta'. I located the 10,000 acres grant in this locality"

A 'fine view', was the Aboriginal word for 'Collungatta,' a description that Berry found difficult to dispute. On 1 July 1822, Alexander Berry climbed Mt. Coolangatta to view his vast estate. He spent the night atop this ancient mountain, pondering the future of his settlement and possible uses of its fertile land.

'Aboriginal Corroboree,' painted by S. T. Gill (National Museum of Australia).

Painting of the long loop known as 'Long Point on the Shoalhaven River', by Samuel Elyard (Shoalhaven Regional Gallery, Nowra).

Encounters with Aboriginal People

Upon arrival, Berry found the local Aborigines to be ferocious and initially they were driven away by the sawyers and woodcutters. Several weeks after the first arrival of the party at Shoalhaven about 20 came down and camped near Berry's settlement, and for a year or two they stole maize and potatoes. Their two chiefs were Wagin, chief of Numba or Shoalhaven, and Yager, chief of Jervis Bay. Berry later took these two on as part of the crew of a cutter in which he voyaged to Sydney and return. Berry recalled the following account of that initial settlement period:

> "I went to Shoal Haven in June 1822 in order to form an establishment. At that time the Natives at that place bore a very bad character and were considered very hostile to the whites. Some years previously the Shoalhaven River was frequented by cedar cutters from Sydney. In the end the natives either killed all the sawyers or forced them away."
>
> One day my friend James Norton thus addressed me... "I hear you are going to take a farm near Jervis Bay. Is it true?" I replied in the affirmative. "Are you mad," he retorted. "The natives will eat you."
>
> *Alexander Berry* [1]

Despite the initial conflicts, Berry later employed local Aboriginal people on his estate, integrating them into his workforce alongside convicts, free settlers, and indentured laborers. Some Aboriginal people took on key roles in timber cutting and farming, helping to shape the estate's success. Their involvement in estate operations was complex, blending cooperation and tension as they navigated a rapidly changing landscape.

A homestead was swiftly established, and despite allegations of harsh treatment towards convicts, Berry always insisted that "only mild measures and moral influences were of use in controlling men." Significantly, many of his workers remained with him even after the expiration of their penal terms, indicating a fair level of treatment.

Berry's approach to estate management was both methodical and innovative. He implemented a structured system where convicts were assigned specific tasks based on their skills. Blacksmiths, carpenters, and agricultural labourers worked in designated sections, ensuring the estate's rapid development. This system not only benefited Berry, but also allowed convicts to gain valuable skills, increasing their chances of a better life post-sentence. The government monitored the estate's progress, recognizing Berry's methods as a model for penal settlements across the colony. As a result, Coolangatta became a hub of economic and agricultural activity, setting a precedent for future landowners who sought to develop self-sustaining estates.

Berry's initial years at Coolangatta were filled with challenges, including sourcing materials, managing labor, and establishing reliable transport routes. Despite these difficulties, he successfully developed a thriving agricultural and timber enterprise. As the estate expanded, its influence grew, shaping the broader economic landscape of the developing Shoalhaven region.

Evolution of the Coolangatta Estate

As time flowed on, Berry sought to combine his merchant business with farming, drawing on his farming roots in Fife, Scotland. To prepare the land for farming, his laborers

Alexander Berry (1781-1873)

For initiative, courage and sheer wild adventure there would be few careers to rival that of Alexander Berry. Born at Cupar in Fifeshire, Scotland, on St. Andrews Day 1781, his father planned for him to become a surgeon and to that end sent him to St. Andrews and Edinburgh Universities. While studying his thoughts turned to a life at sea and he accepted a commission with the East India Company, and made a number of voyages as a ships surgeon to China and India. Whilst on the job he taught himself navigation and business principles, but resigned from this role soon after as he was determined to follow a future in commerce.

After his first commercial venture to the Cape of Good Hope in 1807, he heard of a serious shortage of food in New South Wales. Investing all his resources in the purchase of a ship, which he renamed the "City Of Edinburgh" and stocking it with provisions, he set sail for Sydney on 4th September 1807. The voyage took 14 weeks and the ship was twice dismasted in furious seas, but it eventually limped into Sydney on the 14th January 1808. Berry had offloaded most of the cargo at Port Dalrymple and the remainder was mostly spirits, which apparently aroused the anger of Governor Bligh as the Rum Rebellion was in full swing in Sydney at this time.

Following a trip to Norfolk Island and Van Diemans Land, Berry set out for New Zealand seeking spars and sandalwood. Attacked by hostile Maories in Koroaika he left for Tevenuni in the Tongan Group. Here he almost met with disaster and only his quick thinking saved him and his crew from becoming the main course at a cannibal feast. Loading sandalwood in Fiji, the "City Of Edinburgh" reached the Bay of Islands where Berry heard of a British ship being attacked and the crew taken prisoners at Whangaroa. With two armed boats he set out at once and found the remains of a convict transport ship "The Boyd", which had been returning to England and learned from local tribesman that the ships company were being eaten at a rate of two per day. Berry was able to arrive in time to rescue four survivors.

A month later in January 1810 saw Berry enroute for England via Cape Horn. Approaching the notorious passage, terrific storms played havoc with sails and steering gear, and the "City Of Edinburgh" drifted helplessly for several days. In his reminiscences, Berry tells of opening a Bible and reading the passage in Ecclesiastes 9: "Whatever thy hand findeth to do, do with all thy might." This he took as a message for him to act and not to despair. His changed attitude had its effect on a crew on the point of mutiny and with only a makeshift rudder and rig they finally reached Callao in Chile, where his ship was repaired.

With his ship ready for sea again and loaded with produce, he set sail for Cadiz in Spain and this time rounded Cape Horn in safety only to meet such constant bad weather in the Atlantic that the vessel became water-logged and foundered not far from the equator. Two boats were launched, but only that carrying Berry and his party reached safety in the Cape Verde Islands, from where he eventually got to Lisbon and Cadiz. Here, a bout of yellow fever nearly cost him his life, and on recovery Berry signed on as a crew member of a ship bound for England only to be captured by a privateer! After more adventures and much journeying Berry eventually found himself back in Lisbon where he met his future partner and friend Edward Wollstonecraft, son of a London lawyer and nephew of Mary Wollstonecraft, wife of the poet Percy Bysshe Shelley (1792-1822).

Reaching London in 1815 Berry stayed with the Wollstonecrafts at Greenwich for three years. Having established a legal partnership with Edward they chartered the "Admiral Cockburn" and took a cargo to Sydney, which arrived in July 1819. Berry wasted no time in getting the business going and built a wharf and commenced trading in timber, wool, sealskins and whale oil at what is now Berry's Bay, North Sydney.

While the business grew Berry explored the coast as far as the Hunter River and inspected the Bong Bong (Southern Highlands) district. They returned to London and applied for a grant of land in the colony, which was refused because only permanent residents were eligible. Berry and Wollstonecraft therefore decided to return to Sydney to fulfil the condition and sailed on the "Royal George" along with Governor Macquarie's successor, Sir Thomas Brisbane.

Early in 1822, at the request of the governor, Berry explored the south coast in the "Snapper" and entered every inlet between Wollongong and Bateman's Bay. His reports of the surrounding country were both accurate and interesting, but the area in the vicinity of Shoalhaven impressed him so much that he decided to settle there. Six months later he was sleeping at the foot of the hill he called 'Cullengatty' and began erecting buildings.[17]

Berry applied to the NSW Government for a grant of 10,000 acres and 100 convicts, and Wollstonecraft was granted 500 acres in the Sydney suburb that now bears his name, building a house on a hill overlooking the harbour called 'Crows Nest Cottage', which is today on the site of the current North Sydney Public School.

Not surprisingly, the government granted Berry's land request since it was estimated that by maintaining 100 convicts, Berry and Wollstonecraft would save the authorities £16,000 over the next ten years. The homestead was quickly established and despite charges of harshly treating his convicts, Berry always maintained that only mild measures and moral influences were of use in controlling men and it is of interest that a number of men stayed with him when their penal terms expired.[#19] The date 23 June 1822 has since been recognised as the first European settlement on the South Coast of NSW. Alexander Berry wrote:

"For my headquarters I fixed on the north side of the river at the foot of a hill called by the natives 'Collungatta'. I located the 10,000 acres grant in this locality"

'Collungatta' was the Aboriginal word for fine view, a description that Berry found difficult to dispute. On 1 July 1822, Alexander Berry climbed Mt. Coolangatta to view his vast estate. He spent the night atop this ancient mountain, pondering the future of his settlement and possible uses for its fertile land.

REF. https://www.coolangattaestate.com.au/history

(These entries not listed in the index)

'Coolangatta Mountain,' by Conrad Martens, showing the Berry Estate on the right, c.1860.

cleared trees to open up grazing land. In the early 19th century, red cedar (Toona ciliata), a native deciduous tree, grew abundantly along the New South Wales coast. This valuable wood was used for building, furniture, and boat construction, much of it being exported to Europe. Knowing that cedar was scarce around Sydney, Berry saw an opportunity to profit, as timber from his land was exempt from government taxes. On the return journey of the "Blanche" to Sydney, it carried a load of cedar wood bound for Europe.

Berry was drawn to the area by its rich alluvial soils, ideal for farming and grazing, though much of the low-lying land was swampy. To make the land productive, he devised a drainage system to channel water from the swamps into the river. Convicts, using basic tools, dug channels between one and three meters deep. The main channel draining Coomondery Swamp into the Shoalhaven River is still in use today and runs through the village of Shoalhaven Heads, parallel to Bolong Road. By the end of the work, around 200 kilometers of drainage channels had been dug.

Later in 1822, Hamilton Hume brought cattle to the area, marking the beginning of the district's primary industry. Mills and workshops were established, where tradesmen worked on cask-making, building repairs, leather treatment, condensed milk, gelatine, and shipbuilding. By 1824, the first vessel they called "Coolangatta" had been launched, and his influence was such that the town of Coolangatta in Queensland was even named after this first schooner, which was wrecked there in 1846.

Berry married Elizabeth (1781-1845), the sister of his business partner, Edward Wollstonecraft, on September 21, 1827. They established their headquarters at the foot of Coolangatta Mountain, north of the river, surrounded by tools, provisions, and mostly convict laborers who formed the first community. With further land purchases from the

John Frawley ("JAVA") at the Berry Estate - Coolangatta

Assigned Servants Punishment Book Berry Estate, 1835 [8]

Name:	Frawley, John
Ship:	Cahafer [JAVA]
Sentence:	Seven years
Trade:	Labourer
Age:	17
Religion:	Catholic
Date of Arrival:	[18th Nov] 1833
Date of Assignment:	December, 1833
Notes:	Free, flash gambler, very lazy.

Assigned Servants Punishment Book Berry Estate, 1835 [9]

June, 1st - John Frawley lazy, remained in his bed, the 1st plea, due for shoes etc.

July, 28th - John Frawley sent to Wollongong for drowning a mare when crossing the river, through neglect. Unfortunately, the charge could not be proved, and John Frawley was acquitted.

November, 30th - John Frawley sentenced to 36 lashes for disobedience of orders and insolence to ????? [*unclear*].

1837 - General Return of Convicts [10]

Number:	9527
Name:	Frawley, John
Age:	20
Ship:	JAVA
Year:	1833
Where Tried:	Limerick
Master:	Alexander Berry Esq.
District:	Illawarra
Page:	88

Assigned Servants Day (Slop) Book Berry Estate, 1834-1840 [11]

1834 (p.139)
January 12th	1 pr shoes, R (exchanged)
April 12th	1 pr shoes
June 7th	5 yd prs, 1 shirt
August 3rd	A new pr boots
October 4th	A new shirt
December 20th	A new pr shoes

1835
January 10th -	Shirt, duck trousers & frock
June 15th	A new pr boots
Sept 12th	1 striped shirt
October 17th	1 pr shoes

1836
June 16th	Duck frock, trousers and shirt

February 20th	1 pr boots
May 21st	1 new rug, BW #43, fruit stops
August 6th	1 pr boots
August 27th	1 shirt
November 12th	1 pr boots, 1 suit slops

1837
January 27th	1 rug #79, bed linen 18
March 10th	1 pr boots
June 2nd	1 pr boots
July 8th	1 blanket # 48
Sept 2nd	1 pr boots #40

1838
March 19th	1 pr of boots #255
March 19th	pr of duck trousers
March 24th	returned
March 28th	pr of cord trousers
May 11th	1 shirt, 1 pr trousers, 1 jacket
July 18th	1 pr of boots #423 stamped
October 13th	1 pr boots #497
December 20th	1 pr boots #552

1839
April 18th	1 pr boots
April 20th	1 rug #197
May 24th	1 frock, shirt & trousers
Sept 2nd	1 shirt (5)
Sept 22nd	1 pr boots, 1 blanket #166

1840
January 4th	1 pr boots

Various entries regarding John Frawley at the Berry Estate (From the 'Berry Papers', Mitchell Library, Sydney).

Crown and private transactions, the Coolangatta Estate expanded, eventually covering land from Gerringong in the north to Jervis Bay in the south, and even beyond the town of Berry to the west.

The Coolangatta Estate village, at the base of Coolangatta Mountain, grew into a self-sustaining township with up to 600 people. The community included builders, carpenters, blacksmiths, stonemasons, tinsmiths, bootmakers, and livestock keepers for pigs, sheep, and cattle. The estate also bred thoroughbred horses for export to India. The partners employed both convict labor and free workers to drain swamps and grow crops such as tobacco, maize, barley, and wheat, as well as raise pigs and cattle for hides, milk, and cheese. These products were transported to Sydney via ships purchased or built by the estate.

Coolangatta Estate's produce was sold in Sydney, and the estate's shipbuilders constructed vessels for transportation. The estate also supplied salt beef to the government and exported cedar to Europe. In 1823, the estate's first tobacco crop brought in substantial profits, as it was highly sought after in the Sydney market. The estate was home to a diverse population of convicts, ex-convicts, free settlers, and Aboriginal families, and his distribution of free goods to many of these helped improve their morale.

John Frawley at Coolangatta

By 1833, convict assignment had become a fairly efficient process, enabling John Frawley to be placed under Alexander Berry's charge. This likely required him to embark on another voyage, though a much shorter one south from Sydney to the Shoalhaven. The voyage would only have taken around a day or two and the vessels, which were plying this minor route at that time were smaller coastal sailboats. To be selected by a respected member of the colony at the time in the identity of Alexander Berry, proved to be providential for John Frawley in more ways than one. By the time John Frawley arrived at Berry's Coolangatta homestead in late 1833, the estate had already been functioning for 11 years, so so accommodation and out-buildings had already been erected and daily routines firmly established.[2]

On the Berry Estate most of the day to day operations were recorded and live on today in the 'Berry Papers', which are held at the Mitchell Library, at the State Library of New South Wales, Sydney. Entries for all workers including assigned servants on Berry's Estate were listed alphabetically, with the initial arrival entry for John Frawley making for interesting reading.[3]

A 'Flash' Reputation

Upon his arrival at Coolangatta in December 1833, John Frawley would no doubt have been surprised at the beauty of the rural property. He gave his age as 17, which confirms the information given by him on the Convict Indents, and fixes his birth year as somewhere in the year 1816. The other notable feature was that the convict overseers at Coolangatta categorised John Frawley as a 'free, flash gambler', with the added note that he was 'very lazy'![4] Undoubtedly, this attitude and work ethic would have to change if he was to survive in his new environment.

'FLASH'
Convicts of the early colony had their own 'flash' language, made up of slang words developed by criminals in London. Outsiders couldn't understand the language, so convicts were often able to undermine the authorities with their own jargon.

Discipline and Punishment

After 18 months of work, often enduring harsh treatment, John likely became quite familiar with the Coolangatta homestead, the work routine and life in general. However, he

TOP (Left): Engraving of the road leading to the Berry Homestead at Coolangatta, c.1835. (Right): Coolangatta Homestead, looking down from the mountain. ABOVE (Left): Alexander Berry viewing his accomplishments at Coolangatta. (Mid): Old timber wagon, likely produced on site at Coolangatta. (Right): Main entrance to the Coolangatta Estate.

TOP: Early panoramic photograph of Coolangatta Estate, c.1896. ABOVE (Left): 'Fairwaters - Shoalhaven River near Berry', NSW, c. 1896 (SLNSW-a6292008) (Right): The Great Hall on the Coolangatta Homestead.

was slow to change his habits and his old reputation soon snagged more difficulties with the estate overseers. Infringements of any kind on Berry's Estate were noted, and John Frawley is recorded in the 'Berry Estate Punishment Book' on three separate occasions during 1835.

He received 36 lashes on the 30th November, for 'disobedience of orders and insolence', which certainly would have made a psychological and physical impression on him, as there is no further mention of punishment for John Frawley thereafter.[5] Furthermore, signs that John's run of bad luck was drawing to a close became apparent when he was scheduled to receive his Certificate of Freedom in March 1840, although his actual certificate has not been found to date.

Following ten years of constant urging, Alexander Berry's three brothers, John, William

ABOVE (Left): Coolangatta House, on the Berry Estate, NSW, c. 1896 (SLNSW-a6292020) (Right): Members of the Hay Family, Coolangatta Estate, Shoalhaven River, N.S.W, 1891 (SLNSW-a3683008)

and David as well as his two sisters, arrived from Scotland to reside at the Coolangatta Homestead. Berry now left much of the daily running of the homestead to his brothers, although how much this affected the labourers is not known.

In 1837 the New South Wales Government conducted a General Return of Convicts in an attempt to accurately locate the whereabouts of the convict population at that time. John Frawley is recorded in the return as residing and working with Alexander Berry in 'Illawarra'.[6] The day to day work continued on the Berry Estate, but resources were always scarce, especially in regard to supplies handed out to the convicts. The masters of the day recorded all transactions in the Assigned Servants 'Day or Slop Book,' where John Frawley is recorded as receiving a number of items of clothing and supplies over the period from 1834 to 1840.[7]

The Coolangatta Estate After 1850

After convict transportation to New South Wales ceased in 1850, labour shortages worsened, compounded by the gold rush of the 1850s, when many workers left for the goldfields. To address this, Berry began bringing immigrant workers from China and Germany as indentured laborers and also employed local Aboriginal people and some Pacific Islanders.

In the mid-1800s, Berry began leasing small farms, requiring tenants to clear and fence the land. By 1863, the estate had expanded to over 40,000 acres. By 1869, there were around 370 tenant farmers, many of whom were the pioneer settlers who contributed to the development of the Shoalhaven District.

Alexander Berry passed away in 1873, leaving an estate valued at £1,252,975. His brother David, who had been managing the estate since 1836, inherited it. To cover three large bequests left by Alexander, David was forced to sell much of the land. The sale began in 1892, starting with the Gerringong farms and eventually including other estates.

By the late 1870s, most of the cedar had been harvested, and the estate turned increasingly to dairying to supply products like cheese and butter to the Sydney market. Dairy farming was further encouraged by the failure of wheat crops due to rust disease.

Upon David Berry's death in 1889, the estate passed to his cousin, Dr. John Hay, and later to his half-brother, Alexander Hay. Under their management, the estate became a Government Stud Farm and school in 1900. Dr. Hay traveled to Europe to study the latest methods in dairy production and imported the best dairy cattle breeds to improve milk yield. In 1895, Dr. Hay established the Jersey Milk Company at Shoalhaven Heads to produce tinned milk, which was exported to markets including China, Africa, and New Zealand. The factory was known for its strict hygiene standards, with workers required to bathe daily.

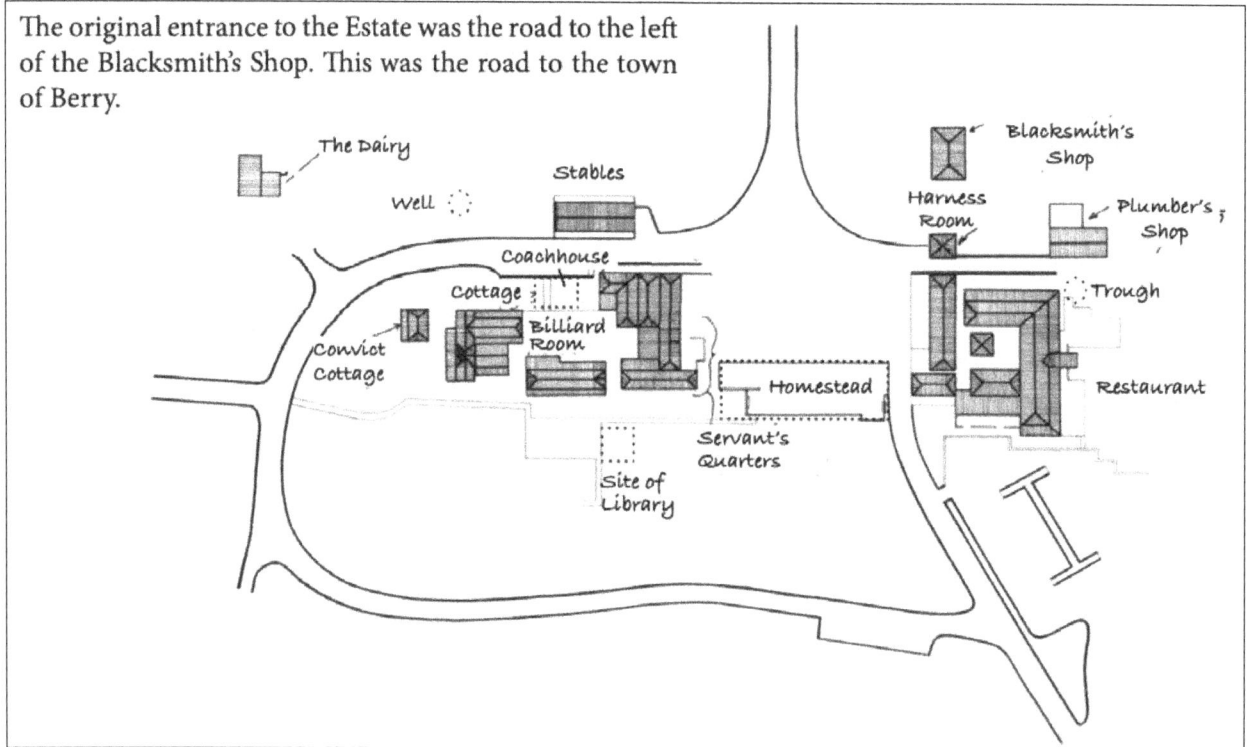

M10. Map of Coolangatta Homestead. Behind the residence at Coolangatta were numerous small dwellings, workshops, stores, coach houses etc., which were built over the years. The complex was served by a well sunk in 1827 and a large exceedingly productive kitchen garden.

TOP: 'Exploring Party', (plate 1), in James Atkinson's 'An account of the state of agriculture & grazing in New South Wales'..., London, J. Cross, 1826. (DL 82/95).
ABOVE: Farmhouses No. 5 & 2, at Shoalhaven, painted by Samuel Elyard (Shoalhaven Regional Gallery, Nowra).

Dr. Hay died in 1909, and Alexander Hay continued managing the estate until his death in 1941. His son, Alexander Berry Hay, inherited the estate, but under their management, it declined into neglect. Buildings fell into ruin, and by 1946, a fire destroyed the homestead, along with much of the estate's history. The fire was considered suspicious, and the estate was insured.

Following the fire, his second wife Elizabeth Hay began selling off the property. Over the years, Col Bishop, born on a neighbouring farm, bought parts of the estate, ultimately restoring the remaining buildings. In 1950, he purchased the former servant's quarters and made it his family home. By the 1960s, Col and his wife, Norma, had acquired all 300 acres of the estate.

In 1968, the Bishops began restoring the property for commercial use, transforming it into accommodation. Col financed the restoration himself, purchasing furniture from the Metropole Hotel in Sydney, which was due for demolition. The Coolangatta Historic Village Motel opened in 1972, on the 150th anniversary of Alexander Berry's arrival.

Today, the Coolangatta Estate remains a picturesque site overlooking the ocean and surrounded by vineyards, preserving its historic legacy amidst modern development.

For further details of the founding of the settlement at Coolangatta and to read Berry's fascinating account of his interactions with the Aboriginals, read the "Reminiscences of Alexander Berry', (*see Appendix D*).

Few lives could match the initiative, courage, and sheer adventure of Scottish born Alexander Berry, who trained as a surgeon but soon turned to trade and exploration, embarking on daring ventures across the Pacific. Eventually, he settled in New South Wales, where he became a prominent landowner and entrepreneur.

In 1822, Berry established the first European settlement on the Shoalhaven River, securing an enormous land grant of 10,000 acres, five times the typical allocation. The grant came with a strict condition: he had to employ, feed, and clothe one convict for every 100 acres for a decade, meaning he was responsible for 100 convicts. Many of these men had been sentenced to transportation for life due to serious crimes. The arrangement, however, benefited both parties, reducing the government's burden while supplying landowners with much-needed labor.

Berry's sharp business instincts and resilience enabled him to build immense wealth, but his later years were overshadowed by legal battles and personal tragedies. He passed away in 1873, leaving a lasting mark on Australian colonial history.

For our ancestor John Frawley, life as a convict at Alexander Berry's Coolangatta estate was one of toil and hardship. Sentenced to a life far from his homeland, he laboured under the harsh conditions of colonial New South Wales, shaping the very land that would become

The Schooner "Coolangatta" & Coolangatta, QLD [13]

LEFT: The "Coolangatta", Alexander Berry's ship that was wrecked off Kirra Beach in Queensland. RIGHT: Anchor from the "Coolangatta" wreck site memorial.

The Queensland Gold Coast township of Coolangatta was named after a ship, the "Coolangatta", which was built in 1843 on the Coolangatta Estate in Shoalhaven, New South Wales. The vessel met its fate just three years later, wrecking on Kirra/Bilinga Beach near a creek during a storm in 1846.[12] The Coolangatta was a topsail schooner, measuring 83 feet (25 meters) in length and weighing 88 long tons. It was built by John Blinksell for Alexander Berry at his property, Coolangatta Estate, which bordered Coolangatta Mountain on the northern bank of the Shoalhaven River. The ship primarily transported produce to Sydney for sale.

On July 6, 1846, under the command of Captain Steele, the "Coolangatta" departed from Brisbane, carrying two convict prisoners—George Craig (in irons) and William George Lewis. The ship was bound for the Tweed River to collect red cedar logs for transport to Sydney. However, upon arrival, Steele found the river entrance blocked by a sandbar and anchored the ship in the lee of Point Danger off Kirra Beach. Since the logs could not be loaded directly onto the vessel, they were hauled overland from Terranora Inlet and rafted from the beach. Despite six weeks of effort, fewer than half of the contracted 70,000 feet of cedar had been loaded, while five other ships remained trapped inside the river due to the bar.

On August 18, while Steele was ashore, a southeast gale struck. His boat was damaged in the surf, leaving him stranded as he watched the storm intensify. As conditions worsened, the "Coolangatta" began dragging anchor. Realizing the ship was doomed, the prisoners were freed, and the crew abandoned ship, swimming to shore just before it broke apart near what would later be called 'Coolangatta Creek'.

The survivors then embarked on a grueling six-day, 110-kilometer trek north to Amity Point. Along the way, they were provided food each night by various groups of friendly Indigenous Australians before being rescued and transported to Brisbane aboard the "Tamar". Over time, the wreckage of the Coolangatta was buried by sand, and in 1883, the area was officially named in its honor.

TOP: Looking south across 'Broughton Creek and Coolangatta Mountain from Boxsell's Farm', painted by Samuel Elyard. ABOVE: 'Shoalhaven River Boats', painted by Samuel Elyard (Shoalhaven Regional Gallery, Nowra).

his reluctant home. The days were grueling, the work unending, and his hope of freedom a distant dream. Yet, in the midst of his struggles, fate had something unexpected in store.

However, as the year 1838 drew to a close, John's world changed with a single glance. Among the convicts toiling on the estate was a young Irishwoman, someone who, like him, had been torn from her homeland and sentenced to an uncertain future on the far side of the world. She was Mary Ann McGarry, a fellow Limerick native, and like John, she carried the weight of exile on her shoulders. Their shared pasts, their shared loss, and the bond of their homeland forged an unbreakable connection.

But who was Mary Ann McGarry before she became a convict? What circumstances led her to this distant shore? To understand her journey, we must turn back the pages of history and uncover the story of her ancestors, a tale that begins far from the rugged coast of Shoalhaven and deep in the heart of Ireland…

'The Shoalhaven River at its junction with Broughton Creek', painted by Julian Ashton.

References

1. Bayley W. A. (1965). 'Shoalhaven: History of the Shire of Shoalhaven', pp.24-25.
2. Anderson, J. (ed.). (1990). 'Guide to the papers of the Berry, Wollstonecraft and Hay Families.' Mitchell Library, Sydney.
3. Berry Papers. John Frawley, in 'List of Assigned Servants'. Mitchell Library, Sydney (MSS-315/62).
4. Ibid.
5. Berry Papers. John Frawley in 'Assigned Servants Punishment Book.' Mitchell Library, Sydney (MSS-315/62).
6. John Frawley in 'General Return of Convicts in 1837.' Mitchell Library, Sydney, p.227.
7. Berry Papers. John Frawley, off the 'Chafer' [sic. "Java"] in 'Assigned Servants Day (Slop) Book.' Mitchell Library, Sydney.
8. John Frawley in the Berry Papers (Mitchell Library/MSS-315/37).
9. John Frawley in the Berry Papers (Mitchell Library/MSS-315/62).
10. John Frawley in the Berry Papers, Mitchell Library, p.227.
11. John Frawley in the Berry Papers (Mitchell Library/MSS-315/62).
12. Gold Coast Bulletin, 'Could Coolangatta's History Be Rewritten If A Maritime Mystery Is Solved?,' by Andrew Potts, 29th March 2014, p.1.
13. Wikipedia - Wreck of the "Coolangatta" [https://en.wikipedia.org/wiki/Coolangatta].

Chapter Seven

THE McGARRY ANCESTORS
(Antecedents of Mary Ann McGarry)

Although Mary Ann McGarry was not born until 1813, her story begins long before then, shaped by the turbulent history of Ireland and the struggles of her ancestors. The period between 1780 and 1838 was one of profound change in Ireland, particularly in County Limerick, where her family resided. This era witnessed major events that reshaped Irish society, affecting the political, economic, and social conditions that would ultimately influence Mary Ann McGarry's path and her fate as a convict.

One of the most significant events of this period was the Act of Union (1801), which formally united Ireland with Great Britain, dissolving the Irish Parliament and intensifying tensions between Irish nationalists and the British Government. The economic hardships that followed were exacerbated by lingering effects of the Penal Laws, which disproportionately impacted Catholic families like the McGarrys. These restrictive laws suppressed Catholic rights, limiting land ownership and access to education, thereby perpetuating poverty and social division.

Limerick, a key city in western Ireland, was deeply affected by these national struggles. The Napoleonic Wars from 1803 to 1815, had both positive and negative consequences for the region. While they created temporary economic opportunities through military recruitment and increased demand for goods, they also led to trade disruptions and greater

A clear Autumn day at St Mary's Cathedral, in Limerick, Ireland (Protestant Church of Ireland), photograph by Tracy Rockwell (Oct. 2018).

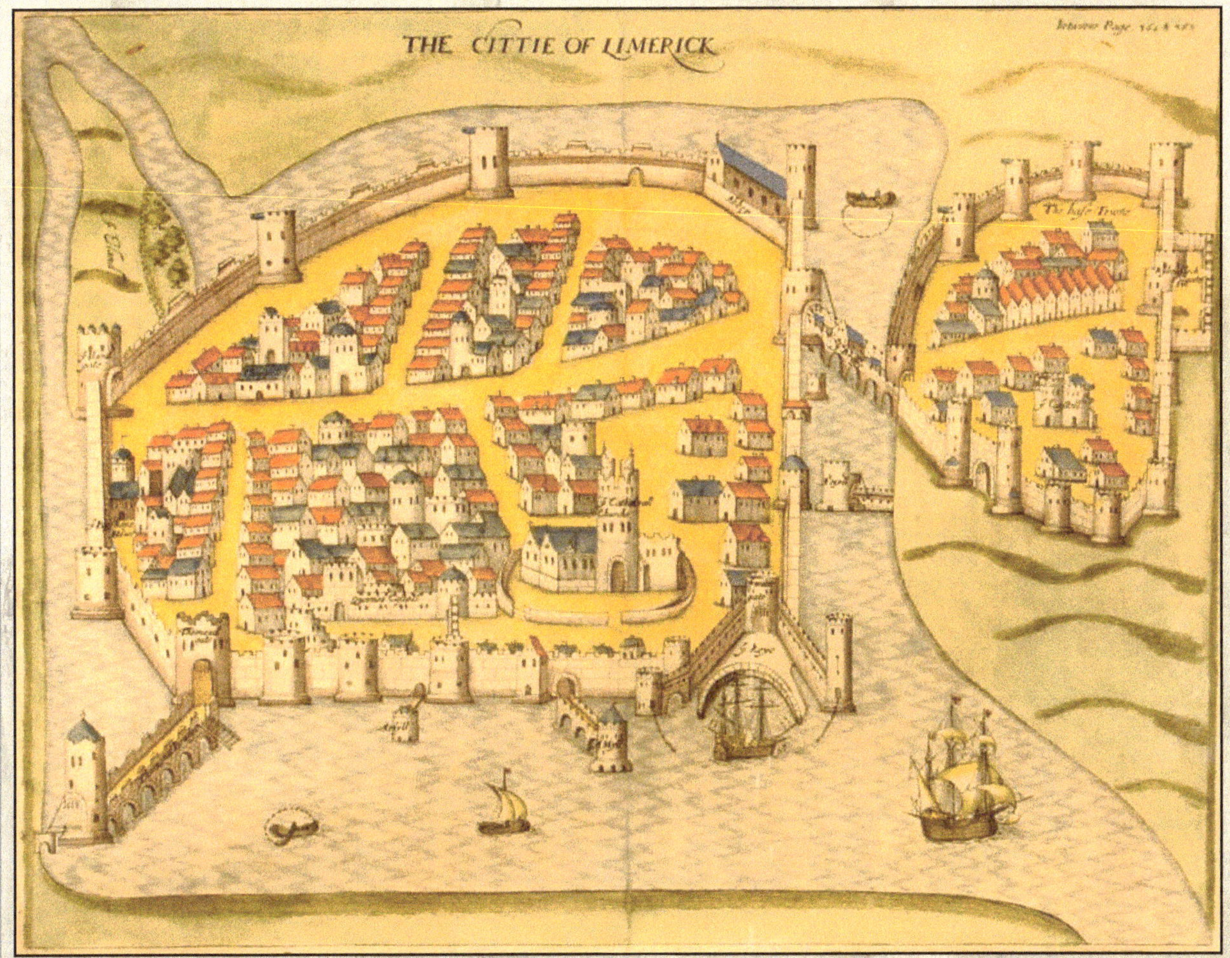

TOP: M11. 1587 Map of Limerick City, showing 'English Town' to the left. ABOVE (Left): A typical Irish crofter hut of the 18th & 19th century. (Right): Typical gaelic clothing as worn in the 16th century.

hardship for rural communities. In response to economic distress and oppressive landlord policies, secret agrarian societies such as the 'Whiteboys' and the 'Rockites' emerged, engaging in resistance against landlords and British authorities. This period of unrest and rebellion reflected the desperation of many Irish families who faced eviction, starvation, and persecution.

Within this historical backdrop, this chapter delves into the origins of the McGarry

St Mary's Cathedral of the Church of Ireland in Limerick, was founded in 1168 and is the oldest building in Limerick still in daily use. It has the only complete set of 'misericords' left in Ireland. (A misericord is a folding seat which, when folded up, is intended to act as a shelf to support a person in a partially standing position during long periods of prayer).

surname and explores Mary Ann McGarry's earliest known ancestors, who were farmers in County Limerick. Their lives, shaped by agricultural traditions and the changing political landscape, provide vital context for understanding the world Mary Ann was born into. By examining their struggles and resilience, we gain deeper insight into the circumstances that led to her eventual transportation as a convict.

Ireland in the 16th & 17th Centuries

The McGarry ancestors lived through turbulent times including the American Revolution, which ignited strong sympathy in Ulster, particularly among the Presbyterians. Having been denied the right to hold public office, they sought widespread emancipation that included Roman Catholics. In 1778, the Irish Parliament responded by passing the Relief Act, easing some of the harshest restrictions imposed by the Penal Laws. Meanwhile, Irish Protestants, using the pretense of protecting the country from a potential French invasion, formed volunteer militias, swelling to nearly 80,000 members. Empowered by this force, they demanded legislative independence for Ireland. This push for autonomy gained momentum when British statesman Charles James Fox successfully moved for the repeal of Poynings' Law and significant anti-Catholic legislation. However, despite these advances, the Irish Parliament remained firmly under Protestant control and resisted extending voting rights to Catholics.[1]

The influence of the French Revolution found its most fervent supporters in Ireland through the Society of United Irishmen, who orchestrated the 1798 Irish Rebellion. Though poorly armed, Irish peasants rose in Wexford, staging a valiant effort that briefly threatened

Dublin. However, they were ultimately defeated by Crown forces at Vinegar Hill. A French force of 1,100 men later landed at Killala Bay, but their arrival came too late to turn the tide. Observing the unrest, British Prime Minister William Pitt the Younger concluded that only a legislative union between Great Britain and Ireland, alongside Catholic emancipation, could stabilize the situation. To achieve this, he employed a mix of financial incentives and political patronage, persuading the Irish Parliament to pass the Act of Union.

In 1800, both the Irish Parliament and the Parliament of Great Britain passed the Act of Union, which came into effect on the 1st January 1801. This abolished the Irish legislature and merged the Kingdom of Ireland with Great Britain to form the United Kingdom of Great Britain and Ireland. The Union Flag was modified to include Saint Patrick's Cross, which was counterchanged with Saint Andrew's Cross to symbolize Ireland's inclusion. However, King George III vehemently opposed Catholic emancipation, forcing Pitt to abandon his promise and resign in frustration.[2]

Post-union Irish history was dominated by the struggle for civil and religious freedom, as well as the ongoing desire for independence from Britain. Dissatisfaction with the union quickly boiled over, leading to the armed rebellion of July 23, 1803, led by Irish nationalist Robert Emmet. The uprising was swiftly crushed, and for a time, armed resistance subsided. However, the fight for Catholic rights continued through peaceful means. In 1823, the Catholic Association was founded, relentlessly advocating for full emancipation. Their efforts bore fruit in 1828, when Catholics were granted the right to hold local office, followed by the landmark 1829 decision allowing them to sit in Parliament.

With religious restrictions easing, attention turned to another major grievance, the compulsory tithes paid to support the Anglican Church of Ireland. The so-called "Tithe War" erupted as Irish Catholics resisted these unjust payments. Violent clashes ensued, with atrocities committed by both sides. Alongside the tithe protests, the call for repealing the Act of Union grew louder, giving rise to various nationalist groups, including the Ribbon Society, which operated on the fringes of law and order.[3]

The 1832 reform of the British Parliament brought a modest victory for Ireland, increasing its parliamentary representation from 100 to 105 seats. More significantly, it empowered the middle class, weakening the dominance of the pro-English aristocracy. In 1838, Parliament passed a bill converting tithes into rent charges paid by landlords, momentarily easing tensions over the issue.

Just as one struggle seemed to settle, a catastrophic disaster reshaped Ireland's landscape. Between 1845 and 1850, a devastating famine struck, caused by widespread potato crop failure. The impact was catastrophic, millions either perished from starvation or fled the country. Emigration to America surged, with entire communities uprooted in search of survival. It is estimated that Ireland's population declined by over two million due to famine and forced displacement.

Amidst this period of upheaval, the McGarry ancestors endured. Coming from the southwestern city of Limerick, they lived through these turbulent times, witnessing firsthand the fight for Irish independence, religious equality, and economic survival. The reforms of 1838 had briefly alleviated tensions, but the famine's devastation overshadowed any progress, leaving an indelible mark on the history of Ireland and its people.

The resilience of the Irish spirit, tested through centuries of struggle, would continue to shape the nation's history in the years to come. Through rebellion, reform, and resistance,

The 1801 Act of Union [8]

At the start of the 19th century, Ireland was still reeling from the aftermath of the 1798 Irish Rebellion. Prisoners were being deported to Australia, and sporadic violence continued in County Wicklow. Another failed uprising, led by Robert Emmet, took place in 1803. The Act of Union, which formally merged Ireland with Britain, was largely an effort to address the grievances behind the 1798 rebellion and to prevent future unrest from threatening Britain or inviting foreign intervention.

In 1800, both the Irish Parliament and the Parliament of Great Britain passed the Act of Union, which came into effect on the 1st January 1801. This abolished the Irish legislature and merged the Kingdom of Ireland with Great Britain to form the United Kingdom of Great Britain and Ireland. The Union Flag was modified to include Saint Patrick's Cross, which was counterchanged with Saint Andrew's Cross to symbolize Ireland's inclusion.

The act's passage in the Irish Parliament, like the 1707 Acts of Union between Scotland and England, was ultimately secured through widespread bribery. Many Irish MPs were granted British peerages and other incentives in exchange for their support.

During this period, Ireland was governed by officials appointed by the British government. The Lord Lieutenant of Ireland, who represented the King, and the Chief Secretary for Ireland, appointed by the British Prime Minister, were the key figures. Over time, as the British Parliament assumed more executive power from the monarchy, the Chief Secretary gained prominence, while the Lord Lieutenant became largely symbolic. With the abolition of the Irish Parliament, Irish representatives were now elected to the United Kingdom's House of Commons at Westminster.

The British administration in Ireland, often referred to as "Dublin Castle," remained dominated by the Anglo-Irish elite until its withdrawal from Dublin in 1922.

TOP: The Castle of King John, traditional refuge of the English inhabitants of Limerick. ABOVE (Right): The 'Union Jack' before above... and below, with the addition of the red saltire of Saint Patrick, after the 1801 Act of Union with Ireland.

Ireland's long road to self-determination was far from over.

In weaving this family history with Ireland's historical past, this chapter sets the stage for Mary Ann McGarry's journey. Whether by forced exile, voluntary migration, or transportation as convicts, countless Irish laid the foundations for new communities in Australia. Mary Ann McGarry, the 'colleen' from Limerick, was part of this story of Irish resilience and survival. What better way to begin this section than by tracing the origins of the McGarry name and uncovering the history of the ancestors and family that came before her?[4]

THE McGARRY ANCESTORS

The McGarrys were the paternal ancestors of Mary Ann McGarry, but unfortunately, little is known about them. The earliest confirmed mention of Mary McGarry's paternal ancestors was written into her 1889 death certificate, registered in Queensland. On that document, Mary's father was identified as Patrick McGarry, who was a farmer likley working in and about Limerick. While we face the same frustrating lack of information about John Frawley's ancestors, we can nevertheless dive into the origins of the McGarry surname and uncover its history.

The Surname of McGarry

The surname of McGarry is found in various spellings which include MacCarry, McHarry, McGarrie, McGarry, MacAree, M'Garry and Megarry. This latter form is a strange anglicised corruption, which resulted from the similarity of the sound 'Mac an Ri', meaning 'the son of king', although there is no logical connection.[5] It is said that the

Birthdates from Family Search.org
For Patrick McGarry

Death	Age	Place	Birth	Source
		Dublin (bap.)	1783	Catholic Parish Registers
1844	60	Annelly	1784	Catholic Parish Registers
		Ireland	1790	Find A Grave
		Wicklow (bap.)	1792	Catholic Parish Registers
1868	67	Belfast	1792	IGI
		Cloonguish (b.)	c.1793	UK Pension - Solder Service
		Kilmon (b.)	c.1794	Canada - British Regiment
1865	70	Mohill	1799	IGI
		Longford (b.)	1799	UK Pension data
		Wicklow (bap.)	1800	Catholic Parish Registers
		Manchester (b.)	c.1800	1861 English Census

For Mary McGarry (nee Heffernan)

Death	Age	Place	Birth	Source
1841	70	Mohill	1771	Wife residing 1841 Census
1866	86	Dublin North	1780	IGI
1866	73	Mullingar	1793	IGI
1865	70	Dublin South	1795	Widowed...IGI
1866	71	Manorhamilton	1795	IGI
1865	70	Nenagh	1795	IGI
1865	70	Rathdown	1795	IGI
1866	70	Dublin South	1796	IGI
1867	70	Dublin South	1797	IGI
1865	67	Granard	1798	IGI
1867	65	Mohill	1802	IGI

Thomas William McGarry, whose family came from Ireland, became a Canadian politician. He served as a Conservative Member of the Legislative Assembly of Ontario for Renfrew South from 1905 to 1919, and later as provincial treasurer from 1914 to 1919. He was born to Thomas McGarry and Mary Dowdall, and died in 1935.

RIGHT: Possible birth dates for Mary McGarry's parents... Patrick McGarry & Mary Heffernan.

McGarrys form part of the clan MacHugh of Leitrim and Roscommon, although again this has not been proven as the derivation of the surnames are quite different. Examples of recordings for this complex surname include Grizzel McHarry at Killyleagh, County Down, on April 28th 1742; Mary McGarry, christened at Downpatrick, County Down on July 8th 1779; and Mary McCarry, who was a passenger on the ship "Marmion of Liverpool", which sailed from Belfast to New York on May 25th 1846, during the 'Great Famine' of 1846-1848.[6]

The first known recorded spelling of the family name of McGarry may be that of Nickolas Magheree, which was dated September 28th 1625, at the church of St John the Evangelist, in Dublin, during the reign of King Charles I (1625-1649), otherwise known as 'The Martyr'.[7]

Famous & Notable McGarrys

The surname McGarry, has been associated with a number of notable individuals across various fields. Some distinguished bearers of the McGarry name (all from Wikipedia) are:

Seán McGarry (1886–1958, no known relation): An influential Irish nationalist and politician, Seán McGarry was a senior member of the Irish Republican Brotherhood (IRB) and served as its president from 1917 to 1918. He played a significant role in Ireland's struggle for independence, participating in the 1916 Easter Rising and later serving as a Teachta Dála (TD) in the Irish parliament.

Bill McGarry (1927–2005, no known relation): An English international football player and manager, Bill McGarry had a notable career in football, both on the field and from the sidelines. These individuals exemplify the diverse achievements of those bearing the McGarry surname, making significant impacts in their respective fields.

Mary Ann McGarry's father, Patrick McGarry was a farmer in the early to mid 19th century, likely in and about County Limerick.

THE HEFFERNAN ANCESTORS

The Heffernans were the maternal ancestors of Mary Ann McGarry. The Heffernan family crest came into existence many centuries ago. This ancient Irish name of Heffernan is an Anglicized form of the Gaelic surname "O'hIfearnain", the "O" prefix indicating "male descendant of", and the personal name "Ifearnan", being a diminutive formation from the nickname "Ifreannach", or demon, being from "ifreann", or hell.[10]

The Surname of Heffernan

There is some confusion as to the meaning of this name, but some believe it to mean Horse-Lord, or 'eachearnan', where 'eich' was 'horse' and 'Thigearnán' meant lord' and that the name Aherne, who are from the same area is the anglicised variation of this name. Traditionally, Irish family names were taken from the heads of tribes, or from some illustrious warrior, and were usually prefixed by "O", as above, or "Mac", denoting "the son of." The original territory of the Heffernan sept was near Corofin in County Clare, called Muintirfernain after them, but they established themselves early on in eastern County Limerick, on the Tipperary border, and were chiefs of Owneybeg. The O'Heffernans are still found mostly in those areas. Old manuscripts such as the "Book of Rights" describe the O'Heffernans as one of the "four tribes of Owney", the others being MacKeogh, O'Loingsigh (Lynch), and O'Calahan. The modern surname of Heffernan can be found recorded in a number of variations such as Heffernan, Hiffernan, Heffernon and Hefferan.[11]

Famous & Notable Heffernans

A notable bearer of the name was William Dall O'Heffernan (1715-1802), the Gaelic poet. One of the first recorded spellings of the family name is shown to be that of Aeneas O'Heffernan, the Bishop of Emly, which was dated 1543, during the reign of King Henry VIII (r.1509-1547), otherwise known as "Bluff King Hal," of England. Notable persons with the Heffernan surname include the following...[12]

William Daniel Heffernan (b.1943), more commonly known as Bill Heffernan, is a former Australian politician who was a member of the Liberal Party in the Senate representing the state of New South Wales, and serving from 1996 to 2016. Christy Heffernan (b.1957) is an Irish retired hurler who played as a full-forward for the Kilkenny senior team. William J. Heffernan (1872-1955), was an American politician and member of the New York State

TOP: The Lisburn & Lambeg Volunteers firing a 'Feu de Joie' in honour of the Dungannon Convention, 1782. ABOVE (Left): Photograph of George's Quay at Limerick, by Tracy Rockwell, 2018. (Right): Photograph of Bill Heffernan (b.1943), Liberal Party politician from Australia.

Senate (5th District) from 1913 to 1918, sitting in the 136th, 137th, 138th, 139th and 140th New York State Legislatures.[13]

Beyond the Heffernan surname, no further details are known about Mary McGarry's maternal ancestry at this time.

PATRICK McGARRY & MARY HEFFERNAN

Around 900 years before the McGarrys and Heffernans set foot in Limerick, the region was known as 'Luimneach.' It encompassed the general area along the banks of the Shannon Estuary, then referred to as 'Loch Luimnigh.' The earliest recorded settlements on King's Island during the pre-Viking and Viking eras were called 'Inis Sibhtonn' and 'Inis an Ghaill Duibh' in historical annals.[14]

Mary Ann McGarry's parentage is fortunately well-documented. Her death certificate, recorded at the Dunwich Benevolent Asylum in Queensland in 1889, lists her parents as Patrick MacGarry, a farmer, and Mary Heffernan of Limerick, County Limerick, Ireland.[15] However, due to the lack of surviving records, tracing her ancestry beyond this point remains an exceedingly difficult task.

A 2014 blog post by 'GenealogyBank' titled "Why Do You Love Genealogy?" highlighted the widespread passion for family history research. Bu the sub-question, "what most frustrates people about genealogy", resonated with my own experiences of hitting research roadblocks. The post received over 200 responses, many of which echoed my own struggles with the Frawley and McGarry lines, dead ends, missing information, and the occasional inaccuracy in shared genealogical data.[16]

The Arms and motto of Limerick, depicted in stained glass, which translates to "There was an ancient city, very fierce in the skills of war."

As the daughter of Patrick MacGarry and Mary Heffernan, Mary Ann McGarry was undoubtedly a native of Limerick. Her parents likely had other children, and records from the International Genealogical Index (IGI) list Patrick McGarry (1821-1878) and Michael McGarry (born 1833) as potential siblings. Michael married Johanna FitzGerald, daughter of James FitzGerald, on February 25, 1865, in Croom, County Limerick.

Patrick McGarry, the Patriarch

Little is known about Mary's father Patrick MacGarry, who was likely born around 1790. Mary Ann recorded his occupation as a farmer and noted that the McGarry family hailed from Limerick, or possibly from Loughmore, slightly to the south. A death registration in the IGI lists a Patrick McGarry of Aghalust, born around 1788, but there is no way to confirm whether he was Mary Ann's father.

Mary Heffernan, the Matriarch

Similarly, very little is known about Mary Heffernan, Patrick MacGarry's wife, and Mary Ann McGarry's mother. She was probably born around 1790 and resided in County Limerick. One possible record in the IGI lists a Mary Heffernan of Mitchelstown, County Cork, about 60 kilometers south of Limerick, born around 1790. However, there is no definitive proof linking her to Mary Ann McGarry.

A baptism record for a Maria (Mary) Heffernan was discovered on the FamilySearch website, dated July 4, 1790, at St. Mary's Church in Clonmel, close to Mitchelstown, and this record lists her parents as Joannis (John) Heffernan and Catharine Hennessy, with William Meehan and Maria Kelly as godparents. However, this connection requires verification.[17]

TOP (Left): 1870 Death registration for a Patrick McGarry, possible father of Mary Ann McGarry (1788 birthyear, from Family Search.org). (Right): 1816 Possible baptism for Mary Ann McGarry (1816 birthyear, from Family Search.org). ABOVE (Left): Possible baptism for Mary Heffernan on the 4th July 1790 at St Mary's, Clonmel, co. Tipperary, Ireland. (Catholic Parish Registers, 1655-1915, Waterford and Lismore - St Mary's, Clonmel 1790 - 1797). (Right): The coat of arms of the Hennessy family.

The Protestant Ascendancy [18]

The Protestant Ascendancy, often referred to simply as the Ascendancy, was the political, economic, and social dominance of Ireland by a small Protestant elite from the 17th to the early 20th century. This ruling class consisted mainly of wealthy landowners, Protestant clergy, and professionals, all of whom belonged to the Church of Ireland or the Church of England.

The Ascendancy systematically excluded most of the Irish population, primarily Roman Catholics, but also Presbyterians and other religious minorities, including Jews, from political power and high society. Even the majority of Irish Protestants were largely excluded due to property requirements that prevented them from voting until the Reform Acts (1832-1928). The privileges enjoyed by the Ascendancy were widely resented, particularly by Irish Catholics, who made up the majority of the population.

The dispossession of Catholic landowners in Ireland occurred gradually, beginning in the reigns of Queen Mary I and her Protestant half-sister, Elizabeth I. A series of unsuccessful Irish uprisings against English rule, including the Nine Years' War (1595-1603), the Irish Rebellion of 1641-53, and the Williamite Wars (1689-91), resulted in widespread land confiscation by the Crown. These lands were then granted or sold to individuals deemed loyal to the English monarchy, most of whom were English and Protestant. Over time, English soldiers, traders, and landowners formed a new ruling class. The wealthiest among them were elevated to the Irish House of Lords and eventually gained control over the Irish House of Commons. Collectively, they became known as the Anglo-Irish.

By the 1790s, the term Ascendancy took on different meanings depending on political perspective. For Irish nationalists, who were mostly Catholic, it became a symbol of oppression and resentment. For unionists, who were predominantly Protestant, it evoked a sense of lost prestige and influence. The vast majority of Ireland's population were Catholic peasants, many of whom lived in extreme poverty and had little political influence during the 18th century. Some Catholic leaders even converted to Protestantism to avoid severe legal and economic penalties. Despite this, a growing Catholic cultural awakening was beginning to take shape.

Tensions eventually erupted in the Irish Rebellion of 1798, culminating in the Battle of Vinegar Hill on June 21, 1798. In this decisive conflict, more than 13,000 British troops attacked Vinegar Hill, near Enniscorthy in County Wexford, which served as the largest camp and headquarters of the Wexford United Irish rebels. The battle, which took place both on Vinegar Hill and in the streets of Enniscorthy, marked a turning point in the rebellion. It was the last major attempt by the Irish rebels to hold and defend territory against the British military.

The tranquil morning beauty of the River Shannon, County Limerick, Ireland.

At this stage, further investigation into the McGarry and Heffernan family lines has been unproductive. Although multiple birth registrations exist for individuals named Patrick McGarry and Mary Heffernan, none provide definitive proof of lineage. Rather than clarifying the picture, the available data only deepens the mystery, leaving the search for Mary Ann McGarry's ancestors an ongoing challenge.

Patrick McGarry and Mary Heffernan's legacy carried on through their children, including a daughter born in Limerick around 1813. Named after her mother, young Mary's life took a devastating turn when she was convicted of 'receiving stolen goods', a crime that ripped her from her home and condemned her to exile on the far side of the world.

In 1838, she arrived in Sydney aboard the convict transport "Diamond", sentenced to seven years of servitude. But as the ship's anchor dropped, her true journey was just beginning. Forced to navigate the brutal realities of a fledgling colony, Mary's story became one of resilience, survival, and fate's unexpected twists.

In the next chapter, we uncover the trials she faced, the choices that shaped her destiny, and how the ghosts of her past would forever shape the woman she would become.

References

1. Wikipedia - History of Ireland (1801-1823) [https://en.wikipedia.org/wiki/History_of_Ireland_(1801–1923)].
2. Ibid.
3. Ibid.
4. Ancestry - McGarry Family History [https://www.ancestry.com.au/name-origin?surname=mcgarry].
5. SurnameDB - McGarry [https://www.surnamedb.com/Surname/McGarry].
6. Ibid.
7. Ibid.
8. Wikipedia - Acts of Union 1800 [https://en.wikipedia.org/wiki/Acts_of_Union_1800].
9. Wikipedia - Thomas McGarry [https://en.wikipedia.org/wiki/Thomas_McGarry].
10. Wikipedia - Heffernan [https://en.wikipedia.org/wiki/Heffernan].
11. SurnameDB - Heffernan [https://www.surnamedb.com/Surname/Heffernan].
12. Ibid.
13. Wikipedia - Heffernan, op. cit.
14. Wikipedia - History of Limerick [https://en.wikipedia.org/wiki/History_of_Limerick.
15. Queensland Dept of BDM. (1889). Death Certificate for Mary Frawley (nee McGarry) at Dunwich Benevolent Asylum, 1889/3633-1695.
16. Harrell-Sesniak, Mary, (2014). 'Your Top Genealogy Challenges & Frustrations', GenealogyBank Blog, October 28, 2014.
17. Possible baptism for Mary Heffernan on the 4th July 1790 at St Mary's, Clonmel, co. Tipperary, Ireland. (Catholic Parish Registers, 1655-1915, Waterford and Lismore - St Mary´s, Clonmel 1790 - 1797).
18. Wikipedia - Protestant Ascendancy [https://en.wikipedia.org/wiki/Protestant_Ascendancy].

Chapter Eight

MARY ANN McGARRY, CONVICT

Mary Ann McGarry's journey began in the heart of Ireland, likely around the year 1813, in the bustling city of Limerick.[1] Born to Patrick McGarry and Mary Heffernan, she was one of many caught in the tides of hardship that swept through early 19th-century Ireland.[2] While little is known of her childhood, by the mid-1830s, she was working as a housemaid in Limerick, a position that offered stability, but little protection from the grinding realities of life.

Fate, however, had a different path in store for Mary. In July 1837, she found herself standing in a courtroom, accused of receiving stolen goods, a crime that, minor as it seemed, carried severe consequences in an era of unforgiving British law. It wasn't her first run-in with the authorities; records indicate a previous conviction that had already landed her behind bars for three months. Whether out of desperation or misfortune, Mary had crossed a line that the judicial system did not take lightly.[3] The verdict? Transportation beyond the seas, a seven-year sentence to the penal colony of New South Wales.

Desperate to alter her fate, Mary took the only option available to her, she petitioned for clemency.[4] Her plea landed on the desk of none other than Richard Wellesley (1760-1842), 1st Marquess Wellesley, the Lord Lieutenant of Ireland, and elder brother of the Duke of Wellington.[5] In a time when mercy was rarely granted, prisoner petitions were meticulously reviewed, their merits weighed by judges, constables, and gaol governors. Mary's petition,

Prisoner Petition for Mary Ann McGarry

Surname:	McGarry
Other names:	Mary
Age:	16
Sex:	F
Alias:	-
Place of trial:	Limerick City
Trial date:	00/07/1837
Place of Imprisonment:	-
Document date:	-
Crime description:	Receiving stolen goods
Sentence:	Transportation 7 yrs
Ship:	"Diamond" 15/11/1837
Petitioner:	-
Relationship:	-
Document references:	TR 2, p.77 (F)
Microfilm references:	-
Comments:	Record 10 of 17

LEFT: Sample prisoner petition to the Lord Lieutenant & Governor of Ireland, for a commutation of sentence. RIGHT (Top): Prisoner petition for Mary McGarry. (Above): A convict ship pulls away from Ireland, with most poor souls never to see their homeland again.

however, was sparse. She claimed to be just sixteen years old, perhaps an attempt to evoke sympathy, but beyond that, there was little to strengthen her case.[6,7]

With the weight of the British judicial system against her and her fate hanging by a thread, Mary's journey was only just beginning. What lay ahead was a world unknown, one of hardship, resilience, and the unyielding will to survive.

Transportation

Unfortunately, the appeal was unsuccessful and Mary was transported under guard in a gaol wagon along with other prisoners from Limerick to Dublin, and was later embarked on board the female convict ship "Diamond", which was then moored in Kingston Harbour.

The "Diamond" was a relatively new and large schooner of 573 tons, having been built in 1835 on the Isle of Man, the master being James F. Bissett.[8] The ship was loaded with 162 female prisoners and 27 of their children, who were received from the Penitentiary at Dublin, probably in October or early November of 1837.

There was also 18 female passengers aboard the "Diamond", most of whom were the free wives of convicts already in New South Wales together with 36 of their children. One cabin passenger also came aboard in Mr. Goodwin.[9] The newspapers reported that the ship was to depart at the first opportunity, however their actual departure was delayed from Kingston Harbour until the 29th November 1837, and sailed just a day after the "William Jardine".

> "Two hundred female convicts have been embarked on board the Diamond convict-ship, now in Kingston Harbour, for New South Wales. She sails on the first fair wind."
>
> *The Morning Post, 15th November 1837* [10]

Mr. William McDowell, the surgeon superintendent, who was going out on his third such convict voyage, was required to keep the ships journal.

> "Receipts for convicts, clothes etc received on board, 16 November 1837; Memorandum of convicts families recommended to be sent to New South Wales at Public expense, with observation on character, situation etc; List of Free Settlers embarked; Scale of the Proportion of Medicines and Necessaries for 200 Convicts for voyage (printed); Manifests of Stores received; Return of names and ages of the children of Convicts embarked; and List of money belonging to Convicts given into the charge of the Surgeon Superintendent."
>
> *William McDowell, Surgeon* [11]

McDowell kept the medical journal from the 20th October 1837 to 20th April 1838. However, it seems few if any unusual events confronted any of the female convicts, the ships company or the ship itself en route to New South Wales.

> "I beg leave to acquaint you agreeable to my instructions that the number of female convicts embarked on board the ship Diamond for a passage to New South Wales were in all 162 received from the Penitentiary in Dublin all in tolerable good health with twenty-seven of their children of different ages."
>
> *William McDowell, Surgeon* [12]

Once at sea, the women suffered severely from seasickness and constipation during the voyage, with Mr McDowell supposing this was made worse by the great change they experienced in their rations and lack of exercise. According to the surgeon's sick book, McDowell remarked that there were seven confinements, which expended most of the medical comforts and hospital clothing, with three deaths on the voyage, although only

TOP (Left): Mary Ann McGarry likely came from humble origins in County Limerick, Ireland. (Right): A description of the Dublin Female Penitentiary as it was in 1821, (from 'An Historical Guide to Ancient and Modern Dublin', by George Newenham Wright, 1821). ABOVE (Left): On voyages from Ireland to Australia, authorities sometimes struggled to contain the depravity on board. (Right): Female convicts often showed solidarity and defiance of authority.

\multicolumn{2}{c}{List of 162 female convicts by the Ship "DIAMOND" James F. Bissett – Master; William McDowell – Surgeon. Arrived from Ireland March 28, 1838.}
Standing Convict No:	47-38
Indent No:	47
Name:	McGarry, Mary
Age:	25
Education:	None
Religion:	Roman Catholic
Single or Married:	Single
Children:	None
Native Place:	County Limerick
Trade or Calling:	House Maid
Offence:	Receiving Stolen Goods
Tried Where:	Limerick City
When Tried:	July 1837
Sentence:	7 Years
Former Conviction:	3 Months
Height:	4' 11.25"
Complexion:	Ruddy & Freckled
Hair Colour:	Brown
Eye Colour:	Hazel Grey
Marks or Scars:	Eyebrows Meeting
Cert. of Freedom:	*Unsure* (44/1183 or 45/848)

TOP: The convict ship "Diamond" departing Kingston Harbour, Dublin in late Nov. 1838. ABOVE (Left): A convict transport drops anchor in Sydney Harbour. (Right): Convict Indent for Mary Ann McGarry, off the "Diamond", March 1838. (NSW Archives Convict Indents Fiche# 735, p.226; Film# 908, Shelf# X641).

one was a prisoner, and considered that illnesses aboard were otherwise "mostly trifling." A violent gale blew up on the 14th December during which the prisoner Catherine Raygan (Regan), was injured by a cask rolling about the deck, and she was afterwards treated by the surgeon for almost six weeks for her sufferings.

According to the masters log on route, the "Diamond" spoke with the "Hyacinth", bound for the Cape of Good Hope in latitude 4°6' north and longitude 18°15' west. Also on the 1st February the "Duchess of Northumberland" from London to Sydney in latitude 32°5', and longitude 21°30' west, near the Cape of Good Hope; and on the 3rd January exchanged numbers with the "Alacrity", 30 days out from London in latitude 5° north, and longitude 18°40' west, bound for Port Jackson.[13]

The "Diamond" arrived at Port Jackson on the 28th March 1838 after a voyage of

114 days. However, the women were kept on board for almost two weeks before being landed on Thursday 12th April, but at Fort Macquarie instead of at the dockyard. Fort Macquarie was designed by Francis Greenway, and built in 1817, but was demolished in 1901. The superlative site then became a tram shed until the 1950s when Jan Utzon won a competition to design the world famous Sydney Opera House that occupies the site today.

Just six months later, Caroline Chisholm (1808-1817) arrived in Sydney with her husband Captain Archibald Chisholm, who had been granted a two-year furlough from Madras, India on the grounds of ill health. Rather than return to England, the Chisholms decided the climate in Australia would be better for his health so they set sail for Sydney, aboard the "Emerald Isle", and arrived at Port Jackson in September 1838, later settling at Windsor.[14]

Upon disembarkation on the 12th April 1838 the female convicts were recorded by the authorities in the Convict Indents and the listing for Mary Ann McGarry was very informative. A committee of ladies was in attendance at Fort Macquarie for the purpose of pointing out to the newly arrived prisoners the necessity of their behaving themselves in the different situations they may be placed in, so as to merit any future indulgence. Governor Sir George Gipps (1790-1847) was also in attendance, and exhorted the women to behave themselves in their new capacities. They were also addressed by the Bishop before being distributed to various people who had applied for convict labour.[15]

The 'Sydney Monitor' carried the following news on the 16th April 1838...

NEWS OF THE DAY

"At the time of landing the women by the "Diamond", at Fort Macquarie on Wednesday last, a circumstance occurred which is likely to give employment to some of our gentleman learned in the law. The matter of dispute was between two gentlemen well known in the town, and both holding Government appointments. As the facts will most probably come to light in the Supreme Court, we abstain from at present mentioning names or particulars."

The Sydney Monitor, 16th April 1838.

Sydney Harbour around the time Mary Ann McGarry arrived at the end of March 1838, painted by Conrad Martens about 1836.

Standing No. of Convicts	Indent No.	Name	Age	Education		Religion	Single, Married or Widow	Children		Native Place	Trade or Calling	Offence	Tried	
				R. Reads	W. Writes			Male	Female				Where	When
		M:												
101-38	102	M'Call, Bridget	24	None		Rom. Cath	Single			County Antrim	Country servant	Stealing money	Antrim	18 October,
83-38	84	McCloy, Mary	20	R		Rom. Cath	Single			Londonderry	Country servant	Arson	Londonderry	26 July, 18
86-38	87	M'Corkill, Anne	19	R		Protestant	Single			Londonderry	Country servant	Vagrancy	Londonderry	24 July, 18
47-38	47	M'Garry, Mary	23	None		Rom. Cath	Single			County Limerick	House maid	Receiving stolen goods	Limerick City	July, 1837

TOP: Convict Indent for Mary Ann McGarry, off the "Diamond", March 1838. (NSW Archives Convict Indents Fiche# 735, p.226; Film# 908, Shelf# X641). ABOVE: Wood engraving of the "St Vincent" being towed in by a paddlesteamer, with 'bounty' emigrants. (Illustrated London News 1844).

Although we know not the exact reason, the dispute was apparently between Colonel Wilson and the clerk to the Superintendant of Convicts at the time, and a Mr. Thomas Ryan, which involved the distribution of two of the women who disembarked the "Diamond".[16]

Details taken directly from Mary McGarry's 'indent' show that she declared herself to be a Catholic, and was working as a housemaid prior to her arrest in Limerick.[17] However, an interesting feature of Mary's information was that despite her 'Prisoner Petition,' which was submitted in Ireland just nine months earlier, stating her age to be just 16, her true age may actually have been as high as 28, according to her 1889 certificate of death.[18]

WALES, 1838. (227)
WILLIAM McDONALD, Surgeon-Superintendent Arrived from IRELAND, March 28, 1838.

Former Conviction.	Height		Color of			Particular Marks or Scars Remarks.	Colonial History.				
	Feet.	In.	Complexion	Hair.	Eyes		Colonial Sentence.	Ticket of {Emancipation Leave.	Conditional Pardon {Absolute Colonial.	Certificate of Freedom.	Dead or left the Colony.
None	5	3½	Ruddy	Brown	Dark hazel	Full featured, diagonal scar on centre of forehead, perpendicular scar on left eyebrow, scar on back of fore finger of right hand.					
None	5	3	Ruddy and much freckled	Red	Grey	Arms and hands much freckled.					
None	4	11½	Fair ruddy and freckled	Sandy	Light hazel	None.				44/1183	
3 months	4	11½	Ruddy and freckled	Brown	Hazel grey	Eyebrows meeting.					

View of the 3-storey dormitory building known as the Female Factory complex at Parramatta, prior to its demolition in the 1880s (Parramatta Heritage Centre).

The Female Factory

Most female convicts were directly assigned to a colonist for work as a domestic servant, while the more troublesome, hardened or 'useless' prisoners were mostly sent to the 'Female Factory' in Parramatta, as it was then known. Although some convict women were classed as depraved and irredeemable prostitutes, most had been in domestic service in England and had simply stolen from their employers or shops, and were therefore being transported for the most menial of crimes. Upon arrival, the system of selection of servants often meant that the gentry and officers could choose the prettiest young convict girls, while others had to take up prostitution to survive.[19]

After being processed by the authorities, Mary Ann McGarry was not officially recorded as an inmate of the Female Factory at Parramatta, but she may very well have spent a short time there or nearby. The first 'Female Factory' was built at Parramatta in 1804 and initially consisted of a single long room with a fireplace at one end for the women to cook on. Women and girls made rope, spun and carded wool. Their accommodation was very basic and they often slept on the piles of wool. An upgraded three-storey barracks and Female Factory was built in 1821, which was mainly used to house women convicts who had committed local offences, or women with children and convict girls who were unsuitable for work with the settlers. In time, the work done in the Female Factory transformed to be less difficult with needlework and laundry becoming the main duties. Some women consigned to the Female Factory did not actually take up residence in the Parramatta building itself, but resided nearby and came in every day to work. Many also remained only for a day or so before being assigned to free settlers or even emancipated convicts, while others were very quickly married off.

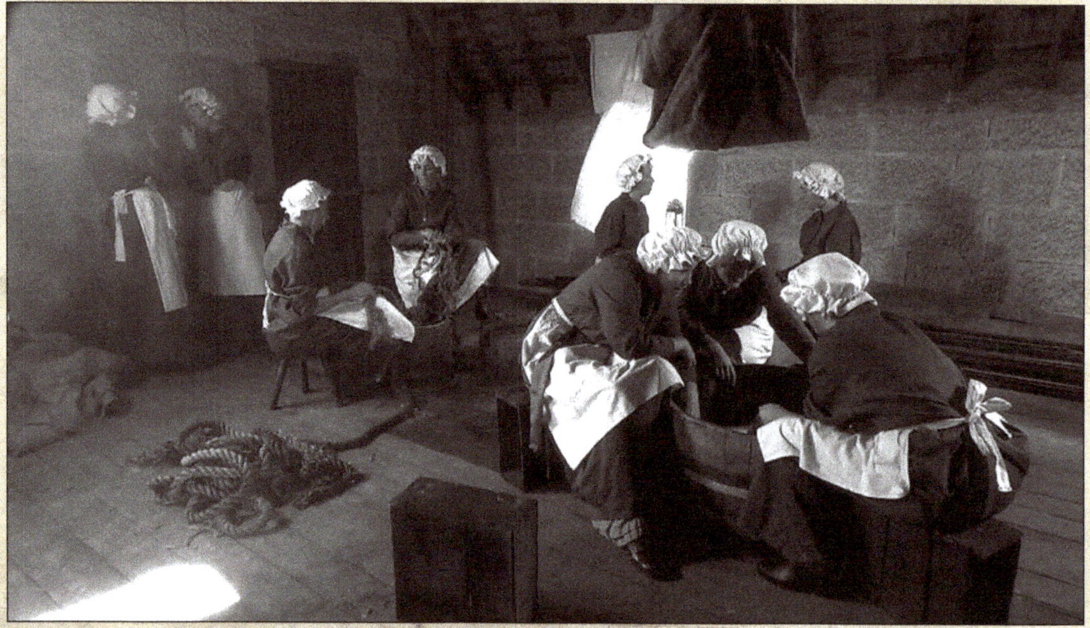

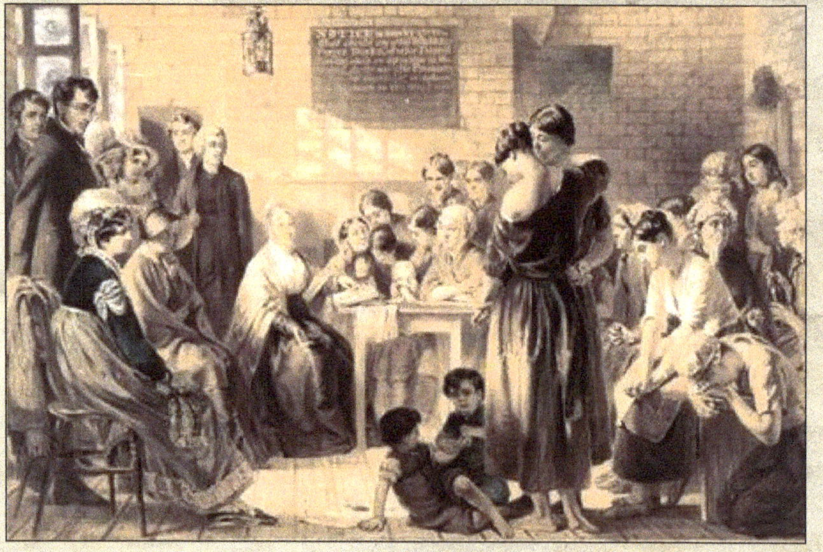

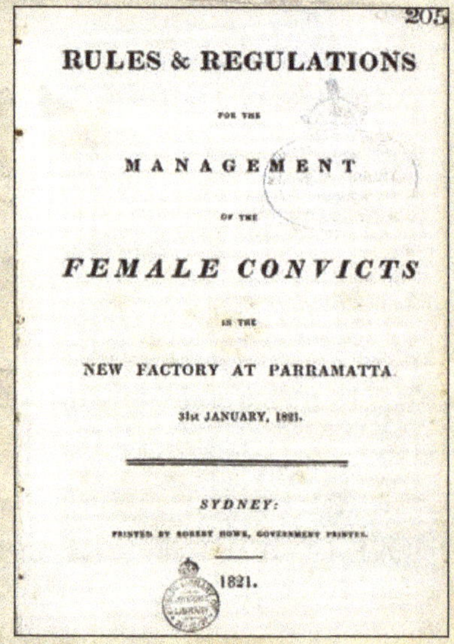
205

RULES & REGULATIONS

FOR THE

MANAGEMENT

OF THE

FEMALE CONVICTS

IN THE

NEW FACTORY AT PARRAMATTA.

31st JANUARY, 1821.

SYDNEY:

PRINTED BY ROBERT HOWE, GOVERNMENT PRINTER.

1821.

TOP (Left): A Convict women and their children checking into the Female Factory at Parrmatta about 1840. (Right): Copy of the 1821 Rules & Regulations for Female Convicts at the Parramatta Female Factory. ABOVE: The female convicts performed most of the daily domestic chores.

List of Assigned Servants - Berry Estate Assigned Servants Day (Slop) Book Mary McGarry, [DIAMOND]			
1838 [26]		Nov 6th	3½ yds print @ 1/1½
July 5th	1 [pirn], cotton 2½	Nov 12th	1 pair blk stockings 2/6,
August 31st	3 yrds calico, 8d/yd 2½		1 pr shoes
	7 yds stripe [yours] piece @ ½	December 6th	1⅓ yds check @ 1/6
Sept 10th	3 yds calico @ 8d	December 7th	3⅓ yds calico @ 1/
	9 yds print @ ½ per yd	December 18th	1 yard calico @ 1/
Sept 20th	6 yds calico @ 8d	**1839** [27]	
	4/3 yds flannel @ 2.6d	January 3rd	6½ yards calico
October 9th	1 cotton handkerchief,	Name:	[Megarry], Mary
	1 pr shoes	Notes:	Returned to government.

TOP: Sketch of 'Coolangatta Homestead' (From... 'Album of drawings of New South Wales views,' by Georgiana Lowe (NSW Library). ABOVE: Mary McGarry was assigned to the Female Factory at Parramatta, and had arrived at Alexander Berry's 'Coolangatta' Homestead, in Shoalhaven by early July of 1838.'

One if the Female Factory's moralistic features was that any man could apply to marry one of the girls. The procedure involved the women being lined up at the Factory while the men would walk along the line and drop a scarf or handkerchief at the feet of his woman of choice. If she picked it up, the marriage was virtually immediate... so much for getting to know one another! Children of convict women either stayed with their mothers or were moved to an orphanage.[20]

Convict women generally left little trace of themselves, and their movements in early Sydney were rarely if ever recorded. This was most certainly the case for Mary, so after disembarking from the "Diamond," where did she go and what did she do? A few clues reveal snippets of evidence that better piece together Mary's movements from the time she arrived in Sydney in April 1838 until her marriage at Wollongong in July 1840.

To The Coolangatta Estate

Records show that our ancestor Mary McGarry, was selected by Alexander Berry for his Coolangatta Estate by pure chance, where she was either put to work as a housemaid, or

Tom Thumb's Lagoon, Illawarra, which much later became the Port Kembla Steelworks, painted by Capt. Robert March Westmacott, c.1838.

given the regular supplies of fabric she withdrew from stores, she may also have worked as a seamstress. It was almost certain to have been at Coolangatta where Mary met and developed a relationship with her future husband John Frawley, which was likely a case of mutual attraction that could very well have come from their both being natives of the same town.

However, being of similar age, it is also possible that Mary McGarry and John Frawley already knew one another from Limerick. If this were the case, might it have also been possible that John Frawley somehow knew of her impending arrival in the colony, in which case he could have somehow played a part in having her assigned to Coolangatta? We may never know the answer to this question, but all options remain a possibility.

Mary was soon placed on board a coastal vessel from Sydney to the Shoalhaven wharf and then brought to Berry's Estate by wagon. At Coolangatta the day to day operations were recorded in the Estate journals with all workers on Berry's Estate being listed alphabetically.

The initial entry for Mary McGarry recorded little information, perhaps because she was later returned to the government. Why this initial Coolangatta Estate entry in the records that Mary Ann McGarry was 'returned to the government' is unclear, but if she was returned, it couldn't have been for long as she is soon after listed as receiving supplies at the Berry Estate, in records kept in the supply (slop) books.[21]

Although no evidence of her assignment has been found, it appears that Mary McGarry arrived at Coolangatta sometime between her disembarkation from the "Diamond" in Sydney in April, and the 5th July 1838, as it was then that she was first recorded in the 'Assigned Servants Day (Slop) Book', and began to regularly draw supplies of cotton, calico and flannel from the Estate stores.[22]

But the Berry Estate entries for Mary McGarry concluded on the 3rd January 1839, when she was transferred to the service of the Rev. Matthew Devenish Meares (1800-1878), in Wollongong. This assignment was confirmed by Mary herself, and recorded on her death certificate that about this time she worked for a period of 18 months at Wollongong, in the service of the Rev. Meares,[23] the first Anglican Minister of the Illawarra-Shoalhaven District.[24]

Meares was a fervent anti-papist, but despite railing against the Catholics and taking issue in 1840 at the building of a Catholic Church by outright refusing them the use of a quarry on his property, he was evidently happy to select Mary McGarry, a Catholic from Limerick, as a house servant. Following a raft of back and forth correspondence on the Wollongong Catholic Church issue, the final say of the colonial Catholics was poisonous... and may have even had something to do with Mary's eventual departure:

Rev. Matthew Devenish Meares (1800-1878) [36]

▲LEFT: *Portrait of Reverend Matthew Devenish Meares, who took Mary McGarry on assignment for domestic service from January 1839 to July 1840 at Wollongong (Image published by Meare's descendant Marion Hall in 'The Morning Bulletin', Cairns, QLD, 16 July 2018). RIGHT: Rev. Meares at the Coolangatta Estate (The Colonist, 11 July 1838, p.2)*

Well knowing, however, that Mr. BERRY is no *local preacher*, and that he has just given himself as little trouble about the moral and spiritual improvement of his assigned servants as nineteen-twentieths of the landed proprietors of the colony, the Attorney-General very good-naturedly ascribes the interesting moral condition of the Shoalhaven establishment to the pastoral visits of the pious clergyman in the neighbourhood, the Rev. Mr. MEARES, of Wollongong. But we can inform Mr. ATTORNEY-GENERAL, that the fair condition of the Shoalhaven estate is just as little to be ascribed to the clerical visitations of Mr. MEARES, as to the local preaching of Mr. BERRY.

Matthew Devenish Meares was born in 1800 in Meares Court, Westmeath, Ireland, the son of William Devenish and Deborah Coghlan and the brother of John Devenish Meares (1795-1875). Matthew married his cousin Georgina Augusta Devenish (c.1802-1881) on 23rd June 1822 in St. Anne's Church, Dublin, County Dublin, Ireland.[28] Their oldest child was born in Dublin Ireland, which at that time was part of the United Kingdom.

Matthew emigrated aboard the "Mariner" which arrived Sydney, in the colony of N.S.W. on the 10th July 1825. Matthew was accompanied by his wife and two children, William being under two years old and their daughter Elizabeth who was born enroute.[29] Matthew had graduated in Arts at Trinity College, Dublin, Ireland and later qualifying for Holy Orders. The family lived at Windsor, NSW for about 2 years then moved to Pitt Town, where he performed weekly services at Wilberforce. On every other Sunday he held service at Pitt Town and Sackville and every three months at Wiseman's Ferry. He moved the family to Wollongong in 1837 where he stayed until 1858 when he resigned his position and moved to Sydney to become Rector of St. Thomas' Enfield until he retired about 1860. The following was printed in the Sydney Gazette on the 14th July 1825.

"KNOW YE, that we have nominated and appointed, and do hereby nominate and appoint, Our trusty and well loved Matthew Devenish Meares, Clerk, to be one of our Chaplains within our said colony; he, the said Matthew Devenish Meares, being a Priest in holy order of the established church of England and Ireland, And it is Our Will, that the said (Matthew) shall hold such his office during our pleasure, and no longer, And We do further direct and command, that the said (Matthew) so long as he shall retain his office, shall officiate as a Minister of the Church."[30]

Rev. Meares was the first incumbent of the Illawarra-Shoalhaven District where he served from 1838-1857.[31] He died on the 5th December 1878 in Olivia Terrace, Bourke Street, Surry Hills, New South Wales,[32,33] at age 78, and was buried in St. Thomas' Anglican Cemetery, Enfield, New South Wales.[34,35] His wife Georgina was born in 1802 in Dublin, Ireland, United Kingdom and died on 28 June 1881 in Sydney, Colony of New South Wales at age 79. Their children were William Devenish Meares, Elizabeth Devenish (Meares) Ellis, Henry Douglas Devenish-Meares, John Devenish Meares, Alfred Devenish-Meares, Catherine Ann (Meares) Ellis, Augusta Ann Devenish (Meares) Osborne, Alexander Sparke Meares, Frederick Potter Devenish-Meares and Thomas Barker Septimus Meares the younger.

(These entries not listed in the index)

'Seven Mile Beach at Gerroa, NSW, with Coolangatta Mountain in the distance.' Panorama made up of three vintage silver gelatin photographs, postcard format, 8.8 x 13.8cm (approx. each), c.1933.

> "On this subject we trust we are 'sans peur et sans reproche' (without fear and without reproach), but we do not see the necessity of carrying the war into the heart of the peaceful Protestant camp, because a few of the 'awkward squad' have the folly to batter their heads against our ramparts. Mr Meares' own letter was the most terrible blow that he could give his own reputation, a blow which could not be strengthened by any comment of ours.
>
> *Australasian Chronicle, 4 June 1840, p.2*

We do know that Rev. Meares was in the habit of making regular visits to Coolangatta for the 'moral and spiritual improvement' of the assigned servants there.[25] Although as a covict she couldn't marry without permission, and couldn't write, Mary likely received letters from her suitor John Frawley, at Coolangatta via her 'master.' Or she may even have accompanied him on occasion, with the intersection of these circumstances providing every possibility of visiting her future husband.

Mary McGarry's early years in the colony had been filled with hardship, but as time passed, her fortunes began to change. Having been assigned at Coolangatta, and later worked in the service of Rev. Meares in Wollongong, she had carved out a place for herself in the growing settlement of Wollongong. After just two years in New South Wales, life for Mary looked much brighter than it had since she first stepped off the convict ship. But a new chapter was about to begin, one that would transform her life completely.

At the same time, another figure in Coolangatta's convict ranks was reaching a turning point. John Frawley had served his full seven-year sentence on the Berry estate, with his last recorded entry on January 4, 1840. By then, he was a well-known figure in the settlement, possibly granted a cottage or even promoted within the estate. But freedom meant change. No longer bound to the estate without pay, he was likely no longer needed. Yet, instead of moving on immediately, John remained at Coolangatta a little longer. Perhaps it was because something, or someone, was keeping him there.

And so, as he stood at the threshold of his new life, John Frawley found freedom and a new future all at once. In March of 1840, he and Mary Ann McGarry applied for permission to marry in Wollongong, marking the beginning of a life together, one of the earliest unions in the town's history. Their story, and the challenges and triumphs that lay ahead, is the subject of the next chapter...

References

1. Queensland Dept of BDM. (1889). Death Certificate for Mary Frawley (nee McGarry) at Dunwich Benevolent Asylum, 1889/3633-1695.
2. NSW State Archives & Records. (1838). Mary McGarry off the "Diamond," arrived Sydney 28th March 1838, in 'Convict Indents.' (Fiche #735, p.226; Film #908; Shelf #X641).
3. NSW State Archives & Records. (1838). Mary McGarry, op. cit.
4. The National Archives. (15/11/1837). 'Prisoner Petition for Mary McGarry of the "Diamond." [http://www.nationalarchives.ie/cgi-bin/naisearch01]. The National Archives, Kew, Surrey. (Record 10 of 17/PPC - TR2, p.77).
5. Wikipedia. 'Richard Wellesley.' [https://en.wikipedia.org/wiki/Richard_Wellesley,_1st_Marquess_Wellesley]. Retrieved 8th June 2021.
6. The National Archives. (15/11/1837). 'Prisoner Petition for Mary McGarry of the "Diamond," op. cit.
7. National Archive of Ireland, 'Convict Reference Files and Prisoners' Petitions and Cases', [https://www.nationalarchives.ie/topics/transportation/transp8.html].
8. Jen Willetts. (1838). 'Convict Ship "Diamond." [https://www.freesettlerorfelon.com/convict_ship_diamond_1838.htm]. Retrieved 9th June 2021.
9. Jen Willetts. (1838). 'Convict Ship "Diamond." op. cit.
10. Departure of the "Diamond" (The Morning Post, 15th November 1837).
11. The National Archives. (1838). Journal of William McDowell off the "Diamond." UK Royal Navy Medical Journals, 1817-1857, The National Archives, Kew, Surrey.
12. The National Archives. (1838). Journal of William McDowell off the "Diamond," op. cit.
13. The National Archives. (1838). Journal of William McDowell off the "Diamond," op. cit.
14. Australian Dictionary of Biography - Caroline Chisholm [https://adb.anu.edu.au/biography/chisholm-caroline-1894/text2231.
15. Jen Willetts. (1838). 'Convict Ship "Diamond," op. cit.
16. 'Police Incidents'. The Sydney Gazette and New South Wales Advertiser, 19 Apr 1838, p.2.
17. Convict Indent for Mary Ann McGarry, off the "Diamond", March 1838. (NSW Archives Convict Indents Fiche# 735, p.226; Film# 908, Shelf# X641).
18. Queensland Dept of BDM. (1889). Death Certificate for Mary Frawley (nee McGarry), op. cit.
19. Nicholas, T. H. (2019). The Place That Had No Heart: a Memoir. Parramatta Factory Precinct Memory Project.
20. Cobb, J. E. (1958). The History of the Female Convict Factory at Parramatta. Published by The Author.
21. Mary McGarry in the Berry Papers, op.cit. (MSS-315/37).
22. Berry Papers. Mary McGarry, off the "Diamond" in 'Assigned Servants Day (Slop) Book. Mitchell Library, Sydney.
23. Queensland Dept of BDM. (1889). Death Certificate for Mary Frawley (nee McGarry), op. cit.
24. Davis, Joseph L. (2019). 'The Spotless Reputation of the Reverend Matthew Devenish Meares, 1800-1878 At Wollongong' [www.academia.edu/39765539/].
25. Rev. Meares at Coolangatta (The Colonist, 11 July 1838, p.2).
26. Mary McGarry in the Berry Papers (Mitchell Library/MSS-315/62, p.108).
27. Mary McGarry in the Berry Papers, op.cit. (MSS-315/37).
28. Matthew Devenish Meares & Georgiana Augusta Devenish marriage licence, 1822 ("Dublin, Ireland, Probate Record and Marriage License Index, 1270-1858").
29. New South Wales And Tasmania: Settlers And Convicts 1787-1859. (From... FindMyPast). First name(s): Richd M. D. - Last name: Meares - Age: 28 - Birth year: 1797 - Arrival year: 1825 - Ship name: "Mariner" - Occupation: Clergyman - Residence: Pitt Town, New South Wales. With... Georgiana Meares (Age: 28, born 1797); William Meares (Age: 5, born 1820); Elizabeth Meares (Age: 3, born 1822); Henry Meares (Age: 1/2, born 1825).
30. By Appointment of the King: "Appointment by King George the Fourth: GIVEN at Our Court, at Carlton-house, this Twentieth Day of December, One thousand eight hundred and twenty-four, in the Fifth Year of Our Reign."
31. Memorial: "Rev Meares started St Michael's Anglican Church: In April 1938, at St Michael's Anglican Church, a special service was held to unveil a memorial plaque in honour of the Reverend Matthew Devenish Meares and his wife. This memorial recognises that Rev. Meares was the first incumbent of the Illawarra-Shoalhaven District from 1838-1857." (By Carol Herben, OAM, in the 'The Illawarra Mercury', 10th Nov 2014).
32. NSW Dept of BDM. (1878). Death certificate for Matthew Devenish Meares, # 2170/1878.
33. Death Notice: Rev. Matthew Devenish Meares - December 5, at Olivia-terrace, Bourke-street, in the 79th year of his age (The Sydney Morning Herald (NSW) Sat, 7 Dec 1878, p.1).
34. Burial: Rev Matthew Devenish Meares - Birth: 1800 Meares Court, Westmeath, Ireland - Death date: 5 Dec 1878 (aged 77–78) - Place: Surry Hills, New South Wales, Australia - Burial: St. Thomas Anglican Cemetery, Enfield, Burwood Municipality, New South Wales, Australia - Portion: 11 Row, 15 (Find A Grave: Memorial #123534395).
35. FamilySearch, Australia Cemetery Inscriptions (1802-2005). Name: M. D. Meares, Death date: 05 Dec 1878; Age: 78; Burial Place: Enfield St Thomas; Spouse's Name: Georgina Augusta, citing Jim and Alison Rogers (Various cemeteries, Australia; FHL microfilm).
36. Wikitree - Rev. Matthew Devenish Meares [https://www.wikitree.com/wiki/Meares-316].

Further Reading

Bateson, C. (1974). The Convict Ships 1787 – 1868. Sydney, Reed.
Cousins, A. (1994). The Garden of NSW: A history of the Illawarra and Shoalhaven districts. Wollongong: Illawarra Historical Society.
Felton., M. (1986). Coolangatta; Shoalhaven Heads 1861-1986. Shoalhaven Heads Parents & Citizens Association.
Flower, C. (1981). Illustrated History of NSW. Adelaide, Rigby.
Hawkins, I. (1977). Shipping Arrival and Departures Sydney 1826 – 1840: Volume 3, Canberra, Roebuck.
Sealy, M. (2000). The Journeys to Coolangatta. Glebe, Book House.
Willetts, Jen [https://www.jenwilletts.com/convict_ship_diamond_1838.htm].
www.academia.edu/39765539/The_Spotless_Reputation_of_the_Reverend_Matthew_Devenish_Meares_1800-1878_At_Wollongong.
'Women Transported: Life In Australia's Convict Female Factories', by Parramatta Heritage Centre & Univ. of Western Sydney (undated).

Chapter Nine

JOHN & MARY ANN FRAWLEY

As the year 1840 began, John Frawley had reached a turning point in his life at Coolangatta. For seven years, he had laboured on the estate, becoming a familiar figure within its operations. However, the records of his service begin to wind down from the beginning of that year. What became of him afterward remains unclear, perhaps he was granted a cottage elsewhere on Alexander Berry's vast property, or maybe he was elevated to a managerial role. Yet, the most plausible outcome is that, having completed his term and now entitled to wages, his continued employment was no longer required.

Despite the common perception of convict servitude as brutal and oppressive, life on the estate was more nuanced. Referred to as 'government men,' the assigned convicts were not shackled, dressed in prison garb, or regimented into tightly controlled work units. They were not supervised by soldiers, nor were they subjected to the inhumane conditions often associated with penal labor. Nevertheless, discipline was strictly enforced. Infractions were met with corporal punishment or deprivation, and oversight fell to former convicts who had firsthand knowledge of the tricks and tendencies of reluctant labourers.

Alexander Berry, often accused of treating his convict workforce with excessive severity, consistently defended his methods, claiming that mild measures and moral persuasion were the key to maintaining order. His assertions hold some merit, as evidenced by the number of men who chose to remain in his employ even after earning their freedom. John Frawley Jr.'s continued presence at Coolangatta beyond his term suggests that, while the system was undoubtedly one of control, it was not entirely devoid of opportunity or choice.

The Aboriginal Population at Shoalhaven

The years 1833-42 are some of the historically richest, in terms of the study of Illawarra and South Coast Aborigines, for during this period the first census information of the local Aboriginal inhabitants was compiled in connection with the issue of blankets. This survey

TOP (Left): A convict's rendition of work in the penal colony of New South Wales. (Right): 'Flogging prisoners, in Tasmania', by James Reid Scott (Trove, PIC Drawer 3841 #R454, undated). ABOVE: Convicts, also known as 'government men' who worked with timber were known as 'splitters', by S.T. Gill.

revealed a great deal of personal information on the native population. Though blankets had been issued earlier, it is only from 1833 that returns have survived for the Illawarra and South Coast people. With such detailed information many of the Aborigines mentioned in the historical accounts were brought to life for the first time *(see Appendix C)*. The family history value of this material is also significant, as Aborigines were not again included in Australian census returns until the 1960s.

While most Europeans found their customs abhorrent, the Aboriginal people were just as often revolted by some of the customs of the Europeans. Aboriginal methods of punishment for example seemed to be barbaric, especially spearing, while Aboriginals were horrified by some of the white man's ways of punishing offenders like flogging.

This period also saw the issue of a significant collection of reminiscences on the Aboriginals of Shoalhaven, by Alexander Berry *(see Appendix D)*. But it was their nomadic lifestyle, and their lack of ingenuity that made them easy targets for colonisation:

> "...at no stage did Aboriginal civilisation develop substantial buildings, roadways or even a wheeled cart... I would strongly make the point that rightly or wrongly dispossession of the Aboriginal civilisation was always going to happen."
>
> *Tim Fischer (Deputy P.M, 1995)*

John Frawley's Freedom

John Frawley was just a small cog in the vast machine that was the Coolangatta Estate, where the whole was truly greater than the sum of its parts. As one of many convicts assigned to the estate, he played his role in the daily operations, likely performing hard labour under the oversight of the Berry family's strict management. Yet even within the rigid structure of convict life, personal connections and aspirations for a better future still flourished.

It was in this environment, sometime in 1838, that John Frawley either met or reconnected with his fellow Shannonsider, Mary Ann McGarry. Their paths may have first crossed at the Coolangatta Homestead, where she might have been employed, or perhaps in Wollongong, where they could have encountered one another while running errands or attending church services. Whatever the circumstances, a bond formed between them, strong enough that they soon agreed to marry.

But John's situation was still uncertain, as records indicate that he remained at the Berry Estate until at least early 1840. His last documented mention at Coolangatta comes from

TOP: 'Coolangatta Estate, Shoalhaven,' visited and drawn in the 1840s by Georgiana Lowe, from her 'Album of drawings of New South Wales' [Courtesy of Mitchell Library, NSW]. ABOVE (Left): As Aboriginal nomadic life gradually faded, many struggled to assimilate on the outskirts of growing towns, often falling into hardship and suffering from the effects of alcohol, by A.H. Fulwood. (Right): Artist unknown.

TOP: Photographs of delapidated but actual wagons, likely made and used on and about the Coolangatta Estate. ABOVE: Employees of the Coolangatta Estate, Shoalhaven River, N.S.W, 1891 (SLNSW- a3683017).

a routine but telling request, another pair of boots from 'slops,' the convict clothing and supplies store. This suggests that as of that moment, he was still under the control of the estate and had not yet secured his freedom. However, John Frawley was well aware that liberty could be obtained through several legal avenues, each with its own restrictions and conditions.

Convicts in the colony had four primary paths to freedom:

- A Ticket of Leave, which allowed early release but restricted the convict's movements to a designated area within the colony. Holders of a Ticket of Leave were still required to report regularly to local authorities and, whenever possible, attend divine worship on Sundays.

- A Certificate of Freedom, issued once a convict completed their full sentence. This document confirmed they were no longer under any penal obligations and granted them unrestricted travel within the colony and beyond. While some ex-convicts chose to return to the United Kingdom or Ireland, doing so was often financially difficult. Those who managed to make the journey back frequently found the "convict stain" to be a far heavier burden in their homeland than in Australia, where former prisoners could more easily integrate into society.

- A Conditional Pardon, granted to convicts serving life sentences. This allowed them freedom within the colony but forbade them from ever returning to the United Kingdom. For many, this was an acceptable trade-off, as Australia provided opportunities unavailable to them in their homeland.

- An Absolute Pardon, the most coveted form of clemency. It granted complete freedom, lifting all restrictions and allowing the former convict to travel wherever they pleased, including back to Britain if they wished.

Regardless of the method of release, all ex-convicts were required to carry their discharge papers at all times. Failure to present a Ticket of Leave, Certificate of Freedom, Conditional Pardon, or Absolute Pardon when demanded, particularly at muster time, could result in being classified as a 'Prisoner of the Crown' once more and returned to government service. These documents essentially functioned as passports for former convicts, proving their legitimacy as free individuals in a society where their past was never entirely forgotten.

Although no direct records confirm the exact manner of John Frawley's release, circumstantial evidence strongly suggests that he obtained either a Ticket of Leave or a Certificate of Freedom before mid-March of 1840. His likely window of release falls between January, when he would have completed his required sentence at Berry Estate, and March, when he formally submitted a "request to marry," an official declaration of his free status. This process would have required legal documentation proving he was no longer bound by the constraints of servitude, reinforcing the likelihood that his freedom had been secured just weeks or months prior.

Meanwhile, Mary Ann McGarry's circumstances in the lead-up to their wedding remain

Coolangatta Homestead, Shoalhaven NSW

1 Convict Cottage
THIS PARTICULAR COTTAGE WAS USED TO HOUSE THE MAIDS ATTENDING TO THE MISS HAYS' IN THE ADJOINING 'COTTAGE'. IDENTICAL BUILDINGS WERE SCATTERED OVER THE ESTATE, HOUSING THE CONVICTS. THIS IS THE ONLY ONE SURVIVING. THIS BUILDING IS NOW ONE MOTEL UNIT.

3 Original Coolangatta Homestead Site
ALEXANDER BERRY SETTLED COOLANGATTA IN JUNE 1822. THE CONSTRUCTION OF THIS HOME BEGAN IMMEDIATELY AND WAS COMPLETED IN 1825. THE FREE STANDING WALLS MARK ITS EXTREMITIES. IT WAS DESTROYED BY FIRE IN 1940 UNDER SUSPICIOUS CIRCUMSTANCES. THIS WAS BERRY'S ACTUAL BEDROOM.

4 Original Coach House Site
A RESTORED COOLANGATTA COACH CAN BE SEEN AT VAUCLUSE HOUSE IN SYDNEY. COACHMEN WERE HOUSED IN THIS SECTION OF THE MAIN BUILDING WITH THE RECEPTION AREA ORIGINALLY SIX STABLES. THE MAIDS' QUARTERS, LAUNDRY AND CONVICT RATION STORAGE OCCUPIED THE REMAINDER.

CONVICT RATION - TEN, TEN, TWO AND ONE QUARTER.
TEN lbs. MEAT. TEN lbs. FLOUR. TWO lbs. SUGAR. ONE QUARTER lb. TEA.

Photographs of various structures on the Coolangatta Estate, at Shoalhaven, by Tracy Rockwell, c.2000.

somewhat unclear. The marriage certificate records her residence as Shoalhaven, which suggests she was likely working at Coolangatta at the time. However, it is also possible that she remained in the employ of the Reverend Meares, a situation that could have extended even beyond her nuptials. Domestic service was one of the most common occupations for women in colonial Australia, and if she had been working in a household such as that of Reverend Meares, she would have had some stability, though likely little personal freedom.

For John, the reunion with Mary Ann and the transition from convict to free man

Few 'Certificates of Freedom' have survived, as was the case for John Frawley, but above is an example of the document issued this on for Thomas Siderson on the 25th July 1832.

TOP: John Frawley & Mary McGarry (March 1840) listed in the 'Register of Convict Applications to Marry' (1826-1851)'. ABOVE (Left): The marriage certificate of John Frawley and Mary McGarry on 6th July 1840 (NSWBDM #25-123/1840). (Right): 1841 Census Return for Coolangatta Homestead.

would not have been without its challenges. To reach her, he would have needed to make his way from Shoalhaven to Wollongong, an arduous journey by any means available. He could have booked passage aboard a small coastal cutter bound for Kiama or Wollongong, a common but often unpredictable mode of transport along the colony's rugged eastern coastline. Alternatively, if no boat was available or if he lacked the necessary funds, he would have been forced to make the grueling 60-kilometer overland trek on foot.

At the time, no proper roads connected Shoalhaven to Wollongong, only a series of rough coastal tracks carved through dense bushland and treacherous terrain. These paths were not for the faint-hearted, requiring careful navigation and considerable endurance.

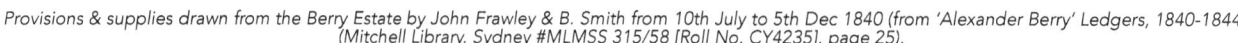

Provisions & supplies drawn from the Berry Estate by John Frawley & B. Smith from 10th July to 5th Dec 1840 (from 'Alexander Berry' Ledgers, 1840-1844 (Mitchell Library, Sydney #MLMSS 315/58 [Roll No. CY4235], page 25).

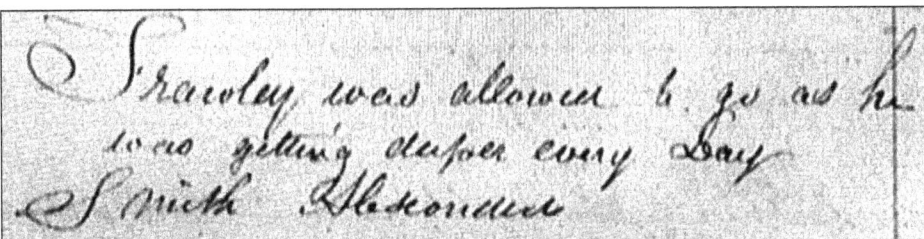

Provisions & supplies drawn from the Berry Estate by John Frawley & B. Smith from 19th Dec 1840 to 19th July 1841 (from 'Alexander Berry' Ledgers, 1840-1844 (Mitchell Library, Sydney #MLMSS 315/58 [Roll No. CY4235], page 98).

He would have had to traverse forests, cross rivers, and contend with the unpredictable elements of the Australian wilderness, all while carrying whatever meager belongings he possessed. For a man recently freed from servitude, it was perhaps a small price to pay for the promise of a new life with Mary Ann.

Though many details of John Frawley's journey remain lost to history, one thing is certain, by mid-1840, he had successfully left his past as a convict behind. Whether by land or by sea, he reached his destination, claimed his freedom, and prepared to embark on the next chapter of his life as a husband and, eventually, a man free from the constraints of his past.

> "By 1849 a new road was cleared from Kiama to Gerringong to replace the old track along the beaches and headlands. It rose to a point midway up the hillsides winding around the spurs to meet the top of the range at Mt. Pleasant. After descending to the south of Mt. Pleasant it crossed the flats and rose to the village site of Gerringong on the hill and then almost straight along the ridge to Crooked River near Black Head."[1]

The Marriage of John Frawley & Mary Ann McGarry

As Mary was still serving her sentence in the months leading up to their July 1840 wedding, the couple had to wait for official approval to marry. Their application for 'permission to marry' was submitted to Governor Sir George Gipps on March 26, 1840.[2,3] At the time, Mary had five years remaining on her sentence and was listed as 'bonded' for seven years aboard the "Diamond", while John Frawley was recorded as 'free.'

The next documented reference to the couple is their marriage, which took place on July 6th, 1840, in the Roman Catholic Parish of Wollongong. Their marriage certificate states that Father John Rigney of Wollongong, who was then the priest for Illawarra certified the wedding of John Frawley and Mary McGawly [sic. McGarry] both of Shoalhaven. The ceremony was witnessed by Dudley Morris and Patrick Keogh and signed by both the bride and groom.[4] Early governors and clergy encouraged marriage due to its 'presumed reformatory and moral advantages.' For female convicts, marriage provided a path to respectability, as they were assigned to their husbands and allowed to live freely, provided they maintained good behavior. Additionally, land grants were offered to married convicts, with extra land allocated for each child born.

Given the circumstances, John and Mary likely traveled back to Coolangatta by boat from Wollongong or Kiama. At the time, Kiama was a small but developing port.[5] Although a few houses existed there as early as 1829, the first land purchase wasn't recorded until 1840, followed by the establishment of the Post Office on January 1, 1841. Over time, Kiama grew into a modest yet productive regional port. While mail was transported overland, local produce was shipped to Sydney two or three times a month via small coastal

'Wollongong from the stockade with Mt Kiera in the distance', by Capt. Robert Marsh Westmacott, 20th April 1840. The Roman Catholic Church (erected c.1836), which was the site for John & Mary Ann's 1840 wedding, can be seen on the distant hill at right.

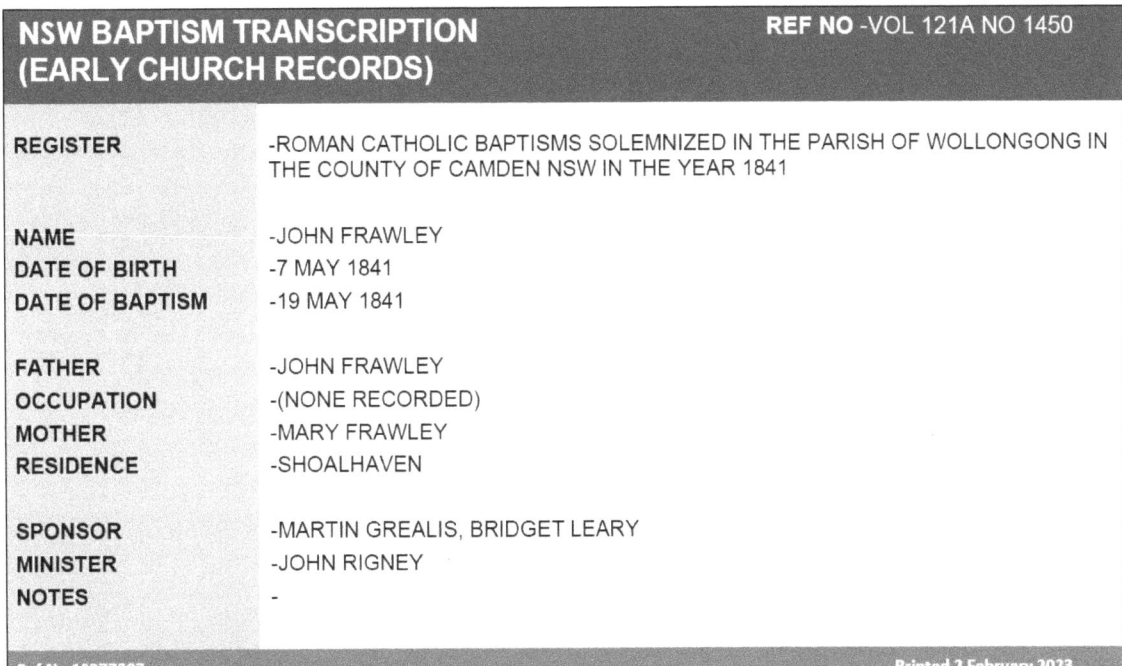

The 1841 birth & baptism transcription of John Frawley Jr., ceremony administered by Father John Rigney, showing 'Shoalhaven' in the County of Camden as their residence, with Martin Grealis & Bridget Leary as witnesses (NSW BDM #V121A, 1450).

sailing vessels, with each trip taking one to two days. Ships such as the "Bee", "Charles", "Pedlar", and "Dolphin" all regularly traveled the route before 1847, though sailors had been navigating those waters long before then.

The region's first steamer, the "Tamar", arrived from Sydney in 1841, but did not operate for long. Until the 1850s, smaller sailing vessels remained the primary means of transport for settlers in the area.[6]

Beginnings of Wollongong

During their years at Shoalhaven, John and Mary Frawley would have been witnesses to the development of the town of Wollongong. On 26 November 1834, the town of Wollongong was first gazetted and George Brown erected the first court house. The main road down the escarpment through through Westmacott Pass later renamed Bulli Pass was built by convict labour in 1835–6, although other passes were built during the 19th century as well, such as O'Briens Road and Rixons Pass. By 1836, a small wooden church with seating for 250 people was built for the Catholics of Wollongong. Shortly afterwards, the pioneer priest, Monsignor John Rigney established St Francis Xaviers Church in 1838, and that structure remains the oldest church of any denomination in the Illawarra region.[7]

While the first settlers in the Illawarra in the early 19th century were cedar cutters, they were followed by graziers in 1815 when Charles Throsby established his stockman's hut near Wollongong.[8] By 1830, a military barracks had been constructed near the harbour, and with further settlers constantly arriving, the town of Wollongong was first gazetted on the 26th November 1834.

In 1831 the "Sophia Jane" became the first steamship to visit Wollongong and in 1839 the first regular service commenced from Sydney with the establishment of the Illawarra Steam Packet Company. Mr. Thomas Shadforth (c.1771-1862), an ex-soldier and trustee of the company, bought the paddlesteamer "Maitland" from Edye Manning (1807-1889), and she began sailing to the South Coast on the 15th June 1839.[9] While the newly formed company

'View of Wollongong with Mount Keira in the distance', drawn by J.R. Roberts (Illustrated Sydney News, 16 March 1866).

commenced the Wollongong service with the "Maitland", it later added the "William The Fourth", both of which were built in New South Wales on the Williams River.[10] Just three months after its inception, the Illawarra Steam Packet Company merged with the Brisbane Water Steam Passenger Co. to become the General Steam Navigation Company,[11] and that company then serviced the Hunter River along with the South Coast.[12]

By 1841 the Census of that year revealed that there were 468 males and 296 females residing in northern Illawarra, 637 males and 294 females in Wollongong, 233 males and 143 females on the small farms around Dapto whilst the Lake Illawarra area had a sizeable population of 588 males and 340 females.[13] The 1841 Census listed 659 houses in Illawarra of which 571 were of wood and 88 of brick.[14] The road from Sydney to Wollongong began in 1843, and traversed to the south via Georges River.

The first coal mine in the Illawarra was opened at Mt Keira by Mr James Schoobert in 1849, and some of these coal mines built jetties so that the coal could carried by horse and loaded directly onto ships before being sent to other places within Australia or other countries.

Most travellers and settlers to Wollongong either walked or journeyed by horse from Liverpool, Campbelltown or Appin along rough tracks before reaching the dangerous Illawarra escarpment. Others came by paddlesteamer as by the 1850's there were two steamers running almost daily between Sydney and Wollongong. In 1852 a new road was built from Appin through Broughton's Pass down Mount Keira to Wollongong, on which carriages could drive for the first time. The Illawarra Mercury newspaper was established by Thomas Garrett and W. F. Cahill in 1855.

By 1858, a court house had been built, a horse-drawn tramway from Mount Keira to the harbour was completed in 1861, and in 1862 a telegraph line was opened between Wollongong and Bellambi. By 1865 the first gas supply in Wollongong was provided from a gas plant in Corrimal Street, and in 1868, extensions to the harbour were opened.

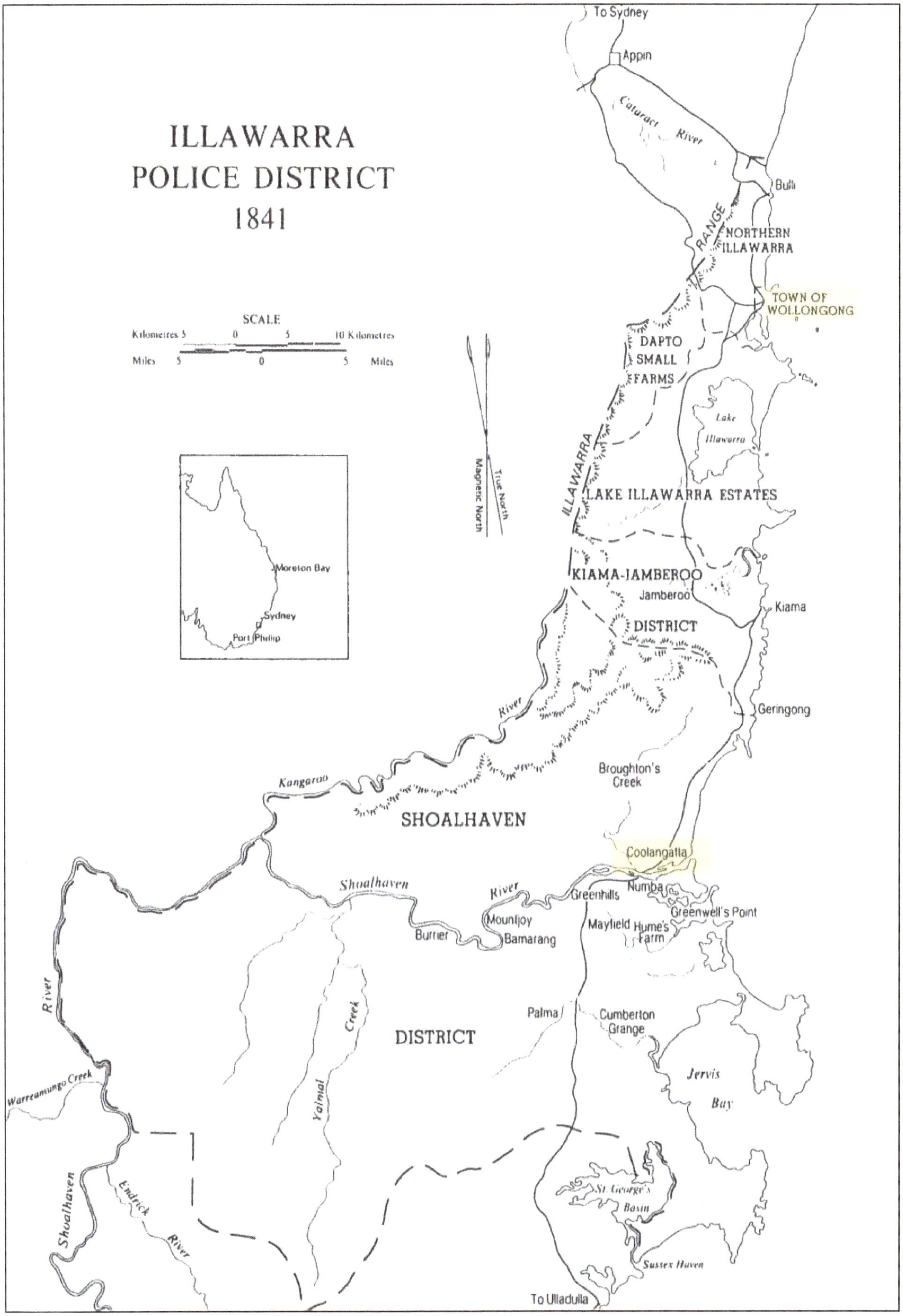

M12. Map of the Illawarra Police District in 1841, showing the Coolangatta Estate in relation to the town of Wollongong (Henderson, 1983).

Return to Coolangatta

After returning to Coolangatta, records indicate that John Frawley began drawing more heavily on estate provisions and supplies.[15] He partnered with B. Smith to carry out "burning off" operations, accumulating an account of £14.9.1 by the end of 1840. The clearing work continued into 1841, but their demands on estate supplies nearly tripled, placing an even greater strain on resources.

Their first child, John Frawley Jr., was born on May 7th, 1841, while they were still residing at Coolangatta. He was baptized in Wollongong by Father John Rigney on May 19th, with Martin Grealis and Bridget Leary serving as sponsors.[16] That same year, the New South Wales Government conducted a colony-wide census. Although not listed by name, John, Mary Ann, and their infant son were recorded in return #618 for the County of Camden, Illawarra District, under the household of John Berry (brother of Alexander) at the Coolangatta Homestead. Berry provided the census information to officials on March 13th, 1841.[17]

While the census does not specify their identities, it is not difficult to deduce where John and Mary Ann were recorded. They were a married couple, aged between 21 and 45, Roman Catholic, and either privately employed or holding a ticket of leave. Based on John's later occupation, it is likely that he worked as a shepherd or stockman at the homestead, a theory supported by evidence that he handled horses while at Coolangatta.[18]

The Berry Estate ledgers record that sometime after August 19th, B. Smith absconded. Meanwhile, John Frawley was allowed to leave the homestead, as his debts were mounting daily. One final reference to John Frawley appears in the Berry Papers for 1842, though its precise details remain unclear. However, it appears to be of a financial nature, possibly related to his departure from the Coolangatta Estate.[19]

'Wollongong Hotel' with Mount Keira in the background, painted by James G. Sawkins, c.1852-53.

Government notice to 'Ticket of Leave' men, Hobart, 1842.

The Frawleys' exact movements between late August 1841 and September 1842, the month their daughter Ellen was born at Warraguberra on the far South Coast, are unclear. They may have either have traveled south to Twofold Bay or remained in the Shoalhaven or Illawarra District, possibly finding work there.

During his last days and weeks at Coolangatta, John Frawley likely heard of new opportunities on the far South Coast, where labourers were being drawn in increasing numbers. Ever resourceful, he somehow secured employment before September 1842, with the Imlay Brothers at Warragaburra Station.[20]

By the summer of 1841, the Frawleys had become accustomed to a life at Coolangatta that was a far cry from their convict beginnings. The once-untamed land had been transformed into an ordered, civilised community, with the comforts and stability that came with hard-earned progress. They had grown familiar with the solid buildings, regular routines, and the ease of a life now firmly rooted in the colony's growing prosperity.

Yet, as they left Coolangatta behind, they were about to step into a starkly different world, a world where civilization had not yet touched the land. Ahead lay the untamed wilderness of the far South Coast, a region so remote that few even dared to dream of settling there. The Frawleys would soon find themselves surrounded by dense forests, wild rivers, fierce Aboriginal tribes and vast expanses of isolation that would challenge everything they had come to know.

With the comforts of Coolangatta fading into the distance, they faced an uncertain future. Would the wilderness prove to be a new beginning, or would it be a harsh reminder of the very hardships they had hoped to escape? The life they had left behind might have been comfortable, but the true test of their resolve was only just beginning.

References

1. Bayley, W. A. (1960) Blue Haven: Centenary History of Kiama Municipality NSW. Kiama Municipal Council, Halstead Press.
2. NSW State Archives & Records. (1840). John Frawley and Mary McGarry in 'Convicts Permission to Marry 1826 to 1856.'
3. NSW State Archives - John Frawley & Mary McGarry, 'Convicts Applications to Marry 1825-1851' (NRS 12212 [4/4510 p.045]; COD 13; Reel 713; Fiche 786-788 | Place: Wollongong).
4. NSW Dept of BDM. (1840). Marriage Certificate for John Frawley & Mary McGarry, 6th July 1840 at Wollongong, #25/123.
5. Bayley, W. A. (1960) Blue Haven: Centenary History of Kiama Municipality NSW. op. cit.
6. Ibid.
7. Piggin, Stuart., et al. (1984). Faith of Steel: a History of the Christian Churches in Illawarra, Australia. University of Wollongong.
8. Wikipedia - Wollongong [https://en.wikipedia.org/wiki/Wollongong].
9. Kolsen, Helmut (1959). 'Company Formation in NSW: 1828-1851,' Bulletin of the Business Archives Council, Vol. 1, No. 6.
10. Inglis, Brian (2000). "Transport". In Fellows of the Australian Academy of Technological Sciences and Engineering (ed.). Technology in Australia 1788-1988. Melbourne: Australian Science and Technology Heritage Centre. ISBN 0-908029-49-7. Retrieved 1 February 2009.
11. Coroneos, Cosmos (2005). "Steamer Bega (1883–1908): Conservation Plan" (PDF). Parramatta, New South Wales: NSW Heritage Office. Retrieved 1 February 2009.
12. Ibid.
13. Henderson, K. & T. (1983). 'Early Illawarra - People, houses, life', History Project Inc, Canberra, p.19 & 24.
14. Jervis, James, (1942). op. cit., p.273.
15. NSW Dept of BDM. (1841). Birth & Baptism Certificate for John Frawley Jr., op.cit..
16. NSW Dept of BDM. (1841). Birth & Baptism Certificate for John Frawley Jr., #1450/1841 (V18411450 121A).
17. NSW State Archives & Records. (1841). '1841 Census of the Colony of NSW: John & Mary Frawley in 'Return #618 for Coolangatta.' County of Camden, District of Illawarra.
18. Berry Papers. John Frawley in 'Assigned Servants Punishment Book.' Mitchell Library, Sydney (MSS-315/62).
19. Berry Papers. John Frawley in 'Index to Persons on the Berry Estate - Financial Records.' Mitchell Library, Sydney (MSS-315/62).
20. NSW Dept of BDM .(1842). Birth & Baptism for Ellen Frawley, 2nd Sept 1842 at Warigubera, #1772/1842 (V18421772 62).

Further Reading

Andrews, G. (1984. South Coast Steamers. Maritime History Publications.

Assigned Servants Punishment Book, Berry Estate (Berry Papers MLMSS 315/62).

Bayley, W. A. (1960). Blue Haven: Centenary History of Kiama Municipality NSW. Kiama Municipal Council, Halstead Press.

Bayley, W. A. (1964). Behind Broulee. Eurobodalla Shire Council.

Bayley, W.A. (1975). Shoalhaven: History of the Shire of Shoalhaven, NSW. Nowra: Shoalhaven Shire Council.

Bradshaw, N. T. (1972). Coolangatta. Self-published.

Cousins, A. (1994). The Garden of NSW: A history of the Illawarra and Shoalhaven districts. Wollongong: Illawarra Historical Society.

Cox. P. (1978). South Coast of New South Wales. Melbourne, Macmillan.

Davis, Joseph L. (2019). 'The Spotless Reputation of the Reverend Matthew Devenish Meares, 1800-1878 At Wollongong' [www.academia.edu/39765539/].

Felton., M. (1986). Coolangatta; Shoalhaven Heads 1861-1986. Shoalhaven Heads Parents & Citizens Association.

Financial Ledger Record for John Frawley in 'Index to Persons on the Berry Estate'.

Flower, C. (1981). Illustrated History of NSW. Adelaide, Rigby.

Hawkins, I. (1977). Shipping Arrival and Departures Sydney 1826 – 1840: Volume 3, Canberra, Roebuck.

Index to Certificates of Freedom, 1823-69. John Frawley, July 1836, No: 36/0601.

NSW State Archives & Records. (1840). Convicts Permission to Marry 1826 to 1856 for John Frawley and Mary McGarry.

Sealy, M. (2000). The Journeys to Coolangatta. Glebe, Book House.

Chapter Ten

THE MANEROO & TWOFOLD BAY

The Frawley family's journey to the remote and largely unexplored region of the Maneroo in 1842 marks a pivotal chapter in the history of early Australian settlement. Having already carved out a place for themselves in the growing colonies of Shoalhaven and the Illawarra, they had witnessed the transformative power of civilization and progress in areas like Berry's Coolangatta Estate and the township of Wollongong. These settlements, though still young, were already imbued with the trappings of colonial life: government infrastructure, established roads, and the steady rise of European influence in the region. In contrast, the path the Frawleys were now embarking upon would take them far beyond the safety and structure of these burgeoning communities.

Their move into the Maneroo, an area largely unknown to the wider population of New South Wales in 1842, would place them on the frontier of European settlement. At this time, the Maneroo was still a wild and untamed land, dominated by dense forests, rugged terrain, and Indigenous peoples whose presence and way of life had remained largely undisturbed by European settlers. To understand the significance of the Frawleys' decision to venture into this unknown wilderness, it is essential to explore the origins of the Maneroo region itself, its early exploration, and the challenges it presented to those daring enough to settle there.

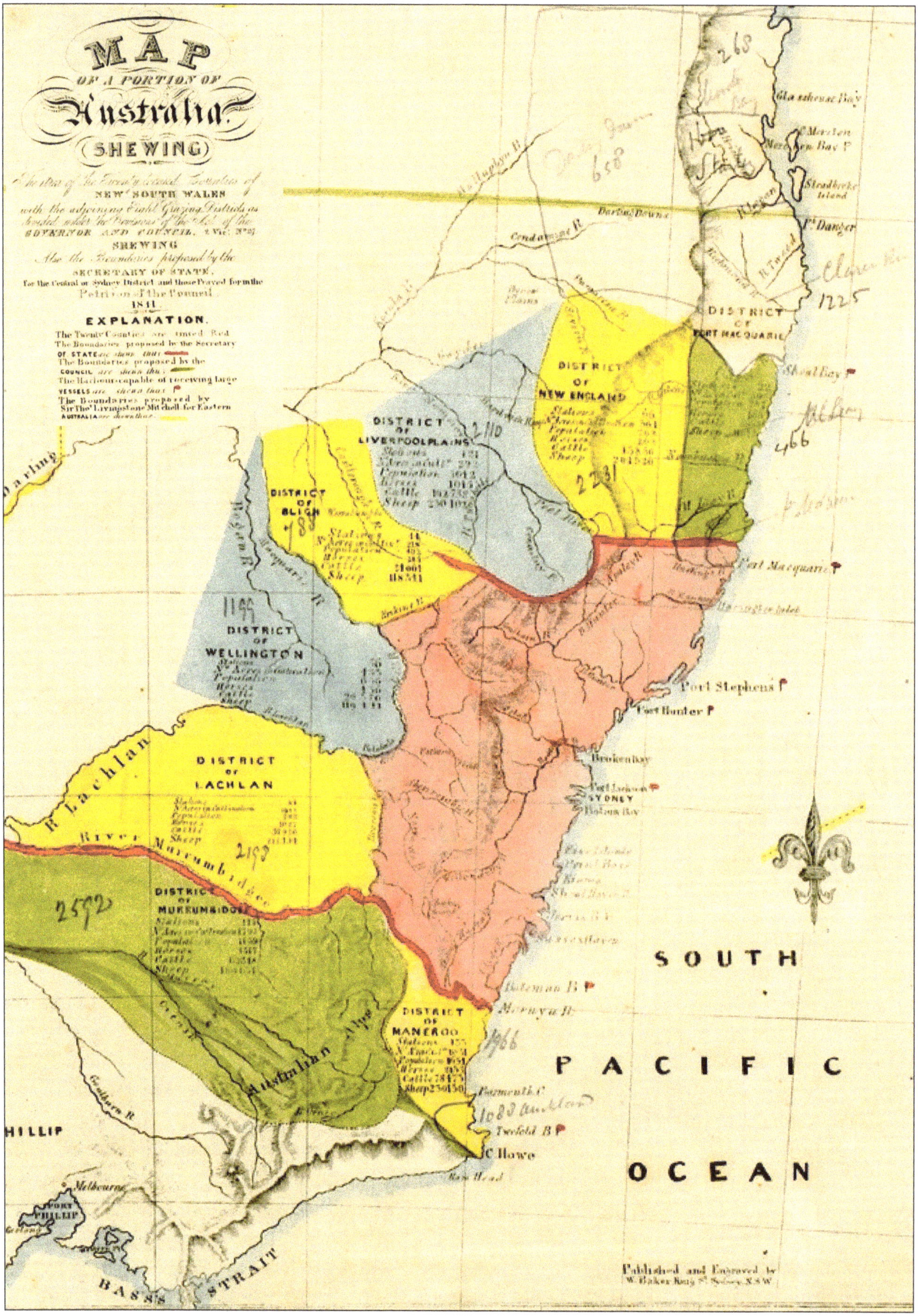

M13. William Baker's 1841 map of the Southeast coast of Australia showing the districts of New South Wales beyond the 'Limits of Location' as designated by Gov. Sir Ralph Darling in 1826 (NLA MAP NK 5348).

This chapter delves into the early history of the Maneroo, examining its geographical, cultural, and historical significance within the context of colonial expansion. By understanding the region's origins and the motivations behind the Frawleys' bold move, we gain a deeper appreciation of the challenges they faced, as well as the pioneering spirit that drove them to push further into the frontier.

Twofold Bay & The Maneroo

Prior to European settlement the local Aborigines, the Katungal of the Thawa tribe who were part of the Yuin language group, had lived in the area for thousands of years. But the first European to sight Twofold Bay was Lt. James Cook in April, 1770.

The first known white men to pass through the South Coast and Bega district on foot were a group of 17 survivors from the wreck of the "Sydney Cove", which was beached on what became known as Preservation Island in Bass Strait, on the 9th February 1797. The small group had been despatched by their captain in a longboat to seek help, but were themselves wrecked in a storm west of Point Hicks. They had to trek nearly 500 miles (800km) north to Sydney, through completely unknown, often dense bush and across numerous rivers, lakes and around other obstacles including mountain ranges and hostile natives. Only three of the original party managed to reach Sydney. However, little more was heard about this area of New South Wales for another 30 years.[1]

Hearing the reports of the survivors, George Bass, travelled down the coast in December of 1797. On his return in early 1798 he entered Twofold Bay and named Snug Cove, where Eden wharf now stands, because he believed it was suitable as a resting place for passing vessels. Later in 1798, Bass with Matthew Flinders headed south to Van Diemen's Land. This time a more detailed and accurate survey of Twofold Bay was made and the duo made

Early squatters and settlers built bark slab huts on the far South Coast of NSW.

Early newspaper announcements of the Maneroo. **LEFT COLUMN:** 1-News from Maneroo Plains (The Sydney Herald, 24th March 1834). 2-Snow Storm at Maneroo about Guyandra (17th Sept 1834). 3-Mail service between Reid's Flat and Queanbeyan (Undated). **CENTRE COLUMN:** 1-Mr. Edwin J. Abraham's Maneroo Store (The Sydney Herald, 6th June 1836). 2-Mr Abraham Moses on the road with stores to Maneroo Plains (The Sydney Monitor, 16th November 1836). 3-Mr Thomas Jones' Maneroo Stores (The Sydney Herald, 15th January 1837). **RIGHT COLUMN:** 1-Mail service by Mr. Abraham Moses (???, 16th February 1838). 2-Flood at Maneroo (???, 3rd January 1839). 3-John Gray, Subscription Postal Agent from Queanbeyan to Maneroo (???, 17th February 1838).

contact with the local Aborigines. Flinders recounted an amusing and friendly incident where he offered a local some biscuits and in turn the local offered Flinders some fat. After tasting the fat Flinders explained that while "watching an opportunity to spit it out when he should not be looking, I perceived him doing precisely the same thing with our biscuit".

The Whalers

As early as 1791 whalers were seen in the area, which was the reason the area was initially settled. The migration, mostly of right whales, to and from the Antarctic resulted in large numbers passing Twofold Bay between May and November. The first European whaler in Twofold Bay was evidently Capt. Thomas Raine (1793–1860), in 1828, and although whaling stations were already set up on Van Diemen's Land and Kangaroo Island, he established the first shore-based whaling station on the Australian mainland. The Twofold Bay area became a well known whaling ground and the bay was a natural harbour for ships.[2]

Then in 1829, some Braidwood squatters came down Eurambene Mountain into Wandella and the Maneroo to explore the kangaroo grasslands and open forests. William

Duggan Tarlington (1806-1893), found a route down to the sea at Bermagui, and later that year pushed through from Cobargo to Biggah (Bega).³ Tarlington chose Cobargo for his run and returned with cattle in 1832. Other squatters included John Campbell, Henry Badgery, Captain Raine, Thomas Cowper, Major William Elrington, the Pollack Brothers, the Alsops, and Dr Thomas Braidwood Wilson, who did not settle in the valley. Other squatters followed and soon a second party was sent from Thomas Cowper's 2,000 acre squattage at Braidwood with 300 head of young cattle to take up Brogo.⁴ Cowper's squattage expanded rapidly to include Yarranung, and Tarraganda on the north east side of the Bega River, and Brianderry on the north western side of the river about two miles due west and opposite the present site of Kingswood. Joseph Bartley with Michael Dunn as hut-keeper took up the land on the south west side of the river below the eventual site of the Bega township, on behalf of Henry Badgery and this squattage became known as 'Warragaburra'. Otherwise the entire region was basically unpopulated.⁵

The 'Maneroo' was the early reference for what is now known as the far South Coast region of New South Wales. By the early 1830s the Imlay Brothers had also started whaling at Twofold Bay, and trained local Aborigines to become whalers. Peter Imlay (1797–1881), arrived at Twofold Bay around 1833 and decided to settle. Unfortunately the depression

"TOP "Whales amusing themselves - not at all exaggerated", c.1848 (artist unknown). ABOVE (Left): Early photograph of Eden whalers in the 1880's, with the fabled killer whale named 'Old Tom' swimming alongside a whaling boat, being towed by a harpooned whale. (Right): Boat fastened to a whale by harpoon and line, and killing the whale with a bomb lance, painting by J.S. Ryder.

of the 1840s destroyed the family financially. The Imlays and others reported considerable activity between Twofold Bay and Wolumla, about 10km south of Brianderry and 16 km south of Bega.

The year 1834 saw the visit of Governor Bourke, which was followed soonafter by the arrival of the Imlay brothers. They acquired over 65,000 acres of land by squatting and began permanent settlement of the 'Biggah' region, which included a few assigned convict servants, who became the district's pioneers. But the area was so remote that Governer

The Imlay Brothers [20]

George (1794–1846), Peter (1797–1881), and Alexander Imlay (1800–1847) were Scottish landowners and speculators born in Aberdeen. They were the sons of Alexander Imlay, a farmer and merchant, and his wife, Agnes Bron.

Alexander, an army surgeon, arrived in Sydney in December 1829 aboard the "Elizabeth" and was appointed to the colony's medical staff in March 1830. Peter, a naval surgeon, reached Hobart Town in February 1830 on the "Greenock". George arrived in Sydney in February 1833 as the surgeon superintendent of convicts on the "Roslyn Castle" and later joined Alexander at the Sydney Infirmary.

In 1832, Alexander explored the South Coast and County of Argyle with Governor (Sir) Richard Bourke. By the following year, he held 1,280 acres (518 ha) on the Breadalbane Plains. That same year, Peter visited Twofold Bay and saw potential for shore-based whaling and stock-raising. He soon settled there, and in 1835, George joined him. Despite managing pastoral interests, George remained in his naval post until 1841. Meanwhile, Alexander resigned from his army medical post in 1833 after ten years of service. He moved to Hobart in January and became primarily responsible for the brothers' properties in Van Diemen's Land.

In 1834, Alexander secured support from Governor Bourke and Lieutenant-Governor (Sir) George Arthur for his plans to develop trade in cattle and salted provisions between Twofold Bay and Van Diemen's Land. He also proposed introducing steam navigation and expanding the wool trade from the Monaro district. The brothers acquired several properties in Van Diemen's Land, including a 2,560-acre (1,036 ha) grant on Forestier Peninsula, the site of one of their whaling stations. Despite government objections to their use of convict labour, the Imlays were among the top six producers of whale products by 1837. In 1841, Alexander attempted to diversify their interests by drilling for coal on his New Town property near Hobart, but the effort was unsuccessful.

In January 1838, Alexander transported 120 cows from Twofold Bay to Adelaide by sea. Shortly after his arrival, he traveled across the Mount Lofty Ranges to the Murray River with a servant and an Aboriginal guide. His journey diary was later published in the 'Adelaide Register' in June and July 1838. David McLaren, manager of the South Australian Company, found the expedition significant enough to report it to his London headquarters.

The Imlay brothers' most substantial holdings were in the Bega district, where George and Peter managed pastoral and whaling operations. Peter also expanded their trade into New Zealand, acquiring land at New Plymouth. Despite holding 1,500 square miles (3,885 km²) of prime land, their financial fortunes collapsed. By late 1844, they had surrendered most of their holdings to creditors, retaining only four runs totaling 37,400 acres (15,135 ha) near Bega and Cobargo. In November, Alexander attempted to sell his Forestier Peninsula property to the government, but Lieutenant-Governor Sir John Eardley-Wilmot declined the offer. The following year, all their Van Diemen's Land properties were put up for sale as Alexander prepared to join his brothers at Bega.

Tragedy struck in July 1846 when Peter's chartered vessel, the "Breeze", was shipwrecked at Upolu while traveling from Tahiti to New Zealand in search of oil. Later that year, on 26 December, George, who was unmarried and suffering from an incurable disease, took his own life atop a mountain overlooking Bega, now known as Dr. George Mountain.

Alexander married Sophia Atkins in Hobart, and they had a son born in New Town on 2 September 1843. However, the child died in March 1847, and Alexander passed away later that year.

Peter, the last surviving brother, migrated to New Zealand in 1851. He married Jane Maguire at St. Andrew's Church, Sydney, on 23 February 1853, in a Presbyterian ceremony. Settling in Wanganui in 1857, he oversaw trading interests in the southwest Pacific. He died there on 8 March 1881, survived by Jane and three daughters.

Early drawing of pelicans being speared with whaling ships and longboats in the background, which operated out of Twofold Bay from about 1828.

TOP (Left): The Pambula River provided access tor the South Coast pioneers. (Right): Built of timber slab walls and bark roofing, the slab hut was popular with early settlers. ABOVE (Left):Dr Alexander Imlay was an early doctor in New South Wales. (Mid): Early settler Dr Peter Imlay, who, along with his brothers, Dr George and Dr Alexander Imlay, some of Twofold Bay's first settlers. (Right): Close-up of Peter Imlay, an early settler in Eden-Twofold Bay area of NSW.

Bourke recognised the futility of collecting the government 20/- per 100 acre squattage fee and did not enforce it. Bourke actually visited the district twice in 1834 and was so impressed by its fertility that he recommended to the Colonial Office that the land be made available for sale, and that a town be built at Twofold Bay. Soon after Bourke's visits, Eden was gazetted as a town in 1836.

The Imlay Brothers

The Imlay brothers, Drs. Alexander, George and Peter prospered at Twofold Bay, they diversified from whaling into the pastoral industry, and in the process they obtained an extensive land holding in south eastern New South Wales.

They established themselves at Panbula and extended their Bega holdings, which were used as pastoral properties for grazing sheep and cattle. However, drought and bushfire in 1839 and 1840 caused grave problems and dealt them a serious financial setback. Fortunately, they were saved from financial ruin by bankers in Hobart Town by the name of James, Sydney and Edward Walker, who were wealthy men at the time. With backing from the Walkers, the Imlay brothers prosperity again increased such that by 1844 they owned 72,500 acres of land (30,000 ha) in the immediate district. This holding was part of a total of 960,000 acres that they held between Twofold Bay and the Clyde River.[6]

The Imlay brothers' biggest interests were in the Bega district, where George and Peter controlled the pastoral and whaling activities. Peter also opened up trade with New Zealand where he had acquired land at New Plymouth. Although he and his brothers held 1500 sq miles (3885 km²) of the colony's best land, their fortunes once again declined disastrously. By the end of 1844 they had surrendered to their creditors all their land except four runs totalling 37,400 acres (15,135 ha) around Bega and Cobargo.[7]

These early settlements were all outside and well beyond the 'limits of location' for settlement as decreed by Governor Sir Ralph Darling (1772-1858), in 1824, which meant there was no military protection against the Aborigines, no land survey provided and no deeds to land, so disputes over land were frequent. Slab huts with stringy bark roofs were erected and generally occupied by two shepherds or stockmen and a hut keeper. They took the sheep or cattle to pasture in the morning and returned them to pens at night to prevent their straying and becoming lost in the bush, or being killed by natives.[8]

> Imlay, George (per P. Imlay). Name of run: Bega. Estimated area: 20,000 acres. Estimated grazing capabilities: 640 cattle, 4,000 sheep. Bounded on the north and east by Mumbla Range; on the south by Bega River and Grossis Creek, being the boundary lines with the Warragaburra and Brichago stations occupied by William and James Walker; and on the west by a swamp running parallel to the east side of the Numbugga swamps and nearly joining the Double Creek.

TOP: A ship finds shelter and drops anchor in Twofold Bay, in the midst of the pristine district of Manaroo. ABOVE (Left): An Aboriginal corroboree as witnessed and drawn by William Gardner, 1854. (Right): Frontier clashes between settlers and Aboriginals occurred often during the colonial period.

TOP (Left): 'A country house, Eden, 1847, by Sir Oswald Brierly' (From Voyage of "H.M.S. Rattlesnake", Vol. I, by Owen Stanley, R.N.). (Right): Shanties and huts constructed of bark slabs, were the first types of dwellings erected on the South Coast. ABOVE: 1855 lithograph of Snug Cove, one of the deepest harbours in the southern hemisphere, at Eden by Elizabeth Hudspeth, showing the Crown & Anchor Hotel towards the top of the hill on the left, In 1828, Capt. Thomas Raine established the first shore based whaling station at Snug Cove. A small pier was erected by Raine, as well as slab huts for a home and for the whaling try-works. The first purpose built wharf for shipping was constructed in 1860.

Prior to 1840, the only practical way in and out of Twofold Bay and Eden was by ship. Later attempts were made overland from Braidwood and a Mr. Nicholson gave an account of his trip over the coast ranges from Broulee to Maneroo in 1841, which hitherto, had been considered impassable:

> "It gives me great pleasure in being able to inform you of the full success of my trip from Broulee to Maneroo, over the heretofore considered impassable coast ranges. I started on the 26th ult, from the coast, with a team of eight bullocks, containing nearly fourteen hundred weight, I reached Braidbo on the ninth instant, four days out of which was occupied in resting the bullocks, so that my journey would have been completed in 11 days, had it not been for the density of the scrub, and live and dead timber which we had either to cut down or remove from the road.
>
> I had, when I left the range on the New Country, upwards of ten hundred weight on the dray, and the bullocks drew it over easy enough, owing much to the management of the drivers. The possibility of bringing a dray over the ranges is now set at rest. The Maneroo people are willing to cooperate with the Broulee folks, as it will save a distance of 100 miles; even now, twelve or fifteen hundred weight of dry goods can be easily conveyed between these two places by drays."
>
> *Mr. Nicholson, Driscoll's Inn, Maneroo, 16 Sept 1841* [9]

The Township of Eden [10]

The Australian botanist, Allan Cunningham (1791-1839), landed at Snug Cove in December 1817 so that he could collect botanical specimens from the district.[11] However,

TOP: Marombet [sic.] River, Twofold Bay, by Capt. Robert Marsh Westmacott. ABOVE (Left): Ben Boyd's Tower, used for whale-spotting. (Right): Commemorative plaque for Benjamin Boyd at Ben Boyd Road, Neutral Bay, NSW, Australia.

Peter Imlay and his brothers George and Alexander Imlay are credited with erecting Eden's first building, a small bark slab hut at Snug Cove. Sketches of the hut were made by Sir Oswald Brierly in 1842 and by Captain Owen Stanley from "HMS Rattlesnake" in 1843.[12]

The graziers, who had taken up squattages in the Monaro district inland from Twofold Bay, were seeking a better way to transport their cattle to Hobart, Tasmania. It was therefore decided to establish cattle-handling facilities and an accompanying township on an appropriate site at Twofold Bay. Thus the government authorised the captain of "HMS Alligator" to seek an appropriate site for a settlement at Twofold Bay.[13] Early in 1835 the governor of New South Wales, Sir Richard Bourke, visited Twofold Bay and the site of the

The opening of the post office at Eden, 1848 by Frederick Garling (1806-1873).

proposed new settlement on board "HMS Hyacinth".[14]

Permission was given by the governor to establish a town at Twofold Bay in 1834, when Eden was named after George Eden (1784-1849), 1st Earl of Auckland, the British Secretary for the Colonies.[15] The area for the proposed town of Eden was surveyed in 1842 by Mr Thomas Townsend, the government surveyor. The main thoroughfare was named after the Imlay brothers who were the earliest pioneers to the district. Other streets were named after Lieutenant Flinders, George Bass, Queen Victoria and her consort, Prince Albert. A wharf was built out into a cove, now named Cattle Bay, from a site on the western edge of Eden, where cattle could be grazed prior to their being loaded onto the ships. Cattle were also

Benjamin Boyd & Twofold Bay [21]

▲ Twofold Bay, by Capt. Robert Marsh Westmacott (Dixson Library, SLNSW). ▼ Portrait of the flambouyant and visionary Benjamin Boyd (State Library of New South Wales, Australia, ML1461).

Benjamin Boyd (1801-1851) was a Scottish entrepreneur born on August 21, 1801, in Penninghame, Wigtown, Scotland. He was the second surviving son of Edward Boyd, a London merchant from Merton Hall, Wigtownshire, and his wife, Janet Yule of Wheatfield, Midlothian. By 1824, Boyd had established himself as a stockbroker in London and held an interest in the St. George's Steam Packet Company.

In October 1840, Boyd wrote to Lord John Russell, outlining his ambitious plans to develop the resources of Australia and its surrounding islands. He believed that efficient communication between settlements required large steamships and informed Russell that he had already dispatched one to New South Wales, with another soon to follow. Seeking official support, Boyd requested permission to select five or six coastal locations for harbors and coaling stations, along with the right to purchase nearby land. While he was assured of assistance for his navigation proposals, the Colonial Office remained non-committal regarding his broader plans for the Pacific Islands.

Boyd's ventures were financed by the Royal Bank of Australia, established in London in 1839 with a nominal capital of £1,000,000. He personally carried £200,000 in debenture sales to Australia. Additionally, in November 1841, he formed the Australian Wool Company, depositing £15,000 of its debentures with the Royal Bank. Boyd, a director of the bank, was supported by his brother Mark, who served as its manager.

Sailing from Plymouth aboard his schooner, "Wanderer", a vessel of the Royal Yacht Squadron, Boyd arrived at Port Phillip on June 15, 1842, and reached Port Jackson on July 18. His arrival generated much excitement, with crowds gathering to witness the "Wanderer" and a welcoming salute from the schooner "Velocity". Among his passengers were his brother James, marine artist Oswald Walters Brierly, and future whaling captains Adam Bogue and Downes. Boyd's steamers had begun arriving ahead of him, with "Seahorse" in June 1841, Juno in March 1842, "Velocity" in May, and "Cornubia" in June, all bringing supplies for his enterprises.

Wasting no time, Boyd launched multiple ventures. Partnering with Joseph Phelps Robinson, he established the Sydney office of the Royal Bank at Church Hill, offering financial services, including Scotch Bank acceptances payable in London. His steamships primarily serviced the southern route to Twofold Bay and Hobart Town. By May 1844, Boyd had become one of the colony's largest landholders, controlling fourteen stations in Monaro and four in the Port Phillip District, covering 426,000 acres (172,398 ha). His pastoral holdings, often purchased from previous owners, were described by Governor Sir George Gipps as "well-watered and in the best parts of the Colony." By 1844, he managed 20,000 sheep and 10,000 cattle in Monaro.

The Royal Bank, or Boyd & Robinson, oversaw more than 160,000 sheep and controlled over 2,500,000 acres (1,011,715 ha) in Monaro and Riverina, secured at minimal annual license fees. However, Boyd struggled to recruit suitable labor. In testimony before the select committee on immigration on September 27, 1843, he revealed that he employed around 200 shepherds and stockmen but saw the colony's prosperity as dependent on cheap labor. He advocated lowering shepherd wages to £10 per year with rations, excluding luxuries such as tea and sugar. Despite his claims of concern for the unemployed,

▼ Benjamin Boyd's famous yacht the "Wanderer" was built in England, but was wrecked in 1851 at Port Macquarie, NSW.

critics like Samuel Sidney saw Boyd as representative of a "haughty, gentlemanly, selfish class."

With labor shortages persisting, Boyd proposed using convicts with tickets-of-leave from Van Diemen's Land in New South Wales, but the government rejected the idea. He then turned to the Pacific Islands, recruiting approximately 200 laborers from Tanna (New Hebrides), Lifu (Loyalty Islands), and other islands in 1847. However, most were sent back by year's end following protests from workers and humanitarian objections. Allegations arose that some islanders had been brought against their will, but a subsequent investigation by the attorney-general found no evidence of wrongdoing.

Boyd selected Twofold Bay as his coastal base, facilitating the shipment of livestock, wool, and tallow from Monaro. He planned two townships: Boyd Town, featuring a hotel, church, houses, stores, salting and boiling-down works, a jetty, and a lighthouse, and East Boyd, where he established a whaling station. He also set up facilities in Port Jackson, including ship fittings at Mosman Bay and a wool-washing establishment at Neutral Bay.

As tensions over land policy mounted in the 1840s, Boyd sought to protect his interests by entering public life. In 1844, he became president of the newly formed Pastoralists' Association, which sent Archibald Boyd to London to advocate their cause. From September 1844 to September 1845, Boyd represented the Port Phillip District in the Legislative Council.

However, his complex and opaque financial dealings led to overextension and financial difficulties. In 1846, he lost a costly legal battle over a £25,000 insurance claim for his damaged steamer, "Seahorse". He misrepresented financial reports to London investors, inflating profits to £36,071 for 1845. Suspicious shareholders ousted him in 1847 in favor of his brother William Sprott Boyd, who also failed to stabilize affairs. In 1849, the Royal Bank of Australia entered liquidation.

Following his financial collapse, Boyd sought fortune in the Californian goldfields. Departing on "Wanderer" on October 26, 1849, he lamented the loss of an anchor on departure, calling it a "parting legacy" to a colony where he had "hoped for much, succeeded in part, but ultimately failed." His American ventures proved unsuccessful, and he turned to the Pacific Islands, envisioning a "Papuan Republic or Confederation."

In June 1851, "Wanderer" and its tender, "Ariel", left San Francisco for the Hawaiian Islands before reaching Guadalcanal in the Solomon Islands. On October 15, Boyd went ashore to hunt but never returned. His companions heard two gunshots and later searched in vain. Concluding he had been killed by locals, they retaliated before sailing for Australia. Less than a month later, "Wanderer" was wrecked in a gale off Port Macquarie on November 12, 1851.

Rumors that Boyd had survived persisted, prompting expeditions by "Oberon" and "H.M.S. Herald" in 1854, but no trace was found. In May 1864, his estate, valued at under £3,000, was granted to the London manager of his creditor, the Royal Bank of Australia.

Boyd was known for his striking appearance and charisma. Artist Georgiana McCrae, who dined with him in 1842, likened him to Rubens and recalled how he once attended a masquerade as the painter. In his prime, Boyd entertained lavishly in Sydney and Boyd Town. A visionary and adventurer, he constantly devised new business or pleasure pursuits. He never married, and the remnants of his ventures now stand as ghost town relics, the only enduring testament to his grand ambitions in Australia.

grazed on Lookout Point until 1853, but was later subdivided for housing.[16] After the town plan was finalised the first blocks were auctioned off on 9th March 1843, when the land was sold to Thomas Aspinall, Benjamin Boyd, S. Clinton, Lewes Gordon, W. Hirst, James Kirwan, J.P. Robinson and T.A. Townsend.[17]

The first postmaster was appointed in 1843, but the first post office did not officially open until 1847. The first customs officer was appointed in 1846, but he was located at East Boyd initially, until the customs house was constructed in 1848. Eden grew in the 1850s following the decline of nearby Boydtown, and the discovery of gold in Kiandra, which led to the 1859–1860 gold rush.

The discovery of alluvial gold at Kiandra in 1859-1860 led to the development of Eden as a port for prospectors heading to the goldfield. At one point there were some 4,000 people living in the town. But the rush ended by 1866 when the port failed to develop. Around 1900 Eden was even mooted as a possible future national capital. This was partly because it was recognised at the time as having the third deepest natural harbour in the

TOP: Boydtown Beach at Nullica Bay, remains today almost as it was when Benjamin Boyd arrrived in 1842, photo by Tracy Rockwell, 2023. ABOVE (Left): The Seahorse Inn at Boydtown opened its doors to tourists after WWII. (Right): The Seahorse Inn in 2023 following extensive renovation.

world. Whaling died off in the late 1920s and slowly replaced by other industries. There was a need for wattlebark, a source of tannin, and dairying, timber and brickmaking became important. Today tourism, commercial fishing, and the woodchip industry are the town's economic base.

The Arrival of Ben Boyd

Around this same time, Benjamin Boyd (1801-1851) arrived at Twofold Bay, and established Boydtown in late 1842. He also took up large holdings in the Monaro District in addition to establishing his own whaling station on the south side of Twofold Bay, away from the Imlay's smelly try-works on the northern shore. Boyd had sound financial backing from London and established such a strong settlement that by 1848 the immigrant ship "Bermondsey" sailed directly from Plymouth to Twofold Bay, bringing 111 immigrants into the district.[18]

Governor Sir George Gipps mentioned in a dispatch dated 17th May 1844 that Boyd had become one of the largest squatters in the country, with 14 stations in the 'Maneroo' district and four in the Port Phillip district, amounting altogether to 381,000 acres (1,540km^2) of land. At about the same period the firm of Boyd and Company had three steamers and three sailing ships in commission. Large sums of money were also spent on Boydtown at Twofold Bay, with the building of a jetty 300 feet (91m) long, and a lighthouse tower of some 75 feet (23m) in height.

Boydtown featured a Gothic church with a spire, commodious stores, well-built brick houses, a whale watch tower, and "a splendid hotel in the Elizabethan style." At this time Boyd had up to nine whaling ships working out of Twofold Bay. He was also elected to the New South Wales Legislative Council for the Electoral District of Port Phillip in September 1844, a position he held for just 11 months.[19]

Twofold Bay became a focal point of settlement in the early 19th century, its deep harbour and abundant whale populations drawing enterprising settlers to the region. The Imlay brothers, Alexander, Peter, and George, arrived in the 1830s, establishing vast pastoral holdings and a thriving shore-based whaling operation. By the late 1830s, they were among the colony's leading producers of whale oil and baleen, despite government restrictions on convict labour. Their success helped lay the foundations for the small but growing settlement of Eden, which emerged as a crucial hub for maritime trade and industry.

In the early 1840s, Scottish entrepreneur Benjamin Boyd arrived with grand ambitions, expanding the whaling industry, establishing Boydtown, and attempting large-scale commercial ventures. However, his reliance on indentured South Sea Islander labour and speculative investments led to financial collapse, leaving his once-promising empire in ruins.

Amidst this landscape of booming industry and shifting fortunes, John Frawley and his family arrived on the far South Coast in 1842, and was hired to work on the Imlays' remote pastoral property, 'Warragaburra'. As they stepped onto this rugged frontier, they found themselves in a land of opportunity and hardship, where fortunes could be made, or lost, on the whims of the sea and the struggles of the land. Their journey into this untamed world was just beginning…

References

1. Jeffreys, Max. (1997). The Wreck of the 'Sydney Cove.' New Holland Publishers Pty Ltd.
2. History Cooperative. (2 March 2017). 'History of Whaling in Twofold Bay.' [https://historycooperative.org/history-whaling-twofold-bay/]. Retrieved 9th June 2021.
3. Bayley, W.A. (1942). History of Bega. Sydney, Brooks, p.10.
4. Weebly, "A Brief Early History of Bega Valley", [https://begapioneersmuseum.weebly.com/a-brief-early-history-of-bega-valley.html.
5. Higgins, J. (1982). Pambula's Colonial Days: A short history of the period 1797-1901. The Merimbula – Imlay Historical Society.
6. Swinburne, H. & Winters, J. (2001). 'Bega Valley Shire: Pictorial History.' Kinsclear Books & Bega Valley Shire, p.19.
7. Australian Dictionary of Biography - Peter Imlay, by H.B. Wellings [https://adb.anu.edu.au/biography/imlay-peter-2259].
8. Parbery, D.G. (1992). Fabric Of A Family. Self-Published. Mont Albert, Vic.
9. Mr. Nicholson's Overland Trip to Maneroo (Sydney Monitor & Commercial Advertiser, 24 Sep 1841, p.2)
10. Aussie Towns - Eden, NSW [https://www.aussietowns.com.au/town/eden-nsw].
11. Wellings, H.P. (1996). 'Eden and Twofold Bay: Discovery, Early History and Points of Interest 1797–1965' (Second ed.) [ISBN 0-646-29410-5].
12. Ibid.
13. "HMS Alligator" at Twofold Bay (The Australian, 3 June 1834).
14. Gov. Bourke Visits Twofold Bay (The Australian, 13 February 1835 & 13 March 1835).
15. "Eden, New South Wales" Travel (Sydney Morning Herald, 8 February 2004).
16. Wellings, H.P. (1996). 'Eden and Twofold Bay, op. cit.
17. Wellings, H.P. (1996). 'Eden and Twofold Bay, op. cit.
18. Bayley, W.A. (1942). History of Bega, op. cit., pp.16-17.
19. "Mr Benjamin Boyd (1803-1851)". Former members of the Parliament of New South Wales. Retrieved 7 April 2019.
20. Wellings, H.P. (1967). 'Imlay, Peter (1797–1881)', Australian Dictionary of Biography, National Centre of Biography, Australian National University, published first in hardcopy 1967, accessed online 18 May 2016. [http://adb.anu.edu.au/biography/imlay-peter-2259/text2887].
21. G. P. Walsh, 'Boyd, Benjamin (Ben) (1801–1851)', Australian Dictionary of Biography, National Centre of Biography, Australian National University, http://adb.anu.edu.au/biography/boyd-benjamin-ben-1815/text2075, published first in hardcopy 1966, accessed online 18 May 2016.

Further Reading

Bach, J. (1976). A Maritime History of Australia. Sydney, Pan Books.
Bayley, W. A. (1964). Behind Broulee. Eurobodalla Shire Council.
Cox. P. (1978). South Coast of New South Wales. Melbourne, Macmillan.
Elias, S. (Ed.) (1986). Tales of the Far South Coast. Vol.3., Bega Valley Shire Bi-Centennial Committee.
Flower, C. (1981). Illustrated History of NSW. Adelaide, Rigby.
Hawkins, I. (1977). Shipping Arrival and Departures Sydney 1826 – 1840: Volume 3, Canberra, Roebuck.
Hueneke, K. (1976). 'The high country gold rush', in Canberra Times, 28 August, p. 11.
McKenzie, J. A. S. (1991). The Twofold Bay Story.
Monaro Pioneers Group. 'Monaro.' [http://www.monaropioneers.com/towns/Pambula.htm]. Retrieved 6 July 2021.
Moye, D.G. (1972). Historic Kiandra: a guide to the history of the district. Sydney, Cooma-Monaro Historical Society.
Stegemann, W.C. (1980). Kiandra: goldfield and community. Canberra Historical Journal, No. 6, Sept., pp. 1-9.

Chapter Eleven

WARRAGABURRA HOMESTEAD

The year was 1842, and John Frawley, his wife Mary Ann, and their infant son, John Jr., stood on the deck of their ship as it sailed into Twofold Bay. The vast, untamed Australian coastline stretched before them, a world apart from the familiar landscapes of their homeland. Growing up in Ireland, they had walked the stone streets of Limerick, where the grandeur and comfort of King John's Castle and St. Mary's Cathedral stood as towering reminders of a medieval past. Seven centuries of history had shaped those structures, their stone walls echoing the footsteps of countless generations. Now, as they disembarked, they faced a stark contrast, a land where the comforts of civilization were exchanged for the crude bark slab huts and dirt floors of New South Wales settlers.

District	Stations	Acres Cultivated	Population	Horses	Cattle	Sheep
Bligh	44	218	402	241?	24,064	118,341
Lachlan	84	1,945	792	1,027	37,920	114,134
Liverpool Plains	121	292	1,042	1,045	102,758	230,102
Maneroo	132	1,031	1,651	2,133	78,473	230,150
Murrumbidgee	147	1,795	1,139	1,517	62,348?	183,654?
New England	56	361	702	262	13,850	201,926
Port Macquarie	22	590	287	169	5,833?	14,642?
Wellington	56	433	656	436	26,370	119,441

Statistics for the Eight Grazing Districts, Lying Outside of the 'Limits of Location' in New South Wales, 1841[24]

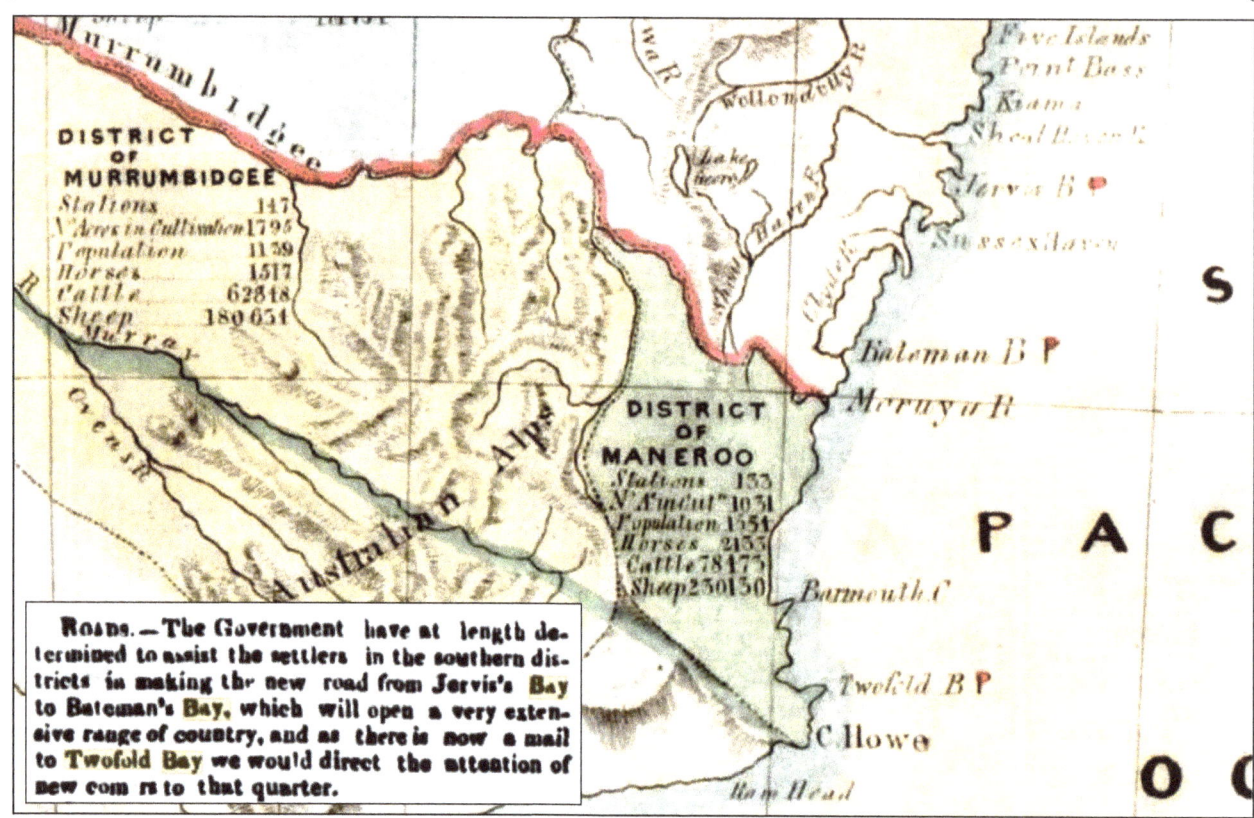

M14. William Baker's 1841 map of the District of Maneroo showing the location of Twofold Bay, Shoalhaven and the Illawarra (NLA MAP NK 5348).
INSET: The road between Jervis Bay and Batemans Bay - News (Sydney Herald, 4th March, 1840, p.2).

The Frawleys had come in search of opportunity, a future carved out of the unforgiving wilderness. Their journey overland would take them from the sleeping hamlet at Twofold Bay to the remote Imlay brothers' 'Warragaburra Station', a place where survival required resilience and determination.

Like many who ventured into the frontier, they were met with formidable challenges. The harsh Australian landscape was as merciless as it was beautiful, searing heat, relentless bushfires, and devastating floods tested their endurance at every turn. Even more perilous was the ever-present tension between settlers and the Aboriginal inhabitants, who fiercely resisted encroachment on their ancestral lands.

John Frawley and his wife, Mary Ann, likely arrived on the far South Coast in response to an advertisement from the Imlay Brothers, who were seeking a husband-and-wife team or a shepherd for their pastoral property, called Warraguburra. With the skills and experience John had gained at the Coolangatta homestead, he was probably hired as a general hand or hutkeeper. Meanwhile, Mary likely took on essential domestic duties such as sewing, mending, laundry, and cooking, tasks highly valued by the other workers.

For the Frawleys, there was no turning back. They were true pioneers, battling the harsh realities of survival while building a new life in an unfamiliar and grueling land. Their story is one of hardship and adversity but also of resilience, courage, and determination.

In the early days of settlement, the region surrounding Eden and Bega was completely devoid of roads, making transportation of supplies an arduous challenge. Even the most basic necessities had to be carried by pack-bullocks, significantly limiting access to essential goods. Twofold Bay, located 332 kilometers south of Sydney, was remote and difficult to reach. While no direct records confirm their exact route, the Frawley family likely traveled by ship from the Illawarra to Sydney, then continued on another vessel to Twofold Bay after a brief stopover.

In 1842, the port of Eden had a population of only about 30 people, and the idea of a South Coast road had not yet been considered. Traveling beyond the officially designated 'Limits of Location' was not only difficult but also extremely dangerous. The Bega Valley, in particular, posed significant risks, with deaths from snake bites, starvation, exposure, and conflicts with Aboriginal groups being harsh realities of life.[1] Early settlers in the Maneroo region faced extreme isolation and had to rely entirely on the land for survival until they could cultivate their own food. Their homes were simple huts made from slabs of stringy bark, and they often encountered hostility from Indigenous groups. Without roads, public transport, regular mail, or church services, self-reliance was essential for survival.[2]

Due to the dangers of the wilderness, settlers were only allowed to take up land within the officially gazetted 'Nineteen Counties', the designated boundaries of the colony. These limits had been established in 1826 by Governor Ralph Darling in accordance with an order from Henry Bathurst (1762-1834), 3rd Earl Bathurst, the Secretary of State. Counties had been used for administrative purposes since the very first year of settlement, with Cumberland County, the first being officially proclaimed on June 6, 1788. William Baker's map provides data on the grazing district of Maneroo. Since Maneroo lay beyond the 'Limits of Location' in 1841, its statistics were not drawn from the census but instead compiled for an 1840 report to the Legislative Council of New South Wales regarding proposed boundaries within the colony.

The Spearing Of Michael Dunn

Prior to 1850 on the far south coast, and throughout the Bega district, the pioneers struggled to co-exist with the Aboriginals. Not least among their problems was the ferocity of the local 'Jellat Jellat' tribe of Aborigines near Bega, whose camp was nearby to both Warragaburra and Brianderry Stations. The murder of Michael Dunn at Warragaburra in 1835 served to illustrate the dangers of remote living:

South Coast settlers under attack by spear carrying Aboriginals, the likes of who murdered Michael Dunn at 'Warragaburra' in 1835.

From Prisoners To Pioneers

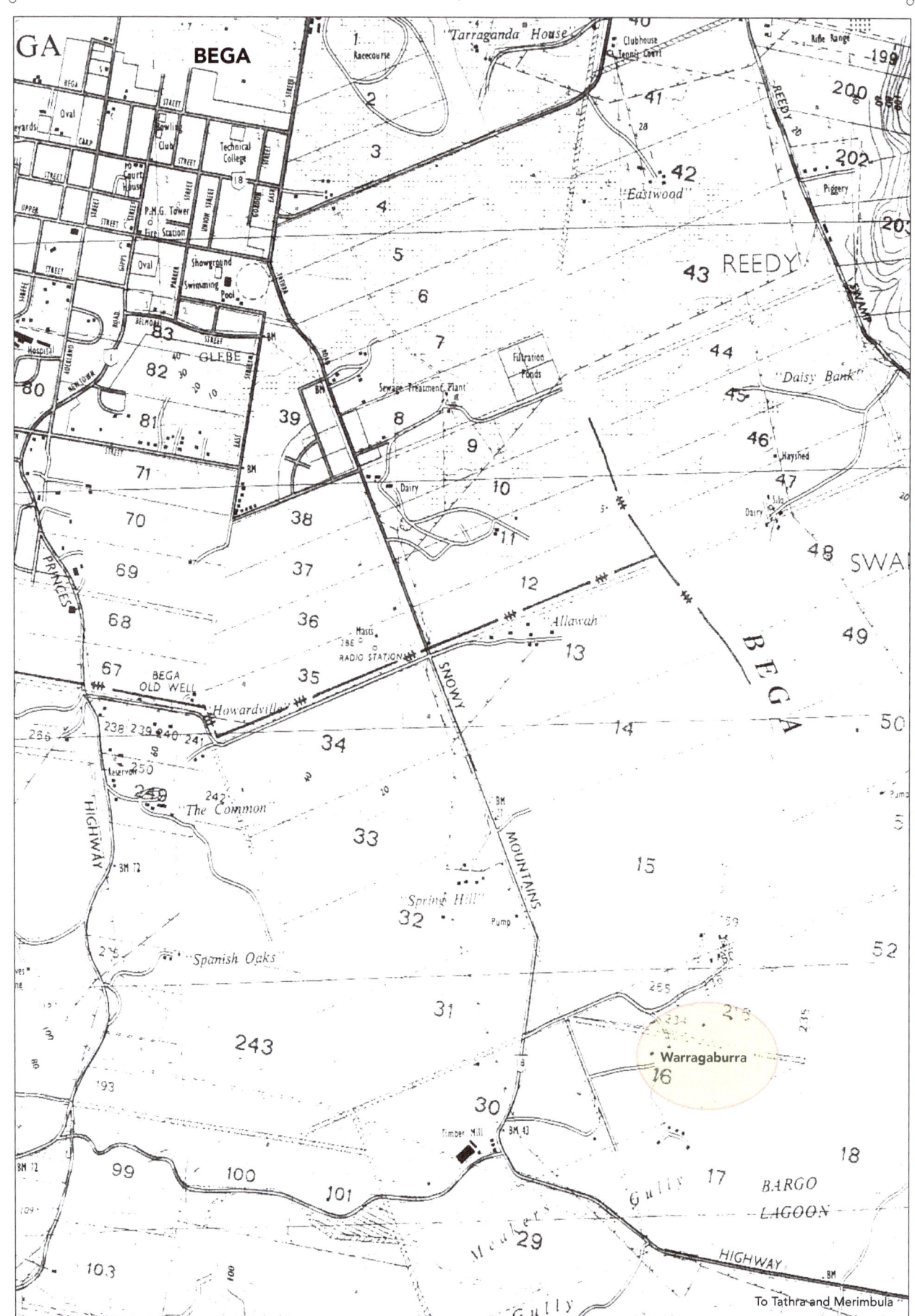

M15. Modern map of the Bega area, showing the location of the Warragaburra Homestead at bottom right.

> "The men from these two stations went around together for mutual protection. One day in 1835 when Bartley had left Warragaburra to visit Brianderry, the blacks attacked the hut at Warragaburra, speared Dunn to death and threw his body into a waterhole. When Bartley returned he found the hut ransacked, blood on the floor and Dunn missing. He barricaded himself in and spent a worried but quiet night. The following day when Bartley tried to leave, the tribesman again attacked the hut preventing him from doing so. Later in the day he again attempted to leave and succeeded only after sooling his dog onto the nearest warriors. He made for a white man's camp at Wandella, north west of Cobargo, about thirty miles away and the Badgery settlement was subsequently abandoned. Higgs and a party from Brianderry buried Michael Dunn in an unmarked grave the following day."
>
> D. G. Parbery [3]

Coastal Shipping

Coinciding with the relocation of John Frawley and family to Warraguberra, who likely knew little of its history, was the arrival of the intrepid Benjamin Boyd with his various enterprises. While Boyd sailed into Port Jackson in his yacht "Wanderer" on the 12th July 1842,[4] John, Mary and their infant son John Frawley Jr. were preparing to sail out, taking the momentous step of accepting a pioneering position in the Maneroo District.

Realistically, the Frawleys could have arrived at Warraguberra anytime after the birth of their son John Jr. on the 7th May 1841, until the birth of their daughter Ellen on the 2nd September 1842, which was is an unaccounted window of some 18 months.

From 1841, Broulee was increasingly becoming the preferred port for loading and unloading of goods on the South Coast, with an average of 2.3 ships arriving and departing from there each month. However, Twofold Bay had been the preferred port for the Imlay's since the early 1830s, with their ships mainly transporting livestock, and by 1841, it also began to receive commercial ships from Sydney. Considering the overland track from Broulee to Warragaburra was 140km, it made more sense for the Frawleys to sail south

Ships Departing Sydney for Twofold Bay & Broulee in 1842

Date	Ship	Tons	Capt	Port
January				
04	"Industry"	19	Woods	Twofold Bay
13	"Water Witch"	27	Evans	Broulee
14	"Brothers"	44	Millie	Twofold Bay
15	"Star"	20	Thompson	Broulee
20	"Alligator"	20	Walters	Broulee
28	"Alligator"	29	Walker	Broulee
February				
04	"Star"	12	Thompson	Broulee
05	"Brothers"	44	Melville	Twofold Bay
17	"Industry"	19	Woods	Twofold Bay
24	"Water Witch"	37	Evans	Broulee
March				
12	"Industry"	14	Wright	Broulee
19	"Bee"	12	Sugden	Broulee
21	"Star"	12	Thomson	Broulee
24	"Rover"	10	Thomson	Broulee
30	"Eliza Ann"	32	Gaunson	Broulee
April				
04	"Water Witch"	37	Evans	Broulee
(Lacuna in reporting from - 14th April to 8th July)				
July				
21	"Mary Hay"	75	A. Volum	Twofold Bay
	(with Mr. Imlay a passenger)			
23	"Star"	16	Thomson	Broulee
28	"Eliza Ann"	32	Gaunson	Broulee
August				
04	"Mary Hay"	75	A. Volum	Twofold Bay
05	"Industry"	14	Wright	Twofold Bay

Shepherds Wanted.
WANTED, two Shepherds, to proceed to Twofold Bay, and two to remain in this Colony.—None need apply but those who can produce satisfactory testimonials of character, and knowledge of the management of sheep.—Apply to the Undersigned.
A. IMLAY.
59, Campbell-street, April 6, 1837. (1000

TO SHEPHERDS.—WANTED. Two Free or Ticket-of-Leave Men as SHEPHERDS, to whom liberal wages will be given. None need apply who do not thoroughly understand the management of sheep. Apply to Marlborough, May 17. JOHN CLARK.

WANTED, Shepherds, Hutkeepers, Bullock Drivers, Splitters. Apply between the hours of Twelve and Two, to
MR. A. BROADRIBB,
70 Royal Hotel.

For Jervis Bay, Ulladulla, and Broulee.
THE regular trader cutter STAR, will leave for the above ports on Monday night next, positively. For freight or passage apply to the Captain on board, or to
E. M. STORKY,
February 18. Union Wharf.

TOP (Left): Advertisements such as these... 'Shepherds Wanted' notices in various newspapers of the time, likely attracted John Frawley to relocate to the Maneroo District in 1842. (Right): A list of ships departing for Twofold Bay and Broulee in 1842 shows fewer sailings during the winter months. However, the "Mary Hay" voyage on July 21st from Sydney to Twofold Bay appears to be the most likely option for the Frawley family's passage.

TOP (Left): Advertisement 'Wanted - Superintendant or Overseer' of the kind that likely attracted John Frawley to relocate to the Maneroo District in 1842 (SMH, 23 July 1842, p.3). (Right): Painting of the barque "Mary Hay", captained by Alexander Volum out of Peterhead, Scotland, which likely conveyed the Frawley family to Twofold Bay, about July 1842 (from Arbuthnot Museum, Peterhead, Scotland). ABOVE: 'Encamping for the night at the foot of the Maneroo range of mountains', by Capt. Robert Marsh Westmacott (Dixson Library, SLNSW).

via Twofold Bay, which meant only a 53km journey to Warragaburra. Interestingly, that route passed right by Imlay's 'Panbula Station', which was to become the future township of Pambula. We don't know exactly when the Frawleys sailed south from Sydney, but there were then a few vessels operating the Sydney to Twofold Bay route in 1842.

In an attempt to identify the actual ship the Frawleys might have sailed on, evidence reveals that there were only three possible vessels that sailed from Sydney to Twofold Bay in 1842. So the Frawleys were either aboard the "Brothers", "Industry", or most likely, the "Mary Hay", the latter of which, departed from Sydney on the 21st July, and carried on board one of the owners of 'Warragaburra', in a Mr. Imlay.[5]

Arrival at Warragaburra

Exactly when John and Mary Ann Frawley, and their infant son John Jr. arrived at 'Warragaburra' is uncertain, but the "Mary Hay" arrived in mid-winter at Twofold Bay, around the 23rd July 1842. Whichever route they travelled, the Frawleys evidently arrived safely at Warragaburra after what would have been quite a journey. Mary Ann, who was heavily pregnant at the time, and her husband, likely set themselves up in nothing more than a tent in the wilderness, or a dirt floored slab hut if they were fortunate. The property was situated exactly at the tidal extent of what was later named the Bega River, so travel to and from was often conducted by navigating the river. Above the tidal limit was fresh water, which was used to irrigate crops, making Warragaburra an excellent place to situate the original hut in the mid 1830s.

The term 'warragaburra' is a mild corruption of the aboriginal word 'warragubbra', which means, 'the turning of the tide'.[6] Warragaburra, has been variously spelt as 'Warragubera', 'Warragubra', 'Warigubra' and even 'Warigaberra'. That property today is situated around 5kms southeast of today's town of Bega, and was located precisely at the point on the Bega River, where the flow becomes tidal and then empties into the sea just north of today's town of Tathra.

The Frawleys likely arrived at Twofold Bay about six weeks prior to the birth of their second child Ellen Frawley, which occurred at 'Warigubara Station' on the 2nd of September 1842,[7] with her father working as a labourer. Consequently, Ellen is believed to be one of the first, if not the very first white child born on the far South Coast.

The birth and baptism registration for Ellen Frawley at 'Warigubara', Twofold Bay, by Father Michael Kavanagh (NSW BDM # #1772/1842 (V18421772 62).

TOP: Panorama of the Warragaburra property in 2023, by Tracy Rockwell. ABOVE (Left): The name of the fierce Aboriginals known as the 'Jellat Jellat' tribe lives on in the local signage. (Right): The long dirt road to the now sub-divided property of Warragaburra.

Until 1862, squatters occupied all the land in the Monaro and coastal districts except for some land sold near government townships. So far as the white population was concerned, the area was almost entirely occupied by squatters, their assigned servants and employed persons. However, few immigrant families ventured into the district of Twofold Bay until the 1840s. Indeed, the family of James Kirwan's wife objected to their Elizabeth accompanying James to the Monaro, at that time, because there were no white women there.

First White Child Born in the Monaro

In those early days, the hardships and privations borne by these worthy pioneers was really indescribable, but here arises the disputed issue as to who was the first white child born in the Monaro District. Ellen Frawley was one amongst a shortlist of contenders, but if she wasn't the very first white child born in the region, there was obviously only a short space of time between her and the rival claimants.

There are many claims regarding which European women and which child was first born in the isolated areas. A white woman, a widow named Ritchie, was reported to be with the Imlays at Twofold Bay, in 1840, after her husband, a ship's carpenter died there. When the Anglican Rev E. G. Pryce visited Bega in 1844, he baptised Henry the son of Thomas and Jane Underhill born there in 1842. William Bartley was born at Dry River in 1841. Father Michael Kavanagh of Queanbeyan baptised a child at Kiah in 1844 and also John Jr. and Ellen Frawley at Warrigubura. From this information it can be deduced that the first family groups entered the district in the 1840s. Reporting on conditions in the Queanbeyan - Canberra districts in 1839 Rev. Pryce stated, "There is no school of any description in the district... here is no church, no school, no place where the decencies of public worship can be observed.' Concerning Twofold Bay which he referred to as the 'Untouched District' he wrote:

ABOVE (Left): The dirt road to the original property of Warragaburra Station. (Right): Road sign on Tathra Road, pointing to the location of Warragaburra Station, photos by Tracy Rockwell, 2023.

> "The popular neighbourhood of Braidwood and all the country as far as Bateman's Bay are I believe unprovided for. Menaroo also, extending 150 miles in another direction, beyond the limits with a scattered population of 1600 is totally without the means of grace."
>
> *John B. Cornell* [8]

Ellen had been preceded in her family by her older brother John Frawley Jr, but he had been born in May of the preceding year, and baptised while the Frawley's were still working at Alexander Berry's Coolangatta homestead. In any case, by November of 1843, John and Mary Ann Frawley's third child, James Frawley, had arrived at Warragaburra.[9]

Although the Frawley's had by now become accustomed to the rigours of the untamed Australian bush, this attribute hadn't yet extended to other members of colonial society and in particular the clergy. Indeed it wasn't until the 18th March 1844 that Father Michael Kavanagh, the roving parish priest for Queanbeyan and the Monaro District, arrived for the very first time, to administer to the outlying Catholic pioneers. Baptismal record state that John Jr., Ellen and James Frawley were all baptised at that time, with the ceremonies being conducted in 'Parish Unnamed' in the County of Murray and in the District of Manaroo (aka Monaro) of New South Wales. The father, John Frawley was recorded as working as a labourer and living with Mary (McGarrey) at Warragaburra, with Twofold Bay being the nearest settlement.[10]

> "When Bishop Polding [1794-1877] came to Sydney in 1835, he set up parishes to cover the populated areas of the country. Among them was Queanbeyan, with Father Heston in charge in 1842. The Bega Valley was in this vast Parish, which stretched from west of the Dividing Range to the sea, and from Moruya to south of Twofold Bay. So Catholics who had come down

> with William Duggan Tarlington from Braidwood or made their way from Ben Boyd's camp in Twofold Bay belonged to the Queanbeyan parish. Once a year Rev. Michael Kavanagh, who was appointed to Queanbeyan in 1843, visited the coastal fringe of the Queanbeyan parish. On the 18th March 1844 he baptised John Jr. Ellen & James Frawley of Warrigubura...So the Sacraments were administered and probably the Holy Sacrifice offered in somebody's slab hut?"

Gerard Monaghan [11]

The fact that their oldest child John Frawley Jr. had already been baptised in 1841, didn't seem to matter... as in the wilderness, they likely concluded that "the more protection, the better." While the actual record of his baptism has not been accessed, the Queanbeyan baptismal records for both Ellen (18 months) and James Frawley (5 months), provide sufficient information.

Reminiscences of a Bush Family

The book "Recollections of the Early Days of Moruya", by Mrs Celia Rose of 'Gundary', Moruya, mirror similar experiences of the Frawley family at Warragaburra, and she gives an account of her interactions with the Aborigines of that district, after she had arrived there as a child with her family in the late 1830s...

> "There was only one sailing vessel, named the "Waterwitch", that called at Broulee about once a month, bringing provisions from Sydney, and the shortage was acute. Aboriginals saved the settlement several times from starvation by supplying fish and oysters. I think the Aboriginals numbered about four hundred. They were quiet and harmless, and the elders of them were very kind, and would put their hands on our heads and say, "Buderree", or fellow white picaninny. There were no other white children but my brother and myself, and we used to play with the blacks, and were never frightened of them. My mother was the only white woman here at the time. The first hotel was built on the northern bank of the Moruya River, and when the blacks got drunk there they would fight and kill each other, and now there is not one full-blooded black left in this district."

Mrs Celia Rose of 'Gundary', Moruya [12]

The Walker Brothers

The year 1844 brought the collapse of the beef industry, and having over-extended themselves the Imlay brothers were unable to repay their debts. The combination of a severe drought and depression saw the foreclosure of the Imlay properties by their bankers, the Walker brothers. Consequently, the Imlays were forced to sell-up most of their holdings with ownership of 'Warragaburra' passing to William Walker & Co.

A typical pioneer's bark slab hut, with external kitchen and cleaning facilities on the NSW South Coast.

TOP: 'Whales in Sight, Twofold Bay, NSW, 1844', painted by Oswald Brierly (State Library of New South Wales V1-FL1083061).
ABOVE: An Aboriginal corroboree by the banks of a South Coast river (artist unknown).

William Walker (1787-1854), merchant, was the second son of Archibald Walker, the laird of Edenshead, Fife in Scotland, and his second wife Isabel, daughter of the laird of Falfield. In 1803 William joined the London branch of a Scottish bank and after a few years joined Fairlie, Ferguson & Co., merchants, whose headquarters were in Calcutta. He was soonafter sent to Calcutta and in July 1813 voyaged to Sydney in the "Eliza" as agent for his firm, with the immediate task of collecting debts owed to it by Robert Campbell (1769-1846). After sailing back to Calcutta, Walker resigned from the firm and in March of 1820 he returned to Sydney in the "Haldane".[13]

William Walker had already formed William Walker & Co., while his eldest brother James, a half-pay naval officer, followed him to Sydney on the 24th September 1823,[14] joining two nephews, Thomas and Archibald Walker, who were also in the colony as shareholders. The firm became engaged in coastal shipping and whaling, and operated out of their wharf and warehouse at Dawes Point in Sydney. William had already received a grant of 1000 acres (405ha) from Governor Lachlan Macquarie in 1821, and another 1000 acres (405ha) from Governor Sir Thomas Brisbane at 'Lue', near Mudgee in 1825.

Settlers with capital were favoured by the land and immigration regulations of the 1820s, since these 'capitalists' could support themselves and relieve the government of

The Walker Brothers & William Walker & Co.
James Walker (1785-1856)

Eldest son of Archibald Walker, Laird of Edenshead, Fife, and merchant of Perth, Scotland, and his second wife Isabel Walker, daughter of the Laird of Falfield. Married Robina Walker in 1832. Presbyterian.

Joined the Royal Marine Artillery and arrived in Sydney in September 1823 as an officer on half-pay and a shareholder with his brother William Walker and two nephews in William Walker & Company; merchants, coastal shippers and whalers. Was soon granted 2000 acres at Wallerawang and settled there in 1824. Visited London with his brother in 1831, founding Walker Bros. & Company; in which in the late 1830s exported large quantities of wool to London. In the 1840s joined the squatting rush, acquiring large holdings. In 1854 his interests included sixteen runs totalling 256,000 acres in the Bligh District, four runs totalling 70,500 acres in the Wellington District, and Baradean, 19,840 acres on the Liverpool Plains. He was a Member of the NSW Legislative Council for six months, just prior to his death in Sydney in 1856.[25]

"In 1823, James Walker arrived in Sydney from Scotland, joining his younger brother, William Walker. Together the two brothers developed Walker and Co., engaging in coastal shipping and whaling from their wharf and warehouse at Dawes Point. During the late 1830s the company exported large quantities of wool to London. Walker established himself at Wallerawang in 1824, taking its name from an Indigenous word meaning "place of plenty of wood and water". Wallerawang was a sheep and cattle station which also served as a major stop-over location for travellers between Sydney, Mudgee and Bathurst.

In 1836, Charles Darwin visited the district and specifically Wallerawang, after which he wrote, "this place offers an example of one of the large farming or rather sheep grazing establishments of the colony". In correspondence to the Colonial Secretary, Alexander McLeay, dated 1837, Walker outlines his status: "I beg you will be pleased to submit to his Excellency the Governor's consideration the following grounds upon which I venture to solicit an extension of my present grant of land of 2000 acres which I received when I first came into this country in 1823, as a free settler. I brought out with me 18 merino sheep (having lost nine on the voyage), a free man as overseer, who is still in my employment, agricultural implements and workmen's tools to the amount of £200 and I have purchased sheep in this colony to the amount of £1500, and although I suffered the severe loss of upwards of 400 head last winter".

Wallerawang was a sheep and cattle station which also served as a major stop-over location for travellers between Sydney, Mudgee and Bathurst. James Walker continued to build both property and livestock numbers over the following two decades including Loowee (Lue) about 70 miles from Wallerawang, Biambil on the Castlereagh River, Yooloondoory, Coonamble, Barradean, and Mobilla near the Warrumbungle Ranges."[26]

James Walker was known to have squatted on the majority of his lands prior to officially claiming them. His wife, Robina Walker, is registered within the NSW Squatting Directory (1871) as holding six stations within the Bligh District for a total of £245 rental. These properties were Yarragrin, Wallambrawang, Yoolangra, Round Hills, Wallangolang and Dilly-Dilly. Earlier, in 1844, Governor George Gipps wrote to Lord Stanley, stating:

"...by a return received only yesterday I find there is an individual in the Bligh district who holds 27 stations under a single licence, Mr James Walker of Wallerowang. The commissioner returns his run as having 5,184,000 acres, but I conclude that the greater part of it must consist of barren or mountain land. The individual has 3,000 head of cattle and 13,000 sheep and pays no more rent for the land they feed on than is paid by another person in the same district who holds only 12,000 acres and has on them 1,000 cattle.[27]

In 1832, Walker had returned home to Scotland to marry his cousin Robina Ramsay who accompanied him back to Wallerawang. The Walkers had four children in Allison (born at Wallerawang in 1834), Wilhemina (born in London), and Archibald James (1841) and Georgina Lyon Wolgan (1843) both born in Australia. The male line of the Walker family ceased when Archibald, died in 1858 in Glasgow. Allison married a New Zealander and moved to London after selling her share of the estate, and died in 1912, aged 78. Wilhelmina married a cousin and died in childbirth aged 28 in 1854. Georgina married Edwin Barton, a surveyor who was employed to map out the route for the railway to the west.

James was patron of the committee of the Bowenfels National School and laid the foundation stone in 1850. By 1854, Walker was the holder of 16 stations with an area of 4,700,000 acres. After Walker died in 1856, aged 71, his widow Robina held licenses for 15 stations. Robina died in 1867. The following notice appeared in the Sydney Morning Herald on 22 January 1867:

"She was one of the pleasure party who lately attended at Bowenfels (Lithgow Valley) on Saturday, 5th instant witness the great blasting explosion on the railway works. She was accompanied by her daughter, Mrs. Barton, the wife of the engineer in chief, and it is said received a fright and died a week later."[28]

Edward Walker (1815-1899) was a 'sleeping partner' of William Walker & Co., and only briefly occupied historic 'Oaklands Manor' at Pambula.

'Redleaf Mansion', now the Woollahra Council Offices at Double Bay, was originally built by William Benjamin Walker, who was also the first Commodore of the Royal Sydney Yacht Squadron.

William Walker (1787-1854)[29]

William Walker, merchant, was the second son of Archibald Walker, laird of Edenshead, Fife, Scotland, and his second wife, Isabel, daughter of the laird of Falfield. In 1803 he joined the London branch of a Scottish bank and after a few years joined Fairlie, Ferguson & Co., merchants, whose headquarters were at Calcutta. He was soon sent to Calcutta and in July 1813 went to Sydney in the "Eliza" as agent for his firm, with the immediate task of collecting debts owed to it by Robert Campbell. After his return to Calcutta he resigned from the firm and in March 1820 came back to Sydney in the "Haldane".

William Walker's eldest brother James, a half-pay naval officer, arrived in Sydney in September 1823. Walker had already formed William Walker & Co., with James and two nephews, Thomas and Archibald Walker, who were in the colony, as shareholders. The firm had a wharf and warehouse at Dawes Point and engaged in coastal shipping and whaling. William received a grant of 1000 acres (405 ha) from Governor Lachlan Macquarie in 1821 and in 1825 another 1000 (405 ha) from Governor Sir Thomas Brisbane at Lue, near Mudgee. James received 2000 acres (809 ha) at Wallerawang and settled there in 1824.

In May 1826 William sailed in the "Mangles" for London. On his return to Australia in the "Numa" in July 1828 he brought 160 Saxon merino ewes from Stettin. On the 20th October 1828 in Sydney he had married Elizabeth Kirby; they had nine sons and two daughters. While in England he had applied for an increased grant as he now had capital of approximately £25,000 invested in the colony. He was given another 1000 acres (405ha) and later obtained more land in the central west of NSW and at Twofold Bay. In February 1831 both brothers chartered the "Forth" and returned to London to establish the firm of Walker Bros. & Co., which during the late 1830s exported large quantities of wool to London. Their men moved stock to the upper Castlereagh River and squatted on several runs. David, William and Thomas Archer, sons of William Archer and Julia Walker, daughter of William's half-brother Archibald, had arrived at Wallerawang and remained there from 1834-38 when David Archer began managing the Walkers' properties. News of losses in the depression and drought brought William Walker to Australia again in 1843, but his permanent residence remained in England until he died on the 8th July 1854.

William Walker played an active part in public life during his long residence in New South Wales. He was a director of the Bank of New South Wales in 1820-24, a member of committees appointed to examine the bank's affairs in 1844 and 1845, and was on its first London board in 1853-54. He was president of the Chamber of Commerce and treasurer of the Agricultural Society, a strong supporter of the Scots Church and a subscriber to charitable institutions.

Edward Walker (1815-1899)

Edward Walker was educated at Pembroke College, Cambridge, he spent most of his boyhood in Perth, Scotland. He lived at Loowie Station in the Blue Mountains, NSW around 1839. He was a sleeping partner in David Archer & Co. with his younger brother William Benjamin Walker, at "Oaklands" on the Pambula Flats, Twofold Bay area, where he owned a lovely house in 1852-3. He sold his run the Twofold Bay Pastoral Association to his brothers. By 1855 he had returned to England and was residing at "Oxted Cottage", Oxted, and by 1859 at Orme Square, London; then "Carey House", Brockenhurst, Hampshire; and "Araluen" at Eastbourne in Sussex, and finally at "Mayer House", Symondsbury, Dorset. He had 9 children by each of his two wives, 18 in all.

William Benjamin Walker (1820-1889)[30]

William Benjamin Walker (1820 - 9 January 1889) was a politician, merchant, pastoralist and yachtsman from New South Wales, Australia. He was the second son of William Walker, a prominent merchant in early colonial Australia. W.B. Walker was originally a pastoralist, operating a series of stations in the Bega region, based out of the Kamarooka Estate near Bega. He was later a merchant in Sydney, operating the firm of William Walker & Co. He built and resided in the 'Redleaf Mansion' at Double Bay, which he named after his parent's house in England.[31,32] The property survives, and now serves as the council chambers for the Municipality of Woollahra. He served in the New South Wales Legislative Council from 1863 until his resignation in 1867. He was involved in the establishment of the Royal Sydney Yacht Squadron in 1863, and served as its Commodore until resigning in 1867.[33] In 1870, he was reported to have been cruising the Mediterranean and to be preparing for the racing season in England. He had also been president of the Anniversary Regatta Committee. He married Corentia (née Browne), sister of Rolf Boldrewood. Their second son, Cecil, died in the shipwreck of the "Avalanche" off Portland in 1877. W. B. Walker died in 1889, aged 69.

(These entries not listed in the index)

expenditure by employing convicts. As a result, half-pay navy and army officers and well-to-do middle-class merchants and farmers formed an increasing proportion of the population at that time. In addition, the first part of Commissioner Bigge's report on the state of the colony in New South Wales, had aroused a great deal of interest in Britain.[15] Following the publication of William Charles Wentworth's (1790-1872) book in London in 1819,[16] which glowingly described the colony and emphasised the prospects for men of capital regarding the farming of sheep, James Walker joined his younger brother William, who was then prospering in New South Wales. James Walker's career had been in the navy until 1822, when he was retired on half-pay as Britain reduced the armed forces, following its long drawn-out wars against France.[17]

But James Walker made up his mind to become a pastoralist in New South Wales rather than to join his brother in commercial life. He was then thirty-seven years old with no experience of agriculture, but he brought with him a free labourer named Andrew Brown who had been born at 'Tibbermuir' near Perth, Scotland, who was then 25 years old.[18] By 11th November 1824 James Walker was back in Sydney and had received from Governor Brisbane a promise of the usual grant of 2,000 acres (809 ha),[19] at the site he had selected, which was known by the Aboriginal name of 'Wallerawang', near Lithgow.[20]

By 1844, the Walkers were the third largest share holders in the Bank of New South Wales, so when they foreclosed on the Imlay's, they took most of their land in the process. This left George and Alexander Imlay only with 'Tarraganda Station', which Peter Imlay, who later moved to New Zealand, re-purchased following the death of his brothers in 1846-7.

The Birth of Pambula

On the South Coast, James Walker established his head station at 'Kameruka' with a series of out-stations like 'Warragaburra', while his younger brother Edward established a grand residence in Pambula, known as 'Oaklands House'.[21] The Oaklands property was originally owned by the Imlay brothers (1833-1844), who transferred it, with the manor house built by William Walker & Co, to the 'sleeping partnership' of Edward Walker

The rustic welcome sign to Pambula, which began in the late 1830s, from the Imlays pastoral property called 'Panbula'.

(1844-1853). Ownership was transferred again to the Twofold Bay Pastoral Association from 1853 to 1863, whose proprietors included William Montagu Manning (1811–1895), James A.L. Manning (1814–1887), Edye Manning, Thomas Sutcliffe Mort (1816–1878), John Croft (1792–1863), Robert Tooth (1821–1893) and Edwin Tooth (1822–1858).

The Walker's continued with the Imlay's practice of exporting cattle to Sydney and Hobart Town. The procedure used by the shepherds and graziers to get these cattle to market at that time was rather unique:

> "For loading, the cattle had a sling placed around them and were then forced into the sea off a shallow beach at Cattle Bay and led by a horseman to the side of a ship, often the "Aron", where sailors hooked onto the sling and winched the beast aboard".
>
> *D. G. Parbery* [22]

Essentially the Imlay Brothers, followed by Ben Boyd and the Walker Brothers were the first developers to draw settlers and employees to the region, and the dealings of these land barons no doubt coincided with and affected the lives of the Frawley family. And so, as living in almost complete isolation at Warragaburra would have been extraordinarily difficult, John and Mary Ann Frawley likely looked around and took on work wherever it presented itself, so that within a few years of Ellen's birth, they had moved into the newly developing township of Panbula (now called Pambula). The Frawleys eventually moved on, and by around 1845 they were residing in a new growing township...

> "The Walkers made Panbula and Kameruka their head stations. The Panbula station of the Imlays had no buildings other than four stockmens huts so the Walkers built 'Oaklands' in 1842, a single storey residence of four big rooms and made of convict brick. The bricks were made on the property and the timber pit-sawn half a mile to the north. The Walkers also built many other solid structures including boiling-down works for tallow, a store managed by Mr. Bell and the Governor Fitzroy Hotel."

> "Oaklands was surrounded with English gardens, trees and orchards. An enormous oak tree with a girth of more than seven metres stands in front of the house today! William Walker Sr. also kept an extensive aviary of English birds, which were released into this area and contribute to our broad exotic bird population.
>
> *Panbula 'News Weekly', 27th Sept 1995* [23]

In 1845, a census of Aborigines revealed a total of 158 blacks living in the 'Biggah' area, some of who were employed as stockmen, sheep-washers and farm labourers. By December 1848, the "Bermondsey" disembarked immigrants at Eden in Twofold Bay, to work at 'Kameruka' or 'Tarraganda'. Then in March of 1855, another ship called the "Caesar" brought German emigrants directly from Hamburg to Twofold Bay, who also took up positions at 'Kameruka,' and many descendants of these families remain landowners today.

May 1851 saw a disastrous flood sweep many families down the Bega River, with 17 souls dying and being buried at 'Corridgeree' near Tarraganda. The government surveyor Samuel Parkinson had just laid out a township at North Bega, on the site of the present Bega Cheese Factory, but was forced by the flooding to move to higher ground on the southern side of the river where a new town was founded. In 1852 the Walker brothers sold out to the Twofold Bay Pastoral Association. The first town allotments were surveyed in February 1854 and sold at Eden in August of that year. Eden was the only port for communication and transport in the Monaro District, until the port of Merimbula was opened by the proprietors of Kameruka in 1855.

The Frawley family endured the harsh isolation of Warraguberra Station, far from the settled communities of Coolangatta and Wollongong, for two full years, where life on the far South Coast proved to be unforgiving with rugged terrain, relentless weather, and total dependence on the landholders, William Walker & Co. But hardship breeds resolve, and by the summer of 1844, the Frawleys had seized an opportunity, leaving the remote station for the budding township of Pambula. Here, determined to establish a home and a future for themselves, they would carve out a new life, one built on their own terms...

References

1. Death from Exposure (The Teetotaller & General Newspaper, 26 March 1842, p.1)
2. Wikipedia - 'Benjamin Boyd.' [https://en.wikipedia.org/wiki/Benjamin_Boyd]. Retrieved 12th January 2020.
3. Parbery, D.G. (1992). Fabric Of A Family, op.cit.
4. Arrival of Ben Boyd in the "Wanderer" (The Australasian, 20 July 1842, p.2)
5. 'Shipping Intelligence.' Sydney Morning Herald, 1st January to 10th August, 1842.
6. Higgins, J. (1982). Pambula's Colonial Days: A short history of the period 1797-1901. The Merimbula – Imlay Historical Society.
7. NSW Dept of BDM .(1842). Birth & Baptism for Ellen Frawley, 2nd Sept 1842 at Warigubera, #1772/1842 (V18421772 62).
8. Cornell, J. B. (1994). Most Obedient Servants on the Monaro and Far South Coast. Cheltenham, NSW.
9. NSW Dept. of BDM. (1843). Birth & Baptism for James Frawley, #1773/1843 (V18431773 62).
10. NSW Dept of BDM .(1842). Birth & Baptism for Ellen Frawley, op. cit.
11. Monaghan, Gerard. (1985). 'Vision For A Valley': Catholic People In The Bega Valley 1829-1985: A History. Self-published.
12. "Recollections of the early days of Moruya." Journal of the Royal Australian Historical Society, 8 (Supplement)(1923), pp. 375–376.
13. Parsons, Vivienne (1967). 'William Walker (1787–1854)', Australian Dictionary of Biography, National Centre of Biography, Australian National University, https://adb.anu.edu.au/biography/walker-william-2767/text3931, published first in hardcopy 1967, accessed online 26 January 2023.
14. Sydney Gazette, 25 Sept. 1823.
15. Crew, B.H. (1963). The History of the Walker and Archer families (M.A. thesis, Australian National University), pp.24-26.
16. Wentworth, W.C. (1819). "A Statistical, Historical and Political Description of the Colony of New South Wales".
17. John Leslie: "From Stockyards to Streets (The Story of the Founding of Coonamble) (1955). Jack Stephens (ed.) "Coonamble" (1955). Anny Lists - Great Britain and Ireland, 1785-1835; 27 July, 1808; 16 Feb. 1814; 25 Dec. 1818.
18. Leslie: op. cit. Report of the Select Committee· on Secondary Punishments. P.P. 1831, VII, 276. Evidence of James Walker pp.56-63.
19. N.S.W. Government Gazette, 24 Oct. 1832 p.356.
20. Ibid.
21. Parbery, D.G. (1992). Fabric Of A Family, op. cit.
22. Parbery, D.G. (1992). Fabric Of A Family, op. cit.
23. 'Oaklands House.' Panbula 'News Weekly', Historical Feature, 27 September 1995.
24. William Baker's 1841 map of a the District of Maneroo showing Bateman's Bay, Shoalhaven and the Illawarra (NLA MAP NK 5348)
25. Crew, B.H. (1963). The History of the Walker and Archer families, op.cit.
26. Leonard Joel - A Look Back In Time: James Walker (Scottish, 1785-1856) [https://www.leonardjoel.com.au/newsletter/a-look-back-in-time/].
27. Winchester F, 1972; James Walker of Wallerawang, cited in Lithgow and District Historical Society, Occasional Papers No.11, p.3.
28. Holt I, 2004; Opening the Gateway: the Birth and history of the Lithgow District, Lithgow District Historical Society Inc. p. 66.
29. Parsons, Vivienne (1967). 'William Walker (1787–1854)', op. cit.
30. Wikipedia - William Benjamin Walker (1820-1889, New South Wales colonial politician), [https://en.wikipedia.org/wiki/William_Walker_(New_South_Wales_colonial_politician)].
31. [https://apps.environment.nsw.gov.au/dpcheritageapp/ViewHeritageItemDetails.aspx?ID=2711246]
32. Wikipedia - Redleaf [https://en.wikipedia.org/wiki/Redleaf].
33. Royal Sydney Yacht Squadron - Commodores of the Squadron by John Maclurcan #1. William Walker 1862-1867, [https://www.rsys.com.au/wp-content/uploads/2021/10/I-William-Walker.pdf].

Further Reading

Andrews, G. (1984. South Coast Steamers. Maritime History Publications.
Bayley, W. A. (1964). Behind Broulee. Eurobodalla Shire Council.
Cox. P. (1978). South Coast of New South Wales. Melbourne, Macmillan.
Elias, S. (Ed.) (1986). Tales of the Far South Coast. Vol.3., Bega Valley Shire Bi-Centennial Committee.
Flower, C. (1981). Illustrated History of NSW. Adelaide, Rigby.
McKenzie, J. A. S. (1991). The Twofold Bay Story.
Monaro Pioneers Group. 'Monaro.' [http://www.monaropioneers.com/towns/Pambula.htm]. Retrieved 6 July 2021.
Moruya and District Historical Society (1979). Mining: gold and silver on far south coast and adjacent island areas of N.S.W. Moruya, Moruya and District Historical Society.
Wikipedia - Oaklands, Pambula [https://en.wikipedia.org/wiki/Oaklands,_Pambula]

Chapter Twelve

PIONEERS OF 'PAMBOOLA'

John Frawley's journey from convict to free settler was one marked by resilience, adaptability, and an unwavering determination to provide for his family. Transported to Australia as a government-assigned servant, he endured seven years of servitude before transitioning into employment with some of the most influential pastoralists of the region, first with the Imlay brothers and later with the Walker Brothers at Warragaburra. Though never self-employed, Frawley's skills as a labourer ensured he remained a valued worker in an era when manpower was scarce and industrious hands were in high demand.

His years of toil in isolated and often unforgiving conditions were a testament to his endurance. For two years, Frawley and his family lived in the wilderness, a period that tested their resourcefulness and fortitude. Yet, the harsh realities of remote life also underscored the necessity of community. When the opportunity arose to move into the developing township of Pambula, the family embraced the change. The shift from isolation to settlement life brought them into closer contact with others, allowing them to engage socially, build friendships, and integrate into the growing community.

For John Frawley, Pambula offered more than just a place to live, it provided a sense of belonging, a reprieve from solitude, and the prospect of a more stable future for his young

The 'Jiggama River' was renamed the 'Pambula River', near Pambula on the South Coast of NSW', by Capt. Robert Marsh Westmacott (Dixson Library, SLNSW).

family. While he struggled to own land or business, his contributions as a hardworking labourer played a small yet significant role in the economic and social fabric of the region. This chapter explores the life of John Frawley and his family, tracing their struggles, triumphs, and the legacy they left in the evolving landscape of colonial Australia.

Oaklands Manor House

Majestic oak trees, some planted in the mid-19th century and others naturally sprouting from fallen acorns, stand as enduring sentinels of the estate's history. It is from these very trees that the property derives its name of "Oaklands". Today, it remains one of the oldest working properties on the far south coast, with a legacy dating back to the first permanent European settlement in the Pambula district.

The estate's history is deeply intertwined with the pioneering Imlay brothers, Peter, George, and Alexander, who were drawn to the region by the whaling opportunities of nearby Twofold Bay. They quickly expanded their interests, establishing vast pastoral holdings that stretched beyond what is now the Victorian border, north to Bega and Cobargo, and west to the mountain escarpment. Following the enactment of Governor Bourke's 'Crown Lands Occupation Act' in 1836, they secured licenses covering extensive areas of the far south coast, including a 17-square-mile property known as 'Pampoolah' or 'Pamboola".[1]

By the 1830s, the Imlays had consolidated land spanning from Broulee to south of Twofold Bay and westward into the mountains. They established cattle runs along the fertile Pambula River flats, making their head station on its banks. By 1833, the brothers were actively developing the rich alluvial soil, grazing cattle for beef production, engaging in dairying for butter and cheese, breeding sheep, and cultivating crops such as potatoes and turnips, essential supplies for the survival of the Australian colonies.

By 1835, the Imlays had initiated trade with Hobart, Port Arthur in Van Diemen's Land,

South Australia, and New Zealand, a network that flourished into the 1840s. A description from 1839 details their Panbula Station as spanning 17 square miles, with four slab huts, a stockyard, and 150 acres under wheat and barley cultivation. The station was home to ten residents, with Peter Imlay overseeing operations. The nearest settlement lay 12 miles away.[2]

The Imlays were among the first to export local produce internationally, dispatching the schooner "St. Heliers" to London in 1843. Its cargo included tallow, salted meats, beef, neatsfoot oil, wattle bark extract, and mutton hams. However, by the late 1830s, the unforgiving forces of nature took their toll. A devastating drought, followed by bushfires in 1840, wreaked havoc on their holdings. While Governor Gipps was moving toward granting squatters greater security of tenure, the relief came too late for the Imlays. Unable to recover from their losses before the onset of the colony's first major economic depression, they were forced to cede their Pambula property and most of their other assets to creditors William Walker & Co.

With the Imlays gone, William Walker & Co. emerged as the largest landholders in the

TOP (Left): The Oaklands Manor House features fine cedar joinery, including a highly unusual set of finely glazed entrance doors with corresponding antechamber doors, original fire surrounds, floorboards, plasterwork and french doors with fine glazing bars. The house retains a high degree of integrity and intactness and is considered to have one of the finest Georgian colonial interiors on the South Coast, painted by Mary Jane Bennett. (Right): The ornate fanlight above the entrance to Oaklands House, Pambula. ABOVE (Left): The front driveway to Oaklands House, Panbula. (Right): Oaklands House in Panbula, built for the Walker Brothers around 1844.

Twofold Bay district. In 1844, the original 160-acre freehold "Portion Five" of the Panbula estate was formally granted to William Walker, with additional parcels acquired by various family members over the years. James Walker, William's elder brother, managed the Panbula property, while his son, William Benjamin Walker, focused on securing Kameruka.

In response to the slump in meat prices, the Walkers established a boiling-down works at Panbula in 1847, rendering livestock into tallow, bones, hides, and other valuable by-products, which proved more profitable than selling live animals. Around the same time, James Walker constructed a homestead at Panbula, while the Governor Fitzroy Hotel, licensed to Charles Robertson, opened its doors. The hotel's namesake, Governor Sir Charles Fitzroy (1796-1858), was at least an acquaintance of the Walkers and had visited their Kameruka Estate.

Following the Colonial Government's establishment of a public education system in 1848, James Walker provided a slab hut on his Panbula property for use as a school in 1849. He also played a role in securing two and a half acres within the township for a permanent school building. The Walker estate in Pambula also featured a blacksmith's shop and a general store operated by Charles William Bell.

James and Louisa Walker, along with their three children, remained at Panbula until William Benjamin Walker returned to England to join William Walker & Co.'s head office. At that point, the family shifted their focus to Kameruka. Arthur Manning leased the Panbula property until Edward Walker arrived in April 1853 to finalize its sale to the Twofold Bay Pastoral Association, marking the end of an era for the Walkers in Pambula.

Pambula Is Born

Today's town of Pambula is a small, but historic town on the far South Coast, and is located 456 km south of Sydney via the Princes Highway and 525 km via the Hume

Sketch of 'Nangutta Station' in the Manaroo District, NSW, showing the farm with the creek in foreground and Nangutta Peak in background, engraved by Samuel Calvert [1828-1913], engraver. (State Library of Victoria).

'The Drovers', a typical farming scene from the South Coast, painted by Robert John Lovett (1931).

Motorway, through Canberra and Cooma. Prior to the arrival of Europeans the land was inhabited by the Dyirringany and Thaua Aborigines, with 3,000 year old middens in the area. The Princes Highway passes through the middle of Pambula and makes the town, with its cafes and shops, a convenient stopping point for people wanting to break their journey north or south. The town spreads across the Pambula River Valley and has a sweet, unspoiled charm, with its principal attraction being the tranquil, but picturesque Pambula Beach.

The Pambula area was first visited by survivors of the wreck of the "Sydney Cove" in 1797, and a year later by navigator and explorer George Bass, who journeyed south from Sydney in a 28 foot open whaleboat, expanding Cook's observations with more detailed chart of the east coast of New South Wales. Taking shelter in an inlet during a gale, Bass travelled up the Pambula River noting the beauty of the spot in his diary. Bass recorded the beauty of the location in his log book:

> "...were it not for the extreme shallowness of this bar this little harbour would be a complete harbour for small craft....the upper part of this place is a kind of lagoon, or at least a flat, but the lower part downwards as far as the bar is one of the prettiest harbours....every small bite has its little sandy beach and every turning its trim, rocky point....I have named this place Barmouth Creek."
>
> *George Bass, 18th February 1798* [3]

Bass was describing the 'Jigama River', known today as the Pambula River, with 'pambula' or 'panboola', probably being named by the Thaua speaking clan of the Yuin nation, to mean 'twin waters.' The region was popular amongst the Aborigines for thousands of years due to an abundance of oysters, shellfish and the seasonal 'bardi' grub. Disease and a clash of white and Aboriginal cultures led to social disintegration and a rapid depopulation of the natives, with only a few Aborigines resident in Pambula by 1848.

The early squatters and pioneers were attracted to the area by land, and when they

Photographs of the entrance to the Pambula River, on the far south coast of NSW.

managed to obtain it, their axes rang out as the trees were felled and the timber was shaped for the primitive slab and bark huts. The village quickly developed to serve the early settlers in the locality and Mary Ann Frawley was one of them...

> "At first it meant that cooking was done out in the open, with water carried up from the creek. Dimly, against this rugged backdrop, we see women struggling to make a home in this hostile environment. Women were called upon to face the larger dangers of drought, bushfire and flood, and were forced to hide their fears of childbirth, accident, illness and molestation."
>
> *Jule Higgins* [4]

The town of Pambula was first charted in 1843, when assistant surveyor Thomas Scott Townsend surveyed the land on the river flats. Following his work, F. McCabe drew up the first full town survey in 1847, but there were some unforeseen difficulties...

> "Lack of foresight resulted in the township of Pambula being laid out on the southern side of the flood prone flats, and the Governor Fitzroy Hotel was washed away... along with it's 'splendid cedar fittings'.
> In 1851 the Sydney Morning Herald reported severe floods, stating... "the township of Pambula became a lake. The whole of the tenants of the frail Australian huts, who could do so, had to seek safety in the two substantial taverns in the town." This flood nearly wiped out the same settlement, which was ultimately re-sited to higher ground on the present site of Pambula town centre.
> The Anglican (1855) and Catholic (1851) 'slab' churches were reconsecrated in solid stone on their present sites in 1866 and 1867 respectively. The town cemetery was also moved due to the flooding and at least 53 graves had to be exhumed from the Pambula Bridge site.
> After a census showed that 62% of the population under 21 could neither read nor write, Mr. James Walker supplied a newly repaired hut as a temporary school and Mr. Grearly started teaching on July 23rd 1849, with 37 pupils. It was the seventh school established in NSW, only nine months after the first school. By the following year a four room brick and shingle building had been erected and attendance had risen to a high of 51 pupils.
> Three quarters of Pambula's settlers were free at a time when 65% of the colony were convicts or had convict origins."
>
> *Jule Higgins* 5

In 1844 retired naval officer Lt. John Lloyd RN, was granted 300 acres upon which he built 'The Grange'. He employed two local men to help build his substantial homestead and may also have had two convicts assigned to assist with construction.

In 1845 a road was completed between Eden and the Monaro Plains, which exactly passed through the small, but developing village of Pambula. Around this time the Governor Fitzroy Hotel was built by the Walker Brothers.

By the late 1840s, opportunities in the Pambula District picked up considerably with a marked increase in available work being advertised by the Walkers and other land holders. This brought on a corresponding increase in the number of ships servicing the area, with many calling directly at Pambula. Being open to the sea the shallow river was an issue, but they use small boats to offload passengers and supplies.

In 1848, 'persons' were given an opportunity to object to the large holdings of the squatters, but few could challenge such powerful men?

> Colonial Secretary's Office, Sydney, September 27.—His Excellency the Governor [Sir Charles A. Fitzroy] directs it to be notified, for the information of all persons interested, that in pursuance of her Majesty's Order in Council, of the 9th March, 1847, the under mentioned persons have demanded leases of the several runs of Crown Land, particularised in connexion with their respective names.
>
> Persons, who object to any of these claims, either wholly or in part, should lodge caveats at this office within two months - from the present date, specifying the lands to which their objections extend, and the grounds on which their objections are based.
>
> It is to be distinctly understood that the Government does not pledge itself to the issue of a lease in any case until due enquiry has been made into the validity of the claim, and whether or not it may be necessary to reserve any portion of the land claimed, for any of the public purposes contemplated in the Order in Council.
>
> By His Excellency's Command
> E. Deas Thomson.[6]

A detailed and in depth history of Pambula's colonial days has been written by Jule Higgins (1982), which covers the exploration and origins of the region.[7]

Births & Baptisms for John & Mary Frawley

John Frawley Jr.
Born 1841
District Born Illawarra, Wollongong
Birth Cert. No. 1450/1841 V18411450 121A
Baptised 18th March, 1844
Parents John Frawley & Mary McGarrey
Residence Warigubura, Twofold Bay
Sponsors Fenton Brien & Bridget McNamara
Priest Michael Kavanagh

Ellen Frawley
Born 2nd September, 1842
District Born Maneroo, Twofold Bay
Birth Cert. No. 1772/1842 V18421772 62
Baptised 18th March, 1844
Parents John Frawley & Mary McGarrey
Residence Warigubura, Twofold Bay
Sponsors Den Connor & Bridget McNamara
Priest Michael Kavanagh

James Frawley
Born 14th November, 1843
District Born Maneroo, Twofold Bay
Birth Cert. No. 1773/1843 V18431773 62
Baptised 18th March, 1844
Parents John Frawley & Mary McGarrey
Residence Warigubura, Twofold Bay
Sponsors Fenton Brien & Bridget McNamara
Priest Michael Kavanagh

Stephen Frawley
Born 26th December, 1844
District Born Maneroo, Twofold Bay
Birth Cert. No. 1168/1844 V18441168 63
Baptised 11th May, 1846
Parents John Frawley & Mary McGarry
Residence Pampula, Twofold Bay
Sponsors John Farrell & Mary Coleman
Priest Michael Kavanagh

Patrick Frawley
Born 17th March, 1848
District Born Maneroo, Twofold Bay
Birth Cert. No. 1415/1848 V18481415 65
Baptised 8th September, 1848
Parents John Frawley & Mary McGarry
Residence Panbula, Twofold Bay
Sponsors William Shea & Honoria Ryan
Priest Michael Kavanagh

Letitia Frawley
Born 17th March, 1848
District Born Maneroo, Twofold Bay
Birth Cert. No. ?
Baptised 8th September, 1848
Parents John Frawley & Mary McGarry
Residence Panbula, Twofold Bay
Sponsors John Collins & Catherine Ryan
Priest Michael Kavanagh

Thomas Frawley
Born 24th June, 1849
District Born Maneroo, Twofold Bay
Birth Cert. No. 1519/1849 V18491519 66
Baptised 18th October, 1849
Parents John Frawley & Mary McGarry
Residence Pampula, Twofold Bay
Sponsors Thos Clancy & Catherine Cusack
Priest Michael Kavanagh

Births and baptisms for the surviving seven children of John & Mary Frawley, of Pambula.

The Frawley Family

The question at this point is whether our ancestor John Frawley, remained in the employ of the Walker's, or were the Frawley's enticed into Panbula Station for some other purpose? Perhaps John Frawley was hired by the Walkers or John Lloyd as a labourer to assist in the construction of their manor houses? In terms of accommodation, there wasn't too much on offer in Panbula at that time, and most residential structures were simple 'bark slab' huts.

> "In Panbula during the twenty years from 1842 there appears to have been an extensive use of home-made bricks. Except for one residence, The Grange, all homesteads and public buildings were erected with brick construction, tending to create a definite brick era. Good clay deposits were close at hand and the lime needed for the mortar was derived from ground-up oyster shells, enormous deposits of these having accumulated due to the aboriginals partiality for oysters over many hundreds of years. This type of construction could also have resulted from an influx of tradesmen from Boydtown around 1847. The 'Grange' was constructed of imported stone and was erected under the supervision of Lt. John Lloyd after he purchased the land in 1843. He was given a grant of land by the Government on his retirement from naval service, in which he had fought alongside Lord Horatio Nelson at the Battle of Trafalgar on the 21st of October 1805."
>
> J. Shannon [8]

The first buildings to be erected on the Panbula flats were simple stockman's slab huts located on the Imlay brothers land. Despite the survey by Thomas Townsend, who toured the area in 1842, no indications of buildings occur on his map of 1847, and no homestead is evident.

If John Frawley did move to Panbula to work in and around the Walkers new 'Oaklands

Lt. John Lloyd, R.N. (c.1782-1868)

Born in Ireland, John Lloyd entered into a career in the Royal Navy at just 12 years of age and was by all reports in attendance at the Battle of Trafalgar in 1805.

Much later he moved to Panbula about 1840 becoming one of the original pioneers of that town, and proceeded to build one of the most beautiful homes, a striking two storey Georgian and Edwardian stone residence known as 'The Grange,' which has been a local landmark for almost 170 years and is now one of the oldest buildings in the district.

After securing 302 acres for his Grange Farm in January 1844, Lloyd added further land in 1856, his property at one point embracing the land between the pristine Pambula and Yowaka Rivers. His appointment as a magistrate of the town of Pambula was announced in May of 1848.[22] His eldest son Arthur Lloyd Esq., married Elizabeth Lucy Lloyd at Durdham Down, Clifton in January of 1859, at which time he was still in residence at Pambula. John Lloyd Esq, R.N. died on the 15th December 1868, late of Pambula in the 86th year of his age.[23]

A much different dwelling to the mostly bark slab huts that were being erected around it, 'The Grange' homestead at Panbula (c.1844), was built by Lt. John Lloyd (1782-1868), who once fought with Lord Nelson at the Battle of Trafalgar in 1805.

Syms Covington (1816-1861)[24]

Syms Covington was a well known resident and the Post Master of Pambula, and sailed as a fidler and cabin boy on Charles Darwin's voyages of natural discovery on board "HMS Beagle". Part way through the voyage, Covington became Darwin's assistant, preserving, labelling and packing hundreds of specimens, many new to science, and he was appointed as his personal servant in 1833, continuing in Darwin's service after the voyage until 1839.

Originally named Simon Covington, he was born in Bedford, Bedfordshire, England, the youngest child of Simon Covington V, and Elizabeth Brown. After Covington's trip on the "Beagle", he then emigrated to Australia and settled as a postmaster, marrying Eliza Twyford. The Covington house is still standing in the main street of Pambula and is now used as a restaurant.

By STEVE MEACHAM

RESTAURATEUR and cook Dara Jaroenwong only arrived in Australia in 1989, from Bangkok. But ask her what is the connection between Pambula on the state's South Coast and one of the most profound thinkers in history, and she answers without a beat.

She names Syms Covington, fidler, companion, and personal assistant to Charles Darwin on the HMS Beagle which sailed into Sydney Harbour on January 12, 1836.

Darwin's experiences on that five-year voyage changed the course of human knowledge, resulting in the publication of *On The Origin Of Species*, 150 years ago. Commemorative events will be held around the world this year because it is the 200th anniversary of Darwin's birth.

Yet Covington's equally adventurous life won't be marked beyond a weekend of activities in April at Pambula, the gold rush town he made his home.

Dr Michael Pickering, one of the curators of the National Museum of Australia's Darwin exhibition, said Covington was a 15-year-old cabin boy when the Beagle left England in 1831, and was initially distrusted by the young and inexperienced Darwin.

But the amateur scientist came to rely on Covington to excavate fossils, collect specimens, and generally aid his botanical and geological studies.

Unlike Darwin, however, Covington was so impressed by their few days in Sydney that he decided to emigrate.

He arrived back here in 1840, and married Eliza Twyford from Stroud, initially setting up home in Sydney. But by 1854 the couple and the first of their eight children had moved to Pambula, where Covington became postmaster.

From Pambula, he kept up a warm correspondence with Darwin. And in 1849, Darwin wrote asking his friend to collect specimens of barnacles from Twofold Bay. The resulting study won Darwin acclaim as a biologist, paving the way for his epic book challenging the Biblical account of creation.

Olwen Morris, president of the local historical society, says Covington built a new stone-and-brick building in 1857 which contained not only the town post office, but a store and a pub called the Forest Oak Inn.

That same building still stands, though Covington died in 1861 "of paralysis". Today the heritage-listed building is home to Covingtons Thai, run by Ms Jaroenwong and brother Larry.

Ms Jaroenwong said she is proud to be associated with "a building that has so much character and history", and believes Covington would be honoured his former home reflects contemporary Australia.

"Thai food is about as authentically Australian as it gets now," she said.

"The only way to survive in this very small town is with local patronage all through the year."

Syms Covington

Charles Darwin

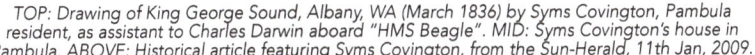

TOP: Drawing of King George Sound, Albany, WA (March 1836) by Syms Covington, Pambula resident, as assistant to Charles Darwin aboard "HMS Beagle". MID: Syms Covington's house in Pambula. ABOVE: Historical article featuring Syms Covington, from the Sun-Herald, 11th Jan, 2009.

Manor House', the experience gained might explain why he later went on to become a builder/labourer of sorts, as he could have learnt many of the required skills while working on the Oaklands property.

> "A large homestead built of handmade bricks was that of Oaklands in Panbula which was on 160 acres bought by the Walkers in 1844. The date of the homestead's actual erection is not known, but correspondence between the Walker and Archer families in 1847 stated that James Walker's wife was 'thrilled as it [the house] was nearly ready for occupation."
>
> J. Shannon [9]

Regardless of the reasons for their move, sometime before December 1844 when their fourth child Stephen Frawley was born,[10] the Frawley family had already moved from 'Warragaburra' into the developing hamlet of Pambula, bequeathing them the honour of being amongst the very first residents, and pioneers of that early New South Wales town.

Bonded by the mutual difficulties experienced by these intrepid pioneers, it didn't take long for the Frawleys to establish friendships. As the Roman Catholic priests made such infrequent visits to the south coast at this time, the settlers often conducted their own religious ceremonies when they had the opportunity, and a number of baptisms were held on the 11th May 1846, when John and Mary Frawley became godparents at the baptism of Elizabeth, the daughter of their new friends Edward and Elizabeth Kennedy at Pambula.

In March of 1848 the young

Frawley family was increased considerably by the birth of their twins Letitia and Patrick Frawley again at Pambula.[11] Although unsure as to the exact address of the Frawleys in Panbula, their last child Thomas Frawley was also born there in June of 1849.[12]

In 1849 too, there was a severe financial crash in the colony, which greatly affected the south coast region. The Boydtown venture failed and Ben Boyd sailed off into the Pacific in his yacht "Wanderer", and disappeared on the island of Guadalcanal. Peter Imlay handed what was left of his Bega Estates in the hands of tenants and resettled in Wanganui, New Zealand. The financial crash also rendered the Walker's cattle trade uneconomic and by 1850 they were faced with the prospect of selling out their holdings for only £20,000. Even though the discovery of gold and the resulting influx of migrants soon created a boom market for cattle and other agricultural products in the colonies, by 1851 the Walkers had decided to sell off their pastoral interests.

Following the failure of Ben Boyd's venture in 1849 and the sale of Walker's holdings,

Early Developments In Pambula

LEFT COLUMN: 1-New line of road completed from Maneroo to Eden, by way of Pambula (SMH, 2 Jan 1845, p.1); 2-Posted rewards for theft of horse and dray (SMH, 1 March 1845, p.3). **CENTER COLUMN:** 1-Runaway servants (SMH, 18 March 1846, p.2); 2-Village of Pambula (NSW Govt Gazette, 28 Sep 1847, p.1023). **RIGHT COLUMN:** 1-William & James Walker, open a Boiling Down Works at Pambula (SMH, 30 Jan 1847, p.1); 2-Wanted Blacksmiths (SMH, 16 Nov 1847, p.4); 3-Opening of Pambula Pound (SMH, 26 April 1848, p.3); 4-Lt. John Lloyd, R.N. appointed magistrate for Pambula (Sydney Chronicle, 6 May 1848, p.3); 5-Apprehension of Collins at Pambula, for murder (SMH, 29 Nov 1849, p.2).

TOP (Left): John Frawley - Secretary for Roman Catholic Church Building Committee (The People's Advocate & NSW Vindicator, 26 August 1854, p.15). (Right): St Peter's Catholic Church, Pambula. ABOVE (Left): Roman Catholics of Pambula (Empire, 2 Oct 1854, p.3). (Right): John Frawley's considerable donation to St Peter's Church, Pambula (Freeman's Journal, 12th May 1855, p.10).

the Twofold Bay Pastoral Association was established with James Manning as manager. The business was based at 'Kameruka' as the main station, with 'Warragaburra' as one of several outstations.[13] Whether John Frawley had any further association with the Imlay's or the Walker Brothers after he left 'Warragaburra' is unknown, but by then the Frawleys were well and truly established in the growing township of Pambula.

By 1856 the newly sited township was prospering with five licensed hotels. The foundation stone for the Pambula Court House was thereafter laid in 1860, but Pambula wasn't officially proclaimed as a town until 1885.

St Peter's Catholic Church, Pambula

Being of Irish descent, the Frawleys were quite involved in the local Catholic community, and a public meeting was convened on the 7th August 1854, where John Frawley became the secretary of a committee of seven residents… "for the purpose of gathering subscriptions for buying a piece of land, for the the erection of a Roman Catholic Chapel."[14]

Over the years, the Frawleys had often donated toward the erection of a Catholic Church in Pambula,[15] with St. Peters Catholic Church eventually being completed in 1867/68. John and Mary Ann had both been active in collecting money for the building of this church, so we can safely assume that they were regular worshippers. The original St. Peter's Church was smaller than the 1868 church, and had a shingled roof. On completion of the latter in July 1868, both Mary and John Frawley were published in the Bega Gazette along with a list of other parishioners to acknowledge their donations.

Ships to Twofold Bay & Pambula (1842-1850)

1842

SH, 12 Apr

For Broulee, Bermagua River, and Twofold Bay, touching at Wollongong, Jervis Bay, and Ulladulla, to land Passengers and Goods.

THE FINE SCHOONER *HOPE*, 60 tons, now loading at F. M. Storey's, Union Wharf, and being under engagement, will sail on Wednesday Evening positively. For freight or passage apply on board, or to E. M. Storey.

4580 W. H. SAWYER, Agent.

1844

SMH, 16 Sep

For Wollongong, Kiama, Jervis Bay, Ulladulla, Bateman's Bay, Broulee, Bermagui, and Pambula.

THE well-known, fast-sailing schooner, *BARD'S LEGACY*, coppered and copper fastened, and has superior accommodations for passengers, will sail for the above ports on Wednesday next, the 18th instant. For freight or passage apply to the master, on board, at the Union Wharf, late Dalgarno's; or to

G. WHITFIELD.

Gunmaker, King-street West, three doors from George-street.

Sydney, September 14. 3583

1845

SMH, 12 Dec

FOR ULLADULLA, PAMBULA, AND TWOFOLD BAY.

THE Packet Schooner *GIPSY* will leave the Commercial Wharf, for the above ports, To-Morrow Evening. For freight or passage apply to the Master, on board; or to

DAVID WARDEN, Commercial Wharf.

December 12. 9236

FOR TWOFOLD BAY, OR ADJACENT HARBOURS, IF SUFFICIENT FREIGHT OFFERS,

THE fast-sailing Cutter *ELIZABETH*. For freight or passage apply to the master, on board, at the [illegible] Wharf.

Will sail on or about Saturday, the 13th instant. 9201

SMH, 12 Dec

FOR JERVIS BAY, BATEMAN'S BAY, BROULEE, BARMAGUA, PAMFULA, AND TWOFOLD BAY.

THE fine fast-sailing cutter *HARRIET* will sail for the above ports on Monday, December the 15th.

For freight or passage, having superior accommodation for passengers, apply to the master, on board; or to

Mr. WILLIAM WEBB, Union Wharf.

1846

FOR BOYD, TWOFOLD BAY.

THE FINE CUTTER *JAMES AND AMELIA*, having the principal part of her cargo engaged will meet with immediate despatch. For freight or passage apply on board, at the Flour Company's Wharf, to

484 MOWBRAY MEGGET.

SMH, 9 Jan

FOR ULLADULLA, PAMBULA, AND TWOFOLD BAY.

THE Packet SCHOONER *GIPSY* will leave the Commercial Wharf To-Morrow Evening for the above ports. For freight or passage apply to the master, on board.

Commercial Wharf, January 9. 603

FOR ULLADULLA, BROULEE, PAMBULA, AND TWOFOLD BAY.

THE Packet Schooner *GIPSY* will leave for the above ports To-morrow Evening. For freight or passage apply to the master, on board, at Walker's Wharf; or to

DAVID WARDEN, Commercial Wharf.

March 10. 4122

SMH, 10 Mar

FIRST VESSEL FOR MELBOURNE, LANDING PASSENGERS AT TWOFOLD BAY.

THE SCHOONER *VANGUARD*, Captain Thompson, will clear at the Customs This Day, Tuesday. For freight or passage, having excellent accommodations, apply on board, at the Circular Wharf; or to

SHEPPARD AND ALGER, Packet Office, 468, George-street.

SMH, 2 Jun

FOR PAMBULA AND TWOFOLD BAY.

THE Packet Schooner *GYPSY*. For freight or passage apply to the master on board, at the Union Wharf, Sussex-street.

June 2. 8730

SMH, 17 Sep

FOR PAMBULA AND TWOFOLD BAY, CALLING AT BROULEE.

THE SCHOONER *COLL CASTLE*, will sail for the above places on Saturday next.

For freight apply to

THOMAS BARNETT, Union Wharf, Sussex-street

[illegible]tember 17. 4411

SMH, 20 Oct

FOR PAMBULA AND TWOFOLD BAY.

THE SCHOONER *RAMBLER*, 36 tons, will sail for the above place on Thursday, 22nd instant. For freight or passage apply to the Master, on board 6198

FOR BOYD TOWN.

THE regular trader *James and Amelia*, Captain Megget, will sail on Friday, the 23rd instant.

FREIGHT 10s
CABIN PASSAGE .... 30s.
STEERAGE DITTO .... 20s.

Apply to

W. S. MOUTRY, Duke's Wharf.

6362

SMH, 26 Oct

STEAM TO MELBOURNE AND LAUNCESTON, CALLING AT EDEN, TWOFOLD BAY.

THE Iron Steam Ship *SHAMROCK*, G. Gilmore, Commander, will sail for the above ports, on Monday, the 2nd November, at 5 p.m.

JAMES PATERSON, Secretary.

H. R. S. N. Company's Wharf. 6566

FOR JERVIS BAY, ULLADULLA, BATEMAN'S BAY, BROULEE, PAMBULA, AND TWOFOLD BAY.

THE SCHOONER *BROTHERS*, to sail on Wednesday next. For freight or passage apply to the master, on board, at Stillwell's Wharf; or to John Stillwell. 6540

SMH, 19 Nov

FOR PAMBULA, CALLING AT BROULEE TO LAND PASSENGERS.

THE Packet Schooner *GIPSY* will sail for the above places on Saturday, the 21st instant. For freight or passage apply to the master, on board; or to

HENRY CLARKE, Union Wharf.

November 19. 7986

1847

SMH, 1 May

FOR PAMBULA AND EDEN.

THE SCHOONER *RAMBLER*, Captain Goldsworthy, will positively sail on Tuesday, 4th May, for Pambula and Eden. For freight or passage apply to the Master, on board

April 30 7024

SMH, 1 May

STEAM TO MELBOURNE AND LAUNCESTON, CALLING AT EDEN, TWOFOLD BAY.

THE Iron Steam-Ship *SHAMROCK*, G. Gilmore, Commander, will be dispatched for the above ports on WEDNESDAY, 5th May, at 6 p.m.

JAMES PATERSON, Secretary.

H. R. S. N. Company's Wharf. 6791

SMH, 15 Sep

FOR TWOFOLD BAY AND PAMBULA.

THE FINE SCHOONER VIXEN, 45 tons, will sail for the above ports on FRIDAY, the 17th instant. For freight or passage apply to the Captain, on board, at Stilwell's Wharf; or, to

JOHN STILWELL, Coasting Packet Agent.

September 14. 4341

SMH, 2 Oct

FOR TWOFOLD BAY AND PAMBULA.

THE new coppered and copper-fastened clipper Schooner O P S, 65 tons, Captain Easton, is ready to receive cargo at the Commercial Wharf, and will sail positively on Wednesday next. For freight or passage apply to

5589 T. C. THOMAS AND CO.

SMH, 4 Oct

FOR TWOFOLD BAY AND PAMBULA.

THE FAST-SAILING SCHOONER LADY MARY FITZ ROY, Abraham Barter, Master, will sail on Wednesday, 6th instant. For freight or passage apply on board, at Walker's Wharf. 5589

SMH, 18 Oct

FOR TWOFOLD BAY AND PAMBULA.

THE new clipper Schooner CECILIA, 80 tons, Robert Williams, Commander, is now loading at the Commercial Wharf, and will sail on Tuesday next; has room for a few tons of goods, for which, or passage, apply to

T. C. THOMAS AND CO., Commercial Wharf.

6297

FOR TWOFOLD BAY AND PAMBULA.

THE fine Schooner VIXEN will sail for the above port on Thursday, 21st instant. For freight or passage apply on board, at Stilwell's Wharf; or, to

JOHN STILWELL, Coasting Packet Agent.

6325

SMH, 20 Oct

FOR PAMBULA DIRECT.

THE fine schooner V I X E N, being under engagement to Messrs. W. Walker and Co., will sail To-morrow, 21st instant. For freight or passage apply on board, at Walker's Wharf; or, to

JOHN STILWELL, Coasting Packet Agent.

6484

SMH, 20 Oct

FOR BOYD TOWN, PORT PHILLIP, AND ADELAIDE.

CALLING OFF BELFAST AND PORTLAND BAY TO LAND AND RECEIVE PASSENGERS, WEATHER PERMITTING.

THE STEAM-SHIP J U N O, E. J. F. Kirsopp, R.N., Commander, will sail for the above ports TO-MORROW MORNING, (Tuesday), at 10 precisely.

The Juno will continue to run regularly between Sydney, Boyd Town, Port Phillip, and Adelaide.

SMH, 11 Nov

THE FIRST AND ONLY VESSEL FOR TWOFOLD BAY AND PAMPULA.

THE remarkably fast-sailing schooner LADY MARY FITZ ROY will sail for the above ports on Friday, the 12th instant. For freight or passage apply on board, at Walker's Wharf.

ABRAHAM BARTER, Master.

7474

SMH, 7 Dec

FOR PAMBULA DIRECT.

THE fast-sailing Schooner LADY OF THE LAKE, under engagement to sail This Afternoon. For light freight or passage, apply to

JOHN STILWELL, Coasting Packet Office.

December 7. 9038

SMH, 27 Dec

FOR EDEN, TWOFOLD BAY, AND PAMBULA.

THE fine powerful Cutter JAMES AND AMELIA, Captain Piggins, will positively sail for the above ports on Wednesday Evening next.

For freight or passage apply to

T. C. THOMAS AND CO., Commercial Wharf.

10268

1848

SMH, 9 Mar

FOR TWOFOLD BAY AND PAMBULA.

THE fast-sailing schooner ELIZABETH, (formerly Lady Mary Fits Roy), will sail for the above ports on Saturday, the 11th instant. For freight or passage apply on board, at Walker's Wharf.

ABRAHAM BARTER, Master.

4168

SMH, 10 Mar

FOR ADELAIDE AND PORT PHILLIP, VIA BOYD TOWN.

CALLING OFF BELFAST AND PORTLAND BAY TO LAND AND RECEIVE PASSENGERS, WEATHER PERMITTING.

THE STEAM-SHIP JUNO will be despatched for the above ports, on Monday, the 3rd of April, at three o'clock p.m.

SMH, 6 Jun

FOR TWOFOLD BAY AND PAMBULA.

THE fast-sailing schooner ELIZABETH, (formerly Lady Mary Fits Roy), will sail for the above ports on Saturday, the 11th instant. For freight or passage apply on board, at Walker's Wharf.

ABRAHAM BARTER, Master

4193

SMH, 23 Jun

FOR TWOFOLD BAY AND PAMBULA,

THE fine powerful Cutter JAMES AND AMELIA, will have immediate despatch. For freight or passage (for which early application is necessary) apply to

T. C. THOMAS AND CO., Albion Wharf.

10467

SMH, 14 Jul

FOR TWOFOLD BAY AND PAMBULA.

WILL POSITIVELY SAIL ON SUNDAY MORNING.

THE powerful Cutter JAMES AND AMELIA, 40 tons. For freight or passage apply to

T. C. THOMAS AND CO., Packet Office, Albion Wharf.

765

SMH, 1 Aug

FOR PAMBULA AND TWOFOLD BAY.

IN consequence of the inclemency of the weather, the BARD'S LEGACY will not sail till to-morrow afternoon, at 5 o'clock.

For freight or passage, apply to the Master, on board, at Walker's Wharf, Lower Fort-street; or to

G. WHITFIELD, Gunmaker, No. 85, King-street West.

Sydney, August 1. 1781

SMH, 8 Aug

FOR TWOFOLD BAY AND PAMBULA.

THE fast-sailing cutter JAMES AND AMELIA, 40 tons, Captain Giles, will sail *this evening*, at 5 o'clock.

For freight or passage apply to

T. C. THOMAS AND CO., Albion Wharf.

2155

SMH, 29 Aug

FOR TWOFOLD BAY AND PAMBULA.

A REGULAR TRADER.

THE powerful cutter JAMES AND AMELIA, Giles, master, will sail for the above ports on Saturday next.

For freight or passage apply to

T. C. THOMAS AND CO., Albion Wharf.

3477

FOR PAMBULA AND TWOFOLD BAY.

THE Packet Schooner BARD'S LEGACY will leave Walker and Co's Wharf, Lower Fort-street, for the above ports, To-morrow Afternoon, at five o'clock. For freight or passage apply to the Master, on board; or to G. WHITFIELD, gunmaker, No. 83, King street West.

August 29. 3499

SMH, 6 Sep

FOR TWOFOLD BAY AND PAMBULA.

THE fine powerful packet cutter JAMES AND AMELIA, 40 tons, Charles Giles, master, will positively sail for the above ports on Saturday next. For freight or passage apply to

T. C. THOMAS AND CO., Albion Wharf.

3925

SMH, 9 Sep

FOR TWOFOLD BAY AND PAMBULA.

THE fast-sailing and favourite cutter JAMES AND AMELIA, 40 tons, will sail on Tuesday evening next, positively. For freight or passage, apply to the master, on board, or to

T. C. THOMAS AND CO., Albion Wharf.

September 8. 4101

SMH, 15 Nov

THE FIRST VESSEL FOR PANBULA AND TWOFOLD BAY.

THE SCHOONER MARIA PRUDENCE will leave Walker and Co.'s Wharf, Lower Fort-street, for the above ports This Afternoon, at 5 o'clock. This vessel has superior accommodations for passengers. For freight or passage apply to the master, on board; or to G. WHITFIELD, gunmaker, No. 33, King-street West.

Sydney, November 15.

1849

SMH, 14 Feb

FOR PAMBULA,

THE packet-schooner ELIZABETH will sail on Saturday next. For freight or passage, having [illegible] accommodation, apply on board, at Walker's Wharf; or to

ABRAHAM BARTER, Master.

February 14. 2758

SMH, 3 Mar

FOR PAMBULA AND TWOFOLD BAY.

THE packet schooner BARD'S LEGACY, will leave Walker and Co.'s Wharf, Lower Fort-street, for the above ports, on Tuesday next, the 6th instant. This vessel has superior accommodations for passengers. For freight or passage apply to the master on board, or to G. Whitfield, Gunmaker, No. 83, King-street West.

Sydney, March 1. 3445

SMH, 15 Mar

FOR TWOFOLD BAY AND PAMBULA.

THE fast sailing Schooner MIDAS, John Benaud, master, now loading at the Circular Wharf, will positively sail for the above ports on Saturday, the 17th instant.

For freight or passage apply to the master, on board; or

W. S. MOUTRY, Circular Quay Office.

4260

SMH, 19 May

FOR TWOFOLD BAY AND PAMBULA.

THE well known fast-sailing Schooner ELIZABETH will sail on Monday Evening, the 21st instant, for the above ports. For freight or passage apply to the Master, on board, at Walker's Wharf. 8227

SMH, 9 Jul

FOR TWOFOLD BAY AND PAMBULA.

THE clipper brigantine FANCY will sail for the above ports, on Wednesday next, the 11th instant. For freight or passage, apply on board; or, to

470 Messrs. WALKER AND CO.

1850

31 Jan

FOR PAMBULA.

THE fast-sailing schooner ELIZABETH, now loading at Cunningham's Wharf, Soldiers' Point, and will sail on Saturday morning. For freight or passage, apply on board. 2076

An Appeal for the Release of Land at Pambula (1852)

FOUNDATION OF BEGA.

We have received the following communication from a gentleman holding a respectable official position in Sydney, who appears, by his statement, to establish an irrefutable claim to the honor of being the Founder of our promising settlement, as also a claim to consideration for his early work, anticipatory to Free Selection, to which, it would seem, he committed himself almost single handed.

NARRATIVE OF 'PLEBS.'

"We left London, wife and I, in October, 1852, the day after our marriage, at our own expense, and we arrived at Sydney in April, 1853. We went to Pambula in June, 1853, and took up our quarters on the flat, where a scouring but yet alluvium-yielding flood had lately occurred. Being, as I am, the son of a skilful Nottinghamshire farmer and Lincolnshire grazier, I enquired for FARMS, but found none. There were a few still held office. I conferred with a number of settlers, and brought them to a promise to help forward an appeal to Home Authorities. Accordingly, I wrote out the following; and the document was signed at the solicitation of agents; but I was not seen in the transaction. The appeal, or memorial, was as follows:—

"'To his Grace the Duke of Newcastle, &c, &c, &c, &c, her Majesty the Queen's Chief Secretary of State for the Colonies.

'Your Grace,—We, the undersigned, being occupiers of land in the parish of Pambula, district of Eden, Twofold Bay, New South Wales humbly and respectfully beg leave to urge upon your Grace the following considerations:

We beg leave to subscribe ourselves your Grace's most faithful servants,

James Egan	Henry Schaback
John Egan	Daniel Duncan
Anthony Dunlane	John Mackay
Syms Covington	John Clynick
John Whelang	Thomas Newlyn
Joseph Berry	Wm. Gibson
Stephen Collier	Michael Cusack
Thomas Bray	Samuel Thompson
J. J. Grealy	Nath. Thompson
John Hayes	James Furnier
William Moore	J. Lloyd, Lieut., R.N.
B. Carracher	Henry Shipway
Frederick Moore	John Woods
George Barclay	John Davis
S. C. Boyland	Thomas Clancy
Wm. McNevin	Charles Fairman
Duncan Cameron	William Woods
Prince Champion	J. F. Whelan
Wm. Shea	Frank Woods
John Frawley	James Reid
William Dickenson	Richard Birkett
John Schaback	

'1. Our cramped condition as cultivators of the soil, and the difficulty and annoyance attending every attempt to stretch out our operations, render imperative a speedy alteration of the mode for accomplishing the settlement of the lands about us.

'3. We do not presume to offer any specific measure for the guidance of your Grace in this grand work of State founding, but would humbly and respectfully seek your authority for the throwing open of the adjacent Bega country for purchase at the upset price of £1, in blocks not exceeding 100 acres, and subject to actual occupation.

Mr Nicholson duly sent my memorial to the Duke. My mother duly sent to his Grace a communication from me on the subject of the memorial, and received a gracious autograph answer from the Duke, which signified that "her son "would be aware that at the time when he sent "his dispatch, he (the Duke) had ceased to hold "office; but that he had moved his successor, "Earl Grey, in the matter, and trusted to see the "the object carried out."

An appeal for the opening up of land by the Pambula pioneers. (Republished by... The Bega Standard & Candelo, Merimbula, Pambula, Eden, Wolumla and General Advertiser (11th November 1876, p.2).

ST. PETER'S CHURCH, PAMBULA

Mrs. J. Schaback, Mrs. Bickelmire, and Mrs. Frawly, for glazing one window of the church - £3,13,0. Collected by Mr. Behl, Mr Frawly, and Mr. McPhee, for altar - £12.

Bega Gazette, 18th July 1868

In 1853 an interesting letter to the editor of the newspaper 'Empire', described the township and geography of Pambula:

'PANBULA AND ITS NEIGHBOURS'

Panbula lies about 30 miles east of the magnificent tableland district of Monaro, wherein it is estimated with very much confidence that gold exists in great abundance of which the enterport is Panbula. It consists of a plain, or flat, in extent resembling an ordinary rural parish in England, and comprising an extensive government reserve (central), with a contiguous tract of nine acres for a future industrial school, an acre for the national school, an acre of burial ground, a horse-shoe shaped lagoon, which yields fresh water supplies in the dry seasons, several 'streets', 100 links wide... and many five acre allotments, one of which was purchased at 16 pounds an acre. A considerable slope of pleasing aspect under cultivation occupies the open space southwest of the plain, and here are several freehold homesteads. Obliquely across the plain, in a cleared recess of the bush on rising ground, is situated the township, close to which is a supply of good water as inexhaustable as is that of the lagoon half a mile distant. Of the half-dozen brick built houses (the residences of Messrs Walker and Bell, Mr. Bell's store-overseer, the school house and two public houses), one of the last named is, for neatness of style and humble elegance of finish throughout, an ornament to the bush [ie. Oaklands Manor House]. The parish numbers a population of forty to fifty families of Irish, Scot, English, coloured, American and German, and all are too prosperous to know poverty any longer, or feel the fear of it. They form a spirited and stirring community and perhaps worse neighbours might be found in a search for better, taking them on average.

Panbula News Weekly, 29th Sept 1853 [16]

Another letter at this time, sent by an unknown pioneer that arrived in Pambula in June of 1853, was addressed to Henry Pelham-Clinton (1811-1864), 5th Duke of Newcastle, who was at that time the minister for Foreign Affairs in London. It was apparently the privilege of the author to know and be known by the Duke, so by way of a complaint he proceeded to lament that all the district land was held in the possession of either Peter Imlay or the Twofold Bay Pastoral Association, and called for the opening up of reasonably priced blocks of land. Adding weight to the request, he attached the names of occupiers of land, who he regarded to be pioneers of the Parish of Pambula.[17] This letter may actually have had some effect as 'blocks for sale' were opened up in Pambula in 1856, two of which were selected by John Frawley. Apparently William Shea was at that time the anonymous author's tenant and the signatures were obtained by John Whelan, the poundkeeper.[18]

Early photograph of the township of Pambula, c.1855.

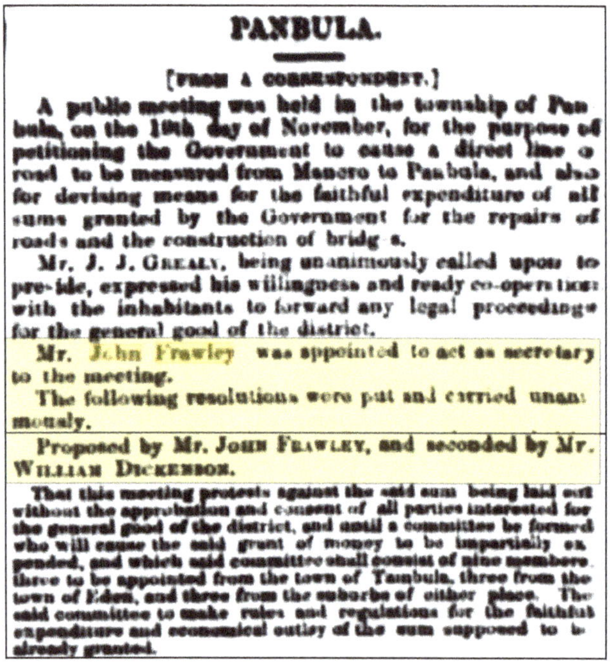

PAMBULA.

[FROM A CORRESPONDENT.]

A public meeting was held in the township of Pambula, on the 19th day of November, for the purpose of petitioning the Government to cause a direct line of road to be measured from Manero to Pambula, and also for devising means for the faithful expenditure of all sums granted by the Government for the repairs of roads and the construction of bridges.

Mr. J. J. Grealy, being unanimously called upon to preside, expressed his willingness and ready co-operation with the inhabitants to forward any legal proceedings for the general good of the district.

Mr. John Frawley was appointed to act as secretary to the meeting.

The following resolutions were put and carried unanimously.

Proposed by Mr. John Frawley, and seconded by Mr. William Dickenson.

That this meeting protests against the said sum being laid out without the approbation and consent of all parties interested for the general good of the district, and until a committee be formed who will cause the said grant of money to be impartially expended, and which said committee shall consist of nine members, three to be appointed from the town of Pambula, three from the town of Eden, and three from the suburbs of either place. The said committee to make rules and regulations for the faithful expenditure and economical outlay of the sum supposed to be already granted.

On the 15th of October 1854, John Frawley is recorded as sponsoring the baptism of both James Dunn and Mary Ann Collins in separate ceremonies conducted by Father William Xavier Johnson at Pambula.

But discontent was foaming across the colony at this time and just six weeks later, between 22 to 60 diggers, many of them Irish, were killed by troopers at the 'Eureka Stockade' on the 3rd December 1854. The rebellion was instigated by gold miners at Ballarat, Victoria, who under their new fashioned flag called the 'Southern Cross' revolted against the colonial authorities.[19]

In December 1855 and on the 19th

LEFT: *John Frawley - Appointed Secretary of the Pambula Roads Committee (Empire, 13th December 1856, p.3).*

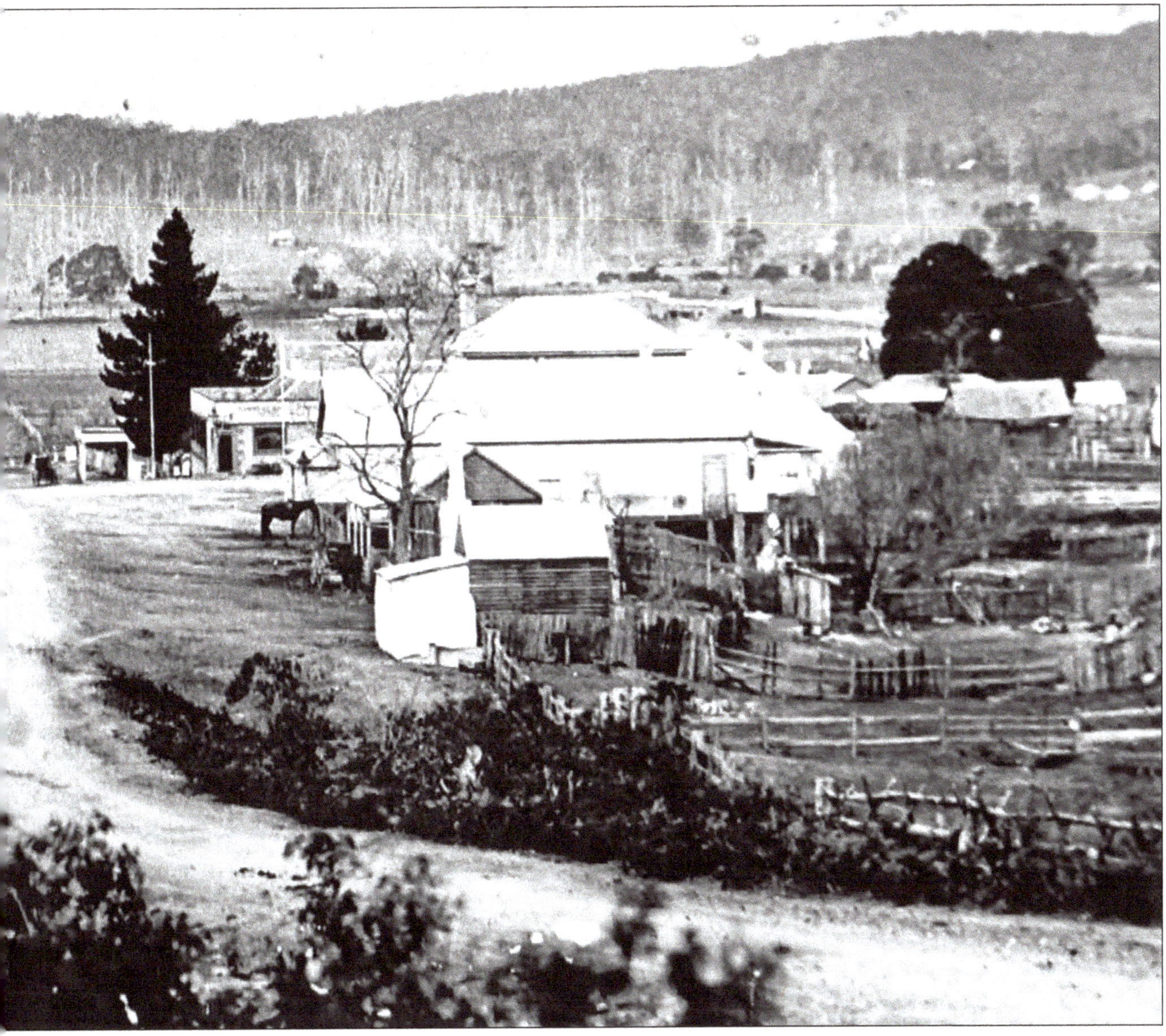

November 1856, we find John Frawley, a concerned citizen of the new town, acting as secretary for town meetings petitioning the government "to cause a direct line of road from Monaro to Pambula, and devise expenditure for the repair of roads and construction of bridges," at which both John Frawley and Syms Covington were the proposers of motions.[20,21]

Thus, by the mid-19th century, John Frawley had firmly established himself as a pioneer of Pambula. His contributions to the town's development, perhaps even to the construction of the historic 'Oaklands Manor House' and Lt. John Lloyd's 'Grange Manor',

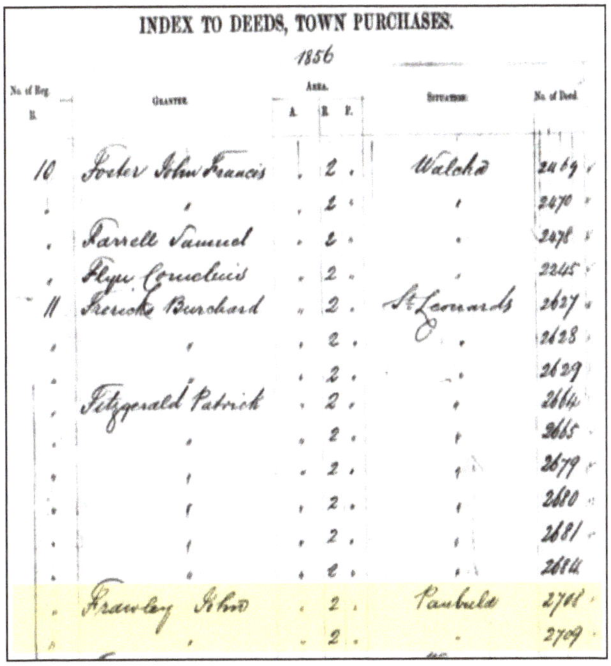

INDEX TO DEEDS, TOWN PURCHASES.

1856

No. of Reg. B.	Grantee	Area A.	R.	P.	Situation	No. of Deed
10	Foster John Francis	.	2	.	Walcha	2469
.	"	.	2	.	"	2470
.	Farrell Samuel	.	2	.	"	2478
.	Flyn Cornelius	.	2	.	"	2245
11	Frericks Burchard	.	2	.	St Leonards	2627
.	"	.	2	.	"	2628
.		.	2	.	"	2629
.	Fitzgerald Patrick	.	2	.	"	2664
.	"	.	2	.	"	2665
.	"	.	2	.	"	2679
.	"	.	2	.	"	2680
.	"	.	2	.	"	2681
.	"	.	2	.	"	2684
.	Frawley John	.	2	.	Pambula	2708
.	"	.	2	.	"	2709

RIGHT: John Frawley, land purchaser in 1856 from Index to Deeds - Pambula Town Purchases (NSW, Land Records, 1811-1870).

were significant. His children followed in his footsteps, supporting the construction of St. Peter's Catholic Church, while John himself played a key role in shaping the region's infrastructure as secretary of the roads committee. He successfully applied for a conditional land purchase in the township and was a strong proponent of good education, helping to lead the effort to establish a school for the growing community.

But while John was building a future in Pambula, he was not the only Frawley making a fresh start in Australia. In the next chapter, we turn our attention to another branch of the family, his Frawley cousins, who began arriving in Victoria from about 1854. Their journey was one of determination, hope, and an enduring family bond, one strong enough to span continents. As they sought to reconnect with John, they proved that, despite the vast distance, the Frawley family remained united.

References

1. Bega Shire Hidden Heritage - 101 Objects Revealed - 'Oaklands' Oak Trees, Pambula', [https://hiddenheritage.com.au/heritage-object/?object_id=82].
2. Lambie, John (1839). Commissioner for Lands. (Extract from. Higgins, J. (1982). Pambula's Colonial Days: A short history of the period 1797-1901. The Merimbula – Imlay Historical Society).
3. Bayley, W.A. (1942). History of Bega. op. cit., p.10.
4. Higgins, J. (1982). Pambula's Colonial Days: A short history of the period 1797-1901. The Merimbula – Imlay Historical Society.
5. Ibid.
6. Claims To Leases Of Crown Land Beyond The Settled Districts - Maneroo District (SMH, 6 October 1848 & 7 October 1848, p.8).
7. Higgins, J. (1982). Pambula's Colonial Days, op.cit.
8. Shannon, J. (1969). Buildings of Pambula, Twofold Bay. Unpublished Thesis.
9. Ibid.
10. NSW Dept. of BDM. (1843). Birth Certificate for Stephen Frawley, 1844 at Panbula, 1168/1844 (V18441168 63).
11. NSW Dept. of BDM, Birth Certificates for Letitia & Patrick Frawley (twins), 1848 at Panbula, 1415/1848 (V18481415 65).
12. NSW Dept. of BDM, Birth Certificate for Thomas Frawley at Panbula, 1849 at Panbula, 1519/1849 (V18491519 66).
13. Bayley, W.A. (1942). History of Bega, op. cit., p.20.
14. John Frawley - 'Secretary of Committee to Purchase Land for RC Church.' The People's Advocate & NSW Vindicator', 21 August 1854, p.15.
15. John Frawley - RC Church Subscriptions. Freeman's Journal, 12 May 1855, p.10.
16. Panbula News Weekly, 'Signed R. B.' 29th September, 1853. (Reprinted in News Weekly).
17. The 'Foundation of Bega' (The Bega Standard & Candelo, Merimbula, Pambula, Eden, Wolumla and General Advertiser (11th November 1876, p.2).
18. John Frawley, purchaser in 1856 from Index to Deeds - Pambula Town Purchases (NSW, Land Records, 1811-1870).
19. National Museum of Australia. 'Eureka Stockade' [https://www.nma.gov.au/defining-moments/resources/eureka-stockade]. Retrieved 10th June 2021.
20. John Frawley - Petition for Line of Road (Empire, 13 December 1856, p.3).
21. Pambula Meeting - Illawarra Mercury, 1856.
22. Lt. John Lloyd, R.N. - Magistrate (Sydney Chronicle, 6 May 1848, p.3).
23. Death of Ret. Lt. John Lloyd, R.N. (SMH, 16 December 1868, p.1).
24. Wikipedia - "Syms Covington" [https://en.wikipedia.org/wiki/Syms_Covington].

Further Reading

Andrews, G. (1984). South Coast Steamers. Maritime History Publications.
Bach, J. (1976). A Maritime History of Australia. Sydney, Pan Books.
Cox. P. (1978). South Coast of New South Wales. Melbourne, Macmillan.
Elias, S. (Ed.) (1986). Tales of the Far South Coast. Vol.3., Bega Valley Shire Bi-Centennial Committee.
Flower, C. (1981). Illustrated History of NSW. Adelaide, Rigby.
Monaro Pioneers Group. 'Monaro.' [http://www.monaropioneers.com/towns/Pambula.htm]. Retrieved 6 July 2021.
Wikipedia - Oaklands, Pambula [https://en.wikipedia.org/wiki/Oaklands,_Pambula]

Chapter Thirteen

THE FRAWLEYS OF VICTORIA

The story of the Frawley family is not confined to a single path or destination. While John Frawley remained central to our branch of the family's journey, his brother Patrick and wife Susan Cody took their own bold steps toward a future far from their home in Doora, County Clare. Unlike some emigrants who ventured into the unknown with little connection to those who had gone before, Patrick and Susan's family seem to have been well aware of John's whereabouts. Over a period of several years, from 1854 to 1858, they made the life-altering decision to leave Ireland, undertaking a staggered migration to Australia.[1]

Among their children, Richard Frawley's journey stands out. He did not simply arrive in Australia, but he put down roots. Settling in Pambula, New South Wales, alongside our John Frawley, Richard married and had a son there, ensuring that this branch of the Frawley name would be carried forward in a new land. His presence in Pambula raises intriguing questions: Did he join John Frawley or another relative already established there? Was his path shaped by family letters, guidance, or the pull of opportunity?

However, Richard's time in Pambula was not permanent. Like many Irish migrants drawn by the promise of fortune and new prospects, he later moved away, eventually settling in Ballarat, Victoria. It was there, in 1864, that his life came to an early end. His story, though brief, reflects the restless movement and determination of his family, always seeking, always adapting to the changing landscapes of their adopted country.

This chapter explores the lives of Patrick and Susan's descendants, tracing their migration, settlement, and the impact they had on the communities they joined. Their story, like so many Irish emigrants of the 19th century, is one of resilience, ambition, and the enduring strength of family ties that spanned oceans.

The Irish Origins of Patrick Frawley

Evidence reveals that John Frawley had a brother, Patrick Frawley a tenant farmer who lived in the townland of 'Ballyvonnavavn', near Doora, County Clare, Ireland.

Patrick John Frawley was born around 1790 in Doora and Kilraghtis, County Clare, Ireland. In 1821, he married Susan Cody, the daughter of Dennis and Margaret Cody, in County Clare. The 1826 tithe list records that Patrick owned seven and a half acres of land and was required to pay a tithe for the upkeep of the Protestant clergy.

Susan was born in 1796 at 'Jasper's Pound' near Quin, County Clare, Ireland. She emigrated to Australia in May 1858 aboard the "Parsee", accompanied by her daughter Bridget Catherine, and son Patrick. Susan passed away from chronic bronchitis on 19 December 1864 at Warrenheip, Victoria, aged 68. She was buried on 22 December 1864 in the Old Ballarat Cemetery, where she rests alongside her sons Richard and Michael, and Michael's wife, Bridget. Susan was of Roman Catholic faith.

At the commencement of the Irish Famine in 1845, Patrick would have been at least

The Frawley cottage at Doora in County Clare, was still standing in 1997, and was similar to the above structure.

M16. Map of Ennis and surrounds, County Clare, showing the location of Doora, and Quin in relation to the larger town of Limerick.

45 years old. By 1855, land records list Susan as a widow, indicating Patrick had died sometime between 1840 and 1855, and well before Susan's 1858 emigration. The cause of his death remains unknown, perhaps due to famine, accident, or political turmoil.

In 1992, a search conducted by the Clare Heritage Centre at Corofin provided baptismal records for five of the seven children, Patrick, Michael, Richard, Eliza, and Sarah, but failed to locate records for Bridget Catherine and John. These records confirm that the Frawleys were baptized in what is now known as the Parish of Doora, Barfield, County Clare. Unfortunately, Catholic church records before 1864 were often incomplete, leaving many gaps in historical documentation.

Life in Doora and the Famine's Impact

The Frawleys lived in a one-room, earthen-floored cottage in Doora. The structure had a single window and door, additional windows were taxed at the time, making light and ventilation a luxury. Susan and her seven children endured incredibly harsh conditions. It is unknown whether they owned animals or how they survived during the famine. The family's survival suggests they either had enough food or received aid from relatives.

The famine devastated County Clare, with more than 150,000 people perishing or emigrating. Some of the Frawleys may have emigrated as a direct result of these hardships. In 1992, a visit to the remains of Susan's cottage revealed that it had stood until 1997 before being replaced by a modern home.

The Frawley Family's Journey to Australia (1854-1858)

Between 1854 and 1858, the Frawleys left Ireland for Australia aboard three different ships:

In 1854, the "Rodney", a ship of London; Alex Maclean, Master and burthen weight of 877 tons, sailed from the port of London, arriving on the 15th March 1854, at Sydney, New South Wales with 250 adults and 87 children - Government Immigrants. These included Michael Frawley, and his sister Sarah, who arrived in Sydney on March 15, 1854, as assisted immigrants.[2]

In 1855, the "Chowringhee", a ship of Belfast; D. Ferguson, Master and burthen weight of 893 tons, sailed from the port of London, and arrived on the 26th November, 1855, at Sydney, New South Wales with 235 adults and 49 children - Government Immigrants. These included, Anne Frawley (c.1807-1872), who brought with her five of her family members: Patrick, Richard, John, and Bridget, the wife of Michael Frawley, who arrived the year earlier, and another younger Michael (II) Frawley.[3]

In, the "Parsee", a ship of London; Edwin E. Thomas, Master and burthen weight of 1,050 tons, sailed from the port of London, via Southampton, and arrived on the 14th May

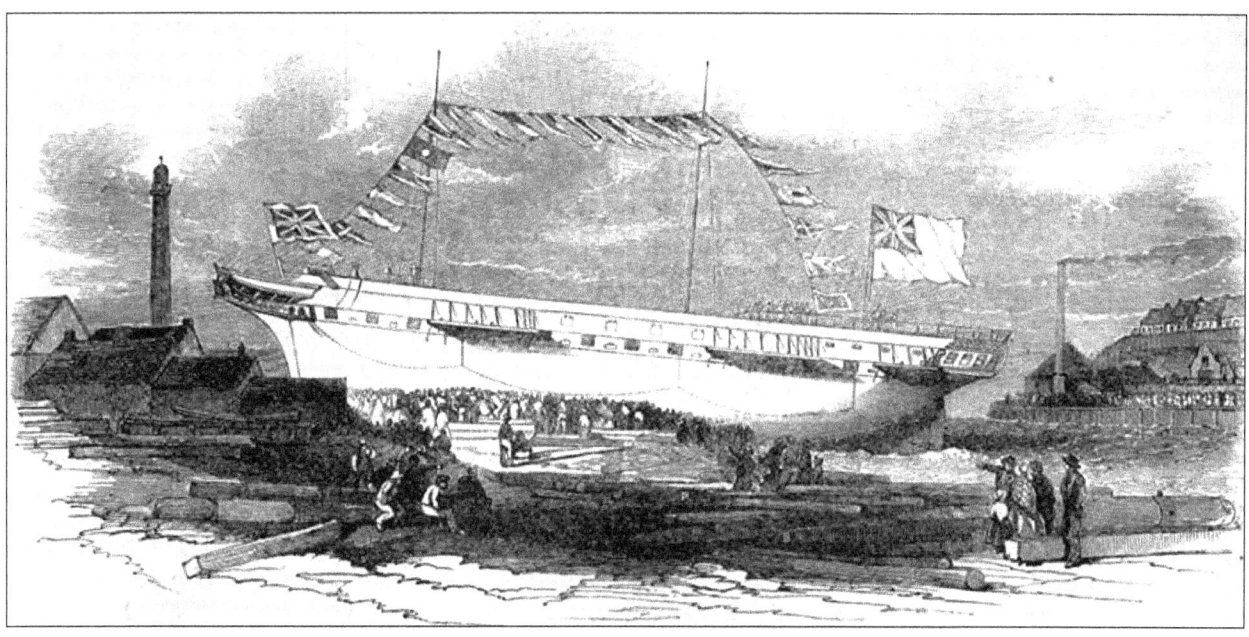

ABOVE: Launch of the "Chowringhee" at Sunderland (London Illustrated News, 22 March 1851). LEFT: Rodney - Arrival (The Maitland Mercury, 18 March 1854, p.2); Chowringhee - Arrival (The Shipping Gazette et al, 19th Nov 1855, p.257). BELOW: Parsee - Arrival (The Argus, 15 May 1858, p.4)

Arrival registrations for Frawley family off the Chowringhee, which arrived 16th November 1855 (from Assisted Immigrants Index 1839-1896, Reel 2137 & 2469). These arrival records for Anne Frawley (b.1807); Patrick Frawley (b.1828); Bridget Frawley (b. 1830), the wife of Michael Frawley, who was already in Australia; Richard Frawley (b.1833); John Frawley (b.1838); and another younger Michael Frawley (b.1843), which are confusingly different to the baptismal records.

1858, at Melbourne (Hobsons Bay) with 437 passengers - Government Immigrants. These included the mother, Susan Frawley (nee Cody), who arrived with her daughter Bridget Catherine, and son Patrick, in Melbourne on May 14, 1858.[4]

The reasons for choosing Australia over the United States remain speculative. However, the presence of relatives, specifically some of Susan's Cody family, who had settled in Warrenheip, Victoria, likely influenced their decision. Additionally, the Frawleys arrived as assisted immigrants, meaning they were likely to have been financially sponsored by relatives or other community networks in Victoria.

Establishing a New Life in Leigh Creek/Bungaree

Upon arrival, the Frawleys settled in Leigh Creek and Bungaree, near Ballarat. This area, part of the Parish of Warrenheip, was rich in Irish Catholic immigrant communities. The Frawleys quickly integrated, purchasing land and raising families. It remains unclear how they funded their passage and land acquisitions, but support from the Cody family or an inheritance from Susan's father, Dennis Cody, may have played a role.

The Frawley family resided at Leigh Creek and Bungaree, alongside the old Bungaree homestead, painted by S.T. Gill.

The Eureka Stockade, a defining moment in Australian history, occurred on November 30, 1854, amidst the emigration of the branch of the Frawley family. Though it is unknown whether they were directly involved, the rebellion marked a period of great social and economic upheaval in the gold-mining regions of Victoria.

The Death and Legacy of Susan Frawley

Susan Frawley (nee Cody) passed away in 1864 at the age of 68. For over 126 years, she lay in an unmarked grave in the Old Ballarat Cemetery until 1991, when family members, including Monica Burke (nee Frawley), raised funds to erect a headstone. Her grave, located in Section E1, Row 12, Grave 14, also holds her sons Michael and Richard, and Michael's wife Bridget (nee McMahon).

The McMahon sisters, who married Michael and John Frawley, were also from County Clare. It is possible the families knew each other in Ireland before emigrating to Australia.

The Frawley name remains prominent in various parts of the world, particularly in Ireland, in Boston in the United States, and Australia. Many Irish Frawleys trace their lineage to famine emigrants, while in Ireland, the name has a particular concentration around Kilrush, County Clare.

In an effort to trace the family's roots, every Frawley listed in the Irish telephone directory was contacted in 1992. Out of more than 200 letters, we received 13 responses and maintained regular correspondence with eight individuals. Many had become successful in various trades, including farming, hospitality, and transportation. Several family members also joined religious orders.

The Quest for Answers

Despite extensive research, including four trips to Ireland between 1992 and 1999, the exact details of Patrick Frawley's birth, marriage, and death remain elusive. Extensive searches in churches, cemeteries, and records have yielded little concrete evidence. Some theories suggest Patrick may have died of natural causes or political violence, as Ireland experienced significant upheaval from the 1798 Irish Rebellion through the mid-1800s.

Future family historians may uncover more through additional research in 'Ballyvonnavavn' and surrounding areas. Questions remain about the family's journey, did they depart from Cork or travel to London before boarding their ships? How did they finance their emigration? Did they receive financial help from the Cody family?

The Frawley family's journey from Ireland to Australia was one of hardship, resilience, and determination. Their story, like that of many Irish emigrants, is interwoven with the broader history of famine, migration, and settlement. While many questions remain unanswered, their legacy continues through generations who seek to preserve and honor their history.

The Next Generation

In the quiet countryside of County Clare, Ireland, in the early 19th century, Patrick John Frawley and Susan Cody raised a large family. Life in Ireland was harsh, and as the years passed, their children sought opportunities beyond the rolling green hills of home. The seven children of Patrick John Frawley and Susan Cody, all Roman Catholics were:[5]

1. Patrick Frawley (1822-1901), the eldest, was born in 1822 in co. Clare and christened two years later on 23 January 1824. With Bridget and Patrick Frawley as his sponsors, his future seemed promising. A farmer by trade, he never married. When the call of a new land beckoned, he set sail for Australia in 1858 aboard the "Parsee", accompanied by his

The death certificate for Susan Frawley (nee Cody), who died in 1864.

13.1 Descendants of Patrick Frawley & Sussanah Cody

Patrick John Frawley (c.1790-c.1858), married in 1821 at County Clare to Susan Cody (1796-1864), with issue:

1. Patrick Frawley (1822-1901), was born in 1822 in co. Clare and christened two years later on 23 January 1824. He set sail for Australia in 1858 aboard the "Parsee", accompanied by his mother, Susan, and sister, Bridget. Patrick lived with his brother Michael until his death in Warrenheip, Victoria, on 10 October 1901, aged 78. No issue.

2. Bridget Catherine Frawley (1826-1914), born in 1826 in County Clare, Ireland, was a devoted daughter and sister. Arrived in Australia aboard the "Parsee" on 24 May 1858. She later married Matthew Jenkin, a bookmaker from Cornwall, England, in 1866. Died in Ballarat, Victoria, in 1914 at the age of 86.
2.1 Patrick James Jenkins

3. Michael Frawley (1829–1883), born in 1829 in County Clare, Ireland, shared his brother Patrick's pioneering spirit. He and his sister Sarah braved the long journey aboard the "Rodney", arriving in Australia on 15 March 1854. A hardworking farmer and labourer, Michael married Bridget (1833–1882), daughter of James McMahon and Anne Hillard perhaps at St Mary's in Geelong? Michael died on the 25 January 1883 in Ballarat, Victoria, aged 55, just a year after losing his wife, and buried on the 28 January 1883 in the Old Ballarat Cemetery, with issue
3.1 Patrick Frawley
3.2 James Frawley
3.3 Elizabeth Ann Frawley
3.4 Susan Frawley (1862–1903), married John O'Donohue (1842–1902) in 1884
3.5 Michael Frawley
3.6 Annie Frawley
3.7 Mary Jane Frawley
3.8 Thomas "Little Daddy" Frawley
3.9 Catherine Alma "Kate" Frawley
3.10 Bridget Frawley (1874–1903), married Francis Kavanagh in 1902, but tragedy struck when she passed away the following year.

4. Richard Frawley (1831–1864), was born in 1831 in Doora, Ennis, County Clare, Ireland. In 1858 he reunited the Frawley family by journeying to reside alongside his cousin John Frawley and family in Pambula, where he also married Catherine Penderghast, but their happiness was short-lived; and their infant son, John Frawley, also passed away the same year. Richard was a labourer, but his own life ended abruptly in 1864, when he died on the 10 June 1864 in Ballarat, Victoria, at the age of 33, and was buried 13 June 1864 in Ballarat General Cemetery. Catherine later remarried William Wexted in 1875, but Richard's memory lived on in the land he had sought for a better future. They had one child:
4.1 John Frawley (1858–1858).

5. Sarah Frawley (1836–1897), born in 1836 in County Clare, Ireland and baptised on 12 June 1836, shared her brother Michael's adventurous nature. They made the voyage aboard the "Rodney" together on 15 March 1854. On 28 April 1859, she married Maurice Bruton (1836–1917). Their family grew over the years, with children like Susan "Suze," Francis "Jack," and Patrick Henry bringing both joy and responsibility. Sarah's life came to an end on St Patricks Day, 17 March 1897 in North Melbourne, aged 60, with issue:
5.1 Susan "Suze" Bruton
5.2 Francis John Augustus "Jack" Bruton (1861–1921)
5.3 Patrick Henry Bruton
5.4 Anna Maria "Annie" Bruton (Nurse)
5.5 Maurice Bruton (1866–1931)
5.6 Elizabeth Mary "Betsy" Bruton
5.7 Mary "Polly" Bruton
5.8 Catherine "Kate" Bruton (1872–), matron, WWI nurse, awarded the Royal Red Cross
5.9 Isabella Rose Bruton
5.10 William Bruton (1876–1877)

6. Eliza Frawley (1839–1927), was born and baptised on 23 August 1839 in Quinn, County Clare. As a young woman, she journeyed to Australia, where she found work as a servant. On 25 February 1865, in the small township of Happy Valley, she married Patrick McCormack (1830/1840–1909). She died on 11 August 1927 in South Melbourne, Victoria, at the age of 88, with issue:
6.1 Mary Susan Rose McCormack
6.2 Richard Joseph McCormack
6.3 Elizabeth Ellen McCormack (Twin)
6.4 Patrick Michael McCormack (Twin)
6.5 Alexander John McCormack
6.6 Hugh Henry McCormack (1876–1951)

7. John Frawley (1840-?), was born in 1840 in County Clare. On 20 April 1865, he married Catherine McMahon (1840–1872) at St Patrick's Cathedral in Ballarat, with issue:
7.1 Susan Mary Frawley
7.2 Sarah Jane Frawley (1869–1918)
7.3 Patrick Frawley (1871–1872), died an infant

* Died before adulthood - d.s.p.
(Some names not listed in the index).

---

mother, Susan, and sister, Bridget. Patrick lived with his brother Michael until his death in Warrenheip, Victoria, on 10 October 1901, aged 78. He was laid to rest in the New Cemetery, Ballarat on the 12 October 1901.

2. Bridget Catherine Frawley (1826-1914), born in 1826 in County Clare, Ireland, was a devoted daughter and sister. She, too, arrived in Australia aboard the "Parsee" on 24 May 1858. She later married Matthew Jenkin, a bookmaker from Cornwall, England, in 1866. Together, they had a son, Patrick James Jenkins. Bridget lived a long life, passing away in Ballarat, Victoria, in 1914 at the age of 86.

3. Michael Frawley (1829–1883), born in 1829 in County Clare, Ireland, shared his brother Patrick's pioneering spirit. He was baptised on the 27 January 1829 in Doora and Kilraghtis, County Clare. He and his sister Sarah braved the long journey aboard the "Rodney", arriving in Australia on 15 March 1854. A hardworking farmer and labourer, Michael married Bridget (1833–1882), daughter of James McMahon and Anne Hillard at St Mary's in Geelong on 11 September 1855 . They had several children, including Patrick, James, Elizabeth Ann, and Susan, who later married John O'Donohue. Their daughter Bridget wed Francis Kavanagh in 1902, but tragedy struck when she passed away the following year. Michael himself died on the 25 January 1883 in Ballarat, Victoria, aged 55, just a year after losing his wife, and was buried on the 28 January 1883 in the Old Ballarat Cemetery. They produced ten children.

4. Richard Frawley (1831–1864) was born in 1831 in Doora, County Clare, Ireland and christened on 13th February that year. In 1858, he married Catherine Penderghast, in Pambula, New South Wales, confirming that there was commincation between the Frawley cousins. But sadly, their happiness was short-lived as their infant son, named John, after our John Frawley of Pambula, passed away the same year. Richard was an agricultural labourer, but his own life ended abruptly in 1864, when he died on the 10 June 1864 in Ballarat,

Victoria, at the age of 33, and was buried 13 June 1864 in Ballarat General Cemetery. Catherine later remarried William Wexted in 1875, but Richard's memory lived on in the land he had sought for a better future. They had one child, John Frawley (1858–1858).

5. Sarah Frawley (1836–1897), born in 1836 in County Clare, Ireland and baptised on 12 June 1836, shared her brother Michael's adventurous nature. They made the voyage aboard the "Rodney" together on 15 March 1854. Four years later, on 28 April 1859, she married Maurice Bruton (1836–1917). Their family grew over the years, with children like Susan "Suze," Francis "Jack," and Patrick Henry bringing both joy and responsibility. Their daughter Catherine "Kate" Bruton later became a WWI nurse and was awarded the Royal Red Cross for her service. Sarah's life came to an end on St Patricks Day, 17 March 1897 in North Melbourne, aged 60, and she was buried in the Melbourne General Cemetery on the 19 March 1897. They produced ten children.

6. Eliza Frawley (1839–1927) entered the world in 1839 in Quin, County Clare, and was baptised on 23 August 1839. As a young woman, she journeyed to Australia, where she found work as a servant. On 25 February 1865, in the small township of Happy Valley, she married Patrick McCormack (1830/1840–1909). Together, they raised a family, welcoming children Mary Susan Rose, Richard Joseph, twins Elizabeth Ellen and Patrick Michael, Alexander John, and Hugh Henry. Eliza worked as a servant and lived a long and full life, passing away on 11 August 1927 in South Melbourne, Victoria, at the age of 88, and buried on 12 August 1927. They produced six children.

7. John Frawley (1840-?), the youngest of the siblings, was born in 1840 in County Clare. On 20 April 1865, he married Catherine McMahon (1840–1872) at St Patrick's Cathedral in Ballarat. They had three children: Susan Mary, Sarah Jane, and Patrick, the last of whom died in infancy. Catherine's own life was cut short in 1872, and little Patrick's remains were later moved to rest beside her. They produced three children.

The Frawley family's story is one of resilience, sacrifice, and new beginnings. From the shores of Ireland to the goldfields and farmlands of Victoria, their legacy endures, carried forward by the generations that followed.

 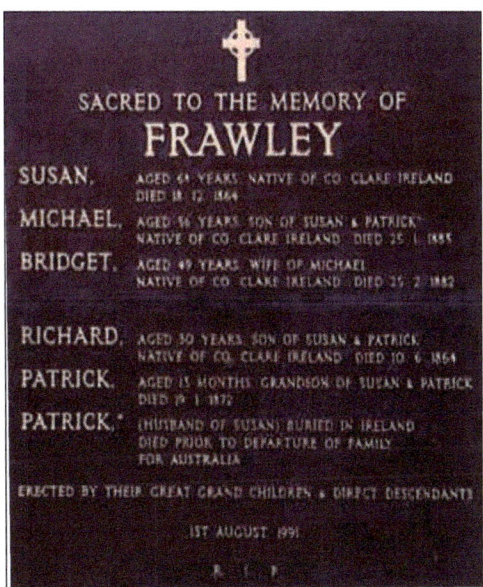 

LEFT: Bridget Frawley (nee McMahon) - wife of Michael Frawley. CENTRE: Frawley family memorial plaque, produced and funded by the Frawley Reunion of 2000. RIGHT: Michael Frawley (son of Patrick Frawley & Susan Cody).

Danny Patrick Frawley (1963-2019), played 240 games with the Saints, and was captain from 1987 to 1995 for a total of 173 games, becoming the longest-serving St Kilda Australian Football Club captain.

Danny Frawley

Another descendant to achieve recognition, but in a totally different field is Danny Frawley, son of Brian and Shirley Frawley, of Bungaree. He has made his mark on the football field, beginning his playing days with local club Bungaree in the Central Highlands Football League before graduating to East Ballarat in the Ballarat Football League.

Danny was later recruited by St Kilda and went on to play 240 games with the Saints. He was captain from 1987 to 1995 for a total of 173 games, becoming the longest-serving St Kilda captain. He won the St Kilda best and fairest award in 1988. He played 11 state games for Victoria, was named in the All Australian team in 1988 and was vice-captain of the All Australian team in 1990.

After he finished playing in 1995, he accepted a coaching role with Collingwood Football Club for four years before being appointed senior coach of the Richmond Football Club. He has just completed his first year in that position.

Special Thanks

Family history is an ongoing journey, and the reunion booklet represented an important step in that process. As time goes on, new information will undoubtedly come to light. While some omissions, discrepancies, or inaccuracies may exist, we hope they are minimal. This booklet should be seen as a foundation for a more comprehensive publication in the future.

Compiling details about people and events from 150 years ago, especially in a distant country where record-keeping was not as meticulous as today, is no small feat. We owe a great debt of gratitude to Ivan Frawley for his thorough investigative work and to Trish Lette for her exceptional family history research skills. We encourage other family members to visit Ireland, our ancestral homeland, to deepen their appreciation of our heritage. Such a trip may even uncover missing pieces of our family history puzzle. At the very least, visitors will experience Ireland's warm hospitality and see historic sites significant to our family, such as the location of Susan's cottage in Doora, which stood until 1997.

The year 2004, brought the 150th anniversary of the arrival of Michael Frawley and his sister Eliza in the Bungaree district. This milestone presents a fitting opportunity to hold another family gathering and perhaps publish a more extensive family history book. We welcome all comments and suggestions to help make that possible.

This booklet is the result of many people's efforts, and we sincerely thank everyone who contributed. A special acknowledgment goes to Patricia Lette, who has dedicated countless hours over many years to this project. Her unwavering commitment has been instrumental in both the reunion celebrations and the creation of this booklet. Another invaluable contributor is Ivan Frawley, who is passionate about passing family history on to future generations. He has traveled to Ireland four times, tirelessly researching and uncovering our family's past.

We also extend our gratitude to Monica Burke, whose remarkable memory has been invaluable in preserving details of our ancestors. She recalls names, burial sites, causes of death, marriages, and family connections, insights that many of us wish we had at our fingertips.

The organizing committee has shown tremendous enthusiasm in bringing this event to life, and we are grateful to everyone who played a role, whether in recording family history, planning the reunion, or producing this booklet. Many individuals have worked tirelessly behind the scenes to make this gathering a reality, and we hope their dedication is recognized and appreciated.

One person who deserves special mention is Patricia Lette of Cooma, New South Wales. Trish is the great-great-granddaughter of Maurice Bruton and Sarah Frawley (daughter of Susan and Patrick), who married on April 28, 1859. Sarah passed away on St. Patrick's Day in 1897 at the age of 60, while Maurice lived until 1917, reaching the age of 81. Trish, a true "computer wiz," has spent years reaching out to countless descendants, investing not only her time but also her own resources in phone calls, faxes, postage, and stationery. We also extend our appreciation to her family for their patience and support throughout her research journey.

We hope this booklet offers valuable insights into our family history and that this reunion is both memorable and meaningful for all. Thank you to everyone who has contributed in ways big and small, your efforts ensure that our family's legacy will be preserved for generations to come. For more information contact Ray Frawley (Author) at RMBE 325 Killarney Road, Warrenheip ,Victoria, 3352 Phone (03)5334 7389.

And so, Susan Frawley (née Cody) left behind the rolling green fields of Doora, County Clare, in Ireland, for the uncertain promise of a new world. Widowed and determined, she gathered her children and embarked on the long, perilous voyage by sailing ship to Australia in the mid-1850s. From there, they pressed onward to Leigh Creek and Bungaree in Victoria, where hardship gave way to opportunity. In this fresh land, her family took root, her children thrived, and the generations that followed would multiply, forging a new legacy far from the famine-stricken soil of Ireland.

But while Susan and her children found prosperity, not all of the Frawley family's journey in Australia was smooth. Hundreds of miles away, another chapter of the Frawley family story was unfolding, one marked by struggle, conflict, and the relentless weight of the law. Back in Pambula, our John Frawley was about to face a battle of a very different kind...

References

1. Frawley, Ray (2000). "From Clare to Bungaree", For the occasion of the reunion of descendants of Patrick Frawley and Susan Cody, 7-8 October 2000 at Ballarta & Bungaree.
2. State Records Authority of New South Wales: Shipping Master's Office; Passengers Arriving 1855 - 1922; NRS13278,[90] reel 399. Transcribed by Joyce Pickup, 2004.
3. State Records Authority of New South Wales: Shipping Master's Office; Passengers Arriving 1855 - 1922; NRS 13278, [X93] Reel 402. Transcribed by Tricia Miller, 2003.
4. "Shipping Intelligence" (The Argus [Melbourne], Sat 15 May 1858, Page 4).
5. Frawley, Ray (2000). "From Clare to Bungaree", For the occasion of the reunion of descendants of Patrick Frawley and Susan Cody, 7-8 October 2000 at Ballarta & Bungaree.

Chapter Fourteen

PROPERTY & PROSECUTIONS

By 1856, John Frawley was a man of standing in the thriving town of Pambula. A respected figure in the community, he had his hands in many of the town's most vital affairs. As secretary for the roads committee, he helped shape the infrastructure that would connect Pambula to the wider world. He lent his voice to the appeal for the release of land, ensuring the town had room to grow. He reached into his own pocket to support the construction of St Peters Roman Catholic Church and worked tirelessly to improve local education. With property now to his name, it seemed that Frawley's future was set on a steady and prosperous course.

But fortunes, like the tides that lapped at the shores of Pambula Beach, have a way of turning. What began as minor civil disputes soon escalated into a series of legal battles that would test Frawley's resilience and reshape his fate. As accusations mounted and claims against him grew, the man who had helped build the town found himself at risk of losing everything. By the time criminal charges entered the fray, it was clear, John Frawley's run of good luck had come to a sudden and dramatic halt.

Having survived transportation, a seven year sentence as a convict with hard labour, the trials of bush living at 'Warragaburra', hostile aboriginals and floods, one might think John

Frawley and his young family had seen the worst that life could throw at them. But no, his life now took a downward spiral as he became entangled in one court case after another. This is the story of how a man who had once stood among Pambula's most valued citizens found himself entangled in the unforgiving grip of the law.

Court Matters I - Frawley v Hayes

By 1855 John Frawley became entangled in court proceedings at the Police Office in

▲ The District Courthouse on Imlay Street, Eden. ▼ Court proceedings for John Frawley v John Hayes, 9th January 1855.

John Frawley v John Hayes (1855)

New South Wales - To Wit:

John Hayes of Panbula appears on summons to answer the complaint of John FRAWLEY and William Shea for that he the said John Hayes refuses to pay certain wages due to them for the erection of a building at Panbula and pleads not guilty.

William Shea being duly sworn states by a written agreement made on the 13th February 1854, John FRAWLEY and myself undertook to build a dwelling for Hayes we completed according to agreement for which we were to received 55 pounds all was paid except a balance of £19,8,8d. which Hayes refuses to pay on the plea that the roof is badly built and not weather tight. Hayes entered into possession before the building was finished we put on fresh spouts at his request. He then said he would pay us the balance of our wages.

Cross examined by plaintiff. We agreed to erect a building as good as Mr Covingtons which we did.

William Shea, Sworn before us at the Police Office Eden this 9th day of January 1855.
A.W. Manning P.M. - Stewart Mowle J.P.

John Hayes states in his defence that the roof is badly built with shingles three feet long which does not keep out the rain and the wind has already blown some off in consequence of this not being properly nailed.

James McMann states I have examined the hut erected for Hayes at Panbula. The shingles are not properly laid or closed.

James McMann, Sworn before us at the Police Office Eden this 9th day of January 1855.
A.W. Manning P.M., Stewart Mowle J.P.

The case adjourned to the 16th January 1855.

A.W. Manning P.M.
Stewart Mowle J.P.

New South Wales - To Wit:

John Hayes of Panbula appears on summons to answer the complaint of John FRAWLEY and William Shea for that he the said John Hayes refuses to pay certain wages due to them for the erection of a building at Panbula and pleads not guilty.

John FRAWLEY being duly sworn states I am in partnership with William Shea. We agreed to put up a building for John Hayes for the sum of 55 pounds we completed the building according to agreement. I produce the agreement. We received £35,11,4d. on account of the work. The balance £19,8,8d. Hayes refuses to pay.

John Frawley, Sworn before us at the Police Office Eden this 16th day of January 1855.
A.W. Manning P.M. Stewart Mowle J.P. Defence

John Hayes states in his defence the agreement made with the plaintiffs specified that the building to be erected for me was to be as good as the one Mr Covington had built. I object to paying the balance claimed as they did not complete the work according to contract. The roof and the shingles are badly put on not being water tight and some of the shingles having already fallen off. There is a door post deficient and one they did put up I was obliged to pay a man to remove and replace.

John Hayes

William McNiven being duly sworn states I live at Panbula and am a farmer. I do not consider the hut built by FRAWLEY and Shea properly finished and should not be satisfied with such a building myself. I do not consider the shingling properly done. If such work were done for me I would not pay for it.

W. McNiven, Sworn before us at the Police Office Eden this 16th day of January 1855
A.W. Manning P.M. Stewart Mowle J.P.

John Charles Davis being duly sworn states I am a blacksmith living at Panbula. I have seen the building put up for Hayes by FRAWLEY and Shea. I consider it all very good but the shingling. I saw one shingle off. The shingles are three feet long; when I looked up at the shingling I saw it was badly done and said it was scandalous. I do not think the roofing as well done as Mr Covingtons.

Cross examined by plaintiff. I do not consider the rafters properly placed, the ends of the full layer of shingles pointing inside the house under the battens in consequence. If the shingling had been done for me. I should not have paid for it.

J.C. Davis, Sworn before us at the Police Office Eden this 16th day of January 1855.
A.W. Manning P. M. Stewart Mowle J.P.

The case dismissed with costs three pounds.

A.W. Manning P.M., Stewart Mowle J.P.

Wolumla, a nearby township which developed around a watering place for bullock teams, was later buoyed by the discovery and mining of gold, c.1880.

Eden on the 9th of January. In partnership with William Shea, he was a co-defendant in a claim lodged over their workmanship in the building of a cottage for Mr. John Hayes. The cottage was in Monaro St, Pambula.

> **Before Judge Manning and Mowle.**
>
> James McMann (policeman) stated he'd inspected the hut erected for John Hayes, Panbula and found the shingles not properly laid or closed, as claimed by Hayes. Builders John Frawley and William Shea were summonsing Hayes for payment. Hayes stated he wanted his hut "to be as good as the one Mr Covington had built". Blacksmith Davis and Wm McNevin gave evidence that the shingles were bad. Case dismissed with costs three pounds.
>
> *Eden Bench Books, 9th January 1855* [1]

It seems that John Hayes wasn't satisfied with the quality of the shingling so withheld part payment. It would appear in those days that court cases were a regular happening, and many records of the proceedings have survived. In this case, Mr. Hayes insisted that "he wanted his house to be as good as Mr. Covingtons."

A full transcript of the court proceedings between John Frawley, William Shea and Mr. Hayes has been preserved. Mr. Hayes argument and witnesses were obviously convincing and accepted by the judges, the end result being that not only did Frawley and Shea lose the case, but they had to pay £3 in costs! Unfortunately, Mr. Hayes' house has not survived the test of time, the absence of which today adds weight to his argument, that it had not been built anywhere near as good as Covington's house.

In 1856 New South Wales received responsible government when a number of land grants were offered to assist with settlement of the rural areas. Taking advantage of these 'selections', John Frawley applied for and was granted land in the township of Panbula on the corner of Toalla and Quondola Streets, on the 10th of September 1856.[2] John Frawley later sold this land to innkeeper, John Behl in 1872 for just £10,[3] which has since become recognised as 'Toad Hall'.

John Martin v John Frawley (1857)

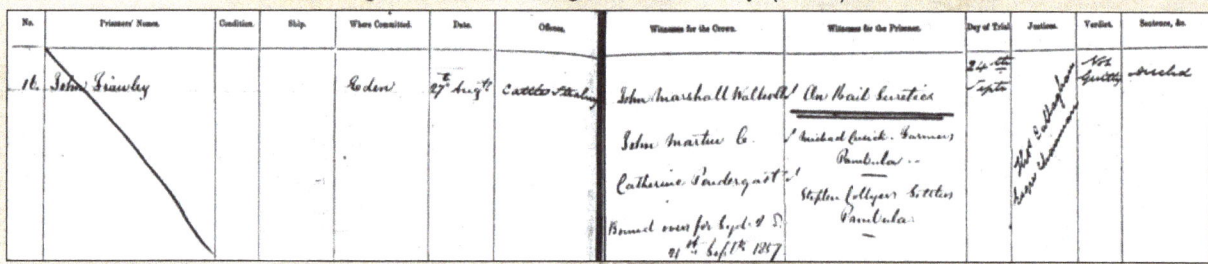

SYDNEY QUARTER SESSIONS.
Monday, September 21.
Before the Chairman.

The Crown Prosecutor conducted the following cases on behalf of the Crown:—

THURSDAY.

John Frawley was indicted for stealing a heifer, the property of John Martin. At the close of the case for the Crown, the Chairman expressed his opinion that there was not sufficient proof of a taking in law by the prisoner; the taking relied on being the branding of the heifer with the prisoner's brand, without proof that that brand was put on by him, or by his directions. Under the chairman's direction, therefore, the jury acquitted the prisoner, and he was discharged. Mr. Roberts appeared for the prisoner.

▲ Court proceedings for John Martin v John Frawley, 27th August 1857. TOP: John Frawley was charged with cow stealing on 27th August 1857 (NSW, Criminal Court Records, 1830-1945, Quarter Sessions). ABOVE (Left): John Frawley indicted, but acquitted of stealing a cow (SMH, 28 Sept 1857, p.4. (Right): Early photograph of drovers on horseback. ▼ Court proceedings for John Martin v John Frawley, at Eden Courthouse, Aug & Sept 1857.

New South Wales - To Wit:

The information and complaint of John Marshall Walker of Eden, Chief Constable, taken this 24th day of August, 1857, before the undersigned, one of Her Majesty's Justices of the Peace in and for the said Colony who saith that I have reason to believe and do believe that John FRAWLEY of Panbula did felonously steal a calf and ear mark and brand the said calf with JF his own brand some time in the month of July last past which calf was and is the property of John Martin of Yowaka in the said Colony.

Signed Jno M. Walker
Sworn before me at Eden the day and year first above mentioned
Signed G.P. Keon P.M. (58)

New South Wales - To Wit:

The examination of John Marshall Walker of Eden in the said Colony, Chief Constable John Martin of Yowaka in the said Colony, ordinary Constable, and Catherine Pendergast of Yowaka in the said Colony, servant, taken on oath this 27th day of August 1857 in the presence and hearing of John FRAWLEY of Panbula in the said Colony who is this day charged before me for that he the said John FRAWLEY did felonously steal a calf and ear mark and brand the said calf with JF his own brand some time in the month of July, last past, which calf was and is the property of John Martin of Yowaka in the said Colony.

This deponent John Marshall Walker being only sworn with as follows:

I am Chief Constable in the Eden Police on the 21st of July last I was going to Bega on duty when passing Boggy Creek my attention was drawn by Constable Martin to a number of cattle amongst which were some calves, some of the latter bearing the brand of defendant JF. Constable Martin then pointed one out to me and said Mr Walker there is a calf of mine which I have missed for some time and FRAWLEY has branded it, I saw the calf and believed it to have been branded only a few days as it was quite fresh, I replied to Martin that it was not possible for FRAWLEY to brand his calf as he was not returned from the Murrumbidgee. Martin then told me that he (FRAWLEY) had been back some days. I gave Martin directions to get the calf in if he was quite sure it was his, on the 22nd of this month I saw the same calf in Mr Gwynn's yard it bore the fresh brand JF besides on examining further I saw an old brand on the side JML which was Martin's brand. The letter M was not plain but I am quite sure it was M. The first day I saw the calf I only saw on it your brand quite fresh.

Signed Jno M. Walker
Sworn before me this 27th day of August 1857,
Signed G.P. Keon P.M.

This deponent John Martin being duly sworn saith as follows:

On or about the 21st day of July last past I was going to Bega on duty with Mr Walker and Constable Balantine at this side of Boggy Creek and my attention was drawn to a number of cattle amongst the herd I saw a white heifer yearling calf of mine it had been recently branded JF on the milking side rump with an ear mark in square hole cut in it, it must have been very recently done as I saw blood on it. I was not able to drive home the calf then as I had to go to Bega on duty but drew Mr Walkers attention to the affair. I have since that day frequently looked for the calf but did not succeed in finding it until the 21st of this month. I received information to the effect that if I went to Boggy Creek I would find a calf of mine fresh branded accordingly next day I went with Constable Balantine to the place mentioned where we found the calf which we drove to Panbula and put in Mr Lloyd's yard. I have since roped the calf and swear that it is my property it bears my brand which is JML on the ribs at the milking side. I had not seen the calf for about three months previously, I have before seen it with some of the defendants cattle on the Flat.

By Deponent...
You were at the Murrumbidgee when I missed the calf. The day I met you at Boggy Creek I told you I was waiting to see Mr Walker, we spoke about cattle, I cant say that you told me you couldn't see the brands on your cattle distinctly and you branded two a second time, I saw my brand distinctly on the calf the first day at Boggy, and to me it was quite legible but perhaps it may not have been to a stranger. It is possible that a stranger may brand the calf through a mistake.

Signed John Martin
Sworn before me this 27th day of August 1857,
Signed G.P. Keon P.M.

By Defdt.
John Martin recalled you told me that my calf was frequently at your place.

Signed John Martin
Sworn before me this 27th day of August 1857,
Signed G.P. Keon P.M.

This deponent Catherine Pendergast being duly sworn with as follows:

I am a servant in Mr Martins employ. I have been in the habit of milking a cow at Mr Martins. She had a white heifer calf. It would be about a year old now. I assisted Mr Martin to brand the calf with his own brand JML on the milking side ribs. I saw this calf on the 22nd of this month in a yard at Panbula it then bore the brand of John FRAWLEY the defdt which is JF it was ear marked and was only recently done.

Catherine 'X' Pendergast (her mark).
Witness P. Murray
Sworn before me this 27th day of August 1857,
Signed G.P. Keon P.M.

The defendant John FRAWLEY having been duly cautioned states as follows:

I have a white heifer calf the same as Mr Martins running on the same run which was branded by me and am quite sure the brand is illegible which must have ensued the mistake as I have branded two of my own a second time I think it quite probable that at this time of the year persons should make such mistakes.

Signed John Frawley
Declared before me this 27th day of August 1857,
Signed G.P. Keon P.M.

John FRAWLEY committed to take his trial at the next court of Quarter Sessions of the Peace to be holden at Sydney on Monday the 21st day of September next.

Signed G.P. Keon P.M.

John Marshall Walker, John Martin and Catherine Pendergast

bound over in the (penal?) sum of ten pounds such to appear at the same time and place for the prosecution.

Signed G.P. Keon P.M.
From Eden Bench Books

New South Wales - To Wit:

The examination of John Marshall Walker of Eden Chief Constable, Adam Balantine of Panbula ordinary Constable, Francis Turner cattle overseer and Thomas Smith of Panbula Innkeeper taken on oath this first day of September 1857 in the presence and hearing of John FRAWLEY who is this day charged for that he the said John FRAWLEY did on the sixth day of August last past steal and kill a cow the property of the Twofold Bay Pastoral Association.

This deponent John Marshall Walker being duly sworn deposes:

I am Chief Constable in the Eden Police on the ninth of August last I received information that the defendant now before the court had committed a breach of the Slaughtering Act by giving notice to the assistant Inspector that he was about to kill a certain beast and then substituted another for it from what I could learn I believe it to have been a cow the defendant killed which cow was the property of the Twofold Bay Pastoral Association. I can produce the hide if required bearing the AD brand which now belongs to the Twofold Bay Pastoral Association.

Signed Jno M. Walker
Sworn before us this first day of September 1857.
Signed G.P. Keon P.M. John Lloyd RN JP

This deponent Adam Balantine being duly sworn deposes:

I am a constable in the Eden Police stationed at Panbula on Tuesday the sixth of August last the defdt. came to my house and gave me the brand of a bullock he was about to kill. I went to his yard about three or four o~clock that evening he pointed out a white bullock that he was going to kill branded JA which brand I took. I then left the yard and went away on the Sunday following I received information that the defendant had not killed the bullock he showed me but instead killed a cow branded AD which was formerly that of Armstrong McCausland but has since been purchased by the Twofold Bay Pastoral Association.

By Chief Constable

It was on Thursday the sixth of August I took the brand at FRAWLEY'S yard my first statement as to the day of the week was a mistake though I said Tuesday I meant Thursday. I received the hide from the defendant at his own place as being that of the last beast he had killed and also the same beast for which he had been sued under the Slaughtering Act.

By the Bench:

I saw a hind quarter of beef at Smiths public house which was that of a cow Smith told me he received from defendant.

By Defdt.

You said that the last beast you killed was that of the hide now produced I was in bed when I heard you come to my house to give notice. You spoke to my wife, when I heard you speaking to my wife I suspected at the time that you were out looking for some of my bullocks, that you were about to purchase from me ?? I came to your yard to (take?) the brand I saw two cows and two calves the property of McCarthy and a white bullock you pointed out to me and said you were going to kill it was on Thursday the sixth of August I took the brand of the bullock at your yard you asserted to me that you turned out the bullock the same night I saw only the stock above named in the yard I cant say where you got the hide from.

By Chief Constable

I received no notice from the defdt this year until I got the one with reference to this bullock.

Signed Adam Balantine
Sworn before us this first day of Sept. 1857
G.P. Keon P.M. John Lloyd R.N. J.P.

This deponent Francis Turner being duly sworn deposes:

I am cattle overseer to the Twofold Bay Pastoral Association. I am aware that the cattle known as the AD cattle are the property of the Company. A great many of those cattle run about Panbula and Boggy Creek generally on the Wolumla Runs. Wolumla is about twelve miles from Panbula and Boggy Creek is about five. I have seen a hide the same now before the Court it bears the same brand as that AD cattle on the station. I believe the cow of which the hide now produced to be the property of the Company from the A leaning to the D which is the same in all the other cattle of the same brand. I have carefully examined the hide as well as the brand. I never sold the defendant any cattle bearing the AD brand I let him have a cow branded with the Twofold Bay brand.

By Defdt.

I can't swear to the brand of the cow I let you have but the cow I bargained with you for I swear is not the AD cow you told me at the time it was a Twofold Bay cow I gave no delivery of the cow further than letting you ?? could take her I wont know of any of the AD brand having been sold to anyone at or near Panbula I was not at the delivery of the cattle since I have been on the station some of the AD cattle bear other brands I am not aware whether any of those cattle were given away.

By the Bench:

I have known the defdt to be on the Company run several times I have made complaints to Mr Manning about several people being on the station without leave.

Signed Francis Turner
Sworn before us this first day of September 1857
Signed G.P. Keon P.M. John Lloyd J.P.

Francis Turner recollects:

I recollect telling FRAWLEY that I would not consent to his taking the cow alluded to in the former part of my evidence until a circle M should be put on the cow. The Company always have this brand put on all cattle sold except those for killing.

By Defdt

I have put circle M on some cows sold, I cant say how long it is since I exchanged? the cow with you.

Signed Francis Turner
Sworn before us this 1st day of September 1857.
Signed G.P. Keon P.M. John Lloyd R.N. J.P.

This deponent Thos Smith being duly sworn deposes:

I am a Licensed Innkeeper at Panbula, I bought a quarter of beef from the defendant John FRAWLEY on the sixth or the seventh of last month I am not sure which date but it was on a Friday I was sent to by FRAWLEY to know if I would take a quarter of beef. I said if it was good I would take it and next day I was sent down a hind quarter of a cow.

Signed Thos Smith
Sworn before us this 1st day of Sept. 1857
Signed G.P. Keon P.M. John Lloyd R.N. J.P.

Remanded for further evidence to the 5th of September.

The examination of Adam Balantine of Eden, ordinary Constable and Armstrong McCausland of Lochiel farmer taken on oath this fifth day of September 1857 in the presence and hearing of John FRAWLEY who stands charged with stealing a cow and was remanded to this day.

By Chief Constable - This deponent Adam Balantine being duly sworn saith as follows.

I am ordinary Constable residing at Panbula. I know the cows quite well that Mr Arthur Manning had milking for the use of his house at Panbula. They were all branded with a single M on the shoulder. I never saw an AD cow at his place. I have reason to believe that James Collins of Panbula assisted the prisoner to kill the cow for which he now stands charged. Collins is under prohibition as a confirmed drunkard by this Bench. I have reason to believe that Collins tried to induce a man of colour at Yowaka to steal the hide after it was in my possession.

By Dep.

You had an opportunity of making away with the hide before and after I saw it, you told me the beast was yours but I told you I would be answerable for the hide while it was in my possession. Mr Arthur Manning had no cows but those bearing the Twofold Bay brand during the four or five years I knew him. I am not aware that he had any of Mr Bells?. I have seen some AD cattle on the flat but I cant swear to whom they belong.

Signed Adam Balantine
Sworn before me this 5th day of Sept 1857.
Signed G.P. Keon P.M.

This deponent Armstrong McCausland being duly sworn ??

I have known the owner of the AD brand they now belong to the Twofold Bay Pastoral Association I have seen in Eden in the possession of the police. I believe it is the original brand I have no recollection of the beast but now I can only recognize the brand. I have some cattle bearing the AD brand but they are all rebranded with AM. The Company are now the owners of the AD brand. I have not been solicited to come and give evidence. I have no recollection of giving Mrs FRAWLEY a cow but I would not swear that I have not done so, I am not in the habit of giving away cattle though. I have given away a few. There are a few AD cattle running about Panbula some have been got from me and some from Mr Walker they are all rebranded by their owners.

By the Bench:

I could see no other than the AD brand on the hide produced by Constable Balantine.

Signed A. McCausland.
Sworn before me this 5th day of September 1857.
Signed G.P. Keon P.M.

The defendant John FRAWLEY being duly cautioned states as follows.

I got the cow for the stealing of which I am charged in exchange from Mr Francis Turner I request that I may be allowed to call on Mr Turner.

Francis Turner being duly sworn saith:

I could have no entry in the books of the exchange with you. I am satisfied that we agreed to exchange a cow as soon as the circle M would be put on you asked me to change with you a Twofold Bay cow that was at Panbula for one of (yours?) that was running at Wolumla which I agreed to I have seen plenty of Twofold Bay cows at Panbula but I wont know the one I exchanged myself with you.

Signed Francis Turner
Sworn before me this fifth day of Sept. 1857.
Signed G.P. Keon P.M.

By Defdt. This deponent James Collins being duly sworn deposes:

I reside at Panbula. I recollect your stating to me that you exchange a cow with Mr Turner I don't recollect that you mentioned any particular brand I remember seeing a Twofold Bay cow on the flat I am not quite sure whose she is now ?? the brand W on the shoulders which is the Companys brand.

By Chief Constable

I have been out in the bush with FRAWLEY and his son but I cant say what date I went out with FRAWLEY to look for two bullocks of Constable Balantine. We drove in two cows and one calf of William McCarthy, a cow of James Egans and a bullock of FRAWLEYS it was late when we got into Panbula that night I assisted FRAWLEY to kill a cow last month.

DISMISSED.

Signed James Collins
Sworn before me this fifth day of September 1857.
Signed G.P. Keon P.M.

Despite the scrutiny, it appears that John's choice to reside in Panbula was sound, as a letter published in the Illawarra Mercury of 1856 described the growing township at that time:

> '...a very pretty, flourishing township...there are four or five public houses, as many more stores, a Crown Land Commissioner's office, a Church of England place of worship, two or more schools, about three dozen well erected weatherboard houses together with as many rough huts.'
>
> *Illawarra Mercury, 1856* [4]

Court Matters II - Martin v Frawley

On the 3rd of March 1857 John Frawley was granted a slaughtering licence by the Eden Bench of Magistrates. Unfortunately, by August of 1857, and perhaps caused by his new enterprise, he was back in the local court, this time for stealing and branding a calf, on charges brought by Constable John Marshall Walker of Eden.[5] The court proceedings for this incident, John Martin (plaintiff) against John Frawley (defendant), have also survived. Fortunately, the charges in this trial against John Frawley were dismissed by the magistrate.

Family Reunion

While John Frawley had got himself out of trouble in 1857, on the charge of cow stealing, one of the key witnesses against him was Catherine Penderghast,[6] who, later that same year, went on to marry a member of the Frawley family in Panbula.[7]

This Richard Frawley was John's first cousin from Ireland. He had arrived in Sydney as an assisted immigrant aboard the "Chowringhee" on November 16, 1855, at the age of 22. Travelling with his aunt, Anne Frawley (48), as well as his siblings: Patrick (27), Bridget (25), John (17), and Michael (12).[8] This Anne Frawley was therefore likely to have been an aunt of John Frawley. According to the "Chowringhee"'s passenger records, Anne

LEFT (Top): Group of Aboriginal trackers. (Above): John Frawley was involved in a court case against Wyman (aboriginal), John McAllister (constable, Broulee) and John Walker (constable, Eden) for having his horse stolen (Illawarra Mercury, 1 Nov 1858, p.2). RIGHT: Aboriginals gather around a 'gunyah'.

14 - Property & Prosecutions

Ponsonby v John Frawley (1860)

Eden District Court

Ponsonby v Frawley for work done and performed. The plaintiff is a plasterer, the amount claimed was £78. Defendant pleaded a contra account. Verdict for plaintiff £53,4,0d. Forbes for defendant; plaintiff conducted his own case.

Twofold Bay & Maneroo Observer, 23 March, 1860

Ponsonby v Frawley

The Registrar of the said Court will cause to be Sold by Public Auction at Panbula
On Thursday, the 15th day of November instant, All the right, title, and interest of the Defendant's in this case, in and to all that piece or parcel of Land Situated at Panbula and known as Allotment No.3 of Section No.16(?) together with a Six Roomed House erected thereon. Also a quantity of Household Furniture.

The Observer, 9th November, 1860

Ponsonby v Frawley

A quantity of Household Furniture will be sold by Auction, on the Premises of John Frawley, at Panbula, on Saturday next, the 1st December.

The Observer, 27th November, 1860

Frawley v Ponsonby

18th December 1860
Verdict for plaintiff. £148,0,7d.
FRAWLEY v Ponsonby.
No appearance of plaintiff. Ordered to stand over.
FRAWLEY v Ponsonby
Recalled. Cash advanced, work and labour done, as per account rendered. Defendant did not appear. John FRAWLEY swore to the correctness of the account, and that he had rendered a bill of particulars to defendant. In answer to a question from His Honor, he said, that he had not made any arrangement with defendant that morning, nor had any conversation with him about the matter. Order for the amount with costs.

The Observor, 21 December, 1860

LEFT: The Colonial Police often used native troopers. RIGHT: The Police Station & Courthouse at Pambula, c.1900.

Frawley was born around 1807 in Quin, County Clare, while Richard and the rest of the family were born and baptized in Doora, just east of Ennis, County Clare, Ireland.[9] These locations, Ennis, Doora, and Quin, are situated just 35 kilometers northwest of John and Mary Frawley's hometown of Limerick.

Tragically, the newborn son of Richard and Catherine Frawley passed away at just 17 days old on December 20, 1858, in Panbula. The child had been given the name John Frawley, after his cousin, who then was regrettably recorded as a witness at the infant's burial.[10]

By 1859, both John and Richard Frawley were still residing in Panbula and were listed on the Eden District Electoral Roll:

1859 EDEN DISTRICT - ELECTORAL ROLL
#232 John Frawley (Panbula)
#233 Richard Frawley (Panbula)

A year or so later, Richard Frawley followed the footsteps of his own siblings and trekked south to Leigh Creek and Bungaree in Victoria, where he tragically passed away just a few years later, at just 30 years of age.[11] For many years, little was known about the Victorian branch of the Frawley family. However, in 2023, a chance encounter with another Frawley family member unexpectedly revealed new connections between Richard's descendants and our Frawley ancestors of Pambula.

Surprisingly, the tables were turned on John Frawley soon afterwards when he apparently had his own horse stolen by a local Aborigine, named Wyman:

The Township of Pambula

▲LEFT: Line drawing of Pambula's early days, featuring the two storied Toad Hall. RIGHT: The Police Station & Courthouse at Pambula. ◄Main street weatherboard house in Pambula. ▼Looking up the main street of Pambula about 1870.

▲LEFT: Old weatherboard cottage from Pambula's early days. RIGHT: 'The Royal Willows Hotel', one of the Pambula's original pubs. ▶John Frawley originally owned the land in Panbula upon which 'Toad Hall' was later built.

Pambula National School

TOP (Left): Pambula Public School teacher, W. S. Apsey and students in front of the 2nd permanent school building, c.1880. (Right): Teachers Residence, Pambula. ABOVE (Left): List of NSW National Schools by August of 1850 (The Maitland Mercury & Hunter River General Advertiser, 7 Aug 1850, p.3). (Right): John Frawley enquiring about the cost of education (Illawarra Mercury, 21 March 1859, p.2).

COURT OF PETTY SESSIONS
Moruya - 21st October 1858
Wyman an aboriginal native, appeared, charged with stealing a horse, the property of John FRAWLEY of Panbula in the police district of Eden. John McAllister chief constable of Broulee, stated that he had received a letter from Mr Walker, chief constable of Eden, directing him to apprehend Wyman and forward him to Eden. He was remanded to the Bench of Magistrates at Panbula on the above charge.

Illawarra Mercury, 1st November 1858 [12]

Court Matters III - Ponsonby v Frawley

In early 1860, John Frawley ran into more difficulty with proceedings in the Eden District Court, this time with a plasterer by the name of Mr. Ponsonby. By November, ongoing proceedings from this tragic case had a devastating effect on the Frawley family, when not only their house, but all their household furniture were scheduled to be auctioned off.

John and Mary Frawley, their children, friends and neighbours would have witnessed the dreadful sight of their hard earned and valuable possessions being carried off by the Sheriff and his officers. However, by December of that year, John Frawley was back in court against Mr. Ponsonby, and this time the tables were turned with the magistrate ordering Mr Ponsonby to repay the full £148.0.7d. in addition to the costs, but by then, Ponsonby had dissapeared, so whether or not John Frawley and family actually received those monies is another matter.

Pambula National School

The origins of the Pambula School are interesting, as the Frawley children likely all enroled and attended as pupils during this period. Certainly John Jr. (9), Ellen (8), James (6) and Stephen Frawley (5) would have been eligible to attend, when the school opened its doors in November of 1849, which at that time had an enrolment of 20 boys and 17 girls.

> "Following the National Education Act of 1848, Pambula became the seventh public school in the colony and by 1999 was the fourth oldest still in operation.
> A temporary teacher, Mr. J. Grealy, took charge of the new school supplied with books worth £2,1-. Two and a half acres in Section 4 of the township was claimed by Messrs Walker, Jones and Bell for a permanent school. Construction of the brick and shingle school commenced in November 1849. Mr. Grealy remained in charge of the school until the first permanent teacher, Henry Fowler, arrived to take over.
> Attendance at the school rapidly increased however, as the local industry was predominantly agricultural and pastoral, but spring and summer brought a marked decrease with children required to help with the planting and harvesting."
>
> *Angela George* [13]

But there were a number of potential issues, and top of the list was that the school had been built on Pambula Flat, and was therefore vulnerable to flooding. The following description of the devastation inflicted by the flood of 1860 meant that the location of the school had to be re-assessed:

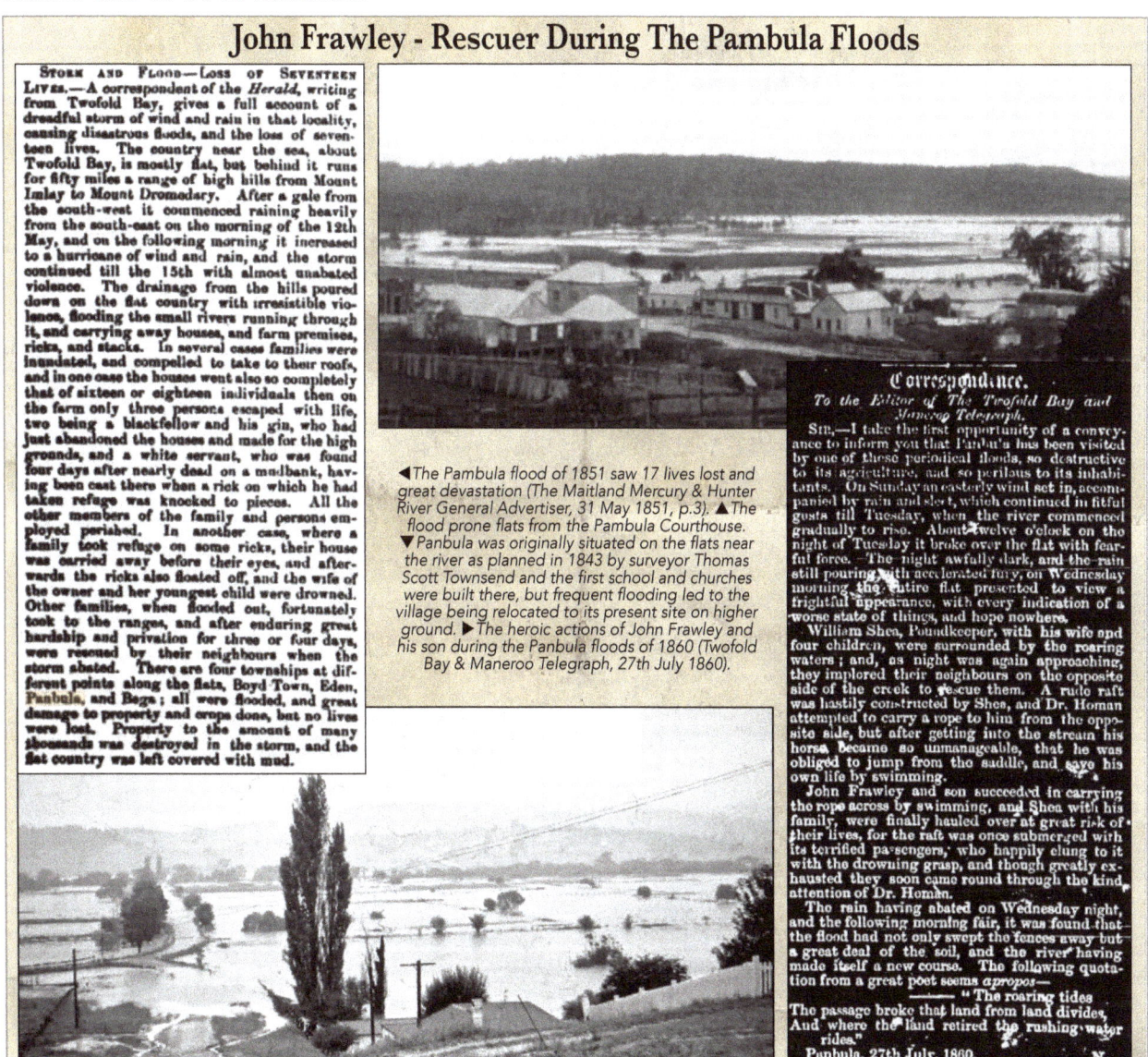

◀ The Pambula flood of 1851 saw 17 lives lost and great devastation (The Maitland Mercury & Hunter River General Advertiser, 31 May 1851, p.3). ▲ The flood prone flats from the Pambula Courthouse. ▼ Pambula was originally situated on the flats near the river as planned in 1843 by surveyor Thomas Scott Townsend and the first school and churches were built there, but frequent flooding led to the village being relocated to its present site on higher ground. ▶ The heroic actions of John Frawley and his son during the Panbula floods of 1860 (Twofold Bay & Maneroo Telegraph, 27th July 1860).

1860 Kiandra Gold Rush

In November 1859, gold was discovered by the Pollock brothers, mountain cattlemen, and by March 1860, some 10,000 miners and storekeepers had raced to Kiandra, where initial returns were very good. A 9kg nugget was discovered in river deposits under what became known as New Chum Hill. Kiandra post office opened on the 1st June 1860[26] and it is estimated that the area at its peak accommodated around 15,000 people, served by 25 stores, 13 bakers, 16 butchers, 14 pubs, several banks and four blacksmiths.[27,28] Nevertheless, by 1861, the Sydney Morning Herald was reporting a "mass exodus" after the easy pickings had been exhausted.[29]

Significant numbers of Chinese people worked the Kiandra goldfields. Chinese miners built Three Mile Dam in 1882 to assist with sluicing operations at "New Chum Hill". The scenic lake still exists and now supplies Selwyn Snowfields with its snow-making water requirements. The last mining operations at Kiandra finally ceased around 1905. Official total production recorded was 48,676kg of gold.[30]

TOP: View over Kiandra from nearby hill. MID (Left): A postcard of the Kiandra Gold Diggings, 1860. (Right): Prospector's display their gold nuggets. ABOVE (Left): Panning for gold at the Kiandra diggings, by S.T. Gill. (Centre): Kiandra Police Station in the depth of winter. (Right): Advertisement for transport direct from Eden to the Kiandra goldfields (SMH, 31st July 1860, p.8).

> "The school building is sometimes surrounded by floods to a height of three feet. The organization is defective. The children are neither punctual nor regular. Much noise and disorder. The walls are dirty and damp. None but the ordinary subjects are taught, and of those, the smallest quantity possible. The few children present are deficient in acquirements."
> In 1860... "the National School at Panbula was full in the stream, the doors were burst open and a quantity of mud, sand and timber occupied the place of the teacher for several days. It is a wonder that the Board of Commissioners do not see to this matter as I fear very much that the teacher and the building will make a moonlight flit."
>
> *Angela George* [14]

By 1861, in excess of 30 scholars were recorded on the school roll with an average daily attendance of just 19. The school situation eventually became so bad that something had to be done and after much agitation on the part of the community and local education authorities, the new public school was relocated to its present site on higher ground, and opened in April of 1869.[15]

The Floods of 1851 and 1860.

The old village of Panbula including the first school and churches had all been erected on the flats near the Pambula River, which was planned in 1843 by surveyor Thomas Scott Townsend. But following a gale in early May of 1851, heavy rains commenced and continued almost unabated until the 15th, when drainage from the surrounding hills poured down onto the flat carrying away houses, haystacks and anything else in its path. In several cases families were inundated and compelled to take to their roofs. The settlers living on the flats at Boydtown, Eden, Pambula and Bega all experienced the devastating flood, with some 17 lives being lost.[16] In Pambula, the residents subsequently had to move the entire village to higher ground.

Another more devastating inundation struck in 1860 when John Frawley made the news after he and his son John Jr., assisted in the rescue of the Shea family during the most severe moments of that Pambula flood. This was the same William Shea with whom he had been in partnership when building the house for Mr. Hayes, so they were obviously close friends. The report of the courageous rescue was published in the form of a well composed letter to the editor by an unknown author, written on the 27th July 1860 at Pambula.[17]

The Kiandra Gold Rush

In November of 1859, gold was discovered by mountain cattlemen, the Pollock brothers, and by March 1860, some 10,000 miners and storekeepers had raced to the scene. Initial returns were very good, and a 9kg nugget was discovered in river deposits under what became known as 'New Chum Hill'. Kiandra post office opened on 1 June 1860,[18] and it is estimated that the area at its peak accommodated around 15,000 people, served by 25 stores, 13 bakers, 16 butchers, 14 pubs, several banks and four blacksmiths.[19] Nevertheless, by 1861, the Sydney Morning Herald was reporting a "mass exodus" as the easy pickings had been exhausted.[20] Pambula benefitted from being one of the closest towns to the diggings.

Medical Gentleman For Pambula

Pursant to advertisement, a public meeting was held at the Swan Inn, Panbula, on Monday evening 26th inst., for the purpose of inviting a medical gentleman to reside in the district.

Mr Shea was voted to the chair, and the following resolutions were carried unanimously.

Proposed by Mr John FRAWLEY, and seconded by Mr James Egan, "That in the opinion of this meeting the services of a second medical gentleman are required for this place." Carried.

Proposed by Mr James Egan, and seconded by Mr P. O'Neill, "That the people at this meeting pledge themselves to use every means in their power to further the object named in the first resolution." Carried.

Proposed by Mr Ploughright, and seconded by Mr Thomas Smith - "That a requisition be forwarded to each householder, with the amount that each is willing to pay placed opposite his name, and also, that the people of Eden be requested to lend their assistance to the object." Carried.

Mr FRAWLEY said that he could not let the meeting disperse without saying a few words. "It might appear strange he said, that a public meeting should be called for the purpose of inviting another medical gentleman to reside in the district, but he could tell them it was no way strange if the people came to consider the manner in which they had been dealt with. Since the arrival of the present doctor amongst them, it was a very short time, yet it seemed an age; he first commenced impounding the neighbours cattle, and then overran the place with a stock of breeding sheep. But, worse than all, he commenced to question the way in which justice had been administered in the district by Mr. Murray. This was simply a piece of barefaced impudence. He would like to know from Dr. Homan where were all the pretensions of friendship he made to Mr Murray some time back. Were they all melted like snow, or turned to acid, giving the doctor the heartburn? How had all that come to pass in such a short space of time? The people in the district could answer by saying that even-handed justice had been dealt out between man and man. The aspect of affairs would be different if the position of certain people could influence the decisions of Mr Murray, but such not being the case Mr Murray had secured what Dr. Homan, nor his powerful neighbour, never had nor never would have - the sympathies of the people." (Cheers)

The following memo, was unanimously agreed to - "That this meeting particularly wishes it to be made known for general information, that they regret the absence of Mr R. Beck Jr. from the meeting, as he has been one of the mainsprings in moving it round."

Signed William Shea, Chairman and William Stritch, Secretary. A vote of thanks was returned to the Chairman, and the proceedings terminated.

The Observer, 30th November, 1860 [79].

LEFT: Recent photograph of the restored cottage of Syms Covington at Pambula. RIGHT: A quaint colonial cottage in Pambula, NSW.

> As travelling was slow, many public houses for nourishment and beverages sprang up in the area, many served the miners trying their luck on the extensive local goldfields around Pambula. It is estimated there were more than 20 hotels during the late 1880's in the districts from Eden to Merimbula, today only five remain. The Royal Hotel in Pambula (now known as the Royal Willows Hotel) was built in 1864 and the Commercial Hotel built in 1878 are the last two operating hotels in Pambula today.
>
> *A.T. Shakespeare* [21]

Not being involved in some way or another with the rush to the gold fields would have been hard to avoid, but whether John Frawley tried his luck is unknown. In Pambula, we know that John Frawley had cleared himself of legal difficulties levelled at him by the plasterer known as Ponsonby.

During this difficult time, John Frawley still involved himself in local issues and volunteered his time as committee chairman to publicly thank Dr Richard Bligh, for his work as the town medical practitioner, upon his departure for Sydney on 12th November 1859.

> To Richard Bligh, Esq, Pambula
> Dear Sir, We, the undersigned inhabitants of the district of Twofold Bay, knowing that it is your intention to remove from hence to Paddington, in Sydney, wish to convey to you our expression of very sincere regret for the loss we shall individually and collectively sustain by your removal from amongst us after your sojourn here for five years. During your residence amongst us we have become attached to you by your asiduous and kind attention to the sick, by your urbanity of manner, and by your excellent and christian like conduct in your private life. You may rest assured that you will always be most kindly remembered by us, and that you will ever have our best wishes for your own and your family's happiness and prosperity."
> We remain, dear Sir, yours very sincerely,
> John Frawley, Mrs Frawley, John Frawley Jr, & Ellen Frawley (amongst other residents)
> *The Sydney Morning Herald, Saturday 12 Nov 1859* [22]

By July of 1860, John Frawley had acquired two more Crown Land allotments in the names of his son John Frawley Jr. and daughter Ellen Frawley, in the village of Wyndham:

> CROWN LANDS SALE AT PANBULA
> The following allotments of land were sold on Thursday 19th inst., and are situated in the township of Wyndham, about 25 miles from Eden. A list of lots, prices, and names of purchasers are given below:-
> Town Lots At Wyndham - Lot 53. - John Frawley Jr., 7s. & – Ellen Frawley, 4s.
> *Twofold Bay & Maneroo Telegraph, July 1860* [23]

He also expressed support for Mr. Daniel Egan on 7th December 1860, who was then a candidate for local member of Parliament:

> To Daniel Egan, Esq.
> Sir, - We the undersigned, electors of Panbula and its adjoining Vicinity, having taken particular notice of your late parliamentary career, it is with pleasure we saw you record your vote on the Government side of the Land Bifl. We earnestly request that you allow yourself to be nominated for this electorate, and we pledge ourselves to secure your return to the utmost of our power. Dear Sir, we tender you our most respectful thanks for your late parliamentary career.
> John Frawley, Chairman
> *Twofold Bay & Maneroo Telegraph, 7th Dec 1860* [24]

LEFT: A weatherboard cottage in Pambula, NSW. RIGHT: The two-storey 'Toad Hall', situated on the land once owned by John Frawley.

As 1860 drew to a close, the proceedings from the Ponsonby case brought devastating consequences upon the Frawley family, with the Sheriff openly removing their property and all their belongings from their home. How the family got through this dreadful incident can only be imagined. Despite the litigation, his convict past and the mounting setbacks, it would appear that John Frawley still remained a respected member of the local community. Although he had appeared before magistrates for a number of matters, he remained supportive of the community he lived amongst, and lent his support at a public meeting to request a second doctor for the town from the relevant authorities, in 1860.[25]

Interestingly, Daniel Egan eventually won the election. Despite being an emancipist and a defendant in court proceedings on a number of occasions, John Frawley was nevertheless included on a list of all persons within the District of Eden who by nature of his land holdings was now eligible to serve as a juror on court sessions.

LIST OF ALL PERSONS WITHIN THE DISTRICT OF EDEN
LIABLE TO SERVE ON SESSIONS FOR 1860
John Frawley, Settler from Panbula
Nature of qualification to serve on sessions – 'Real and personal estate'.

By the dawn of the 1860s, John Frawley had carved out a name for himself in the growing township of Pambula, becoming a man of action, flexibility, and ambition. He had fought to improve local education, championed the need for a doctor, and stood as an advocate for his fellow townsfolk, whether through letters of gratitude or direct acts of heroism in the devastating flood of 1860. His influence stretched from civic affairs to political circles, supporting Daniel Egan's election and even serving as a juror in Eden's Petty Sessions. Yet, for all his accomplishments, shadows loomed over his reputation.

Accusations of shoddy workmanship, unpaid debts, and even an allegation of cattle theft, though it was dismissed, marked a turbulent period between 1856 and 1860. Despite his efforts to establish himself as a respected builder and community leader, legal troubles and financial struggles continued to haunt him.

But if these years had been difficult, they were nothing compared to what lay ahead. John Frawley's fortunes were about to take a catastrophic turn. Stripped of the fragile respectability he had worked so hard to build, he would soon find himself once again a prisoner, bound by the chains of his past.

References

1. John Frawley Sr. - Eden Bench Books, 9th January, 1855.
2. John Frawley - Land Grants Panbula, 1856. NSW Land Titles Office. (1856). .
3. John Frawley - Index to Deeds, Town Purchases, 1856. NSW Index to Registers of land Purchases, 1811-1870.
4. Pambula - Illawarra Mercury, 1856.
5. John Frawley - Indicted for Cow Stealing (Sydney Morning Herald, 28 September 1857, p.5).
6. Eden Bench Books, Court proceedings for John Martin v John Frawley, at Eden Courthouse, Aug & Sept 1857.
7. NSW Dept. of BDM. (1858). Marriage of Richard Frawley & Catherine Pendergast, 1858 at Panbula, #1714/1858.
8. NSW State Archives & Records. (1855). Frawleys on the "Chowringhee." Assisted Immigrants Index 1839-1896 (Reel 2137, [4/4792]; Reel 2469, [4/4946]).
9. Richard Frawley - Baptised at Doora, Ennis, County Clare on 13th Feb 1832 with parents Pat Fraly & Johana [sic. Susan] Cody ("Ireland, Catholic Parish Registers, 1740-1900", database, FamilySearch).
10. NSW Dept. of BDM. (1858). Birth Certificate [#6890], and Death Certificate [#3448] for John Frawley.
11. Victorian Dept. of BDM. (1864). Richard Frawley (son of Patrick & Susan Frawley) - Death Certificate [#2808/1864].
12. John Frawley - Plaintiff re Stolen Horse (Illawarra Mercury, 1 November 1858, p.2).
13. George, Angela (1999). From Bark Hut To Brick Veneer: 150 Years of Education at Pambula Public School. Pambula Public School.
14. Panbula News Weekly, 'Signed R. B.' 29th September, 1853. (Reprinted in News Weekly).
15. Ibid.
16. Storm & Flood - Loss of Seventeen Lives (The Maitland Mercury & Hunter River General Advertiser, 31 May 1851, p.3).
17. John Frawley and son - rescuers during the 1860 Panbula Flood (Twofold Bay & Maneroo Telegraph, 27th July 1860).
18. Brown, Alan G. & Campbell, Hugh M. (1963). New South Wales Numeral Cancellations Victoria: The Royal Philatelic Society of Victoria, Australia, and London: Robson Lowe Ltd.
19. Wikipedia - 'Kiandra, NSW.' [https://en.wikipedia.org/wiki/Kiandra,_New_South_Wales]. Retrieved 15th May 2021.
20. Traveller. 'Guide to Kiandra in NSW.' [https://www.traveller.com.au/kiandra--places-to-see-6df6] Retrieved 17 December 2017.
21. Shakespeare, A.T. (1958). The Kiandra Gold Rush and its impact on surrounding districts. Canberra & District Historical Society, Canberra.
22. Richard Bligh - Farewell (The Sydney Morning Herald, Saturday 12 Nov 1859).
23. John Frawley Jr. - Twofold Bay Land Sale at Wyndham (Twofold Bay & Maneroo Telegraph, 31 July 1860).
24. John Frawley, supporting Daniel Egan (Twofold Bay & Maneroo Telegraph, 7th December 1860).
25. John Frawley at Medical Practitioner at Panbula (The Observor, 30th November 1860).
26. Brown, Alan G. and Campbell, Hugh M. (1963) New South Wales Numeral Cancellations Victoria: The Royal Philatelic Society of Victoria, Australia, and London: Robson Lowe Ltd.
27. "Kiandra landmark brought back to life". Cooma Monaro Express. 19 March 2009. Archived from the original on 10 November 2010. Retrieved 26 August 2022.
28. "Kiandra". Archived from the original on 13 September 2009. Retrieved 22 July 2009.
29. "Guide to Kiandra in NSW". Archived from the original on 31 October 2010. Retrieved 17 December 2017.
30. Ibid.

Chapter Fifteen

FRAWLEYS UNDER FIRE

After enduring the brutal 14,500 mile journey of transportation, serving seven years of hard labour as a convict, and battling the harsh realities of life in the wilderness, which included the dangers of the untamed bush, hostility from Aboriginal groups, and devastating floods, one might assume that John Frawley and his young family had overcome the worst that life could throw at them. But just as the spectre of a sustainable existence seemed within reach, temptation led him astray. What he thought was easy money would soon drag him into the depths of despair, and setting the stage for his next downfall...

Pambula Post Office

In 1861 John Frawley added his name to a list of supporters for Robert Beck, who was at that time the incoming postmaster for Pambula.

POST MASTER GENERAL, SYDNEY
Panbula, August 19th 1861

Sir, We the undersigned inhabitants of the township of Panbula, beg to express our entire confidence in Mr. Robert Beck Senior as a fit and proper person, to discharge the duties of Post Master in this place, and also that he is perfectly solvent, having no interest in the business of his son.

We are sir, your obediant servants
Signed - John Frawley (amongst another 19 residents) [1]

No.	Prisoners' Names	Where Committed	Date	Offence	Witnesses for the Crown	Witnesses for the Prisoner	Day of Trial	Chairman	Verdict	Sentence, &c.
			1862							
31	John Frawley	Eden	17 Nov.	cattle stealing and receiving	James Manning, William Shea, John Nadin, James Atkins. Bound fr Eden 25	On bail. Sureties William Feeney, James Egan.	24th April	J Spearing Esquire Chairman of Court	Guilty of Cattle Stealing	5 years hard Labor on the Roads or other Public Works of the colony.

THE QUEEN AGAINST JAMES FRAWLEY. — In this case the prisoner was called upon to answer a charge of horse-stealing, but the chief evidence not being obtainable, an application was made by the Crown Prosecutor, and granted, for postponement till next sittings. Bail allowed as on the committal of prisoner.

John Frawley was indicted for stealing a cow and calf, the property of Mr. James Manning, of Kameruka; and perhaps no case occupied the attention of the people here more than this, from the fact of Mr. Manning being a well-known squatter in this district, and the prisoner also having lived here some time, and having become a free selector adjacent to the Wolumla station of Mr. Manning. It was given in evidence that the prosecutor, believing that the prisoner had branded the animals, the subject of the enquiry, with his own brand, JF, and having also defaced what is known as a bible brand, or that of the Twofold Bay Company, had caused the animals to be impounded, with the view of discovering the thief in the claimant. The prisoner released the cattle as his own; his attention being particularly called to those alleged to have been stolen. At one stage of the case for the Crown, the Judge asked the jury whether they would like to inspect the cattle, upon which they retired from Court, and examined the brands, which were scarcely visible. The Crown Prosecutor having gone out of Court with them and observing this difficulty, adopted a somewhat novel expedient, and in returning to Court made application to the Judge that the animals be shaved, for the purpose of clearly discerning the brands. This having been done the Twofold Bay brand was clearly perceptible, and defaced, as represented on behalf of the Crown. The Crown Prosecutor, in reply, dwelt at some length upon the prevalence of the crime of cattle stealing, and the desirability of its suppression, and concluded an eloquent address by expressing a hope that the jury would solely be influenced by the evidence on either side, and not by any previous knowledge of the parties. The jury, after a few minutes' consideration, found the prisoner guilty, and he was sentenced to five years' hard labour on the roads.

John Frawley, the son of the last prisoner, was charged with having obtained money under false pretences by reason of having fraudulently passed a spurious piece of paper purporting to be a bank note, and alleging it to be genuine. Verdict, guilty; sentence, twelve months' hard labour in Parramatta gaol.

TOP: Trial for John Frawley at Eden Court House, April 1863, with witness list: James Manning, William Shea, John Nadin, James Atkins for the Crown, and William Feeney & James Egan for the prisoner. ABOVE: Three Frawleys in the dock, with James Frawley charged with horse stealing, John Frawley being convicted of cattle stealing and imprisoned for five years, and John Frawley Jr. being convicted of fraud and imprisoned for 12 months (SMH, 29th April 1863, p.5).

Desperate Times

But not all was well within the Frawley household as various members of the family came under closer scrutiny, as events were about to play out in 1862 and 1863. At a time when the Civil War was raging in the American States, members of the Frawley family were unfortunately engaged in their own battles, and began to fall like nine pins as they were at first suspected, then gradually rounded up by the local authorities.

First to come under suspicion was John Frawley Jr (21), Letitia Frawley (14) and their mother Mary Frawley (49), who were all three charged with 'intent to defraud' on the 15th October 1862. The case concerned a promissory note and bank note to the value of just one pound. The names of the people involved were Joseph Twyford, constable; Isaac Chapple, farmer; Adam Ballantyne, constable; Margery Cameron wife of Duncan Cameron, storekeeper; Llewellyn Heaven, innkeeper; and Ely Heaven.[2]

One month later, John Frawley, then aged about 46, who since receiving his 'Certificate of Freedom' in 1840, had otherwise been a responsible and respected member of the Pambula community, was charged with cattle stealing on the 17th November 1862.[3] This was followed soonafter by his son James Frawley (aged 19) being charged with stealing a horse owned by Frank Boller at 'Tantawangalo', on the 15th December 1862.[4] James went into custody at Eden, but was released on bail:

BAIL RECEIPT
25th April 1863

James Frawley in Custody on committal to take his seat at the next Court of General Quarter Sessions of the Peace to be holden at Eden on a charge of Horse Stealing.
Admitted to Bail in the sum of £50 himself, with two sureties in twenty five pounds cash for his appearance at the sessions as above:

Stephen Collier   £25
Daniel (Purther)   £25

P.J. Murray (P.W.)
Taken and acknowledged this 25th day of April 1863.

The trials for all five members of the Frawley family came up for hearing on the same day at the Eden Court House, on Friday 24th April 1863, which was apparently followed with great interest by all the townsfolk of Pambula. In the first case, despite the mother and daughter, Mary and Letitia Frawley being discharged, John Frawley Jr. was found guilty of 'intent to defraud' and sentenced to 12 months imprisonment with hard labour at Parramatta Gaol.[5] In the next case against James Frawley, proceedings were postponed and he remained free on bail, apparently avoiding a gaol sentence due to lack of evidence.[6]

TOP: Watercolour of prisoners breaking stone at Darlinghurst Gaol about 1890, by H.L. Bertrand, 1891. ABOVE: John Frawley & John Frawley Jr. in the Darlinghurst Gaol Entrance Book - 27th April 1863.

Darlinghurst Gaol

▲Clockwise from top left: The imposing Forbes Street entrance to Darlinghurst Gaol; Henry James O'Farrell, who shot and wounded the Duke of Edinburgh at Clontarf, in Darlinghurst Gaol in 1868; Prison Staff at Darlinghurst Gaol, undated; Darlinghurst Gaol from Burton Street in 1870. ▼A lineup of inmates at Darlinghurst Gaol (c.1880).

Cockatoo Island Gaol [36]

Before the arrival of Europeans, Cockatoo Island was used by the indigenous Australians of Sydney's coastal region, but laid largely undisturbed until 1839 when Governer Gipps chose it for the site of a new penal establishment to alleviate overcrowding on Norfolk Island. Convicts were put to work initially quarrying stone for various projects around the colony. They also built stone prison barracks, a military guardhouse, granary silos, official residences and commenced work in 1847 on the Fitzroy Dock, which took ten years to complete. By 1842, the rock-cut silos on the island stored approximately 140 tonnes of grain for the colony's grain supply, all now part of the island's heritage.

Escape from Cockatoo Island was rare, not least because few prisoners could swim. Supposedly shark-infested waters around the island also tested the resolve of those bent on escape. The prisoner's accommodation was appalling. Living conditions on Cockatoo Island were barely satisfactory, even by the standards of the day. The convict-built barracks were soon overcrowded. Congestion and its attendant ills became a perennial feature of the prison and a constant spur to critics. At times, 500 convicts were crammed at night into the inadequate barracks. A police inspector once described convicts squeezed up against the bars of the prison in an attempt to breathe. With "double tiers of double sleeping berths," prisoners were crammed in "coffin-like apertures" and locked up for 12 hours at night with the stench of the "night tubs" (buckets for excrement).

The convicts themselves provided all the services required to run the penal establishment's infrastructure. In addition to labouring, quarrying and conducting various trades such as bricklaying and carpentry, convicts were gatemen, overseers, messengers, servants, gardeners, hospital attendants, cooks and constables.

In 1869 the prison was closed and the prisoners transferred to Darlinghurst Gaol, which marked the close of the island's convict period. However, the complex was soon put to another use as an industrial school for girls and reformatory. In 1888, the girls moved to Parramatta and the old penal settlement reverted to a gaol for a time to ease the crowded conditions at Darlinghurst Gaol. When the prison finally closed in 1908, it marked the end of an era.

▲ TOP: Convicts writing letters at Cockatoo Island Gaol, about 1849, by Mrs Allan MacPherson (from 'Cockatoo Island- Scenes in New South Wales' [1856-7], Mitchell Library). ABOVE: Early painting of Cockatoo Island Gaol, Sydney. ▼ The Dry Dock on Cockatoo Island, c.1872.

Parramatta Gaol [37]

The current complex, completed in 1842, was the third gaol built in Parramatta. The first was built in 1796 on the north bank of the Parramatta River, near the southern boundary of the present Prince Alfred Park. It was designed by Governor John Hunter to house robbers, and the plan, with its single cells, followed contemporary English penal concepts. It was constructed of double log and thatch, but on 28th December 1799, the flammable structure was torched by arsonists, and several of the incarcerated inmates were 'shockingly scorched'.

Work began in August 1802 on the second gaol. It was built on the original site, and was supervised by the Parramatta magistrate, Reverend Samuel Marsden. He was famously known in Sydney as 'the flogging parson'. The building was financed by a tax on spirits, which probably led to the increased use of illicit stills.

This second gaol was completed in December 1804. A linen and woollen manufactory had been included, and the Dundee weaver and political prisoner George Mealmaker, became the superintendent of both male and female convicts. Floggings took place within the gaol yard, while executions were public affairs held outside. Stocks at the entrance were used to expose minor offenders to public scorn. Separate yards were provided for male and female prisoners, but other facilities were shared. Having survived another incendiary attack in December 1807, the three-room gaol quickly became overcrowded and continued to deteriorate over the next 30 years.

After his arrival in 1831, Governor Richard Bourke appealed to the Colonial Office in London for a new gaol, and colonial architect Mortimer Lewis submitted a design for the third penitentiary in 1835. However, it was a design by the new commanding royal engineer Captain George Barney that was used by the builders James Houison and Nathaniel Payten at a new site to the north of the town. In 1842 economic depression halted construction of the gaol, however a perimeter wall, a governor's house-cum-chapel, and three of the proposed five double-storied radiating wings had been finished. Governor George Gipps proclaimed the incomplete prison open on 3 January 1842. The first gaoler was Thomas Duke Allen. He spent most of his 20 years in charge trying to requisition sufficient facilities to make the gaol habitable. His wife Martha acted as matron for the female prisoners.

From the late 1850s, with better economic times, the gaol area was doubled, workshops and a cookhouse were built, two of the original cell wings were converted to male and female hospital wings, and a new stone perimeter wall surrounded the enlarged enclosure. Between 1883 and 1889, three additional cell wings were built, largely by prison labour. One of these wings was reserved for prisoners certified insane.

By 1897, Parramatta was the second largest gaol in the colony, with 364 men and eight women inmates. Under William Frederick Neitenstein, the Comptroller General of prisons from 1896, the prison system became more efficient and economical. By June 1899, all double cells were converted to single cells, electricity was installed, the prisoners' circumambulatory walks were replaced by physical drill, and a sixth wing was completed.

TOP: John Frawley at Cockatoo Island Gaol - Return of Prisoners, 9th August, 1866. MID (Left & Right): Photographs of Parramatta Gaol. ABOVE: John Frawley - Discharge from Parramatta Gaol (NSW Police Gazette, 26 June 1867, p.203). NB: John Frawley was mistakenly recorded as arriving on the "Lord Lyndoch."

Back In Chains

However, the father John Frawley wasn't so lucky and the proceedings in his case resulted in him being found guilty of 'stealing and branding of a cow' that was owned by James Manning of the Twofold Bay Pastoral Association, from 'Kameruka Station'. John was sentenced by Judge Dowling to five years 'hard labour on the roads or other public works of the colony.'[7] Adding insult to injury, John lost another case that very same day against a Mr. Harte in the amount of £15, incredibly because his incarceration disabled his ability to appear in court as the plaintiff... how very unfair?[8]

It must have been an extraordinary sight as both John Frawley and his son John Frawley Jr. were placed in irons and led out of the prisoner dock at Eden Court House that day. From Eden the two felons were loaded aboard a coastal steamer, from whence they were transported to Sydney and initially admitted to Darlinghurst Gaol.[9] John Sr. couldn't have helped but recall his first appearance in chains in Sydney, when he was temporarily housed in Hyde Park Barracks on Macquarie Street, some 30 years previously.

Hard Labour

In 1865, being sentenced to 'hard labour' meant being forced to perform physically demanding, repetitive, and often pointless tasks in prison, usually involving machinery like treadmills, crank machines, or breaking rocks, with the primary goal of punishment through exhaustion and discomfort, often under harsh conditions with poor sanitation and limited food. Essentially, it was a brutal form of forced labour designed to deter future criminal activity.

Common jobs included 'treadmill walking' where prisoners would continuously climb a large wheel, 'picking oakum', separating strands of old rope, or breaking stones with a hammer, all requiring constant physical exertion with little productive output. Prison regimes were typically very strict, with harsh punishments for not meeting work quotas, including solitary confinement or reduced rations. Prisons at this time were typically overcrowded and unsanitary, with inadequate ventilation and poor quality food, contributing to the overall hardship of the sentence. The monotony and lack of purpose in hard labour could have a significant psychological impact on prisoners, leading to depression and feelings of hopelessness, although this experience led John Frawley to became a 'shoemaker.'

TOP (Left): John Frawley v Mr Harte in Eden Court - lost the case due to his non-appearance (SMH, 29th April 1863, p.5). (Right): John Frawleys - also lost his 40 acre Conditional Purchase in the Eden District due to his inability to improve the property while incarcerated (NSW Govt Gazette, 10 Oct 1865, p.2245). ABOVE: John Frawley - Released from H.M. Goal Parramatta (NSW Police Gazette, 12 June 1867).

TOP: Upon his release, returning to the pristine landscape of Twofold Bay and Pambula, would have been of great consolation for John Frawley. MID (Left): John Frawley - Witness in a Perjury Trial (Sydney Mail, 6th March 1869, p.14). (Right): John Frawley contributed to the Irish Prisoner Relief Fund in August 1869 (Freeman's Journal, 7th Aug 1869, p.10). ABOVE: John Frawley - Timber License (NSW Govt Gazette, 11 Jan 1870, p.29).

After serving his time, John Frawley Jr. was released from Parramatta Gaol in April of 1864.[10] But in that very same month his younger brother Stephen Frawley aged 20, was charged with stealing a horse, the property of John Carpenter, although luckily, this case seems not to have been pursued.[11] On the 1st of May 1865, the Frauley [sic. Frawley] name again came up in the District Court at Pambula. Firstly as a defendent against a Mr. Wheeler for a breach of contract, and again on the same day as a defendant against Mr. Page, the storekeeper at Merimbula, for the balance of a store account. Unfortunately, both cases were lost and had to be paid, presumably with costs.

PANBULA COURT OF REQUESTS
Monday May 1st, 1865
Wheeler v Frauley for £5 breach of contract. Verdict for plaintiff.
Page v Frauley for £4,13,7 - 1/2 store account. Verdict for plaintiff.

Bega Gazette, 6th May 1865 [12]

But that wasn't the end of it as two more Frawley boys, Stephen again and Patrick were charged in September of 1866, the latter being brought up on trial and convicted of 'horse stealing' on the 31st January 1867. Patrick Frawley was sentenced by Judge Heffernan to 'five years on the roads',[13] and sent initially to Darlinghurst Gaol, but he was transferred in June 1867 to Parramatta Gaol.[14]

Patrick may have even crossed paths with his father as by that time, John Frawley had been transferred from Cockatoo Island as an 'invalid' to Parramatta Gaol on the 9th August 1866.[15] Likely due to his invalidity and good behaviour, John Frawley was released from Parramatta during the month of June 1867, having served four years and three months of his five year term.[16,17] He had been initially sent to Darlinghurst Gaol in 1863, then transferred to Parramatta Gaol, but it seems the majority of his incarceration was spent at Cockatoo Island Gaol, in Sydney Harbour, where he was described as a 'shoemaker' of 'good' character.[18]

Exhibit 'A" - the forged petition for Post Master produced by John Frawley in mid-January 1870.

TOP: John Frawley - On Bail to appear when called upon (NSW, Criminal Court Records, 1830-1945). ABOVE: John Frawley - discharged from remand & bailed (The Monaro Mercury & Cooma and Bombala Advertiser, 26th March 1870, p.8).

John Frawley then boarded a coastal steamer for the trip down the coast back to Eden, before travelling overland to be reunified with his family at Pambula. But the law wasn't finished with the Frawley's just yet as John Frawley Jr. and his brother-in-law Robert Little, were fined £10 each for 'illegally riding horses'. Despite being a minor crime, neither of them could afford the fine, and had no option other than to accept imprisonment with hard labour, for three months at Darlinghurst Gaol.[19]

Incredibly, the only members of the entire Frawley family, not to have been charged with an offense (that we know of), was the eldest daughter Ellen, who by the mid 1860s had gravitated to Sydney and the youngest brother Thomas.

Rejoining the Pambula Community

Despite his ordeal, but having rejoined his neighbourhood, John Frawley's community-minded spirit came to the fore once again in late 1867 as he signed his name to a petition requesting that the local Post Office be moved into the main township of Pambula.

> To The Honorable
> The Post Master General, Sydney
> Received 23rd December 1867
>
> Sir, we the undersigned residents in and about Panbula, beg to bring under your notice, the great inconvenience arising from the Post office not being in Panbula, it being at present one mile distant from the Township and across a creek which some months in the year is unfordable, and the bulk of the inhabitants numbering about two hundred, also the Court House, Police Offices, Churches etc. are in the Township, there only being a few straggling houses, numbering between forty and fifty inhabitants near the present P.O.
>
> We also beg to bring under your notice that the former Post Master, Mr. Robert Beck, lived in the Township and on his leaving Panbula, there was no other eligible person living in Panbula at the time to keep it. Since then there are additions to our population, one of whom is a Mr. George King, a storekeeper, who we would beg to recommend to your favourable considerations, as a fit and proper person to keep the Post Office in Panbula. We also beg to say that the above arrangements will not interfere with the duties of the Mail Carrier. Trustful this our humble petition will meet with your approval and we beg to ascribe ourselves.
>
> Yours Gladly
> John Frawley (Settler), Panbula (amongst 44 other petitioners)[20]

A follow up letter was written by the Panbula residents on the 27th February 1868 again urging the Post Master General in Sydney to re-locate the Pambula Post Office to the main township as a matter of urgency. They also recommended Mr. Charles H. Baddeley Esq. J.P., as being available to take charge. A further 43 residents signed their names to this second petition with John Frawley amongst them.

John Frawley - Charged With Forging Signatures To A Petition

CASE OF FORGING SIGNATURES TO A PETITION.—On the 25th ultimo this singular case was proceeded with by the Panbula Bench, the prisoner, John Frawley, was brought up on remand, charged with forging signatures to a petition praying for the appointment of a postmaster at Panbula, when the following evidence was taken (as reported in the *Bega Gazette*):— J. H. Bennett sworn: Deposed to having on Monday, the 17th January, received the document marked A from the General Post Office, Sydney, to report upon; knows prisoner; showed him the document on the 18th, when he stated that the petition was not for taking the post-office away from him (witness) but to get an additional one in Panbula; witness is well acquainted with all the signatures attached to the document, and has no hesitation in saying that they are all forgeries, except the third one which is John Frawley, senior; with that exception, there is not one written by the person whose name is mentioned; I know the handwriting of John Frawley, and have no hesitation in saying that the petition and twenty-four names attached to it are all in Frawley's handwriting; I consider prisoner to be a most improper person to be appointed postmaster; I have known him about fifteen years; about two years since he returned from serving a sentence of five years at Parramatta gaol for felony; he has since then been in goal here once or twice; his general character is bad, and he is a man that no person could place any confidence in. John Woods sworn: I am a shoemaker and reside at Panbula; I know prisoner; I never saw the paper marked A before this morning; I see the name of John Woods in the list; I did not write it; I knew nothing about the petition recommending Frawley as a postmaster. I was asked a month ago to sign a petition for a post-office at Panbula; but I never signed it or saw it. John Cusack, sworn, states: I am a labourer and live at Boggy Creek; I know the prisoner; I know nothing of the paper marked A; I never saw it before; I never wrote the words "John Cusack" in the list; and did not authorise anybody else to do it for me; I cannot write myself; I have known prisoner about twenty years; I think him to be a very honest man; he was in Parramatta gaol four or five years, once for cattle stealing; but I think it was a mistake; he might have been innocent; he has been in gaol here two or three times this last twelve months; I do not know what for; I only remember once for an assault, and the next time for brutally treating his wife; my memory is very bad; I think he would make a good postmaster; I think none the worse of him having served a sentence for felony; he might have been innocent. James Lovell, sworn, states: I am a blacksmith and live at Panbula; I know the prisoner; I have seen the document marked A; I see the name "James Lovell" written among a list of names; I never wrote it; I did not authorise any one else to do so; I would have signed it if he had asked me to do so as I think prisoner is a very good man for a postmaster; I have only known him about six years; I know he served a sentence of five years or about for cattle stealing in Parramatta gaol within the six years; and I know he has been in gaol once or twice since he came home from Parramatta; once for assaulting John Egan, and again for hammering his wife; I think both times within the last twelve months. Committed for trial at Bega on the 7th March; bail allowed, self £300, two sureties £150 each.

CURIOUS CHARGE OF FORGERY.—At the Panbula Police Court, on the 21st ultimo, a man named John Frawley, was charged with having written a letter to the Postmaster-General, applying for the situation of Postmaster at Panbula, purporting to be a petition from the residents of Panbula, in which he describes himself as a person of good character, and every way calculated to fill the office: such petition having appended thereto twenty-four names purporting to be the signatures of twenty-four residents, the whole of which were forgeries. The evidence of two witnesses was taken, who deposed that the signatures attached to the petition as theirs were forged; the defendant was then remanded.

John Frawley, sen., charged on warrant with forging signatures to a petition to the Honorable the Postmaster General, with a view to obtain the appointment of Postmaster at Panbula, has been arrested by Senior-constable M'Kee and Constable Woods, Panbula Police. Committed for trial at the next Quarter Sessions to be holden at Bega. Bail allowed, self in £300, and two sureties £150 each.

BEGA.

We extract the following items from the *Bega Gazette* of Thursday:—

FORGERY.—At the Panbula Police Court on the 2nd instant:—John Frawley, senior, was charged with forgery. Senior-constable McKee, sworn, states: I received the document branded C from the postmaster at Yowaka; it is a letter addressed to Daniel Egan, Esq., Postmaster-General, of Sydney, and dated from Eden; it is signed P. Slattery, recommending John Frawley, senior, as a fit person to be appointed postmaster at Panbula, and requesting that a good salary may be appropriated for his benefit; from my knowledge of prisoner's handwriting, and by comparison with other letters and documents I now produce and written by him, I have no doubt but prisoner wrote the letter signed P. Slattery, marked "C." John Henry Bennett, sworn: I am postmaster at Yowaka; on or about the 8th January last I received some papers from the General Post Office, Sydney; among others the letter marked "C," being a letter dated from Eden, purporting to be signed by P. Slattery; it is a recommendation of John Frawley, senior, to the office of postmaster of Panbula, and requesting a good salary may be allowed him as such; from my knowledge of Frawley's handwriting I have no hesitation in saying that the letter marked C was written by him; I have compared it with other letters and writings of his, and am certain of it; I know prisoner to have served a sentence of five years in Paramatta Gaol for felony, and I believe he has been twice in gaol at Panbula since his return from Parramatta. Patrick Slattery, sworn, states: I am a Catholic clergyman and reside at Eden; there is no other person living in or near Eden of the same name; I know the prisoner; the document marked C now handed to me I never saw before; I see the signature P. Slattery to it; it is not my handwriting; I never signed the letter, nor did I authorise prisoner or any body else to sign it for me; I know nothing whatever about the document; if I had been asked to do so, I certainly would not have recommended the prisoner for such a situation, unless after mature deliberation, a more fitting person was not to be found; I believe from letters that I have received from prisoner that the letter marked C was written by him. Committed for trial at Bega on the 7th March; bail allowed, self in £80, two sureties £40 each.

FORGERY.

John Frawley was charged with having forged the signatures of several residents to a document purporting to be a petition to the Postmaster-General, recommending the prisoner as a proper person for the appointment of postmaster at Panbula.

The details of the case have already been published in these columns.

Prisoner pleaded not guilty, and was defended by Mr. James.

The jury gave a verdict of not guilty, and the prisoner was discharged.

LEFT COLUMN: 1-John Frawley - Forgery allegation by John Henry Bennett (*Freeman's Journal*, Sat 12th Feb 1870, p.10). **RIGHT COLUMN**: 1-John Frawley - Placed on remand in Forgery Case (*SMH*, 5th Feb 1870, p.6); 2-John Frawley - Charged with Forgery (*NSW Police Gazette*, 9 Feb 1870, p49); 3-John Frawley - Charged with Forgery (*The Monaro Mercury, & Cooma and Bombala Advertiser*, Sat 19 Feb 1870, p.5); 4-John Frawley - Not Guilty of Forgery (*The Monaro Mercury & Cooma and Bombala Advertiser*, 26th March, p.8).

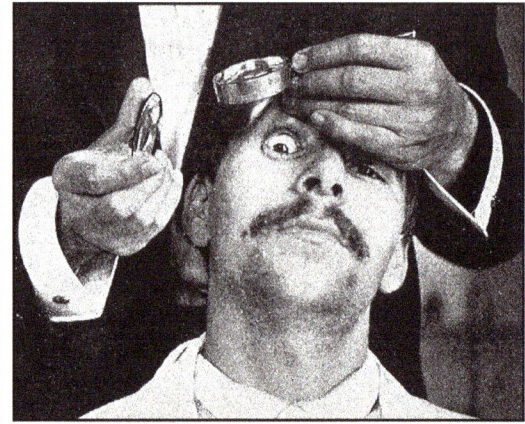

LEFT (Top): A John Frawley - curing eyesight (The Gundagai & Tumut, Adelong & Murrumbidgee District Advertiser, 8th March 1873, p.2). (Above): John Frawley - mentioned in the 'Foundation of Bega' (The Bega Standard & Candelo, Merimbula, Pambula, Eden, Wolumla and General Advertiser (11th November 1876, p.2). RIGHT: A John Frawley advertised occular treatments (The Gundagai & Tumut, Adelong & Murrumbidgee District Advertiser, 3rd August 1872, p.2).

Next, John Frawley was twice imprisoned locally in 1869, probably in Pambula or Eden, first for an assault against John Egan, and secondly for "brutally hammering" his wife, although his prison stays this time around, were just a day or two.

John Frawley most likely returned to work as a labourer, but by 1869 was back in court as a witness in a perjury trial, an outcome of which may have given him an idea for the future.[21] John Frawley also contributed funds to the 'Irish State Prisoners' (Fenians) upon their release in July 1869,[22] and in searching for work wherever he could get it, he applied for a 'Timber License', which was approved in early January of 1870.[23]

In Trouble Again

With monotonous consistency, John Frawley once again fell into trouble with the authorities when he was this time, charged with forgery. The case was in relation to the collection of a petition at Pambula, involving Father P. Slattery, the Catholic priest at that time. If proven, a conviction would confirm John Frawley's guilt in signing the parish priests name, and the names of others to a petition nominating himself for postmaster!

He was remanded by the magistrate, but permitted to post bail in the substantial amount of £300 by himself, or with two sureties of £150 each, and was committed for trial at the next Quarter Sessions to be held at Bega. The correspondence is set out below:

Informing that petition forwarded to him for report is a forgery naming
Jn. Frawley Sr. for Postmaster
Stamped Feb 3rd 1870, P.O. at Panbula

Sir, I beg to acknowledge receipt of a petition signed by residents of Panbula – also a letter signed 'P.Slattery'. I suspected the whole to be a forgery and handed the papers over to the Police, which resulted in Frawley being committed to take his trial for forgery.
I remain your most obt. serv.
J.H. Bennett, P.M., Panbula

POST OFFICE RECEIPT
To the Postmaster at Panbula

The Registered Paper No. 521 relative to having the P.O. at Panbula & naming J. Frawley for P.M. sent to you on the 14th January last has not been returned to this office – I request you will send it back without delay.
S.H. Lambton, Secretary, General Post Office [24]

Police Panbula 11th August, 1870
Memo, The document referred to is in hands of Crown Law Officers for purpose of Prosecuters,
David McKee, The Postmaster Yowaka – Panbula [25]

This issue might seem petty to most, but in fact the charge was a blatant case of forgery (although non-fiscal), in which John Frawley was most fortunate to be found not guilty by the jury and discharged at the Bega Quarter Sessions on the 8th March 1870.[26] In June

1870, John Frawley was back in court, this time as a 'key witness' at the Supreme Court in Sydney over an action for 'slander' between Charles H. Baddeley and John H. Bennett, both residents of Pambula and magistrates of the Monaro District.[27]

By the late-1860's the Frawley children were mostly young adults and the two daughters Ellen and Letitia had by this time, moved to Sydney, where on the 3rd of August 1869, aged 27, Ellen married James Mahony O'Sullivan at St. Mary's Cathedral in Sydney, according to the rights of the Roman Catholic Church.[28] No wedding can be found for Letitia, but she produced two children in quick succession named Patrick who died, and Charlotte E. Frawley,[29,30] although no further information can be found for the latter.

Map of the South Coast of NSW

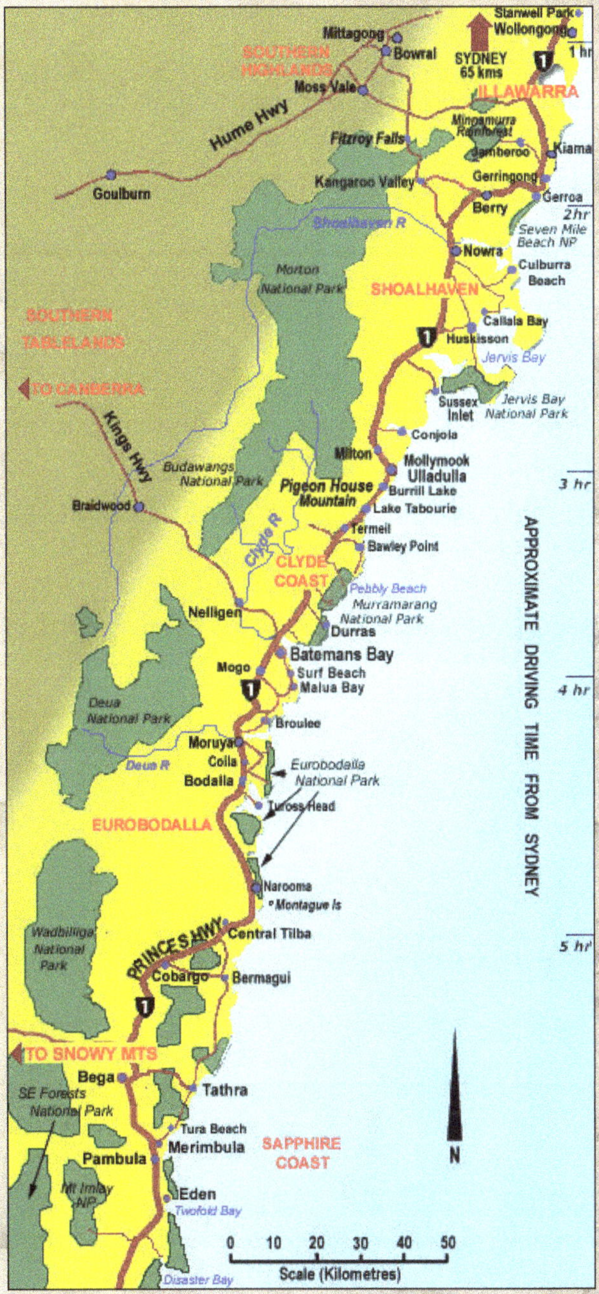

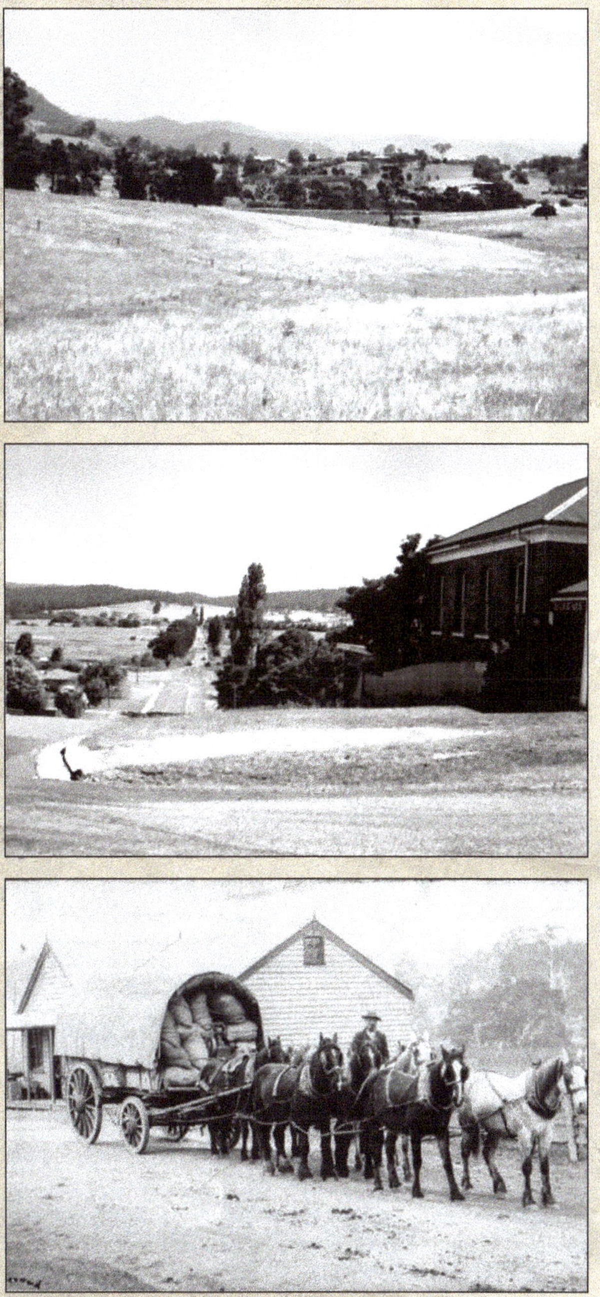

LEFT: M17. Road map of the South Coast of NSW, showing the massive amount of development since 1840, when there had only been a few settled places. RIGHT (Top): John Frawley Jr. owned land at Wolumla. (Mid): The view from Pambula looking south over Pambula Flat. (Above): Horses were a valuable commodity to the squatters and settlers.

In October 1871 four letters for John Frawley of Pambula, were returned from the country to the Sydney GPO.[31] Then in 1872, John Frawley sold his vacant land on the corner of Toalla and Quondola Streets in Pambula to a Mr. John Behl, who had previously accused Frawley of forgery, and who soon built a two storey building on the site, which became known as the iconic 'Toad Hall'. This building is now a craft shop and residence. The land can be found at the roundabout, opposite the Commercial Hotel, which was also owned by John Behl.

> "John Frawley (settler) and called "the elder" was granted land on September 10th 1856 and later sold it to John Behl (innkeeper) in 1872 for ten pounds."
>
> Bernie Cornell

By August 1872 and into 1873, a John Frawley was reported as healing occular defects in Tumut. The town was 313km away from Pambula, which likely seems implausible without other verification to substantiate if this was the same John Frawley.[32] Two years later, both John Frawley now aged 60, and John Frawley Jr. aged 34, were listed on the rolls of the Eden Electoral District for 1875. John Frawley Jr. was also listed in the Post Office Directory as residing at 'Three-Mile Water Hole' near Wolumla from 1875 to 1877.[33]

1875 EDEN DISTRICT ELECTORAL ROLL

Eden - #274, John Frawley (Panbula/Res.)
Bega - #283, John Frawley (Wolumla/Res.)

Despite their frequent run-ins with the law, the Frawley family have nevertheless been recognised as amongst the earliest of pioneers not only of Pambula, but also of Bega.[34]

John Frawley's second incarceration, this time for rebranding and cattle stealing, saw him endure harsh sentences in Darlinghurst, Cockatoo Island, and Parramatta Gaols. Meanwhile, his family's petty crimes, like obtaining money under false pretenses, only reinforced their reputation as troublemakers. When John and his sons eventually returned to Pambula, they tried to rebuild their lives, but the community was unwilling to forget. The Frawleys were ostracised, their presence a lingering reminder of a past that respectable settlers wanted to leave behind.

ABOVE (Left): Renovated cottage in Quondola St, Pambula. (Right): Mural of the town of Pambula, in Quondola St, Pambula.
TOP: The actual signature of John Frawley (Jan, 1870).

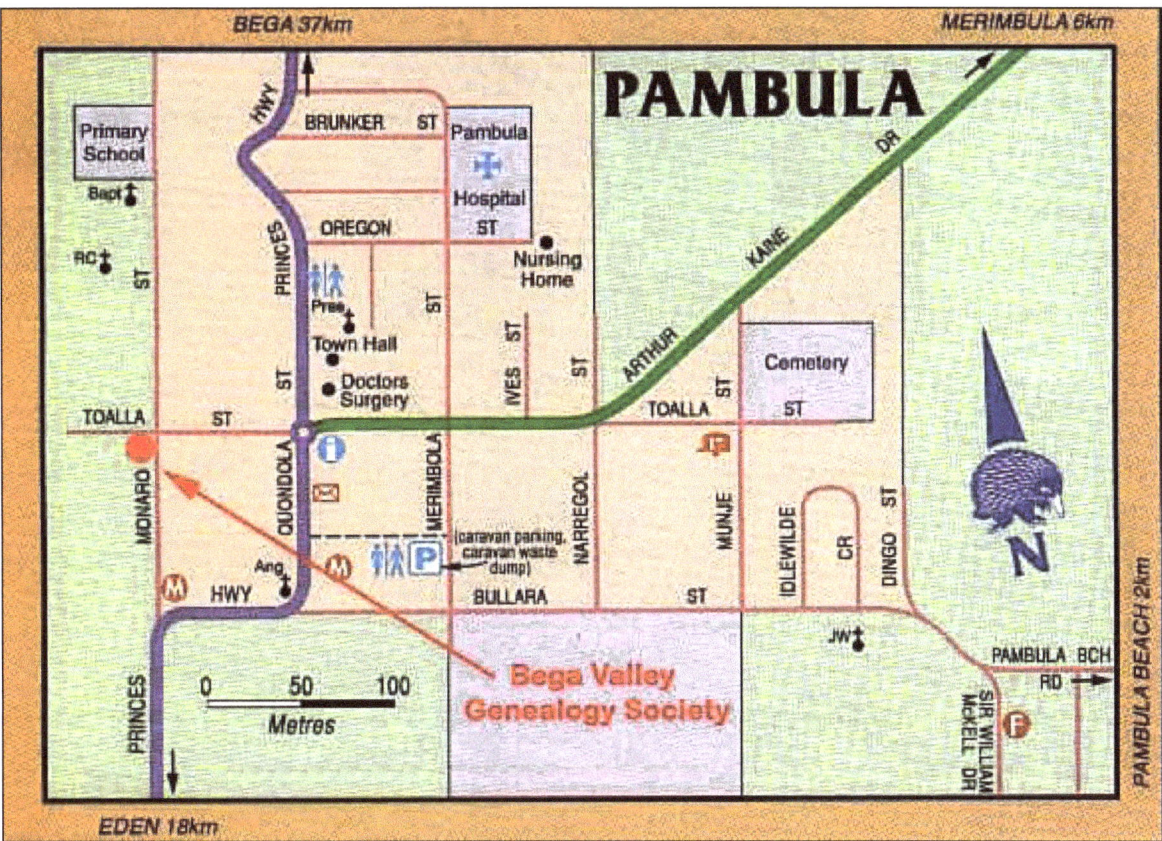

M18. Map of the town of Pambula, showing the location of Bega Valley Genealogy Society.

Like all emancipists, the Frawleys struggled to overcome the convict stain, a burden made heavier by their Irish heritage in a colony still dominated by the English. Though religious freedom was technically upheld, Catholics remained objects of suspicion and scorn, and the Frawleys' long history of legal troubles only cemented their low standing. In Pambula, they were fighting a losing battle.

The need for a fresh start was undeniable, and all it took was a small push. That nudge came from their son, James Frawley. After more than three decades of hard work, amongst neighbours who never fully accepted them, the family saw an opportunity. With little more than determination, they sold up what meagre possessions they had and set their sights on a new home, a place where their past could not follow.

References

1. John Frawley, on the petition list for a postmaster at Panbula (Twofold Bay & Maneroo Telegraph, 19th August 1861).
2. NSW Criminal Court Records. (1862). Letitia, Mary & John Frawley Jr., in Register of Criminal Cases Tried at Eden, NSW 1862-1869.
3. Ibid.
4. NSW Criminal Court Records. (1862). James Frawley in Register of Criminal Cases Tried at Eden, NSW 1862-1869.
5. NSW Criminal Court Records. (1862). Letitia, Mary & John Frawley Jr, op.cit.
6. NSW Criminal Court Records. (1862). James Frawley, op. cit.
7. John Frawley Sr. - convicted of cattle stealing and sent to prison for five years 'hard labour' (SMH, 29th Apr 1863, p.5).
8. John Frawley Sr. - plaintiff v Harte at Eden Court (Sydney Morning Herald, 29th April 1863, p.5).
9. NSW State Archives & Records. (1863). John Frawley Sr. & John Frawley Jr. in the Darlinghurst Gaol Entrance Book, 27th April 1863.
10. John Frawley Jr. - released from Parramatta Gaol (NSW Police Gazette, April 1864).
11. Stephen Frawley - charged with Horse Stealing (NSW Police Gazette, April 1864).
12. Frauley [sic] in Pambula Court of Requests (Bega Gazette, 6th May 1865).
13. NSW State Archives & Records. (1867). Patrick Frawley, in Return of Prisoners Tried At Eden (Different Circuit Courts & Quarter Sessions, January 1867).
14. NSW State Archives & Records. (1867). Patrick Frawley, in Admission Book, Parramatta Gaol, NSW Gaol Description & Entrance Books, Parramatta, 1863-1873.
15. NSW State Archives & Records. (1866). John Frawley Sr., in Return of Prisoners, Cockatoo Island Prison, 9th August 1866.
16. John Frawley, Released from H.M. Goal Parramatta, NSW Police Gazette & Weekly Record of Crime, 12 June 1867, p.191.

17. Ibid.
18. NSW State Archives & Records. (1866). John Frawley Sr.,op.cit.
19. John Frawley Jr & Robert Little (brother-in-law), Imprisoned for Three Months in Darlinghurst Gaol, NSW Police Gazette & Weekly Record of Crime, 9 Oct 1867, p.297.
20. John Frawley Sr., in Post Office petition (Twofold Bay & Maneroo Telegraph, 23rd December 1867).
21. John Frawley - witness in Perjury Trial (Sydney Mail, 6th March 1869, p.14).
22. John Frawley - donations to the Irish Prisoner Relief Fund (Freeman's Journal, 7th Aug 1869, p.10).
23. John Frawley,- Timber License (NSW Govt Gazette, 11 Jan 1870, p.29).
24. Lambton, S.H., Secretary, General Post Office, Sydney, 29th July,1870.
25. McKee, David. (1870). [Regisse] & 'Frawley Forgery,' The Post Master Yowaka, Panbula, 11th August 1870.
26. John Frawley - charged with 'Forging & Uttering' (NSW Returns of Criminal Cases Heard at Bega Quarter Sessions, 1870).
27. John Frawley Sr. - witness in a Slander Trial at the Supreme Court of NSW (Sydney Morning Herald, 1 June 1870, p.2).
28. NSW Dept. of BDM. (1869). Marriage Certificate for Ellen Frawley & James Mahony O'Sullivan, 3rd August 1869 at Sydney, #757/1869.
29. NSW Dept. of BDM.(1869). Death Certificate for Patrick Frawley, #5776/1868.
30. NSW Dept. of BDM.(1869). Birth Certificate for Charlotte E. Frawley, #2676/1869.
31. John Frawley - Pambula - 'List of Letters Returned From The Country, and Now Lying At The GPO, Sydney (NSW Govt Gazette, 3rd October 1871).
32. John Frawley - providing occular treatments (The Gundagai & Tumut, Adelong & Murrumbidgee District Advertiser, 3rd August 1872, p.2).
33. John Frawley Jr,. - resident at Three Mile Water Hole, nr. Wolumla, Post Office Directory, 1875-77.
34. John Frawley - the Foundation of Bega (The Bega Standard & Candelo, Merimbula, Pambula, Eden, Wolumla and General Advertiser, 11 Nov 1876, p.2).
35. Wikipedia - Darlinghurst Gaol [https://en.wikipedia.org/wiki/Darlinghurst_Gaol].
36. Wikipedia - Cockatoo Island Gaol [https://en.wikipedia.org/wiki/Cockatoo_Island_(New_South_Wales)]. Retrieved 12th June 2021.
37. Wikipedia - Parramatta Correctional Centre. [https://en.wikipedia.org/wiki/Parramatta_Correctional_Centre]. Retrieved 12th June 2021.

Chapter Sixteen

FINAL DAYS IN QUEENSLAND

A new beginning was not just a desire, it was a necessity. All the Frawleys needed was a spark to set their plans in motion, and that spark came from their son, James Frawley. After more than thirty years of toil in a place where they were always outsiders, the family finally saw a way forward. With little more than sheer grit, they gathered what they could, left the rest behind, and set out in search of a place where their history wouldn't cast a shadow over their future.

It was around the year 1876 that the entire Frawley family moved themselves and their possessions from Pambula to Toowoomba in Queensland, a rapidly advancing new community 150km inland from Brisbane. In the years ahead they would move around southeast Queensland, chasing opportunities wherever they could find them. But their journey would be anything but easy, hardship seemed to follow them, testing their resilience at every turn.

The History of Toowoomba

Toowoomba's history can be traced back to 1816 when English botanist and explorer Allan Cunningham, arrived in Australia from Brazil where he had been collecting botanical specimens for Sir Joseph Banks. In June 1827, Cunningham was rewarded for his many

To build up the town and attract more people to the area, 'The Swamp' was drained to become the foundation for the establishment of Toowoomba.

explorations when he discovered four million acres (16,000 km²) of rich farming and grazing land bordered on the east by the Great Dividing Range and situated 100 miles (160 km) west of the settlement of Moreton Bay, which later became Brisbane. Cunningham named his find the 'Darling Downs' after Ralph Darling (later Sir Ralph), who was then governor of New South Wales.[1]

However, it was not until 13 years later when George and Patrick Leslie established 'Toolburra Station' some 56 miles (90km) south-west of Toowoomba that the first settlers began arriving on the Downs. Other settlers quickly followed and a few tradesmen and businessmen also settled and established a township of bark-slab shops called 'The Springs', which was soon renamed Drayton.

Towards the end of the 1840s Drayton had grown to the point where it had its own newspaper shop, general store, trading post and the Royal Bull's Head Inn, which was built by William Horton (<1817-1864) and still stands today. Although he was not the first man to live there, Horton is regarded as the real founder of Toowoomba. Early in 1849 Horton sent two of his men, William Gurney and William Shuttlewood, to cut away reeds in a marshy swampland area a few miles away that nobody from Drayton ever visited. When Gurney and Shuttlewood arrived they were surprised to find a pitched tent among the reeds. The tent's owner was bush worker Josiah Dent who was the first man to live in 'The Swamp'. This extraordinary news was the main talking point in Drayton for weeks and people became interested in developing the swamp as useful farming land.[2,3]

Plans were drawn up for 12 to 20 acre (49,000 to 81,000m²) farms, which in the hope of building up the town and attracting more people to the area, which was later drained to become the foundation for the establishment of Toowoomba. Two years later people began purchasing the land and the new farm holdings attracted buyers from Drayton. The

16 - Final Days In Queensland

M19. Squatting map of the Darling Downs District, Queensland showing the proposed line of pre-emptive purchases, townships, reserves, roads and approximate boundaries of runs, with head stations (Compiled and published by J.W. Buxton, 1864).

year 1851 saw the establishment of a National School at Drayton, which later became Drayton State School. On the 29th August 1852 the town's only churchman, the Rev. Benjamin Glennie who had lived in Drayton since 1848, christened two children at 'Alford'. It was the first Church of England service held in Toowoomba and the first day the word 'Toowoomba' was written on a public document. How the name Toowoomba was derived is still a point of debate with several theories, including:[4]

- that it was derived from the Aboriginal word for swamp which is 'tawampa' as the Aborigines had no "s" in their vocabulary.
- that the aboriginal interpretation for reeds in the swamp 'woomba woomba' was used as the original source.
- that the word Toowoomba was taken from the aboriginal term for a native melon 'toowoom or choowoom' which grew plentifully in the township.

Toowoomba - Railway Hub

TOP: The railroad station at Toowoomba opened in 1872. MID (Left): Train descending the main lione from Toowoomba about 1880. (Right): Locomotive A14-No.281 in the train sheds at Ipswich, about 1890. ABOVE (Left): Spring Bluff Station, located on the main line between Ipswich and Toowoomba, c.1891. (Right): Two storey railway station building at Toowoomba, c.1872, by Frisco Photo Company (John Oxley Library, State Library of Queensland).

Toowoomba [26]

Toowoomba's colonial history dates back to 1816 when English botanist and explorer Allan Cunningham arrived in Australia from Brazil. In June 1827, he discovered the vast, fertile plains of the Darling Downs, an area spanning 4 million acres (16,000 km²), bordered by the Great Dividing Range to the east and located about 100 miles (160 km) west of Moreton Bay.

European settlement in the region began in 1840 when brothers George and Patrick Leslie established 'Toolburra Station', 56 miles (90 km) southwest of present-day Toowoomba. Soon after, a small township emerged, initially called The Springs before being renamed Drayton. Land surveys for the town took place in 1849 and again in 1853. By the late 1840s, Drayton had developed into a thriving settlement with a newspaper, a general store, a trading post, and the Royal Bull's Head Inn, built by William Horton. While Horton wasn't the area's first settler, his contributions were instrumental in shaping the town's growth, earning him recognition as the true founder of Toowoomba.

Word of Toowoomba's expansion spread quickly among drovers and wagon masters, drawing more settlers to the area. By 1858, the town had a population of 700, three hotels, and several stores. Land values surged from £4 per acre (£988/km²) in 1850 to £150 per acre (£37,000/km²) within just a few years. In response to this rapid growth, Governor Sir George Bowen (1821–1899), the first of Queensland's governors, officially declared Toowoomba a municipality on 24 November 1860. The town's first council election followed on 4 January 1861, with William Henry Groom elected as its first mayor.

The arrival of the railway from Ipswich in 1867 further fueled economic and commercial development. By 1892, Toowoomba and its surrounding districts were officially recognized as a township, and in 1904, it was declared a city. Over time, pastoralism overtook agriculture and dairying as the dominant industry, shaping Toowoomba into the prosperous community it remains today.

The 'Shell Series' of postcards were released from 1905 until 1915, and were beautifully coloured cards produced from photos taken all around Queensland, Australia. They were a high quality postcard and very popular at the time. TOP (Left): Postcard of Herries Street, Toowoomba. (Right): Postcard of Russell Street, Toowoomba. ABOVE (Left): Postcard of Ruthven Street, Toowoomba. (Right): Postcard of Ruthven Street at Show time, Toowoomba.

Drovers and wagon masters gradually spread the news of the new settlement at Toowoomba and by 1858 the town was growing rapidly with three hotels, a number of stores, and a population of 700. Land selling at £4 an acre (£988/km²) in 1850, was now £150 an acre (£37,000/km²).

On the 30th June 1860 a petition of 100 names was sent to the governor requesting that Toowoomba be declared a municipality. Governor Sir George Ferguson Bowen (1821-1899) granted their wish and a new municipality was proclaimed on the 24th November 1860. The first town council election took place on the 4th January 1861 and William Henry Groom (1833-1901), who had led the townspeople in their petition for recognition, polled the most votes. On the 12th August 1862, Alderman Groom was elected to State Parliament as the member for Drayton and Toowoomba. Telegraphic communication was also opened between Toowoomba and Brisbane in August 1862, and Toowoomba Gaol had

Toowoomba Township

TOP: (Left): Carlton House, Toowoomba (Right): A residence in Herries Street Toowoomba about 1880. MID (Left): St. James Church of England opened for services in December 1869. The towns foundation stone was laid by Governor Samuel Blackall on 1 May 1869 (John Oxley Library, State Library of QLD). (Right): The 'Harp of Erin Hotel' in Toowoomba (Local History Library). ABOVE: Ruthven Street, Toowoomba about 1881.

opened by 1864, which later became a woman's reformatory and laundry (1883-4), before closing in 1900. The first State School in the town was Toowoomba South State School, which opened in 1865. By April of 1867 a railway line had been built and Toowoomba's rail link with Ipswich and Brisbane was opened.

In 1870 Alderman Spiro replaced William Henry Groom as Mayor. By 1873 Council was granted control of the swamp area and offered a prize of £100 for the best method of draining it. The Toowoomba Gas and Coke Company was floated in 1875 and the Council pledged to erect street lamps to assist with the establishment of the fledgling company. Due to its financial situation Council leased part of the swamp to town brickmakers and also approved construction of the Toowoomba Grammar School, with the school's foundation stone also being laid that year.[5]

First founded as a village in 1849, Toowoomba officially became a town in 1858, a municipality in 1860, and was declared a city in 1904. Situated in southeastern Queensland, on the Great Dividing Range, the town quickly became the principal inland city in the state. Its role as a rail and road junction, a tourist resort, a service centre for the large livestock, grain and dairying businesses in the Darling Downs, and a site of the Perseverence Creek Water Supply Scheme, ensured its future. The city was well planned with many parks and has become an educational centre. The city's industries today include engineering works, railroad shops, and food processing. On the 10th January 2011, severe flash flooding caused by heavy rains engulfed Toowoomba, devastating the city and leaving dozens dead or missing.[6]

The Frawleys Move To Toowoomba

Following his being charged and imprisoned for horse stealing in 1863, John and Mary Ann's son James Frawley, must have thought it best to remove himself from Pambula and district. He likely investigated several potential options, but by 1863 he found himself in

TOP: Farms around the Toowoomba vicinity in 1884. TOP: An early photograph of a very rough Ruthven Street, Toowoomba about 1870.

The 19th century iron paddlesteamer "City of Brisbane", launched in Glasgow in October 1863, could very likely have been the ship taken by the Frawley's from Sydney to Brisbane, during their relocation to Toowoomba in 1876.

the developing township of Toowoomba on the Darling Downs in Queensland, where he was successful in winning a tender for the 'construction of a foot bridge' in November 1863.[7] By 1873 James had gained a firm foothold in the growing district and going from strength to strength, he had secured 120 acres of Crown Land at Meringandan.[8]

Besides riding on the good fortune of their son James Frawley, who was gaining an

Scenic views out over the surrounding farmlands contribute to the setting of Meringandan, QLD.

Early photograph of Russell Street, Toowoomba about 1875.

influential footing in the Darling Downs, the Frawley family's relocation to Toowoomba likely came about from a combination of factors. John Frawley's legal problems had weighed heavily upon him, possible ostracising of the family by Pambula residents, and rumour mongering within a small rural community would all have contributed to their decision to move on.

The Benevolent Asylum, Dunwich, North Stradbroke Island [27]

The Dunwich Asylum admitted 21,000 people over its 80 years of operation. From the 1890s to 1946 there were around 1,000 inmates present at any one time with 1,600 in its peak year of 1903. The Asylum had over twenty wards including a distinct women's section and a separate ward for 'Asiatics'. By the 1930s, it included a police station and lock up, visitor centre, public hall, bakery, kitchen, laundry and ancillary service buildings, ward buildings, tent accommodation and recreational facilities. It was only electrified in 1926 with its own power station using oil generators. It also had its own dairy herd and piggery.

Inmates were predominately old, though not exclusively. People could be assigned to the asylum by a hospital, by police order or by their families. It seems that many of the inebriate men were confined by their spouses. Inmates came from across Queensland with a very detailed process of getting them by boat and/or rail from the north and the west to the Yungaba Immigration Depot at Kangaroo Point, and then by boat to Dunwich.

Six times as many men as women were inmates. The backgrounds were mainly rural and urban workers with, in the nineteenth century, a considerable number of people who had been transported to the Australian colonies as convicts. There was however, a sprinkling of middle class people fallen on hard times or drink. One was John Filhelly, Deputy Leader of the ALP under Theodore and one of the founders of the Queensland Rugby League who is listed in the Australian Dictionary of Biography. Another was Johnny Cassim, who was of Indian origin and transported as a convict from Mauritius to become a hotelier and respected citizen of Cleveland.

The Asylum was always inadequately staffed and funded. In current (2013) values Queensland Government funding was $1,900 per person/per year in 1900 and $2,900 in 1932. In the twentieth century, inmates who received a Commonwealth old age pension paid part of this to the Asylum. The operating principle was that able-bodied inmates were meant to perform work and staff the Asylum. Unfortunately, apart from some of the inebriates, age prevented most inmates doing a full day's labour. In addition, as the Brisbane Courier of 1874 reported 'These old gentlemen at Dunwich do not as a rule approve of being asked to work. They meet every request to do with the categorical retort... "Why should I work ! If so be I could work, why be I sent here?"

From the 1880s to the 1920s there were rarely more than 20 official staff to 900 or 1,000 inmates. The Asylum needed cheap and permanent labour, which they found from the 'Quandamooka' Aboriginal people of the island who lived at One Mile outside Dunwich, and who did what Goodall says was "heavy and unpleasant work" from the 1870s. By the 1920s up to 30 aboriginal men were in the 'outside gang', which included the dairy and piggery. Some aboriginal men were in trade, skilled and semi-skilled jobs including carpentry and operating the power station. Around 15 aboriginal women were employed as cooks, nursing assistants and domestics including in the houses of the senior staff of the Asylum. The aboriginal workers formed a substantial part of the total work force for the Asylum, at times over half, right up to its closure in 1946. Aboriginal workers were originally paid in rations, but from the 1920s onwards took action to be paid wages.

The Dunwich dormitories, and two views of the Benevolent Asylum at Dunwich on North Stradbroke Island.

Those who supported the creation of the first early 19th century public and private hospitals recognized that one important mission would be the care and treatment of those with severe symptoms of mental illnesses. Like most physically sick men and women, such individuals remained with their families and received treatment in their homes. Their communities showed significant tolerance for what they saw as strange thoughts and behaviors. But some such individuals seemed too violent or disruptive to remain at home or in their communities.

But the opening decades of the 19th century brought to Australia new European ideas about the care and treatment of the mentally ill. These ideas, soon to be called "moral treatment," promised a cure for mental illnesses to those who sought treatment in a very new kind of institution—an "asylum." The moral treatment of the insane was built on the assumption that those suffering from mental illness could find their way to recovery and an eventual cure if treated kindly and in ways that appealed to the parts of their minds that remained rational. It repudiated the use of harsh restraints and long periods of isolation that had been used to manage the most destructive behaviors of mentally ill individuals. It depended instead on specially constructed hospitals that provided quiet, secluded, and peaceful country settings; opportunities for meaningful work and recreation; a system of privileges and rewards for rational behaviors; and gentler kinds of restraints used for shorter periods.

By the 1890s, however, these institutions were all under siege. Economic considerations played a substantial role with local governments avoiding the costs of caring for the elderly residents in almshouses or public hospitals by redefining what was then termed "senility" as a psychiatric problem and sending these men and women to state-supported anylums. Unsurprisingly, the numbers of patients in the asylums grew exponentially, well beyond the capacity and willingness of government.

TOP: Admission paper for Mary Ann Frawley to the Benevolent Asylum, Dunwich, 21 October 1880, which mentions Patrick McGarry (her father), Mary Heffernan (her mother), the "Diamond", (her convict ship), her children and Rev. Meares (her first employer at Wollongong). ABOVE: Mary Frawley was buried in an unmarked grave in Dunwich Cemetery, on 8th November 1889.

Whatever their reasons, by 1876 John and Mary Ann Frawley accompanied by their son John Jr, his wife Sarah and their children, had sold up most of their Pambula and Wolumla holdings and moved to Toowoomba in Queensland to join up with their son and brother James Frawley.

The quickest route to Toowoomba at that time was by coastal steamship through Sydney and Brisbane, which was best undertaken initially from either Eden or Tathra to Sydney, where regular shipping services had commenced from the latter in 1862. The Tathra Wharf, built on turpentine supports and set into solid rock, was recently restored by the National Trust, and local residents, and is the only remaining coastal steamer wharf in New South Wales.[9]

After arriving in Sydney, the Frawley's would not have stayed long before re-embarking on another coastal steamer for Brisbane. Once on the dock in Brisbane, their best option for travelling to Toowoomba was by the relatively new rail line. Toowoomba Railway Station with just one platform and a passing loop had opened in 1867, but in due course it

Queensland Electoral Rolls (1860-1884)

James Frawley
First name(s)	James
Last name	FRAWLEY
Year	1876
Residence	Meringandan
Electoral district	Toowoomba/Aubigny
Qualification	Leasehold
State	Queensland
Fiche	46

Patrick Frawley
First name(s)	Patrick
Last name	FRAWLEY
Year	1876
Residence	Meringandan
Electoral district	Toowoomba/Aubigny
Qualification	Freehold
State	Queensland
Fiche	46

John Frawley Jr.
First name(s)	John Jr.
Last name	FRAWLEY
Year	1878
Residence	Meringandan
Electoral district	Toowoomba/Aubigny
Qualification	Residence
State	Queensland
Fiche	67

John Frawley (Sr.)
Field	Value
First name(s)	John Sr.
Last name	FRAWLEY
Year	1878
Residence	Meringadan
Electoral district	Toowoomba/Aubigny
Qualification	Residence
State	Queensland
Fiche	67

John Frawley (Sr.)
Field	Value
First name(s)	John Sr.
Last name	FRAWLEY
Year	1880
Residence	Highfields
Electoral district	Highfields/Aubigny
Qualification	Residence
State	Queensland
Fiche	93

John Frawley (Sr.)
Field	Value
First name(s)	John Sr.
Last name	FRAWLEY
Year	1881
Residence	Highfields
Electoral district	Highfields/Aubigny
Qualification	Residence
State	Queensland
Fiche	106

John Frawley (Sr.)
Field	Value
First name(s)	John
Last name	FRAWLEY
Year	1882
Residence	Highfields
Electoral district	Highfields/Aubigny
Qualification	Residence
State	Queensland
Fiche	119

Thomas Frawley
Field	Value
First name(s)	Thomas
Last name	FRAWLEY
Year	1884
Residence	Meringandan
Electoral district	Highfields/Aubigny
Qualification	Residence
State	Queensland
Fiche	145

Thomas Frawley
Field	Value
First name(s)	Thomas
Last name	FRAWLEY
Sex	Male
Occupation	Farmer
Residence	Meringandan
Year	1903
Polling place	Meringandan
Division	Darling Downs
Country	Australia
State	Queensland
Number	116

NOTE: John Frawley (Sr.) remained at 'Highfields' in 1883 and 1884. No electoral rolls are shown for the late 1880s or 1890s.

LAND SELECTIONS, DARLING DOWNS NORTH.

The usual sitting of the Crown Lands Court was held by Mr. A. M'Dowall, at Toowoomba, on Monday last. There was a large attendance, and great interest was exhibited in the "drawing" for the Drayton land, which fell, as noted below, to Mr. Caskelly. Two applicants were fined for non-attendance. The following selections were conditionally approved:—

HOMESTEAD SELECTIONS.

John Hegarty, 320 acres pastoral, parish Tooth
James Frawley, 120 acres pastoral, parish Meringandan

TUESDAY, 7th APRIL.

Cottage and Land in Eton-street, near Messrs. Ryan and Hutchison's Hotels.

J. S. M'INTYRE

HAS received instructions from Mr FRAWLEY to Sell by Auction, at his Rooms, Ruthven-street, on Tuesday, the 7th April, at 12 o'clock.

All that Cottage and Land in Eton-street, being at present occupied by Mr Frawley. The Cottage contains Three Rooms, and is built on an area of two allotments.

Title Guaranteed Correct.

TOP: Frawley's on the Queensland Electoral Rolls for Meringandan and Highfields, in Queensland (1860-1884). ABOVE: (Left): James Frawley - Land Selections at Meringandan (The Brisbane Courier, 14 March 1873, p.3). (Right): Mr. Frawley - Cottage & Land for sale in Eton Street, Toowoomba (????, 4th April 1874, p.2).

LEFT (Top): Death notice for Mary Ann Frawley (The Queenslander, 23rd Nov 1889, p.5). (Above): The Sydney mail train ascending the Toowoomba Range. RIGHT: Death certificate for Mary Ann Frawley (nee McGarry), at Dunwich Benevolent Asylum on 7th Nov. 1889 (Queensland Dept of BDM, 1889/3633-1695).

became the junction for the Western, Main and Southern Queensland lines.[10]

The Frawleys first house was in Herries Street, the main street of Toowoomba. But sadly, much hope and confidence for their relocation sunk when John Frawley Jr. died from an infection of the lungs on the 9th October 1878, aged just 37 years.[11]

This devastating and unexpected event placed the entire Frawley family at risk. John and Mary Frawley were both over 60 with limited work capacity. John Frawley Jr. had died with four children under the age of 12, and from all accounts, his wife Sarah wasn't able to cope with either rearing the children or bringing forth an income. In short, John Jr.'s untimely death dealt a catastrophic blow, from which the family found it hard to recover. However, their other son James Frawley seemed to be making a success of himself through land acquisition, and perhaps by becoming a publican with an interest in horse racing.

Examing the electoral rolls for that period reveals that John Frawley resided in the township of Highfields from 1878 to 1884, while his sons James, Patrick and Thomas resided at nearby Meringandan.[12] By this time, their daughter Ellen O'Sullivan had produced a family of her own, adding three sons and two daughters to John and Mary Frawley's growing pride of grandchildren.[13] Ellen and her husband James Mahony O'Sullivan were residing at Dalmorton until 1883, when they moved to Moonee Creek, just north of Coffs Harbour.

John and Mary Frawley would certainly have supported their widowed daughter-in-law Sarah, and their four grandchildren, but as the children grew, the lack of a disciplined father began to affect their upbringing. However, events came to a head in 1880 when the matriarch, Mary Ann Frawley had to be committed to the Benevolent Asylum at Dunwich,[14]

TOP: Horse and carts make their deliveries on Herries Street, the main street of Toowoomba about 1897. ABOVE (Left): John Frawley of Maryland, Tenderfield, in 1891 Census, New South Wales, Mitchell Library, Sydney. (Right - Top): John Frawley in 'Index to Prisoners Tried' (offense unknown), Toowoomba, 1892. (Mid): John Frawley elected Trustee of Maryland Temporary Common from 1895 to 1898. (Above): Death notice for John Frawley Sr. (Tenterfield Intercolonial Courier, 5th Feb. 1901, p.3).

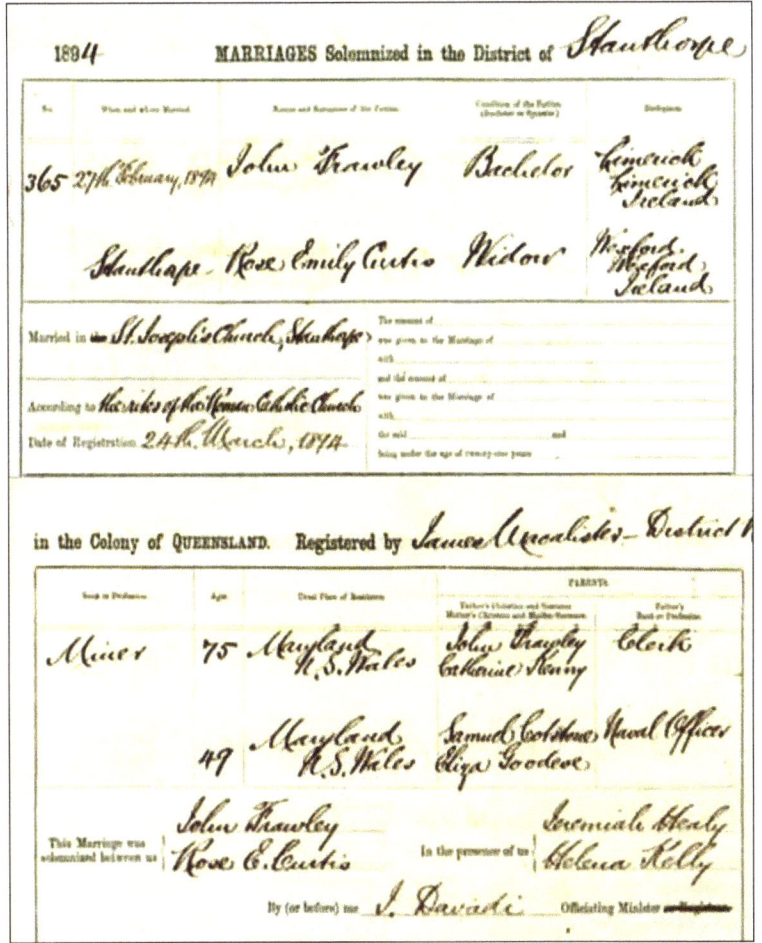

TOP: Tin miners and their dogs in the Stanthorpe District, c.1872. ABOVE: Maryland St, Stanthorpe about 1900. ABOVE: Marriage Certificate for John Frawley and Rose Emily Curtis, 27th February 1894 (QLD BDM #1894/C/1672)

after which their daughter-in-law Sarah, became totally unable to cope, and the children had no one to keep them in check. Young Agnes Maude Frawley was the worst affected when at just 14 years old, she turned to associating with larrikins and prostitutes. Following in her grandmothers footsteps, Agnes fell foul of the law, was charged and sent to the Toowoomba Industrial and Reformatory School for Girls in 1887, for seven long years.[15]

The Committment of Mary

As an inmate at the Dunwich Asylum, the matriarch of the family Mary Ann Frawley, experienced oppressive institutional conditions, which would normally have hastened her

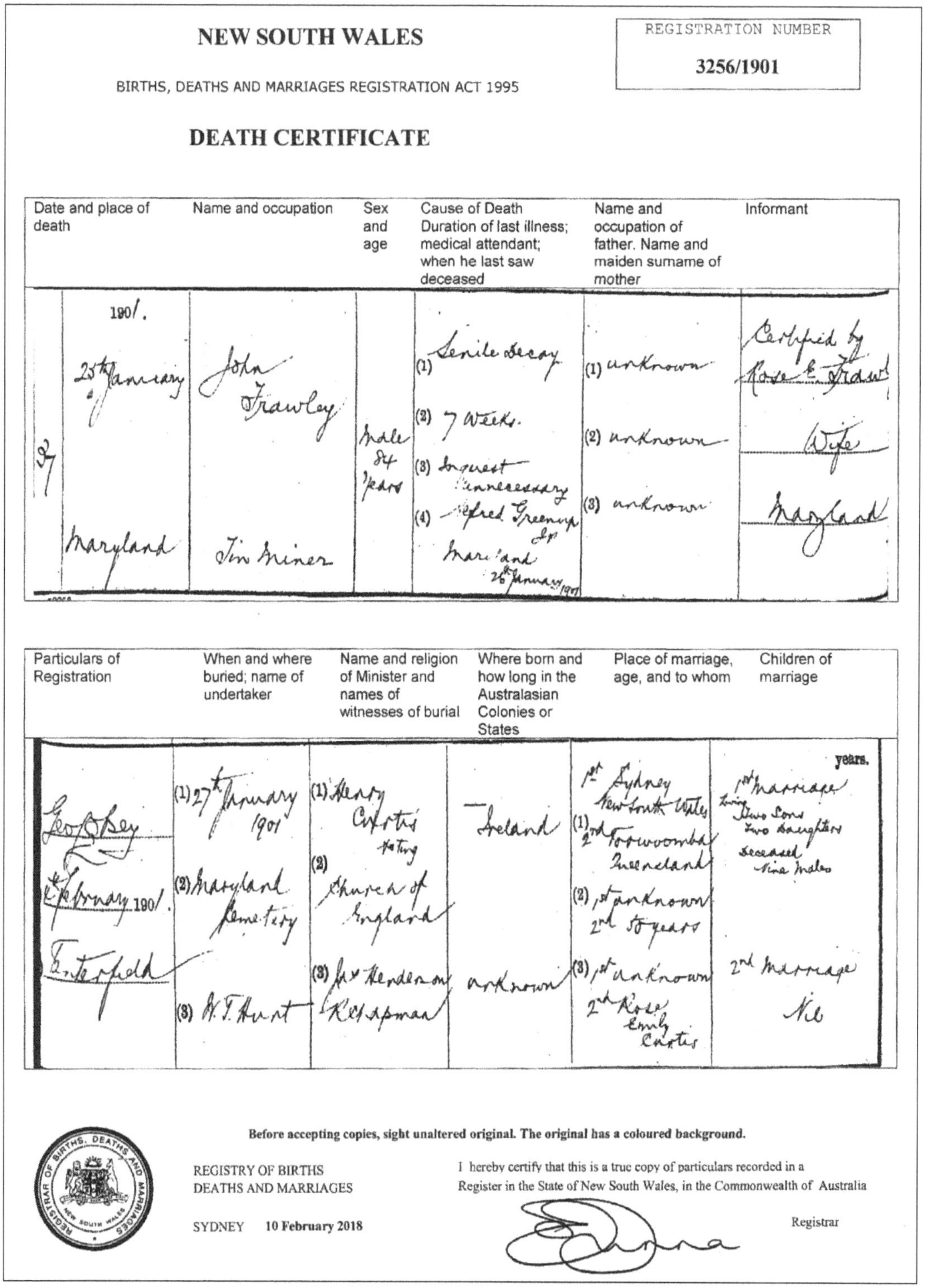

NEW SOUTH WALES

BIRTHS, DEATHS AND MARRIAGES REGISTRATION ACT 1995

REGISTRATION NUMBER
3256/1901

DEATH CERTIFICATE

	Date and place of death	Name and occupation	Sex and age	Cause of Death Duration of last illness; medical attendant; when he last saw deceased	Name and occupation of father. Name and maiden surname of mother	Informant
87	1901. 25th January Maryland	John Frawley Tin Miner	Male 84 Years	(1) Senile decay (2) 7 weeks. (3) Inquest unnecessary (4) Alfred Greenup Jr Maryland 26th January 1901	(1) unknown (2) unknown (3) unknown	Certified by Rose E Frawley Wife Maryland

Particulars of Registration	When and where buried; name of undertaker	Name and religion of Minister and names of witnesses of burial	Where born and how long in the Australasian Colonies or States	Place of marriage, age, and to whom	Children of marriage
Geo Bey 4th February 1901. Tenterfield	(1) 27th January 1901 (2) Maryland Cemetery (3) W. T. Hunt	(1) Henry Curtis acting (2) Church of England (3) Jas Henderson R Chapman	Ireland unknown	1st Sydney New South Wales (1) 2nd Toowoomba Queensland (2) 1st unknown 2nd 50 years (3) 1st unknown 2nd Rose Emily Curtis	years. 1st marriage Living Two Sons Two Daughters Deceased Nine Males 2nd marriage Nil

Before accepting copies, sight unaltered original. The original has a coloured background.

REGISTRY OF BIRTHS DEATHS AND MARRIAGES

SYDNEY **10 February 2018**

I hereby certify that this is a true copy of particulars recorded in a Register in the State of New South Wales, in the Commonwealth of Australia

Registrar

The death certificate for John Frawley, 25th January 1901 (NSW BDM, #03256/1901).

end, but she somehow doggedly clung to life for a further nine years, before succumbing to the inevitability of senile decay on the 7th November 1889.[16]

Interestingly, her death certificate stated that she had lost four boys and two girls. John Jr most certainly died in 1878, and its possible that Patrick, who changed his name to Marr, might also have been thought to be deceased, but when and where the other two deceased males and two deceased females came and went is unclear. John Frawley was arrested and charged again in 1892, but was apparently exonnerated... offense unknown.[17]

The Deaths of... John & Mary Frawley

Without his wife, John Frawley later moved to Maryland Station near Tenterfield,[18] where he may have been present at the 'Tenterfield Oration' a speech in favour of federation, delivered by Sir Henry Parkes (1815-1896), Premier of New South Wales, at the Tenterfield School of Arts in Tenterfield, New South Wales, on 24 October 1889.[19][1]

Throughout this period, Mary Ann was doggedly hanging onto life at the Dunwich Benevolent Asylum, which was established under the Benevolent Asylum Wards Act of 1861 to provide accommodation and care to poor people unable to care for themselves due to illness or infirmity.

The Asylum had opened on 13 May 1865 with the initial transfer of patients from the Benevolent Ward of the Brisbane General Hospital.[20] Over 21,000 people were admitted to the Dunwich Asylum during its operation, with around 1000 to 1600 in residence at any one time. Those who died in the asylum were generally buried in the Dunwich Cemetery, unless families made other arrangements. In the 80 years spanning 1867-1947, 8,426 former inmates of the Dunwich Benevolent Asylum were buried in the Dunwich Cemetery.

But Mary Ann Frawley's death inevitably occurred at the age of 79, at the Benevolent Asylum on the 7th November 1889, and we hope that some of the Frawley family were in attendance at the burial of their dear mother.[21]

John Frawley's 2nd Marriage

For reasons that are unclear, John Frawley then moved south from Toowoomba to Stanthorpe and the area called Maryland in NSW, by the 1890s. John outlived his dear and long suffering wife by a further 12 years, and by the time of his own death at 84 years of age, he was still working as a miner.[22] He even found the energy to take on a new partner, some 30 years younger and remarried on the 27th February 1894 to a widow by the name

Postcard of Ruthven Street, Toowoomba about 1905 (The 'Shell Series' of postcards, 1905-1915)

From Prisoners To Pioneers

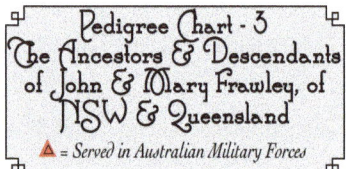

Pedigree Chart - 3
The Ancestors & Descendants of John & Mary Frawley, of NSW & Queensland
△ = Served in Australian Military Forces

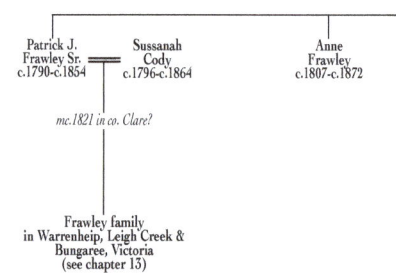

Patrick J. Frawley Sr. c.1790-c.1854 === Sussanah Cody c.1796-c.1864 — Anne Frawley c.1807-c.1872

mc.1821 in co. Clare?

Frawley family in Warrenheip, Leigh Creek & Bungaree, Victoria (see chapter 13)

John Frawley Jr 1841-1878 === Sarah Maud Little 1850-1911 | James Mahoney O'Sullivan 1837-1891 === Ellen Frawley 1842-1909 | James Frawley 1845<1901

mc. 1865, Panbula, NSW | *m. 1869, St Mary's, Sydney*

Children of John Frawley Jr & Sarah Maud Little:
- William Frawley 1865-1876 *Child*
- Male Frawley 1869-1869 *Infant*
- Male Frawley 1870-? *Infant*
- Charles Frawley 1874>1925 *d.s.p.*
- Anna Gilmour Frawley 1867-1946 m. 1888 at Brisbane John Cuddihy 1871-1894
- Agnes Maude Frawley 1872-? m. 1896 at Brisbane Robert Edward Clarke 1874-1938
- Eden 'Edith' Alice Frawley 1875-1937 m. 1894 at Brisbane Mark Raymond Sanders 1863-1935

Children of James Mahoney O'Sullivan & Ellen Frawley:
- Female O'Sullivan 1873-183 *Infant*
- Male O'Sullivan 1875-1875 *Infant*
- Mary Zenobia O'Sullivan 1879-1879 *Infant*
- Ellen Therese O'Sullivan 1880>1932 1m. 1909 at Auckland James Ernest Gear 1881-1961 *d.s.p.*
- William O'Sullivan 1884-1884 *Infant*
- Female O'Sullivan 1888-1888 *Infant*
- Humphrey Joseph O'Sullivan 1871-1905 m. 1900 at Sydney Lenore Mackie 1866-1945
- James Alexander O'Sullivan 1872-1938 m. 1897 at Grafton Emily Ann Jordan 1868-1934
- John Washington O'Sullivan 1877-1947 m. 1902 at Paddington Sarah A. Bridger 1876-1943
- Blanche Zenobia O'Sullivan 1875-1937 2m. 1927 at Sydney John MacKinlay 1873-1953
- Rupert C. O'Sullivan 1886-1886 *Infant*
- Zenobia O'Sullivan 1891-1891 *Infant*

Grandchildren:
- John Cuddihy 1889-1974 m. 1915 at Brisbane Elsie Margaret Abrahams 1885-1947
- James A. Cuddihy 1893-1894 *Infant*
- Evelyn May Clarke 1897-1989 m. 1919 at QLD William G. Foote 1892-1936 △
- Hilda Maude Clarke 1909-1980 w-Aboriginal m. 1930 at QLD William Malcolm 1904-1985
- William Raymond Sanders 1895-1930 *d.s.p.*
- Arthur Carew Sanders 1899-1940 △ *d.s.p.*
- Edna Alice Sanders 1906-2000 m. 1926 at Brisbane Percy Marshall 1901-1970
- Melecca O'Sullivan 1901-1901 *Infant*
- Sylvia Veronica O'Sullivan 1902-1914 *Child*
- Myrtle Helena O'Sullivan 1898-1991 m. 1925 at Norman Pk James W. Lewis 1891-1963 △
- Victor James O'Sullivan 1908-1990 △ 1m. 1955 at Nth Sydney Louisa Groves 1909-1960 2m. 1961
- Claude Hope O'Sullivan 1897-1961 △ m. 1925 at Leeton Florence Ada Pitt 1904-1969 — Changed name to Claude Patrick Wilson

Great-grandchildren:
- Evelyn May Cuddihy 1891-? m. 1913 at Brisbane George P. Doyle 1886-?
- Agnes Ann Clarke 1899-? with Albert F. 'Kid' Lloyd 1891-1959 with Aboriginal
- Harold Robert Sanders 1897-1961 △ m. 1925 at Brisbane Elizabeth M. Riggs 1895-1949 *d.s.p.*
- Dorothy May Sanders 1904-? m. 1925 at Brisbane John A. McIntosh 1902-? div. 1937 *d.s.p.*
- Octavia Corelli O'Sullivan 1902-1976 m. 1926 at Glebe Robert A. Rockwell 1904-1966
- Goldie Alathea O'Sullivan 1905-1982 m. 1927 at Sydney Patrick J. Mulroy 1903-1961
- Gladys O'Sullivan 1903-1930 1. with Maurice 'Jack' Evans 1895-1981 2. m.1922 at Cooparoo Charles A. Rogers 1897-1981
- John William O'Sullivan 1913-1974 m. 1941 at Sydney Minnie L. Pardey 1897-1974 *d.s.p.*

1. Janet A. Malcolm (1950-1991)

1. Edward A. Lloyd (1919-1979) △
2. Pearl Clarke (?-?)
3. William Clarke (?-?)

1. Hope C. Foote (?-2015)
2. Hilda Foote (1921-2015)
3. William G. Foote (1921-1921)
4. Doris E. Foote (1924-2007)
5. William H. Foote (1925-1997) △
6. Natalie S. Foote (1929-1929)
7. Norman M. Foote (1931-2016)

1. Leila E. Marshall (1927-1997)
2. Esme J. Marshall (1929-1951)
3. Raymond T. Marshall (1933-1947)

1. Joy C. Rockwell (1927-2018)
2. Robert H. Rockwell (1929-1984)
3. Elwood L. Rockwell (1933-1987)
4. Lindsay A. Rockwell (1937)
5. Ronie M. Rockwell (1945-2000)
6. Janet L. Rockwell (1946)

1. Lionel R. Mulroy (1928-2010)
2. Leslie A. Mulroy (1938-1999)

1. Myrle Lewis (1926-2001)
2. Joan Lewis (1928-2005)
3. Valma Lewis (1930)
4. Darcy J. Lewis (1931-1945)
5. Samuel G. Lewis (1934-1995)

1. Janice O Sullivan (1936)
2. Robyn G. O'Sullivan (1942-2006)

1. Daphne R. O'Sullivan (1917-2009)
2. Gloria M. Rogers (1923-2012)

1. Patrick C. Wilson (1926-?)
2. Peter J. Wilson (1928-?)
3. Ellen P. Wilson (1951-1951)
4. Mary T. Wilson (1953)
5. Joseph B. Wilson (1937)
6. Alice Z. Wilson (1940)
7. Anne M. Wilson (1942)

1. John E. Doyle (1914-1975)
1. John Cuddihy (1923-1997) △

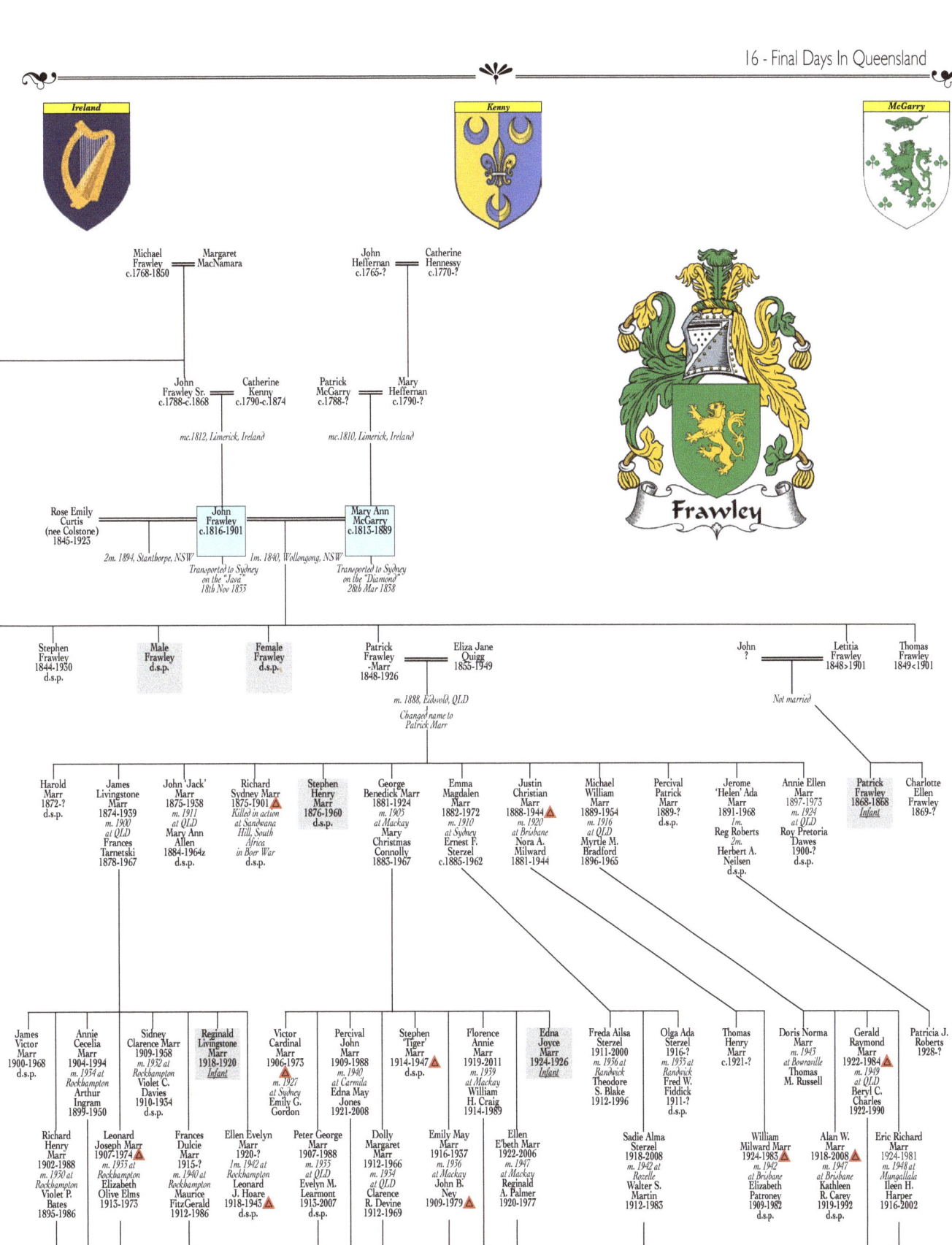

16 - Final Days In Queensland

The historic Meringandan Hotel, established in the early 1870s by German immigrants, has been serving patrons since its construction during that era.

of Rose Emily Curtis (1845-1923), the daughter of Samuel Colstone and Eliza Goodeve.[23] By that time, all of John's grandchildren had come of age and so he moved away to a small and quieter community called Maryland, close to Stanthorpe in south-east Queensland, which was on the New South Wales border. These were the days before pensions and so despite his advanced age, in order to survive and support his new wife, John Frawley continued to work wherever he could, so the intrepid old soul turned to 'tin mining'.

John Frawley was even elected 'Trustee of the Common' at Maryland,[24] and while he survived into the 20th century, his inevitable death came at the age of 84, on the 25th of January 1901, a labourer until the very end. He was buried in an unmarked grave at the bush cemetery at Maryland.[25] His second wife, Rose Emily Frawley (nee Curtis), being much

Maryland Bush Cemetery is now closed, with no remaining headstones or markers. It is managed by the Environmental Services Department of Tenterfield Shire.

younger, survived until the 15th December 1923, and was buried at Toowong Cemetery in Brisbane aged 78, without any additions to John Frawley's issue.

The lives of John and Mary Frawley were defined by adversity, resilience, and an unyielding determination to carve out a better life, which speaks to the strength of the human spirit. Despite their turbulent pasts, their journey from convicted criminals to respected pioneers of the Australian frontier exemplifies the capacity to rebuild and thrive in the face of overwhelming odds. In the end, their story was continued through the lives of their descendants, those who would carry the weight of their legacy forward.

In the final chapter of this book, we turn our attention to the next generation: the children of John and Mary Ann Frawley. What became of them? How did the struggles and triumphs of their parents shape their own lives, and what imprint did they leave on the communities they helped build? Join us as we explore the lives of the Frawley descendants, revealing the remarkable continuities and changes in the family's journey, and the legacy of two pioneering souls who, against all odds, helped shape the history of a young nation.

References

1. T. M. Perry, 'Cunningham, Allan (1791–1839)', Australian Dictionary of Biography, National Centre of Biography, Australian National University, [https://adb.anu.edu.au/biography/cunningham-allan-1941/text2323], published first in hardcopy 1966, accessed online 1 February 2023.
2. Hall, Thomas, 1845-1928. (1920). The early history of Warwick district and pioneers of the Darling Downs / Thomas Hall. [Toowoomba? : s.n [http://nla.gov.au/nla].obj-37325731.
3. Hall, Thomas, 1845-1928. (1920). The early history of Warwick district and pioneers of the Darling Downs / Thomas Hall. [Toowoomba? : s.n [http://nla.gov.au/nla].obj-37325731.
4. Wikipedia - "Toowoomba" [https://en.wikipedia.org/wiki/Toowoomba.
5. Kids Kiddle - Toowoomba [https://kids.kiddle.co/History_of_Toowoomba,_Queensland].
6. Brittanica - Toowoomba [https://www.britannica.com/place/Toowoomba].
7. James Frawley - Payment for Construction of Foot-Bridge (The Toowoomba Chronicle & Queensland Advertiser, 12 Nov 1863, p.2.
8. James Frawley - Land Selections at Darling Downs North (The Brisbane Courier, 14 March 1873, p.3).
9. James Frawley - Land Selections at Darling Downs North (The Brisbane Courier, 14 March 1873, p.3).
10. Wikipedia - 'Tathra Wharf.' [https://en.wikipedia.org/wiki/Tathra_Wharf]. Retrieved 13th June 2021.
11. Queensland Dept of BDM. (1878). Death Certificate for John Frawley Jr., 9th October 1878 at Herries St, Toowoomba, #878/C/896.
12. John Frawley - Carrier at Meringandan (Queensland PO Directory, 1894, p.483).
13. NSW Dept of BDM. (1909). Death Certificate for Ellen O'Sullivan, 4th August 1909 at Newcastle, #10250/1909.
14. Queensland State Archives. (1880). 'Mary Frawley, Admission Paper to the Benevolent Asylum, Dunwich', 21st October 1880.
15. Agnes Frawley - Neglected (The Telegraph [Brisbane], 10 May 1887, p.5).
16. Queensland Dept of BDM, (1889). Death Certificate for Mary Frawley (nee McGarry) at Dunwich Benevolent Asylum, 1889/3633-1695.
17. Queensland Govt. (1892). John Frawley - Arrested Toowoomba, 12 July 1892 (in Index to Prisoners Tried, Toowoomba, 1864-1903, #3/104859/PRI4/1).
18. NSW State Archives & Records. (1891). John Frawley of Maryland, Tenderfield, in 1891 Census, New South Wales." Mitchell Library, Sydney.
19. Henry Parkes Tenterfield Oration 1889". Friends of Sir Henry Parkes School of Arts. Archived from the original on 17 May 2014. Retrieved 23 October 2018.
20. Wikipedia. 'Benevolent Asylum, Dunwich,' op. cit.
21. Queensland Dept of BDM. (1889). Death Certificate for Mary Frawley (nee McGarry), op. cit.
22. NSW Dept of BDM. (1901). Death Certificate for John Frawley, 25 January 1901 at Maryland, NSW, #03256/1901.
23. Queensland Dept of BDM. (1894). Marriage Certificate for John Frawley & Rose Emily Curtis, 27th February 1894, #1894/C/1672.
24. NSW Dept of Mines & Agriculture. (1895). John Frawley, Trustee of Maryland Common.
25. NSW Dept of BDM. (1901). Death Certificate for John Frawley, op. cit.
26. Wikipedia - "Toowoomba" [https://en.wikipedia.org/wiki/Toowoomba].
27. Wikipedia. 'Benevolent Asylum, Dunwich.' [https://en.wikipedia.org/wiki/Dunwich_Benevolent_Asylum]. Retrieved 13th June 2021.

Further Reading

Maurice French, Maurice & Duncan Bruce Waterson (1982). 'The Darling Downs: A Pictorial History, 1850-1950,' Darling Downs Institute Press [ISBN 9780909306267].

Hall, Thomas (1988). 'The Early History of Warwick District and Pioneers of the Darling Downs,' Vintage Books [ISBN 9780731636402].

Chapter Seventeen

THE DESCENDANTS OF JOHN & MARY ANN FRAWLEY

As we reach the final chapter, our journey turns to the next generation, the children of John and Mary Ann Frawley. What paths did they carve for themselves? How did the trials and triumphs of their parents shape their futures? And what mark did they leave on the communities they helped to build? In these pages, we uncover the stories of the Frawley descendants, tracing the threads of resilience, ambition, and change that wove their family's legacy into the fabric of a young nation. What is known of John and Mary Ann Frawley's children is as follows:

1. John Frawley Jr. (1841-1878)

Their first born, John Frawley Jr. arrived on the 7th May 1841 at Alexander Berry's Coolangatta homestead, and was baptised by the Rev. John Rigney at Wollongong on the 19th May 1841, with Martin Grealis and Bridget Leary as the sponsors.[1] But it appears he may have also been baptised a second time on the 18th March 1844 at 'Warragaburra Station' on the far South Coast of New South Wales, this time by the Rev. Michael Kavanagh with Fenton Brien and Bridget McNamara as the sponsors.[2]

After likely attending the school at Pambula from its opening in 1850,[3] John Frawley

Incarcerations of John Frawley Jr.

1st Imprisonment - 12 months Hard Labour at Parramatta Gaol, 1863

1st IMPRISONMENT: TOP (Left): Letitia Frawley & John Frawley Jr. - Eden Quarter Sessions List, 24th April 1863. (Right): John Frawley Jr. in court on exactly the same day as his father, convicted of obtaining money under false pretences and sent to prison for 12 months (SMH, 29th Apr 1863, p5). MID #1: Trial for Letitia Frawley & John Frawley & Witness list at Eden Court House, 24th April 1863. MID #2: John Frawley Jr. - Released from his 1st Incarceation at Parramatta Goal (NSW Police Gazette, April 1864). **2nd IMPRISONMENT:** *LEFT: John Frawley [Jr.] - Transcript of Darlinghurst Gaol - Description Book, Oct, 1867. RIGHT (Top): John Frawley Jr. - Imprisonment for Default of Fine (NSW Police Gazette, 9 Oct 1867, p.297). (Above): John Frawley Jr. - Discharged from Darlinghurst Gaol (NSW Police Gazette, 4 Dec 1867, p.358).*

Jr. later began a relationship with Sarah Maud Little (1850-1911) although, no record can be found of their marriage in the New South Wales Births, Deaths & Marriages Index. Regardless, they soonafter began a family with the birth of their son William Frawley on the 23rd May 1865, who was registered as being born in Wolumla, but was unnamed in the official records.[4] Next was Anna Gilmour Frawley who was born at Wolumla on the 12th July 1867, but was also unnamed in the official registers.[5]

In October of 1862, John Frawley Jr, along with his mother Mary Ann Frawley and sister,

Letitia Frawley were charged with intent to defraud, which concerned a promissory note and bank note to the value of one pound. The writing in this case is difficult to understand, and translation of these court proceedings has not been undertaken. However, although the mother and daughter, Mary Ann and Letitia Frawley were discharged, John Frawley Jr. was convicted and sentenced to Parramatta Gaol for 12 months.[6] Later in 1867, John Frawley Jr. was listed in the National Directory of NSW as residing at Wolumla.[7] However, October 1867 saw John Frawley Jr. once again charged by the local police. This time for illegally riding a horse with his brother-in-law Robert Little, which was the property of one Archibald Spence.[8] Frawley and Little were fined £10, but had to serve three months in Darlinghurst Gaol for default of payment, being released on 23rd December, 1867.[9]

Another son arrived in 1869 to John Jr and Sarah, who was again unnamed in the register,[10] and another unnamed child came along in 1870, both of who died in infancy.[11]

Documents for John Frawley Jr.

TOP (Left): John Frawley Jr. in Court against his tenant Mr. Collins (Bega Gazette etc, 26th April 1872, p2). (Right): Death Certficate for John Frawley Jr, 9th October 1878. ABOVE (Left): John Frawley Jr. - Accident (C&RE, 21 Apr 1874, p.6). (Right): John Frawley Jr. - Government Property Deeds - Panbula (The Bega Standard & Candelo etc, 20 Sept 1879, p.2).

4. Descendants of John Frawley Jr. & Sarah Little
(Data from NSW Births, Deaths & Marriages Index, Ancestry.com & Newspapers).

John FRAWLEY Jr. (1841-1878), was seemingly never married, but partner of Sarah Little (1850-1911). He died in Toowoomba in 1878 and was buried alongside his son William in the Drayton & Toowoomba Cemetery, with issue:

1. William FRAWLEY (1865-1876)*, was charged with killing a 'fowl' at the age of '9', the property of a Margaret Ettinger. He died in Toowoomba and buried in the Drayton & Toowoomba Cemetery, soon after his 11th birthday.

2. Anna Gilmour Frawley (1867-1946), married in 1888 at St Stephens Cathedral, Brisbane, QLD to John CUDDIHY (1871-1894). Anna Cuddihy left Rockhampton in August 1894 after her husbands death. She died on the 31st Dec 1946, in Queensland (registered in 1947 at Queensland, #B009864 - p.498), with issue:

2.1 John CUDDIHY (1889-1974) married in 1919 at Brisbane to Elsie Margaret Abrahams (1885-1947), with issue:
 a. John CUDDIHY Jr. (1923-1997) married to Therese Joan Stewart (1928-2016), issue unknown.
2.2 Evelyn May Cuddihy (1891-1978), married in 1913 at St Stephens Cathedral, Brisbane, QLD to George Patrick DOYLE (1886-1960), with issue:
 a. John Edward DOYLE (1914-1975), issue unknown.
2.3 James Augustus CUDDIHY (1893-1894)*, died an infant.

3. Male FRAWLEY (1869-1869)*, died an infant.

4. Agnes Maude Frawley (1872<1911), born in Bega, she was apparently a lost girl during her teen years and was placed in the Industrial and Reformatory School for Girls, Toowoomba, for seven years. The institution was run by the Queensland Government, and was established on 1 April 1881. It was previously the Toowoomba jail. The superintendent and matron of the jail were appointed superintendent and matron of the school under the Industrial and Reformatory Schools Act of 1865. Under the Act, children under the age of fifteen who were unmanageable or incorrigible, or with convictions, were sent to reformatories while those from unwholesome environments were sent to industrial schools to be trained for employment. The school was re-named 'The Industrial School for Girls, Toowoomba', around 1890.
Agnes must have reformed herself and changed her ways as she married in 1896 in Queensland, at age 24 to Robert Edward CLARKE (1874-1938), with issue:

4.1 Evelyn May Clarke (1897-1989) married in 1919 at Queensland to William George FOOTE (1892-1936) with issue:
 a. Hilda Foote (1921-2015), issue unknown.
 b. William George FOOTE (1921-1921)*, died an infant.
 c. Doris Evelyn Foote (1924-2007) married in 1944 at Glebe to Herman J. C. Harris (1921-2006) US Army Corp. Doris departed Australia as a war bride in 1945 to reside in Arkansas. She divorced in 1966 and died in Little Rock, Arkansas in 2007, with issue:
  a1. Kenneth Clarence HARRIS (1947-1982), married in 1968 at Pulaski, Arkansas to Fonda Gay Lambert (1950-?).
  a2. Shirley Ann Harris (1948-?)
 d. William Hugh FOOTE (1925-1997) was with Dorothy Louisa Scrivens. No issue.
 e. Natalie Shirley Foote (1929-1929)*, died an infant.
 f. Norman Mervyn J. FOOTE (1931-2016) married to Patricia Hough (1935-1985), with issue:
  f1. Stephan Brett FOOTE (1965-2000), issue unknown.
  f2. Patrick FOOTE (1967-1967)*, died an infant.
 g. Hope Charlotte Foote (?-2015), issue unknown.
4.2 Agnes Ann Clarke (1899-?), She apparently had an affair circa 1918 in Townsville with Albert Francis 'Kid' LLOYD (1891-1959), who won the Australian Heavyweight Boxing Championship in 1918, 1920 and 1921... and she delivered an illegitimate son:

 a. Edward Albert R. LLOYD (1919-1979) married on the 10th August 1947 at Marrickville to Shirley Joan Flynn (1926-2021),with issue:
  a1. Gayle Lloyd (c.1948), married 1971 to Stan Clarence BYRNE (div. 1988), with issue:
   a1.1 Veronica Lee Byrne (1970), married Shane BLACKSELL, with issue:
    a1.1.1 Jade E. Blacksell
    a1.1.2 Patrick M. BLACKSELL
   a1.2 Nicole Ann Byrne (1974), with Warren HOGDEN, with issue:
    a1.2.1 Tyler HOGDEN
    a1.2.2 Mackenzie J. HOGDEN
    a1.2.3 Jake J. HOGDEN
   a1.3 Jess BYRNE (1977), married Margaret Fallon, with issue:
    a1.3.1 Heaton BYRNE
    a1.3.2 Ryan BYRNE
Agnes also met an unknown Aboriginal man, from which she delivered a daughter (a half-sister to Janet):
 b. Pearl Clarke (?-?)
After this, Agnes fell pregnant again to yet another unidentified man and delivered a second son:
 c. William Clarke (?-?)
4.3 Hilda Maude Clarke (1909-1980) married in 1930 at Queensland to William MALCOLM (1904-1985). However, it appears she fell pregnant to the same Aboriginal man as her sister Agnes, and delivered a daughter (a half-sister to Pearl):
 a. Janet Agnes M. Malcolm (1930-1991) married firstly bef. 1957 to David Edward KOOSACHI/CAVELL (1924-1991) with issue:
  a1. Mark David CAVELL (1957-2015)
Janet may have married secondly or been with Ronald James GOWARD (1928-2008). No issue.

5. Charles FRAWLEY (1874>1939), recorded in the 1891 NSW Census, at Lismore (Parish of Bexhill), County Rous. In 1902 Charles was in South Brisbane Court as the owner of a stolen horse. On 14th Sept 1915 he was arrested at Babinda for drunkeness, for which he was subsequently convicted on numerous occasions, but by 1939 had turned to painting and actually won awards for his art at the Mackay Show (Daily Mercury, 27th June 1939, p.4). Charles Frawley died sometime after 1939, issue unknown.

6. Eden 'Edith' Alice Frawley (1875-1937), married on the 15th May 1894, in Queensland to Mark Raymond SANDERS (1863-1926). Mark Sanders was a valet to the Premiers of Queensland and travelled both interstate and internationally on numerous political occasions. Mark Raymond SANDERS died in 1926, in Brisbane, Queensland, with issue:

6.1 William Raymond SANDERS (1895-1930) No issue.
6.2 Robert Harold SANDERS (1897-1961) married in 1925 at Brisbane to Elizabeth Mary Riggs (1895-1949),without issue.
6.3 Arthur Carew SANDERS (1899-1940) No issue.
6.4 Dorothy May Sanders (1904-?), married firstly to John Alexander McINTOSH (1902-?), but divorced in 1937. Dorothy married secondly in 1938 to Allan Hindmarsh BLACK (1916-?). No known issue.
6.5 Edna Alice Sanders (1906-2000), married 1926 at Queensland to Percy MARSHALL (1901-1970), but were divorced in 1937, with issue:
 a. Leila Edith Marshall (1927-1997), married in 1948 at Enoggera, QLD to Cecil George D. FORRESTER (1922-2001) with issue.
 b. Esme Joan Marshall (1929-1931)*, died an infant.
 c. Raymond Thomas MARSHALL (1935-1947)*, died a child.

* Died before adulthood - d.s.p.
(Some names not listed in the index).

Evelyn May Clarke (1897-1989)

Hilda Maude Clarke (1909-1980)

Robert Edward Clarke (1874-1938)

William George Foote (1892-1936)

William Hugh Foote (1925-1997)

George Patrick DOYLE (1886-1960), John Edward DOYLE (1914-1975) & Evelyn May Doyle (nee Cuddihy, 1891-1978)

Cecil George D. Forrester (1922-2001)

Albert Francis 'Kid' Lloyd (1891-1959)

Faces & Documents for Descendants of John Jr. & Sarah Frawley

William Raymond Sanders
(1895-1930)

Robert Harold Sanders
(1897-1961)

Mark Raymond Sanders
(1863-1926)

Edna Alice Sanders
(1906-2000)

LEFT COLUMN: 1-Baptisms for the children of John Frawley Jr. and Sarah Little (Bega Baptisms, St Patricks Roman Catholic Church); 2-W. Frawley - Charged with Vagrancy (Darling Downs Gazette, 9 Dec 1875, p.3); 3-Agnes Frawley - Neglected Child (The Telegraph Brisbane, 10 May 1887, p.5); 4-Marriage announcement for Anna Gilmour Frawley & John Cuddihy at St Stephens Cathedral, Brisbane (Queensland Figaro and Punch – 5 May 1888, p.3). **CENTRE COLUMN:** 1-Marriage announcement for Evelyn May Cuddihy & George Patrick Doyle at St Stephens Cathedral, Brisbane (Brisbane Courier, 22 August 1913, p.9); 2-Charles Frawley - Charged with Stealing (NSW Police Gazette, 30 January 1924, p.646); 3-Charles Frawley - Drunkeness (Daily Mercury, 23rd March 1925, p.7). **RIGHT COLUMN:** 1—William George Foote - Charged with Wife & Child Desertion (Townsville Daily Bulletin, 9 September 1931); 2-Divorce announcement for Dorothy May Sanders & John A. McIntosh (The Courier Mail, 7 August, 1937); 3-George Patrick Doyle - Funeral notice (N'paper?, 27 April 1960).

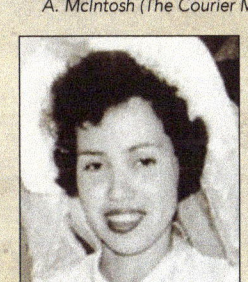
Janet Agnes M. Malcolm
(1930-1991)

William Malcolm
(1904-1985)

Leila Edith Marshall
(1927-1997)

Percy Marshall
(1901-1970)

Arthur Carew Sanders
(1899-1940)

Robert Edward Clarke (circled), was the husband of Agnes Maude Frawley, played football for Rockhampton v New South Wales in 1895.

This was followed by a second daughter named Agnes Maude Frawley in 1872.[12] Another son arrived in 1874 in Charles Frawley. These children were all born at Wolumla, just 16km north-west of Pambula, although seemingly without official registration as no baptismal records have been found to date *(see Table 4. Descendants of John Frawley Jr. & Sarah Little)*. By March of 1872 John Frawley Jr. was in the news again as a defendant at the District Court in Bega, up against a Mr. James, for an unknown matter.

> **Bega District Court - James v Frawley**
> Mr. Rawlinson drew his Honor's attention to the unavoidable absence of Mr. James and the case was allowed to stand over.
>
> *Bega Gazette, 19th March 1872*

John Frawley Jr. was listed in the NSW Post Office Directories of 1872 and 1875-77 as residing at 'Three-Mile Water Hole' near Wolumla.[13,14] By 1876, he was listed on a petition of 'Free Selectors' for the foundation of the township of Bega,[15] and in 1879, John Jr. was listed in the NSW Government Gazette as having 'favor deeds' with the government.[16]

Despite being officially registered as residing at 'Three-Mile Water Hole' near Wolumla, by 1876 John Jr., and his family had moved to Toowoomba in Queensland as it was there that he died on the 9th October 1878 at his residence in Herries St, Toowoomba.[17] His unexpected death wrought devastation upon the Frawley family at that time, although some of his descendants still likely reside in the Toowoomba area. John Frawley Jr. was buried in the Drayton and Toowoomba Cemetery.[18] The following pages contain memorials from Australian Service Records, for descendants of John Jr. and Sarah Frawley, who enlisted in the Australian forces.

Albert Francis 'Kid' Lloyd (1891-1959)
Heavyweight Boxing Champion of Australia

Albert Francis 'Kid' Lloyd, won the Australian Heavyweight Boxing Championship three times in 1918, 1920 and 1921. He had a dalliance with Agnes Ann Clarke (1899-?), the great grand-daughter of John and Mary Ann Frawley, which led to the birth of an illegitimate son in Edward Albert Lloyd (1919-1979).

'Kid' Lloyd was somewhat of a rogue, both in terms of his pugilistic business and with his relationships, but there was no doubting his ability or his record. However, it seems 'Kid' Lloyd wasn't the only 'tiger' to occupy this branch of Frawley tree.

"A bit of gossip for you... my grandmother Agnes never married, but produced my father Edward after her affair with the boxer 'Kid' Lloyd, and after another affair with an unknown aboriginal man produced my Aunt Pearl, Uncle William came from yet another man, so as far as I know, she had three children to three different men."

Gayle Lloyd (grand-daughter)

BOXING.
LLOYD V. GEORGE.

The return match between Albert "Kid" Lloyd, of Victoria, and "Kid" George, of Kalgoorlie, is causing a deal of interest locally, and there should be a large crowd at the Goldfields Athletic Club tomorrow (Saturday) night, when the men enter the ring. They are very evenly matched physically, and judging by their battle early in the week there is little to choose between them. On this occasion the contest is for £100 aside, the winner also taking the whole of the gate receipts. Both men are sanguine of victory, and an exciting battle is promised. Popular prices will be charged.

Australian Heavyweight Champions 1915-1921

Harold Hardwick	6 Mar 1915 – 19 Feb 1916
Les Darcy	19 Feb 1916 – 16 Aug 1916
Dave Smith	26 Dec 1916 – 26 May 1917
Jimmy Clabby	26 May 1917 – 1 Jan 1918
Albert 'Kid' Lloyd	1 Jan 1918 – 22 Mar 1918
Ern Waddy	1918 – 15 Feb 1919
Albert 'Kid' Lloyd	1 Mar 1919 – 21 Feb 1920
George Cook	21 Feb 1920
Billy Shade	7 May 1921
Ern Waddy	7 May 1921 – 8 Sep 1921
Albert 'Kid' Lloyd	8 Sep 1921

ALBERT LLOYD V. CHICH WIGGINS.

SYDNEY, Dec 14. By Telegraph. Albert Lloyd, heavyweight champion, was defeated on points by the American Chich Wiggins, at the stadium last night. The weights were Lloyd. 12st. 11lb, Wiggins. 12st. 1lb. (Townsville Daily Bulletin, 16 December 1919, p.5).

PREMIERLAND
BACK CHURCH LANE, COMMERCIAL ROAD. E.1
Boxing Manager — JOE MORRIS

THURSDAY, NOV. 16TH
Doors Open at 7.30   Commence at 8

THE NIGHT OF BIG MEN

£100 IMPORTANT 20 ROUND CRUISER-WEIGHT CONTEST FOR £100

ALBERT LLOYD
Cruiser-Weight Champion of Australia
versus
HARRY DRAKE

Three Great Special Middle-Weight Contests

TED COVENEY	v.	FRED RICHMOND
BILL BATES	v.	CHARLIE CROXON
YOUNG HEALEY	v.	HARRY GOLD

AND OTHER 6-ROUND CONTESTS

POPULAR PRICES   1/3   2/4   3/6   5/9 & 8/6

Girl "Cousin" Broke Up The Home
WHEN BOXER RETURNED WITH RITA
"SHE TURNED OUT NO GOOD," HE CONFESSED
HEAVYWEIGHT LLOYD DIVORCED

When Albert Francis Lloyd, ex-heavyweight champion boxer of Australia, returned to Australia in 1924, from a tour of Great Britain, he brought back with him, according to his wife's story in the Divorce Court, a young lady—Rita by name—whom he introduced to his wife, when she went to the boat to meet him, as his "cousin."

"She treated me in a contemptuous manner," said Mrs. Lloyd. Her husband and Rita took their departure from the Lloyd home; and when the wife, at a subsequent interview, asked him what had become of Rita, he naively remarked, "She turned out no good."

EX-CHAMP DIES

Albert Lloyd, ex-heavyweight champion of Australia, died in Melbourne last Sunday.

Albert won the vacant title beating Colin Bell in Sydney in 1917, after Dave Smith had retired.

He was born in Carlton, Melbourne, but broke into the fight game winning a heavyweight tournament in New South Wales in 1912.

Albert was a good boxer for a big fellow.

By 1915 he was fighting top boxers like Americans Walter Coffey and Fritz Holland and Australian Jerry Jerome.

Eddie McGoorty, KO Brown, Jimmy Clabby, Chuck Wiggins and George Cook are a few other top liners he fought before he went to England in 1921.

Albert stayed on fighting in England until the middle of 1924 where he toed the scratch against such names as Bombadier Wells, Jack Bloomfield and Phil Scott.

But a lot of hard fights in England took toll of Albert. He was only a shadow of his former self when he returned to Australia.

He retired in 1926.

#QX25523 Edward Albert Lloyd (1919-1979)

Stretcher bearers attending a wounded 2/24 AIF Battalion soldier on Tarakan Island, Borneo, 4th May 1945.

Edward Albert Lloyd (Sergeant); Service Number - QX25523; Date Of Birth - 05 Apr 1919; Place Of Birth - Townsville QLD; Place Of Enlistment - Enoggera QLD; Next Of Kin - Lloyd, Agnes (mother); Unit: 2/24 AIF Battalion. He was a great grandson to John and Mary Frawley.

World War Two Service

SERGEANT EDWARD LLOYD QX25523

SERVICE	AUSTRALIAN ARMY
DATE OF BIRTH	5 APRIL 1919
PLACE OF BIRTH	TOWNSVILLE, QLD
DATE OF ENLISTMENT	27 JUNE 1940
LOCALITY ON ENLISTMENT	SOUTH BRISBANE, QLD
PLACE OF ENLISTMENT	ENOGGERA, QLD
NEXT OF KIN	LLOYD, AGNES
DATE OF DISCHARGE	7 NOVEMBER 1945
POSTING AT DISCHARGE	2/24 AUSTRALIAN INFANTRY BATTALION
ADDITIONAL SERVICE NUMBERS	Q55

Australian Government — Department of Veterans' Affairs

#QX51786 John Cuddihy (1923-1997)

John Cuddihy; Service Number - QX51786; Date Of Birth - 21 Feb 1923; Place Of Birth - Brisbane QLD; Place Of Enlistment - Cairns QLD; Next Of Kin - Cuddihy, Elsie (mother). He was a great grandson to John and Mary Frawley.

World War Two Service

SIGNALMAN JOHN CUDDIHY QX51786

SERVICE	AUSTRALIAN ARMY
DATE OF BIRTH	21 FEBRUARY 1923
PLACE OF BIRTH	BRISBANE, QLD
DATE OF ENLISTMENT	2 APRIL 1943
LOCALITY ON ENLISTMENT	SPRING HILL, QLD
PLACE OF ENLISTMENT	CAIRNS, QLD
NEXT OF KIN	CUDDIHY, ELSIE
DATE OF DISCHARGE	18 SEPTEMBER 1946
POSTING AT DISCHARGE	35 S/B OP SECTION

Australian Government — Department of Veterans' Affairs

#QX60925 William Hugh Foote (1925-1997)

William Hugh Foote; Service Number - Q218381; Date Of Birth - 27 Jul 1925; Place Of Birth - Townsville QLD; Place Of Enlistment - Townsville QLD; Next Of Kin - Foote, Evelyn (mother). He was a great grandson to John and Mary Frawley.

World War Two Service

PRIVATE WILLIAM HUGH FOOTE QX60925

SERVICE	AUSTRALIAN ARMY
DATE OF BIRTH	27 JULY 1925
PLACE OF BIRTH	TOWNSVILLE, QLD
DATE OF ENLISTMENT	18 JULY 1944
LOCALITY ON ENLISTMENT	TOWNSVILLE, QLD
PLACE OF ENLISTMENT	COWRA, NSW
NEXT OF KIN	FOOTE, EVELYN
DATE OF DISCHARGE	23 OCTOBER 1946
POSTING AT DISCHARGE	2/14 AUSTRALIAN INFANTRY BATTALION
ADDITIONAL NUMBERS	Q272725

Australian Government — Department of Veterans' Affairs

OPPOSITE (Counter clockwise from top left): Photo of William 'Ray' Sanders (circled) with fellow soldiers of the 26th Battalion, c.1916; The Military Medal; British Expeditionary Force 'Despatch' for Ray Sanders, 10th Dec. 1920; AIF Military Medal 'Despatch' for Ray Sanders; Court Martial Preceedings for Ray Sanders; Action for award of the 'Military Medal', 17th-18th July 1918 (signed E.A. Wisdom, Brig-Gen., Commanding 2nd Aust. Div.); Citation for award of 'Bar to the Military Medal', 8th August 1918 (signed C. Rosenthal, Major-Gen., Commanding 2nd Aust. Div.); Colour patch for the AIF 26th Battalion (centre).

#148 William Raymond Sanders (1895-1930)

William Raymond Sanders (1895-1930) was working as a Labourer when he enlisted in the AIF at Brisbane on the 19th March 1915. On the 24th May he embarked for active service abroad, but was returned to Australia aboard the "Port Lincoln" with 'gonorrhoea' on the 2nd September. He was then allocated to the 17th Reinforcements of the 26th Battalion and departed from Brisbane aboard the "HMAT Marathon" on the 27th October 1916. They disembarked at Plymouth on the 9th January 1917 and were marched into a training Battalion at Rollestone, by which time he had been charged with three offences for drunkeness and AWL.

On the 15th February 1917 he proceeded to Etaples, France, but was 'wounded in action' on the 26th March and sent back to Kitchener Military Hospital in Brighton. He recovered and was discharged on 21st April, given two weeks furlough, then was reorganised at Perham Downs before proceeding to Le Havre, France, where he rejoined the 26th Battalion on the 12th June 1917 for a further seven months. Following another short AWL event, he was given two weeks leave in Paris where he contracted V.D., but returned for another month with his unit. By then his venereal infection had reached such a stage that he was transferred to England. He was then Court Martialed for 'Failing to report to R. T. C. on 17th March 1918 and remaining AWL until the 3rd April 1918', for which the finding was 'Guilty'. His punishment was to be reduced in the ranks and fined 44 days pay.

He was discharged from hospital on the 22nd April 1918, and rejoined the 26th Battalion in France on the 8th May. The main Allied offensive of the war came around Morlancourt on 10th June 1918, while another was undertaken around Monument Wood, near Villers-Bretonneux, on 17th July. It was during this raid that Lieutenant Albert Borella earned the battalion's second Victoria Cross of the war. On 22nd July, thirteen men of the battalion accompanied 23 men of the British 1st Gun Carrier Company in taking possession of and towing away the abandoned German A7V tank "Mephisto" from within Allied lines. In August, the Allies launched their 'Hundred Days Offensive', which ultimately brought an end to the war. On the opening day of the offensive, the 26th led the 7th Brigade's attack around Villers-Bretonneux, where Ray was mentioned in despatches.

Ray Sanders was severely 'wounded in action' on the 29th August, transferred soonafter to England and admitted to the King George Hospital, London. It was while convalescing here that he was awarded the 'Military Medal' for his actions on the 17th July, and a 'Bar to the Military Medal' for his actions on the 8th August 1918. However, his injuries were so severe that he was unable to rejoin his unit, but from hospital he had recovered enough to go AWL just three days before the end of the war, and remained so until the 20th April 1919... some 163 days!! He then surrendered himself and faced a second Court Martial for 'AWL from hospital from 8th November 1918 to 20th April 1919', for which the finding was 'Guilty', and was handed a sentence of 150 days in detention. He was marched out to Lewes Detention Barracks, but later admitted to Kitchener Hospital at Brighton, then back into detention. On the 26th July 1919, the unexpired portion of his sentence was remitted (71 days). Following his release he immediately took another two days AWL, before his re-admittance to hospital.

Ray Sanders was embarked for Australia via South Africa aboard the "Nestor" on 1st November 1919, but in Cape Town he took another five days AWL and had to entrain to Durban to catch up with his ship. He was medically discharged on the 8th February 1920. He died of his war injuries on the 14th January 1930 at the Prince of Wales Hospital, Randwick... a character, a hero and a true blue Australian! He was a great grandson to John and Mary Frawley.

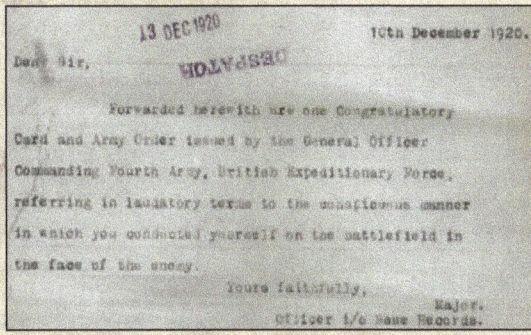

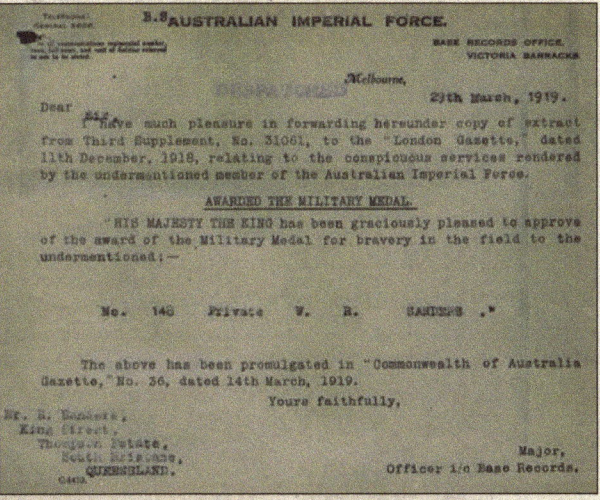
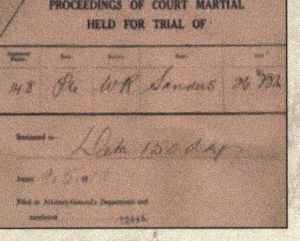
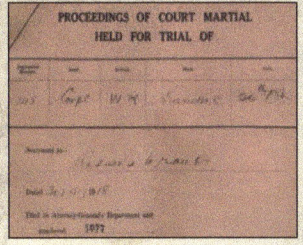

#5120 Robert Harold Sanders (1897-1961)

Harold Robert Sanders (1897-1961), aka 'Harry' was a Railway Porter, but enlisted at Brisbane on the 23rd May 1917 and was allocated to the 14th Reinforcements of the 31st Battalion. He departed from Sydney aboard the "HMAT Hororata" on the 14th June 1917. They disembarked at Liverpool on the 26th August and was marched into Hurdcott, then proceeded to Le Havre, France on the 20th March 1918, and into operations with the 31st Battalion.

In 1917, the 31st Battalion was involved in the Allied advance towards the Hindenburg Line, although because it was employed mainly in the flank protection role in this time, the only major fighting that it was involved in was at Polygon Wood during the Battle of Passchendaele in the Ypres sector in September 1917. It was here that Private Patrick Joseph Bugden, an original member of the Kennedy Regiment, performed the actions that led to him receiving the Victoria Cross.

On 15 May 1918, Sergeant David Emmett Coyne was nominated for the Victoria Cross for throwing himself on a hand-grenade that he had thrown after it had accidentally bounced back off a parapet, in order to protect other soldiers. However, as this was not in the face of the enemy, the posthumous nomination was changed to that of the Albert Medal in Gold, the only such medal issued to a member of the AIF (it was later superseded by the George Cross). Later, in August 1918, the 31st Battalion was involved in the last Allied offensive of the war when it took part in the fighting that resulted in the capture of Villers Bretonneux and then Bullecourt. Later, in September, the battalion was involved in the attack on the St Quentin Canal. This proved to be their last involvement in the war as they were out of the line when the Armistice occurred on 11th November.

By wars end Harold Sanders was still in the field, but was hospitalised 'dangerously ill' with influenza on the 9th January 1919. He eventually recovered and was embarked for Australia aboard the "Port Sydney" on 22nd September 1919 and discharged on the 23rd December 1919. He was a great grandson to John and Mary Frawley.

#7548 Arthur Carew Sanders (1899-1940)

Arthur Carew Sanders (1899-1940) was working as a Carter, but enlisted at Brisbane on the 5th February 1917 and was initially allocated to the 25th Reinforcements of the 9th Battalion. He departed from Sydney in company with his brother Harry, aboard the "HMAT Hororata" on the 14th June 1917. They disembarked at Liverpool on the 26th August and was marched into Durrington, but was hospitalised in November to Sutton Henry, before recovering and proceeding to Le Havre, France on the 7th March 1918, and was transferred into operations with the 15th Battalion.

In early 1918, the collapse of the Russian Empire enabled the Germans to transfer a significant number of troops to the Western Front and in March, having amassed 192 divisions, they launched an offensive against the British forces in the Somme. Heavily outnumbered, the British and Dominion troops were pushed back by the initial onslaught and the Australian Corps was thrown into the line in an effort to stem the tide. The 15th Battalion was moved initially to Bavincourt before securing Hebuterne late in the month, where they experienced a heavy artillery bombardment before turning back a German attack. Later, after being relieved by a battalion of the Royal Fusiliers, they moved to Rossignol Farm. Throughout April, while the 13th and 15th Brigades fought significant actions around Villers-Bretonneux, the 15th Battalion received several drafts of reinforcements, bringing it up to a total of 57 officers and 955 other ranks as it prepared to move up to replace the 15th Brigade in late April. Following their arrival, they undertook a support role, constructing defences before moving on to Freschencourt on 22 May, remaining there until they marched at the end of the month to Hamelet near Corbie, where they conducted several patrol actions.

However, on the 1st June 1918 Arthur Sanders was hospitalised with an abcess to the chest and 'trench fever', and was sent back to Devonport Military Hospital in England. He recovered and was returned to France, being transferred to the 26th Battalion on the 2nd November, just a week before the wars end. He embarked for Australia aboard the captured "SS Frankfurt" on 20th August 1919 and discharged on the 26th September 1919. Arthurs Sanders was a great grandson to John and Mary Frawley.

"SS Frankfurt"

The amazing fern smothered blue gum forests of the far South Coast of New South Wales, were a playground for the Frawley children.

2. Ellen Frawley (1842-1909)

John and Mary Ann Frawley likely arrived at Twofold Bay about six weeks prior to the birth of their second child Ellen Frawley, which occurred at 'Warragaburra Station' on the 2nd of September 1842.[19] John Frawley was then employed on that remote property by the Imlays as a shepherd or labourer. Consequently, Ellen Frawley is believed to have been one of the first, if not the very first white child born on the far South Coast, with her baptism taking place on the 18th March 1844 at 'Warragaburra'.[20] She would almost certainly have attended the public school at Pambula, which opened in 1850.[21]

Her husband James Mahony O'Sullivan arrived in Melbourne, from Rathmore, Co. Kerry, Ireland aboard the "Ocean Chief", which docked in Port Phillip Bay on the 25th February 1859.[22,23] He was a gold miner, and married firstly at the goldfields town of Donnellys Creek in Victoria's Gippsland region,[24] to a countrywoman from County Kerry, who sadly died of typhus during the first year of their marriage.[25]

While this was happening, Ellen Frawley left Pambula and drifted to Sydney before meeting and later marrying James Mahony O'Sullivan on 3rd August

TOP: John Frawley Jr. (Lot 51) & Ellen Frawley (Lot 63) - Wyndham Land Sale (Twofold Bay Telegraph, 31 July 1860). ABOVE: Memorial photograph of Ellen O'Sullivan (nee Frawley), buried 1909 at Sandgate, Newcastle.

5. Descendants of Ellen Frawley & James Mahony O'Sullivan
(Data from NSW Births, Deaths & Marriages Index, Ancestry.com & Newspapers).

Ellen Frawley (1842-1909)

Ellen Frawley (1842-1909), married on the 3rd August 1869 at St Mary's Cathedral, Sydney to James Mahony (c.1837-1891), son of Thadeus O'SULLIVAN & Zenobia Mahony of 'Coombe Cottage', County Kerry, a gold miner, with issue:

1. **Humphrey Joseph Vincent O'SULLIVAN (1871-1905)**, was born at Fish River Creek near Bathurst, and married on the 11th July 1900 at St Mary's Cathedral, Sydney to Lenore (1866-1945), the daughter of Thomas Eastman Shoveller & Susan Hann, with issue:

   1.1 Melecca O'Sullivan (1901-1901)*, died an infant.
   1.2 Octavia Corelli O'Sullivan (1902-1976), was born in Leichhardt and married on the 21st Sep 1926 at St John's Church, Glebe to Robert Archibald (1904-1966), son of William Henry ROCKWELL & Elizabeth Carpenter (nee Bantin), with issue:
     a. Joy Corelli Rockwell (1927-2018), born 13th Apr 1927 at Naremburn. She married on the 9th Apr 1966 at St Cuthbert's Church, Naremburn to William HYDE (1925-2000), with issue:
       a1. Robert William HYDE (1967-2016)
     b. Robert Hunter ROCKWELL (1929-1984), born 25th Jun 1929 at Naremburn. He married on the 15th Jan 1954 at Sydney to Betty Jean (1935-1996), daughter of William W. Wardle & Mary A. Cummings, with issue:
       b1. Tracy Paul ROCKWELL (1955)
       b2. Robert Wayne ROCKWELL (1959-1963)*
       b3. Sandra Kay Rockwell (1964)
     c. Elwood Lorraine ROCKWELL (1933-1987) born 9th Dec 1933 in Naremburn. He had partners, but never married, with no issue.
     d. Lindsay Archibald ROCKWELL (1937) born 2nd Nov 1937 in Naremburn. He married on the 14th Sep 1957 at St Cuthbert's Church, Naremburn to Lynette Ellen (1939-2006), daughter of Hugh & Alice Watson, with issue:
       d1. Rhonda Janine Rockwell (1960)
       d2. Glen Lindsay ROCKWELL (1962)
     e. Ronie Malcolm ROCKWELL (1943-2000), born 26th Feb 1943 at Naremburn. He married firstly in 1961 to Coral Joy Stretton (1942-1981), with issue:
       e1. Brett Anthony ROCKWELL (1961)
       e2. Mark Malcolm ROCKWELL (1962)
       e3. Paul Steven ROCKWELL (1965)
     Ronie married secondly in 1981 to Cheryl Joy Pooley (1945-2013), with issue:
       e4. Samuel Joshua ROCKWELL (1974)
       e5. Jessica Molly ROCKWELL (1977)
     f. Janet Lenore Rockwell (1946), born 22nd Feb 1946 at Naremburn. She married firstly on the 19th Jun 1965 at St Cuthbert's Church, Naremburn to Roland Lawrence WHITING (c.1945-1982), with issue:
       f1. Michelle Lena Whiting (1965)
       f2. Stephen Hunter WHITING (1968)
       f3. Adam Roger WHITING (1971),

NB. The family of Octavia Corelli O'Sullivan & Robert Archibald Rockwell are featured in Volume 8 of the Rockwell Genealogies - "Nostagia For Naremburn".

1.3 Sylvia Veronica O'Sullivan (1903-1914)*, died a child.
1.4 Goldie Alathea O'Sullivan (1905-1982), was born in Glebe, and later married on the 9th July 1927 in Sydney to Patrick Joseph (1903-1961), son of Patrick Joseph MULROY & Johanna Rooney, with issue:
  a. Lionel Raymond MULROY (1928-2010), was a companion to Shirley ?, no issue.
  b. Leslie John MULROY (1938-c.1999), married in 1958 to Judith Anne Clancey in Sydney (#15130), with issue:
    b1. Lionel Raymond MULROY (1959) married to Anne ?, with issue:
      b1.1 Stella Mulroy (1995)
      b1.2 Unknown Mulroy?
    b2. Leslie Allan MULROY (c.1962), worked as a lifeguard with Waverley Council, married to ?, with issue:
      b2.1 Unknown Mulroy?
      b2.2 Unknown Mulroy?

2. **James Alexander O'SULLIVAN (1872-1938)** was born at Grafton and married on the 31st July 1897 at the Cathedral Church, Grafton to Emily Ann (1868-1934), the daughter of Thomas Jordan (blacksmith) and Mary Jane Harper, with issue:

   2.1 Myrtle Helena O'Sullivan (1898-1991), was born at Grafton in 1898 (#21399), and married in 1925 at Norman Park, QLD to James Wallis LEWIS (1891-1963), with issue:
     a. Myrtle Lewis (1926-2001) married in 1947 to Arthur PARKINSON (1926-1979), issue unknown?
     b. Joan Lewis (1928-2005) married in 1958 to John CRAIG (1928-2001), issue unknown?
     c. Valma Lewis (1930) married in 1948 at Taree, NSW to Reginald George BUCKMAN, with issue:
       c1. Gary Edward BUCKMAN (1950)
       c2. Janette Mary Buckman (1953)
       c3. Beverley Buckman
       c4. Greg BUCKMAN
     d. Darcy J. LEWIS (1931-1945)*, died a child.
     e. Samuel G. LEWIS (1934-1995), issue unknown?
   2.2 Gladys Victoria O'Sullivan (1901-1930), was born at Powell St, Grafton on the 8th Jan. 1901. She delivered Daphne Rosalind O'Sullivan to Jack EVANS at the age of just 15, with the child being brought up by her parents, James and Emily O'Sullivan to avoid shame:
     a. Daphne Rosalind O'Sullivan (b. 4/9/1917-?) born at 110 Fry St, Grafton, and married on the 22nd May 1937 at St. George, QLD to Edgar A. LEGGATT (1917-1971) with issue:
       a1. Daphne Ann Leggatt (b. 5/9/1937) at St. George, QLD, marr. 22/11/1958 at Yeronga to Donald Mervyn MEREFIELD (1934-1998), with issue:
         a1.1 Nichole Maree Merefield

Lionel Raymond Mulroy (1928-2010)

Claude Patrick O'Sullivan (changed to Wilson 1901-1969)

Gladys Victoria O'Sullivan (1901-1930)

DEATHS.
News reached town yesterday of the death of Mr. Humphrey O'Sullivan, which took place in Sydney from pneumonia. He leaves a widow and three children, and a number of his relatives are resident on the Clarence and in the vicinity of Coff's Harbour.

O'SULLIVAN.—In loving memory of our dear brother, Humphrey Joseph O'Sullivan, who departed this life 30th June, 1905.
May his soul rest in peace.
Inserted by his loving mother, sisters, and brothers.
3555

ROGERS v. ROGERS.
Charles Albert Rogers, storeman and packer, residing at Rocklea, petitioned for a divorce from his wife, Gladys Victoria Rogers, on the ground of misconduct with Carmelo Barbera, who was joined as co-defendant, and from whom plaintiff claimed £500 damages.
Mr. P. K. Copley (instructed by Mr. Max Deacon) appeared for the plaintiff.
There was no appearance on behalf of the defendant.

Goldie Alathea O'Sullivan (1905-1982)

James Alexander O'Sullivan (1872-1938)

John W. O'Sullivan (1913-1974) & Victor J. O'Sullivan (1908-1990)

Myrtle Helena O'Sullivan (1898-1991)

Octavia Corelli O'Sullivan (1902-1976)

17 - Descendants of John & Mary Frawley

a1.2 Myles Raymond MEREFIELD
a1.3 Kylie Ann Merefield
a2. Dawn Leggatt (b. 16/11/1938) at Dalby Hosp, QLD, marr. 27/12/1958 at Acacia Ridge Pres. Church, Bris. to Bernard George POPE (1932), with issue:
   a2.1 Daniel Terence POPE
   a2.2 Francis Edgar Albert POPE (b. 12/6/1940) at Dalby, marr. Sharon Sanburg, with issue:
     a2.2.1 Jason POPE
     a2.2.2 Marcus POPE
a3. Anthony Darryl LEGGATT (19/8/1946) at Cleveland, QLD, marr. Shirley Ann Ryan (8/4/1946) at Sydney, with issue:
   a3.1 Catherine Elizabeth Leggatt
   a3.2 Kellie Maree Leggatt
   a3.3 Emma Louise Leggatt
a4. Phillip John LEGGATT (b. 16/10/1952) at Brisbane, marr. 21/12/1970 to Jennifer Anthony (1950) of Brisbane, with issue:
   a4.1 Sacha Leggatt
   a4.2 Sheridan Leggatt
   a4.3 Gretchen Leggatt
a5. Linda Maree Leggatt (b. 31/12/1956) at Brisbane, marr. 7/7/1979 to Chris W. OSBORNE (1958) of Brisbane (Changed name to PETHERICK (12/10/1967) in Sth Aust.), with issue:
   a5.1 Candice Petherick
   a5.2 Anthony PETHERICK
a6. Suzanne Rosalind Leggatt (b. 6/9/1960) at Brisbane, marr. 4/11/1978 to Geraint O. MORGAN (1957) with issue:
   a6.1 Kate Rosalind Morgan
   a6.2 Michael Owen MORGAN
   a6.3 Stephen James MORGAN

Gladys then married in 1922 at Cooparoo, QLD to Charles Albert ROGERS (1897-1991), with issue:
  b. Gloria Mavis Rogers (1923-2012) born in Brisbane, marr. in 1946 at Brighton, VIC to Francis Albert DEAN (1920-?), issue unknown?

Gladys later met and married secondly in 1930, at Cardwell, QLD to Carmelo BARBERO (1900-1901), after divorcing her husband Charles Rogers, but she died in childbirth soonafter, at just 29 years of age.

3. Female O'SULLIVAN (1873-1873)*, died an infant.
4. Male O'SULLIVAN (1875-1875)*, died an infant.
5. John Washington O'SULLIVAN (1877-1947), was born at Dalmorton, NSW, and married on the 25th January 1902 at St Matthias Church, Paddington, Sydney to Sarah Amelia (1876-1943), the daughter of William Bridger and Amelia Jennings of Surry Hills, with issue:
5.1 Victor James O'SULLIVAN (1908-1990) ▲ was born at St Leonards (#29464), and married in 1933 at North Sydney, NSW to Louisa Groves (1909-1960), with issue:
  a. Janice Lenore O'sullivan (1936) born at Crows Nest, NSW, married in 1957 to Graham John McGUINNESS (1935-2003), with issue:
    a1. Peter John McGUINNESS (1958) born at Young, NSW, married 1986 to Christine Anne Lloyd (1960), divorced 1993, d.s.p.
    a2. Michelle McGuinness (1960) born in Sydney, married Geoff PALMER, with issue:
      a2.1 Amelia Palmer, marr. Scott NICHOLLS, with issue:
        a2.1.1 Angus NICHOLLS
      a2.2 Rachel Palmer, marr. Jono McGUIRE, with issue:
        a2.2.1 Owen McGUIRE
        a2.2.2 Lucky McGUIRE
        a2.2.3 Tomas McGUIRE
  b. Robyn Gail O'Sullivan (1942-2006) born at North Sydney, married in 1962 to Richard Nelson Worsley GRAY, AM., (1938), with issue:
    b1. Joanne Helen Worsley Gray (1965), married to James SUTER, with issue:
      b1.1 Jack SUTER
    Joanne married secondly to Mr. THOROUGHGOOD, with issue:
      b1.2 Luke THOROUGHGOOD
    b2. David Mark Worsley GRAY (1969), born in Wagga Wagga, NSW, married to Tamara Jane Reynolds (1972), divorced 2017, with issue:
      b2.1 Jasper Reynolds GRAY (2007)
      b2.2 Astrid Robin Gray (2009)
      b2.3 Araminta Lily Gray (2011)
    b3 Karen Louise Worsley Gray (1971), born in Wagga Wagga, NSW, committed in 2014 to Glenn Andrew ROBERTSON (1965).

Victor married secondly in 1961 at Chatswood, NSW to Joyce Vera Smylie (nee Brown) (1918-2007). No issue.

5.2 John William O'SULLIVAN (1913-1974) ▲ was born at St Leonards (#19289), and married in 1941 at Sydney, NSW to Minnie Laurel Pardey (1897-1974), who was 16 years his senior. No issue.

Later in life, John Washington O'Sullivan was with Augusta Mattie Peyton (?-1954), without issue.

6. Mary Zenobia O'SULLIVAN (1879-1879)*, died an infant.
7. Ellen Theresa O'SULLIVAN (1880>1932), known as 'Nellie', she was born at Dalmorton, NSW and married firstly on the 9th February 1909 at Auckland, NZ to James Ernest Gear (1881-1961). She married secondly on the 14th Sept 1917, at Honolulu, Hawaii to Marion Alvin Mulrony (1886-?) and became a citizen of the United States. No known issue.
8. Blanche Zenobia O'SULLIVAN (1882-1942), known as 'Bessie', she was born at Dalmorton, NSW and delivered her only child illegitimately in 1901. She married firstly on the 1st October 1904 at St. Andrews Presbyterian Manse, Newcastle to Charles Stanborough (1875-1927), no issue. She married secondly in 1927 at Sydney to John McKinlay (1873-1953), no issue.
8.1 Claude Hope O'SULLIVAN (1901-1969) ▲ was born on the 21st Nov 1901, (father unknown) at Newtown (#34239). He changed his name to Claude Patrick WILSON sometime before 1925, and married under that name on the 9th March 1925 at Leeton, NSW to Florence Ada Pitt (1904-1969) with issue:
  a. Patrick Claude WILSON (19/3/1926) - Nil marriages on NSW BDM?
  b. Peter John WILSON (27/6/1928) - 15 possible marriages on NSW BDM?
  c. Ellen Patricia Wilson (6/6/1931-3/9/1951), married in 1948 at North Sydney to Edward HEARNE (#3718/1948), issue unknown?
  d. Mary Teresa Wilson (21/11/1935) - 3 possible marriages on NSW BDM?
  e. Joseph Bruce WILSON (17/10/1937), married in 1961 at Wyong to Denise Margaret Frewin (#12300/1961), issue unknown?
  f. Alice Zenobia Wilson (13/5/1940) - 5 possible marriages on NSW BDM?
  g. Anne Margaret Wilson (10/7/1942), married in 1967 at Parramatta to Wayne Brian LEE (#21287/1967), issue unknown?
9. William O'SULLIVAN (1884-1884)*, died an infant.
10. Rupert C. O'SULLIVAN (1886-1886)*, died an infant.
11. Female O'Sullivan (1888-1888)*, died an infant.
12. Zenobia O'SULLIVAN (1891-1891)*, died an infant.

* Died before adulthood - d.s.p.
(Some names not listed in the index).

Lenore Shoveller (1866-1945)

Ronie Malcolm Rockwell (1943-2000)

Robert H. Rockwell (1929-1984) & Betty J. Wardle (1935-1996)

O'SULLIVAN.—The Friends of Mrs. M. H. Lewis, Mrs. J. McKinlay (Sydney), Mr. J. O'Sullivan (Sydney) are invited to attend the Funeral of their deceased Father and Brother, Mr. James Alexander O'Sullivan, late 9th Batt., A.I.F., to leave the Funeral Parlour, 45 Adelaide Street, City, This (Tuesday) Morning, at 10.30 o'clock, for the Toowong Cemetery.
CANNON & CRIPPS, Funeral Directors.

McKINLAY—The Friends of Mr. John McKinlay, of 87 Muston Street, Mosman, are invited to attend the Funeral of his late beloved Wife, Blanche Zenobia (Bessie); to leave the Private Chapel of Motor Funerals Limited, 389 Pacific Highway, Crow's Nest, This Morning, at 11 o'clock, for the Northern Suburbs Crematorium. Friends may attend the Service at the Crow's Nest Chapel, Motor Funerals Limited, 389 Pacific Highway, Crow's Nest. Tele. XB4015.

◄LEFT: Humphrey J. O'Sullivan - Death notices (Clarence & Richmond Examiner, 1 July 1905, p.5). RIGHT: Rogers v Rogers Divorce (Newscutting, Sep 1929) ▲LEFT: James A. O'Sullivan - Funeral notice (Courier Mail, 21 June 1928). RIGHT: Blanche Zenobia McKinley - Funeral notice (SMH, 31 Dec 1942, p.8).

Robert Archibald Rockwell (1904-1966)

Robin Gail O'Sullivan (1942-2006)

Elwood Lorraine Rockwell (1933-1987)

Janet Lenore Rockwell (1946)

Joy Corelli Rockwell (1927-2018)

Lindsay Archibald Rockwell (1937)

1869 at St Mary's Cathedral in Sydney.[26] Ellen didn't list an occupation on her marriage papers and was a spinster at the time of her wedding. Shortly after their wedding, the O'Sullivans departed Sydney for the Fish River gold diggings near Oberon, where their first son Humphrey Joseph O'Sullivan (1871-1905) was born on the 5th May 1871.[27]

After toiling for 18 months with little success, they travelled back to Sydney and boarded a coaster paddlesteamer for the town of Grafton on the Clarence River. The O'Sullivans initially set themselves up at Villiers St, Grafton, where their second son, James Alexander O'Sullivan was born on the 22nd August 1872.[28] However, they didn't remain in Grafton long, as James likely brought his wife and two infant sons out to his next mining venture. The family next travelled overland to Dalmorton, a new gold town, perhaps via Pinkerton's Coaches, which had commenced a weekly service from Grafton to the goldfields in July of 1872.

It is believed that gold was discovered in the greater Dalmorton area in the 1860's by a Cunglebung Station leaseholder. Thereafter, gold was worked sporadically on the tributaries of the Mann and Boyd Rivers until the main 'rush' was precipitated in early 1871 by the discovery of a gold bearing quartz reef called 'Union Reef' at Quartz Pot Creek, located south of Dalmorton. This piqued the interest of prospectors and lead to the rapid discovery of over 50 workable reefs in the greater Dalmorton area. By March of the same year the rush to the Boyd River and Dalmorton had begun and as per any new gold discovery, prospectors flocked there from all over the country.[29]

In Dalmorton, James O'Sullivan would have quickly converted their tent accommodation into a slab hut dwelling, having gained valuable experience from his mining days in Victoria. After solving their housing problems the next hurdle facing the early miners was obtaining food, which they initially had to bring with them, but it wasn't long before a store opened. The O'Sullivans remained in Dalmorton from 1872 until 1883, and produced more children including John Washington O'Sullivan (1877-1947),[30] Ellen Theresa O'Sullivan (1880>1932)[31] and Blanche Zenobia O'Sullivan (1882-1942)[32] amongst three others that died in infancy *(see Table 5. Descendants of Ellen Frawley & James O'Sullivan)*. But the population of Dalmorton inevitably began to decline, and settlers like James Mahony O'Sullivan realised that the township wasn't really growing. Added to that was the difficulty of bringing up a family amidst the poor health, behaviour and vices of the mostly single miners in the community.

James was obviously in touch with regional developments and he likely heard of a new community opening up on the coast, 50 miles to the south east of Grafton. With the Dalmorton School closing, and the village in decline, James and Ellen O'Sullivan thought it best to move on, which in benefitting their family, still allowed James to travel back and forward to his gold leases in Dalmorton. So they piled up their belongings and moved the family, likely by horse and cart to Moonee Creek, just north of todays Coffs Harbour where they arrived as pioneers of that region well before Christmas of 1883.[33]

Together they produced 12 children, although only five lived to adulthood.[34] The extent to which Ellen kept in contact with her parents and wayward siblings in both Pambula and Toowoomba is unclear, but her life events and descendants are recorded in more detail in the book "The Path That Few Travel" *(see Volume 4 of the Rockwell Genealogies)*. James Mahony O'Sullivan died in 1891 and Ellen O'Sullivan survived until the 4th August 1909, aged 67 and is buried in Sandgate Cemetery at Newcastle, NSW.[35] The following pages contain memorials from Australian Service Records, for descendants of Ellen and James O'Sullivan, who enlisted in the Australian forces.

#2189 James Alexander O'Sullivan (1872-1938)

James Alexander O'Sullivan (#2189) enlisted in the AIF at a rate of five shillings per day, on the 12th August 1915 and was initially assigned as a private to the 25th Battalion, 4th Reinforcements. He was 42 years of age at the time and was working as a 'timber-getter'. His address was given as Kadanga in the Mary Valley, Queensland where he resided with his wife Emily Ann O'Sullivan. He embarked from Brisbane aboard "HMAT Armadale" A26 on the 18th September 1915, and his rate of pay increased to 11 shillings per day after embarkation.

The 25th Battalion was raised at Enoggera in Queensland in March 1915 as part of the 7th Brigade. Although predominantly composed of men recruited in Queensland, the battalion also included a small contingent of men from Darwin. At Gallipoli the 7th Brigade reinforced the depleted New Zealand and Australian Division, but had a relatively quiet time as the last major Allied offensive had been launched, and turned back, in the previous month. They left the Gallipoli peninsular on 18 December 1915.

Clockwise from right: 25th Battalion colour patch. During the world wars and the years in between, Australian soldiers wore cloth patches of various shapes and colours on their upper sleeves to indicate which unit or formation they belonged; James Alexander O'Sullivan proudly sports his AIF uniform from WWI, photo taken at his daughters wedding in 1922; A company of AIF diggers encamped near the Sphinx and the Pyramids in Egypt, which was a training area for all units arriving from Australia via the Suez Canal; AIF Camp at the Pyramids WWI; AIF soldiers of the 9th Battalion at Bir el Habeita, Egypt, Feb. 1916; James Alexander O'Sullivan embarked from Brisbane aboard "HMAT Armadale" A26 on the 18th September 1915.

James was soonafter transferred to the 9th Battalion on 28th February 1916 at Bir el Habeita, Egypt. They proceeded to Alexandria with the British Expeditionary Force on 27th March 1916, and disembarked aboard the "Saxonia" for Marseilles on the 3rd April. On arrival, the 9th Battalion deployed to the Somme, experiencing its first major action at Pozières in July 1916, where Private John Leak earned the Victoria Cross. Following this, the 9th Battalion moved to the Ypres sector, in Belgium, before returning to the Somme where they manned the trenches throughout winter. In 1917, the 9th Battalion was engaged in operations against the Hindenberg Line.

But James O'Sullivan missed most of the action as he was hospitalised with gastritis on the 3rd June 1916 and sent to Reading War Hospital, Berkshire in England. Once recovered he was marched back into France through the French port of Etaples on the 9th February 1917, but was re-admitted to hospital in early March, ahead of being sent back for a second time to England on the 21st April, where he was hospitalised at both Cowley and Milton Hill Hospitals, from 23rd April to 12th July 1917 with 'trench foot and severe varicose veins'. His war ended when he was returned to Australia via New Zealand aboard the "Pakeha", which embarked from England on the 28th August 1917. He disembarked in Sydney on the 24th October, thence traveled overland by train to Brisbane, where he was given a 'medical discharge' and reunited with his family on the 22nd December 1917.

#VN15581 Claude Patrick Wilson (1901-1969)

Claude Hope O'Sullivan, who changed his name to Claude Patrick Wilson (#VN15581), was accepted into the RAAF on the 11th June 1940. He was 38 years of age at the time and had previously worked as a steward, car driver, foreman, tractor driver, roof tiler and cook. His address was given as 16 Ross St, Waverton where he resided with his wife Florence Ada Wilson and his family of six children.

He was initially assigned as a cook to Bradfield Park (West Lindfield), which from 1940 was an RAAF station built to house a number of RAAF and WAAAF units. During World War II, more than 200,000 members of the RAAF and the WAAAF received training at Bradfield Park, on their way to war service in World War II. He was soonafter sent to Wagga RAAF Base for training, but in April of 1942 was posted to Richmond RAAF Base, before being returned to Bradfield Park in May of 1943. In December 1944 he was posted to Narromine RAAF Base, where he was stationed for the remainder of the war, and was discharged on the 2nd November 1945.

Claude was promoted to the rank of Corporal on the 1st December 1941, but due to the essential nature of his work as a cook/caterer, he perhaps fortunately spent the entirety of the war at home in Australia.

Anti-clockwise from top right: Portrait of Claude Patrick Wilson; RAAF Service Certificate; Bombers lined up at the Wagga RAAF Base; Cooks working at the Wagga RAAF Base; Application letter to the RAAF.

World War Two Service

LEADING AIRCRAFTMAN
CLAUDE PATRICK WILSON
15581

SERVICE	ROYAL AUSTRALIAN AIR FORCE
DATE OF BIRTH	21 NOVEMBER 1901
PLACE OF BIRTH	NEWTOWN, NSW
DATE OF ENLISTMENT	11 JUNE 1940
LOCALITY ON ENLISTMENT	WAVERTON
PLACE OF ENLISTMENT	SYDNEY, NSW
NEXT OF KIN	WILSON, FLORENCE
DATE OF DISCHARGE	2 NOVEMBER 1945
POSTING AT DISCHARGE	RAAF STATION NARROMINE

Australian Government
Department of Veterans' Affairs

#NX136906 Victor James O'Sullivan (1908-1990)

O'Sullivan Victor James: Service Number - NX136906; Date Of Birth - 30 Jun 1908; Place Of Birth - North Sydney NSW; Place Of Enlistment - Narellan NSW; Next Of Kin - O'Sullivan Louise (wife). He Was A Great Grandson Of John And Mary Frawley.

World War Two Service

LANCE SERGEANT
VICTOR JAMES O'SULLIVAN
NX136906

SERVICE	AUSTRALIAN ARMY
DATE OF BIRTH	30 JUNE 1908
PLACE OF BIRTH	NORTH SYDNEY, NSW
DATE OF ENLISTMENT	8 NOVEMBER 1942
LOCALITY ON ENLISTMENT	WILLOUGHBY, NSW
PLACE OF ENLISTMENT	NARELLAN, NSW
NEXT OF KIN	O'SULLIVAN, LOUISE
DATE OF DISCHARGE	18 JANUARY 1946
POSTING AT DISCHARGE	AUSTRALIAN NEW GUINEA ADMINISTRATIVE UNIT
ADDITIONAL SERVICE NUMBERS	N171856

Australian Government
Department of Veterans' Affairs

#NX81887 John William O'Sullivan (1913-1974)

O'sullivan John William: Service Number - NX81887; Date Of Birth - 07 Apr 1913; Place Of Birth - Sydney NSW; Place Of Enlistment - Paddington NSW; Next Of Kin - O'Sullivan Minnie (wife). He was a great grandson of John and Mary Frawley.

World War Two Service

SERGEANT
JOHN WILLIAM O'SULLIVAN
NX81887

SERVICE	AUSTRALIAN ARMY
DATE OF BIRTH	7 APRIL 1913
PLACE OF BIRTH	SYDNEY, NSW
DATE OF ENLISTMENT	3 JANUARY 1942
LOCALITY ON ENLISTMENT	MANLY, NSW
PLACE OF ENLISTMENT	PADDINGTON, NSW
NEXT OF KIN	O'SULLIVAN, MINNIE
DATE OF DISCHARGE	21 MARCH 1946
POSTING AT DISCHARGE	1 AUST ARMOURED BRIGADE A I F

Australian Government
Department of Veterans' Affairs

Elwood L. Rockwell

The four Rockwell boys, all great great-grandsons of John and Mary Frawley were too young for WWII, but Elwood was in the CMF, although he apparently spent most of his time in the base lock-up for over-imbibing.

Lindsay A. Rockwell

Lindsay Archibald Rockwell was a member of the CMF for 6 months in 1955, but never saw action. He recalls that members of the regular army had a name for the CMF boys, who they called 'Chocko's' or chocolate soldiers.

Robert William Hyde

Robert joined the regular army straight after school about 1985 and served in a motorised division, although he never saw action. After leaving the army he became an active member of the reserve forces and joined in on many training exercises.

The Australian Army Reserve is a collective name given to the reserve units of the Australian Army. Since the Federation of Australia in 1901, the reserve military force has been known by many names, including the Citizens Forces (CF), the Citizen Military Forces (CMF), the Militia and, unofficially, the Australian Military Forces (AMF).

3. James Frawley (1843<1901)

James Frawley was born on the 14th November 1843 and baptised on the 18th March 1844 by Father Michael Kavanagh at 'Warragaburra' homestead on the far South Coast of New South Wales.[36] He was the third child of John and Mary Ann Frawley, and would have attended the public school at Pambula, which opened in 1850.[37] But like his father and older brother, he became entangled with the local authorities as a youth.

In late 1862, at age 19, James Frawley was charged with stealing a horse from Frank Boller at Tantawangalo, and found himself placed in custody at Eden Police Station on the 15th December 1862.[38] He was summonsed by the Eden District Court to defend the allegations, with a trial date set down for the 24th April 1863, but was bailed for £50.

> **BAIL RECEIPT - 25TH APRIL 1863**
> James Frawley in custody on committal to take his seat at the next Court of General Quarter Sessions of the Peace to be holden at Eden on a charge of Horse Stealing.
>
> Admitted to Bail in the sum of £50 himself, with two sureties in twenty five pounds cash for his appearance at the sessions as above: Stephen Collier (£25/0/0); Daniel [Purther] (£25/0/0). Taken and acknowledged this 25th day of April 1863.
>
> *P. J. Murray, Clerk, Eden Court*

Unfortunately, the outcome of this case is unknown, as it appears that the chief evidence in the case viz, the horse, could not be found, therefore the charge was likely dropped, with James narrowly avoiding a gaol sentence. After this close call, what happened to James Frawley next is uncertain, but he likely sought to avoid such events in the future and left Pambula.

In attempting to put space between himself and the long arm of the law, James travelled to Queensland, where a contractor of that same name appears in Toowoomba on the 12th November 1863, receiving payment for the construction of a foot-bridge.[39] As John and Mary Ann Frawley, together with their son John Frawley Jr., his wife Sarah and their five children William (11), Anna (9), Agnes (4), Charles (2) and Eden (1), all relocated to Toowoomba about 1876, there had to be a reason why they chose that town? Compelling the entire family to relocate north was likely the good fortune of James Frawley, who was likely the trailblazer for his parents and his older brother's family.

To avoid further scandal in Pambula, James Frawley likely journeyed north, about

Colour postcard of the Post Office, on Margaret Street, Toowoomba, c.1910.

Photograph of drovers on their horses in the Goondiwindi area c.1875.

the same time that his father and brother were imprisoned in Darlinghurst Gaol in 1863. About that time, a James Frawley does appear in a number of newspapers in South East Queensland from late 1863, especially in the Toowoomba and Meringandan Districts. For example, a James Frawley obtained good acreage as a selector at Meringandan in 1873, and a James Frawley even established a hotel at Meringandan, although it later burnt down in 1900. Could this have been the same James Frawley?

The Queensland Post Office Directory for 1894 listed a number of Frawley's including three brothers named James, Patrick and Thomas, all farmers, while a John Frawley was conducting a 'carrying' business at Meringandan in Queensland. But muddying the trail somewhat is the presence of two other Frawley's also living in the Toowoomba area at that time. A James Frawley 'selector' at Withcott, and a Thomas Frawley 'farmer', at Cawdor. Were these people the same family from Pambula, or another Frawley family? Somewhat confusingly, it seems that there was indeed, another James Frawley residing in Toowoomba at this very same time, which has confounded the research, and made it difficult to follow.

At the death of John Frawley (Sr.) in 1901, his death certificate stated that he was survived by two daughters who were Ellen and Letitia, but only two of his five sons, who could only have been Stephen and Patrick. While the death indexes have been unsuccessfully searched for James Frawley in New South Wales, Queensland and Victoria, it seems certain that he died sometime before 1901. No other information is known about any possible issue or his death, although possible marriages for a James Frawley held in Queensland Dept of Births, Deaths and Marriages were:

1865 to Ellen Murphy (#C78)
1876 to Ellen Hegarty (#C206)
1883 to Ann Doran (#C1756)

Unfortunately, without a verified marriage or descendants the trail for James Frawley goes cold at this point, but these leads may at some future stage assist further research and help untangle this branch.

Documents for James Frawley

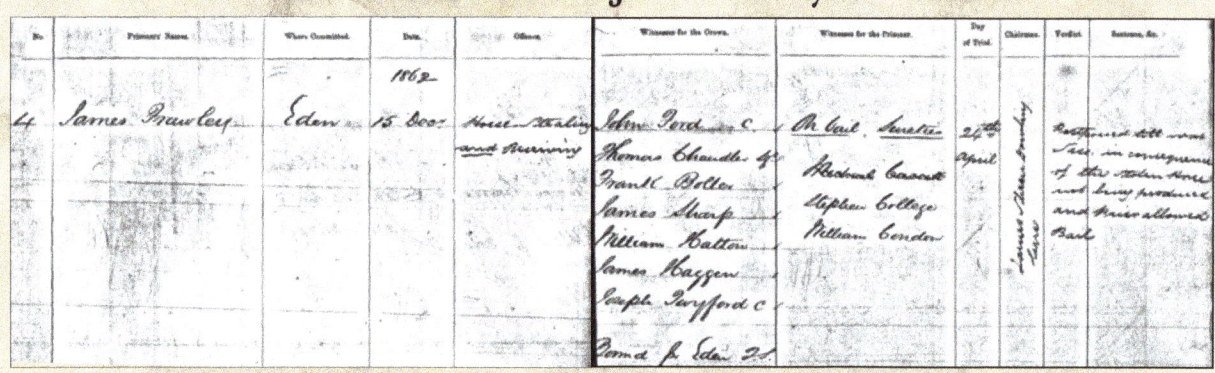

THE QUEEN AGAINST JAMES FRAWLEY.— In this case the prisoner was called upon to answer a charge of horse-stealing, but the chief evidence not being obtainable, an application was made by the Crown Prosecutor, and granted, for postponement till next sittings. Bail allowed as on the committal of prisoner.

TOOWOOMBA MUNICIPAL COUNCIL.
MONDAY, NOVEMBER 10, 1862.

PRESENT: His Worship the Mayor, and Aldermen Campbell, Flori, Ryan, and Groom.

The minutes of the preceding meeting having been confirmed, the following letters were read:—

Report of the Finance Committee, recommending payment of the following sums:—To James Frawley for construction of foot-bridge, £60; to Meldon, balance for clearing north-street, £30; to Dennis, for forming watercourse and dam near Shuttleworth's Bridge, £3, and £3 5s. for cutting drains in Stephen-street; to Inspector of Works, three months' salary to 4th November, £12 10s.; and to Town Clerk, one month's salary, £16 13s. 4d. Total, £135 8s. 4d.

TOOWOOMBA MUNICIPAL COUNCIL.

The Council met at the usual hour on Monday afternoon. Present—The Mayor and Aldermen Fraser, Cooper, Flori, Groom, and Ryan.

The minutes of the last meeting were read and confirmed.

The Town Clerk drew attention to the fact that there was a dead carcase near Southerden's paddock; but as it appeared that no complaint had been made to the Corporation the matter was allowed to drop.

CORRESPONDENCE.

A letter was read from the Postmaster-General, acknowledging the receipt of the application of the Council for three iron letter receivers in certain parts of the town, and stating that those applications should receive consideration.

James Frawley, £30; James Jackson, £11; James Gasper, £35; W. Brennan, £29; Henry Lang and Martin Fox, £20; Martin Kelly, £43; John Hollands, £30; Hugh Ferrett and Co. (five months), £24.

On the motion of Alderman Groom, seconded by Alderman Cooper, the tender of W. Brennan was accepted.

ANNE STREET.

John Collins, three months, £43; J. M'Inerney, three months, £49; John Daley, three months, £10; Hugh Ferrett, five weeks, £50; James Frawley, three months, £60; Martin Kelly, £8; Joseph Riley, £50.

On the motion of Alderman Fraser, seconded by Alderman Flori, the tender of Daley was accepted.

TOOWOOMBA MUNICIPAL COUNCIL.
MONDAY, OCTOBER 16.

Present—His Worship the Mayor, and Aldermen Ryan, Groom, Cooper, Fraser, and Flori.

The minutes of the meeting held on the 2nd instant were confirmed.

	£	s.	d.
NEIL-STREET.			
Martin Kelly, to be completed in four months	50	0	0
James Jackson, ditto three months	50	0	0
Hugh Ferrett and John Kaney, ditto five months	30	0	0
James Frawley, ditto four months	45	0	0
John Daley, ditto three months	55	0	0

Alderman Groom moved that the tender of James Frawley be accepted, which was seconded by Alderman Flori.

PHILLIP-STREET.	£	s.	d.
James Frawley, to be completed in two months	30	0	0

HUME-STREET.			
James Frawley, ditto three months	60	0	0
Martin Kelly, ditto three months	80	0	0
Joseph Riley	50	0	0

Alderman Fraser moved, and Alderman Flori seconded, that John Daley's tender for Hume-street be accepted, which was put and carried unanimously.

Alderman Groom then moved, and Alderman Fraser seconded, that James Frawley's tender be accepted, provided he undertook to do the work within three months, which was put and passed.

Mr. Frawley undertook to bind himself to complete the work in that time, and his contract was accepted.

Only one tender was sent in for the erection of the Market Sale Yards and Auctioneer's Shed.

Alderman Groom moved—seeing there was only one tender, that fresh tenders be called for.

TOOWOOMBA MUNICIPAL COUNCIL.

On Thursday afternoon, a special meeting of the Council was called. Only the Mayor and Alderman Groom were in attendance, and at half-past four o'clock it was agreed to adjourn until Saturday afternoon.

SATURDAY, JANUARY 6, 1866.

Present—His Worship the Mayor, and Aldermen Benjamin, Groom, Cooper, Flori, Ryan, and Cranley.

The minutes of the previous meeting were read. Alderman Groom moved, and Alderman Flori seconded their adoption, which was put and carried.

FINANCE REPORT.

	£	s.	d.
Martin Kelly, for forming and draining Stuart-street, and making and draining road to well in Herries-street	40	0	0
M'Inerny and Callaghan, 2nd payment on account—Erecting market yards	30	0	0
William Brennan, for repairing three wells, clearing Phillip-street, fencing, &c.	19	0	0
Hugh Swann, one months' salary	21	13	4
John M. Flynn, ditto	5	6	8
Assistant to Town Surveyor, 5 days, at 6s. per day	1	10	0
James Carey, burning 4 carcasses	2	0	0
J. W. Bennett, chains supplied for two wells	2	2	0
James Frawley—balance of contract for clearing Neil street	20	0	0
	£142	2	2

TOOWOOMBA MUNICIPAL COUNCIL.
MONDAY, NOVEMBER 13.

Present—His Worship the Mayor, and Aldermen Groom, Cranley, Ryan, Fraser, and Flori.

The minutes of the meeting held on the 30th October were read and confirmed.

A letter was read from his Excellency, acknowledging receipt of a letter of condolence to Mrs. Lincoln on the death of her husband, with a promise that it should be forwarded.

A letter from the Lands Department, stating that the Minister for Lands would shortly visit Toowoomba, when he would be happy to learn what were the wishes of the Council respecting the public park.

Also, a letter of similar import respecting a reserve for the townspeople.

The Finance Committee recommended payment of the following sums:—William Brennan, clearing Phillip-street, £20; James Frawley, clearing Neil-street, £10; James Carey, burning off cattle, £1 15s.

Alderman Groom moved and Alderman Ryan seconded, that the recommendation be adopted. Carried.

To this report an addendum was made, to the effect that Frawley, according to the opinion of the Town Surveyor, had not done his work according to contract. He had offered to deduct £2 if his work was not approved of. This matter related to some damage alleged to have been done to a fence on private property in the performance of his contract. It was agreed that the Improvement committee should inspect the work and decide upon the course to be pursued in the matter. In the course of discussion on this report it was stated that the sheep and cattle yards would be completed by the end of January. The Finance Report was adopted without opposition.

TOOWOOMBA PETTY DEBTS COURT.
MONDAY, MARCH 11, 1867.
[CONTINUED.]
(Before the Police Magistrate.)

FRAWLEY v. HOGAN.

Plaintiff, on the oath being administered, did not kiss the Bible, for which he was severely reprimanded by the Police Magistrate, and told that his evidence would be considered untrustworthy, and if his statements were disputed he should place little reliance on them.

James Frawley deposed: I agreed with the defendant to stump eleven trees for me at 4s. per tree; I went to Warwick, and when I returned he had not done it; I agreed to let him have rations; he was three weeks over the job, and his rations amounted to £3, being 16s. more than the value of the work done; he took it at 4s. per tree, and I knew d—d well it wouldn't pay him.

The Police Magistrate: Don't swear here—wait till you are outside.

The evidence of defendant being here taken, his Worship remarked that he did not wonder at Frawley's kissing his thumb instead of the book when he stated that a single man consumed 150 lbs. of flour in three weeks.

Verdict for plaintiff 24s.

TOP: James Frawley - Charged with Horse Stealing at Eden Criminal Court, 15th Dec, 1862 (Eden Court, NSW Criminal Court Records, 1830-1945). **LEFT COLUMN:** 1-James Frawley, charged with horse stealing (SMH, 29th Apr 1863, p.5).; 2-James Frawley - Construction of Foot-bridge (Toowoomba Chronicle, 12 Nov 1863, p.2); 3-James Frawley - Contractor (The Darling Downs Gazette & Gen. Advertiser, 9 Jan 1866, p.3); The rough streets of Toowoomba in 1870. **CENTRE COLUMN:** 1-James Frawley - Contractor (The Darling Downs Gazette & Gen. Advertiser, 19 Oct 1865, p.3); 2-James Frawley - Construction of Foot-bridge (Toowoomba Chronicle, 11 Jan 1866, p.3). **RIGHT COLUMN:** 1-James Frawley - Contractor (Toowoomba Chronicle, 16 Nov 1865); 2-James Frawley - Remedial Work (Toowoomba Chronicle, 9 Jan 1866, p.3); 3-James Frawley v Hogan (Toowoomba Chronicle, 16 Mar 1867, p.3).

TOP: James & Miss Frawley - Arrive Sydney form Brisbane aboard the paddlesteamer "City of Brisbane" on the 19th October 1868 (NSW Unassisted Immigrant Passenger Lists, 1826-1922). **LEFT COLUMN:** 1-Ellen Frawley - Charged with Assault (The Darling Downs Gazette & Gen. Advertiser, 7 Nov 1868); 2-James Frawley - Crown Lands Selections at Highfields (Toowoomba Chronicle, 15 March 1873, p.3); 3-James Frawley - Crown Lands Selections (Brisbane Courier, 14 Mar 1873, p.3). **CENTRE COLUMN:** 1-James Frawley - Crown Lands Selections (The Darling Downs Gazette & Gen. Advertiser, 12 Mar 1873, p.3); 2- J. Frawley - Crown Lands Selections (The Darling Downs Gazette & Gen. Advertiser, 9 Jan 1875, p.5); 3-James Frawley - Unregistered Dog (Toowoomba Chronicle, 15 Mar 1873, p.3); 4-James Frawley - Fine for Unregistered Dog (Toowoomba Chronicle, 15 Mar 1873, p.3); 5-James Frawley - Hotel Fire at Meringandan (The Darling Downs Gazette & Gen. Advertiser, 26th May 1900, p.2). **RIGHT COLUMN:** 1-James Frawley - House Fire (Queensland Times, 24 May 1888, p.5); 2-William Murphy Frawley & Mary Sharkey - Marriage announcement (Queensland Times, 10 Sep 1892, p.4); 3-James Frawley & Miss Brady (Toowoomba Chronicle, 8 Sep 1900, p.3).

NEW SOUTH WALES POLICE GAZETTE.
APRIL, 1864.

Apprehensions.

A man named Stephen Frawley, charged on warrant with stealing a horse (found in his possession), the property of one John Carpenter, has been arrested by Constable Ward, Bega police.

The mare No. 15 in this week's list, the property of Thomas Jones, is supposed to have been taken to Bega or Panbula by Stephen and Patrick Frawley. The former is about 25 years of age, 5 feet 9 inches high, dark complexion, round features, black hair, worn native fashion, black goatee, no whiskers; the other is about 20 years of age, 5 feet 8½ inches high, dark complexion, round features, good looking. No warrant issued.

2 May 1913

MR. HIGGS'S NOMINATORS.

Ruby Vale.

John H. Moore Stephen Frawley

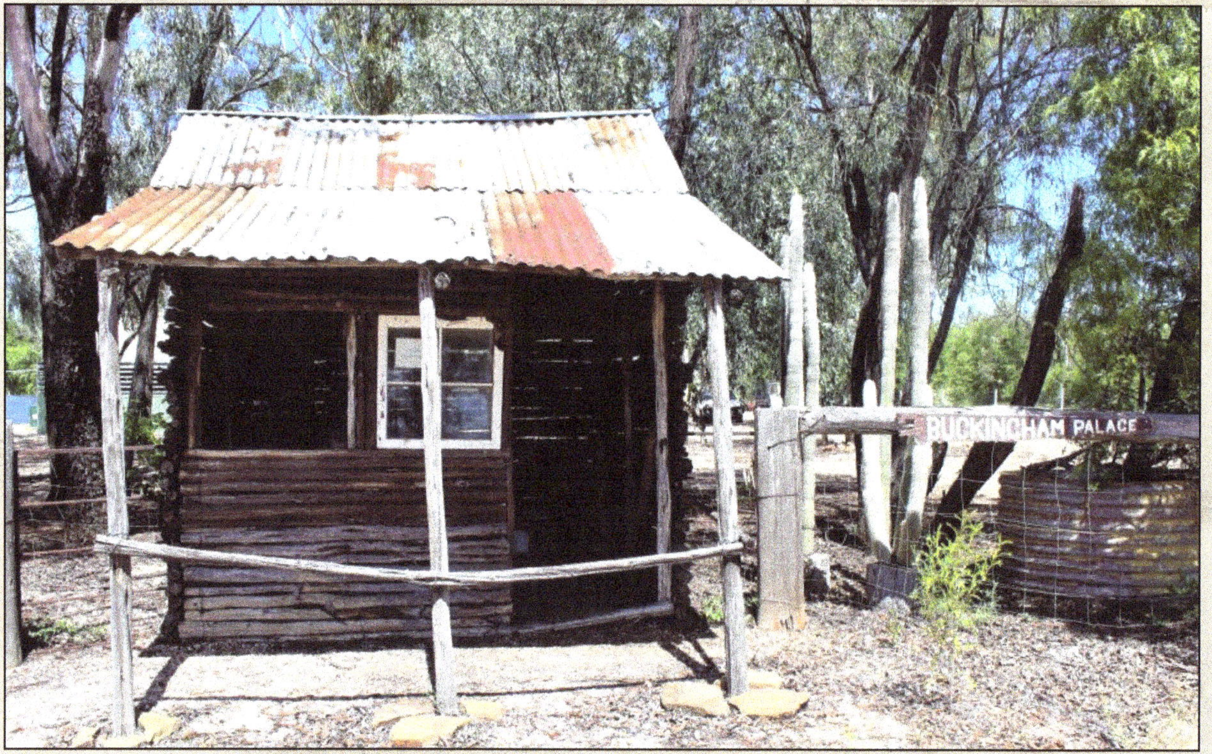

TOP (Left): Stephen Frawley - Charged with Horse Stealing (NSW Police Gazette, 11 May 1864). (Centre): Stephen & Patrick Frawley - Wanted for Horse Stealing (NSW Police Gazette, 5 Sept 1866). (Right): Stephen Frawley nominated a Mr. Higgs as the local member for Rubyvale, 2 May 1913. MID: An old miners shack at Rubyvale, QLD.

4. Stephen Frawley (1844-1930)

Stephen Frawley was born on 26th December 1844 and baptised by Father Michael Kavanagh on the 11th May 1846 at the family residence in Pambula.[40] He was the fourth child of John and Mary Ann Frawley, and would have attended the public school at Pambula, which opened in 1850.[41] Like his two older brothers, Stephen Frawley also fell foul of the law and was charged with horse stealing in April 1864 (aged 19) and again in 1866, although fortunately for him, no convictions were seemingly recorded in either case.[42,43]

Stephen moved to Queensland and may have worked as a carrier for a time. From 1912, as the last surviving member of his family, was listed on electoral rolls as residing at Rubyvale, west of Emerald in Queensland. The name Rubyvale was derived from a ruby weighing 5 to 6 pennyweights (0.27 to 0.33oz; 7.8 to 9.3g) found near the town by miner William Dunn in the early 1900s. Dunn was very proud of the ruby and did not sell it, but showed it to people he trusted, although after his death the ruby could not be found. Stephen apparently never married, preferring a remote and isolated existence over marital domesticity. Living relatively close to one another, Stephen likely maintained contact with his brother Patrick in Townsville, but no other information is known about a marriage or issue for Stephen Frawley, who lived the longest of all his siblings before dying on the 14th July 1930, aged 86. He was buried at 'Norman Gardens' in the North Rockhampton Cemetery.[44]

5. Patrick Frawley/Marr (1848-1926)

The fifth surviving child of John and Mary Ann Frawley was Patrick Frawley, born on St Patricks Day, the 17th March 1848 and baptised with his twin sister Letitia, by Father Michael Kavanagh on the 8th September 1848, at the family residence in Pambula.[45] Along with his brothers and sisters, he attended the public school at Pambula, which opened in 1850.[46]

Patrick grew up in Panbula, and like his father and three older brothers John Jr, James and Stephen, Patrick also became a rebel, and as a young man was a well known figure in the eyes of the local police. He initially tried his hand as a prospector at what was then known as the 'Gulf Diggings' at Deep Creek in the vicinity of Mount Dromedary, just to the west of Tilba Tilba, New South Wales. But unfortunately for Patrick, while unsuccessful at finding gold, while there he inadvertently became a witness to a shooting and robbery.

In the 1800s horses were of course the primary mode of transport in the colony, and were comparable back then to the motor vehicles of today. Although horse stealing was a serious crime, it proved to be a popular pastime amongst the Frawley boys as they were all, save young Thomas, charged with that offence at some time or other, and this also included Patrick Frawley.

Incarceration

The police eventually caught up with Patrick on the 20th October 1866 when he was arrested and charged with horse stealing.[47] He appeared before the bench at Eden Court House on the 21st January 1867, where he was found guilty and sentenced to five years hard labour on the roads.[48] At just 19 years old Patrick was removed from Eden by coastal steamer and admitted to Darlinghurst Gaol.[49]

DARLINGHURST GAOL DESCRIPTION & ENTRANCE BOOKS
Record for Patrick Frawley[50]

Name:	Patrick Frawley
Birth Year:	Abt 1848
Age:	19
Arrival Date:	1865
Vessel Arrive In:	Born In Colony
Date Of:	1867
Goal:	Darlinghurst
Goal Location:	Darlinghurst, NSW
Record Type:	Description Book

Prisoners line up in single file in the yard at Darlinghurst Gaol c.1885.

HORSE AND CATTLE

The mare No. 15 in this week's list, the property of Thomas Jones, is supposed to have been taken to Bega or Panbula by Stephen and Patrick Frawley. The former is about 25 years of age 5 feet 9 inches high, dark complexion, round features, black hair, worn native fashion, black goatee, no wiskers; the other is about 20 years of age, 5 feet 5 1/2 inches high, dark complexion, round features, good looking, no warrant issued.

NSW Police Gazette, 5 Sep 1866

Witness Against Bushrangers

It was while in Darlinghurst Goal that Patrick Frawley testified as a witness to a robbery that had occurred the year before. He stated that he was present on the 9th April 1866, at Deep Creek when bushranger Thomas Clarke, together with his uncles Patrick and Thomas Connell and four other criminals, William and Joseph Berriman, Bill Scott and

Incarceration of Patrick Frawley

TOP: Patrick Frawley in the Admittance Book for Parramatta Gaol, June 1867. MID (Left): Patrick Frawley - Baptism Certificate, 8th Sept 1848. (Right): John & Thomas Clarke, bushrangers - locked up and in irons at Darlinghurst Gaol. ABOVE (Left): Patrick Frawley - Return of Prisoners Tried at Eden Quarter Sessions, 21st Jan.1867. (Right): Patrick Frawley - Witness for the Crown (The Empire, 16th Feb. 1867).

Bushrangers 'Sticking Up The Gundagai Mail', about 1867.

William Fletcher, robbed a Chinaman, who was on the way to the bank from the 'Gulf gold diggings'.[51] They took all of the Chinaman's savings, with several others being held up including a small boy, and they called upon Mr. John Emmott, the storekeeper from Moruya to surrender. But Emmott wasn't about to lose his £100 and a parcel of gold dust, so he put spurs to his horse and galloped away.

Both Thomas Clarke and Patrick Connell fired at Emmott with their revolvers with one of the shots wounding him in the thigh, and the other killing his mount from under him. After relieving Emmott of his valuables, he and the other prisoners who had already been bailed up were marched off in the direction of Mrs. Groves store. Because of his wound Emmott could not walk quickly so the bushrangers pistol-whipped him over the head and left the poor man lying semi-conscious and helpless on the road.[52]

Patrick Frawley's testimony may have reduced his sentence as after a few months at Darlinghurst, he was transferred to Berrima Gaol for a time, before his removal again to Parramatta Gaol, arriving there on the 15th June 1867. In a coincidental twist of fate, Patrick may very well have arrived at Parramatta Gaol just before the release of his father, John Frawley, which occurred that very same month. If so, his father's gaol connections may well have helped Patrick in his new prison environment, where he likely also received visits from his two sisters, Ellen and Letitia.

Unfortunately, no record of Patrick's release from any New South Wales gaol has been found, but his incarceration couldn't have extended beyond 1871. After gaining his freedom, he likely returned to Pambula, where under difficult circumstances he tried at first to blend back into the town. However, lending creedence to the theory that his older brother James Frawley, had already pioneered the move to the Darling Downs District, Patrick later travelled to south-east Queensland, where he made his next recorded appearance.

Daring Escape From Police Custody

It was around this time that Patrick decided to change his surname to 'Marr', and relocate to Queensland, but there was seemingly no change in his behaviour as four years later, he was brought before the Police Magistrate at Roma, Queensland, about 350km west of Toowoomba, on the 20th October 1875, on the charge of cattle rustling![63] A group of prisoners including James Montgomery, Samuel Thompson and Patrick Marr were all brought up on remand, charged with stealing certain cattle, the property of John Town, who deposed the following circumstances:

> BEFORE THE POLICE MAGISTRATE.
> Wednesday October 20.
>
> Mr. Thompson appeared for the prisoner Thompson. I John Town deposed I am a grazier residing at Berarba, in New South Wales. I was at the pound yard yesterday morning, and saw twenty nine head of my cattle there; there are four or five head I can swear positively to without the brands; I saw the cattle in the middle of July last at Berarba on the Gil Gil; I swear to the balance of those cattle by the brands, the brand is — over JT over oo -near rump; it is registered in New South Walbs, and belongs to my father and myself; I have never sold any of those cattle, or authorised any one else to do so; I missed some of the cattle now here when I was mustering the fat cattle; I have known prisoner, Montgomery upwards of ten years; I saw him' last on the Gil Gil at his brothers, whose place joins mine; he knows our brand well; it is about 250 miles from here to the Gil Gil.
>
> *Western Star and Roma Advertiser, 23 Oct 1875.*

The three prisoners were committed to take trial at the next sitting of the Roma District Court. Thompson and Marr were admitted to bail, themselves in £100 each, and two sureties of £50 each respectively, with events being closely followed in the newspapers...

> At the hearing Patrick Marr pleaded "Guilty" to a charge of using threatening language to Terence Byrne. He was fined £1, but in default of immediate payment, was sentenced to four weeks imprisonment.
>
> *Western Star and Roma Advertiser, 30 Oct 1875.*

> Roma - 29 February 1876
>
> Patrick Marr, one of the three men on bail charged with cattle stealing in New South Wales, has been again arrested for horse-stealing. March 1. Marr, charged with horse-stealing, has been acquitted. Smith, a witness in the case, has been committed for trial on the same charge, and also for perjury.
>
> *The Queenslander, Brisbane, 4 March 1876*

> Roma - 18 March 1876
> (From our Correspondent - March 13).
>
> A STRANGE case of turning the tables occurred at the Police Court on the 1st instant. A man, named Patrick Marr, was arrested for stealing a horse from one Owen Mullavey. Among the principal witnesses against him was a man named William Smith. Several other witnesses deposed that they saw Marr buy the horse from Smith. A receipt was produced in Court by the prisoner Marr, which he said he got from Smith. The receipt was denied by Smith in open Court. The Police Magistrate, to make the matter sure, asked Smith to write a receipt. The two receipts were compared, and found to be in the same handwriting. Marr was accordingly discharged, and Smith was arrested for perjury and horse stealing. He was committed next day for trial, bail allowed, four at £40 each, and himself £80.
>
> *The Queenslander, Brisbane, 18 March 1876.*

> Roma - 6 April 1876
>
> At the District Court sittings, the following cases have been tried: Montgomery and Marr, charged with stealing cattle from New South Wales, were discharged, but again taken into custody to be tried in New South Wales.
>
> *The Queenslander, Brisbane, 8 April 1876.*

> 22 April 1876
>
> Patrick Marr, James Montgomery, and Samuel Thompson, charged with cattle-stealing, in New South Wales, were discharged, the Court having no jurisdiction. Marr and Montgomery were at once re-arrested on a warrant from New South Wales. Samuel Thompson, on a second charge of cattle-stealing, was sentenced to eighteen months' hard labor in Brisbane Gaol. I presume he will be sent to New South Wales to take his trial with Marr and Montgomery.
>
> *The Queenslander, Brisbane, 22 April 1876.*

If Patrick intended to conceal his identity with the change of surname, the ruse obviously failed as he was soon identified as Patrick Frawley! What occurred next was either extraordinarily brave or foolhardy on the part of Patrick. While in police custody, he made a daring but calculated break for freedom, and the newspapers had a field day:

▲ LEFT: Patrick Marr - Apprehended & Released (NSW Police Gazette, 27 Dec. 1876). RIGHT: Patrick J. Marr - Escaped from Police (The Queenslander, 29 April 1876).

ROMA
(From our own Correspondent).

A man named Frawley, charged with horse-stealing, has been brought here for trial his defence being that he bought the horse in question. Patrick Marr, remanded for horse-stealing to New South Wales, has escaped from the police escort.

The Brisbane Courier, 2 May 1876.

ONE day last week news (says reached town The Western Star) that Patrick Marr, who was remanded from Roma to New South Wales on a charge of cattle stealing, had escaped from Constable Kelly, who was escorting him. Kelly states that about forty miles below St. George, Marr struck him on the head with the handcuffs, the blow completely stunning him. Marr then galloped away on the Government horse he was riding handcuffed as he was, with leg-irons on also and has not since been heard of. As this is the second prisoner that has escaped from this escort in this district within the last few months, it is time some action was taken by the authorities to make such a thing next to impossible. In this case there seems to have been negligence somewhere, as there were two constables together, as well as a black trooper, escorting two prisoners, and surely the one that was unhurt could have secured his prisoner, and started off in pursuit.

Rockhampton Bulletin, 10 May 1876.

On Tuesday last, a man known as Marr, and supposed to be a brother of Patrick Marr, who escaped from Constable Kelly a few days ago, rode into the police yard in this town, and delivered up the horse on which Patrick Marr escaped, with saddle and bridle. As he would not account for the animal being in his possession, he was arrested, brought up before the Bench on Monday last and remanded for the, arrival of Constable Kelly. On being taken to the lock-up he gave the name of Rawley Patrick Marr, who escaped from his escort a few days ago, has not yet been re-arrested, and as he is known to be a good bushman chances of his capture are small.

Western Star and Roma Advertiser, 6 May 1876.

St George - 28 April 1876

(From our own Correspondent), PATRICK J. MARR, a prisoner on remand from Roma to New South Wales, on a charge of cattle stealing, escaped from the custody of Constable Kelly, on the 18th instant, while en route to his destination. The two prisoners, Marr and Montgomery, left here in charge of Constables Dargin and Kelly; Kelly having charge of the former and Dargin the latter. They stayed at 'Nindy Gully Station' on the Monday night, and started for Kunopia, on the Weir River, on the Tuesday morning. When they had got about twelve miles from Nindygully, they took a bridle track through a scrub, and Marr made some excuse for getting off the horse he was riding. The constable got off also to assist him, as he was handcuffed. When Marr got into the saddle again, Constable Dargin and the black boy, with the other prisoner, were out of sight. Marr called the constable's attention to the fact, and said, "Where are the tracks?" Kelly leant forward on the saddle and was seized with a fit of coughing; Marr took advantage of the opportunity, and struck him on the back of the neck with his manacled hands, partially stunning him, then pulled the reins of the bridle from him and darted off into the scrub. The constable followed him for some time, but did not succeed in finding him, and returned here 'for assistance'. He started next day with a black tracker, but up to this no tidings of the fugitive have been received.

The Queenslander, Brisbane, 13 May 1876.

We learn that the enquiry into the escape of Patrick Marr has resulted in the dismissal from the force of Constable Kelly, who had the escaped prisoner in charge. The prisoner Montgomery, who was sent from Roma at the same time as Marr, was committed last week to take his trial for cattle-stealing in New South Wales.

Western Star and Roma Advertiser, 20 May 1876.

APPREHENSIONS

Patrick Marr, who escaped from the Queensland Police whilst on escort on remand to Moree, on a charge of stealing 41 head of cattle, the property of John Town, has surrendered himself to the Moree Police Remanded. Patrick Marr charged with stealing cattle the property of John Town, has been discharged by the Moree Branch on his own recognisance in £40 to appear when called upon.

NSW Police Gazette, 1876, p.170.

But it seems that after May 1876 nothing more was printed about this case or the extraordinarily bold escape, and no evidence has been found about any subsequent trials or incarceration. Therefore, we can only assume that Patrick Marr (Frawley) abided by the bond he made with the Moree Police, and lived out the remainder of his life without further incident.

From Prisoners To Pioneers

▲James Patrick Marr - Funeral Notice (Townsville Daily Bulletin, 25 August 1926). ◀Marriage Certificate for Patrick Marr (Frawley) & Eliza Jane Quigg, 11 Feb. 1888. BELOW: Eidsvold Catholic Church, about 1900.

Patrick Frawley Becomes Marr

Perhaps as a result of his time spent in prison, Patrick Frawley now made the conscious decision to keep the name change from Frawley to 'Marr'. The exact reason for choosing the surname of Marr is unclear, but it was likely done to block any association with prior felonious activities.

After his release from prison, Patrick Marr fell in with a woman by the name of Eliza Jane Quigg, by whom he was soon delivered of a son who arrived in 1872 and was named Harold Marr. Eleven more children were to arrive over the next 27 years with all of them being christened under the surname of Marr, which extinguished the Frawley surname from that branch of the family.

At the age of 40, Patrick James Marr became a 'carrier', and after producing seven children, he finally married his long time partner Eliza Jane (1862-1949), daughter of John Quigg and Mary Jane Hamilton, on the 11th February 1888 at the Roman Catholic Church, Eidsvold, in Queensland.[53] His marriage certificate reveals that his

304

The Sydney Morning Herald
DEATHS
MARR, Eliza Jane.—May 11, 1949, at a private hospital, Coogee, dearly beloved mother of William (Wutul, Qld.), Madge (Mrs. Sterzel), Thea (Mrs. Dawes), Nell (Mrs. Nielson), grandmother of Freda, Olga, Sadie and Patricia, aged 87.

▲ *Death notice for Eliza Jane Marr (nee Quigg), (Sydney Morning Herald, 11 May 1949).* ▶ *Death Certificate for Patrick Marr (Frawley), 24 August 1926. BELOW: Sketch of Roma, Queensland, c.1875, showing the Court House and Gaol in the distance (artist unknown).*

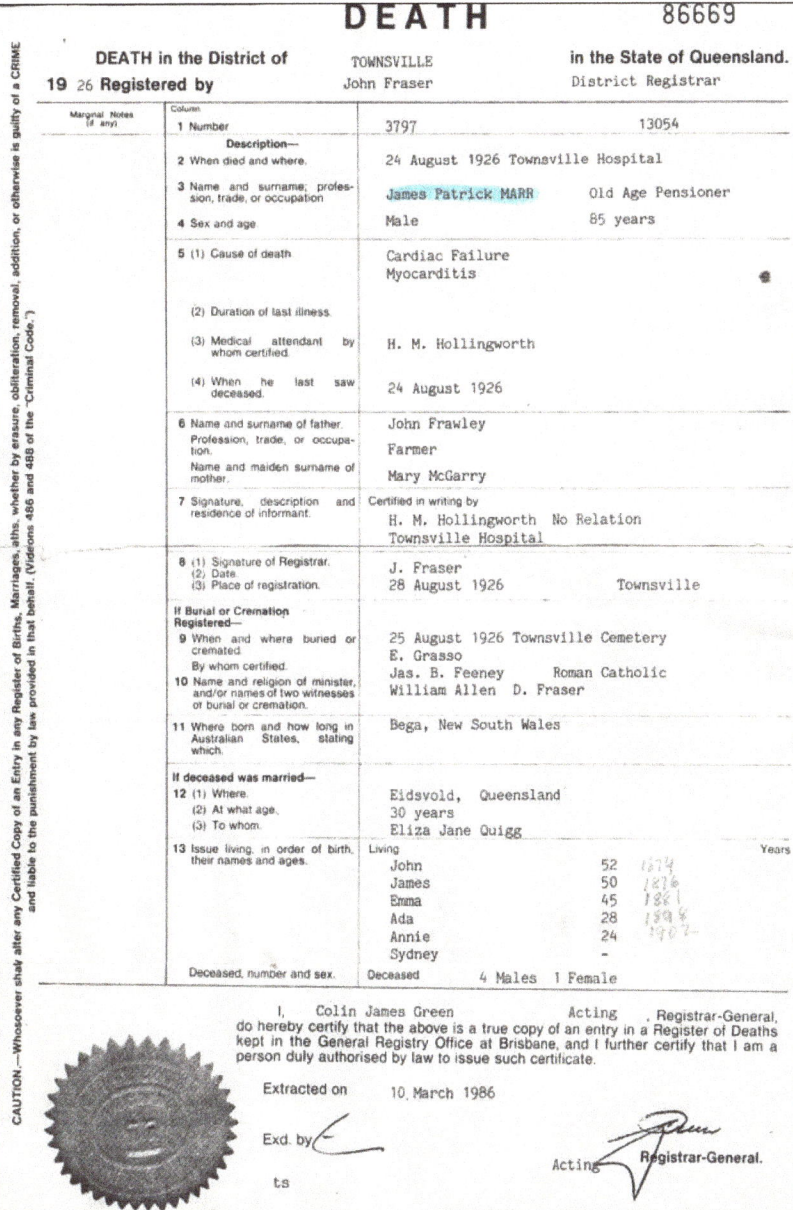

age lines up exactly with details on his 1848 certificate of baptism, and his mother was listed correctly as Mary McGarry although, there was no mention of his father, which he likely witheld so as not to divulge his new identity.

SMALL DEBTS COURT.
Thursday, 12th December.
Before the Acting Police Magistrate.
- Undefended Cases. In the following undefended cases verdicts were given for the plaintiffs for the amounts claimed with costs :

P. J. MARR v W. STENHOUSE & CO.
In this case the plaintiff claimed £5 2s. 6d, as agistment for horses. Mr. R. A. Brumm appeared for the plaintiff, and Mr. J. Pattison for the defendant.

A verdict was given for the plaintiff for the 15s. paid into Court, and for the balance a verdict was given for the defendant with £1 1. professional costs and 2s. costs of Court.
Morning Bulletin, 13 December 1895

Patrick continued on in his work as a 'carrier' as we hear little more of him until his death on the 24th August 1926 at Townsville Hospital,[54] by which time he had re-located the family to Townsville *(see Table 6. Descendants of Patrick Frawley & Eliza Jane Quigg).*

Funeral Notice
The friends and relatives of the late James Patrick Marr (Oonoonba) are respectfully invited to attend his funeral which will move from the general hospital this (Wednesday) morning at 10.30 o'clock.

F. Heatley And Sons, Ltd, Undertakers.
Telephones: 162 Day, 998 Night
Townsville Daily Bulletin, 25th August 1926

6. Descendants of Patrick Frawley/Marr & Eliza Quigg
(Data from NSW Births, Deaths & Marriages Index, Ancestry.com & Newspapers)

Patrick FRAWLEY (1848-1926), changed his name to MARR about 1872 and fathered seven illegitimate children before marrying on the 11 Feb 1888 at Eidsvold, QLD to Eliza Jane (1862-1949), daughter of John Quigg and Mary Jane Hamilton, producing five more children, totalling 12 in all:

Theodore S. J. Blake (1912-1996)

1. **Harold MARR (1872-1949)**, apparently died a bachelor in Maitland, NSW. No issue.

2. **James Livingstone MARR (1874-1939)**, was killed in a level crossing smash with a train in 1939. He married in 1900 at QLD to Frances Tametski (1878-1967), with issue:
   2.1 James Victor MARR (1900-1968). No issue.
   2.2 Richard Henry MARR (1902-1988) married in 1930 at Rockhampton, QLD to Violet P. Bates (1895-1986) with issue:
      a. Val Richard MARR (1931)
      b. Desma Patricia Marr (1932)
   2.3 Annie Cecelia 'Ciss' Marr (1904-1994) married in 1934 at Rockhampton, QLD to Arthur INGRAM (1899-1950) with issue:
      a. Beryce Lorriane Ingram (1939-1952). No issue.
   2.4 Leonard Joseph MARR (1907-1974) ▲ married in 1933 at Rockhampton, QLD to Elizabeth Olive Elms (1913-1973), with issue:
      a. Bryan William MARR (1934)
   2.5 Sidney Clarence MARR (1909-1958) married in 1932 at QLD to Violet C. Davies (1910-1934). No issue.
   2.6 Frances Dulcie Marr (1915-?) married in 1940 at Rockhampton to Maurice FitzGERALD (1912-1986), with issue:
      a. Warren James FitzGERALD (1943-1982)
   2.7 Reginald Livingstone MARR (1918-1920)*, died an infant.
   2.8 Ellen Evelyn Marr (1920-?) married firstly in 1942 at QLD to Leonard John HOARE (1918-1943) ▲, killed in action. No issue. Following the death of her husband in the war, Ellen married secondly in 1945 to William DAHMS (1917-1985), with issue.

Alan William 'Lofty' Marr (1918-2008)

3. **John 'Jack' MARR (1875-1938)**, married in 1911 at QLD to Mary Ann Allen (1884-1964). No issue.

4. **Richard Sydney MARR (1875-1901)** was killed in action in the Boer War at Sandwana Hill, South Africa. Never married and no issue.

5. **Stephen Henry MARR (1876-1960)**, died a bachelor. No issue.

6. **George Benedick MARR (1881-1924)**, married in 1905 at Mackay, QLD to Mary Christmas Connolly (1883-1967), with issue:
   6.1 Victor Cardinal MARR (1906-1973) ▲ married in 1927 at Sydney to Emily G. Gordon. Issue unknown.
   6.2 Peter George MARR (1907-1988) married in 1935 at QLD to Evelyn May Jones (1913-2007) with issue:
      a. Raymond Peter G. MARR (1936-2002) married Doreen Joyce Wells (1936-2011). Issue unknown.
   6.3 Percival John MARR (1909-1988) married in 1940 at Carmila, QLD to Edna May Jones (1921-2008) with issue:
      a. Mervyn P. E. Marr (1941-2006)
      b. Trevor K.G. Marr (1946-1992)
   6.4 Dolly Margaret Marr (1912-1966) married in 1934 at QLD to Clarence R. DEVINE (1912-1969) with issue:
      a. Joyce M. E. Devine (1938-1938)*, died an infant.
      b. Dorothy M. R. Devine (1941-2017), married in 1965 to Leslie Ronald (Les) KIESEKER (1932-1999), with issue.
      c. Douglas Victor G. DEVINE (1945-1968), may have married Yvonne ???, with a son he never knew, named Darren?
   6.5 Stephen 'Tiger' MARR (1914-1947), was an outstanding sportsman and enlisted in the AMF prior to WWII and was attached to the 42nd Battalion, bachelor, no issue.
   6.6 Emily May Marr (1916-1937) married in 1936 at Mackay to John B. NEY (1909-1979) ▲ with issue:
      a. John B. Ney (1937-1937)*, died an infant.
   6.7 Florence Annie Marr (1919-2011) married in 1939 at Mackay, QLD to William H. CRAIG (1914-1989) with issue:
      a. Desmond W. F. CRAIG (1939-2003) ▲ married, with issue
      b. Annie E. Craig (1943-1999), married in 1965 to John Desmond BOSEL (1941-2022), with issue.
   6.8 Ellen Elizabeth Marr (1922-2006) married in 1947 at Mackay, QLD to Reginald A. PALMER (1920-1977), with issue.
   6.9 Edna Joyce Marr (1924-1926)*, died an infant.

Dolly Margaret Marr (1912-1966)

7. **Emma Magdalen Marr (1882-1972)**, married in 1910 at Sydney to Ernest F. STERZEL (c.1885-1962), with issue:
   7.1 Freda Ailsa Sterzel (1911-2000) married in 1936 at Randwick to Theodore S. BLAKE (1912-1996) ▲, with issue.
   7.2 Olga Ada Sterzel (1916-?) married in 1935 at Randwick to Fred W. FIDDICK (1911-?), issue unknown.
   7.3 Sadie Alma Sterzel (1918-2008) married in 1942 at Rozelle to Walter S. MARTIN (1912-1983), with issue:
      a. Rhondda Lyn Martin (1946)

8. **Justin Christian MARR (1888-1944)** ▲ married in 1920 at QLD to Nora A. Milward (1884-1944) with issue:
   8.1 Thomas Henry MARR (c.1921-?), issue unknown.
   8.2 William Milward MARR (1924-1983) ▲ married in 1942 at Brisbane, QLD to Elizabeth Patroney (1909-1982), issue unknown.

9. **Michael William 'Bill' MARR (1889-1954)**, married in 1916 at QLD to Myrtle M. Bradford (1896-1965) with issue:
   9.1 Doris Norma Marr, married in 1943 at Bowraville to Thomas M. RUSSELL, issue unknown.
   9.2 Alan William 'Lofty' MARR (1918-2008) ▲ married in 1947 at Brisbane, QLD to Kathleen R. Carey (1919-1992), issue unknown.
   9.3 Gerald Raymond MARR (1922-1984) ▲ married in 1949 at QLD to Beryl C. Charles (1922-1990) with issue:
      a. Raymond MARR (1943-2008)
      b. Terrence MARR (1947-1987)
      c. Gary W. MARR (1955-1986)
      d. Janelle Marr (?)
      e. Sheryl Marr (?)
   9.4 Eric Richard 'Bluey' MARR (1924-1981) married in 1948 at Mungallala, QLD to Eileen H. Harper (1916-2002) with issue:
      a. Annette Marr (?)
      b. John MARR (?)
      c. Colin MARR (?)

10. **Percival Patrick MARR (1889>1904)**, apparently died a bachelor. Issue unknown.

11. **Helen Ada Marr (1891-1968)**, married firstly to Reginald ROBERTS, with issue:
    11.1 Patricia J. Roberts (1928-?)
    Helen married secondly to Herbert Alfred NEILSEN. No issue.

12. **Annie Ellen 'Thea' Marr (1897-1973)**, married in 1924 at QLD to Roy Pretoria DAWES (1900-?) - divorced in Sept. 1939. No issue.

* Died before adulthood - d.s.p.
(Some names not listed in the index.)

Dolly M. Marr (1912-1966) & Clarence R. Devine (1912-1969)

Ellen E. Marr (1922-2006) & Reg A. Palmer (1920-1977)

Ellen Evelyn Marr (1920-?) & Leonard J. Hoare (1918-1943)

Emily May Marr (1916-1937) & John B. Ney (1909-1979)

Eric Richard Marr (1924-1981)

Florence A. Marr (1919-2011) & William H. Craig (1914-1989)

17 - Descendants of John & Mary Frawley

Faces & Documents for Descendants of Patrick & Eliza Marr

Sadie Alma Sterzel
(1918-2008)

Farmer Killed In Level Crossing Smash
Companion Seriously Injured

One man was killed, another was seriously injured and the utility truck in which they were travelling was smashed to pieces in a collision with a mixed train at a level crossing near Archer, on the southern line, about 6 p.m. yesterday.

The victim was James Livingstone Marr, 66, married, a farmer at Upper Ulam and the injured man was Jack Hawk, 57, single, who is understood to have been employed on Marr's farm.

As Hawk was admitted to the Rockhampton General Hospital in a serious condition and was unable to make a statement, the police last night could learn little of the accident. However, it was ascertained that Marr and Hawk were in Rockhampton yesterday and left for home about 5.30 p.m., Marr being at the wheel of the truck.

The collision occurred at a level crossing on the Upper Ulam Road, which branches off the main road to Gladstone about two miles from Archer and 13 miles from Rockhampton. The engine of the train, which was travelling to Rockhampton, struck the rear part of the truck and hurled the vehicle against the guard posts of the cattle grid, throwing the two men out. The truck was then caught in the undercarriage of a wagon and dragged a further distance. The vehicle was completely wrecked.

Marr apparently died instantly, his injuries including a broken neck.

Hawk sustained a fractured left forearm, a lacerated wound on top of the head, an injury to the left shoulder and shock.

While the news of the accident was being sent to Rockhampton through the railway telegraph system a man named Ross, from the road construction camp nearby, had the two men placed in his utility truck and set out for the city. He was met on the road by ambulance bearers and a doctor, who pronounced Marr to be dead. Hawk was treated and hurried by the ambulance to the General Hospital, where he was admitted in a serious condition.

WEDDING.
MARR—BATES.

The Rev. Father Dolan officiated at the wedding of Violet Patricia, daughter of Mr. and Mrs. C. Bates, Murray street, Rockhampton, and Richard Henry son of Mr. and Mrs. J. L. Marr, of Archer, which was celebrated at St. Joseph's Presbytery on the 22nd instant.

Mr. Ray Bates gave his sister away. A dainty and becoming frock of ivory silk crepe, with a cape from the shoulders, was chosen by the bride. The skirt, which had panels of guipure lace

FIVE SUFFER IN TRUCK SMASH

ROCKHAMPTON, April 21
A utility motor truck, out of control crashed into a tree on the Gladstone road about 3.15 a.m. to-day, and the five occupants were thrown on to the bitumen roadway. Three were injured, two seriously. The party was returning to Rockhampton from Bouldercombe. Seated in front with Sidney Marr (26), the driver, were Miss Doreen Hill (23), of Park Avenue, and Miss Evelyn Rodekirchen (22), who resides in Davis Street. Two men sat in the back of the truck. When near the Nicholson Street intersection, a motor cyclist and a girl riding pillion, drew level with the truck. In some manner the girl struck Marr's arm, and the truck swerved and dashed into a tree in the centre of the roadway. Marr suffered internal injuries and shock, and Miss Hill injuries to the back and head, and shock. Both were admitted to the General Hospital. Miss Rodekirchen suffered an injury to the left leg, and after attention by ambulance bearers, she was taken to her home.

A dance was held in the C.W.A. Hall at Archer, in aid of the Upper Ulam School to provide funds for the annual picnic.

The music was supplied by Mr. S. Marr (violin) and Miss Dulcie Marr (piano). Extras were played by Miss M. Crawford, Mrs. S. Marr and Miss E. Marr, Mr. J. L. Marr was M.C.

A ten shilling note was won by Mrs. J. Thompson, Archer. Mrs. Myers and Mr. J. Leyden, were the winners of the Monte Carlo. A chocolate one-step was won by Miss E. Marr and Mr. J. Greenough.

THE Friends of Mr. and Mrs. J. L. MARR (of Archer), are respectfully invited to attend the Funeral of his deceased beloved SON (Reginald Livingston) to move from Finlayson and M'Kenzie's Parlour, William-street, THIS (Thursday) FORENOON, at 10.30 o'clock, for the Rockhampton Cemetery.

MARRIAGE NOTICE.

HOARE—MARR.—At St. Peter's Roman Catholic Church, Dawson Road, on April 4th, by Rev. Father Murtagh, Ellen Evelyn, youngest daughter of the late Mr L. J. Marr and Mrs F. Marr, Archer, to Corporal Leonard John, second son of Mr and Mrs A. J. Hoare, John Street, Rockhampton.

POLICE ESCORT.

Constables H. C. Miller and H. Cofee left yesterday by the mail train for Brisbane escorting John Marr, who was sentenced at the last sitting of the Supreme Court at Rockhampton to eighteen months' imprisonment with hard labour in Brisbane Gaol for horse-stealing at Mount Morgan, and two lunatics.

CARMILA.
(From Our Own Correspondent.)

A sad accident, which terminated fatally occurred on Friday. Mr. G. Marr, a well-known and respected farmer, of Carmila, whilst riding, was thrown from his horse and was picked up unconscious. The Sarina ambulance bearers were immediately summoned and responded as quickly as the state of the road would allow. The sufferer was conveyed to Mackay for medical attention, but succumbed to his injuries on Sunday afternoon. Mr Marr was prominent in all sports, and took a great interest in the development of this district. He could always be depended upon to assist the community in any way way he could. His death comes as a blow to his many friends. The sympathy of the district is extended to Mrs. Marr and her children in their sad bereavement.

Steve Marr, affectionately known as "Tiger" to the whole of Carmila and district, passed away on October 22 after a long illness, and left the district poorer by his death. He had grown up with the district, and was only a young man when death claimed him. Until his illness, he was one of the foremost figures in sport—a promising tennis player, cricketer and football—from his boyhood days. He also trained his own racehorses, and was a well-known figure at the Sarina Diggers' races. He was a sportsman, clean and keen.

Prior to the outbreak of war, deceased served with the 42nd Btn. AMF. He was a good soldier. Owing to physical disabilities, he was unable to join the AIF, but gave freely of his time and money to assist any function organised to further the interests of the lads who enlisted from the district.

His father was killed at Carmila, and "Tiger" and his young brothers knew what it was to toil long hours in the canefields. The farm was practically in the pioneering stage, and it was heavy going for young lads. Even when he was but a lad, "Tiger" could be relied upon to lend a helping hand to a neighbor in trouble, and no one ever sought his assistance in vain.

He leaves a number of relatives to mourn his passing—his mother, Mrs. M. C. Marr, of Sarina; three sisters, also of Sarina district; and three brothers, of Carmila.

ACCIDENTS.

Justin Marr, a lad of about thirteen years of age, living at Crocodile, was admitted to the hospital yesterday suffering from a dislocated collar-bone, the breaking of two ribs and the arm at the shoulder joint, the result of a horse falling upon him. J. Dickson, a child of six years, was also admitted, his arm being broken at the elbow joint. On inquiry to-day I am glad to be able to state that the boys are doing as well as can be expected.

William Milward Marr
(1924-1983)

Stephen 'Tiger' Marr
(1914-1947)

Richard Sydney Marr
(1875-1901)

LEFT COLUMN: 1-Farmer Killed (Morning Bulletin, 29 April 1939); 2-Marr - Bates Marriage announcement (Morning Bulletin, 30 April 1930). **CENTRE COLUMN:** 1-Truck Smash (The Courier Mail, 22 April 1935); 2-CWA Dance (Archer, 2 October 1933); 3-Reginald L. Marr - Funeral notice (Unreferenced Newscutting - 1920); 4-Hoare - Marr Marriage announcement (Morning Bulletin, 14 April 1942); 5-Police Escort (Morning Bulletin, 3 December 1904). **RIGHT COLUMN:** 1-George Marr Death (Morning Bulletin, 23 January 1924); 2-Stephen Marr Death (Newscutting - November 1947); 3-Justin Marr (Newscutting - 1901).

Gerald Raymond Marr
(1922-1984)

George B. Marr (1881-1924) &
Mary C. Connolly (1883-1967)

Justin Christian Marr
(1888-1944)

Percival J. Marr (1909-1988) &
Edna M. Jones (1921-2008)

Peter G. Marr (1907-1988) &
Evelyn M. Jones (1913-2007)

The informant for Patrick's death certificate was his wife Eliza who outlived him by 25 years, eventually dying in Coogee, NSW on the 11th May 1949, aged 87.[55] The following pages contain memorials from Australian Service Records, for descendants of Patrick and Eliza Marr, who enlisted in the Australian forces.

6. Letitia Frawley (1848>1901)

Despite the well documented exploits of Patrick Frawley, one can't say the same of his twin sister Letitia (1848>1901), of whom very little is known. Letitia Frawley was born a twin to Patrick on 17th March 1848 and baptised by Father Michael Kavanagh, on the 8th September 1848 at the Frawley family residence in Pambula.[56] Attending school in Pambula with her twin brother Patrick from 1853 to 1860, we know little of her former years, except that at age 14, she was implicated with her brother John Frawley Jr. in obtaining monies under false pretences in October 1862, but was discharged.[57]

#904 Justin Christian Marr (1888-1944)

Justin Christian Marr (1888-1944), a grandson of John and Mary Frawley, enlisted in the 5th Light Horse Regiment at Gayndah, QLD on the 23rd Dec. 1914. He departed from Brisbane aboard the "Star of England" on the 8th April 1915, and landed on the Gallipoli Peninsula on the 22nd May. After months of fighting he fell ill and admitted to No. 1 A.C.C. Station at Lemnos on the 16th Sept, then embarked for Malta with dysentery. He was then embarked for England aboard the hospital ship "Regina d'Italia" on the 9th October 1915. After that, Justin's war consisted of either being repeatedly admitted and discharged from hospitals in England, or being disciplined for infractions like showing 'insolence to N.C.Os'. He embarked for Australia aboard the "Berrima" on the 2nd January 1919 and was discharged from the AIF on the 25th April 1919.

The 5th Light Horse Regiment were a mounted infantry regiment of the Australian Army during the First World War. The regiment was raised in August 1914, and assigned to the 2nd Light Horse Brigade. The regiment fought against the forces of the Ottoman Empire, in Egypt, at Gallipoli, on the Sinai Peninsula, and in Palestine and Jordan. After the armistice the regiment was awarded sixteen battle honours.

Regimental number	904
Religion	Roman Catholic
Occupation	Labourer
Address	Elizabeth Jane Marr, 72 Devonshire Street, Sydney, New South Wales
Marital status	Single
Age at embarkation	26
Next of kin	William Marr, Winton, Western Queensland
Enlistment date	23 December 1914
Rank on enlistment	Private
Unit name	5th Light Horse Regiment, 4th Reinforcement
AWM Embarkation Roll number	10/10/2
Embarkation details	Unit embarked from Brisbane, Queensland, on board HMAT A15 *Star of England* on 8 April 1915
Rank from Nominal Roll	Sapper
Unit from Nominal Roll	5th Light Horse Regiment
Fate	Returned to Australia 2 January 1919

▲ Clockwise from top left: Silhouette of Justin Christian Marr in Light Horse uniform; .The 5th Light Horse Regiment Colour Patch; The 5th Light Horse Regiment Badge; Photograph of the 5th Light Horse Regiment, B squadron, C troop at Brisbane's Enoggera Barracks before leaving for World War I.

#119 Richard Sydney Marr (1875-1901)

Richard Sydney Marr (1875-1901), a grandson of John and Mary Frawley, enlisted in the 6th Queensland Imperial Bushmen at Rockhampton. The 6th was a battalion with a grand total of 20 officers, 19 staff sergeants and sergeants, 12 artificers, 3 buglers, 350 rank and file with 40 private, 660 public riding horses, or 404 of all ranks, with 700 horses. Draught horses were supplied by the Imperial authorities in South Africa.

The 6th QIB left for South Africa on the 4th April 1901 aboard the "Victoria", arriving on 2nd May. From Cape Town, they proceeded, by order to Durban and arrived on 7th May, then entrained same day for Pietermaritzburg, leaving horses and 30 men, including farriers and smiths at Durban, under Lieutenants Rich and Vaughan. Arrived at Pietermaritzburg on 9th, entrained on 14th, arrived at Volksrust on the following day, and Standerton on 16th. The horses arrived in six trains on the same day, having been starved and not watered for two and a half days. Transport was drawn on the 18th, consisting of 9 buck wagons, 4 Scotch carts, and 1 water cart.

On the 19th May, the Contingent was posted to Lieut.-Colonel R. Grey's Column, consisting of (in addition) the 7th New Zealand Regiment (six squadrons), some Royal Field Artillery, half-battalion 1st East Lancashire, and detachments of Royal Engineers, Army Service Corps, &c. Lieut.-Colonel Hon. H. F. White (a Jameson raider) commanded the mounted troops. The 6th served side by side with the 7th New Zealanders during the greater part of 1901 and the first three months of 1902 in eastern Transvaal and Free State under Grey.

Like the other oversea Contingents at this stage of the war, the 6th were employed for the most part in constantly trekking over given districts, driving in and harassing the enemy, bringing to the various bases prisoners, horses, cattle, sheep, vehicles, etc., and laying waste the country, a service of much excitement and vicissitude. Fatal casualties = seven killed or died of wounds, five died of disease.

Sadly, Richard Sydney Marr was killed on the evening of the 5th October 1901 while scouting with NZ troops at Sandwana Hill in the Newcastle/Vreheid area, north of Durban. He was one of only seven of the entire 6th Queensland Imperial Bushmen contingent to be killed in action. A statue in memory of the Queensland heroes who fell in the South African Boer War from 1899 to 1902 stands in Anzac Square, Brisbane, and lists the name of Richard Sydney Marr, along with 43 other soldiers who gave their life to the cause. He was posthumously awarded the Queens Medal.

The death of Pte R S Marr

Eyewitness report in a letter from Pvte. J.F. Smith, 6th QIB: "There are about thirty NZ and QIB in the scouts, and we went out about 4 miles from camp to watch a pass at about 1 o'clock in the morning. We went onto a long spur and followed it on to the end. All halted there but four men, and they extended and galloped to some bush about 400 yards away. They fired a volley and Dick fell. Two New Zealanders raced back to him thinking he was only wounded, but when they got there they found he was dead. The New Zealanders were also wounded."

ROLL OF HONOUR
Richard Sydney Marr

Service number	119
Final Rank	Private
Unit	6th Queensland Imperial Bushmen
Service	Colonial Military Forces
Conflict/Operation	South Africa, 1899-1902 (Boer War)
Conflict Eligibility Date	South Africa, 1899-1902 (Boer War)
Date of Death	05 October 1901
Place of Death	Sandwana Hill, South Africa
Cause of Death	Killed in action
Source	AWM142 Roll of Honour cards, War in South Africa, 1899-1902

The Morning Bulletin
8 October 1903

IN MEMORIAM.

MARR.—Sacred to the memory of Sidney Richard Marr, who was killed in South Africa, on the 5th of October, 1901.
Thou art gone from this earth, its toil and its care,
To rest with the Saviour, His blessings to share,
Where sorrow, and sickness, and pain are unknown,
To meet all our loved ones around the great throne.
(Inserted by his loving parents, brothers, and sisters.)

TOP: Photograph of Richard Sydney Marr in Mounted Horse uniform, with the Queens Medal. CLOCKWISE (From Above): Brisbane statue commemorating the Queensland heroes of the Boer War; QIB Badge; Roll of Honour details for Richard S. Marr; 'In Memorium' notice for R. S. Marr.; Report of the death of Private Richard S. Marr.

#Q215472 Victor Cardinal Marr (1906-1973)

Marr, Vic Cardinal: Service Number - Q215472: Date Of Birth - 15 Feb 1906: Place Of Birth - Mackay Qld: Place Of Enlistment - Sarina Qld: Next Of Kin - Marr, Mary (mother). He was a great grandson to John and Mary Frawley.

World War Two Service

PRIVATE
VICTOR CARDINAL MARR
Q215472

SERVICE	AUSTRALIAN ARMY
DATE OF BIRTH	15 FEBRUARY 1906
PLACE OF BIRTH	MACKAY, QLD
DATE OF ENLISTMENT	9 MAY 1942
LOCALITY ON ENLISTMENT	CARMILA WEST, QLD
PLACE OF ENLISTMENT	SARINA, QLD
NEXT OF KIN	MARR, MARY
DATE OF DISCHARGE	21 OCTOBER 1945
POSTING AT DISCHARGE	15 BATTALION VOLUNTEER DEFENCE CORPS (QLD)

Australian Government
Department of Veterans' Affairs

#75930 Leonard Joseph Marr (1907-1974)

Marr, Leonard Joseph: Service Number - 75930: Date Of Birth - 08 Jul 1907: Place Of Birth - Rockhampton Qld: Place Of Enlistment - Brisbane: Next Of Kin - Marr, Olive (wife). He was a great grandson to John and Mary Frawley.

World War Two Service

LEADING AIRCRAFTMAN
LEONARD JOSEPH MARR
75930

SERVICE	ROYAL AUSTRALIAN AIR FORCE
DATE OF BIRTH	7 AUGUST 1907
PLACE OF BIRTH	ROCKHAMPTON, QLD
DATE OF ENLISTMENT	25 MAY 1942
LOCALITY ON ENLISTMENT	EMERALD, QLD
PLACE OF ENLISTMENT	BRISBANE, QLD
NEXT OF KIN	MARR, OLIVE
DATE OF DISCHARGE	30 NOVEMBER 1945
POSTING AT DISCHARGE	EASTERN AREA HEADQUARTERS

Australian Government
Department of Veterans' Affairs

#QX21990 Alan William Marr (1918-2008)

Alan 'Lofty' Marr, great grandson to John and Mary Frawley, enlisted in the Australian Army on 4 July 1941. Next of Kin: Marr, William (father). 'Queensland Country Life' reported on 24th July 1941, that Tara gave a send-off to the people from the area who were home on leave from the AIF, including Alan Marr, and the Tara Patriotic Committee presented them each with a wallet.

On 17th September 1943, Private A. Marr, of Tara, was named on the list of Soldiers Overseas previously reported missing, but now reported missing, and believed to be a prisoner of war. It was later found that Alan was stationed in Malaya with the 2/26th Australian Infantry Battalion when he was captured along with 1,202 other men by the Japanese Army, and were now prisoners of war.

In May 1944, he was one of the 5,000 Australians included in the 11,700 Allied prisoners crammed into less than a quarter of a square kilometre in the environs of Changi Gaol, Singapore.

World War Two Service

PRIVATE
ALAN MARR
QX21990

SERVICE	AUSTRALIAN ARMY
DATE OF BIRTH	2 NOVEMBER 1918
PLACE OF BIRTH	MACKAY, QLD
DATE OF ENLISTMENT	4 JULY 1941
LOCALITY ON ENLISTMENT	LARA, QLD
PLACE OF ENLISTMENT	BRISBANE, QLD
NEXT OF KIN	MARR, WILLIAM
DATE OF DISCHARGE	15 NOVEMBER 1945
POSTING AT DISCHARGE	2/26 AUSTRALIAN INFANTRY BN
PRISONER OF WAR	YES

Australian Government
Department of Veterans' Affairs

#Q89724 Gerald Raymond Marr (1919-1984)

Marr, Gerald Raymond: Service Number - Q89724; Date Of Birth - 20 Sep 1919; Place Of Birth - Mackay Qld; Place Of Enlistment - Brisbane Qld; Next Of Kin - Marr, William (father). He was a great grandson to John and Mary Frawley.

World War Two Service

DRIVER
RAYMOND MARR
QX30017

SERVICE	AUSTRALIAN ARMY
DATE OF BIRTH	20 SEPTEMBER 1916
PLACE OF BIRTH	MACKAY, QLD
DATE OF ENLISTMENT	5 MARCH 1942
LOCALITY ON ENLISTMENT	CROWDERS CREEK, QLD
PLACE OF ENLISTMENT	BRISBANE, QLD
NEXT OF KIN	MARR, BERYL
DATE OF DISCHARGE	12 DECEMBER 1945
POSTING AT DISCHARGE	AUSTRALIAN NEW GUINEA ADMINISTRATIVE UNIT

Australian Government
Department of Veterans' Affairs

#QX51471 William Milward Marr (1924-1983)

Marr William Milward: Service Number - Qx51471; Date Of Birth - 28 Oct 1924; Place Of Birth - Stanthorpe; Place Of Enlistment - Brisbane Qld; Next Of Kin - Marr Elizabeth. He was a great grandson to John and Mary Frawley.

World War Two Service

GUNNER
WILLIAM MILWARD MARR
QX51471

SERVICE	AUSTRALIAN ARMY
DATE OF BIRTH	28 OCTOBER 1924
PLACE OF BIRTH	STANTHORPE
DATE OF ENLISTMENT	9 NOVEMBER 1942
PLACE OF ENLISTMENT	BRISBANE, QLD
NEXT OF KIN	MARR, ELIZABETH
DATE OF DISCHARGE	24 APRIL 1946
POSTING AT DISCHARGE	2/13 ANTI TANK REGIMENT

Australian Government
Department of Veterans' Affairs

#Q59108 Desmond William F. Craig (1939-2003)

Compulsory military training for young Australians was reintroduced in 1951 by the Liberal and Country Party alliance Government. It was the third such scheme to have existed in Australia since Federation. Eighteen-year-old men were required to undertake 176 days of military training as part of the National Service scheme. Desmond remained a soldier in the army for 21 years and received both the ADM & ANDSM medals.

National Servicemen's Association of Australia
Certificate of Service
1951-1972

Private
Desmond William Frederick CRAIG Q59108

Service	Army
Date of Birth	05 09 1939
Place of Birth	Sarina
Date of Intake	5 05 1958
Training	11 NST Battalion / Wacol
Next of Kin at time of Service	Mr W.H. Craig
Medals	ADM / ANSM

Later moving to Sydney, Letitia Frawley co-habited with a partner for a time whose first name was John, and by him had at least two children, but as they didn't marry her issue were born illegitimately and both given the surname of Frawley.

6.1 Patrick Frawley (1868-1868)[58]
6.2 Charlotte Ellen Frawley (1869-?)[59]

While her son Patrick died as an infant, research has failed to find any further mention of her daughter Charlotte. Letitia appeared as a bridesmaid for her older sister Ellen, at her wedding to James Mahony O'Sullivan in Sydney, in 1869.[60] However, after that no other references to a Letitia Frawley have been found. The marriage and death indexes have been unsuccessfully searched for the unusual christian name of 'Letitia' across New South Wales,

Correspondence on behalf of Eden (Edith Sanders (nee Frawley) for the proceeds of her late mother's estate, viz. Sarah Frawley (nee Little).

TOP (Left): Postcard of carriages lining-up in Toowoomba, c.1905. (Right): Postcard of the 'Horse Sales' in Toowoomba, c.1900. ABOVE: Postcard of stock crossing the Condamine River at Killarney on the Darling Downs, c.1905.

Queensland or Victoria from 1869 to 1900. At this stage no other information is known about any marriages, further issue or her death.

7. Thomas Frawley (1849<1901)

Thomas Frawley was the last child of John and Mary Ann Frawley, and was born on 24th June 1849 and baptised by Father Michael Kavanagh on the 18th October 1849 at the Frawley family residence in Pambula.[61] He attended school in Pambula, but little else is known of Thomas, except that he died somewhere between 1889 and 1901, as this fact was stated on his fathers 1901 death certificate. The marriage and death indexes have also been unsuccessfully searched for New South Wales, Queensland and Victoria. Thus at this stage, no further information is known about Thomas Frawley's marriages, issue or death.

Frawley Legacy & Inheritance

With seemingly very little to pass on to beneficiaries, an inheritance issue arose when the estate of John Frawley Jr, who had died 33 years previously, was re-examined in 1911. John Frawley's youngest daughter Eden (or Edith) Frawley, who by then was Mrs Sanders, pressed for her share of two parcels of land, sold for £36, which had been held by her late mother Sarah Frawley, until her death in April 1911. The correspondence states that apparently two daughters and two sons of the marriage were still living and stood to inherit the sum, who were likely to have been Mrs. Anna Gilmour Cuddihy, Charles Frawley and the plaintiff, Mrs. Eden [Edith] Alice Sanders.

The legacy of the Frawleys was memorable, although probably not for the right reasons. Gayle Lloyd, a 3rd great grand-daughter of John and Mary Ann Frawley commented in July of 2020...

> "Ahh... the Frawleys, lots of stories about them... such crooks, but very interesting. One story I recall was when the police came around at Toowoomba, asking if they knew anything about stolen saddles... "Saddles, what saddles?" they exclaimed... then the very next minute, the ceiling collapsed and down came all the saddles."[62]

Summary

John Frawley (c.1816–1901) and his wife Mary Ann McGarry (c.1813–1889) lived lives marked by hardship, resilience, and pioneering spirit. Born in Ireland, both were convicted of petty crimes, John for stealing clothes and Mary Ann for receiving stolen goods. Their punishment was transportation to Australia, where John spent seven long years in servitude under Alexander Berry at Coolangatta homestead, a common fate for many convicts seeking redemption in an unfamiliar land.

In 1840, after completing their sentences, John and Mary Ann married in Wollongong, a fledgling town on the New South Wales South Coast. With great determination, they ventured south to the Monaro District, carving out a life in the untamed wilderness. They found work at Warragaburra Station before joining the earliest settlers of the small coastal hamlet of Pambula. There, they raised a family of seven children and contributed to the growth of their community.

John was a man of strong will and deep involvement in his surroundings, and his unwavering support of the Catholic Church provided a moral anchor throughout his life, reinforcing his commitment to community and family. But his path was not without further trials. Though a respected member of Pambula, he made a costly mistake, convicted of cattle stealing, he was sentenced to five years of hard labour. This second incarceration cast a shadow over the Frawley family, and they faced intense scrutiny and backlash from a judgmental community. Unable to reclaim their place in Pambula, they left behind their hard-earned home and moved north to Toowoomba, Queensland, in search of a fresh start.

The Marr homestead at Mt Alma Station, Calliope District, west of Gladstone, owned and run by descendants of Patrick Marr (Frawley).

Frawley descendants in a four wheel carriage, at Mount Alma Station, 1890s Mrs T.S. Bell of 'Dumgree' about to leave for home.

Mary Ann's final years were marked by sorrow and struggle. She passed away in 1889 at Dunwich Asylum, a tragic end for a woman who had endured so much. Following her death, John Frawley remarried, choosing a much younger wife. Yet, despite a lifetime of toil, his work never ceased. He laboured until his final days, passing away in 1901, a testament to the endurance that had defined his existence.

Though their lives were fraught with hardship, John and Mary Ann Frawley left behind a lasting legacy. Their children carried their story forward, and their pioneering efforts played a role in shaping the communities they once called home. Their journey, from convicted criminals to pioneers of the Australian frontier, epitomizes the spirit of survival and the unbreakable will to build a better life, even in the face of great adversity.

References

1. John Frawley Jr. - Transcription of Birth on the 7th May & Baptism on the 19th May 1841 at Wollongong (NSW BDM #V121A, 1450).
2. NSW Dept of BDM. (1841). Birth & Baptism Certificate for John Frawley Jr., #1450/1841 (V18411450 121A).
3. Pambula School - in a List of NSW National Schools by August of 1850 (The Maitland Mercury & Hunter River General Advertiser, 7 Aug 1850, p.3).
4. NSW Dept. of BDM. (1865). Birth of a Male Frawley to John & Sarah Frawley, 1865 registered at Eden, #8498/1865.
5. NSW Dept. of BDM. (1867). Birth of a Female Frawley to John & Sarah Frawley, 1865 registered at Eden, #9040/1867.
6. NSW Criminal Court Records. (1862). Letitia, Mary & John Frawley Jr., (in Register of Criminal Cases Tried at Eden, NSW 1862-1869).
7. John Frawley Jr, resident at Three Mile Water Hole, nr. Wolumla, (Post Office Directory, 1875-77).
8. John Frawley Jr & Robert Little (brother-in-law), Imprisoned for Three Months in Darlinghurst Gaol (NSW Police Gazette & Weekly Record of Crime, 9 Oct 1867, p.297).
9. John Frawley Jr., Released from Darlinghurst Gaol (NSW Police Gazette, 4 Dec 1867, p.358).
10. NSW Dept. of BDM. (1869). Birth of a Male Frawley to John & Sarah Frawley, 1869 registered at Eden, #10365/1869.
11. NSW Dept. of BDM. (1872). Birth of Agnes Maude Frawley to John & Sarah Frawley, 1872 registered at Bega, #6915/1872.
12. NSW Dept. of BDM. (1872). Birth for Agnes Maude Frawley to John & Sarah Frawley, 1872 registered at Bega, #6915/1872.
13. John Frawley Jr, resident at Three mile Water Hole, near Wolumla (Post Office Directory, 1872).
14. John Frawley Jr, resident at Three mile Water Hole, nr. Wolumla (Post Office Directory, 1875-77).
15. John Frawley Jr. - 'Free Selectors' for the foundation of the township of Bega (The Bega Standard & Candelo etc, 11th November 1876, p.2).
16. John Frawley Jr. - 'Favor Deeds' (The Bega Standard & Candelo etc, 20 Sept 1879, p.2).
17. Queensland Dept of BDM. (1878). Death Certificate for John Frawley Jr., 9th October 1878 at Herries St, Toowoomba, #878/C/896.
18. Find a Grave - John Frawley - Buried on the 9th October 1878. (https://www.findagrave.com/memorial/199235721/john-frawley: accessed 04 February 2023), memorial page for John Frawley (unknown–9 Oct 1878), Find a Grave Memorial ID 199235721, citing Drayton and Toowoomba Cemetery, Toowoomba, Toowoomba Region, Queensland, Australia; Maintained by F.P.McLoughlin (contributor 48316713).
19. NSW Dept of BDM .(1842). Birth & Baptism for Ellen Frawley, 2nd Sept 1842 at Warigubera, #1772/1842 (V18421772 62).
20. Ibid.
21. Pambula School - in a List of NSW National Schools by August of 1850, op. cit.
22. Jas. O'Sullivan & Corn. Healy, Passengers on the "Ocean Chief." (Australia: Inward, Outward & Coastal Passenger Lists 1826-1972).

23. "Ocean Chief," arrived Melbourne from Liverpool, Geelong Advertiser, 24 February 1859, p.2.
24. Victorian Dept of BDM. (1866). Marriage Certificate for James Mahony O'Sullivan & Margaret Buckley, 9th April 1866 at Donnelly's Creek, Vic., #1508/1866.
25. Victorian Dept of BDM. (1866). Death Certificate for Margaret O'Sullivan, 26 October 1866 at Raspberry Creek, Vic, #12-268/1866.
26. NSW Dept. of BDM.(1869). Marriage Certificate for Ellen Frawley & James O'Sullivan, 3 August 1869 at Sydney, #757/1869.
27. NSW Dept. of BDM. (1871). Birth Certificate for Humphrey Joseph Vincent O'Sullivan, 5 May 1871 at Fish River Creek, NSW, #6704/1871.
28. NSW Dept. of BDM. (1872). Birth Certificate for James Alexander O'Sullivan, 1872 at Grafton, #10684/1872.
29. "The Little River Reefs." (Sydney Mail and New South Wales Advertiser, 13 July 1872. p.2).
30. NSW Dept. of BDM. (1877). Birth Certificate for John Washington O'Sullivan,16th November 1877 at Dalmorton, NSW, #12652/1877.
31. Ellen O'Sullivans Family Bible. "Ellen Theresa O'Sullivan, born 3rd August 1880 at Dalmorton." Rockwell Family Tree on ancestry.com.au.
32. Ellen O'Sullivans Family Bible. Blanche Zenobia O'Sullivan, born 22nd February 1882 at Dalmorton." Rockwell Family Tree on ancestry.com.au.
33. NSW Dept. of BDM. (1884). Birth Certificate for William O'Sullivan, 12th April 1884 at Moonie Creek, NSW, #23815/1884.
34. NSW Dept of BDM. (1909). Death Certificate for Ellen O'Sullivan, 4th August 1909 at Newcastle, #10250/1909.
35. Ibid.
36. NSW Dept. of BDM. (1843). Birth & Baptism for James Frawley, #1773/1843 (V18431773 62).
37. Pambula School - in a List of NSW National Schools by August of 1850, op. cit.
38. James Frawley - Horse Stealing (Sydney Morning Herald, 29th Apr 1863, p.5).
39. James Frawley - Payment for Construction of a Foot-Bridge (The Toowoomba Chronicle & Queensland Advertiser, 12 Nov 1863, p.2).
40. NSW Dept. of BDM. (1843). Birth Certificate for Stephen Frawley, 1844 at Panbula, 1168/1844 (V18441168 63).
41. Pambula School - in a List of NSW National Schools by August of 1850, op. cit.
42. Stephen Frawley - Charged with Horse Stealing (NSW Police Gazette, April 1864).
43. Stephen & Patrick Frawley - Wanted for Horse Stealing (NSW Police Gazette, Sept 1866).
44. Queensland Dept of BDM. (1930). Death Certificate for Stephen Frawley, 14th July 1930, #1930/C/3041.
45. NSW Dept. of BDM. (1848). Birth Certificates for Letitia & Patrick Frawley (twins), 1848 at Panbula, 1415/1848 (V18481415 65).
46. Pambula School - in a List of NSW National Schools by August of 1850, op. cit.
47. Patrick Frawley - Prisoners Tried at Eden Quarter Sessions, 21st Jan.1867.
48. Patrick Frawley - Return of Prisoners (NSW Police Gazette, January 1867).
49. NSW State Archives & Records. (1867). Patrick Frawley - Darlinghurst Gaol Entrance Book.
50. Record for Patrick Frawley - Darlinghurst Gaol Description & Entrance Books, 1867 (New South Wales Police Gazette New South Wales, Australia, Goal).
51. Patrick Frawley - Witness for the Crown (The Empire, 16th February 1867).
52. The Sydney Morning Herald, 12th May 1866.
53. Queensland Dept. of BDM. (1888). Marriage Certificate for Patrick Marr & Eliza Jane Quigg, 11th February 1888 at Eidsvold, #1888/C/213.
54. Queensland Dept of BDM. (1926). Death Certificate for James Patrick Marr, 24th August 1926 at Townsville Hospital, #1926/C/3797.
55. Eliza Jane Marr (nee Quigg) - Death Notice (SMH, 12 May 1949, p.18).
56. NSW Dept. of BDM. (1848). Birth Certificates for Letitia & Patrick Frawley (twins), op. cit.
57. Letitia Frawley & John Frawley Jr. - Eden Quarter Sessions List, 24 April 1863.
58. NSW Dept. of BDM. (1868). Death Certificate for Patrick Frawley - son of Letitia Frawley & John Unknown (NSW BDM #5776/1868).
59. NSW Dept. of BDM. (1869). Birth Certificate for Charlotte E. Frawley - dau. of Letitia Frawley (NSW BDM #2676/1869).
60. Letitia Frawley - Witness (NSW Dept. of BDM.(1869). Marriage Certificate for Ellen Frawley & James O'Sullivan, 3 August 1869 at Sydney, #757/1869.
61. NSW Dept. of BDM, Birth Certificate for Thomas Frawley at Panbula, 1849, 1519/1849 (V18491519 66).
62. Gayle Byrne (nee Lloyd), 4th cousin by the name of 'gaggs8,' on Ancestry.com (4 July 2020).
63. Western Star and Roma Advertiser , 23 Oct 1875.

Appendices

Roll of Arms for the Direct Ancestors of

JOHN FRAWLEY & MARY ANN McGARRY

APPENDIX A
Timeline of Exploration on the South Coast of New South Wales

WHEN	WHOM	WHERE
1770-Apr	Lt. James Cook	"HMS Endeavour" sailed north from Point Hicks to Botany Bay recording features and sightings along the way.
1788-Jan	Gov. Arthur Philip & The First Fleet	"First Fleet" sailed north from Van Diemans Land to Botany Bay & Port Jackson recording features and sightings along the way.
1791-Nov	Lt. Richard Bowen & Capt. Weatherhead	Lt. Richard Bowen in the "Atlantic" & Capt. Matthew Weatherhead in the "Matilda" both entered Jervis Bay and recorded depth soundings.
1795-Oct	Dr. George Bass & Lt. Matthew Flinders	Sailed south from Port Jackson in the tiny sailboat "Tom Thumb" and explored the Georges River as far as Bankstown.
1796-Mar	Dr. George Bass & Lt. Matthew Flinders	Again sailed south to explore Port Hacking & the Illawarra in the "Tom Thumb."
1797-May	Survivors of the "Sydney Cove"	After being wrecked on Preservation Island in the Furneaux Group, 17 survivors of the "Sydney Cove" trekked over 500 miles north along the south east coast, with only three being rescued and brought to Sydney.
1797-Dec	Dr. George Bass	Sailed south in a larger open whaleboat he called "Tom Thumb II" to explore Kiama, Shoal Haven, Jervis Bay, Ulladulla, Durras, Tuross River, Twofold Bay, and then explored the Victorian coast as far as Western Port Bay.
1798-Oct	Dr. George Bass & Lt. Matthew Flinders	The "Norfolk" circumnavigates Van Diemans Land and verifies the existence of Bass Straight, and stressed the lack of harbours other than Jervis Bay and Twofold Bay.
1800-Dec	Lt. James Grant	The "Lady Nelson" sailed through and proved that Bass Straight separated Van Diemans Land from the mainland, which was confirmed by the "Harbinger" and the "Margaret" just a few weeks later.
1801-Mar	Lt. James Grant, Barrallier & Cayley	Aboard the "Lady Nelson" they explored Jervis Bay, then sailed to Western Port Bay and returned to Sydney.
1805-Feb	Lt. Bartholemew Kent & James Meehan	Sailing in the colonial cutter "Anne" to explore the Shoal Haven region, but had to anchor in Jervis Bay and walk overland. They explored as far north as 'Berry' and west to 'Burrier' reporting on the landscape.
1811-Nov	Gov. Lachlan Macquarie	Took a return voyage aboard the "Lady Nelson" to Van Diemans Land, staying at Jervis Bay for two days and was so impressed that he commissioned a survey of the region.
1812-Jan	Cedar Getters	Cedar was covertly transported out of the Illawarra by the "Speedwell" and at least nine other ships, with sealers and whalers also beginning to operate along the coast at this time.
1812-Mar	George W. Evans	Sailing aboard the "Lady Nelson", George Evans landed at Jervis Bay and explored a land route through Shoal Haven and the Illawarra to Appin from the 3rd to 17th April.
1813-Apr	Capt. Collins	Sailing in the "Matilda", he began an exploration from Jervis Bay, and possibly reached the southern bank of the Shoalhaven River, but after being deserted by their natives at a distance of 12 or 14 miles from the vessel, they were reduced to the necessity of abandoning the project.
1815-Mar	Messrs Batty & Howell	Accompanied by Aboriginals, they trekked from Shoal Haven to Five Islands (Kembla), Watermoolly [sic. Wattamolla] to Sydney.
1815-	Charles Throsby	Throsby found an overland trail from Appin to Five Islands and weeks later moved his stock in a repeat of the journey, which was followed by a number of other stockholders.
1817-	Dr William Elyard, R.N.	The erection of the Red Point Barracks at Five Islands (Kembla), under Dr William Elyard, R.N. (superintendant).
1818-Apr	Throsby, Meehan, Hume, Grimes, Wild, Bundell & Broughton	Departing from the Moss Vale area, they crossed the Wingecarribee River, and passed though Marulan, Bungonia Creek, but the party split with Meehan's party discovering the Goulburn Plains. Throsby's expedition guided by aboriginals explored Bundanoon Creek, Meryla Pass, Yarrunga Creek and Kangaroo Valley, reaching the Shoalhaven River at Burrier, and Jervis Bay at Huskisson Hill before returning to Exeter.
1819-Oct	Oxley, Meehan, Hume & Broughton	Sailing on the "Emmeline", they set out from Jervis Bay, with Oxley turning about. Meehan and Hume continued north-west, tracing Throsby's route to Burrier, and keeping to the east they came to Fitzroy Falls and the precipitous cliffs, which they climbed to arrive at present day Bong Bong.
1821-Nov	Lt. Robert Johnston	Explored the River Clyde in the "Snapper" taking soundings for a distance of 35 miles, and was enthusiastic about the possibility of settlement.
1822-Jan	Lt. Robert Johnston & Alexander Berry	Sailing aboard the "Snapper" they entered the Crookhaven River and dragged their whaleboat across a narrow neck of land, describing the Shoalhaven River to Burrier. Retracing their steps they also sailed to Jervis Bay and then to Batemans Bay where they once again sailed up the River Clyde. As a consequence of this expedition Berry decided the Shoalhaven River afforded him the best prospects of settlement.
1822-Feb	William Kearns	A party consisting of Messrs. Kearns, Marsh, Packard and Aboriginal guides travelled overland from the southern end of Lake George to near Batemans Bay (Pigeon House Mountain), to investigate the possibilities of a road to the coast and survey the land.
1822-May	Alexander Berry	Establishes a settlement at 'Coolangatta' mountain on the Shoalhaven River.
1824-Oct	Hamilton Hume & William Hovell	Undertook a land journey of exploration over four months from Appin to Port Phillip Bay in eastern Australia, and returned by January 1825.
1827-	H.S. Badgery & Henry Burnell	Settlers and cattlemen began moving down from Goulburn and Braidwood to Moruya & the banks of the River Clyde.
1828-	Whalers & Sealers	At Twofold Bay, whalers set up a tri-works and began whaling.

Compiled by Dr Tracy Rockwell (2023)

APPENDIX B

The Aboriginal Populations of Illawarra & Wollongong (1835-1846)

The Illawarra Blacks

Sir, - We, the Undersigned, have, for a long time past, suffered great and grievous losses from the depredations of the Black inhabitants of this quarter. We have not unfrequently, after our year's toil and anxiety, had the mortification of finding whole acres of our corn, swept away in one night by them, by **them**, we say, because that fact we can clearly ascertain by the peculiar prints of their feet. But although we have suffered much in the loss of all things out of the house, still we have suffered most in the loss of our pigs; of the two farms alone of Mr Campbell and Mr Hindmarsh, no less than twenty have been taken and destroyed in the last three months; and their wonderful adroitness in the art of stealing has baffled all the vigilance up to the 18th of this month, as to the identical individuals, when Mr Otton's stockman met their chief, Black Harry, with a pig of about one hundred weight on his back, and accompanied by another of his tribe, called Captain Brooks, carrying a bunch of spears and a tomahawk.

On being questioned by the stockman, Harry immediately plunged into the bush again, carrying off the pig, while Captain Brooks, with his spear brandished, turned and gave front to the stockman, and so covered Harry's retreat, on which the stockman went and immediately reported the circumstances to Mr Hindmarsh, who, with a few others, followed, and guided by the smoke of their fires, came up to their camp, where a large oven was prepared in a particular way to roast the pig, and where Captain Brooks had arrived, but not Harry. However, next morning early, on our going to the place again, the watchfulness of their dogs gave them alarm in time to get off leaving behind them about one half of the pig, cut up and partly roasted, together with a quantity of Mr Campbell's potatoes and Black Harry's jacket, with some spears &c.

Now Sir, as silence or supineness on our part, in this case would undoubtedly (in their mind) establish their right to plunder and rob us with impunity, and so render our property insecure and our farms of no value, we humbly hope that you will see the necessity of taking such steps as will appear to you best calculated to put a stop to such daring outrages in future; and as we are now able to identify two individuals, we hope we can put the thing within your reach, and we wait ready to co-operate with the Police or Constable under your orders.

We are Sir,
With respect,
Your most obedient humble servants,

To W.N.Gray Esq.,
Police Magistrate,
Wollongong,
Kiama, 26th July 1835

Thomas Campbell,Patrick Marra,
Michael Hindmarsh,John Ritchie,
Prudenc Otton,Michael Hyam,
William Browne,J.M.Gray.

1836

Reward for Black Natives

May 1836: Local Aborigines discover the clothes of a murdered convict and are recommended for reward (Archibald Campbell Papers, Appendix 2)

...Mr W.N. Gray recommended that the reward offered for the murder of the late Patrick Fox in Illawarra be not paid to the parties claiming such. He stated that he did not consider any persons but the Black Natives who found the clothes of the deceased had any claim for a reward - such clothes have been the chief evidence against the murderer - James Tobin.

Wollongong & Kiama Aborigines

20 May 1836: Return of Wollongong and Kiama natives for 1836 (AONSW, 4/2302.1)

Return of Aboriginal Natives
taken at Wollongong on 20th May 1836

No	English Names	Native Names	Prob Age	Number of wives	Child M	Child F	Tribe
1	Old Bundle	-	40	1		1	Five Islands & Kiama
2	Young Bundle	-	23	1			
3	Frying Pan	-	44	1			
4	-	Timbery	40	1			
5	Doctor	Tarang	23	1		1	
6	Billy Hooker	Burwa	24	1			
7	Charley Hooker	Kerwune	24	1		1	
8	Old Man	Quidbally	50				
9	Jo	Trinamill	20				
10	-	Manggy	38	1			
11	Bill	Mullangollo	25	1			
12	-	Wollongong	50	1	1		
13	Tommy	Bitherst	22	1			
14	Charcoal	Taura	40	1		1	
15	-	Chit Tat	45	1		1	
16	Darby	Mittangle	26	1			
17	Thomas	Tomarra	38		1	1	
18	Tommy	Guringong	30	1			
19	Tallboy	Illamoo	26	1			
20	Philip	Mewjalong	30				
21	-	Mangle	50	1			
22	Charly	Miln	20				
23	Puss	Wollangut	20	1			
24	Jack	Kul	32	1	2		
25	-	Buttoe	55	1		1	
26	Caw buwn	Tullinba	38	1			
27	Paddy	Burringalla	20				
28	River Jim	Jimmy jiurra	38				
29	Paddy	Corrang	20				
30	-	Naigoo	20				
31	Thomas	Undelitte	20	1			
32	Johny	Tarranidy	30				
33	Jimmy	Connoe	18				
34	Fisherman	Coromal	13				
35	Jack	Wingillong	20				
36	Old	Tallagh	50	1			
37	Young Man	Timberry	24				
38	Timothy	Corrorjung	22	1	1	1	
39	-	Morrura	50	1			
40	Jacky	Worralla	28	1			

[All the above were designated as belonging to the 'Five Islands tribe and Kiama tribe', with their usual place of resort at 'Wollongong & Kiama']

Summary	Men	40		
	Women	26		
	Boys	5		
	Girls	8	Total	79

Capture of Bushrangers by Aborigines

29 August 1839: (*Sydney Gazette*) Report on the capture of a gang of bushrangers by local Aborigines at Illawarra:

The Poor Blacks

Illawarra. - Extract from a Letter from Wolongong, dated 26th instant, to a gentleman in Sydney.

> A curious scene took place here yesterday - five bushrangers have been committing depredations for the last five or six weeks, and have been the terror of the neighbourhood, excluding the Police, who have been out in all directions after them. To our surprise, the Blacks, in a small party, brought them in prisoners, with their hands tied firmly behind them. They have been committed and will be sent up by the steamer the next trip.

1840

Reverend W.B. Clarke at Illawarra

January 1840: The diary of the Reverend W.B.Clarke records his encounters with Illawarra Aborigines during January 1840 (Mitchell Library, MSS139)

Reverend W.B.Clarke was an Anglican minister and geologist who visited Illawarra early in January 1840, travelling to Wollongong, Kiama, and Shoalhaven to study the local geology. He was accompanied during these travels by members of the Wilkes United States Exploring Expedition.

Clarke's diary includes a description of a corroboree held near Wollongong on the night of Saturday, 4 January 1840; an incident at Kiama concerning the abuse of an Aboriginal woman by both white and black men; comments re the Aboriginal significance of the old figtree at Figtree; and a conversation with the Aborigine "Old Frying Pan" re religion.

The following are relevant extracts from the diary:

Saturday, January 4 - .....On the point [Towradgi] there were pieces of fossil wood, of granite, shale etc. The beach was marked by the impressions of 2 naked feet which had come from Bulli, evidently a black fellow's.....

The evening was spent in instructive converse, till about 9 when Mr Agate, Mr Rich and myself went off to attend a corrobery, a meeting of the blacks, to which we had been invited by 'old Frying Pan', alias Brown Bean, and some others, whom we got to throw the Boomerang for our amusement after dinner.

'Frying Pan' I had seen at Mr Nichol's store yesterday and again today - he was also a guide to Mr Foster. He is a fisherman, but when I asked him to catch me some Dildils, a huge prawn abounding here, he was angry, and said only women took them. Men catch nothing but with a spear.

About 10 we reached the corrobery ground.

It was in the bush where several large Teatrees were growing. Three of four fires made known the spot, to which we are at first directed by the laughter of the blacks. Beside a fire to the right over which sat an old woman whom we had seen in town dressed in a dirty pink gown thrown over her, lay 8 naked fellows, daubing themselves over with white pipe clay, which they first chewed to make soft, and red ochre etc.

They lay on their backs forming bands of white over their chests, arms and legs; and then they rubbed each others backs with red ochre, rising from time to time, that the old lady might see that all was perfectly properly done. They then bound their middles with strips of linen, having a tassle at each end, one of which hung down before, the other behind.

When this was done, during which time their spears stood against a tree, they sipped some liquid from a tin pot which they had got at by means of a piece of rope-yarn. The liquor turned out to be sugar and water.

Around the other fires lay various groups of men and women, some partly and some wholly clad, others quite naked. One fellow who was as black as Erebos wore a large straw hat, and as we came up, said in excellent English "I have nothing to do with getting up this corrobery. I have not been at one for several years." The facility with which the blacks acquire our language is wonderful - several spoke as well as this fellow.

When the ball was ready to be begun they told us to go to a fire which two half-naked women were making. I lent a hand and plucked some of the soft tea-tree bark for them and in a few minutes there was a great blaze, illumining the overhanging arches of the tree and showing their trunks like the column of a cathredal aisle. I could not fail to be impressed with a feeling of wild sublimity, especially as fire after fire blazed up and I found myself amongst at least 100 native savages, many of them in a state of perfect nudity and looking most unearthly. One, a tall, thin fellow without a rag upon him, sat over a solitary fire alone, stirring the ashes with a stick having a hook to it, the machine with which he catches worms and maggots from the trees. By another fire sat a man with his wife and child, the latter ill with fever. I asked how old it was, the answer was "holding up the hands twice and two fingers twice, 2 years or 24 moons."

About five minutes after we had assembled we heard from a dark corner a low melancholy sort of chant, and a beating of a waddy against a shield; the shout grew louder, at first it was sung by two voices, then by several - voice chiming in till it burst out in a most unearthly howl - the noise increasing. 'O Roa' seemed to be frequently repeated. After the first chant, the singers came out into the night and we then saw one man with a reddish cotton pocket handkerchief on his shoulders beating the waddy against the shield, the chief musician who sang with another beside him. The sound appeared to be emitted from the chest with a great straining of muscles, as if it caused pain.

The dancers, 8 in number, then came out, each having in his hand a bunch of fresh leaves, the very bouquet of an English belle - and when the chant began again, in which all seemed to join, they commenced the dance - by moving the right limb first, the left afterwards, backwards and forwards with a low grunting coincident with the kicking out of the limbs. Then one at a time they advanced, opened their legs, stood perfectly erect and stiff, and jerked the whole body by a violent muscular movement in and out by the knees. This was clearly a difficult part, and very painful to continue, as it lasted for a moment, and I observed that they whisked the green boughs about them after it as if to cool themselves.

The song was going on all the while, and the entertainment consisted in repeating the song and dance together. This was done several times when the party who were looking on, reminding me strongly of the old dowagers and aunts and uncles at an English ball, began to express dissatisfaction. Amongst the complainers was Mr Frying Pan, who with a red night-cap on his head, sat beside the first fire. He made a great noise and when, as I was informed by an interpreter, he urged the dancers on and they said they could not get more than themselves to dance - he said "if the man wont dance why don't you take the woman?" which afforded great merriment to all who understood him. I use the word 'understood' because it appears that this corrobery was called by the Sydney Blacks, and the ball given by them to the Blacks of Kiama, Wollongong, Liverpool, Brisbane Water and Newcastle, from which places some came to this meeting. Now, as they are of different tribes and do not speak the same dialect, several did not understand a single word of the song, which was a new one, and therefore no wonder it did not give satisfaction to them.

On enquiry I find the burden of the song to be: "that the white man came to Sydney in ships and landed the horses in the saltwater." It is of such ridiculous subjects that the Blacks of New Holland make their songs - and any trifling event is celebrated by a song.

They appeared to be perfectly harmless, nor was there the slightest indecorum in their conduct on this occasion. There was a degree of quiet and silent gravity I was astonished at, and I could compare their behavior to nothing so much as to that of well-behaved people at a similar Corrobery or Ball in England. On grave occasions the Corrobery has doubtless a different character, varying with circumstances ... the only signs of war here were the spears with which some of the men danced, held upright before them. I recognised one of the dancers as a man with one arm, wearing a plate in the day time as chief of Wollongong; he had told me that he lost his arm in the General Hospital. Another I knew to be the man who had thrown the Boomerang in the morning.

Of the Blacks it may be generally remarked, that they are fond of seeing the whites amongst them ... they have kindness enough to perceive our advantages over them, and they generally ask for a little sixpence as Frying Pan did tonight. It was 12 o'clock before I left, when this Australian opera was not nearly done, as we returned home we heard the noise of song and dance evidently continued with uninterrupted ardour.

Old Frying Pan, whom I had seen before, seemed to have some notions of Religion, but it is certain they are in part borrowed from the whites. I examined him closely on the subject of Cannibalism. He was very angry at the idea, and said none of his people ever ate flesh. But he allowed some bad fellows did up the country far away. I asked him what happened after death. He said "Go up on high tree-then go to great governor. He give bull (drink) plenty kangaroo, plenty opossum, plenty fish." On further enquiry he satisfied me this was not all original, for he used the term "God Almighty."

The Blacks, however, certainly believe in a state after death, for they have an idea that they are turned into white-men, into whales, porpoises, etc., and many of them go so far as to address a whale or other great fish as their Uncle, Father, etc., and call them to come on shore with them. Nay, so far is this carried, that some time ago a white man was asked by a Black to make atonement for an injury done by another, who was dead, because there happened to be a great resemblance between the dead man and the white.

The most extraordinary thing is the perfect way in which they pronounce and express themselves in English. Their own dialects appear to be pronounced thickly, only perfectly clear and well defined, even the harshest sounds.

I observed tonight a great diversity of colour and countenance. There were evidently more than one race......

Monday, January 6 -Rose at 6. Breakfasted with Mr Meares at 7, with Mr Hancock Dana, Drayton and Burnet. Off at 9.

Hancock an Meares accompanying Dana and me and the guide, (Biggs) to Dapto. The road leaves that over Keira to the right, then descends to country much like the coal district of England - through a woody region to Charcoal Creek, which is bridged by palm trees, passing an enormous fig-tree, at the foot of which old Timbery, a black, was born, and which his people venerate. There is another tree which the blacks say contains the names of their tribe and its history, by some hieroglyphical interpretation of its branches: a real genealogical tree......

[To Shoalhaven] Tuesday, January 7 - We came about 5 o'clock to a river, which we crossed, then to the saw-mill established by Mr Berry, which we visited. The machinery is simple and washed by water in the American plan. Here I saw three gins - one woman of about 40 having her shoulders and bosom tattooed (marks of mourning, cut with a glass bottle or stone, the very custom of old time Leviticus XIX 28, XXI 5), the other very young, one with a child extremely small in her blanket behind her. I asked them the name of the waterfall we had seen yesterday. They did not know. I said "where are you going?" - they said "Walkabout". As I knew they were in search of food I gave the old one a shilling which she thanked me for, and putting on her blanket she walked off. The youngest of these women was very good-looking. Their husbands, they said, were at home No doubt asleep, whilst their wives were "raising the wind"......

Thursday, January 9 - Rose at 6. While at breakfast a black fellow, his gin, and child, came to the house, begging. The man afterwards lay down to sleep on the grass and sent the woman to fish.

I first visited the little cove to the right which we passed last night. The rock there was all hard basalt and like what we saw at Boonaira. We then called at Mr Burnett's tent in front of which I found a dyke of porphyritic trap of a red colour running along the shore approximately from N. to S. We then went passed a cottage building for a store, the walls of which were made of palm trees, in which were three black fellows, one making a handle of a hatchet, another acting as servant, and the third as shopman. This fellow was very intelligent and was dressed in a blue jersey frock with a black stock round his neck. He seemed proud of his attire. I understand that he has had the shop in charge for several days at a time and that he is capable of serving out small articles. From him I learned the name of the waterfall- Tsejingouera. He was much pleased when I showed him a sketch of it......

.....As we rode up the steep I saw three blacks, father mother and child, all lying naked together on the beach along our path. Mr Burnett accosted the lady with "Well, Maria?" She replied "Yes Master". Returning a few seconds afterwards the woman following I had left behind I saw her going into the tent of the men, and from their manner they did not like her to be seen. But the picaninny betrayed her.

As I came back again, she was half clad in her blanket outside, and evidently beaten about. Two other black fellows came down the hill, one of whom threw a waddy into the bush nearby. I stopped and took it up. It was shaped thus: and was made of hard wood. I asked if he ever beat his gin with it; he said no, but being further questioned, he said that he would "beat a black fellow who should meddle with her, but would not touch a white fellow - let him do what he might. The fact is, white fellows carry white money as well, black fellows have nothing but black skins to recommend them."

It is a remarkable fact that scarcely a black child is now to be seen. The young ones are now more or less mongrel. I saw one the other day with a pale skin and red hair - a dark red or rose colour.

[Heads north from Kiama to Wollongong]

......On reaching the other side [of the cove] I returned for the horses, and not finding Dana trotted on with Mr Burnett. Our cries were answered by some black fellows fishing, one of whom came past us with a fish nearly as large and much like a salmon.

.....After striking into the bush some distance we came to the side of a hill where we found the ground much cleared and clearing, and at last stopped at a farm house where the good people gave us some new milk. Then again we entered the bush, and passing in view of a great swamp (Terragong Swamp), which appeared on our right, we came to a place called Wintye Wintye where we found ourselves in the midst of an encampment of blacks, in the Fig Tree Forest.

The only protection these people had against wind and sun was a screen of dried palm leaves, and these they lay near their fires, asleep in a burning hot day. Dogs and picaninnies were abundant, and when I spoke to one a child threw a tomahawk at one of the dogs to keep him quiet.

A venerable old man was here with a beard as white as snow. I asked him if they had been at the Corrobberies at Wollongong to which they replied No.

.....After passing the swamp we came to an inn at Jamberoo in front of which sat two well dressed Englishwomen and stood 6 or 7 dirty and naked black gins with their children. A mutual stare was all our salutation; but I think they were quizzing Mr Burnett's beard (which he does not shave in the back) and my dirty legs, for they laughed heartily as we passed.

[Aboriginal people, words, and place names mentioned by Clarke in the Diary include:

Old Frying Pan	alias Brown Bean
Captain Biggs	the Aboriginal guide
Timbery	an old Aboriginal Man
Gin	Aboriginal Woman
Picaninny	Aboriginal Child
Corrobery	Aboriginal song and dance festival
Boomerang	hunting implement
Dildilis	a lobster or large prawn
Waddy	implement
O'Roa	a chant at the corrobery
Marcilla	mountain on the way to Kangaroo Valley and Coolangatta
Barenjewry	mountain on the way to Kangaroo Valley and Coolangatta
Walkabout	
Diddel	Pigeon House mountain
Nunimura	mountains
Boonama	a locality
Borwarri Cove	a bay near Kiama
Boonaira	a locality
Segingouera	a waterfall near Macquarie Pass
Khanternigee	Kiama (blowhole) Point
Pungoilee	Headland opposite Blowhole Point
Wangorang	Headland north of Kiama
Kembla	mountain
Burelli	mountain
Gennigalla	a locality

Clarke was persistent in recording Aboriginal place names during his many years of geological excursions throughout New South Wales.

In a later letter to his mother in England, dated 3 August 1840, he stated:

I have now a very decent number of royal acquaintances, but my greatest affection is for my friend and namesake, Bran Bran, alias Mr. Frying Pan, in the Illawarra country....

For a watercolour of Frying Pan refer under Skinner Prout 1841.

Americans in Illawarra

December 1839 - January 1840: Members of the Wilkes United States Exploring Expedition visit Illawarra, including James Dwight Dana, geologist; Alfred T.Agate, artist with the expedition; and H.Hale, naturalist. They are accompanied during their visit by Rev. W.B.Clarke (refer to Clarke's Diary above).

Aborigines at Wollongong

1 May 1840: Return of Aboriginal Natives at Wollongong for 1840 (AONSW, 4/2479.1, 40/4871)

Police Office Wollongong
12th May 1840

Sir

With reference to your Letter of the first of January last, I have the honor to transmit to you the accompanying return of Aboriginal Natives taken at Wollongong on the first instant, and to whom Blankets were distributed.

I have the honor to be
Sir
Your most obedient Servant
P.Plunkett P.M.

The Honorable
The Colonial Secretary
Sydney

Return of Aboriginal Natives
taken at Wollongong on 1st May 1840

No	English Names	Native Names	Prob Age	Number of wives	Children M	Children F
1	John Bundle	Trumelong	45	1		
2	Parramatta Tom	Undedlight	27	1	1	
3	Charly Hooker	Gerone	30	1		1
4	Frying Pan	Mueamull	50			
5	Joe	Tumble	27			
6	Billy	Wolongolin	30	1		
7	Jack	Winelong	60	1	2	
8	Connor	Nango	27			
9	Paddy	Bulingolong	22			
10	Paddy	Tevirle	22			

1846 Enquiry Into The Condition Of The Aborigines, And The Best Means Of Promoting Their Welfare.

Aborigines at Wollongong

3 May 1842: Letter from Patrick Plunkett re blankets for Aborigines at Illawarra (Wollongong Bench of Magistrate returns, IHS)

Police Office Wollongong
3rd May 1842

Sir

I have the honor to acknowledge rect. of your Letter of the 18th ultimo inclosing receipts in Duplicate for Seventy Blankets forwarded by the Gosford Packet, for distribution to the Native Blacks of this place, and to inform you that the Gosford Packet has not arrived here, and is suposed to have been wrecked in the late Gales. I can obtain Blankets here in lieu of them, I think at as low a rate as they can be purchased in Sydney, if you will sanction my doing so, stating the price I may give.

I have the honor &c
Sd/ P.Plunkett P.M.

A.Rogers
Col. Storekeeper
Sydney

---

27 May 1842. Return of Aboriginal Natives at Wollongong (AONSW. 4/1133.3, 42/4224)

Police Office Wollongong
7th June 1842

Sir

In reply to your Letter of the first of January last, I have the honor to transmit to you, a return of the Aboriginal Natives residing in this District to whom Blankets were distributed on the 27th ultimo.

I have the honor to be Sir
Your most obedient Servant
P.Plunkett P.M.

The Honorable
The Colonial Secretary
Sydney

Return of Aboriginal Natives
taken at Wollongong on 27th May 1842

No	English Names	Native Names	Prob Age	Number of wives	Children M	Children F
1	John Bundle	Treemelong	47	1		
2	Parramatta Tom	Undeddolight	27	1	1	
3	Charley Hooker	Girone	30	1		1
4	Frying Pan	Muramulle	50			
5	Joe	Tumble	27			
6	Billy	Wolongolin	30	1		
7	Jack	Winelong	60	1	2	
8	Paddy	Burngolong	22	1		
9	Paddy	Tiveree	22			
10	Peter	Coodagong	18			
11	Jem	Jenegamem	30		1	
12	William Darby	Medangle	30	1		
13	Paddy	Cooreen	27			
14	Fisherman	Corumblo	18			
15	Jack	Manggy	30	1		1
16	Charcoal	Tourewya	50	1		1
17	Charley	Millen	30			
18	Tommy	Jeerenoo	34			
19	Tall Boy	Illimugo	30	1		
20	Phillip	Mogelong	35	1		
21	Long Jack	Currevoor	65	1		
22	Mickee	Numima	27	1		
23	Jim	Coonel	22			
24	Jimmy	Barrad	23			
25	Bill	Tullen Bar	45	1		
26	Geeagong	Geeagong	35	2		
27	Fallow	Tallow	65			
28	Caobawn Jack	Borregel	55			
29	Greedy Boy	Toorang	35	1		
30	Captain Brooks	Monnagh	55			
31	Maria	Burrigoo	20	*	1	
32	Mary	Beeone	50			
33	Biddy	Nigernagh	27	1		1
34	Mary	Cooramelong	30		3	1
35	Mary	Budiek	35	1		
36	Mary	Norroon	35	1	1	
37	Nelly	Nerreel	35	1		
38	Betsey	Coongall	24			
39	Nanny	Booel	49	1		
40	Molly	Boonan	35	1		
41	Biddy	Moboon	24	1		1
42	Mary	Murereen	40	1		
43	Betsey	Banbaroo	20	1		
44	Polly	Jaujake	18	1		
45	Polly	Murret	35	1		
46	Mary Anne	Mary Anne	18			
47	Ebeek	Coongarah	24	1		1
48	Morgan	Bathhiet	30	1		
49	Doctor	Dherong	40	1		
50	Bob	Chit Tat	30	1		1
51	Thomas	Tomra	30	1		1
52	Lewis	Magath	45			
53	Maria	Good good	30	1		
54	Maria	Yardah	18	1		
55	Cabbage	no native name	15			1
56	Betsey	Wenelong	20	1		2
57	Mary	Coolbelong	17	1		1
58	Sook	Glengawley	20			
59	Charlotte	Coorack	12			
60	Betty	Woorang	15			
61	Billy	Wyalvia	10			
62	Maria	Woorawonga	10			
63	Eliza Hooker	no native name	7			
64	Patrick	Byeul	20			
65	Billy	Dambool	9			
66	Charley	Yambut	30	1	2	
67	Long John	Bungelong	28			1
68	Mary	Moomung	31	1		
69	Charlotte	Nelyat	38	1		
70	Polly	Burrobing	34	1		

Men 70
Women 42
Boys 11
Girls 14 Total 137

[All are designated as members of the Five Islands tribe and resident at Illawarra]

Select Committee on Aborigines

During 1845-6 the New South Wales Legislative Council undertook an investigation into the condition of the Aborigines of the east coast of Australia via the appointment of a Select Committee.

Illawarra Aborigines

*From the Reverend M.D. Meares, M.A., Minister of the Church of England, Wollongong, 6th April, 1846:

1. What is the probable number of Aborigines in your district, distinguishing males, females, and children?

    Males 34, females 40, children 19; of these 8 are black, 11 half-caste.

2. Has the number diminished or increased, and if so, to what extent, within the last five or ten years?

    In 1837 there were I believe upwards of 350 Aborigines in this district.

3. Has the decrease been among the children or adults?

    The decrease has been pretty equal in adults and children.

4. To what cause do you attribute the decrease in your district?

    To the fact of their having from associating much with the worst characters, among the white population, imbibed most of their vices, without any of their redeeming qualities.

5. What is their actual condition and means of subsistence?

    Their moral condition is, from the causes stated above in the reply to query No.4, worse than before they were exposed to the degrading effects of such association.

    Their means of subsistence are fully adequate to their wants; whether derived from their ordinary pursuits of hunting and fishing, or in exchange for such services as they are able and willing to render to the settlers.

6. Has their ordinary means of subsistence diminished, and if so, what part of it, and from what causes; if it has increased, what part, and from what causes?

    The improved parts of the district, afford more extensive hunting grounds than the present diminished numbers of the Aborigines require; the fish are as abundant as ever, and they can earn a something occasionally from the settlers.

7. Have blankets been issued to the Aborigines in your district heretofore, and for what period? What was the effect of giving them? Has the giving of blankets ceased? When did it cease; and what has been the effect of its cessation? Would it be advisable to resume the distribution?

    Blankets have heretofore been issued by the Government to the Aborigines; the effects produced were 1st - an increase of their comforts, and the preservation of their health; 2nd - a partial incitement towards civilization by an increase of their wants.

    No blankets have been issued since 1844; the effects have been an increased mortality, particularly among the males; and much dissatisfaction among the survivors, with considerable suffering from rheumatic affections and colds. I would strongly recommend an immediate return to the former practice of distribution.

8. Have they been allowed or refused Hospital or Medical treatment in case of need; and in what manner; and, if allowed, at whose expense?

    Bundel, a native of Illawarra, died in the Hospital in Sydney some two years ago; in no other instance has medical assistance, within my knowledge, been sought for.

9. What proportion of them are either regularly or occasionally employed by the settlers, and in what way? In what manner are they remunerated?

    There are two or three who are frequently employed by the settlers in Illawarra, but for irregular periods; and they receive wages and rations as other men.

10. What habits have they bearing upon their aptitude for employment?

    They have no habits, of which I am cognizant, bearing upon aptitude for employment of a laborious character; if it were otherwise, I am of opinion that their muscular development would be much greater than I have ever witnessed it, except in rare instances.

11. Are there any, and how many, half-castes in your district? Are they living with or after the manner of the Aborigines?

    There are two or three adult half-castes who live as do the Aborigines, and with them.

12. Is there any disposition on the part of the white labouring population, to amalgamate with the Aborigines, so as to form families?

    There is no desire on the part of the white labouring population to amalgamate, in a legitimate way, with the Aborigines; cases have occurred in which white men, working among the mountains, as cedar cutters, have cohabited with black women for months together; in one instance for two years, but the connexion has always ceased immediately on their return to a settled part of the district.

13. Are the Aborigines in friendly or hostile relations with the settlers in your district; if hostile, how has the hostility arisen, and what collisions have taken place between the two races; what loss of life has there been; and in what manner has it taken place on either side?

    The Aborigines in this district are peaceable in their habits, and generally well disposed.

14. What destruction of property has been occasioned by Aborigines?

    None whatever.

15. What are the relations, hostile or otherwise, of the Aborigines among themselves in your district?

    Generally of a friendly character.

16. Are their numbers directly or indirectly affected by their hostilities, and to what extent?

    One man was killed in a private quarrel by his own brother, about two years ago.

17. Is infanticide known among them?

    It is altogether denied by the Aborigines of this district, and I have never heard of an instance of it among them.

18. Will you be good enough to state any facts relative to the Aborigines that would assist the Committee in its endeavour to promote their welfare?

    From my limited acquaintance with the habits of the Aborigines I cannot state any facts which could assist the Committee in its endeavour to promote their welfare, but I am of opinion that their children, in no way deficient in intellect, are capable of a high state of moral culture.

    I have never met with any people endowed to the same extent with the ability to acquire a knowledge of the English language; indeed, I feel convinced that if that paternal care, which a Government is upon every principle, bound to extend to all classes of its subjects, had been exercised towards them, the moral and physical condition of the Aborigines would have been raised to a respectable level, instead of being sunk, in a great measure from neglect, to a state the most degraded.

    What course is best calculated to benefit them now is not easy to be ascertained, but something at least ought to be attempted. A long debt is due to those people from the inhabitants of European descent; and whatever the legislature can do for their religious improvement, their temporal comfort, or the education of their children, will, I am persuaded, be well and wisely expended.

From the Reverend M. D. Meares, M.A., Minister of the Church of England, Wollongong, 6th April, 1846

1. Males 34, females 40, children 19; of these 8 are black, 11 half-caste.
2. In 1837 there were I believe upwards of 350 Aborigines in this district.
3. The decrease has been pretty equal in adults and children.
4. To the fact of them having from associating much with the worst characters, among the white population, imbibed most of their vices, without any of their redeeming qualities.
5. Their moral condition is, from the causes stated above in the reply to query No. 4, worse than before they were exposed to the degrading effects of such association.
   Their means of subsistence are fully adequate to their wants; whether derived from their ordinary pursuits of hunting and fishing, or in exchange for such services as they are able and willing to render to settlers.
6. The improved parts of the district, afford more extensive hunting grounds than the present diminished numbers of the Aborigines require; the fish are as abundant as ever, and they can earn a something occasionally from the settlers.
7. Blankets have heretofore been issued by the Government to the Aborigines; the effects produced were 1st – an increase of their comforts, and the preservation of their health; 2nd – a partial incitement towards civilization by an increase of their wants. No blankets have been issued since 1844; the effects have been an increased mortality, particularly among the males; and much dissatisfaction among the survivors, with considerable suffering from rheumatic affections and colds. I would strongly recommend an immediate return to the former practice of distribution.
8. Bundel, a native of Illawarra, died in Hospital in Sydney some two years ago; in no other instance has medical assistance, within my knowledge, been sought for.
9. There are two or three who are frequently employed by the settlers in Illawarra, but for irregular periods; and they receive wages and rations as other men.
10. They have no habits, of which I am cognizant, bearing upon aptitude for employment of a laborious character; if it were otherwise, I am of the opinion that their muscular development would be much greater than I have ever witnessed it, except in rare instances.
11. There are two or three adult half-castes who live as do the Aborigines, and with them.
12. There is no desire on behalf of the white labouring population to amalgamate, in a *legitimate* way, with the Aborigines; cases have occurred in which white men, working among the mountains, as cedar cutters, have cohabited with black women for months together; in one instance for two years, but the connexion has always ceased immediately on their return to a settled part of the district.
13. The Aborigines in this district are peaceable in their habits, and generally well disposed.
14. None whatever.
15. Generally of a friendly character.
16. One man was killed in a private quarrel by his own brother, about two years ago.
17. It is altogether denied by the Aborigines of this district, and I have never heard of an instance of it among them.
18. From my limited acquaintance of the habits of the Aborigines I cannot state any facts which could assist the Committee in its endeavour to promote their welfare; but I am of opinion that their children, in no way deficient in intellect, are capable of a high state of moral culture. I have never met with any people endowed to the same extent with the ability to acquire a knowledge of the English language; indeed, I feel convinced that if the paternal care, which a Government is upon every principle, bound to extend to all classes of its subjects, had been raised to a respectable level, instead of being sunk, in a great measure from neglect, to a state the most degraded; what course is best calculated to benefit them now is not easy to be ascertained, but something at least ought to be attempted; a long debt is due to those people from the inhabitants of European descent; and whatever the legislature can do for their religious improvement, their temporal comfort, or the education of their children, will, I am persuaded, be well and wisely expended.

NSW Government, (1846). 'Aborigines' Reply by Rev. M.D. Meares, Church of England Minister at Wollongong, To A Circular Letter Addressed To The Clergy Of All Denominations, By Order of the Select Committee On the Condition of the Aborigines, 6th April 1846, NSW Govt Printing Office'.

APPENDIX C
The Aboriginal Population at Shoalhaven (1833-1842)

Blankets and Alexander Berry's Reminiscences

1833 - 1842

The years 1833-42 are some of the richest, historically, in our study of the Illawarra and South Coast Aborigines, for during this period the first census information of the local Aborigines was compiled in connection with the issue of blankets. They revealed a great deal of personal information on the native population.

The majority of the extant blanket issue forms, from the Archives Office of New South Wales Colonial Secretary Letters, record the following information with respect to individual Aborigines, namely:

- English name
- Native name
- Age
- Number of wives and children
- Place of residence or resort
- Designation of tribe

Though blankets had been issued earlier, it is only from 1833 that returns have survived for the Illawarra and South Coast people. With such detailed information many of the Aborigines mentioned in historical accounts are brought to life for the first time. The family history value of this material is also significant, as Aborigines were not again included in Australian census until the 1960s. The Aborigines Protection Board lists of 1882-1960s merely indicated numbers, not individual names.

This period also saw the issue of a significant collection of reminiscences on the Aborigines of Shoalhaven, by Alexander Berry.

1833

Shooting at Minamurra

22 May 1833: (Archibald Campbell Papers, 4.1) Notes re shooting of some Aborigines at Minamurra, extracted from offical records which no longer survive:

Two blacks found dead, after some shooting at Minamurra - supposed to have speared a bullock night before - shots.....

Blankets for South Coast Aborigines

12 August 1833: Captain Allman, magistrate at Wollongong, writes to the Colonial Secretary re a parcel of blankets for Aborigines at Illawarra which had erroneously been sent to Mr Elyard's (?at Ulladulla). They were subsequently retrieved by Constable Edward Corrigan (AONSW, 4/6666B.3, 33/5289)

Return of Nullandarie Aborigines

8 October 1833: Return of Aborigines at Nullandarie, St Vincent (AONSW, 4/6666B.3), the property of Francis Flanagan near Moruya:

Return of Aboriginal Natives at .... on ... 1833

No	English Names	Native Names	Prob Age	No. of wives	Children M	Children F	Place or District of Usual Abode
1	Warrinda	Warrinda	50	1		1	Burgurgo
2	Snow-ball	Muthar	33	2		1	Kivora
3	Peter	Callumboo	35	2	1		do
4	Jemmy	Abba	20				do
5	Jemmy Buuwin	Buuwin	40	3	2	2	do
6	Paddy	Wambut	25	1			Browley
7	Charley	Thurwood	35	1		1	do
8	Dickey	Kowal	18				do
9	Joe	Alwoonigal	20				do
10	Tommy	Biddimogul	30	1		1	do
11	Browley Dickey	Muddoogali	16				do
12	Paddy	Thaboora	15				do
13	Jerry	Boogal	35	1			do
14	Jackey	Gumboa-a	20				do
15	Thurama	Thurama	60	2	3	4	River
16	Billy	Jugroo	25	1			Moorooya
17	Bumiel	Bumiel	18				do
18	Lazy Sandy	Karbierly	35	1	1		do
19	Coborabull	Yowgooau	35	1			do
20	Joey	Burjungala	18				Mullandaru
21	Warrinda Tommy	Moothooga	20				do
22	Jack	Kovara	30		1	1	Arralooin
23	Big Sandy	Allumroo	35	1		2	Wagunga
24	Jemmy Eagan	Koora	50		1		Kariery
25	Pretty Dickey	Mimmina	20				Burgali

Nullandarie, St. Vincent
8th Octb. 1833

[All are designated as belonging to the 'Burgurgo' tribe]

1833: Assistant Surveyor Elliott records the following Aboriginal place names on his 'Plan of Road through the District of Illawarra' (refer W.G.McDonald *The Oldest Road*, 1979, p.21):

* Ballambi
* Touradgee

Return of Shoalhaven Aborigines

21 June 1836: Return of Aboriginal Natives taken at Shoal Haven. Compiled by Alexander Berry (AONSW, 4/2302.1)

June 21st 1836
Return of Aboriginal Natives taken at Shoal Haven and to whom Blankets have been given

No	English Names	Native Names	Prob Age	No. of wives	Child M	F	Tribe	Blankets
1	Bogeno	Bogeno	33		2		Shoal Haven	1
2	Cobbian Mick	Nooroon	32	1				1
3	Greedy Boy	Towrang	27	1				1
4	Sam	Tool enboy	28	1	2			2
5	Michael	Monkey	14					1
6	Neddy	Noorar	27					1
7	Cobborn Mick	Yaniet	33	1				1
8	Coorooboy	Coorooboy	52		1	2		1
9	Jack Jack	Coombung	47	1				1
10	Mary	Illawora	18					1
11	Paddy	Groonnell	18					1
12	Kennedy	Goonora	22	1				1
13	Charley	Yambet	23	1				1
14	Burnoe	Burnoe	19					1
15	Jirimbunga	Jirimbunga	23					1
16	Good Good	Good Good	42	2	2	1		3
17	Jack	Boolbin	33					1
18	Nurang Jack	Waral	30	1	1			2
19	Tommy Settler	Pautaulic	32	3				4
20	Waterman Jack	Woonawara	27	1				1
21	Burrow	Coombrull	12					1
1	Long Charcoal	Moorunit	37	1	3		Numba	2
2	Friday	Burmin	42	1				1
3	Peckey corn	Toonmoor	53	1				1
4	Blackey smith	Goodbar	62	1				1
5	Bobino	Bobino	32	1				1
6	Ugly Jack	Gerimbell	13					absent
7	Cobboo	Parrawell	32	1				1
8	Jem Charcoal	Nunberry	35					1
9	Harry	Cunnong	31	1				1
10	Cobborn Bill	Pillarra	35					1
11	Walfaby Jack	Batoon	19					1
12	Charley Goodnight	Arbey	51	1	1	2		1
13	Monkey Pe	Perregorong	16					1
14	Dr Wentworth	Tucken	23					
1	Carroll (At Five Islands)	Carroll	30				Gerongong	
2	Billy Roberts	Herenrrell	24					1
3	Water Water	Water Water	28	1				1
4	Harry (At Five Islands)	Yuckier	27					
5	Sawyer	Umberunda	26	1		1		
6	Mickey	Nathoo	16					1
7	Georgey (At Five Islands)	Numerall	17					1
8	Mungelong	Mungelong	51					1
9	Commandant	Commandant	13					
10	Jack Ratley	Terremwer	20					1
11	William	William	18					1
1	Darby Brook ('a notorious thief')	Yacking	32				Broughton Creek	
2	Armor	Sandigong	52	1	1			1
3	Lion	Carman	21					1
4	Jackey	Undigong	23					1
5	Tiger	Toonung	24					1
6	Dick	Buttoong	20	1				1
7	Charley	Tindel	20	1				1
8	Gandy Gandy	Gandy Gandy	40					1
9	Joe	Tamong	11					1
10	Shordar	Shordar	9					1
11	Macarthy	Macarthy	11					1
12	Broughton	Toodwick	38	2				3
13	Billy	Bullboong	8					1
1	Sam (V. Die. Land)	Conduwhite	25				Murroo	
2	Davey	Berrong	27					1
3	Abraham	Cullawar	30					1
4	Sam	Fisherman	40	1	1	1		1
5	Davey	Tunerier	52					1
6	Jemmy	Coongalong	18					1
7	Tinker	Tinker	41	1				1
8	Jemmy	Mejue	23					1
9	Tommy	Wougung	51					1
10	Sam	Warriri	25	1	1			1
11	Toolbiw	Yawra	30	1				1
12	Sam	Minbar	30					1
13	Old Megar	Megar	40					1
14	Johnney	Tilbar	8					
1	Jack	Nuttong	26				Jarvis's Bay	1
2	Monday	Monday	50					1
3	Jack	Barong	40	1				1
1	Joe	Nunguroo	28				Woregy	1
2	Peter	Vordaluck	30	1	1			1
3	Nelson	Naurangully	26					1
4	Jem Cotton	Illett	30					1
5	Tom Bailley	Woolooboroo	28	1				1
6	Joe	Columbin	33	1				1
7	Johnney	Burranong	34					1
8	Pudugong	Minja	52	1	1	1		1
9	Joe	Janbagong	52					1
10	Paddy Bluet	Cuttuck	52			4		1
11	Paddy	Wallau	19					1
12	Nimilite	Nimilite	47	1	1			1
13	Billy	Yammin	16					1
14	Yellowman	Coorooboon	50	2				1
15	Uncle John	Mundjeng	51	1				1
16	Charley	Unumbar	28					1
17	Dick	Jangret	29					1
18	Jackey	Nerremut	28	1				1
19	Noddy	Diegong	30					1
20	Jackey	Jenebiar	27					1

General Total

		Men	Women	Children Male	Female	Genl Total	Number of Blankets to each tribe
1	Shoal Haven	21	14	9	3	47	26
2	Numba	14	7	5	2	28	14
3	Gerongong	11	5	1	1	19	8
4	Broughton Creek	13	5	1	1	19	14
5	Murroo	14	4	2	1	21	13
6	Jarvis's Bay	3	1	4	1	3	
7	Woregy	20	8	5	7	40	20
		94	41	22	14	173	100 issued

Alexr. Berry

APPENDIX D

Reminiscenses of Alexander Berry

Berry, Alexander, 1781-1873. (1912). "Reminiscences of Alexander Berry", with portrait and illustrations. Sydney : Angus & Robertson.

May 1838: 'Recollections of the Aborigines by Alexander Berry 1838' (AONSW, Supreme Court Papers, Cod 294, Part B, pp.557-608)

The following reminiscences by Alexander Berry were initially recorded in May 1838, and later updated for publication in 1871 (refer also under that date).

Alexander Berry was a prominent Sydney merchant who had established a settlement at Coolangatta, on the Shoalhaven River, in 1822. He eventually claimed over 10000 acres of land in the area, and his family held the property until the turn of the century. Berry was relatively accommodating to the local Aborigines in everything but granting them land, and did not chase them away by force of gun as was so common in other areas of Australia.

These reminiscences, combined with the accurate blanket issue / census compiled during the 1830s by both Alexander and David Berry, give a rare glimpse into the post-contact Aboriginal society at Shoalhaven.

The first Native in whom I took an interest was old Bungaree in the year 1819. He was a particular favourite with Governor Macquarie, who created him a chief, gave him a farm, and Government men victualled from the store to cultivate it. Bungaree was a man decidedly of considerable natural talents, very faithful & trustworthy, but had all the defects of his Race, in consequence of which all the trouble & expense bestowed by the humane Macquarie to ameliorate his constitution proved abortive, as in every other instance.

About Christmas in that year, poor Bungaree was severely beaten in a drunken brawl by his countrymen. He was brought to my house with a severe wound in the head and a fracture of the fore-arm. I dressed his wound, bound up his arm, & gave instructions that he might be taken care of in the kitchen. There he remained several days until he recovered from the bruises. The moment however he was able to move he escaped from the house as from a jail, and disconnected the arm from the bandage. Some weeks after he came back. On examining his arm I found that the ends of the fractured bones had healed without uniting, giving the appearance of a joint, and it remained for the rest of his life.

About the same time I had a great deal of conversation with another intelligent native at the country house of Mr Oxley, the late Surveyor General. I asked him if they could not erect houses for themselves like the mens' huts which would afford them better protection from the weather than a sheet of bark. He replied that they no doubt could do so, and that such huts would afford them better shelter, but that it would not suit their mode of life. That it was necessary for them constantly to change their place of residence in search of the means of subsistence, and that their means of subsistence had become more scanty since the country had been occupied by white men. That the sheep and cattle cut all the grass in consequence of which Kangaroos had become very scarce, and that they now lived chiefly on squirrels and opossums & such small animals.

I went to Shoal Haven in June 1822 in order to form an establishment. At that time the Natives at that place bore a very bad character and were considered very hostile to the whites. Some years previously the Shoal Haven River was frequented by cedar cutters from Sydney. In the end the natives either killed all the sawyers or forced them away. One day my friend James Norton thus addressed me:

"I hear you are going to take a farm near Jervis Bay. Is it true?"

I replied in the affirmative.

"Are you mad," he retorted. "The natives will eat you."

I however entertained no fears, and had no doubt would be able to conciliate them. I was even so chimerical as to be sanguine that I would be able to civilize them.

I went down in a small cutter (15 tons) and took along with me two natives - one named Broughton, born at Shoal Haven & who had accompanied the late Mr Throsby on several journeys into the bush; the other a tame native named Charcoal who was a good boatman.

On the evening previous to my departure I observed this fellow moving on stilts with great rapidity past my door as if he had some important business to perform. I considered his earnestness as a mark of intelligence and beckoned to him. He was informed that I was to sail to Shoal Haven in the morning. I asked him to accompany me. He instantly forgot his own business, informed me that he was a good sailor & would be very glad to accompany me. He stopped in the kitchen all night. Next morning he was rugged out in sailors cloathes and appointed pro forma Mate of the cutter Blanch.

When we arrived near the Shoal Haven Heads it fell calm, and we got the boats ahead of the vessel. The River empties itself into the sea through a low sandy beach and there is a bar at the entrance, but I had heard that vessels of 70 or 80 tons had entered, and therefore I imagined there would be water enough for a sloop of 15 tons. When the boats however got to the back of the surf they returned, observing that it would be unsafe as they saw every surf heaving up the sand. On entering the vessel Davidson the Master, a young man whose life I had saved years before at New Zealand, urged me very much to proceed. I directed him however to take the vessel into Crook Haven, a small place 3 miles to the southward, where we would examine the bar at our leisure. He persisted however in saying that the surf was nothing, that it was not near so bad as Dublin bar, and that we were deceived by the glitter of the sun upon the waves.

During the dispute the vessel gradually approached the surf, & Turner, one of the men, observed, "Davidson is right, the nearer we get, the less the surf appears."

I tacked again and there appeared a small channel abreast of the vessel. "Well Davidson," I observed, "since you are so urgent you may take the boat if you can get volunteers, and sound the channel - but take care to keep out of the breakers."

In a moment the boat was manned. I looked at Davidson as he passed over the side - there was a livid flush upon his face. I thought it resembled the purple hue of death and immediately repented the consent I had given. I ran up to the mast head and again saw the surf breaking across what a few minutes ago was a smooth channel. I called out for all hands to shout for the return of the boat, & waved my hat from the mast head for their return. They heard & saw us, and absolutely turned round the boat, but after disputing some time among themselves again turned round the head of the boat toward the surf.

I again went up the mast in breathless anxiety. The passage was again smooth & I saw the boat passing along it with a wall of breakers on the right hand side & on the left. I observed to a person near me they had got into a smooth place & hope it may not prove a deceitful calm. I had ceased speaking when a mighty roller rose up behind the boat. As it moved along the boat was hid from my view, but in a few seconds I saw it on top of the wave. A second wave rolled along and the boat was again invisible. In a few seconds the oars appeared in the air, and as the wave passed the boat appeared upset & the men clinging to her sides.

My first impulse was to leap into the little Dingo and get to their assistance. A moments reflection convinced me it was madness. We then got out our sweeps & pull for Crook Haven and endeavour to assist them by land.

I forgot to mention that a third roller again rendered the boat invisible and when it passed we only saw two men out of five clinging to the boat.

On our way to Crook Haven we saw a lame & naked blackman supported by a stick moving along the beach. He reached Crook Haven at the same time as the cutter - it was Charcoal. We sent the Dingo for him & he came on board.

"It is a bad job," he said. "They are all drowned."

Charcoal informed us that when I called them they were all desirous to come back except Davidson, who strongly urged the men to proceed. Charcoal told them that if they did not go back they would be drowned. At length Turner, the man who spoke before, said: "Davidson is now our master & is the best judge. Let us obey him."

They then put round the boat, when Charcoal stripped of all his clothes and recommended them all to do the same as they would have to swim for their lives; that he was not afraid being a good swimmer; that none of them would take his advice, & that he was sure they were all drowned, particularly Davidson who had on two pairs of Trowsers.

Assistance was immediately sent along the beach, and after some time they brought back two living men, one of whom was Turner, but the bodies of Davidson & the other man were never found.

They confirmed Charcoal's account of the matter - that when the boat was upset Davidson & the other man both left & took to swimming, but they being unable to swim stuck to the boat. That when the 3rd wave struck her it turned her over on her bottom. They then contrived to get inside, & although full of water she still floated & was driven ashore by the surf.

These two men were much bruised by the surf but neither of them were permanently injured, & Turner had since become a very noted character in the Bay of Islands New Zealand.

This tragical adventure upset all my arrangements, & therefore I immediately put spades into the hands of my men and their first operation was to cut a canal between Crook Haven & Shoal Haven River.

The Natives all this while kept aloof. We went one morning to the banks of the Shoal Haven River & observed some Natives on the opposite side. Charcoal immediately stripped himself and held up his hands, when they launched their Canoes & came over to us, & from this time forward the other natives gradually began to show themselves.

Charcoal was my regular boatman, but Broughton on the other hand was my Landman & I must speak of him next.

My intention was originally to have fixed myself upon a high bank to the north side of the River about six miles from the entrance. I therefore determined to explore the country while my men were cutting the canal. Having launched the Dingo into the River I therefore proceeded to the spot with Broughton & another Black whom he called his mate, accompanied by Mr Hamilton Hume.

On reaching the place, I found only a narrow border of dry land with an interminable swamp behind. After this unpleasant discovery I came back to the boat & set down at the fire. In the course of the evening I observed to Mr Hume that the place would not do for an establishment. Hume replied - "If I were in your place I would never give up this piece of land."

Broughton who was listening to the conversation smiled & said - "I wonder to hear you Mr Hume." I replied - "what do you mean Broughton, do you think this place will not do for a farm?"

"No," he replied. "Besides being all swamp, there is no water unless in very deep holes, and when the cattle went to drink they would fall in and drown themselves."

"This is all very singular. You told [me] Broughton, in Sydney, there was plenty of fine land at Shoal Haven."

He replied "& so there is, but this is not the place."

"Why then did you bring me here."

"I did not bring you here, you said you wanted to go to Balang (the name of the place) and I only accompanied."

"Very well Broughton, tomorrow you must take me to the right place," and next day I pit myself under his guidance, & he showed me a different description of country, but the place he recommended was the spot where he was born at the head of a long creek now called Broughton Creek. He told us that at this place the creek became fresh & divided into two branches. That there was an elevated forest range that divides the two branches. That I ought to build my house & stock yard on the range, & that there was a clear meadow in front where I could cultivate maize.

As this was at some distance we returned to our encampment in order to refit ourselves for the expedition. Our plan was to walk with Broughton to the head of the creek in order to examine the whole extent of the country, & I sent up our provisions in the Dingo. The Dingo was put in charge of Billy - a boy of sixteen, Broughton's mate - and he got another Boy of the Natives about the same age to assist. This last had never before seen a white man & I mention the circumstance to show that I began by placing complete confidence in the natives, for I could see that they were proud of the confidence.

It was late in the evening when we reached the head of the creek. We were all very hungry & expected to find the Dingo, but behold no Dingo was there. My foolish confidence was now finely ridiculed for putting so much provisions in charge of two boys, one of whom was a mere savage & quite a stranger. Broughton expressed his hopes that his mate would behave properly, but another Blackman who was along with us gave it as his opinion that the boys after becoming hungry had eaten their bellyfulls & gone to sleep.

We sat down on the bank & made a fire, and I even began to think that we must go supperless to bed. About sun set we observed the Dingo coming round a point. The poor boys were quite tired with their long pull and had touched nothing and gave us a most amusing account of the voyage. They said that the creek was very long and very crooked, and at one place there was a long narrow peninsula, and that they wasted a good deal of time in disputing whether they should haul the boat across instead of pulling round.

Next morning we found the place to agree exactly with Broughton's description. I now made up my mind about the plan of the establishment, but as the district was almost completely barricaded with almost impassable brush it became necessary to find some road to bring cattle, and here again I had recourse to Broughton. He collected 2 or 3 of his tribe and his brother Broger & went accompanied with Mr Hume to cut a road up a range with which he was acquainted. Being furnished with Tomahawks they wrought very hard & in the course of 4 or 5 days cut a road up the mountain.

Before the road was finished Brogher began to tire and threatened to leave. Mr Hume shot a pheasant & gave it to Brogher to his supper to induce him to stop. He appeared to assent, roasted & eat the pheasant. Bye & Bye he looked at the moon which was near the full, observed that it was a fine night and therefore he would take advantage of the moon light and go home to his wife. Broughton was very indignant at him, & told him that he would rather cut all the road himself than have his assistance.

The natives continued very shy and few showed themselves. I gave no concern about it, only treated such as came to us with kindness. One day a large party well armed arrived from Jervis Bay, and sat down in the neighbourhood of our encampment, but did not come near us according to the native custom untill they received an invitation. I went to them, asked for their Chief - an old gentleman of the name of Yager - & we became immediately great friends. He had the organ of devotion highly developed in his head and from his own account had much intercourse with the visionary world.

About this time the Chief of the place where I was cutting the canal - name Wajin - came in. He was a stout elderly gentleman of a mild, sedate appearance & hairy as Esan himself. He informed me that a piece of clear meadow ground on the west of the canal was called Numba. I asked him who cleared it. He replied that all he knew about it was that it was in the same state in the days of his grandfather. Of course I made him my friend and promised to give him a Brass Plate when he came to Sydney.

In about a month I completed the canal so far that a moderate sized boat could pass through into the Shoal Haven River at half tide, cleared a small spot on the ridge on the north shore of the River, and transferred with the assistance of the natives who had now become familiar, my stores to a small log building at that place.

The natives called the range Gilpigong, but as it is at the foot of a hill 930 feet high called Coolangatta, I called the place after the mountain as the more prominent object.

It now became necessary for me to go to Sydney to make ulterior arrangements. My only 2 sailors as before mentioned had been drowned in attempting to enter the Shoal Haven River, and the young man whom I had brought down as an overseer was much alarmed at the idea of being left with a few white men, all prisoners in a corner 50 miles from any other establishment (Wollongong), and surrounded by wild natives.

I therefore determined to take the cutter back to Sydney with a crew of the aborigines, fortunately however, Mr Throsby of Bongbong sent down a white man who was a good bush ranger, accompanied by a friendly native in order to find me out. I therefore engaged this man to go along with me.

My crew consisted of this man, Wajin Chief of Shoal Haven, and my religious friend Yager the Chief of Jervis Bay. Charcoal the tame native also returned with me. Broughton however being a bush native disliked the sea and determined to go back by Land to meet me in Sydney in order to assist in bringing down some cattle. My friend Mr Hume accompanied him to Appin.

Broughton had brought down with him a young man of about 18 named Billy, a relation of his own whom he called his mate, and he left him in charge of the place during his absence, explaining to his tribe that the establishment was formed under his particular protection. That they must all behave in a friendly manner to the white people and obey his lieutenant Mr Billy during his absence.

I got safe to Sydney with my singular crew after a tedious passage occasioned by fowl winds. During the voyage we saw a large ship beating up and making the same tracks as ourselves. My white assistant wished me very much to go along side to beg that they would lend us a sailor to assist us, but the weather being fine I declined doing so, as I had a particular aversion to go along side of a large ship in such a plight. Thereafter always when we neared the vessel I put about and stood in there.

I had been several days without cleaning myself, and went below to do so. At this time we were standing on different tacks. My mate the white man immediately quietly wore the boat. The large ship did the same and stood towards us. I took up a book and began to read. Time passed without observation. The white man called down that the ship was close to us, and on enquiry I found that we were standing on the same tack.

I said "Immediately put about."

"Oh," he says, "they have lowered a boat and it is nearly alongside."

Much mortified - unwashed and unshaven - I packed my head up thru the skuttle, and at the same moment a boat with the Captain came along side.

The ship was the Convict ship Asia, Capt. Reid, with whom I was slightly acquainted. He insisted upon my coming on board, gave a hawser to the Blanch - in order to tow her - sending also some of his sailors on board.

On stepping on board the Asia the first man I saw was Mr or Major Mudie, whom I had seen in London in the house of Sir Charles Forbes, and who was coming out with his family as a settler.

It appeared that being delayed by fowl winds they were naturally anxious to speak to the little vessel, in the expectation of getting some potatoes or other vegetables, but when they found that the boat always stood inshore when they neared it, their curiosity was excited. They thought we must be runaway convicts.
Mudies daughters were quite surprized at my uncouth & wretched appearance and savage & naked crew. I explained that no disaster had happened, that I was a mere settler who had come back after establishing a farm, & that I had slept under a tree for the last month, and that if their papa meant to become a settler he must do the same. They cried all night at the prospect before them. I made very light of it & wondered how they could expect to find homes ready made in the wild bush.

I returned to the place in about a month, and went overland with Broughton by way of Bong Bong. I found every thing well and many natives about and all of them quite friendly.

Mr Billy obeyed his chief and remained with the overseer during Broughton's absence, living in the same hut, and waiting upon the overseer as Cook & House Servant. This however was too much restraint to be long endured, although he was well clothed and well fed, and therefore he left the hut and he took himself to his usual mode of life on the return of Broughton.

Previous to my return Wagin and Yager had returned, with a suit of clothes and Brass plates - black badges of nobility - & with many wonderful stories of the new discovered country of Sydney.

But among the crowd of admiring natives there appeared a testy, shrivelled, & irascible old Gentleman, who claimed the rank of Chief of Shoal Haven, alleging that he was the Feudal Chief of the very place where I had made my huts, and that he also must be invested with an order of nobility. The poor overseer was alarmed at his vehemence, and told him that Wajin being now King, it could not be helped, that it was his own fault in not putting in his claim sooner, and we could not make two Kings. Then he observed - I will not allow you to remain. Pack up your alls and be gone.

The overseer offered to make him a Constable, & assured him that I would get him a Constable's Plate (this is square; a chief's plate is like a half moon). This he indignantly refused. The overseer then offered to make him a settler, observing that I was only a settler myself. He agreed to this on condition that he was made a Free Settler, but such was his impatience that it was necessary to give him a leaden plate until a better could be procured. When I came down I got the blacksmith to make an Iron Plate & to engrave upon it that he was the Free Settler of Shoal Haven, and this plate he wore for the rest of his days, and in future was always known by blacks & whites under the name of Old Settler.

From this time by kind treatment we have been invariably good friends with the natives. It is true that they used to steal for the first years of the establishment, a good deal of any crops of maize and potatoes, and we were obliged to watch them, but the Cockatoos in a year or two discovered that we began to plant maize and proved even more destructive than the blacks, & at least as cunning, for they soon learned the effects of the gun and used to place Watchers on the trees to give notice to the others of the approach of any whiteman. They called out. Their friends continued their depredations with more eagerness. When he came near they again called out, & it is curious that if he had a gun all the natives took flight, but if he was unarmed they continued in defiance.

The Blacks also used to spear our pigs in the bush. I have never heard however that they molested either the cattle or the calves, and for many years their depredations have been so slight as not to be noticed. The Cockatoos however have continued, and experience has rendered them still more expert thieves. There has therefore been a constant necessity to watch the maize when it attains a certain state of maturity, and this no doubt has also protected it indirectly from the depredations of the natives.

After gaining the confidence of the Blacks I tried hard to get them to adopt habits of industry by paying them for their labour, but generally one day's labour was enough to tire them, however slight. I have seen however some of them live with and assist favourite free men for weeks together, and on one occasion Broughton acted as a Bricklayers labourer for some weeks. One day as he was leaving his work, I observed him replying in a very indignant manner to a Black woman. On enquiry he told me she was his cousin, and had been jeering him, & in the end told me with some reluctance that she reproached him with working every day like a prisoner, and that he despised her remarks. Next morning however he disappeared and never more acted in the capacity of a Bricklayers Labourer.

I have mentioned his relation Billy leaving his post of hut keeper to the overseer - after some weeks he came back naked & hungry. I observed:

"Well Billy, I expected you were to have become like a white man but am sorry to find that you have again become a wild bush native."

"Oh no sir, I am no more wild than formerly, but I have become a free man again."

Poor Billy was killed some years after at Parramatta in a drunken fray by some of his country men.

I recollect observing a young native who was assisting some free men to clear a piece of ground. I told him that he wrought as well as any of the whites. "Yes," he replied, "Bye & Bye I mean to make a contract myself to clear a piece of ground, and then I shall go to Sydney & get my money out of the office like the others." In the present instance he lived with the white man, eat with them, and they gave him their old clothes to wear. He at length tired of such a regular life & never made his contract.

Their bodily frame is not fitted for labour and their inherent disposition is to wander, consequently they are very fond of going with messages and deliver them faithfully. They delight very much in pulling in boats as this indulges their locomotive propensities.

When I last came to Sydney from Shoal Haven, the vessel was laying six miles from my house. The tide rendered it necessary for me to leave my house at one o'clock in the morning. My crew consisted of Black people, a great condescension on their part, as they have a great aversion either to early rising or having their nights rest disturbed. They are naturally a kind heated and generous people. They will divide or even give away their last morsel to a stranger, and much as they value cloathing will do the same with their clothes.

One of my men some years ago lost himself in the bush and was nearly starved. He met a native on one of his own journeys. The poor native put him in the road and gave him all his provisions.

Last year I met the same native at Berrima on my way to Goulburn. I was surprized to see him, & the surprize was mutual. He told me that his wife was a Berrimian Lady and that he had brought her up to see her relations. I requested that he would take charge of a letter to Shoal Haven & deliver it on his return. After a few minutes he brought back the letter & requested I would wrap it up in a bit of waste paper to keep it clean. I was afterwards informed that he immediately went to Shoal Haven with the letter & again returned for his wife, thus voluntarily taking a journey of at least 50 miles through a rugged mountainous country.

I saw the same man lately at Shoal Haven. He spoke about the dry weather & great want of rain. Many of the natives were affected with the influenza. He observed they would not get entirely better untill we had plenty of rain. I told him that the Deity - pointing upwards - was so offended with the natives on account of their allowing the white men to cohabit with their women. He replied it is too bad of the Blacks, but that the white men were equally bad. He observed all the blacks now know that there is a God in Heaven, and that there is a future state of rewards and punishments. Some of the blacks told me that the Catholic priest had been baptising their children, but they did not seem to understand the nature of the Ordinance.

For many years I have reaped my harvest on the principle of free Labour. Many of the white men employed Blacks to assist, deriving some small advantage from their labour, but now they have become more knowing and have for some years reaped on their own account, so as to receive the full benefit of their labour. They did not however work any last harvest, observing that they were more or less indisposed with the influenza.

My brother assisted 2 families to build comfortable huts for themselves, but when I was last down I found the huts deserted, and a piece of ground they had farmed in as a garden uncultivated. They were pleased at first with the novelty of the thing, but in the end a fixed residence did not suit their locomotive propensities.

There is certainly a considerable change in their ideas since I first knew them. The men & women used to walk about stark naked without any sense of shame. Now they all contrive to have some covering, and I think the females would have as much shame in appearing in a state of nudity as any white woman.

At the time Colonel Arthur was hunting down the Aborigines in Van Diemans Land, he employed some New Holland Natives to assist - these belonged to the Shoal Haven Tribe. About six years ago a number of them landed in Sydney off a vessel from Hobart Town. They were well dressed & appeared quite respectable and each of them had a trunk or Portmanteau. They immediately came to my house and requested I would give them store room for their luggage. One of them said that they had succeeded in getting in the natives & pacifying the Island, but that the natives of V.D.Land were such a stupid race that there was no hope of civilizing them.

There is great difficulty in the savage state of rearing children, therefore as a wise provision of nature the organ of Love of Offspring is highly developed in the women, who are generally very kind mothers and remarkably fond of their children.

A number of years ago during a very dry season an old Man named Couray installed himself in the office of waterman, to bring good water from a spring at some distance, and was highly indignant when any other native interfered with his office, and his old wife to whom he was much attached also made herself free of the kitchen. About this time a convict woman was sent down as a servant, and this woman had a child in her arms. An immediate attachment sprung up betwixt the child and the old Mrs Couray. When its mother scolded or beat it, it always took refuge with the old Black woman, and if at any time the mother of the child gave it any ill usage the old woman used to cry bitterly.

I used to hear formerly that women used to strangle white children as soon as they were born, but this not the case now, for they are equally fond of the piebald children as of the others, and what is curious the husband of the woman seems equally fond of them as of the black ones. The cross bred are distinctly an improved race.

It is very seldom that any bushrangers appear at Shoal Haven and when they do they are generally brought in by the Natives.

Some months ago 2 men escaped from Mr Sparks place at the Kangaroo. His overseer gave notice of the escape at Shoal Haven and next day they were brought in by the Blacks. They informed me that they had heard of the escape, and suspected the 2 men to be runaways as they could not give a good account of themselves, & observing the men tried to deceive them with a plausible story, but that they ordered them to walk to Shoal Haven and that if they tried to escape they would spear them as they spear Kangaroos. The men confessed and congratulated themselves that they were captured before they had time to do any amount of harm & were much ashamed on being taken by the blacks - it is singular that they have behaved well since then.

The Blacks used to have their medical practitioners. They generally used certain spells but some of their practice was highly judicious.

Shoal Haven was much infested with snakes. One day a man was bitten by a very venemous one. Old Dr Greenwall was near. They applied for his assistance. He examined the sufferer & enquired about the kind of snake. He then replied that he could do nothing, and that the man must die. They requested him to try. Replied it could be of no use, and by making a useless attempt he would risk his medical reputation.

There happened to be a young Doctor present who had still to make his medical reputation. He addressed the sufferer: "I fear you must die, but if you will allow me I will do my best to save your life." The sufferer gladly assented.

The Doctor immediately bound a tight ligature above the wound, and then commenced sucking. He spit the first mouthful into his hand & examined it - the blood was black and he silently & mournfully shook his head. He then renewed his operations & sucked with all his might. After a

considerable interval he started to his feet, probably distinguishing a difference in the taste of the blood. He spit again into his hand. He smiled & addressed his patient: "Bel you die". The cure was complete. The overseer who had been originally tied to the medical profession witnessed the whole and I respect the story as he told it.

Some years ago when I was at Shoal Haven an old man (a native) was found murdered near one of the mens huts. On enquiry I was informed that he had been living there for some days, and that when the men went to their work he remained. That found him dead on their return, and that his body had been taken for interment by his friends, and [I] sent a boat for the body & had it taken out of the coffin (some sheets of bark), that I might examine the wounds. From the appearance I concluded that he had been murdered by a black man. I told this to his friends & mentioned that I was at first afraid he had been murdered by the white people, but they all agreed that it was done by a blackman. We examined the spot. Their acute optics discovered the stealthy foot of a native approaching the place where the old man was sitting, the marks of a struggle and then the marks of the foot of the bush native running away after the act was committed. The murderer was never discovered.

Some of the natives have great personal courage. When last at Shoal Haven I saw an old man whom, not having seen for years, I considered dead. I had often heard his story, but he again told it me.

Nearly 20 years ago, before I went to Shoal Haven, some natives plundered some maize belonging to a convict settler in Illawarra. The settler armed himself with a newly ground cutlass and went in search of the natives. He discovered their camp when they were roasting the maize. They all took to flight. One man alone began to defend himself with a tomahawk, but the white man struck him a blow upon the shoulder which nearly separated the arm from the shoulder blade when the tomahawk fell to the ground. The white savage (man) now aimed a blade at the head of the Black one. The black put up his other arm as a guard to his head and the blow of the cutlass - which must have been very sharp - cut of the forearm as clean as if it had been done by a Surgeon. The poor Black now ran away, but when at a little distance turned round, & shook his bloody stump in the face of the white savage. After some time he dropped from loss of blood, but his friends carried him off bound up and cured his wounds, but he has only a stump on the one side & the other arm hangs nearly powerless.

I observed to him how happens it that your right arm was used as a guard while you fought with the left - "Because," he replied, "I am 'a left handed man'".

The poor fellow spoke without any apparent ill feeling towards his opponent who still lives & thrives - the natives used to call him Saucy William and some of them like him to this day. Both whites & blacks seem kind to the old man, but I believe he never goes to Sydney and seems to think although the greatest sufferer that his own conduct was not free from blame.

I shall now mention a few circumstances of the subsequent fate of my sable friends.

Old Yager continued my friend to the end of his days but for some years has dressed with feathers, and I believe did not have any heir to inherit his honour.

Charcoal, whom I had appointed mate of the Blanch, after a few trips tired of being well cloathed and well fed, and after a few trips left the vessel, but he left it as a friend and used to occasionally to visit Shoal Haven. After some time he married a young woman of the place. There was a considerable disparity in years, but the match was otherwise very appropriate. Charcoal was lame, his leg having been broken to pieces by a cart wheel, and his wife had no toes. It appears that when she was an infant her Mother had gone to sleep one cold night too near the fire, and the toes of the infant were found next morning to have been burnt off.

Charcoal was rather of an irascible temper. One day he found it necessary to give some correction to his wife, in consequence of which she died, and the father of the girl complained to his tribe. Charcoal was summoned to appear on a certain day to stand punishment. I was then at Shoal Haven but the trial took place at some miles distant from my house, and under the circumstances Charcoal did not choose to visit me, but I was informed by the natives (his jury) of the result.

Every thing was prepared. The natives were assembled. Charcoal took his place & the father was there to demand justice. Before the trial commenced Mr Charcoal arose, and requested to say a few words. He acknowledged that he was justly summoned to stand punishment for that he had unfortunately killed his wife, but that in so doing he was more unfortunate than culpable, for that he dearly loved his deceased wife and deplored her loss, and merely intended to give her such gentle correction as a husband is entitled to give his help mate, but that in his passion in consequence of some provocation had got the better of his reason. That he had struck too hard & she died, for which he was now ready to take the consequences, & even to die if it should so happen - a thing but too likely from his being lame and not possessing the activity of another man.

That however he severely felt for the father of his wife who from his want of temper had lost an affectionate daughter and therefore besides giving him all the satisfaction which their Laws and Customs demanded, he now desired to make him any other poor compensation which he had the power of doing. He had therefore brought down a fine new blanket from Sydney which he laid at the feet of his father in Law and requested him to accept.

This speech being ended there was a solemn. At length the father arose and addressed to assembly to the following purpose:

"My friends and countrymen. I am much obliged to you all for the readiness with which you have met my call and assembled here this day to do me justice, but you have all heard what has been said by my son in law, and how he laments the loss of his wife, and I think that you must all agree with me that he has been more unfortunate than culpable. He took up the blanket and displayed it to the court. See what a fine blanket he has given me. He is really a fine generous fellow, and I really feel for his affliction on account of the loss of his wife. I am satisfied and I do not wish the affair to proceed any further, & as my poor son in law is so afflicted for the loss of his wife I desire him to be comforted. I have still another daughter and as soon as she is of age I will give him her for a wife."

The assembled tribe moodily dispersed, and when they told the story at Shoal Haven they sinceringly observed that the father was a mercenary old fellow to sell his daughter for a blanket. I know not whether the second marriage took place. I did not see much of Charcoal after this occurrence. He died a number of years ago.

Old Settler lived a good many years and always wore his Iron plate. He continued to the end of his days a waspish, irascible, but friendly old man. He had a wife & family of children to whom he was much attached.

One morning he was camped with his tribe at the foot of my house. I heard a dreadful screaming and went out to see what was the matter. I saw Old Settler in a frantic rage, with a bark shield in the one hand & a spear in the other and his poor old wife standing trembling at a few paces distance. He was talking to her with great violence, and every now & then threatened to transfix her with his spear. I looked at the frantic old savage, and then at the other natives who were all sitting in groups with their different families, with anxious countenances, but with averted eyes and preserving a profound silence. My presence seemed to disconcert Settler, but I did not appear to notice him. I quietly enquired at one of his tribe what was the matter. The man replied "It is a family affair and not our business." I remained for some time & followed their example. If I had interfered most likely in his rage he would have thrown his spear in defence. After a time his rage expended itself and he sat down. Next day I saw him with his old wife as usual.

Some years after, his oldest son came to my house in Sydney and asked to speak with me. "You know me Mr Berry. I am Tommy Patalick, the oldest son of Old Settler. You know Old Settler was your friend and you gave him a plate. He is now dead. I am his heir and now the Chief of the Tribe and you must give me a plate."

I told Patalick to come back in a few days for his plate, and begun to think what description I could put on it, & determined that he should be designated as the son and Heir of Old Settler. As if he read my thoughts he called me back & said he had one more word to say. That I must not say any thing about his father on his plate. These people never mention the names of the Dead and it is an offence to do so in their presence. Of course I attended to his wishes. Tommy still lives to enjoy his Honours of chief, and as Wajin and Yager have both died without heirs he has rather an extensive authority and is a good deal respected amongst his countrymen.

Wajin lived a good many years happily with his wife, although there was no family. He however, although a quiet good tempered man, had also occasionally his family troubles. One day I looked into a hut and saw Wajin seated by the side of his wife - or the Queen as they used to call her. The Lady looked very sulky, and on looking more closely I saw her face & head covered with blood, and she was cut to the bone.

"What is this Wajin who has dared to touch the sacred face of the Queen?"

He replied "I did it."

"Shame Wajin. Why did you do it?"

"Oh," he says, "it is nothing. I only given her a slight correction, a few gentle taps upon the head with a Waddy. She was very silly and made a great noise with her tongue. She would not erase from scalding untill I broke her head. But I was merciful in the correction I gave her."

The Lady evidently was not accustomed to this kind of discipline, for she looked very sulky, and it cost Wajin a great deal of trouble before he succeeded in making her forget the affair. Poor Wajin some years after got very drunk in Sydney. His tribe carried him to their camp at Woollomolloo, but he died in the course of the night.

Broughton was first appointed a Constable & afterwards the chief of his own tribe, and supplied with slops and rations. He generally staid at Shoal Haven but sometimes he used to disappear without any warning, but his slops and rations were always forthcoming when he chose to claim them.

He had 2 wives Mary & Charlotte. The first was the elder & entitled to all the remains of his principal sustance, but the other was the best beloved. Both were back sliders. He worked at the back sliding of Mary but was very jealous of Charlotte.

One day I looked into his hut and he was sitting at his meal between his ladies. The head of Charlotte was broken and her face was bloody.

"Who has done this Broughton."

"I did it," he replied. "She slept from home last night, but where I cannot find out."

I replied, "this is too bad of Charlotte. I hope she will never do so again. You must not beat her anymore."

Broughton looked displeased at my meddling in his family affairs & I did not interfer further. Next day he disappeared. Some years after some fresh cause of jealousy arrived & he beat her so unmercifully that she died, but he bitterly lamented his loss, and for a long time after when I spoke of the affair he used to cry.

Mary still lives and he has got another wife. He does not like to work but he renders himself useful in many ways and is considered as a kind of priviledged person on the place, and his slops and rations are always forthcoming.
He says that he feels that he is now getting old. That the bush does not suit him as formerly, and boasts he means to build a house. He has one daughter who is married and two other children whom he acknowledges, but they are white.

All the Shoal Haven Blacks consider themselves as my people, but I find it necessary to let do as they please as they cannot be restrained. I might as well attempt to teach the birds of the air not to fly as to restrain their wanderings.

Upon making careful enquiry lately at Shoal Haven both from themselves and from some intelligent white people who have been long on the place, their numbers I am sorry to say have greatly decreased since I came to Shoal Haven.

A good many have died in Sydney in consequence of drinking, a few in their native feuds of violence, and a good many from measles. The natives themselves told me that a good many also had left the Colony in ships. At present there are a good many young people & children amongst them and they seem fine & healthy people.

I enclose a list of their numbers.

One candidate more - Tommy Patalick had a younger brother named Monkey - from his appearance. Upwards of 12 months ago he came to Sydney. One night he dreamt that Red, a Shoal Haven native then at Shoal Haven, bit his throat. On awaking in the morning he had a sore throat. He returned to Shoal Haven and lingered for many months, living under the impression that he would not recover, for that Red had bewitched him. Some weeks ago he died at Shoal Haven. Poor Red was the only native on the spot, and he performed the last offices to the deceased by wrapping up the body in bark, according to their custom, previous to the interment.

Patalick told me that he fully believed that Red had procured the death of his brother by bewitching him, and that he must stand punishment for the supposed offence.

A.Berry

Census of the Natives of the Shoal Haven District

	Married Men	Married Women	Single Men	Single Women	Male Children	Female Children	Total
Gerongong Tribe	4	5	6	1	4	1	21
Broughton Creek	8	9	4	1	-	4	26
Uurro Tribe	8	9	2	1	2	2	24
Shoalhaven Tribe	10	13	2	5	6	3	39
Numba Tribe	5	6	4	2	3	5	25
Wooragee Tribe	11	11	9	3	7	4	45
Jervis Bay	17	18	8	1	11	7	62
	63	71	35	14	33	26	242 Genl. Total

With the exception of 6 old men, the single men are from the age of 13 to 30. The male children are under 13 years of age. The single women are from the age of 12 or 13 to 25. The female children are under 12 years of age.

	242		
Say	25	at Burra	
	267		abt May 1838

A.Berry

Summary of Blankets Issued

[1838] Return of Aborigines at Respective Stations - compiled from lists created for the issue of blankets (AONSW)

District or Station	Men	Women	Boys	Girls	Total
Wollongong	49	25	23	27	124
Shoal Haven, Illawarra	52	38	30	19	139
Shoal Haven, Saint Vincents and Jervis Bay	76	51	43	28	198
				Total	461

APPENDIX E
Map of the South Eastern Portion of NSW in 1838

M20. 1838 Map of the South Eastern portion of Australia, the boundaries of the 'Nineteen Districts' by Major Thomas Mitchell, showing the few coastal settlements between Port Macquarie and Moruya.

APPENDIX F
Frawley Ancestors - AUS Database by First Name & Event Type (1861-1949)
From... Indexes of the New South Wales & Queensland Departments of Births, Deaths & Marriages.

First Name(s)	Surname	Father	Mother	Type	Year	Death Place	State	Order #	Reg#
Agnes Maude	Frawley	Robert Edward	Clarke	Marriage	1896		QLD		C2024
Alice Mary	Frawley	Alexander White	Mary Urquhart	Death	1926		QLD		C3865
Amy Kathleen Maud	Frawley	Daniel Joseph Frawley	Alice Mary White	Birth	1901		QLD	H	C2781
Andrew Patrick	Frawley	Michael Frawley	Ellen James	Birth	1880		QLD	D	C5686
Ann	Frawley	James Frawley	Ann Doran	Birth	1886		QLD	F	C2301
Anne	Frawley	James Doran	Mary Doolan	Death	1931		QLD		B15507
Anne Gilmour	Frawley	John	Cuddihy	Marriage	1888		QLD		B12312
Annie	Frawley	Michael	McNamara	Marriage	1883		QLD		C440
Annie	Frawley	Patrick Joseph	Kate Connell	Birth	1897		QLD	K	C3418
Annie	Frawley	?	Annie Frawley	Birth	1897		QLD	L	C7699
Annie	Frawley	Harry	Devonshire	Marriage	1918		QLD		C3332
Annie Elizabeth	Frawley	Frederick George	Garvis	Marriage	1917		QLD		C1622
Arthur Herbert	Frawley	Daniel Joseph Frawley	Alice White	Birth	1896		QLD	H	C2878
Arthur Hubert	Frawley	Daniel Joseph Frawley	Alice White	Death	1896		QLD	H	C1173
Bartholomew Joseph	Frawley	James Thomas	Bridget Brady	Birth	1904		QLD	M	C3444
Bessie Jane	Frawley	Daniel Joseph Frawley	Alice Mary White	Birth	1900		QLD	H	C2909
Bridget	Frawley	Michael	Gilligan	Marriage	1879		QLD		C344
Bridget	Frawley	James Frawley	Ann Doran	Birth	1895		QLD	F	C3082
Bridget	Frawley	Patrick	Cullinan	Marriage	1898		QLD		C58
Bridget	Frawley	Patrick Joseph	Kate Connell	Birth	1903		QLD	K	C2691
Bridget	Frawley	Richard Dowling	Kirby	Marriage	1910		QLD		C2936
Bridget Johanna	Frawley	James Frawley	Ellen Murphy	Birth	1872		QLD	C	C3114
Bridget Johanna	Frawley	Theodore Thomas	Cannon	Marriage	1909		QLD		B7499
Bruce	Frawley	?	Winifred May Frawley	Death	1943		QLD		C3053
Catherine	Frawley	Patrick Frawley	Margaret Dalton	Birth	1879		QLD	A	O401
Cecily	Frawley	James Thomas	Bridget Brady	Birth	1915		QLD	M	C3561
Charles Augustus	Frawley	?	* Aged 77 years	Death	1947		QLD		B13735
Constance Mary	Frawley	Patrick Frawley	Constance Bridget Mary McKiernan	Birth	1906		QLD	N	C6483
Constance Mary Bridget	Frawley	Michael McKiernan	Catherine Murray	Death	1914		QLD	N	C4699
Cyrus John	Frawley	Daniel Joseph Frawley	Alice Mary White	Birth	1895		QLD	H	C2914
Cyrus John	Frawley	Daniel Joseph Frawley	Alice Mary White	Death	1909		QLD	H	C4054
Daniel	Frawley	Alice Mary	White	Marriage	1891		QLD		C1886
Daniel	Frawley	Michael Frawley	Mary Macke	Death	1914		QLD		C4906
David Paul	Frawley	Thomas Frawley	Lizzie O'Sullivan	Birth	1890		QLD	G	C6150
Denis James	Frawley	Daniel Joseph Frawley	Alice Mary White	Birth	1893		QLD	H	C2785
Denis James	Frawley	Daniel Joseph Frawley	Alice Mary White	Death	1946		QLD	H	C4230
Edith Alice	Frawley	Mark Raymond	Sanders	Marriage	1894		QLD		B16820
Elaine Marie	Frawley	John	Maria Agnes Hammill	Birth	1911		QLD	P	C13996
Elizabeth	Frawley	Daniel O'Sullivan	Bridget Cooney	Death	1936		QLD		C4694
Elizabeth Jane	Frawley	Arthur Colin	Rabbitt	Marriage	1920		QLD		C1958
Ellen	Frawley	Patrick	Manning	Marriage	1873		QLD		C469
Ellen	Frawley	Michael Brogan	Honora Egan	Death	1920		QLD		C4017
Ellen	Frawley	Patrick Murphy	Mary Leahy	Death	1927		QLD		C2648
Ellen Elizabeth	Frawley	William	Mary Sharkey	Birth	1894		QLD	I	C2979
Erin Kathleen	Frawley	Thomas Frawley	Lizzie O'Sullivan	Birth	1909		QLD	G	C10752
Erin Kathleen	Frawley	Thomas Frawley	Lizzie O'Sullivan	Death	1909		QLD	G	C3685
Evelyn Cecilia	Frawley	Thomas Frawley	Elizabeth O'Sullivan	Birth	1905		QLD	G	C2701
Francis Vincent	Frawley	Thomas Frawley	Lizzie O'Sullivan	Birth	1894		QLD	G	C2995
Francis Vincent	Frawley	Thomas Frawley	Lizzie O'Sullivan	Death	1938		QLD	G	C2290
George Robert	Frawley	Patrick Frawley	Elizabeth Greenlees	Death	1947		QLD		S4469
Gladys May	Frawley	Daniel Joseph Frawley	Alice Mary White	Birth	1899		QLD	H	C2735
Hanorah	Frawley	Edwin	Darch	Marriage	1891		QLD		C1454
Herbert	Frawley	Daniel Joseph Frawley	Alice Mary White	Birth	1897		QLD	H	C2840
Honora Jane	Frawley	James Frawley	Ellen Bogan (late Hegarty)	Death	1904		QLD		C1214
Irene Mary	Frawley	William Murphy	Mary Sharkey	Birth	1904		QLD	I	C3066
Jack Hammill	Frawley	John	Maria Agnes Veronica Hammill	Birth	1913		QLD	P	C15906
James	Frawley	Age 22 Yrs	Died Sydney	Death	1861	Sydney	NSW		950
James	Frawley	Ellen	Murphy	Marriage	1868		QLD		C78
James	Frawley	James Frawley	Ellen Murphy	Birth	1873		QLD	C	C3790
James	Frawley	James Frawley	Ellen Murphy	Death	1930		QLD		?
James	Frawley	Ellen	Hegarty	Marriage	1876		QLD		C206
James	Frawley	Anne	Doran	Marriage	1883		QLD		C1756
James	Frawley	Bridget	Brady	Marriage	1900		QLD		C725
James	Frawley	James Patrick	Annie Doran	Birth	1904		QLD	F	C2638
James	Frawley	Thomas Frawley	Ann Hassett	Death	1904		QLD		C1769
James	Frawley	James Frawley	Annie Doran	Death	1908		QLD	F	C4143
James	Frawley	James Frawley	Ellen Murphy	Death	1930		QLD	C	B11637
James Michael	Frawley	James Frawley	Annie Doran	Birth	1897		QLD	F	C2892
James Michael	Frawley	James Frawley	Annie Doran	Death	1929		QLD	F	B8572
James Patrick	Frawley	Michael Frawley	Mary McNamara	Death	1919		QLD		C4934
James Raymond	Frawley	William	Mary Sharkey	Birth	1899		QLD	I	B64903
Jane	Frawley	John	Smith	Marriage	1886		QLD		C663
Jane	Frawley	Patrick Joseph	Kate Connell	Birth	1899		QLD	K	C3638
Jane	Frawley	James Patrick	Annie Maria Doran	Birth	1901		QLD	F	C2634
John	Frawley	Patrick Frawley	Margaret Dalton	Birth	1871		QLD	A	C566
John	Frawley	Michael Frawley	Ellen James	Birth	1878		QLD	D	C5097
John Jr.	Frawley	John Frawley	Mary McGarry	Death	1878		QLD		C896
John	Frawley	Mary	O'Loughlan	Marriage	1894		QLD		C572
John Sr.	Frawley	Rose Emily	Curtis	Marriage	1894		QLD		C1672
John	Frawley	Patrick Joseph	Kate Connell	Birth	1901		QLD	K	C3399
John	Frawley	Maria Agnes Veronica	Hammill	Marriage	1910		QLD		C3465
John	Frawley	Thomas Frawley	Mary Marks	Death	1924		QLD		C190
John	Frawley	?	* Born Caniston, England aged 72 years	Death	1934		QLD		C2420

John	Frawley	Michael Frawley	Ellen James	Death	1941		QLD	D	C189
John Hamilton	Frawley	Patrick John	Mary O'Loughlan	Birth	1907		QLD	O	B15578
John Maurice	Frawley	William Murphy	Mary Sharkey	Birth	1901		QLD	I	C2919
John Victor	Frawley	Thomas Frawley	Lizzie O'Sullivan	Birth	1896		QLD	G	C3048
Kate	Frawley	James Frawley	Anne Doran	Birth	1891		QLD	F	C3094
Kate	Frawley	James	Plant	Marriage	1896		QLD		C550
Kathleen Mary	Frawley	Patrick Frawley	Constance McKiernan	Birth	1907		QLD	N	C7030
Kathleen Mary	Frawley	Patrick Frawley	Constance McKiernan	Death	1907		QLD	N	C2286
Kevin Patrick	Frawley	James Thomas	Bridget Brady	Birth	1913		QLD	M	C13598
Leslie Thomas	Frawley	Thomas Frawley	Lizzie O'Sullivan	Birth	1892		QLD	G	C3473
Letitia	Mitchell	John	Mary	Death	1894	Broken Hill	NSW		3632
Letitia	Howley	John	Mary	Death	1915	Goulburn	NSW		7821
Letitia	Green	John	Mary	Death	1918	Adelong	NSW		9817
Letitia	Clarke	John	Mary	Death	1926	Braidwood	NSW		7840
Letitia	Howard	John	Mary	Death	1931	Gosford	NSW		9180
Letitia A	Byrne	John	Mary	Death	1917	Kiama	NSW		5697
Letitia E	Mildwater	Clarke	Herbert L	Marriage	1901	Woollahra	NSW		7909
Margaret	Frawley	James Frawley	Ann Doran	Birth	1888		QLD	F	C11438
Margaret	Frawley	Thomas	McMahon	Marriage	1894		QLD		B16606
Margaret	Frawley	Patrick Joseph	Kate Connell	Birth	1913		QLD	K	C14076
Margaret	Frawley	Patrick Dalton	Margaret - * born Ireland aged 80 years	Death	1924		QLD		C3209
Martha Josephine	Frawley	William	Mary Sharkey	Birth	1896		QLD	I	C4471
Mary	Frawley	Patrick Mack	Catherine Mack (late Collins)	Death	1873		QLD		C1619
Mary	Frawley	Patrick Frawley	Margaret Dalton	Birth	1879		QLD	A	O400
Mary	Frawley	Patrick MacGarry	Mary Heffernan	Death	1889		QLD		C3633
Mary	Frawley	Daniel Joseph Frawley	Mary Alice White	Birth	1891		QLD	H	C3255
Mary	Frawley	Patrick Joseph	Kate Connell	Birth	1896		QLD	K	C3304
Mary	Frawley	- Markham	Mary O'Hern	Death	1901		QLD		C1159
Mary	Frawley	James Bailey	Hook	Marriage	1910		QLD		C3500
Mary	Frawley	Stanley John Frawley	Mary Alice Campbell	Death	1923		QLD		B40814
Mary	Frawley	John Sharkey	Martha Derbin	Death	1935		QLD		B26863
Mary Ann	Frawley	Michael Frawley	Mary McNamara	Death	1875		QLD		C2866
Mary Ann	Frawley	William Christian	Wockner	Marriage	1896		QLD		C2085
Mary Anne	Frawley	Michael O'Loughlin	Catherine Heffernan	Death	1933		QLD		B20948
Mary Emily	Frawley	John	Scriven	Marriage	1881		QLD		C557
Mary Janet	Frawley	James Frawley	Ann Maria Doran	Birth	1884		QLD	F	C8363
Mary Josephine	Frawley	Patrick Martin James	Purcell	Marriage	1915		QLD		C954
Mary Rose	Frawley	Peter	Healy	Marriage	1898		QLD		C1456
Maud	Frawley	Thomas Mooney	Mary McDade	Death	1938		QLD		C4036
Maureen Monica	Frawley	James Thomas	Bridget Brady	Birth	1910		QLD	M	C11318
Michael	Frawley	Michael Frawley	Mary Mack	Birth	1873		QLD	B	C4191
Michael	Frawley	Michael Frawley	Mary Mack (late Collins)	Death	1873		QLD	B	C1618
Michael	Frawley	James Frawley	Hannah Kensek	Death	1889		QLD		C4470
Michael	Frawley	Martin Frawley	Ellen Dunworth	Death	1905		QLD		C3108
Michael	Frawley	Patrick Joseph	Kate Connell	Birth	1915		QLD	K	C7607
Michael	Frawley	Julia	Walsh	Marriage	1915		QLD		C1904
Michael	Frawley	Maurice Frawley	Mary McInerny	Death	1924		QLD		C2055
Michael Joseph	Frawley	Michael Frawley	Ellen James	Birth	1877		QLD	D	C4925
Michael Joseph	Frawley	?	?	Death	1922		QLD		F3021
Michael Matthew	Frawley	James Frawley	Ellen Brogan	Birth	1886		QLD	E	C3983
Milo Thomas	Frawley	John	Mary Ann O'Loughlan	Birth	1895		QLD	J	C5427
Monica Mary	Frawley	Patrick Frawley	Constance Mary Bridget McKiernan	Birth	1914		QLD	N	C14903
Neive Patrick	Frawley	John	Mary O'Loughlan	Birth	1898		QLD	J	C3635
Nora Isabella	Frawley	Hugh	Milligan	Marriage	1878		QLD		B6169
Norah	Frawley	Patrick Joseph	Kate Connell	Birth	1898		QLD	K	C3668
Patrick	Frawley	James Frawley	Ellen Murphy	Birth	1875		QLD	C	C4076
Patrick	Frawley	Patrick Frawley	Margaret Dalton	Birth	1878		QLD	A	C1561
Patrick	Frawley	Constance Mary Budget	McKiernan	Marriage	1905		QLD		C1378
Patrick	Frawley	Patrick Joseph	Kate O'Connell	Birth	1910		QLD	K	C11879
Patrick	Frawley	Elizabeth	Greenlees	Marriage	1917		QLD		C713
Patrick	Frawley	Patrick Frawley	Margaret Dalton	Death	1923		QLD	A	C4660
Patrick	Frawley	Patrick Frawley	Margaret Dalton	Death	1936		QLD	A	B32640
Patrick	Frawley	James Frawley	Ellen Murphy	Death	1936		QLD	C	B32486
Patrick Burnet	Frawley	James Frawley	Ellen Brogan	Birth	1884		QLD	E	C2446
Patrick Burnet	Frawley	James Frawley	Ellen Hegarty (late Brogan)	Death	1903		QLD	E	C1508
Patrick Clement	Frawley	Patrick Frawley	Constance Mary Bridget McKiernan	Birth	1909		QLD	N	C6370
Patrick James	Frawley	Thomas Frawley	Lizzie O'Sullivan	Birth	1888		QLD	G	C2990
Patrick James	Frawley	Thomas Frawley	Lizzie O'Sullivan	Death	1949		QLD	G	B23934
Patrick James Francis	Frawley	Florence	Sanney	Marriage	1915		QLD		C760
Patrick Joseph	Frawley	Kate	Connell	Marriage	1895		QLD		C581
Patrick Joseph	Frawley	Thomas Frawley	Mary Markham	Death	1944		QLD		C5226
Philomena Mary	Frawley	James Thomas	Bridget Brady	Birth	1905		QLD	M	C5367
Ridgenal Emmet	Frawley	Thomas Frawley	Lizzie O'Sullivan	Birth	1901		QLD	G	C2827
Rose Emily	Frawley	Samuel Colstone	Eliza Goodeve	Death	1923		QLD		B41734
Sarah Maud	Frawley	Robert Little	Ann Gilmour	Death	1911		QLD		C3182
Stanley John	Frawley	John	Mary O'Loughlan	Birth	1897		QLD	J	C3231
Stephen	Frawley	John Frawley	Mary McGarry	Death	1930		QLD		C3041
Susan	Frawley	James Frawley	Ann Doran	Birth	1893		QLD	F	C2833
Terence Michael	Frawley	Stanley John	Alice Campbell	Death	1939		QLD		B45453
Thomas	Frawley	James Frawley	Ellen Brogan	Birth	1881		QLD	E	C2077
Thomas	Frawley	Lizzie	O'Sullivan	Marriage	1887		QLD		C544
Thomas	Frawley	Mary	Hegarty	Marriage	1889		QLD		C556
Thomas	Frawley	?	* Born Ireland aged about 52 years	Death	1899		QLD		C5057
Thomas	Frawley	Patrick Joseph	Kate Connell	Birth	1904		QLD	K	C3705
Thomas	Frawley	Thomas Frawley	Mary Markham	Death	1940		QLD		C2292
Thomas	Frawley	Patrick Frawley	Margaret Dalton	Death	1942		QLD		C2423
Thomas Sylvester	Frawley	Thomas Frawley	Lizzie O'Sullivan	Birth	1900		QLD	G	C3064
Thomas Sylvester	Frawley	Thomas Frawley	Lizzie O'Sullivan	Death	1929		QLD	G	C3546
Victor John	Frawley	Winifred Ann	Abbott	Marriage	1919		QLD		C1299
William	Frawley	John Frawley Jr	Sarah Little - * born NSW aged 11 years	Death	1877		QLD		C579
William	Frawley	James Frawley	Ellen Murphy	Death	1925		QLD		B47333
William Murphy	Frawley	Mary	Sharkey	Marriage	1892		QLD		C1534
Winifred May	Frawley	Thomas Frawley	Lizzie O'Sullivan	Birth	1903		QLD	G	C2387

APPENDIX G
Frawley Research in Toowoomba (1865-1946)

References to Frawley in Toowoomba

1863 (June) Tender By Frawley Accepted (Darling Downs Gazette & Gen. Advertiser, 25 June 1863).

1863 (Nov) James Frawley - Payment for Construction of Foot-Bridge (The Toowoomba Chronicle & Queensland Advertiser, 12 Nov 1863, p.2).

1865 (Oct) James Frawley submitted a tender for clearing Phillip St at Toowoomba (and was successful) (Darling Downs Gazette & Gen. Advertiser, 18 Oct 1865).

1866 (Jul) William Murphy Frawley - Birth son of a James Frawley (Ancestry.com.au).

1875 (Apr) Patrick Frawley - Cottage & Land For Sale (Darling Downs Gazette, 14 April 1875, p.2).

1875 (Nov) Michael Frawley receives 140 acres of 1st class pastoral land at Lucky Valley (Warwick Argus & Tenterfield Chronicle, 18 Nov 1875, p.2).

1876 (Jan) James Frawley v William Hampson - for unlawfully intruding upon closed lands (Toowoomba Chronicle, 5th Jan 1876, p.3).

1878 (Nov) Bridget Frawley - Poisoning Incident (Toowoomba Chronicle, 23rd Nov 1878, p.2).

1878 (Nov) Sarah Frawley - requested her sons James & Patrick Kirby & John Thomas Kirby to contact their mother (Toowoomba Chronicle, 28th Nov 1878, p.1).

1879 James Frawley - selling property (Newscutting, undated).

1879 (Oct) Bridget Frawley, dau. of Thomas Frawley marriage to Michael Gilligan in Toowoomba (Darling Downs Gazette, 23 Oct. 1879).

1882 James Frawley & William Frawley with race horses & show horses (Newscutting, undated).

1889 Michael Frawley - Death (Warwick Argus, 19 Jan 1889, p.2).

1892 (Apr) Frawleys - Alleged Cattle Stealing (Toowoomba Chronicle & Darliong Downs Gen. Advertiser, 23 Apr 1892, p.4).

1892 (Apr) William & John Frawley - Cattle stealing (Queensland Times, 30 April 1892, p.7).

1898 Bridget Frawley m. Patrick Cullinan (Newscutting, undated, #C58).

1900 James Frawley became Vice President of the Darling Downs Amateur Swimming Club (Newscutting, undated).

1901 (Jan) T. Frawley performed particularly well at the Caledonian Sports Society Carnival in Toowoomba. He came 2nd in High Jump and Vaulting with Pole. (Toowoomba Chronicle, 3rd Jan 1901, p.3).

1906 (Apr) Anne & Mary Frawley - Electoral List (Warwick Examiner, 14 April 1906, p.2).

1913 (Nov) Ann & Jas. Frawley - Witness (Truth, 30 Nov 1913, p.8)

1931 (Oct) Ann Frawley - Funeral (The Brisbane Courier, 19th Oct 1931, p.10)

1946 (Feb) John Frawley - Shot Put Record (The Telegragh [Brisbane], 25th February 1946, p.10)

TOP (Left): Listings for Frawley in Queensland Directory, Meringandan, QLD (undated). (Centre): Listings for Frawley in 1894 Queensland Directory, Meringandan, QLD. (Right): James Frawley - Death Notices (SMH, 12 June 1919, p.12). MID: Frawley - Cattle Brands Transferred, Meringandan, QLD (Newscutting, May 1905). ABOVE (Left): The Harristown State School (Toowoomba) Girls' Basketball team was the undefeated, 'A' grade premiers for 1927. On the team were Gwen Lewis, Ivy Swenson, Kathleen Lloyd, Joyce Jones, Daisy Geddes, Ella Robertson, Muriel McGilp, Eileen Swenson, Norah Halligan, and Joyce Chamberlin. Also named in the photograph are Miss Frawley (perhaps the coach or a teacher) and Sally Horner (the mascot). Ella Robertson was the captain and is posing with the trophy. All of the girls are wearing tunics with a shirt of some kind underneath. (Right): The school rpeated the feat in 1929.

APPENDIX H
Frawley
Descendants That Served In Australian Military Forces

Roll of Honour
Frawley
Descendants That Served In
Australian Military Forces

Name	Lifespan	Conflict	Reg. No.	Rank	Unit	Page
Craig, Desmond William	1939-2003	Post WWII	#Q59108	Private	11 NST Battalion	311
Cuddihy, John	1923-1997	WWII	#QX51786	Signalman	35 S/B Op Section	284
Foote, William Hugh	1925-1997	WWII	#QX60925	Private	2/14 Battalion	284
Hyde, Robert William	1967-2016	Post WWII	-	Corporal	?	293
Lloyd, Albert Edward	1919-1979	WWII	#QX25523	Sergeant	2/24 Battalion	284
Marr, Alan William *p*	1918-2008	WWII	#QX21990	Private	2/26 Battalion	310
Marr, Gerald Raymond	1919-1984	WWII	#Q89724	Driver	Aust/New Guinea Admin	311
Marr, Justin Christian	1888-1944	WWI	#904	Private	5th Light Horse Regt	308
Marr, Leonard Joseph	1907-1974	WWII	#75930	Lead. Airman	Eastern Area HQ	310
Marr, Richard Sydney*	1875-1901	Boer War	#119	Private	6th QLD Imp. Bushmen	309
Marr, Victor Cardinal	1906-1973	WWII	#Q215472	Private	15th Battalion	310
Marr, William Milward	1924-1983	WWII	#QX51471	Gunner	2/13 Anti-Tank Regt	311
O'Sullivan, James Alexander	1872-1938	WWI	#2189	Private	25th Battalion	291
O'Sullivan, John William	1913-1974	WWII	#NX81887	Sergeant	1st Armoured Brigade	293
O'Sullivan, Victor James	1908-1990	WWII	#NX136906	Lance Sergeant	Aust/New Guinea Admin	293
Rockwell, Elwood Lorraine	1933-1987	Post WWII	CMF	Private	CMF Holsworthy	293
Rockwell, Lindsay Archibald	1937	Post WWII	CMF	Private	CMF Holsworthy	293
Sanders, Arthur Carew	1899-1940	WWI	#7548	Private	9th Battalion	286
Sanders, Robert Harold	1897-1961	WWI	#5120	Private	31st Battalion	286
Sanders, William Raymond	1895-1930	WWI	#148	Private	26th Battalion	285
Wilson, Claude Patrick	1901-1969	WWII	#VN15581	Lead. Airman	RAAF Narromine	292

* - Died On Active Duty
p - Prisoner of War

INDEX

Symbols

21st Regiment of Foot 97
40th Regiment of Foot 84

A

Aberdeen, Scotland 168
Aboriginal Population at Shoalhaven (1833-1842) 323
Aboriginal Population of Illawarra & Wollongong (1835-1846) 319
Aborigines 24, 30, 42, 43, 44, 50, 60, 71, 77, 79, 80, 86, 105, 106, 110, 114, 116, 147, 148, 149, 161, 163, 165, 166, 167, 170, 180, 181, 183, 186, 188, 189, 192, 199, 202, 228, 239, 243, 258, 264
Abraham
   Edwin J., (storekeeper) 166
Absolute Pardon 150, 151
Act of Union (1801) 39, 55, 59, 66, 69, 119, 123, 124
Adams
   Thomas, (convict, died on "Java") 97
Adelaide, SA 168
Adventure Bay, TAS 52
Aghalust, County Longford 130
"Alacrity" 136
Albany, WA 203
"Alexander" 28
Allan
   Andrew, (grantee) 86
   David, (grantee) 84, 86
Allcot
   John Charles, (artist) 34
Allen
   Thomas Duke, (gaoler) 244
American Revolution 27, 66, 68, 91, 122
Amity Point, QLD 116
Andrew
   Allan, (grantee) 86
Angevin Empire 93
"Anne" 45, 46, 47
Appeal for Land at Pambula (1852) 207
Appin, Sthn Tablelands 75, 81, 84, 158
Apsey
   W.S., (teacher, Pambula) 232
Archer
   Mr, (R.N. officer) 77
Archer family 203
Arklow, County Wicklow 68
"Aron" 193
Arthur
   Lt-Gov. Sir George 168
Ashton
   Julian, (artist) 118
Aspinall
   Thomas, (settler) 176
"Assistant" 51
Assisted Immigrants 214, 215
"Astrolabe" 24, 30
Atkins
   James, (witness) 240
Atkinson
   James, (explorer & author) 115
"Atlantic" 32
Australia Day 31

B

Baal's Bridge, Limerick 57

Baddeley
   Charles H., (magistrate) 248, 251
Badgery
   Henry, (squatter) 167
Badgery settlement, Monaro 183
Baker
   William, (mapmaker) 164, 181
Ballantyne
   Adam, (constable, Panbula) 226, 227, 240
Ballarat Football League 220
Ballarat General Cemetery 219
Ballarat, VIC 212, 215, 218
Ballinahinch, County Galway 68
Ballyvonnavavn (townland), County Clare 212, 217
Bank of New South Wales 192
Banks
   Sir Joseph, (naturalist) 23, 24, 27, 255
Bankstown, Sydney 33
Bantry Bay, County Cork 68
Bard of Thomond 61
Barmouth Creek, Pambula 199
Barney
   Capt. George, R.E. 244
Barrack Hill, Illawarra 86
Barrack Point, Illawarra 79
Bartlett
   William, (artist) 57
Bartley
   Joseph, (settler) 167, 183
   William, (b.1841) 186
Bass
   Dr George, (explorer) 33, 34, 35, 37, 46, 52, 165, 173, 199
Bass Point, Illawarra 78
Bass Strait 37, 39, 165
Bateman
   Capt. Nathaniel, (commander) 24
Bateman's Bay, Shoalhaven 24, 32, 44, 180, 187
Bath, England 32
Bathurst
   Henry, 3rd Earl Bathurst, (politician) 181
Battle of Trafalgar 202
Battle of Vinegar Hill (1798) 68, 69, 123, 131
Beaumont, Shoalhaven 76
Beck
   Robert, (postmaster, Pambula) 239, 248
Bedford, England 203
"Bee" 157
Bega Cheese Factory 193
Bega District Court 282
Bega, Monaro 165, 167, 168, 169, 170, 180, 181, 182, 186, 193, 196, 204, 226, 235, 250, 252, 282
Bega Quarter Sessions 250
Bega River, Monaro 167, 170, 185, 193
Bega Valley Historical Society xiii, 253
Bega Valley, Monaro 181, 187
Behl
   John, (innkeeper, Pambula) 207, 225, 252
Belfast, County Antrim 68, 214
Bell
   Charles William, (storekeeper) 193, 198, 207, 233
Bellambi, Illawarra 158
Bellawongarah, Shoalhaven 76
Bendeela, Shoalhaven 80
Bennelong, (Aborigine) 33
Bennet
   John, (survivor of "Sydney Cove") 35

Bennett
   John Henry, (postmaster, Yowaka) 249, 250, 251
   Mary Jane, (artist) 197
Bentinck
   William, (3rd Duke of Portland) 38
Bercury
   Michael, (convict, died on "Java") 97
Berkeley (homestead) 86
Bermagui, Monaro 167
"Bermondsey" 177, 193
Berriman
   Joseph, (bushranger) 300
   William, (bushranger) 300
Berry
   Alexander, Reminiscenses of 324
   Alexander, (surgeon, explorer & grantee) xvi, 85, 86, 87, 97, 101, 103, 104, 105, 106, 107, 108, 109, 110, 112, 114, 115, 116, 141, 142, 144, 147, 148, 149, 154, 155, 160, 163, 187, 277, 314
   David, (manager) 113, 114
   John, (manager) 112, 160
   William, (manager) 112
Berry Estate, see Coolangatta (homestead) 154, 155, 160
Berry (nee Wollstonecraft)
   Elizabeth, wife of Alexander Berry 109
Berry's Canal, Shoalhaven 105
Berry, Shoalhaven 50, 76, 110
Bertrand
   H.L., (artist) 241
Bickelmire
   Mrs, (Pambula pioneer) 207
Biggah (homestead) 170
Bigge
   John, (commissioner) 98, 192
Billy's Islands, Shoalhaven 47
Birbeck
   Capt., (commander) 43
Bishop
   Capt. Peter (soldier & explorer) 84
   Colin, (owner of Coolangatta) 115
   Norma, wife of Colin Bishop 115
Bissett
   Capt. James F., (master) 134, 136
Blackall
   Gov. Samuel 260
Black-eyed Sue 26
Black Head, Shoalhaven 156
Blake
   Theodore S. J., (descendant of Patrick Frawley/Marr) 306
"Blanche" 104, 105, 109
Bligh
   Dr Richard, (physician, Pambula) 236
   Gov. William 36, 51, 52, 73
Bligh District, NSW 179
Blinksell
   John, (boat builder) 116
Blowhole, Kiama, Illawarra 35, 81
Blue Mountains, NSW 34, 41
Bly
   Thomas, (spearing victim) 44
Boggy Creek, Monaro 226, 227
Boller
   Frank, (farmer, Pambula) 240, 294
Bong Bong, Illawarra 45, 80, 84
Boston Grammar School 33
Boston, Massachusetts 216
Botany Bay, Sydney 23, 25, 26, 27, 28, 29,

30, 34, 37, 43, 47
Bourke
　Gov. Sir Richard 36, 72, 168, 169, 196, 244
"Boussole" 30
Bowen
　Gov. Sir George 259
　Lt. Richard, (commander) 32
Bowen Island, Shoalhaven 32, 73
Boxsell's Farm, Shoalhaven 117
Boyd
　Benjamin, (entrepreneur) 172, 174, 176, 177, 183, 188, 193, 204
Boyd & Company 177
Boyd River, Clarence District 290
Boyd's Tower, Twofold Bay 172
Boydtown, Twofold Bay 176, 177, 204, 235
Bradley
　William, (artist) 28
Braidbo, NSW 171
Braidwood, NSW 166, 171, 187, 188
Brandt
　Dr., (surgeon) 39
Breadalbane Plains, NSW 168
"Breeze" 168
Brianderry (homestead) 167, 168, 181, 183
Brichago (homestead) 170
Brien
　Fenton, (baptism witness) 201, 277
Brierly
　Sir Oswald, (artist) 171, 172, 189
Brisbane 116, 255, 256, 259, 260, 262, 266, 275
　Gov. Sir Thomas 36, 86, 189, 192
Brisbane General Hospital 271
Brisbane Water Steam Passenger Co 158
British Admiralty 22, 25, 28
British Army 55
British Empire 26
British Government 32, 51, 55, 68, 86, 119
British Home Office 27, 28, 31
British House of Commons 26, 73, 124
British Military 131
British Parliament 123, 124
British Royal Navy 22, 33
Broedt
　Edna Louise, wife of William C. Frawley 60
Brogo, NSW 167
Brooks
　Capt. Richard, (grantee) 84, 86
"Brothers" 184
Broughton Creek, Shoalhaven 50, 117, 118
Broughton's Pass, Illawarra 158
Broulee, Shoalhaven 171, 183, 188, 196
Brown
　Andrew, (pastoralist) 192
　George, (grantee) 157
　Mr, (explorer) 52
Brown's Mountain 52
Brundee (homestead) 86
Bruton
　Maurice, husband of Sarah Frawley (Vic) 62, 219, 221
"Buffalo" 46
Bugong Gap, Shoalhaven 80
Bulli, Illawarra 24, 84
Bulli Pass, Illawarra 157
Bundanoon Creek, Sthn Tablelands 80
Bungaree, VIC 215, 216, 220, 221, 229
Bungonia Creek, Sthn Tablelands 80
Burke
　Patrick, (settler) 96

Burrier, Shoalhaven 50, 80
Bushrangers 301
Buxton
　J.W., (mapmaker) 257
Byron
　George Gordon, (6th Baron Byron, poet) 65

C

"Caesar" 193
Cahill
　W.F., (publisher) 158
Calcutta, India 34, 95, 97, 189
Callala Beach, Shoalhaven 47
Cambell
　Yankey, (spearing victim) 43
Cambewarra Lookout 76
Cambewarra Mountain 76
Cambewarra, Shoalhaven 84
Camden, NSW 80
Cameron
　Duncan, (storekeeper) 240
　Margery, wife of Duncan 240
Campbell
　J.F., (colonial secretary) 72, 79
　John, (squatter) 167
　Robert, (merchant) 189
Campbelltown, NSW 158
Canberra, ACT 186
Cape Howe, Monaro 23, 35
Cape of Good Hope 28, 39, 45, 95, 136
Cape St George, Shoalhaven 24
Cape Town, South Africa 25, 39
Carpenter
　John, (Pambula resident) 246
Carthann the Fair, (Eoganachta king) 57
Cash
　Martin, (convict) 97
Cassim
　Johnny, (convict & hotelier) 264
Castlebar, County Mayo 69
Castle Hill, Sydney 42
Catholic Association (1823) 123
Catholic emancipation 123
Cattle Bay, Monaro 173, 193
Cedar cutters 52, 70, 71, 80, 84, 106, 109, 157
Census of Aborigines (1845) 193
Census of Australia (2011) 56
Census of Convicts (1837) 113
Census of England & Wales (1891) 62
Census of New South Wales (1828) 100
Census of New South Wales (1841) 153, 158, 160
Census of New South Wales (1891) 268
Central Highlands Football League 220
Certificate of Freedom 112, 150, 151, 152, 240
Chapple
　Isaac, (farmer) 240
Charcoal Will, (Aboriginal) 105
"Charles" 157
Chinese miners 234
Chisholm
　Capt. Archibald, husband of Caroline 137
　Caroline, (humanitarian) 137
"Chowringhee" 214, 228
Churchill
　John, (1st Duke of Marlborough) 93
"City of Brisbane" 262
Civil War, American 240
Civil War, England 93
Clancy
　Thomas, (baptism witness) 201
Clare Heritage Centre, Corofin 213
Clarence River 290

Clark
　William, (survivor of "Sydney Cove") 34, 35
Clarke
　Agnes Ann,, (descendant of John Frawley Jr.) 283
　Evelyn May, (descendant of John Frawley Jr.) 280
　Hilda Maude, (descendant of John Frawley Jr.) 280
　John, (bushranger) 300
　Robert Edward, husband of Agnes Frawley 280, 282
　Thomas, (bushranger) 300, 301
Clinton
　Mr S., (settler) 176
Clonmel, County Tipperary 130
Clontarf, Sydney 242
Close
　Edward, (artist) 50
Clyde River, Shoalhaven 169
Coalcliff, Illawarra 35, 84
Cobargo, Monaro 167, 168, 170, 183, 196
Cockatoo Island Dry Dock 243
Cody
　Dennis, father of Susan Frawley 212, 215
　Margaret, mother of Susan Frawley 212
Cody family 215, 217
Coffs Harbour, NSW 267, 290
Coledale, Illawarra 78
Coleman
　Mary, (baptism witness) 201
Collier
　Stephen, (bail sponsor) 241, 294
Collingwood Football Club 220
Collins
　Capt., (commander) 77
　David, (judge advocate) 31, 32
　James, (accused) 227
　John, (baptism witness) 201
　Mary Ann, (Pambula, resident) 208
　Mr S.H., (tenant) 279
Colonial Office 169, 244
Colstone
　Samuel, father of Rose Emily Curtis 274
Comerong Island, Shoalhaven 105
Commercial Hotel, Pambula 236, 252
Company of Surgeons 33
Condamine River, Darling Downs 313
Conditional Pardon 150, 151
Connell
　Patrick, (bushranger) 300, 301
　Thomas, (bushranger) 300
Connor
　Dennis, (baptism witness) 201
Convict Applications to Marry 153, 156
Convicts 21, 26, 27, 28, 29, 30, 31, 32, 39, 46, 52, 56, 60, 62, 63, 77, 79, 85, 86, 87, 89, 91, 92, 93, 94, 95, 96, 97, 100, 101, 107, 109, 110, 111, 113, 114, 116, 119, 124, 134, 135, 136, 137, 138, 140, 141, 144, 147, 148, 150, 153, 155, 156, 157, 161, 168, 192, 241, 242, 243, 264, 314
Coogee, Sydney 308
Cook
　Lt. James, (explorer) 22, 24, 26, 27, 29, 30, 32, 165, 199
"Coolangatta" 109, 116
Coolangatta Creek, Shoalhaven 116
Coolangatta Historic Village Motel 115
Coolangatta (homestead) xvi, 84, 86, 87, 89, 101, 103, 104, 105, 106, 107, 109, 110, 112, 113, 114, 115, 116, 141, 142, 143, 144, 147, 149, 150, 151, 152, 153, 156, 159, 160, 161,

163, 180, 187, 193, 277, 314
Coolangatta Mountain, Shoalhaven 50, 103, 104, 105, 109, 110, 116, 117, 144
Coolangatta, QLD 109, 116
Coomondery Swamp, Shoalhaven 109
Cork, County Cork 64, 92, 93, 94, 96, 97, 100, 217
Corofin, County Clare 127
Corridgeree (homestead) 193
Corroboree 43, 105, 170, 189
County Antrim, Ireland 68
County Clare, Ireland 55, 60, 62, 70, 127, 211, 212, 214, 216, 217, 218
County Cork, Ireland 130
County Donegal, Ireland 64
County Down, Ireland 64
County Kerry, Ireland 57
County Limerick, Ireland 65, 66, 119, 122, 129, 130, 131, 135, 136
County of Argyle, NSW 84, 168
County of Camden, NSW 153, 157, 160
County of Cumberland, NSW 181
County Offaly, Ireland 57
County of Murray, NSW 187
County Tyrone, Ireland 64
County Wexford, Ireland 131
County Wicklow, Ireland 124
Coura, Shoalhaven 84
Covington
Elizabeth, mother of Syms Covington 203
Eliza (nee Twyford), wife of Syms Covington 203
Simon V, father of Syms Covington 203
Syms 203, 209, 224, 225, 236
Cowper
Thomas, (squatter) 167
Craig
Desmond William F., great grandson of Patrick Marr 311
George, (convict) 116
Crawley
James, (convict, died on "Java") 97
Croft
John, (pastoralist) 193
Cromwell
Oliver, (Lord Protector of England) 57, 93
Crooked River, Shoalhaven 156
Crookhaven River, Shoalhaven 105
Crookhaven, Shoalhaven 47, 48
Croom, County Limerick 130
Crown & Anchor Hotel, Eden 171
Crown Lands Occupation Act (1836) 196
Cruikshank
George, (artist) 95
Cuddihy
John, (descendant of John Frawley Jr.) 284
Cunglebung (homestead) 290
Cunningham
Allan, (botanist) 171, 255, 256, 259
Cusack
Catherine, (baptism witness) 201

D

Dalcassian Clan 57
Dalmorton, Clarence District 267, 290
Dapto, Illawarra 86, 158
Darling
Gov. Sir Ralph 36, 86, 87, 164, 170, 181, 256
Darling Downs District, QLD 256, 257, 259, 261, 262, 263, 301, 313
Darwin
Charles, (naturalist) 203
Davey
Lt-Col. Thomas 86
Davis
John Charles, (blacksmith & witness) 224, 225
Dawes Point, Sydney 189
Dayes
Edward, (artist) 31, 32
Deep Creek, Monaro 299, 300
Deighton
Robert, (military convict) 97
Delagoe Bay, Mozambique 39
Dent
Josiah, (pioneer) 256
Deptford, England 37
Derwent River, TAS 37
Dharawal Clan 52
"Diamond" 131, 134, 135, 136, 137, 138, 141, 142, 156, 265
Dickson
Robert, (ships surgeon) 95, 96, 97
Dilba, (Aborigine) 34, 35
Dodd
Robert, (artist) 25
"Dolphin" 157
Donnellys Creek, VIC 287
Doora, County Clare 55, 62, 211, 212, 213, 218, 220, 221, 229
Double Creek, Monaro 170
Dowling
Judge 245
Doyle
Evelyn May, (descendant of John Frawley Jr.) 280
George Patrick, (descendant of John Frawley Jr.) 280
John Edward, (descendant of John Frawley Jr.) 280
Drayton, QLD 256, 259
Drayton State School 258
Drayton & Toowoomba Cemetery 282
Dr George Mountain, Monaro 168
Driscoll's Inn, Monaro 171
Dry River, Monaro 186
Dublin Castle, Ireland 124
Dublin-Cork Railway 59
Dublin, County Dublin 68, 91, 123, 124, 134, 136
Dublin Penitentiary 134, 135
"Duchess of Northumberland" 136
Duke of Edinburgh
Albert 242
Dungannon Convention (1782) 128
Dunlop Vale (homestead) 86
Dunn
James, (Pambula, resident) 208
Michael, (hutkeeper & spearing victim) 167, 181, 183
William, (miner) 298
Dunwich Benevolent Asylum 129, 264, 265, 267, 268, 269, 271, 315
Dunwich Cemetery 265, 271
Dyirringany Clan 199

E

Eardley-Wilmot
Lt-Gov. Sir John 168
Earle
Augustus, (artist) 76
East Boyd, Monaro 176
Eden District Court 226, 229, 232, 240, 245, 278, 294, 296, 299, 300
Eden Electoral District 252
Eden, Monaro 165, 167, 169, 171, 172, 176, 177, 180, 181, 193, 201, 204, 227, 232, 235, 236, 237, 240, 241, 245, 248, 266, 299
George, 1st Earl of Auckland 173
Eden Police Station 294
Eden Post Office 173, 252
Edenshead Manor, Fife 189
Egan
Daniel, (Pambula resident) 236, 237
James, (Pambula resident) 235, 240
John, (Pambula resident) 250
Electoral District of Port Phillip 177
"Eliza" 189
"Elizabeth" 168
Elrington
Major William S., (soldier & squatter) 167
Elyard
Dr. William, Sr. 79
Samuel, (artist) 43, 73, 87, 106, 115, 117
William, Jr. 86
"Emerald Isle" 137
Emmet
Robert, (Irish revolutionary) 123, 124
William, (overseer) 80
Emmott
John, (storekeeper) 301
English Town, Limerick 121
Enniscorthy, County Clare 131
Ennis, County Clare 55, 62, 213
Eóganachta Dynasty, Munster 57
Eora Clan 29, 44
Escape from Police Custody 302
Eurambene Mountain, Monaro 166
Eureka Stockade (1854) 208, 216
Evans
George William, (explorer) 45, 46, 50, 73, 74, 75, 76, 81
Thomas, (spearing victim) 43
Exeter, NSW 80
Exmouth (homestead) 86
Eyre
John, (artist) 38

F

Fairlie, Ferguson & Co 189
Farrell
John, (baptism witness) 201
Feeney
William, (witness) 240
Female Factory, Parramatta 139, 140, 141
Ferguson
D., (Master) 214
Fife, Scotland 107, 189
Filhelly
John, (politician) 264
First Fleet 25, 26, 27, 28, 34, 93
Fischer
Tim, (politician) 148
Fish River, NSW 290
Fitzroy
Gov. Sir Charles 201
Fitzroy Dock, Cockatoo Island, Sydney 243
Five Islands, Illawarra 46, 52, 79, 84, 85, 86
Fletcher
William, (bushranger) 301
Flinders
Lt. Matthew, (explorer) 33, 34, 35, 37, 52, 165, 166, 173
"Fly" 43, 44
Foote
William George, (descendant of John Frawley Jr.) 280
William Hugh, (descendant of John Frawley Jr.) 280, 284

Forbes
  Mr, (solicitor) 229
Forestier Peninsula, TAS 168
Forrester
  Cecil, (descendant of John Frawley Jr.) 280
Fort Macquarie, Sydney 137
Fowler
  Henry, (teacher, Pambula) 233
Fox
  Charles James, (statesman) 122
  Michael, (military convict) 97
"Francis" 35
Fraser
  James, (military convict) 97
Frawley
  Agnes Maude, daughter of John Frawley Jr. 269, 272, 280, 282, 294
  ancestors 55, 60, 62, 63, 66, 125, 129
  Anna Gilmour, daughter of John Frawley Jr. 272, 278, 280, 294, 313
  Anne (c.1807-1872), daughter of Michael Frawley 62, 69, 214, 215, 228, 229, 272
  Brian & Shirley, parents of Danny Frawley (Vic) 220
  Bridget Catherine (Jenkin), daughter of Patrick Frawley Sr. (Vic) 62, 212, 213, 215, 218
  Bridget (McMahon), wife of Michael Frawley (Vic) 62, 212, 214, 215, 216, 218, 219, 228
  Catherine (McMahon), wife of John Frawley (Vic) 62, 219
  Catherine (nee Kenny), wife of John Frawley Sr. 62, 63, 64, 66, 67, 69, 70, 273
  Charles, son of John Frawley Jr. 272, 280, 282, 294, 313
  Charlotte Ellen, daughter of Letitia Frawley 251, 273, 312
  Danny Patrick, (descendant of Michael Frawley, Vic) 220
  Eden 'Edith' Alice, daughter of John Frawley Jr. 272, 280, 294, 312, 313
  Eliza Jane (nee Quigg), wife of Patrick Frawley/Marr 273
  Eliza (McCormack), daughter of Patrick Frawley Sr. (Vic) 62, 213, 218, 219, 220
  Ellen (O'Sullivan), daughter of John Frawley 161, 183, 185, 186, 188, 193, 201, 233, 236, 248, 251, 267, 272, 287, 288, 290, 295, 301, 312
  family in NSW 67, 69, 193, 202, 204, 205, 210, 211, 240, 241, 248, 253, 255, 262, 263, 266, 267, 271, 282, 314
  family in Victoria 210, 214, 215, 216, 217
  Ivan, (researcher & Vic descendant) 220, 221
  James Joseph, (director) 62
  James, son of John Frawley 187, 188, 201, 233, 240, 241, 253, 255, 261, 262, 266, 267, 272, 294, 296, 297, 299, 301
  John (c.1816-1901) x, xi, xii, xiii, xvii, 21, 39, 53, 55, 56, 60, 62, 63, 64, 66, 67, 70, 71, 72, 79, 87, 89, 91, 92, 93, 95, 96, 97, 100, 101, 103, 110, 112, 113, 116, 142, 144, 147, 149, 150, 151, 152, 153, 154, 155, 156, 157, 160, 161, 163, 165, 177, 179, 180, 183, 184, 187, 193, 194, 195, 196, 201, 202, 203, 205, 207, 208, 209, 210, 211, 218, 221, 223, 224, 226, 228, 229, 232, 233, 235, 236, 237, 239, 245, 246, 247, 248, 249, 250, 251, 252, 261, 263, 266, 267, 268, 269, 270, 271, 273, 274, 275, 276, 277, 283, 287, 294, 295, 298, 299, 301, 313, 314, 315
  John Jr., son of John Frawley 157, 160, 179, 183, 184, 186, 187, 188, 201, 233, 235, 236, 240, 241, 245, 246, 248, 251, 252, 266, 267, 270, 272, 277, 278, 279, 280, 282, 287, 294, 299, 308, 313
  John, son of Patrick Frawley Sr. (Vic) 62, 213, 214, 215, 216, 218, 219, 228
  John, son of Richard Frawley (Vic) 229
  John Sr., (c.1788-1868), son of Michael Frawley 62, 63, 64, 66, 67, 69, 70, 101, 273
  Letitia, daughter of John Frawley (twin) 201, 204, 240, 241, 251, 273, 278, 279, 295, 299, 301, 308, 312
  Margaret (nee MacNamara), matriarch 62, 63, 273
  Mary Ann (nee McGarry), 1st wife of John Frawley xi, xii, xiii, xvii, 39, 56, 62, 117, 119, 122, 124, 125, 126, 127, 129, 130, 131, 132, 133, 134, 135, 136, 137, 138, 140, 141, 142, 143, 144, 149, 151, 152, 153, 155, 156, 157, 160, 163, 179, 180, 183, 184, 185, 187, 193, 200, 201, 203, 205, 207, 232, 236, 240, 241, 261, 265, 266, 267, 268, 269, 271, 273, 275, 276, 277, 278, 279, 283, 287, 294, 298, 299, 305, 313, 314, 315
  Michael (c.1768-c.1850), patriarch 62, 63, 273
  Michael, mystery? (Vic) 214, 215, 228
  Michael, son of Patrick Frawley Sr. (Vic) 62, 212, 213, 214, 216, 218, 219, 220
  Monica Burke (nee Frawley), (Vic descendant) 216, 221
  Patrick Jr., son of Patrick Frawley Sr. (Vic) 62, 212, 213, 214, 215, 217, 218, 228
  Patrick, son of John Frawley (twin, see also Patrick Marr) 201, 204, 266, 267, 270, 273, 295, 298, 299, 300, 301, 306
  Patrick, son of Letitia Frawley 251, 273, 312
  Patrick Sr. (c.1790-1854), son of Michael Frawley 63, 69, 211, 212, 213, 217, 247, 272
  Ray, (author & Vic descendant) 63, 221
  Richard, son of Patrick Frawley Sr. (Vic) 62, 211, 212, 213, 214, 215, 216, 218, 228, 229
  Rose Emily (nee Curtis), 2nd wife of John Frawley 62, 63, 64, 67, 269, 273, 274
  Sarah (Bruton), daughter of Patrick Frawley Sr (Vic) 62, 213, 214, 218, 219, 221
  Sarah Maud (nee Little), wife of John Frawley Jr. 266, 267, 268, 269, 272, 278, 279, 280, 282, 294, 313
  Stephen, son of John Frawley 201, 203, 233, 246, 247, 273, 295, 298, 299, 300
  Susan (nee Cody), wife of Patrick Frawley Sr. 62, 63, 211, 212, 213, 214, 215, 216, 217, 220, 221, 272
  Thomas, son of John Frawley 201, 204, 248, 266, 267, 273, 295, 313
  Tom, (barman) 60
  William Clement, (actor) 60, 62
  William, son of John Frawley Jr. 272, 278, 280, 294
Freeman
  Charles, (spearing victim) 44
French Revolution (1789) 59, 66, 68, 122
"Friendship" 28
Fulwood
  A.H., (artist) 33, 80, 149
Furneaux Islands, TAS 34, 35

G

Galway, County Galway 64
Gardner
  William, (chronicler & artist) 170
Garling
  Frederick, (artist) 173
Garrett
  Thomas, (publisher) 158
GenealogyBank 129
General Steam Navigation Company 158
"George" 43
Georges Quay, Limerick 128
Georges River, Sydney 158
German emigrants 193
Gernon
  Luke, (magistrate & author) 57
Gerringong, Shoalhaven 110, 114, 156
Gerroa, Shoalhaven 144
Gibraltar 95
Gill
  Samuel Thomas, (artist) 105, 148, 216, 234
Gipps
  Gov. Sir George 36, 137, 156, 177, 197, 243, 244
Gippsland, VIC 35
Giraldus Cambrensus x
Glasgow, Scotland 262
Glennie
  Rev. Benjamin, (Anglican minister) 258
Golden Vale, County Limerick 58
Gold rushes/mining 176, 204, 216, 219, 225, 234, 235, 287, 290, 299, 301
Good Dog Mountain, Shoalhaven 76
Goodeve
  Eliza, mother of Rose Emily Curtis 274
Goodlet
  Robert, (spearing victim) 44
Goodwin
  Mr, (passenger) 134
Gordon
  Lewes, (settler) 176
Gore
  Charles, (artist) 27
Goulburn Plains, Sthn Tablelands 80
Governor Fitzroy Hotel, Pambula 193, 198, 200, 201
Governors of NSW 36
Grafton, Clarence District 290
Grant
  Lt. James, (explorer) 37, 38, 39
Gray
  John, (postal agent) 166
Grealis
  Martin, (baptism witness) 157, 160, 277
Greaney
  Tom, (artist) 56
Grearly
  Mr J., (teacher, Pambula) 200, 233
Great Britain 55
Great Dividing Range 256, 259, 261
Greece 26
"Greenock" 168
Greenway
  Francis, (convict architect) 98, 137
Greenwell Point, Shoalhaven 86
Groom
  William Henry, (mayor) 259, 260
Grose
  Major Francis, (soldier & Lt.Gov.) 32, 33

Index

Grossis Creek, Monaro 170
Guadalcanal 204
Gulf Diggings, Monaro 299
Gundary (homestead) 188
Gurney
  William, (pioneer) 256
Gwynn
  Mr, (poundkeeper) 226

H

"Haldane" 189
Hamburg, Germany 193
Hamilton
  Capt. Guy, (commander) 34
Harp of Erin Hotel, Toowoomba 260
Harte
  Mr, (defendant) 245
Hawkesbury River, Sydney 37, 45, 46
Hawksworth
  Dr John, (editor) 26
Hay
  Alexander Berry, son of Alexander Hay 115
  Alexander, half-brother of Dr John Hay 114, 115
  Dr. John, cousin of Alexander Berry 114, 115
  Elizabeth, 2nd wife of Alexander Berry Hay 115
Hayes
  Capt. John, (commander) 37
  John, (plaintiff) 224, 225
  Mr. 235
Heaven
  Ely 240
  Llewellyn, (innkeeper) 240
Heffernan
  ancestors 127, 129, 131
  Catharine (nee Hennessy), grandmother of Mary Ann McGarry 130, 273
  Christy, (hurler) 127
  Clan xi
  John, grandfather of Mary Ann McGarry 130, 273
  Judge 247
  William Daniel, (Australian politician) 127, 128
  William J., (American politician) 127
Hennessy
  ancestors 130
Heston
  Father, (Catholic priest) 187
Hicks
  Lt. William, (of "HMS Endeavour") 23
Higgs
  Joshua, (convict settler) 183
Highfields, Darling Downs 266, 267
Hirst
  Mr. W., (settler) 176
"HMAT Supply" 28, 31
H.M. Gaol, Berrima 301
H.M. Gaol, Cockatoo Island 243, 247, 252
H.M. Gaol, Darlinghurst 241, 242, 243, 245, 247, 248, 252, 278, 279, 295, 299, 300, 301
H.M. Gaol, Parramatta 241, 244, 245, 246, 247, 252, 278, 279, 300, 301
H.M. Gaol, Toowoomba 259
"HMS Alligator" 172
"HMS Beagle" 203
"HMS Bounty" 51
"HMS Buffalo" 45
"HMS Endeavour" 22, 23, 24
"HMS Hyacinth" 136, 173

"HMS Rattlesnake" 171, 172
"HMS Reliance" 33
"HMS Sirius" 28
Hobart, TAS 37, 51, 161, 168, 169, 172, 193, 196
Hoche
  Gen. Lazare, (French commander) 68
Hoddle
  Robert, (artist) 79
Hoddle's Track, Illawarra 84
Homan
  Dr. (physician, Pambula) 235
Horton
  William, (pioneer & hotelier) 256, 259
Houison
  James, (builder) 244
Howe
  Adm. Richard, (1st Lord Howe) 24
Hudspeth
  Elizabeth, (artist) 171
Hughes
  Robert, (author) 31
  T., (artist) 58
Hume
  Hamilton, (explorer) 80, 84, 104, 105, 109
Hunter
  Gov. John 30, 33, 36, 37, 244
Hunter River, NSW 39, 44, 46, 158
Huskisson Hill, Shoalhaven 80
Hyde
  Robert William, (descendant of Ellen Frawley) 293
Hyde Park Barracks, Sydney 97, 98, 99, 101, 245

I

Illawarra District, NSW 39, 41, 45, 46, 52, 70, 71, 72, 75, 76, 77, 78, 79, 80, 81, 82, 84, 85, 86, 87, 113, 142, 147, 148, 153, 156, 157, 158, 159, 160, 163, 180, 201
Illawarra Farm (homestead) 86
Illawarra Historical Society 75, 81
Illawarra Mercury 158, 228
Illawarra Steam Packet Company 85, 157, 158
Imlay
  Agnes (nee Bron), mother of Imlay Brothers 168
  Alexander, father of Imlay Brothers 168
  Dr Alexander, (surgeon & squatter) 168, 169, 172, 177, 192, 196
  Dr George, (surgeon & squatter) 168, 169, 172, 177, 192, 196
  Dr Peter, (surgeon & squatter) 167, 168, 169, 170, 172, 177, 192, 196, 197, 204, 207
  Jane (nee Maguire), wife of Dr Peter Imlay 168
  Sophia (nee Atkins), wife of Dr Alexander Imlay 168
Imlay Brothers 161, 167, 168, 169, 173, 177, 180, 183, 184, 186, 188, 192, 193, 196, 197, 202, 205, 287
Industrial Revolution 21
"Industry" 184
Insurrection Act, Ireland (1796) 68
International Genealogical Index xiv, 63, 130
Ipswich, QLD 258, 259, 260
Irish Famine (1848) 56, 59, 62, 123, 126, 212
Irish House of Commons 131
Irish House of Lords 131
Irish Militia 122

Irish Parliament 119, 122, 123, 124
Irish Protestants 122
Irish Rebellion (1798) 21, 39, 53, 56, 66, 67, 69, 122, 124, 131, 217
Irish Town, Limerick 91
Iron Gangs & Road Parties 100
Isle of Man 134

J

Jamberoo, Shoalhaven 45, 86
Jasper's Pound, Quin, County Clare 212
"Java" 92, 93, 95, 96, 97, 100, 110
Jellat Jellat tribe 181, 186
Jenkin
  Matthew, husband of Bridget Catherine Frawley (Vic) 218
Jenkins
  Robert, (grantee) 86
Jerrinja Clan 103
Jersey Milk Company 114
Jervis
  Adm. Sir Richard, (Lord St Vincent) 32
Jervis Bay, Shoalhaven 24, 32, 42, 43, 44, 46, 47, 48, 50, 73, 74, 76, 77, 79, 80, 84, 104, 106, 110, 180
Jigama River (see Pambula River) 199
Johnson
  Father William Xavier, (Catholic priest) 208
Johnston
  George, (grantee) 86
  Lt. Robert, (commander) 84, 104
  Melanie, (philosopher) xv
Johnston's Meadows, Illawarra 84
Jones
  Thomas, (storekeeper, Pambula) 166, 233, 300
Jorgenson
  Jorgen, (explorer) 39
"Justitia" 95

K

Kameruka (homestead) 192, 193, 198, 205, 245
Kangaroo Ground, Shoalhaven 84, 86
Kangaroo Island, SA 44, 166
Kangaroo Point, Brisbane 264
Kangaroo River, Shoalhaven 80
Kangaroo Valley, Shoalhaven 76, 80, 84
Katungal Clan 165
Kavanagh
  Father Michael, (Catholic priest) 185, 186, 187, 188, 201, 277, 294, 298, 299, 308, 313
Kelly
  Maria, (baptism witness) 130
Kembla, Illawarra 77, 86
Kennedy
  Edward, (Pambula resident) 203
  Elizabeth, (Pambula resident) 203
  Elizabeth, (the daughter) 203
Kenney
  James, (playwright) 65
Kenny
  Sister Elizabeth, (nurse) 65
  William, (judge & politician) 65
Kenny ancestors xi, 64, 66
Kent
  Capt. William, (commander) 45, 46, 47, 48, 50, 76
Keogh
  Patrick, (marriage witness) 156
Keon
  G.P., (magistrate) 226, 227

Kiah (homestead) 186
Kiama, Illawarra 35, 87, 153, 156
Kiandra, Monaro 176, 234, 235
Kiandra Police Station 234
Kiandra Post Office 235
Kilkenny, County Kilkenny 64
Killala, County Mayo 68, 123
Kilrush, County Clare 216
King
  Gov. Philip Gidley 36, 41, 45, 46, 50, 51, 73
  Mr George, (storekeeper) 248
  Mrs Anna (nee Coombe), wife of Gov. King 51
King Charles I 126
Kingdom of Thomond, County Clare 57
King George III 123
King George Sound, WA 203
King Henry II 93
King Henry VIII 127
Kinghorn Point, Shoalhaven 79
King Island, TAS 42
King James II 57, 93
King John 91
King John's Castle, Limerick 57, 58, 59, 61, 70, 91, 124, 179
King's Island, Limerick 56, 91, 129
Kingston Harbour, Dublin 134, 135, 136
Kingswood, Monaro 167
King William IV xv
King William of Orange 57
Kirra Beach, QLD 116
Kirwan
  Elizabeth, wife of James Kirwan 186
  James, (squatter) 176, 186
Kurnell, Sydney 23, 25

L

Lachlan District, NSW 179
"Lady Nelson" 37, 38, 39, 50, 73
Lake
  Gen. Gerard, (British commander) 68
Lake Illawarra 34, 52, 73, 84, 86, 158
Lambton
  S.H., (secretary GPO) 250
La Pérouse
  Jean-François de, (explorer) 30
Leary
  Bridget, (baptism witness) 157, 160, 277
Lee River, County Cork 93
Leigh Creek, VIC 215, 216, 221, 229
Leslie
  George, (pioneer settler) 256, 259
  Patrick, (pioneer settler) 256, 259
Lette
  Patricia, (genealogist) 221
Levey
  Solomon, (merchant) 85
Lewis
  Mortimer, (architect) 244
  William George, (convict) 116
Limerick, County Limerick xvii, 21, 55, 56, 57, 58, 59, 60, 61, 63, 64, 66, 67, 69, 87, 89, 90, 91, 92, 97, 117, 119, 120, 121, 122, 123, 124, 125, 127, 129, 130, 131, 133, 134, 136, 138, 142, 143, 213, 229
Limits of Location, NSW (1826) 164, 170, 179, 181
Lisburn & Lambeg Volunteers 128
Little
  Robert, brother of Sarah Little 248, 279
Liverpool Plains District, NSW 179
Liverpool, Sydney 52, 85, 158
Lloyd
  Albert Francis 'Kid', (boxing champion) 280, 283
  Arthur, Esq., son of Lt. John Lloyd 202
  Edward Albert, son of Albert Francis Lloyd 283, 284
  Elizabeth Lucy, wife of Arthur Lloyd 202
  Gayle, (descendant of John Frawley Jr.) 314
  Lt. John, (R.N. & magistrate) 201, 202, 204, 209, 227
  Mr 226
London, England 111, 136, 168, 189, 192, 197, 214, 217, 244
London Gazette 33
Lookout Point, Eden 176
Lord Lieutenant of Ireland 124, 133, 134
Loughmore, County Limerick 130
Lovett
  Robert John, (artist) 199
Lowe
  Georgiana, (artist) 77, 81, 141, 149
Lue (homestead) 189
Lycett
  Joseph, (artist) 44

M

MacHugh of Leitrim Clan 126
Maclean
  Alex, (master) 214
MacPherson
  Mrs Allan, (artist) 243
Macquarie
  Gov. Lachlan 36, 50, 73, 76, 79, 80, 86, 98, 99, 189
  Mrs Elizabeth (nee Campbell), wife of Gov. Macquarie 50
Macquarie's Gift (homestead) 84, 86
Madras, India 97, 137
"Maitland" 157, 158
Malcolm
  Janet Agnes, (descendant of John Frawley Jr.) 281
  William, (descendant of John Frawley Jr.) 281
Manly Cove, Sydney 44
Manning
  Arthur 198, 227
  A.W., (magistrate) 224, 225
  Edye, (merchant & shipowner) 157, 193
  James A.L., of Kameruka (squatter) 193, 205, 227, 240, 245
  William Montagu, (barrister & politician) 193
Maori 23
Marr
  Alan William 'Lofty', (descendant of Patrick Frawley/Marr) 306, 310
  Annie Ellen 'Thea', daughter of Patrick Frawley/Marr 273, 306
  Dolly Margaret, (descendant of Patrick Frawley/Marr) 306
  Eliza Jane (nee Quigg), wife of Patrick Frawley/Marr 273, 304, 305, 306, 308
  Ellen Elizabeth, (descendant of Patrick Frawley/Marr) 306
  Ellen Evelyn, (descendant of Patrick Frawley/Marr) 306
  Emily May, (descendant of Patrick Frawley/Marr) 306
  Emma Magdalen, daughter of Patrick Frawley/Marr 273, 306
  Eric Richard, (descendant of Patrick Frawley/Marr) 306
  Florence A., (descendant of Patrick Frawley/Marr) 306
  George Benedick, (descendant of Patrick Frawley/Marr) 273, 306, 307
  Gerald Raymond, (descendant of Patrick Frawley/Marr) 307, 311
  Harold, son of Patrick Frawley/Marr 273, 304, 306
  Helen Ada, daughter of Patrick Frawley/Marr 273, 306
  James Livingstone, son of Patrick Frawley/Marr 273, 306
  John 'Jack', son of Patrick Frawley/Marr 273, 306
  Justin Christian, son of Patrick Frawley/Marr 273, 306, 307, 308
  Leonard Joseph, (descendant of Patrick Frawley/Marr) 310
  Michael William, son of Patrick Frawley/Marr 273, 306
  Patrick, son of John Frawley (twin, see also Patrick Frawley) 302, 303, 304, 306, 308, 314
  Percival John, (descendant of Patrick Frawley/Marr) 307
  Percival Patrick, son of Patrick Frawley/Marr 273, 306
  Peter George, (descendant of Patrick Frawley/Marr) 307
  Richard Sydney, son of Patrick Frawley/Marr 273, 306, 307, 309
  Stephen Henry 'Tiger', son of Patrick Frawley/Marr 273, 306, 307
  Victor Cardinal, (descendant of Patrick Frawley/Marr) 310
  William Milward, (descendant of Patrick Frawley/Marr) 307, 311
Marsden
  Rev. Samuel, (magistrate) 244
Marshall
  Leila Edith, (descendant of John Frawley Jr.) 281
  Percy, (descendant of John Frawley Jr.) 281
Marshall Mount, Illawarra 79
Martens
  Conrad, (artist) 109, 137
Martin
  John, (plaintiff of Yowaka) 226, 228
  Mr, (constable) 226
  William, (surgeon's assistant) 33
Marulan, Sthn Tablelands 80
"Mary Hay" 183, 184
Maryland Bush Cemetery 275
Maryland, NSW 268, 271, 274
"Matilda"
  #1 (1779-1792) 32
  #2 (c.1805-?) 77
Matra
  James, (sailor & diplomat) 27
McAllister
  John, (constable, Broulee) 228, 232
McCabe
  Mr F., (surveyor) 200
McCarthy
  William, (farmer) 227
McCausland
  Armstrong, (farmer of Lochiel) 227
McCormack
  Patrick, husband of Eliza Frawley (Vic) 62, 219
McDowell
  William, (ships surgeon) 135, 136
McFarland
  Alfred, (judge) 82, 85
McGarry
  ancestors 119, 123, 125, 129
  Bill, (footballer) 126
  family 119, 130, 131
  Johanna (nee FitzGerald), wife of Michael

Index

McGarry 130
Mary (nee Heffernan), mother of Mary Ann McGarry 125, 129, 130, 131, 133, 265, 273
Mary, passenger on "Marmion of Liverpool" 126
Michael, brother of Mary Ann McGarry 130
Patrick, brother of Mary Ann McGarry 130
Patrick, father of Mary Ann McGarry 125, 126, 129, 130, 131, 133, 265, 273
Seán, (politician) 126
Thomas William, (Canadian politician) 125

McKee
David, (postmaster, Yowaka) 250
McLaren
David, (overseer) 168
McMann
James, (policeman & witness) 224, 225
McNamara
Bridget, (baptism witness) 201, 277
John, (settler) 97
Michael, (settler) 97
Patrick, (settler) 97
McNiven
William, (witness) 224, 225
McPhee
Mr, (Pambula pioneer) 207
McQuiggan
Hugh, (military convict) 97
Mealmaker
George, (superintendant) 244
Meares
Rev. Matthew Devenish, (Anglican minister) 143, 144, 152, 265
Meehan
James, (explorer) 45, 46, 47, 48, 50, 80
William, (baptism witness) 130
Melbourne General Cemetery 219
Melbourne, VIC 35, 215, 219, 287
Melville
Mr, (whaler & explorer) 32
Merimbula-Imlay Historical Society vi, xiii
Merimbula, Monaro 193, 236
Meringandan, Darling Downs 262, 263, 266, 267, 295
Meryla Pass, Sthn Tablelands 80
Metropole Hotel, Sydney 115
Molle
George, (grantee) 86
Monaro District, NSW 39, 41, 163, 165, 166, 167, 168, 170, 171, 172, 177, 179, 180, 181, 183, 184, 186, 187, 193, 201, 204, 209, 251, 314
Monreel (townland), County Clare 70
Montagu
John, (4th Earl Sandwich, statesman) 27
Montgomery
James, (prisoner) 302
Moonee Creek, NSW 267, 290
Moree Police 303
Moreton Bay, QLD 85, 100, 256, 259
Morris
Dudley, (marriage witness) 156
Mort
Thomas Sutcliffe, (businessman) 193
Moruya Court House 232
Moruya, Eurobodalla 187, 188, 301
Moruya River, Eurobodalla 188
Moses
Abraham, (carrier) 166
Moss Vale, Sthn Tablelands 80
Mount Alma Station, QLD 315
Mount Brown, Illawarra 52

Mount Dromedary, Monaro 24, 299
Mount Gambier, VIC 39
Mount Keira, Illawarra 72, 77, 156, 158, 160
Mount Lofty Ranges, SA 168
Mount Pleasant, Illawarra 156
Mowle
Stewart, (J.P.) 224, 225
Mt Alma Station, QLD 314
Mudgee, NSW 189
Mulroy
Lionel Raymond, (descendant of Ellen Frawley) 288
Mumbla Range, Monaro 170
Mungret Monastery, Limerick 57
Murramarang, Shoalhaven 24
Murray
Mr, (magistrate, Pambula) 235
Murray River, NSW 168
Murrell
Mr, (spearing victim) 42, 43
Murrumbidgee District, NSW 179

N

Nadin
John, (witness) 240
"Nancy" 42
Napoleonic Wars 21, 55, 59, 66, 119
National Directory of NSW 279
National Library of Australia xiii
Neitenstein
William Frederick, (Comptroller General) 244
Nelson
Adm. Lord Horatio 202
Neutral Bay, Sydney 172
New Britain 26
Newcastle, NSW 44, 85
New Cemetery, Ballarat 218
New Chum Hill, Kiandra 234, 235
New England District, NSW 179
New England, USA 26
New Holland 23, 39
New Ireland 26
New North Wales 26
New Plymouth, NZ 168, 170
New Ross, County Wexford 68
New Scotland 26
New South Wales Corps 51
New South Wales Legislative Council 177, 181
New South Wales Penal Colony 69, 71, 73, 89, 91, 96, 133, 148
New South Wales Post Office Directory 282
New South Wales Public Education (1848) 198
Newtown (homestead) 168
Newtown-Pery, Limerick 91
New Zealand 23, 85, 114, 168, 170, 192, 197, 204
Nicholls
Capt., (commander) 52
Nicholson
Mr., (explorer) 171
Ninety Mile Beach, VIC 34
Nine Years' War 131
"Norfolk" 35
Norfolk Island 73, 100, 243
Normans 57, 62
North Rockhampton Cemetery 298
North Stradbroke Island 264
"Northumberland" 24
Norton
James, (solicitor) 106

Nullica Bay, Twofold Bay 176
Numbaa (homestead) 86
Numba Clan 106
Numbugga Swamps, Monaro 170

O

Oaklands Manor House, Pambula 190, 192, 193, 196, 197, 202, 203, 207, 209
O'Brien
Charles, (overseer) 84
Donal Mor, King of Munster 91
"Ocean Chief" 287
O'Farrell
Henry James, (assassin) 242
O'Heffernan
Aeneas, (Bishop of Emly) 127
William Dall, (gaelic poet) 127
Old Ballarat Cemetery 212, 216, 218
Old Tom, (killer whale) 167
O'Neill
Mr P., (Pambula resident) 235
Oonoonba (homestead) 305
Osborne
Henry & Sarah, (Illawarra pioneers) 79
O'Sullivan
Blanche Zenobia, daughter of Ellen Frawley 272, 289, 290
Ellen Theresa, daughter of Ellen Frawley 272, 289, 290
Gladys Victoria, (descendant of Ellen Frawley) 288
Goldie Alathea, (descendant of Ellen Frawley) 288
Humphrey Joseph, son of Ellen Frawley 272, 288, 290
James Alexander, son of Ellen Frawley 272, 288, 290, 291
James Mahony, husband of Ellen Frawley 251, 267, 272, 287, 288, 290, 312
John Washington, son of Ellen Frawley 272, 289, 290
John William, (descendant of Ellen Frawley) 288, 293
Lenore (Shoveller), wife of Humphrey Joseph O'Sullivan 289
Mary Zenobia, daughter of Ellen Frawley 272, 289
Myrtle Helena, (descendant of Ellen Frawley) 288
Octavia Corelli (Rockwell), (descendant of Ellen Frawley) xviii, 288
Robin Gail, (descendant of Ellen Frawley) 289
Rupert Clarence, son of Ellen Frawley 272, 289
Victor James, (descendant of Ellen Frawley) 293
William, son of Ellen Frawley 272, 289
Zenobia, daughter of Ellen Frawley 272, 289
Owneybeg, County Limerick 127
Oxford, England 57

P

Pacific Islanders 114
Paddington, Sydney 236
Page
Mr, (storekeeper, Merimbula) 246
Pambula Beach 199, 223
Pambula Boiling Down Works 204
Pambula Court House 205
Pambula Flat 251

Pambula Floods 233
Pambula, Monaro vi, xi, xii, 190, 193, 194, 195, 196, 197, 198, 199, 200, 201, 202, 203, 204, 205, 207, 209, 210, 211, 218, 221, 223, 224, 225, 226, 227, 228, 229, 230, 233, 235, 236, 237, 239, 241, 246, 248, 250, 251, 252, 253, 255, 261, 263, 266, 282, 287, 290, 294, 298, 299, 301, 308, 313, 314
Pambula National School (1849) 198, 232, 233, 234, 277, 287, 294, 298, 299, 308, 313
Pambula Police Office 224, 229, 230
Pambula Pound 204
Pambula River 169, 196, 199, 200, 202, 235
Panbula (homestead) 169, 184, 197, 198
Parkes
  Sir Henry, (premier of NSW) 271
Parkinson
  Samuel, (surveyor) 193
Parramatta, Sydney 42, 139, 140, 141, 243, 244
"Parsee" 212, 214, 217
Paterson
  Capt. William, (soldier & Lt.Gov.) 33
Payten
  Nathaniel, (builder) 244
"Pedlar" 157
Pelham-Clinton
  Henry, 5th Duke of Newcastle (politician) 207
Penal Laws, Ireland 55, 58, 119, 122
Penderghast
  Catherine, wife of Richard Frawley (Vic) 62, 218, 226, 228, 229
Peron
  Francois, (naturalist) 35
Persevrence Creek Water Supply Scheme 261
Perth, Scotland 192
Peterborough (homestead) 80
Petition for clemency, Ireland 133, 134, 138
Petty
  Sir William, (mapmaker) 65
Pheasant Ground, Illawarra 84
Phillip
  Gov. Arthur 27, 28, 29, 30, 31, 32, 33, 36, 44
Pickersgill
  Richard, (master's mate) 24
Pigeon House Mountain, Shoalhaven 24
Pinkerton's Coaches, Grafton 290
Pitt
  William, the Younger, (Prime Minister) 123
Ploughright
  Mr, (Pambula resident) 235
Plymouth, England 22, 23, 26, 177
Point Danger, NSW 116
Point Hicks, VIC 23, 165
Polding
  Bishop John Bede, (Catholic archbishop) 187
Pollock Brothers 234, 235
Polly
  Robert, (died on "Java") 97
Ponsonby
  Mr, (plasterer, Pambula) 229, 232, 236, 237
Port Arthur, TAS 196
Port Hacking, Sydney 34
Port Jackson, Sydney 30, 31, 32, 34, 35, 38, 39, 45, 77, 96, 97, 100, 136, 137, 183
Port Kembla, Illawarra 79, 87, 142

Port Macquarie District, NSW 175, 179
Port Phillip, Melbourne 35, 177, 287
Portsmouth, England 27, 38
Poynings' Law, Ireland (1494) 122
Pratt
  Charles, (1st Earl Camden, statesman) 50
Preservation Island, TAS 34, 165
Prince Albert, of Saxe-Coburg 173
Prince Alfred Park, Sydney 244
Prospect Hill, Sydney 34
Prostitution 269
Protestant Ascendancy, Ireland 131
Prout
  John Skinner, (artist) 73
"Providence" 51
Pryce
  Rev E.G., (Anglican minister) 186
Ptolemy, (Roman geographer) 57
Pumpkin Cottage (homestead) 79
Purther
  Daniel, (bail sponsor) 241, 294

Q

Qantas xiv
Quandamooka tribe 264
Queanbeyan, Sthn Tablelands 166, 186, 187, 188
Queen Elizabeth I 131
Queen Mary I 131
Queen Mary II 57
Queensland Electoral Rolls 266
Queensland Post Office Directory 295
Queen Victoria 173
Quin, County Clare 212, 213, 219, 229

R

Raine
  Capt. Thomas, (mariner & squatter) 166, 167, 171
Rathmore, County Kerry 287
Redleaf Mansion, Sydney 191
Red Point, Illawarra 79, 80, 84, 87
Regan
  Catherine, (convict) 136
Reid's Flat, Illawarra 166
Relief Act (1778) 122
Ribbon Society, Ireland 123
Richmond Football Club 220
Rigney
  Father John, (Catholic priest) 156, 157, 160, 277
Rio de Janeiro, Brazil 27
Ritchie
  John, (settler & pioneer) 86
River Shannon, Ireland 56, 57, 58, 59, 61, 91, 129, 131
River Thames, England 37, 38
Rixon's Pass, Illawarra 157
Roberts
  J.R., (artist) 158
Robertson
  Charles, (hotelier) 198
Robinson
  Mr J.P., (settler) 176
Rockhampton Football Team 282
Rock Hill, Shoalhaven 87
Rockites, Ireland 55, 121
Rockwell
  Betty Jean (nee Wardle), wife of Robert Hunter Rockwell 289
  Dr Tracy, (author & descendant of Ellen Frawley) vi, xi, 58, 61, 70, 90, 91, 120, 128, 151, 176, 186, 187

  Elwood Lorraine, (descendant of Ellen Frawley) 289, 293
  Janet Lenore, (descendant of Ellen Frawley) 289
  Joy Corelli, (descendant of Ellen Frawley) 289
  Lindsay Archibald, (descendant of Ellen Frawley) 289, 293
  Norman, (artist) x
  Robert Archibald, husband of Octavia C. O'Sullivan xviii, 289
  Robert Hunter, (descendant of Ellen Frawley) 289
  Ronie Malcolm, (descendant of Ellen Frawley) 289
Rockwell Genealogies vi, vii, xi, xiv, xviii
"Rodney" 214, 218, 219
Roma District Court, QLD 302
Roma, QLD 302, 305
Roscommon, County Roscommon 64
Rose
  Mrs Celia, (chronicler) 188
"Roslyn Castle" 168
Ross
  Major Robert, (First Fleet officer) 29
Rowley, (servant) 80
Royal Bull's Head Inn, Drayton 256, 259
Royal National Park, Sydney 52
Royal Red Cross Award 219
Royal Society, London 22, 27
Royal Sydney Yacht Squadron 191
Rubyvale, QLD 298
Rum Rebellion, Sydney 50, 52
Rushworth
  Mr, (commander) 43
Ryan
  Catherine, (baptism witness) 201
  Honoria, (baptism witness) 201
  Mr. Thomas, (settler) 138
Ryder
  J.S., (artist) 167

S

Sadler
  William, (artist) 69
Sadubin
  Penny, (artist) 104
Saint Canice 64
Saint Finbar 93
Saint Munchin 57
Saint Patrick 57, 124
Saint Patrick's Cross 124
Sanders
  Arthur Carew, (descendant of John Frawley Jr.) 281, 286
  Edna Alice, (descendant of John Frawley Jr.) 281
  Mark Raymond, (descendant of John Frawley Jr.) 281
  Robert Harold, (descendant of John Frawley Jr.) 281, 286
  William Raymond, (descendant of John Frawley Jr.) 281, 285
Sandgate Cemetery, Newcastle 287, 290
Sawkins
  James G., (artist) 83, 160
Sawyers & Woodcutters 106
"Scarborough" 28
Schank
  Capt. John, (commander & inventor) 37, 38
Schoobert
  Mr James, (coal mining pioneer) 158
Schubach
  Mrs, (Pambula pioneer) 207

Index

Scott
 Bill, (bushranger) 300
 James Reid, (explorer & politician) 148
Seahorse Inn, Twofold Bay 176
Seven Hills, Sydney 42
Seven Mile Beach, Shoalhaven 144
Shadforth
 Thomas, (shipping proprietor) 157
Shea
 William, (Pambula resident) 201, 207, 224, 225, 235, 240
Sheehan
 Daniel, (settler) 96
Shellharbour, Illawarra 79, 86
Ships to Twofold Bay & Pambula (1842-1850) 206
Shoalhaven District, NSW 39, 41, 45, 46, 48, 70, 71, 74, 75, 77, 81, 97, 103, 104, 106, 107, 110, 114, 115, 116, 117, 141, 142, 148, 149, 151, 152, 153, 156, 157, 161, 163, 180
Shoalhaven Heads 105, 109, 114
Shoalhaven River 37, 46, 47, 50, 52, 80, 85, 87, 103, 104, 105, 106, 109, 112, 113, 116, 117, 118, 150
Shoveller
 Dr. John, (Independent minister) xv
Shuttlewood
 William, (pioneer) 256
Silver Beach, Kurnell 25
Slattery
 Father P., (Catholic priest) 250
Smith
 B., (convict at Coolangatta) 154, 155, 160
 Charles Throsby, (magistrate) 79, 82, 85
 Thomas, (innkeeper, Panbula) 227, 235
"Snapper" 79, 84, 85, 104
Snug Cove, Eden 165, 171, 172
Society of Australian Genealogists xiii
Society of United Irishmen 122
Solander
 Dr Daniel, (botanist) 24
Solomon Islands 30
"Sophia Jane" 85, 157
Southampton, England 214
South Australia 197
South Australian Company 168
South Coast 287
South Coast Exploration Timeline 318
South Coast, NSW 32, 33, 34, 39, 41, 46, 53, 70, 85, 87, 89, 101, 103, 105, 147, 148, 157, 158, 161, 165, 167, 168, 169, 171, 177, 180, 181, 183, 185, 188, 192, 193, 196, 197, 198, 251, 277, 287, 294, 314
Southern Cross (flag) 208
Southern Highlands, NSW 52
South Sea Islands 51
Spence
 Archibald, (Pambula resident) 279
Spiro
 Henry, (magistrate & mayor) 260
Spring Bluff Station, QLD 258
Squatters 53, 70, 71, 166, 167, 172, 177, 186, 199, 251
Standford
 Edward, (military convict) 97
St. Andrew's Cathedral, Sydney 168
Stanley
 Capt. Owen, (commander) 171, 172
Stanthorpe, Darling Downs 63, 64, 269, 271, 274
State Library of NSW xiii
Steele
 Capt. (master) 116
Sterzel
 Sadie Alma, (descendant of Patrick Frawley/Marr) 307
St. Francis Xaviers Church, Wollongong 157
"St. Heliers" 197
Stingray's Harbour, Botany Bay 23, 25
St. Jago, Cape Verde Islands 38
St. James Church of England, Toowoomba 260
St. Kilda Australian Football Club 220
St. Mary's Cathedral, Limerick 57, 59, 90, 91, 93, 120, 122, 179
St. Mary's Cathedral, Sydney 251, 290
St. Patrick's Cathedral, Ballarat 219
St. Patrick's Catholic Church, Eidsvold 304
St. Patrick's Day 219, 299
St. Peter's Catholic Church, Pambula 205, 210, 223
Stritch
 William, (Pambula resident) 235
Sullivan
 John, (settler) 96, 97
Swan Inn, Panbula 235
Sweet Poll, of Plymouth 26
"Sydney Cove" 33, 34, 165, 199
Sydney Cove 28, 29, 30, 31, 32, 38, 104
Sydney GPO 252
Sydney Harbour 100, 136, 137
Sydney Infirmary 168
Sydney, NSW 30, 31, 33, 34, 35, 37, 41, 42, 43, 44, 50, 52, 63, 72, 73, 76, 81, 84, 87, 89, 96, 97, 98, 99, 100, 101, 103, 105, 106, 109, 110, 114, 115, 116, 131, 136, 137, 141, 142, 156, 158, 165, 168, 180, 183, 184, 187, 188, 189, 192, 193, 198, 199, 201, 214, 244, 245, 248, 251, 262, 266
Sydney Opera House 137

T

Table Bay, South Africa 25, 28, 38
Tahiti 23, 168
Talmage
 Algernon, (artist) 29
"Tamar" 116, 157
Tank Stream, Sydney 31
Tantawangalo (homestead) 240, 294
Tapitallee Mountain, Shoalhaven 76
Tarlington
 William Duggan, (explorer & squatter) 167, 188
Tarraganda (homestead) 167, 192, 193
Tasmania 35, 52, 172
Tasman Sea 52
Tathra, Monaro 185, 266
Tathra Wharf, Monaro 266
Tenterfield, NSW 271
Tenterfield Oration 271
Tenterfield School of Arts, NSW 271
Terra Australis 23
Terranora Inlet, QLD 116
Terry
 Samuel, (grantee) 86
Terry's Meadows (homestead) 86
Thaua Clan 199
Thawa tribe 165
The Grange, Pambula 201, 202, 209
Theodore
 Augustus, (artist) 30
The Royal Willows Hotel, Pambula 231, 236
Therry
 Father John Joseph, (Catholic priest) 85
Therry (née Connolly)
 Eliza, wife of John Therry 85
The Springs, Drayton 256
The Swamp, Toowoomba 256
Third Fleet 32
Thomas
 Edwin E., (Master) 214
Thomond Bridge, Limerick 57, 58, 59, 61, 70
Thomondgate, Limerick 57
Thomond Park, Limerick 57
Thompson
 Hugh, (first mate of "Sydney Cove") 34
 Samuel, (prisoner) 302
Three Mile Dam, Kiandra 234
Three-Mile Water Hole, (homestead) 252, 282
Throsby
 Dr Charles, (surgeon & explorer) 52, 80, 85, 157
Tibbermuir, Scotland 192
Ticket of Leave 150, 151, 161
Tilba Tilba, NSW 299
Timor 51
Tithe Wars, Ireland 123
Toad Hall, Pambula 225, 230, 231, 237, 252
Todd
 Capt. John, (master) 95, 96, 97
"Tom Thumb" 33, 34
"Tom Thumb II" 34
Tom Thumb's Lagoon, Illawarra 34, 46, 47, 142
Tone
 Theobald Wolfe, (Irish revolutionary) 68
Toolburra Station, QLD 256, 259
Toongabbie, Sydney 42
Tooth
 Edwin, (merchant & brewer) 193
 Robert, (merchant & brewer) 193
Toowong Cemetery, Brisbane 275
Toowoomba Council 260
Toowoomba, Darling Downs xi, 255, 256, 258, 259, 260, 261, 262, 263, 266, 267, 268, 271, 282, 290, 294, 295, 296, 297, 302, 313, 314
Toowoomba Gas & Coke Company 260
Toowoomba Grammar School 260
Toowoomba Industrial & Reformatory School for Girls 269
Toowoomba Railway 260, 266
Toowoomba South State School 260
Town
 John, (grazier) 302
Townsend
 Mr T.A., (settler) 176
 Thomas Scott, (surveyor) 173, 200, 202, 233, 235
Townshend
 Thomas, (1st Viscount Sydney, statesman) 27, 31
Townsville Hospital 305
Townsville, QLD 298
Transportation Act (1717) 26
Treaty of Limerick (1691) 57, 58, 61
Treaty Stone, Limerick 58
Trustee of the Common, Maryland 274
Tumer
 Francis, (cattle overseer) 227
Tumut, NSW 252
Tupaia, (Tahitian interpreter) 23, 24
Turner
 Francis, (witness) 227
Tweed River, NSW 116
Twofold Bay, Monaro 24, 42, 161, 163, 165, 166, 167, 168, 169, 170, 171, 172, 173, 174, 177, 179, 180, 183,

184, 185, 186, 187, 188, 189, 193, 196, 198, 201, 236, 246, 287
Twofold Bay Pastoral Association 193, 198, 205, 207, 227, 245
Twyford
Joseph, (constable) 240

U

Ulladulla, Shoalhaven 24
Ulster Province, Ireland 67, 122
Underhill
Henry, (b.1842) 186
Thomas & Jane, (settlers) 186
Union Jack 124
United Irishmen 66, 68
United States 215, 216
Upolu, Samoa 168
Utzon
Jan, (Danish architect) 137

V

Van Diemen's Land 33, 34, 35, 37, 38, 50, 51, 52, 73, 165, 166, 168, 196
Vanikoro, Solomon Islands 30
"Venus" 43
Vikings 56, 57, 62, 129
Volum
Capt. Alexander, (mariner) 184

W

Wagin, (Aborigine) 106
Waite
Jack, (convict & explorer) 80
Walker
Archibald, father of the Walker Brothers 189
Archibald, nephew of the Walker Brothers 189
Edward, (banker & pastoralist) 169, 190, 191, 198
Isabel, 2nd wife of Archibald Walker 189
James, (banker & pastoralist) 169, 170, 189, 190, 192, 198, 200, 203, 204
John Marshall, (chief constable, Eden) 226, 227, 228
Louisa, wife of James Walker 198
Mr, (constable) 232
Sydney, (banker & pastoralist) 169

Thomas, nephew of the Walker Brothers 189
William, (banker & pastoralist) 170, 189, 191, 192, 193, 198, 204
William Benjamin 191, 198
Walker Brothers 188, 190, 193, 195, 197, 198, 201, 202, 203, 204, 205, 207, 233
Wallerawang (homestead) 192
Wandella, Monaro 166, 183
"Wanderer" 175, 183, 204
Wanganui, NZ 168, 204
Warragaburra (homestead) 161, 167, 170, 177, 179, 180, 181, 182, 183, 184, 185, 186, 187, 188, 192, 193, 195, 201, 203, 205, 223, 277, 287, 294, 314
Warragamba Dam, Sydney 45
Warragamba River 45
Warrenheip, VIC 212, 215, 218, 221
Waterford, County Waterford 64
Waterford-Limerick Railway 59
Waterhouse
Capt. Henry, (commander) 44
Waterloo (homestead) 86
"Waterwitch" 188
Wattamolla, Sydney 35
Weatherhead
Capt. Matthew, (commander) 32
Wellesley
Arthur, (Duke of Wellington) 133
Richard, (1st Marquess Wellesley) 133
Wellington District, NSW 179
Wentworth
D'Arcy, (surgeon) 80
William Charles, (explorer & statesman) 192
Western Port, VIC 35
West Indies 51, 95
Westmacott
Capt. Robert Marsh, (artist) 45, 46, 47, 72, 81, 84, 142, 156, 172, 174, 184, 196
Westmacott Pass, Illawarra 157
Wexford, County Wexford 67, 122
Wexted
William, 2nd husband of Catherine Penderghast 219
Whalers & Sealers 50, 70, 71, 166, 167, 168, 170, 171, 172, 177, 189
Wheeler
Mr, (plaintiff) 246
Whelan

John, (poundkeeper) 207
Whiteboys, Ireland 55, 66, 121
Wholohan
Conor, (overseer) 84
Wild
Joseph, (convict & explorer) 52, 80
Willemering, (Aborigine) 44
Williamites, Ireland 57
Williamite War, Ireland 57, 61, 131
"William Jardine" 134
William of Orange 61
Williams River, Newcastle 158
"William The Fourth" 158
William Walker & Co 188, 189, 190, 192, 194, 197, 198
Wilson
Claude Patrick, (descendant of Ellen Frawley) 288, 292
Col., (convict superintendant) 138
Dr Thomas Braidwood, (surgeon & squatter) 167
Wilson's Promontory, VIC 35
Windsor, Sydney 137
Wingecarribee River, Sthn Tablelands 80
Wollongong Hotel 160
Wollongong, Illawarra 24, 35, 52, 76, 77, 82, 85, 86, 87, 141, 143, 144, 149, 153, 156, 157, 158, 159, 160, 163, 193, 201, 265, 277, 314
Wollstonecraft
Edward, (grantee) 86, 103, 104
Wolumla, Monaro vi, 168, 225, 227, 251, 252, 266, 278, 279, 282
World War I 21
Wright
William, (settler & pioneer) 86
Wrixon
Lt. John Nicholas, (soldier) 97
Wyllie
John, (grantee) 86
Wyman, (Aborigine) 229
Wyndham, Monaro 236, 287

Y

Yager, (Aborigine) 106
Yarranung (homestead) 167
Yarrunga Creek, Sthn Tablelands 80
Yowaka River, Pambula 202
Yuin Clan 165, 199

THE AUTHOR

Dr. Tracy Rockwell began his career as a teacher in both primary and secondary schools before being appointed to the Dept of Human Movement, where he spent 25 years as a lecturer in the Faculty of Education at Sydney University. He later transitioned into a multifaceted career as an author and artist. As an athlete, he was a competitive swimmer, surf lifesaver, rugby player, and a New South Wales representative in water polo. In 2021, he became the Oceanic indoor rowing champion for his age group. With a deep interest in history, he published "Water Warriors: Chronicle of Australian Water Polo" in 2009 and was awarded the 'Harry Quittner Medal' for his contributions to the sport. A passionate genealogist, he launched his 'Rockwell Genealogies' series in 2020, adding to the list with this latest publication. Dr. Rockwell's other books and illustrated journals are available through Pegasus Publishing.

TITLE	ISBN	GENRE	FORMAT	PUB.	PAGES
Water Warriors: Chronicle of Australian Water Polo	978-0-646488-61-5	Sports History	Hardback	2009	597
The Complete Guide to Rugby World Cup (2015)	978-0-994201-42-3	Sports History	Ebook	2015	161
Play Water Polo: An Interactive Instructional Sports Guide	978-0-994201-40-9	Sports Development	Ebook [interactive]	2016	94
The Unknown Journey, by Joseph Anaman (Edited & pub by TR)	978-0-994201-48-5	Autobiography	Ebook	2016	136
The Unknown Journey, by Joseph Anaman (Edited & pub by TR)	978-0-994201-49-2	Autobiography	Paperback	2016	136
How to Play Water Polo: The Complete Guide to Mastering the Game	978-0-994201-41-6	Sports Development	Paperback	2018	215
Juega Polo Acuático: Guía Interactiva de Deportes de Instrucción	978-0-994201-43-0	Sports Development	Ebook	2018	96
Love Never Lets You Go: Aphorisms about Love Journal [illust.]	978-0-994201-46-1	Sociology	Paperback	2018	216
One Day at a Time: Aphorisms about Life Journal [illust.]	978-0-994201-47-8	Sociology	Paperback	2018	218
Journal of Life's Lessons: With Vintage Images and Aphorisms [illust.]	978-0-994201-44-7	Sociology	Hardback	2019	218
Who's There? Worlds Funniest A-Z Book of 737 Knock Knock Jokes	978-0-994201-45-4	Childrens-Fiction	Paperback	2019	107
Who's There? Worlds Funniest A-Z Book of 737 Knock Knock Jokes	978-1-925909-28-9	Childrens-Fiction	Ebook	2019	107
Australian Seascapes Journal [illust.]	978-1-925909-05-0	Sociology	Paperback	2019	128
Australian Landscapes Journal [illust.]	978-1-925909-06-7	Sociology	Paperback	2019	128
The Complete Guide to Rugby World Cup (2019)	978-1-925909-07-4	Sports History	Paperback	2019	198
My Handy Cruise Journal [illust.]	978-1-925909-10-4	Sociology	Paperback	2019	130
My Handy Travel Journal [illust.]	978-1-925909-11-1	Sociology	Paperback	2019	130
A History of the Ancestors of James Mahoney O'Sullivan and Ellen Frawley	978-1-925909-00-5	Genealogy	Paperback	2020	584
Australian Animals: Through the Looking Glass	978-1-925909-01-2	Childrens-Animals	Paperback	2020	68
Bush Dreaming and Other Plays, by Dr Frank Davidson (Edited & pub by TR)	978-1-925909-02-9	Literature-Drama	Paperback	2020	212
The Spirit of Bronte: A History of Bronte Amateur Water Polo Club 1943-1975	978-1-925909-03-6	Sports History	Paperback	2020	329
Tracy Rockwell: Catalogue Raisonné 2000-2020	978-1-925909-12-8	Visual Arts	Paperback	2021	342
Mystery at Melon Flats, by Dr Frank Davidson (Edited & pub by TR)	978-1-925909-04-3	Literature-Novel	Paperback	2022	192
Mystery at Melon Flats, by Dr Frank Davidson (Edited & pub by TR)	978-1-925909-09-8	Literature-Novel	Ebook	2022	192
The Long Road To Grafton: A Genealogy of Thomas Eastman Shoveller	978-1-925909-08-1	Genealogy	Paperback	2022	362
Nostalgia for Naremburn: The Ancestors of Robert & Corelli Rockwell	978-1-925909-13-5	Genealogy	Paperback	2023	290
Mystery at the Minerva Club, by Dr Frank Davidson (Edited & pub by TR)	978-1-925909-15-9	Literature-Novel	Paperback	2024	128
An Olympic Journey & Beyond, by Robert Menzies (Edited & pub by TR)	978-1-925909-14-2	Autobiography	Paperback	2024	258
From Prisoners to Pioneers: A Genealogy of John Frawley & Mary McGarry	978-1-925909-19-7	History-Genealogy	Paperback	2025	344
The Royal & Noble Blood: Pedigree & Descent of Tracy Paul Rockwell - Vol I	978-1-925909-16-6	Genealogy	Paperback	2025	500
The Royal & Noble Blood: Pedigree & Descent of Tracy Paul Rockwell - Vol II	978-1-925909-17-3	Genealogy	Paperback	2025	530
The Royal & Noble Blood: Pedigree & Descent of Tracy Paul Rockwell - Vol III	978-1-925909-18-0	Genealogy	Paperback	2025	486

www.ingramcontent.com/pod-product-compliance
Lightning Source LLC
Chambersburg PA
CBHW051309110526
44590CB00031B/4354